PLANNING ARMAGEDDON

Planning Armageddon

British Economic Warfare and the First World War

Nicholas A. Lambert

HARVARD UNIVERSITY PRESS
Cambridge, Massachusetts
London, England · 2012

Printed in the United States of America

Library of Congress Cataloging-in-Publication Data

Lambert, Nicholas A., 1967–
Planning Armageddon : British economic warfare and the First World War / Nicholas A. Lambert.
p. cm.
Includes bibliographical references and index.
ISBN 978-0-674-06149-1 (alk. paper)
1. World War, 1914–1918—Economic aspects—Great Britain. 2. Sea power—Economic aspects—Great Britain. 3. Great Britain—Economic policy—20th century. 4. Great Britain—Military policy. I. Title.
HC260.D4L36 2011
940.3'1—dc22 2011006802

For K.K. with love.

Contents

Orkney Islands
Scapa Flow
Christiana (Oslo)
NORWAY
Stockholm
Dagö
Ösel
Nykoping
Oxelösund
SWEDEN
SKAGERRAK
Göteborg
Gotland
KATTEGAT
Öland
BALTIC SEA
NORTH SEA
UNITED KINGDOM
DENMARK
Copenhagen
Malmö
Esbjerg
Bornholm
(Den.)
Danzig
Amrum Light Vessel
Helgoland
Kiel
Borkum
Hamburg
Stettin
GERMANY
RUSSIAN
EMPIRE
NETHERLANDS
Amsterdam
Berlin
Rotterdam
London
Zeebrugge
Oostende
Dover
Antwerp
BELGIUM
0
50
100
150 miles

Introduction

> In the last war the conditions of industrial civilization had made our enemy more susceptible to economic pressure than in the past. And because of geography our navy was better able to apply it. Yet for the first time in our history we made it a subsidiary weapon, and grasped the glittering sword of Continental manufacture.
>
> BASIL LIDDELL HART, 1931

This book offers a radical reinterpretation of the nature and significance of the relationship between economics and sea power before and during the First World War. It focuses on Great Britain's development of a novel and highly sophisticated approach to economic coercion in the event of war against Germany. The British scheme rested upon the discernment that the explosive growth of international trade since the late nineteenth century rested substantially upon the creation of the global credit network, whose inevitable dislocation in the event of war could cripple and conceivably collapse national banking systems. The objective of "economic warfare," as here termed, was to precipitate the rapid collapse of an enemy's financial systems and so disorganize its economy as to produce military paralysis. The perceived benefit of such an outcome was a quick victory at a relatively low cost. Economic warfare, in short, constituted a national strategy of quick, decisive war comparable in function and objectives to Germany's infamous Schlieffen Plan.

It is a matter of common knowledge that the leaders of the European great powers went to war in the confident expectation of a quick outcome.[1] Although the trend in recent scholarship has been to question the prevalence and importance of the short-war assumption, it remains undeniable that the majority of political and military leaders reckoned that the conflict would be measured in months, not years, and that the war plans executed in August 1914 by generals and admirals were based upon this conviction. Certainly in Britain, the expectation of short war underlay the army's General Staff plan calling for the rapid commitment of a military expeditionary force to the Continent to help the French army stem the anticipated German invasion through Belgium. Thus "the glittering sword of Continental manufacture"—better known as the "Continental commitment"—was interlinked with the short-war assumption.

Historians attribute the nearly universal expectation of a short war mostly to warnings from political economists that high-intensity conflict between modern industrial states, if not stopped quickly, would lead to financial, economic, and social disintegration. This belief emerged during the latter part of the nineteenth century with the recognition that the new industrial societies were becoming ever more specialized, ever more dependent upon international trade, and that their interlocking financial systems made them economically interdependent.

Among the first to make such predictions was Ivan Bloch, the Polish banker and railway financier turned strategic analyst. Although best known for his technical arguments on the military implications of the destructiveness of modern weaponry, Bloch had much to say about the economic aspects of warfare. "The future of war," he argued, is "not fighting, but famine, not the slaying of men, but the bankruptcy of nations and the break-up of the whole social organisation . . . in short, the economic results which must inevitably follow any great war in the present complex state of human civilisation."[2] This idea was popularized by Norman Angell, the British newspaperman whose 1910 book *The Great Illusion* sold more than two million copies before the war.[3] The notion that war between the great powers would precipitate an economic Armageddon—a kind of economic mutually assured destruction—possessed a respectable intellectual pedigree and was supported by a considerable body of liberal intellectual thought.

Given the presumption that the global economy was so sensitive, and that 90 percent of the world's trade was carried by sea, one might expect to find naval publicists of the day touting commerce warfare as the fastest way to defeat an enemy—not to mention cheaper than sending vast armies into battle. But they did not. The leading sea power theorist of the time, the American naval officer Alfred Thayer Mahan, while arguing that maritime commerce was essential to the economic prosperity of a great power, assailed the utility of commerce warfare, instead arguing that naval power required command of the sea exercised by battle fleets.[4]

His most famous British counterpart, Julian Corbett, questioned Mahan's focus on battle, pointing out that history showed that decisive fleet actions had been rare because invariably the inferior fleet declined action. Instead, the Royal Navy had mounted a blockade over its enemy's ports. For Corbett, the closing of the enemy's commercial ports represented the apogee of naval power, allowing the dominant navy to "choke the flow" of enemy seaborne commerce.[5] "The primary method, then, in which we use victory or preponderance at sea and bring it to bear on the enemy's population to secure peace, is by the capture of the enemy's property, whether public or private," he wrote, "what may be called economic pressure."[6]

Yet Corbett maintained that such pressure could work only slowly.[7] This argument was indeed correct for the subject that Corbett primarily studied—the Anglo-Dutch wars of the seventeenth century. In the last quarter of the nineteenth century, however, the day-to-day conduct of international trade was revolutionized by the development of transoceanic cable communications, along with the creation of a global credit system associated with modern fractional reserve banking and sophisticated international money markets. This fundamental transformation of the global trading system had enormous strategic implications. Overlooking them, Corbett could agree with Mahan that economic pressure was unlikely to produce decisive results quickly.[8]

The work of naval theorists on this point has influenced generations of naval historians who study British naval planning before the First World War. Perhaps because they lacked full access to naval archives, the first generation of naval historians built their analysis of prewar and wartime naval policy making upon foundations laid down by naval theorists rather than by the actual decision makers. Following Mahan, they tended to focus their attention on the Royal Navy's preparation for battle, treating blockade as almost an afterthought. To the extent that they considered blockade, following Corbett, they tended to assume it must be a slow-acting weapon and, like him, ignored the implications of the fundamental changes in the global trading system of the late nineteenth century. Even after additional archival material became available, subsequent generations of naval historians could not free themselves from the interpretive blinders of their pioneering colleagues or of the naval theorists and as a result overlooked evidence suggesting that the Admiralty developed a *fast*-acting plan for economic pressure.

In the absence of work by naval historians showing that such a plan existed, and perhaps influenced by their knowledge of the Royal Navy's failure to win a decisive battle during the war, other historians naturally concluded that Britain's most credible plan for achieving a quick victory was the military

Continental commitment. This conviction has influenced their comparative judgments about the prewar performance of the Admiralty, the War Office, and the Committee of Imperial Defence (CID), as well as their interpretations of the Anglo-French relationship. It is not too much to say that this lacuna has had profound implications for our ideas about the origins of the First World War.

In actual fact, the Admiralty did have a plan for fast-acting economic pressure. In contrast to the naval theorists, the real naval policy makers were well aware of the important late nineteenth-century changes in the global trading system. In late 1908, the First Sea Lord, Admiral Sir John "Jacky" Fisher, unveiled a grand strategy for war against Germany to Prime Minister H. H. Asquith and his senior ministers that sought to exploit these changes. His plan was predicated upon the twin expectations that the outbreak of hostilities would trigger a countdown toward economic and social Armageddon and that Britain could manage the descent into the abyss. Fisher argued that British naval supremacy, combined with its near monopoly on the infrastructure of the global trading system, would permit the government of the day to slow the effects of chaos upon the British economy while at the same time accelerating Germany's derangement. Rapid economic destruction would be assured for Germany but not mutually assured for Britain. This broadening of war planning beyond the strictly military sphere constituted a revolution in the very definition of strategy.

The Admiralty's ideas provoked considerable resistance. Economic warfare had significant bureaucratic and even constitutional implications that threatened to redefine the relationship between state and society, and thus made implementation fraught with political difficulties. It necessarily entailed massive and unprecedented state intervention into economic and commercial life. For example, the Admiralty requested authority to control the wartime movements of British-flagged merchantmen and to regulate the cargoes they might carry. The admirals also asked for state censorship and control over all cable communication networks as well as the right of supervision over the financial services industry represented by the City of London. Planners not only foresaw that execution of the plan might cause significant collateral damage both to the British economy and to the economies of neutral powers but also warned of the diplomatic complications that in such circumstances would result from the failure of international law to adapt to changes in the methods of world trade.

These impediments notwithstanding, economic warfare was not simply discussed in the abstract before the war but deliberated upon and accepted at the highest levels of government. In late 1912, the British political leadership endorsed the new strategy at a meeting of the Committee of Imperial Defence attended by the prime minister and eight other senior cabinet ministers. The Admiralty was given predelegated authority (itself a major constitutional innovation) to put the plan into immediate effect upon outbreak of war.

Accordingly, on 4 August 1914, the Admiralty began executing the various elements of economic warfare strategy on the basis of these predelegated directives. The implementation quickly ran into trouble, however. The severity of the global financial panic that attended the beginning of the war was such that the added disruption to the global trading system caused by these measures threatened not only the vital financial interests of Germany but also those of neutral countries, especially the United States of America, and hurt powerful groups within Britain as well. The volume of protest from foreign and domestic sources quickly turned both the Foreign Office and the Board of Trade into opponents of economic warfare. In the ensuing departmental squabble, both took steps that effectively countermanded the prewar directives.

Inside a fortnight, the cabinet was asked to adjudicate what should be done. Partially as a consequence of the still unfolding economic crisis and partially because of the continued expectation of a short war, before the end of August the politicians voted for the dilution of economic warfare. In the weeks that followed, the Entente's military position deteriorated and neutral resistance to economic warfare solidified. The government became progressively less willing to take action that added further strain on the global trading system, such as offending important neutral trading partners, upon which the British fiscal and productive war effort depended.

Faced with executive gridlock over its original strategy of economic coercion, the British government improvised. The objective was progressively downgraded from precipitating a total collapse of the German economy to mere trade restriction—and loose restriction at that. By the end of 1914, the last vestiges of economic warfare had been abandoned in favor of what was termed the "blockade," an entirely distinct strategy of economic coercion whose methods, goals, and underlying assumptions differed fundamentally from those of economic warfare. Though technically incorrect (the word had specific legal meaning), "blockade" came to be employed as a convenient term for all the measures taken during the war to exert economic pressure on Germany.

This new strategic approach quickly proved ineffectual, however. During 1915, the transoceanic flow of food and raw materials to Germany—carried in British ships and financed by British banks—grew steadily. The result was bitter political and bureaucratic infighting over the aims, functioning, and control of the blockade. In early 1916, the government created a new department of state, the Ministry of Blockade, and accorded it the power to resolve such quarrels. At the same time the British war cabinet adopted drastic new measures that addressed the strategic requirements of a protracted conflict. These included a reinvigorated blockade, military conscription, and the partial liquidation of accumulated British wealth through sequestration and the sale of privately owned overseas assets.

The narrative outlined above is uncharted territory bordering on several fields. More even than a new perspective from which to view an old story, the tale of economic warfare here told mandates a wholesale reconsideration of British prewar planning, the reaction of the government to the financial and economic crises that accompanied the diplomatic crisis of July 1914, and the strategy adhered to during the critical first six months of hostilities—issues of central importance to the history of the war. This study not only demonstrates how earlier interpretations have subjected the complexities of economic, diplomatic, administrative, and political events to a reductionist narrative of military activity but also represents the first attempt to explain Britain's strategy from exhaustive research in naval, military, diplomatic, economic, and above all political documentation. It also casts new light on Britain's reasons for entering the war, the type of war her leaders expected to fight, the imperatives behind the various strategies they formulated, and the increasing difficulties faced by the government in implementing these as diplomatic and domestic political complications multiplied over time.

It offers a new interpretation of the relationship between the British state and society, showing how prewar planning for economic warfare necessarily entailed (and paved the way for broad political acceptance of) unprecedented state intervention into economic and social life, and how prosecution of the successor blockade policy impelled the government to develop more robust means for gathering information on the internal workings of both national and international economies. Finally, it reveals serious shortcomings in the current interpretation of Anglo-American relations between 1914 and 1916 that should compel scholars to reassess Woodrow Wilson's diplomacy. In the conclusions we will return to consider how proper understanding of prewar plans for economic warfare affects how we see Britain's entry into the war and selection of strategy.

The History of History

Readers may be forgiven for asking how this story, so critical and so dissonant with the commonly held version of events, has escaped detection for near a century. The answer—or at least a partial answer—has to do with government manipulation of the historical record. The controversy surrounding the implementation of blockade policy during the war, as well as continuing sensitivity during the interwar period, led to stringent censorship and a nearly impenetrable shroud of secrecy. Yet this oblivion was not inevitable; government officials initially wanted a much different outcome.

Early in the war the British government made preparations to write comprehensive histories of the conflict. Senior politicians recognized the demand and even the advantage of producing works for public consumption. On 28 June 1916, Prime Minister H. H. Asquith announced to the House of Commons the government's intention to publish the first volumes of "official" history "as soon as possible after the close of the War."[9] These, he went on to explain, would be prepared under the direction of the Historical Section of the Committee of Imperial Defence. He further revealed that the work had been subdivided into three areas: military operations, naval operations, and the blockade. Already two prominent historians had been selected: Sir John Fortescue (1859–1933), widely respected for his monumental history of the British Army, and Julian Corbett (1854–1922), the leading naval historian of the day.[10] Allocation of responsibility for the third portion, "The General Effects of the War on Sea-borne Trade," was less easy to understand. It had been entrusted to the Garton Foundation, a private body founded in 1912 by the industrialist and sugar magnate Sir Richard Garton; the foundation sponsored studies in "the science of international politics" and was best known for its prewar promotion of Norman Angell's pacifistic credo.[11] The prime minister offered no explanation for this unusual—even outlandish—choice, which has gone unremarked upon by historians.

The moving force behind the Garton Foundation was Lord Esher (1852–1930), a curious apolitical figure with a keen interest and considerable influence in prewar defense matters.[12] Since 1905, Esher had been a permanent member of the CID, the forum chaired by the prime minister that brought together senior politicians with admirals and generals to discuss defense policies. Esher held strong views on the importance and utility of reliable official histories and had been chiefly responsible for the creation of the Historical Section within the CID in 1906.[13] Before the war he had also been involved in the framing of government policy toward economic warfare. Another trustee of the Garton Foundation was Arthur James Balfour, the former prime minister (1901–1905) who had been responsible for establishing the CID.[14] In 1916, Balfour, now First Lord of the Admiralty in the coalition government and thus intimately involved in the carrying out of blockade policy, took a keen interest in the production of an official history of the blockade.

In fact, all government departments with a role in administering blockade policy regarded the selection of the official historian as a matter of considerable importance, a fact reflected by the number of minutes written on this seemingly trivial subject by cabinet ministers. There was no shortage of eligible candidates for the job, as the main departments all possessed a stable of thoroughbred academic historians by this stage of the war. In November 1916, Lord Robert Cecil insisted that as minister of blockade, he held responsibility for selection of the official historian of the blockade—and he duly appointed his own department's candidate to author "The Economic Effect of the Naval Operations for the Attack and Defence of Trade."[15]

Henry W. Carless Davis (1874–1928) was a scholar of high standing who before the war had taught medieval history at Balliol College, Oxford. At the beginning of the war he had edited a number of pamphlets for public consumption describing the opening military operations. At the end of 1914, he was recruited to the trade intelligence section of the Postal Censorship Department. In stages this body metamorphosed into the War Trade Intelligence Department, and in 1916 it was subsumed into the newly formed Ministry of Blockade. By this date, Carless Davis had demonstrated a capacity for marshaling enormous quantities of information and so was elevated to become vice chairman of the department. He sat on various high-level interdepartmental committees and produced briefing papers for the war cabinet. It is a measure of his administrative competence that several times after the war he was offered the chance to remain in government, for instance as director of the joint Foreign Office–Board of Trade Department of Overseas Trade. Carless Davis declined these opportunities and in April 1919 returned to Balliol. He was appointed editor of the *Dictionary of National Biography* and six years later became Regius Professor of Modern History at Oxford University.[16]

Carless Davis never finished the official history he began during the war.[17] His personal papers yield no clues as to why he abandoned the project, but it seems likely he fell victim to the government's change of heart toward official histories.[18] Since the announcement of the official history projects in 1916, the editors of the official histories had become subject to steadily closer official supervision and scrutiny.[19] After the war, politicians, generals, and admirals became nervous at what the historians were writing about them and demanded to see the manuscripts before they were set in type. Winston Churchill was particularly obstreperous in complaining that Julian Corbett's first volume on naval operations misrepresented certain decisions he had taken at the beginning of the war (when Churchill had been in charge at the Admiralty) and unfairly tainted his reputation.[20]

In October 1919, Fortescue, the army historian, was dismissed after writing a scathing review of the recently published apologia by Field Marshal Sir John French, who had commanded the army in France during the first year of the war. Fortescue was replaced by a retired army officer, Brigadier James E. Edmonds, who before the war had published a book on the American Civil War.[21] Apprehensive both of further public controversy and of internal acrimony, the cabinet directed the following month that work on the official histories be suspended pending review by a cabinet committee. Production resumed six months later, but the cabinet warned the historians that their work must adhere to newly established guidelines and that there would be no guarantee of ultimate publication. The various authors reacted angrily to these shackles.[22] It was an unlikely coincidence, then, that shortly thereafter relations between the government and the Garton Foundation (and Carless Davis) were severed, though it is unclear which party took the initiative in bringing the blockade history project to an end.

Nevertheless, in June 1920 Carless Davis assembled the notes he had already taken to produce a slim volume entitled *History of the Blockade: Emergency Departments.* As the title implies (and as explained in the preface), its focus was narrow, dealing almost entirely with the "evolution" of the administrative system put into place during the war "either to put the policy of the Blockade into execution or to assist His Majesty's Government in elaborating the details of that policy."[23] Carless Davis made no attempt to define blockade policy, though his account contained hints of the embarrassing intragovernmental friction that had attended its wartime formulation and execution. In March 1921, 250 copies were printed and then promptly classified. Although attempts were repeatedly made to have this stricture lifted, they remained classified until 1959.[24] In his preface, Carless Davis noted that several departments of government had furnished him with copies of their own (semiofficial) internal histories of the blockade.[25] For instance, the Admiralty had commissioned William E. Arnold Forster (1886–1951), who had served for most of the war as deputy naval liaison to the Foreign Office, to produce "The Economic Blockade, 1914–1919."[26] These too were all immediately classified.

In the aftermath, the CID Historical Section hoped that the history of the blockade might be incorporated into Julian Corbett's series on naval operations, or possibly into the newly commissioned series on Seaborne Trade edited by Charles Ernest Fayle (Norman Angell's former private secretary).[27] But this was quickly found to be impracticable.[28] Indeed, the Admiralty became ever more hostile to Corbett and his "official" history, holding up the printing of his third volume for almost a year. The Admiralty, or more specifically Admiral David Beatty, the then First Sea Lord, objected to Corbett's account of the Battle of Jutland, and shamelessly pressured the author to produce a narrative better calculated to quash growing public criticism of his own performance during that action.[29] Corbett died in 1922, leaving the dispute still unresolved. In 1923, the volume was posthumously published after the CID Historical Section agreed to insert a preface stating not merely that the Lords Commissioners of the Admiralty disclaimed responsibility for the views expressed within but also that they actively disputed Corbett's interpretations and conclusions!

After some delay, editorship of the naval histories passed controversially to Sir Henry Newbolt (1862–1938), a former lawyer and novelist better known for his patriotic poetry than for his scholarship.[30] In 1926, Newbolt circulated a draft of the fourth official volume, for the first time incorporating a lengthy section on wartime blockade policy. At the Admiralty, the manuscript was handed for comment to Rear-Admiral Alan Hotham, then director of naval intelligence, who at the end of the war had been in charge of the Naval Staff division responsible for blockade matters. Hotham decried the narrative as perniciously superficial, "really an apologia for the policy of the Foreign Office before and during the war," and likely to "prejudice the exercise of our maritime rights in the future." He strenuously urged the Admiralty to insist that all references to the blockade be expunged.

> The whole question of our blockade policy is very controversial and it seems fundamentally wrong that a history given the use of Admiralty confidential documents and partly financed from the Naval Staff Vote should become a vehicle of propaganda for a policy not only opposed to the full exercise of our maritime rights but running directly counter to the views expressed in 1918 by the Admiralty and HM government.[31]

Hotham received the backing of Oswyn Murray, the Admiralty permanent secretary, and also of Vice-Admiral Sir Frederick Field, the deputy chief of the Naval Staff. Sir Maurice Hankey, secretary to the Cabinet Office and the CID, agreed "the less said the better" about the blockade and supported the Admiralty against the author and the Foreign Office in insisting that the chapters be deleted.[32]

Throughout the 1920s and into the 1930s, discussion of wartime blockade policy remained subject to tight censorship. Cabinet ministers and senior civil servants (such as Hankey) wishing to publish their wartime memoirs were actively enjoined to make no more than passing reference to the subject.[33] Winston Churchill's acclaimed multivolume history of the war, *The World Crisis,* first published in 1923 and purporting to be a full record of his term as First Lord of the Admiralty, made no reference either to the Admiralty's prewar sponsorship of economic warfare or to the ensuing CID and cabinet discussions of the subject in the context of national strategy formulation.[34]

Chronicles by other senior government leaders are similarly uninformative.[35] Hankey's own, which said much more on the subject, remained classified until well after the Second World War. One book, however, somehow slipped through the censorship net.[36] In 1923 Captain Montagu Consett, who during the war had served as British naval attaché to the Scandinavian capitals (and regional head of the intelligence services), created a minor political storm by claiming that for a long time the blockade had proved largely ineffectual owing to Foreign Office interference. Even more explosively, he disclosed that the British government had turned a blind eye to ongoing indirect trade between Britain and Germany. Questions were asked in Parliament and attempts were made to launch official enquiries, but the government eventually agreed that it was best to let sleeping dogs lie.[37]

Beginning in the late 1920s, the march of events caused a revival of official interest in the history of the blockade. Encouraged especially by Hankey, various government committees engaged in formulating contingency preparations for war again looked at a strategy of economic coercion as Britain's best means of offense against Germany and other potential enemies.[38] The strategy was presented as a cheap option, both financially and especially in human terms, that might deliver victory without (much) death. Discussion of economic coercion touched upon several more contemporary—not to say inflammatory—postwar issues including the future of the League of Nations, Anglo-American relations, naval disarmament, and the peace movement.

Whenever debate turned to Britain's experience during the late war, however, heated interdepartmental quarrelling invariably ensued.

In March 1931, the Foreign Office urged the CID to recommence the production of an official history of the blockade that might be used to educate a new generation of government officials on the extraordinary complexities of the subject.[39] To preempt objections, the Foreign Office declared its willingness to bear the full cost. Suspecting nefarious intent, the naval representative to the CID publications subcommittee spoke out against the proposal. He reminded the assembly that this had been—and remained—a sensitive subject. He insisted that if the project was allowed to proceed, "the record should be an impartial one and that the author should not be entitled to arrive at a conclusion in favour of one view or another." Further, the Admiralty must be allowed to critique the draft manuscript to ensure it was an impartial "record of fact" and not simply another departmental hagiography.[40] The Admiralty's objections were noted, approval granted, and the selection of the editor confirmed. This would be Archibald C. Bell, who had served in the Royal Navy during the war and had assisted Sir Henry Newbolt in preparing the later volumes of the official naval operations history project.

In August 1935, Bell circulated his completed manuscript for comment. The Board of Trade refused to touch it. At the Admiralty it was greeted with suspicion, the permanent secretary insisting it must be carefully scrutinized. There was a difficulty, however, in finding someone qualified to "advise whether it is a fair presentation of the case."[41] More than twenty years had passed since the beginning of the First World War, and much corporate memory had been lost. In a sense, the Admiralty intuitively knew they ought to object but could not remember to what they objected. At first a retired officer was tasked to critique the manuscript, but he proved unequal to the task. After six months, the CID high-handedly informed the Admiralty that they had three more months to submit their written comments before the volume went to press regardless. Hastily, Admiralty officials revisited the manuscript and assembled a list of objections, which was duly forwarded. But for the most part their complaints were superficial, highlighting violations of the authorial guidelines issued more than a decade before.

The Admiralty expressed no objection to the various fundamental flaws therein—for instance, to Bell's erroneous assertions that "economic coercion was a secondary object in our naval war plans" upon outbreak of war or that only a handful of officials had "perceived somewhat vaguely" its importance.[42] Indeed, the official history made no reference at all to the prewar plan for economic warfare based upon detailed study of the workings of the global trading system. Bell implied, rather, that the blockade strategy was the prewar plan and that international law had been the determining factor in its conception. These errors, if errors they were, were of critical importance and slanted the entire analysis of the events that followed. After all, evaluation of success or failure must depend upon the original expectations.

Bell's official history of the blockade ran to more than half a million words. Printed in 1937, it remained a confidential document until 1961. By this time almost no one remained alive who was qualified to identify the serious mistakes in critical assumptions; the exceptions were the octogenarians Lord Hankey and Sir Winston Churchill, both of whom were in poor health and unlikely ever to have read it. With no competing explanation of events, subsequent generations of historians have tended to treat it as the definitive study on the subject—despite the fact that an absence of footnotes and restriction of access to original documents made it impossible to verify Bell's narrative of events or retrace the steps that led him to his conclusions.[43]

Now, with access to the original files, we may discern the extent to which Bell submitted to Foreign Office guidance and recognize that he exaggerated his access to the archives of other departments, representing different perspectives.[44] We may also see how Bell shaped his narrative into a form calculated to show Foreign Office actions in the best possible light by skirting around many controversial events (sometime even omitting whole chunks of policy) and minimizing the significance of certain decisions that reflected poorly upon the judgment of senior diplomats. Yet the most glaring weakness in Bell's analysis should have been apparent from the first day of publication, since his narrative is predicated upon the manifestly implausible assumption that wartime blockade policy was set at the departmental level—primarily by the Foreign Office—rather than by the political leadership (i.e., by the cabinet). In other words, this volume purported to be a history of blockade policy—minus the political context.

Directly or indirectly, the official history of the blockade has informed every subsequent account of the subject. Over the years various scholars have identified shortcomings in the official histories (Liddell Hart once quipped they were official but not history) and voiced doubts as to the impartiality of the authors.[45] In the case of Bell's work, though historians have found documents in the archives causing them to query aspects of his story, no scholar has ever challenged its essential validity. The fact remains that to date none of the core histories of the First World War mention the distinction between the strategies of economic warfare and blockade; none have identified economic warfare as the foundation of Admiralty strategy or indeed of its centrality to national strategy in 1914; above all, none have discerned that it was conceived and understood in the context of a short, decisive war.[46]

Then again, few histories of the war devote more than a paragraph or two to the British campaign of economic coercion.[47] As compared with the fighting on the Western Front, the war at sea is widely held to have been of secondary importance, a view buttressed by the conviction that economic pressure could be no substitute for military action.[48] Even naval histories treat the blockade as a secondary and almost exogenous factor in the war at sea, giving readers the impression that it ran continuously (and successfully) throughout the war with minimal input from either the naval command or higher political authority.[49] Such episodic accounts have left readers with a false understanding of what the Royal Navy did during the First World War. Even in the best recent work, discussion of blockade remains cursory, based upon unexamined assumptions and reductionist analysis.[50]

In trying to evaluate the relative importance of the blockade in the eventual Allied victory, moreover, scholars have failed to grasp the sheer magnitude of the enterprise.[51] In effect, the British state sought to monitor and regulate the flow of trade between continental Europe and the rest of the world at the micro level (i.e., down to the level of individual suppliers and consumers). The amount of information required for such an undertaking was staggering—and the objective quickly was found to be too complex an information management task. Throughout the war, certainly until late 1916, the information and statistics available to policy makers were totally inadequate—subjective, error-ridden, and too often massaged for political purposes. The point, as will be shown, is that no one in the government, not even cabinet ministers, possessed more than the haziest picture upon which to make decisions concerning blockade policy. Given these misunderstandings and the unreliability of contemporary statistics, scholarly attempts to measure the efficacy of the blockade are surely akin to making bricks without straw.

In berating Britain's leaders in the world war for grasping the "glittering sword of Continental manufacture" instead of reaching for the traditional British cutlass, Liddell Hart ignored evidence that the blockade strategy had always proved a crude and cumbersome weapon, and that by 1914 it was suspected of brittleness and of having become blunted with age.[52] His remarks, in consequence, lost much of their force. What he did not realize, however, was that in 1914 there had lain in the British armory another blade, newly forged, masterfully tempered, and believed lethal. Its name was economic warfare. When Liddell Hart first voiced his thoughts, in 1931, there was a handful of men still alive who knew of this fearsome weapon and the story of how, on the outbreak of war, the decision had been taken to set it aside. Some may have whispered of it, but none dared utter its name. Years passed, more died, and it became a myth. After thirty more years (and another world war) its very existence had slipped into oblivion.[53] This is its story.

THE PRE-WAR
1901–1914

I

The Emergence of Economic Warfare

> The unmolested course of commerce, reacting upon itself, has contributed to its own rapid development, a result furthered by the prevalence of a purely economical conception of national greatness during the larger part of the century. This, with the vast increase in rapidity of communications, has multiplied and strengthened the bonds knitting the interests of nations to one another, till the whole now forms an articulated system, not only of prodigious size and activity, but of an excessive sensitiveness, unequalled in former ages. . . . The preservation of commercial and financial interests constitutes now a political consideration of the first importance, making for peace and deterring from war.
>
> ALFRED THAYER MAHAN, July 1902

On 24 March 1873, George Goschen, the First Lord of the Admiralty, delivered a speech to the House of Commons in which he likened "our naval expenditure" to a "national premium of insurance—words which must be taken to imply insurance against hostile attack; in fact, the insurance of our power and prosperity."[1] Possession of the largest and most powerful navy in the world not only guaranteed that the British Isles would be safe from invasion, but also safeguarded the nation's commercial prosperity, upon which her economic strength and therefore world political status depended.[2] The analogy was apt and easy to grasp: all businessmen understood the necessity of insurance.

In March 1876, Captain George Price, a backbench Member of Parliament representing the naval town of Devonport, articulated this interconnection yet more explicitly, telling the House that "he regarded the amount of money expended upon the maintenance of the Navy as a premium paid upon the policy of insurance." He went on to censure the government for underinsuring: over the previous fifteen years, whereas naval spending had remained static, the aggregate tonnage of vessels entering and clearing British ports had nearly doubled, and the nation's imports and exports had risen from £375 million to £682 million.[3]

> If, therefore, the premium on the policy of insurance was to be based upon the imports and exports, it was clear, comparing the amount of them with the cost of the Navy, that in 1860 it was at the rate of 3½ per cent and that in 1873 it was not more than 1½ per cent.[4]

For at least the next forty years, the perception that naval expenditures were analogous to "insurance" on Britain's maritime interests remained common currency in parliamentary debates.[5]

Between 1870 and the early 1890s the volume of global trade doubled. The increase has been attributed mainly to a spectacular decline in the cost of transporting goods by sea due to advances in marine technologies. Over the next twenty-odd years, freight costs continued to fall; in combination with transformative developments in monetary systems and especially communication technologies, this kindled another doubling of world trade.[6] The result was the emergence of a globally integrated trading system. The most visible manifestation of this transformation of the world economy was the dramatic convergence of global prices for bulk commodities, such as wheat, cotton, and copper.[7] In 1870, for instance, the price of wheat in Liverpool exceeded Chicago prices by 57.6 percent, in 1895 by 17.8 percent, and in 1913 by just 15.6 percent.[8]

During this forty-year period, furthermore, Great Britain became ever more dependent upon foreign trade and the maintenance of a thriving global trading system for its national well-being.[9] It is difficult to quantify by precisely how much. Between 1875 and 1914, the ratio of British exports (by value) to gross domestic product (GDP) increased from 28.3 percent to 32.4 percent.[10] But these figures relate to values, and at the beginning of this period especially, prices fell steadily, thereby masking the growth in volume of trade. The expansion of trade led to the increasing exposure of regional and national markets to world competition, a development that affected almost every aspect of economic, social, and political life.[11] As one economic historian put it:

> A bigger proportion of the fundamental necessities of life and industrial livelihood was brought from abroad; a wider range of the commodities

> produced at home incorporated directly or indirectly, a certain amount of irreplaceable imports; and the communities of more and more localities found in their midst some export industry whose fortunes appreciably affected the amount of their sales and incomes.[12]

By the 1890s such commentators as Ivan Bloch began discussing the new phenomenon of "economic interdependence" and considering its strategic implications.

For most of the nineteenth century, Britain was consistently responsible for a fifth (at times perhaps more than a quarter) of all international trade. As late as 1880, its output of coal, pig iron, and crude steel was more than twice that of any rival Continental power, and the nation imported more primary commodities than the other European countries combined. However, Britain's economic lead was steadily and substantially reduced as the other European powers (especially Germany) and the United States industrialized. By 1890, Britain's share of global trade had slipped to 18 percent, and by 1914 to 14 percent, with the trend heading inexorably downward.[13] This eclipse was even more pronounced in industrial production. Whereas in 1899, Great Britain produced 20.8 percent of world manufactured output and her share of world manufactured exports was 38.3 percent, by 1914, these numbers had fallen to 15.8 percent and 31.8 percent, respectively.[14]

Historians have employed figures such as these to explain Great Britain's fall from the ranks of the great powers. Perhaps most eloquently, Paul Kennedy traced "the root of Britain's long-term decline" to the last quarter of the nineteenth century, arguing that her "position as an *industrial* power of the first order—indeed in a class of its own—shrank rapidly in the final three decades of the nineteenth century as other nations overtook her in many basic fields of industry and technology, which are after all the foundations of modern military strength."[15] In consequence, the argument follows, "Britain's naval power, rooted in her economic strength, would no longer remain supreme, since other nations with greater resources and manpower were rapidly overhauling her previous industrial lead."[16]

Kennedy's analysis acknowledged but attached little importance to London's position as the financial capital of the world (the world's bank, the world's clearinghouse, the world's greatest stock exchange, the only free market for gold, the chief source of money and credit to facilitate international exchange, and the hub of the global communications network). Financial strength, he insisted, was no compensation for relative industrial decline, and indeed it was likely the source of even greater vulnerability.[17] "The springs of wealth from financial income were less secure, less resilient, more subject to disturbance under the stress of political insecurity abroad or the shock of war than the solid indigenous strength of an efficient system of production and trade."[18]

Accordingly, British foreign and defense policy sprang from weakness: relative industrial decline obliged British policy makers to meet the growing rivalry of a hostile Germany by recutting the strategic coat to fit the available imperial cloth.[19]

Other scholars, however, view the so-called decline thesis as overly deterministic and maintain that Britain's relative "weakness" before 1914 has been "greatly exaggerated."[20] They point out that on the eve of war Britain was still "the *pre-eminent* great power" and her global naval supremacy mostly intact. British industry still led the world in advanced maritime technologies.[21] No insoluble economic, financial, technological, or political obstacles yet existed to the maintenance of a supreme war fleet. In short, relative industrial decline did not automatically equate to technological backwardness or economic decrepitude, nor did it necessarily translate into strategic vulnerability. One recent scholar, Niall Ferguson, has insisted that the general "model of the relationship between economics and power" employed by students of the decline thesis is "deeply flawed." He accuses adherents of misunderstanding how the pre-1914 global economy actually functioned and thereby miscalculating Britain's relative economic strength. Ferguson insists that although undeniably Great Britain was no longer the industrial "workshop of the world" on the eve of the First World War, "in reality the most important factor in early twentieth-century world politics was not the growth of German economic power at all. Rather it was the immense extent of British *financial* power."[22] In short, he argues that it is a mistake to treat finance merely as a subset of economics. Measured by overseas assets, estimates of British financial power and wealth on the eve of the First World War ranged from £3 billion to £5 billion, sums comfortably in excess of annual GDP. It is regrettable that Ferguson did not articulate how this financial power translated into strategic power. But this shortcoming does not necessarily invalidate the basic thrust of his criticisms.

For the purposes of this story, we need not attempt to resolve many of the questions surrounding Great Britain's decline. Whether, in fact, the roots of Britain's decline as a world power reach back to the nineteenth century or whether the First World War either changed the terms of or accelerated the pace of Britain's relative decline are questions not directly germane to the present work. The focus of our interest is upon Britain's domination, before the war, of the industries that were the infrastructure of international exchange.[23]

In 1914, more than half the world's oceangoing steam merchant fleet flew the British red ensign. Additionally, British-registered vessels were generally larger, faster, and more modern than those of its foreign rivals. The building capacity of British merchant yards exceeded that of all other powers in the world combined. It has been estimated that British earnings from the "foreign carrying trade" accounted for about half the "invisible" earnings so vital to covering the chronic shortfall in the balance of trade.[24] At the beginning of the twentieth century, excluding property income from abroad, roughly 20 percent of "export" income was derived from invisible earnings.[25]

Britain accrued additional benefits from possession of the world's largest merchant fleet. Lloyd's of London dominated the maritime insurance industry; the "Baltic Exchange" remained the principal forum for negotiating freight forwarding contracts. In addition, Sterling remained the preferred currency of international exchange as well as the world's reserve currency, accounting for 40 percent of the world's exchange reserves.[26] More than half of global seaborne commerce was transacted through financial institutions based in London, denominated in sterling and financed by British banks. No less important, British firms controlled roughly 70 percent of the world's cable communication network, critical not just in linking vendors with their overseas customers, but also in negotiating and completing transactions.[27] Put simply, Britain reaped enormous invisible benefits from increased foreign participation in international trade. The efficient functioning of the global trading system (and a high level of trade) was critical to the British Empire's prosperity and strength.[28] This said, while the effects of industrialization upon the structure of trade have been well noted, the strategic implications of British control over the infrastructure of international trade have been scarcely explored.

Before the early 1880s, few seriously suggested that Britain's growing dependence upon a thriving system of international trade might prove the source of strategic weakness, simply because there was then no other power capable of threatening its international position.[29] Thenceforward, however, right up until the outbreak of the First World War, this concern became a major factor in British politics. The first to speculate publicly that here lay Britannia's

Achilles' heel was a group of French naval officers, journalists, and politicians known as the *jeune école*.[30] Recognizing the fiscal impossibility of the French Third Republic building a fleet numerically strong enough to challenge Britain's, the *jeune école* advocated an "asymmetrical" approach to the application of naval power. In terms of force structure, this translated into a call for a cessation in battleship construction in favor of building a multiplicity of fast cruisers and small and inexpensive torpedo boats. *Jeune école* theory called for warships to evade combat with the Royal Navy and instead attack Britain's merchant marine. The expectation was not to cut off Britain from her overseas markets and sources of supply, but rather to create a panic in the maritime insurance markets sufficient to paralyze a large proportion of British commercial traffic. For the *jeune école,* ravaging British overseas commerce (in defiance of international law) was an effective means to the end of convincing British merchants that pursuing the conflict would lead to their financial ruin and that they should therefore pressure their government to sue for peace. This went beyond the traditional *guerre de course*—commerce destruction—in that the objective was to attack the underpinnings of the enemy's financial commercial system. This was a novel and very important strategic idea, though few contemporaries (if any) yet understood or recognized the implications.

Beginning in the mid-1890s, given the development of submarines and especially cruisers with side armor impervious to shell thrown by the guns mounted by most British cruisers, Britain's naval leaders began to take *jeune école* theory very seriously.[31] Official concern about the implications of this development was heightened in 1897 after the appointment as French minister of marine of Édouard Lockroy, a known adherent to the *jeune école*. Concern became alarm after Lockroy suspended the construction of battleships in favor of more armored cruisers built for commerce raiding, and appointed the brilliant albeit controversial Admiral François Fournier, a leading *jeune école* theorist, to a senior fleet command.[32] Back in London, the First Lord of the Admiralty outlined his reading of French intent in a paper asking the cabinet to approve a jump in the naval estimates:

> The French, so far as their policy can be gauged, have begun to recognize that it is by cruisers rather then battleships that they can damage us most. What their efforts on battleships have been has been seen from the facts which I have described, but in the new and vast programme which is now awaiting the sanction of the Chamber there is only one

> new battleship to be laid down in 1898. Their first-class cruiser programme, on the other hand, is most formidable.[33]

The British countered with a large cruiser program of their own, seeking to build two to every one laid down by the French and Russian navies. The expense thus entailed was astronomical; armored cruisers were only slightly less expensive to build than battleships yet were far more expensive to maintain in full commission because they required larger crews. In fact, far more than the money, the Admiralty struggled to find sufficient trained manpower. By 1900, British naval expenditures were spiraling out of control and the cost of maintaining Britain's global naval supremacy was approaching the outer limits of what the state could afford.

The above-described change in French naval policy coincided with heightened public concern at Britain's vulnerability to serious dislocation of the global trading system. The nation's increasing reliance upon foreign supplies, especially food, had given rise (rightly or wrongly) to public apprehensions that supply might be interrupted in time of war and that a large section of the population might thus be reduced to want.[34] For most of the mid-nineteenth century Britain had imported about 25 percent of her wheat requirements. But during the final quarter century, home production fell steadily and imports rose. In the 1890s alone, imports, chiefly from North America, nearly doubled, to 3.6 million tons.[35] By the turn of the century, no less than 80 percent of Britain's wheat requirement came from abroad. Furthermore, most was now being ordered "just in time": the nation did not keep significant stocks, and therefore the timely arrival of cargoes with the population's daily bread was a matter of vital necessity.[36] It was no less vital to guard Britain's other trading interests, which crisscrossed the globe. Julian Corbett, the naval theorist, worried that,

> owing to certain well known economic changes, it is far more a matter of life and death to the nation than in the days when food and raw material did not constitute the bulk of our imports. In view of the new conditions it is held that we are more vulnerable through our trade now than formerly, and that, consequently, we must devote relatively more attention and force to its defence.[37]

In short, British well-being depended upon its commerce and transportation being able to move without serious hindrance; any serious disruption to the vast and varied flow of international commerce in any geographical region was predicted to have very serious economic repercussions.[38]

Since the 1880s, the British press and public increasingly questioned the Royal Navy's ability to keep trade losses to manageable proportions.[39] In recent years Great Britain had built relatively few new warships, while Continental powers such as France and Italy had made considerable additions to their fleets. Major war scares in 1884 and 1885 incited public clamor for naval expansion, but the government's response had been equivocal. Small increases in naval expenditures during these two years (financed by borrowing) were followed in the next two years by cuts. Shipowners, meanwhile, called for the state to intervene directly in the underwriting business to guarantee ships and cargoes against war risks. Other concerned citizens proposed that the government should establish state granaries to guarantee food supply. None of these proposals found official favor, mainly because the leaders of both political parties saw the raising of taxes necessary to pay for such programs as a sure path to electoral defeat. In early 1888, however, a war scare with France again led to clamor for naval expansion, which the following year produced more lasting results. While the reasons for this result were complex and varied, the most important were financial and political: George Goschen, then chancellor of the exchequer, had just put through a conversion scheme that substantially reduced the cost of servicing the national debt, allowing the government to raise naval expenditures without recourse to politically unpopular increases in taxation.[40]

Concern that the Royal Navy might not be strong enough to protect British trade was the principal justification for the government in 1889 voting a huge increase in naval expenditures, with a further large rise four years later. Under the 1889 Naval Defence Act, Parliament signaled British determination to maintain a "two-power standard"—committing itself to maintain a battle fleet at least equal in strength to that of the second- and third-ranking naval powers combined. Between 1889 and 1900, effective spending on the Royal Navy more than doubled, from £15.5 million to £33.2 million.[41]

Responsibility for the Royal Navy and advising the British government on the protection of British maritime interests fell to the Right Honourable the Lords Commissioners for Executing the Office of Lord High Admiral of Great Britain, more commonly known as the Board of Admiralty. At their head sat the First Lord. This position was a ministerial portfolio carrying senior rank in the Cabinet of Ministers, the political executive, and throughout this period it was held by a civilian. He was supported by one or more junior Members of Parliament, known as civil lords or by the title of their positions such as parliamentary secretary. The professional naval members of the board were known as sea or naval lords. These were normally four in number. The First Sea Lord always held the rank of full admiral. Although it was the First Lord of the Admiralty who was accountable to Parliament for the Royal Navy and thus the man who held ultimate authority, the others were not his assistants. Power to take decisions was vested in the Board: without the support of the naval lords the civilian head could not act. Quorum for a Board was at least two lords commissioners plus a secretary. There were two secretaries: the head of the civil service department, normally a civilian, and the naval secretary to the First Lord, always a professional naval officer (usually a post-captain). Though technically not a member of the Board, the director of the Admiralty's newly established Naval Intelligence Department a position equivalent to chief of staff to the First Sea Lord, possessed considerable influence in the formulation of strategic policy largely through his control of the information apparatus within the naval bureaucracy.[42]

How to protect the global trading system from serious disruption in time of war was a perennial headache for Britain's naval leadership, which was constantly queried on the subject by political and commercial interests desperate to quantify the probability of commercial losses. Naval historians have portrayed the Admiralty as confused and even complacent on the issue of trade protection. The validity of this assessment may be debated, but there is no doubt that the Victorian Royal Navy's preparations remained substantially incomplete.[43] Part of the problem was that professional opinion was divided on the subject, and the naval leadership was unwilling to air internal disagreements. Testifying before a House of Commons select committee in 1889, the First Sea Lord's blithe assurances that there was nothing to worry about failed to sway an audience convinced that he was in fact resigned to heavy commercial losses. Nor did it help that many senior naval officers saw the attack and defense of trade as an issue of secondary importance, one that ran counter to basic tenets of the navalist philosophy—a distraction, almost, to battle fleet action and achieving "command of the sea."[44] Rear-Admiral Sir Reginald Custance, director of naval intelligence (DNI) from 1899 to 1902, held it was not the navy's job "to defend anything." In 1902, this extremest view was endorsed by the First Lord of the Admiralty, the Earl of Selborne, and incorporated in a published state paper. Custance's successor, Captain Prince Louis of Battenberg (DNI, 1902–1905), was more moderate. Testifying before the Royal Commission on Supply of Food and Raw Material in Time of War in 1903, he admitted under cross-examination that Admiralty assessments of the likely damage a determined enemy could inflict upon British trade were mostly guesswork. "I am inclined to adhere to the views I expressed, but I quite admit all this is vague," he frankly stated.[45]

Internal controversy aside, the government's expectation that the Royal Navy would protect merchantmen meant that the Admiralty could not ignore the problem of trade protection. The lesson was driven home by the clamour arising from the 1898 Fashoda Crisis, when the mere prospect of war with France was sufficient to send maritime insurance rates skyrocketing. The shipping world widely anticipated that British merchantmen would be forced to avoid the Mediterranean in the event of an Anglo-French war, and it was predicted that insurance rates would rise to 18.5 percent.[46] At the end of 1901, the Admiralty finally bowed to demands to prepare a comprehensive scheme for trade defense. Captain Edward Inglefield was assigned to flesh out details of the best recent plan, which had been sketched out some years before but gathering dust ever since. The task was expected to take six months. Inglefield rapidly discovered, however, that the subject was much more complicated than his superiors had imagined, and many of the assumptions underpinning the old Admiralty plan had been based largely upon conjecture.

In reviewing the available data, Inglefield also uncovered serious weaknesses in the official trade statistics provided by the Board of Trade statistical bureau. (Inaccuracies in government economic statistics will be a recurring theme in this study.)[47] Several key questions could not be even attempted because the requisite data simply did not exist. For instance, how much wheat was stored in the country on any particular day? "As far as is known here," the DNI wrote to the prime minister, "nothing approaching accurate figures have ever been produced by any responsible authority. Such knowledge would be of the greatest value to the Admiralty, and to the government as a whole."[48] In July 1902, having barely scratched the surface of the subject, Inglefield's appointment to the Naval Intelligence Division (NID) was made permanent; he was elevated to the status of assistant director of naval intelligence, made head of the newly formed Trade Division, and given additional staff to assist him in his research. Over the next several years, Inglefield scoured London for information on the workings of the global trading system, in the process forging links between the Admiralty and various private maritime concerns. Indeed, he became such an expert on the subject that he later resigned from the Navy to become second secretary (chief executive officer) of Lloyd's.

Inglefield's studies laid the foundation for the notion that in time of war Great Britain might not be uniquely vulnerable to economic dislocation. In recent years, the German economy too had become substantially dependent upon international trade.[49] The lack of surviving evidence makes it difficult to gauge when, precisely, Inglefield first made this connection or just what impression it made on senior naval leaders. The indications are that the Admiralty did not immediately recognize the implications of this possibility and gave him no encouragement to pursue this line of enquiry. There was no discernible change in naval policy or attitudes. But then again, it must remembered that during this period the Admiralty's chief concern was not a war against Germany but rather one versus France and Russia, empires that were much less vulnerable to economic coercion. Inglefield's idea nevertheless took root in minds of several up-and-coming officers then serving in the NID.[50] There were also several others, not then at the Admiralty, thinking along similar lines.

Admiral Fisher and the Kaleidoscopic Strategic Geography of 1904–1905

The appointment of Admiral Sir John Fisher as First Sea Lord in October 1904 has long been recognized by historians as a watershed in the history of the Royal Navy. Until recently, however, the circumstances surrounding his selection as well as the precise nature of the ensuing so-called Fisher Revolution have been seriously misunderstood. Jacky Fisher joined the Royal Navy in 1854. He saw an unusual amount of active service, seeing combat in the Crimean War (1854–1856), the Second China War (1856–1860), and the Anglo-Egyptian War (1882); in the last, until invalided home, he served with distinction (and gained public fame) commanding the naval brigade operating on shore. Between 1885 and 1897, Fisher was given a succession of shore assignments in which he demonstrated his superlative talent and imagination for naval administration. The culmination was his appointment, in 1892, to the Board of Admiralty as controller (Third Sea Lord) responsible for the development and procurement of all naval matériel, a post he held for the unusually long period of six years. Even as a junior flag officer, it should be noted, Fisher's reputation extended beyond the Royal Navy. He maintained unusually close relationships with captains of industry, bankers, and leading politicians. Various private corporations tried to entice him from the service to take a senior management position in their organization. Among the most persistent was Lord Rothschild, the banker, who wanted Fisher to oversee his firm's substantial investments in various armaments companies.

Fisher remained controller of the Navy until 1897, whereupon, after being promoted to vice-admiral, he was given the sinecure of command of the North America and West Indies Squadron. This appeared to spell the end of his career. Then in March 1899, out of the blue, the prime minister handpicked Fisher to serve as British representative to the First International Peace Conference at The Hague. It was simultaneously announced that he would take command of the Mediterranean Fleet, the Royal Navy's premier fighting fleet.[51] At the conference, Fisher probably met Ivan Bloch, the aforementioned Polish banker whose study of modern industrial war led him to predict that any future war between the great powers must be characterized by severe economic and social dislocation as a consequence of the disruption of international trade.[52] Making it even more likely that Fisher was exposed to Bloch's ideas was the fact that several months after the conference Bloch's six-volume work appeared in English, published under the title of *Is War Now Impossible?* by the prominent journalist William T. Stead, a close friend of Fisher's for nearly twenty years.[53] Bloch impressed upon Stead that "every year the interdependence of nations upon each other for the necessities of life is greater than it ever was before."[54] Alas, Bloch's direct influence upon the admiral remains unquantifiable.

Admiral Fisher took command in the Mediterranean in early 1900 and remained there until 1902. At the end of his appointment, Lord Selborne (First Lord of the Admiralty, 1900–1905) appointed him Second Sea Lord specifically to untangle the problem with recruiting and retention of naval personnel. Fisher quickly came to the conclusion that an effective solution required radical reform. Admiral Lord Walter Kerr, the incumbent First Sea Lord (1899–1904), disputed this conclusion; Selborne sided with Kerr, and as a result, Fisher departed the Admiralty (after just a year) to become commander in chief at Portsmouth. Once again his career appeared to be drawing to a close. Shortly thereafter, however, Prime Minister Arthur James Balfour asked Fisher to join the War Office Reconstitution Committee—known as the Esher Committee—set up to reform the Army's administration in the wake of serious shortcomings exposed during the Boer War (1899–1902). Defying the Admiralty's wishes, he accepted. Besides Fisher, there were just two other members of the committee—the chairman, Lord Esher, and Sir George Clarke (a retired colonel of engineers turned colonial administrator, currently serving as governor of Victoria).

The association that Fisher now formed with Lord Esher was crucial. Esher was a rather curious character without political affiliation.[55] Well connected socially, politically, and with the military, he enjoyed considerable influence in defense matters but consistently avoided formal responsibilities. More than once he turned down a seat in the cabinet as secretary of state for war. Esher also played a major role in Balfour's attempts to systematize national defense planning and improve its quality. One of the key recommendations made by the Esher Committee was to create an overarching structure for coordinating departmental defense planning. Theoretically, the existing Defence Committee of the cabinet performed this function, but the Esher Committee advised that its ad hoc approach to problems was dangerously out of date. It also lacked executive authority and thus never could become the instrument of supreme command in time of war. Therefore the Esher Committee recommended reconstituting it under the chairmanship of the prime minister and giving it a permanent secretariat. In May 1904 the Committee of Imperial Defence was established; Sir George Clarke was appointed its first permanent secretary.

At the end of 1905, the prime minister appointed Lord Esher a permanent member of the CID. Between 1906 and 1914, Esher attended practically every meeting of the CID (plus numerous subcommittee meetings), enjoying equal status with the attending cabinet ministers. Successive prime ministers (Balfour, Campbell-Bannerman, and Asquith) solicited his opinion on controversial defense matters, finding that he well enough understood both the technical aspects of particular questions and the likely political ramifications. They also perceived him as willing to offer his thoughts without dissembling.[56]

Fisher's significant contribution to the national defense review process during the winter of 1903–1904, through his membership of the Esher Committee, restored his career fortunes. In May 1904, the darkening national fiscal forecast and growing political pressure upon the Admiralty to achieve savings in naval expenditures (without sacrificing capability or commitments) drove Lord Selborne to accept the need for radical reform. To the surprise of many, he turned to Admiral Sir John Fisher, now 63 years old, offering him the post of First Sea Lord and allowing him to introduce his grand scheme of reform. Selborne did not fully understand what Fisher intended but trusted him to deliver on his boast to cut the financial Gordian knot. The details of Fisher's scheme have been described elsewhere.[57] As for the broader aspects of his vision, historians have long insisted that both Fisher's strategic outlook and his approach to the application of naval power were strictly orthodox. Recent scholarship has demonstrated that nothing could be further from the truth. Fisher's heterodoxy comes across very clearly in his extensive private correspondence with Selborne while serving as commander in chief, Mediterranean. It was during this command, along the central highway of the British Empire (not in the North Sea), that Fisher formed his key strategic views. His letters from this period show that he was alive to the paramount importance of trade to the British Empire and uncommonly interested in the trade defense problem posed by the advent of the armored cruiser.

More than any other senior officer on the flag list, Jacky possessed a broader, better-informed view of the relationship between sea power and the British Empire's commercial lifeblood, along with a much more sophisticated understanding of world economics.[58] Fisher believed that international trade was crucial to the prosperity not just of Great Britain but of all industrial nations and consequently that no modern industrial power could survive for long without access to the global trading system. He understood that the Royal Navy's task in wartime would be not just to protect the national homeland, but also to insulate the economy from the worst effects of war. At the same time, the Royal Navy would be able to exploit a stranglehold over the ocean trade routes to choke an enemy's economy to a point where it would be compelled to sue for peace. Hence his smug proclamation that the Royal Navy held all five keys to lock up the world: Dover, Gibraltar, Suez, the Cape of Good Hope, and Singapore, the key choke points for international trade.[59]

One of the most common misconceptions about Fisher's ideas was that he was fixated upon the threat to the Royal Navy posed by the expansion of the German navy. The enduring perception of an anti-German imperative dominating the formulation of all pre–First World War naval policy remains pervasive.[60] While Fisher certainly recognized the hostile intentions behind the German High Sea Fleet, he did not regard it as a mortal threat to the British Empire (though sometimes he found it politically convenient to say otherwise). He believed that it could be contained within the North Sea by the implementation of a new sea denial strategy, flotilla defense. Relying upon flotillas of torpedo boats and submarines, backed by heavy units of the reserve fleet, to deny European waters to the enemy would allow the Admiralty safely to deploy squadrons of large armored vessels to the outer marches of the empire and secure the trade routes.

In fact, Fisher's long-range plans called for the Royal Navy to discontinue the construction of battleships in favor of a new model of capital ship of his own conception that became known as the battle cruiser. Possessing high speed and long range, in addition to their all-big-gun armament, these warships were far better suited to perform the sort of mission he believed most vital. Throughout his two terms as First Sea Lord (1904–1910 and 1914–1915) Fisher adhered to his controversial ideas on fleet structure, the ideal of a British global supremacy capable of defending interests against all comers, and the necessity of preserving the global trading system. Although he enjoyed mixed results in converting his ideas into policy, thanks largely to internal opposition and changes in technological, domestic political, and diplomatic circumstances, Fisher's underlying strategic vision remained consistent.

Jacky Fisher was fond of boasting that he became First Sea Lord in 1904 on Trafalgar Day, 21 October, the anniversary of Horatio Nelson's greatest victory. By the conventional calendar, he took office on the afternoon of Friday, 20 October.[61] Fisher did not stay long that day, as he was suffering from acute influenza. Because the house that went with his appointment was not ready, he retired to the Charing Cross Hotel, several hundred yards up the road, and remained there in bed for the next two days.[62] Early Sunday morning, 22 October, while Fisher slept, a Russian fleet proceeding through the North Sea blundered into a fleet of British fishing boats. Fearing (they later claimed) that the vessels were Japanese torpedo boats lying in ambush, the Russian warships opened fire, sinking one trawler and killing crewmen on several others. When news of what became known as the Dogger Bank incident reached London on the morning of 23 October, Great Britain stood on the brink of war not only with Russia, but also with France (because of the Franco-Russian alliance) and likely with Germany too. Public opinion was outraged, and the mood of the cabinet was belligerent.[63] Lord Selborne in particular favored war (allegedly being egged on by his DNI, Captain Prince Louis of Battenberg) and pressed for mobilization of the fleet.[64] Belying his firebrand reputation, Fisher urged a less inflammatory response, and ultimately his wishes prevailed.[65] Although the imminence of war quickly subsided, for many months thereafter Anglo-Russian relations continued to smolder and the possibility of conflict remained a worry and a distraction.[66] The Mediterranean Fleet remained on standby to proceed east of Suez, and steam coal was stockpiled at the naval base at Hong Kong.

Once the immediate crisis had passed, the Board of Admiralty turned its attention to evaluating Fisher's proposed scheme of reform. On 21 November 1904, the Board approved the central plank involving the redistribution of the fleet after "taking into consideration the distribution of forces of France, Germany, and Russia."[67] In approving these changes, Lord Selborne, the First Lord of the Admiralty, stressed that "the worst case which can befall us under present conditions is for Germany to throw her weight against us in the middle of a still undecided war between [us and] France and Russia in alliance."[68] A fortnight later, the First Lord explained to the cabinet the strategic rationale behind the proposed changes. In brief, the system of semiautonomous station fleets was to be abolished in favor of centrally located rapid-deployment "flying squadrons" comprised of new-model armored cruisers. The resultant surplus station fleet cruisers and gunboats "too small to fight and too slow to run away" were to be scrapped. The crews released from these old vessels (11,000 men) were to be reemployed as "nucleus crews" for hitherto unmanned warships in the reserve fleet. At a stroke, Fisher had defused the burgeoning personnel crisis, saved millions in maintenance costs, and improved war-fighting capability by enhancing the efficiency of the reserve. In the months that followed, the Admiralty settled upon the design of new-model warships, recast the annual construction program, and redefined their relationship with the armaments industry. At the same time, the groundwork was laid for transforming the Admiralty into a naval command center through heavy investments in new intelligence and communications networks.[69]

The spring of 1905, as is well known, was a time of exceptional diplomatic turmoil and uncertainty. For most historians, especially those engaged on the quest for the origins of the First World War, the most significant strategic development was the prospect of Great Britain becoming embroiled in a war between Germany and France. The story of the First Moroccan Crisis has been told many times before.[70] There is broad consensus that the German government fostered a diplomatic crisis in an effort to shatter the recently negotiated Anglo-French entente. In a move calculated to embarrass the French government while garnering international support, on 31 March 1905 Kaiser Wilhelm II landed in Tangiers to meet with the sultan. He intimated his commitment to Moroccan independence, grumbled that recent French actions had infringed upon German commercial interests in the region, and called for an international conference to discuss the status of Morocco.[71] In aggressively demanding the resignation of the French foreign minister as a precondition to negotiations, however, the German government overreached and induced the British government to offer France diplomatic support under the terms of Article IX of its recently signed entente. In June, after the French government cancelled leave for all military personnel, the fear grew in Britain that Germany and France might come to blows over the Moroccan issue. On 25 June 1905, Admiral Fisher asked the Naval Intelligence Division to prepare a statement "regarding the possibility of manning the existing war fleet in the event of sudden action being necessary in support of France," and also to consider "fleet dispositions in the event of naval action against Germany."[72]

Even as they dealt with possible alliance issues arising from the Moroccan crisis, Admiralty officials still worried about a very different set of alliances arising from the situation in the Far East. There, the Russo-Japanese War was raging, and the operative British alliance was not the 1904 entente with France but the 1902 treaty with Japan. Thus the prospect was not to help France against Germany, as over Morocco, but rather to fight against France (Russia's ally), Russia (Japan's enemy), and possibly Germany as well—precisely the three-power Continental coalition that Lord Selborne had identified as the worst-case scenario when justifying the fleet redistribution scheme in November 1904. In March 1905, Selborne exchanged correspondence with the fleet commander in chief "with regard to the question of our being involved in a war with Germany as well as with France and Russia."[73] The following month the newly appointed DNI, Captain Charles Ottley, implored his superiors to cancel or curtail the upcoming program of fleet maneuvers "in view of the unsettled state of Naval affairs in the Far East" and concern the planned exercises might disrupt fleet readiness.[74] "We have to be prepared," he advised, "for a sharp collision of interests between Great Britain and Japan on the one hand, and the three most powerful European nations on the other." Ottley conceded that conflict seemed unlikely, but given "the highly abnormal and unstable position of our international relationships [t]here never was a time I think when it behooved us to act with greater caution."[75] The Board of Admiralty approved Ottley's suggestion and curtailed the maneuvers. It also incorporated the provision for a war "with Germany, Russia, France, or any combination of these powers" into the new war orders issued several days later (dated 6 May 1905) to the fleet commander in chief.[76]

Given the extreme fluidity of the international situation, Fisher's query of 25 June regarding naval action in support of France against Germany posed a difficult problem for his senior planners. Who were they? As related, Charles Ottley succeeded Prince Louis of Battenberg as DNI in February 1905. He served in this post with distinction for the next two and half years. On 24 August 1907, however, facing mandatory retirement after failing to qualify for promotion to rear admiral, he abruptly resigned from the Navy in order to take up a better-paid position as secretary to the CID.[77] Ottley's failure to gain further advancement was no reflection on his performance; throughout his career he was seen as an officer of exceptional ability. Rather, it was a function of the promotion rules in force at that time, which required naval officers to serve for minimum periods at sea before being raised to the next grade on the active list. Ottley suffered acutely from seasickness; upon being promoted to the rank of captain on 31 January 1899, he resigned command of the sloop HMS *Nymph* (moored at Constantinople as guard ship for the British embassy) the very next day and thereafter declined further sea service.

Ottley's personal financial circumstances would not allow him to sever his connection with the Navy (half pay was just £500 per year), but he was sufficiently well-off (thanks to a good marriage) to volunteer for successive assignments as naval attaché in Washington, Tokyo, Rome, St. Petersburg, and Paris.[78] Another way for a serving officer to remain on the active list (and qualify for promotion) was to be elected to Parliament. In 1903, Ottley was selected as the prospective Conservative candidate for Pembroke Boroughs at the next election. But in May 1904, he relinquished his candidacy to accept the salaried post of assistant (naval) secretary in the newly formed CID secretariat.[79] Captain Ottley discharged his administrative duties so well that he attracted the notice of Admiral Lord Walter Kerr, the current First Sea Lord. Kerr was so impressed with Ottley that the following October he insisted upon his selection as the next DNI, going so far as to amend fleet regulations to achieve this.[80] Considering that Ottley was not scheduled to become DNI until the spring of 1905—well into Sir John Fisher's term as First Sea Lord—this does seem a little curious. Although Fisher and Ottley were both torpedo specialists, they had never before served together and there is no evidence of a prior friendship. It seems unlikely, therefore, that Ottley's appointment was made at Fisher's behest.

As it transpired, however, the tactful and urbane Charles Ottley proved a perfect foil for the sometimes abrasive and volcanic Jacky Fisher, and together they made a formidable administrative team.[81] Very quickly the First Sea Lord began addressing his new DNI in correspondence as "my beloved Ottley." More so than any other officer serving at the Admiralty before the First World War (far more so than Sir John Jellicoe, who is usually seen as Fisher's chief disciple), Ottley's views on strategy mirrored those of Fisher. Throughout his term as DNI (1905–1907) and afterward as secretary to the CID (1907–1912), Ottley wrote enthusiastically and effectively in promoting economic warfare as the cornerstone of British grand strategy. His memoranda on the subject, all beautifully written, as well as his surviving private correspondence show that, like Fisher, he possessed what might be termed a commercialist perspective on global dynamics and the application of naval force.

Probably as the result of his extensive diplomatic experience, Ottley's writings further attest to acute appreciation (exceptionally acute for a naval officer) of the diplomatic and political dimensions of naval policy. His worst shortcoming as a strategic analyst was an "exasperating" reluctance to assert himself or commit to a particular point of view on any controversial subject.[82] It was said he could always see at least two sides to any argument. He was often criticized too for his loquacity—something of a liability in the highly politicized environment he inhabited. As Fisher once complained: "Ottley is very, very clever, and I love him, but he has the *cacoethes loquendi* as well as *scribendi!*"[83] Sir George Clarke (CID secretary from 1904 to 1907) voiced similar criticisms; he acknowledged Ottley's intelligence but thought him "a little flighty" and too unassertive to become secretary of the CID.[84] Ottley nevertheless did succeed Clarke and remained secretary until early 1912, when renewed concern for his personal finances induced him to accept a directorship at the armaments giant Armstrong-Whitworth.[85]

Ottley's principal assistant for strategic planning in 1905 was Captain George Ballard, another important character in our story. Like Ottley, Ballard was a torpedo officer and highly regarded for his intellect and character. He twice (in 1897 and again in 1899) won the Royal United Services Institute gold medal for his essays on strategy.[86] Ottley relied heavily upon Ballard, rating him as "100% the ablest officer of his rank and standing now in the service."[87] Ballard's work also impressed Sir John Fisher—so much so that in early 1907 the First Sea Lord apparently invited him to succeed Ottley as the next DNI. Ballard, however, declined this prestigious appointment, citing concern for his long-term career prospects.[88] Advancement within the service still lay through the fleet, and sea time remained a prerequisite for promotion. So a compromise was devised: Ballard was given successive commands in the reserve fleet at Portsmouth, allowing him to accumulate sea time (his ship firmly anchored), while remaining in close contact with the First Sea Lord in London and available for "special projects." Between January and April 1907, for instance, Ballard chaired a small committee of officers tasked with providing the First Sea Lord with an "independent" appraisal of various naval plans for war against Germany (see below).

After two years in command of a battleship assigned to the Home Fleet, in October 1911 Ballard again was offered the position of DNI and this time accepted.[89] Soon after taking the position, however, Ballard clashed with the First Lord, the brash 36-year-old Winston S. Churchill (who took an instant dislike to him); in a major administrative shake-up, Ballard found himself shunted backward into the number two slot in the reconstituted "naval war staff."[90] In his stead Churchill appointed Rear Admiral Ernest Troubridge, a socially prominent officer who played golf with the prime minister and whom Churchill regarded as "my man."[91] According to one impartial judge who worked alongside both officers at that time, Major Adrian Grant-Duff of the CID secretariat, Ballard "has more brains in his little finger than Troubridge has in his great woolly head."[92]

Archival and historiographical shortcomings mean that reconstructing Ottley's reply to Fisher's request for a strategic appraisal in June 1905 is no easy task. The original Admiralty minutes and correspondence no longer exist. This poses a problem of some magnitude. All scholarly knowledge of the file's content rests upon excerpts quoted by Arthur J. Marder in *The Anatomy of British Sea Power,* first published in 1940.[93] Every subsequent historian with reason to touch upon British naval strategic planning during the 1905–1906 Moroccan Crisis has been forced to rely upon this work for descriptions of the documents and, more critically, upon Marder's interpretations of what they meant in light of those other parts of the file not reproduced.[94] For instance, Marder insisted the lost file showed that Fisher strongly "believed in amphibious warfare."[95] This argument, presented without equivocation or qualification and seemingly supported by the lengthy quotes from one document, has been propagated in numerous subsequent books and articles and has come to inform all understanding of prewar British naval policy.[96] Since *Anatomy* was published, however, additional documents have become available to researchers, including the private correspondence of the principal players (none of which Marder saw at that time). In light of this new evidence (reviewed below), Marder's representation of naval strategic planning during the 1905 Moroccan Crisis, based upon the solitary file he was allowed to see, can be shown to have been seriously inaccurate.[97] More important, Fisher's supposed commitment to amphibious operations—combined with his supposed preoccupation with the German threat—has blinded subsequent scholars to the very existence of the plans for economic warfare. This fundamental error makes it regrettably necessary to examine the subject in some detail.

Fisher's request for a strategic appraisal of war against Germany in June 1905 was not the first time that the Admiralty had considered war against that power—but previously they had considered Germany only as part of a three-power coalition, not as the sole enemy. Although only fragments of the pre-1905 studies (it would be wrong to call them plans) for war against Germany have survived, it is possible to reconstruct them more fully through a letter subsequently written by Ballard to Fisher. Ballard had been one of the key officers involved in their preparation, having served the past three years in the NID. In this letter, Ballard affirmed that one of his first tasks upon joining the department back in 1902 had been to revise a paper drafted the previous year "on the strategic situation in the North Sea with reference to the development of the German Fleet."[98] The DNI (Admiral Custance) had explicitly tasked him "to give due consideration to the conditions which would arise should the Germans adopt an aggressive attitude at a time when Great Britain was already fully occupied in a war with France and Russia."[99] He also told Ballard that the Admiralty envisaged war against Germany as a limited affair fought for limited objectives because only a small portion of the Royal Navy would be available for operations against the German fleet.

Ballard explained that the strategic objective underpinning his 1902 paper had been to "cripple German overseas trade at a minimum of risk and difficulty to ourselves" in the hope that "it might cause such loss to the enemy that the pressure of commercial influence—increasing in Germany—would end the war without further measures on our part."[100] He further insisted that this key underlying assumption, regarding Germany's vulnerability to attack through commercial pressure, serve as "the basis of subsequent papers" written on the subject. This description of the Admiralty's strategic assumptions for war against Germany is substantially corroborated by the formal advice they gave to the CID in February 1904. On that occasion, both Navy and (surprisingly) Army representatives agreed that Germany could be tackled by exploiting Britain's overwhelming naval superiority to capture her overseas colonies and seaborne trade and thereby "induce the enemy to sue for peace on terms advantageous to our interests."[101] Thus the strategic context for this embryonic expression of economic warfare was not war against Germany alone, but war against Germany as part of a Continental coalition. The idea appealed as a way to achieve positive results with limited means.

In framing his recommendations to the First Sea Lord, Captain Ottley unsurprisingly took the embryonic NID studies described by Ballard as his point of departure. On 26 June 1905, the DNI assured Fisher that all preparations for fleet mobilization were complete. The only problem he could see was that "all our pre-supposed [fleet] dispositions will require to be entirely modified in view of the exceptionally favourable circumstances of this moment." By this he meant the possibility of concentrating British naval assets against Germany alone, instead of against Germany as part of a coalition.

> Previous studies of the question of war against Germany have all been based on the assumption that Germany was supported by powerful maritime allies, such as France or Russia, or if not directly supported at least in a position to know that we were so much pre-occupied with them that we could only spare a fraction of our force to deal with the entire German Fleet.
>
> Under the circumstance immediately to be considered the situation is entirely different, and our maritime preponderance would be overwhelming, as we should have the French fleet acting in our own support, and the Russian fleet, even if assisting the enemy, has for the time being ceased to be a factor of importance.[102]

Despite such "exceptionally favorable circumstances," which theoretically would free the Royal Navy to concentrate all its power against Germany, Ottley nevertheless advised the Admiralty not to deviate from the previously agreed plan to limit the naval attack to German sea commerce.[103] The DNI had discussed the matter several days earlier with the historian Julian Corbett, whom he and other naval planners (including the First Sea Lord) sometimes employed as a sounding board on matters pertaining to strategy. In a letter dated 1 June, Ottley emphasized to the historian the vulnerability of German overseas commerce. "Out of a total trade of about [£]572 millions (exports plus imports) carried on by Germany in the year 1903 it would appear that about 60% is sea borne," he noted. Moreover:

> In view of the geographical conditions (the British Isles, lying like a breakwater 600 miles long, athwart the path of German Trade with the west), and remembering the immense strategic advantage of the French harbours so close to the mouth of the Elbe, I believe there would be no practical difficulty in proclaiming and maintaining an effective blockade of the entire German seaboard.

To Ottley, these crude numbers suggested that "the blockade of the German Ports today would sever an artery, essential, it seems to me, to the financial existence of Germany."[104] He made exactly the same point in another letter addressed to the First Lord of the Admiralty.[105]

Of course, we should not read too much significance into a couple of semi-official letters that were long on optimism and short on detail. True, German prosperity now depended heavily upon overseas trade; but Ottley's letters do not explain why severing Germany's links to the outside world would prove so devastating—though his distinction between German commerce and German financial systems is suggestive and tantalizing. Nor did Ottley articulate how the Admiralty envisaged overcoming the inevitable diplomatic and legal obstacles to waging a systematic attack against German trade, which was bound to lead to entanglements with neutrals. It is also not clear why he was so sure "there would be no practical difficulty in proclaiming and maintaining an effective blockade of the entire German seaboard." (And precisely what did he mean by the term "blockade"?) Yet before becoming carried away in our criticism, we must also remember that these letters represent only fragments of an ongoing discussion recorded in official files, since lost.

We ought to keep in mind also that Ottley was new to the position of DNI, and it was therefore hardly his fault if his predecessors had failed to probe German vulnerabilities more closely (which had never been a high priority anyway). The real significance of Ottley's letters is that they represent a statement of his beliefs: first, that the German economy was vulnerable to disruption; second, that the Royal Navy possessed the capability to isolate Germany from the global trading system; and third, that doing so should produce strategically decisive results. The date of these letters, moreover, which were written at the height of the Moroccan Crisis while the Admiralty were making active preparations for war, indicates that Ottley was not contemplating economic warfare as an abstract exercise.

However much the First Sea Lord may have agreed with the thrust of Ottley's recommendation to limit naval operations to systematic attack upon German seaborne trade (and, given Fisher's known views, he probably agreed wholeheartedly), the decision was not his alone to make. Several weeks earlier, Fisher had come to blows with Admiral Sir Arthur Wilson, the fleet commander, over proposed changes in the control of warships in home waters. The First Sea Lord had wanted to introduce flotilla defense.[106] The idea of relying primarily upon the flotilla in home waters and relegating the main battle fleet to a support role flew in the face of orthodox naval theory and was bitterly resisted by Wilson and other senior fleet officers "deadly opposed" to Fisher's radical strategic views.[107] From their perspective, the most objectionable feature of the flotilla defense strategy was Fisher's intention to make the Admiralty in London the principal operational command center, directing by wireless the movements of all cruisers and small craft in home waters.[108] Given the current state of wireless technology and that the Admiralty was already the hub of global intelligence (both strategic and tactical), Fisher's idea made a great deal of sense. But Admiral Wilson insisted that he, as fleet commander, should command all warships in home waters.

Already deeply mired in policy disputes with other senior officers, and believing "he could not afford to alienate the support of a man who carried so great a weight of Service opinion behind him," Fisher cancelled the intended change.[109] In May 1905, the Admiralty formally granted Wilson in time of war full "liberty to dispose the forces under your orders as you think best."[110] It is interesting to note that Ottley had looked askance at giving Wilson unfettered operational control of the fleet—which had major strategic consequences—and regarded it as "usurping one of the most important functions of the Board in general and of the First Sea Lord in particular."[111] He felt so strongly that he inserted into the file a sharply worded minute "that the arrangement is a personal concession to Sir Arthur Wilson as Their Lordships are unwilling to force changes to which he is opposed so long as he retains the command."[112]

Ottley's protestations notwithstanding, the First Sea Lord was thus obliged to consult with Admiral Wilson over strategic policy during the Moroccan Crisis. Accordingly, the DNI immediately couriered him a letter outlining the Admiralty's recent deliberations and inviting him to comment. By return of post, 27 June, Admiral Wilson categorically rejected the limited plan of campaign. "No action by the Navy alone can do France any good," he wrote. The proposed operations

> amount to little more than the capture of a few colonies from Germany which are of no use to her, and the stoppage of direct over-sea trade from her own ports; but as she would probably have free access to the sea through neutral ports this, although a temporary loss to her shipping interests, would not greatly affect her general trade.[113]

Wilson dismissed both the importance and practicability of economic pressure. "In the case of war between this country and Germany," he insisted, "neither nation has much opportunity of doing the other any vital injury," and "if other nations did not intervene, the war might drag on indefinitely, involving great mutual loss to both countries." Three months earlier he had told the First Lord of his doubts that the Navy could exert significant economic pressure upon Germany because the "Scandinavian nations being neutral would make it very difficult for us to effectively stop German and Russian trade as it would be carried on through Danish and Swedish ports principally by American ships, even if not by English ones."[114] In a war between Germany and a Franco-British alliance, he wrote on 27 June, command of the sea would count for little because "the result would depend entirely on the military operations on the French frontier and [therefore] we should be bound to devote our whole military forces of the country to endeavor to create a diversion on the coast of Germany in France's favour." Sir Arthur conceded that making an "effective diversion" would entail "expos[ing] our ships in the Baltic or on the German coast in a way that would not be necessary if we were at war with Germany alone, but under present conditions, with France on our side, this is a risk that can be accepted."[115] For future reference, readers should note the critical qualifying clause: "under present conditions." Wilson closed his letter of 27 June with a request to be placed in direct communication with the War Office so that together they might devise an offensive combined operation "on the largest scale possible."[116]

The practicalities of amphibious operations aside, Wilson's letter of 27 June was extraordinarily brusque. While it is true he had been invited to air his thoughts on the subject, his sweeping dismissal of the Admiralty viewpoint, not to mention his demand to be left alone with the Army planners to work out a strategy, verged on insubordination. Fortunately, because the diplomatic crisis subsided before Wilson's letter reached London, the Admiralty were able to ignore it and thereby avoid confrontation. Thus we can never know if the different strategic outlooks held by the Admiralty and the fleet commander would have proved significant in the event of war. Despite Wilson's objectionable tone, one argument he made struck home. The Admiralty conceded that Wilson was probably right in thinking that the French would demand more active assistance, and given the enormous disparity in naval forces between the two sides, the Admiralty could afford to hazard Royal Navy warships in applying greater pressure.

After again discussing the subject with Julian Corbett, who was a fervent supporter of this sort of combined operation, Ottley grudgingly allowed that the idea merited closer consideration: "You are absolutely right. We should *have* to throw an expeditionary force ashore on the German coast *somewhere* in addition to any naval action we might take. No other attitude would by worthy of our traditions—or would be acceptable to France."[117] The clause to note was "in addition to any naval action"; this indicates Ottley viewed possible combined operations against German territory as a secondary strategy.

Indeed, in subsequent documents Ottley would be explicit on this point. Thereafter, the DNI always qualified his countenance of Wilson's "reckless offensive" (as we shall hereafter term it), insisting that such a strategy could be contemplated only "under the present conditions" or for so long as Britain retained overwhelming naval supremacy over Germany, France remained allied, and Russia stayed at least neutral.[118] In so doing, of course, Ottley implied that the strategic circumstances of the moment were unique and unlikely to recur.

The following week, Ottley prepared a revised appreciation of British strategy in the event of war against Germany, which Sir John Fisher forwarded to the prime minister, Arthur Balfour. The new document unequivocally restated the Admiralty's desire to focus Britain's strategic efforts primarily against German trade. It predicted the "total disappearance of the German mercantile marine, a loss which to a country becoming increasingly dependent upon industrial prosperity would in itself be a serious blow."[119] Clearly anticipating objections, Ottley noted, "It is true that a proportion of German oversea trade might be carried on through neutral ports, but such an arrangement is a much less easy method of evading the consequences of commercial blockade than is sometimes supposed." Besides, he continued, the diversion of German trade must "entail an automatic increase in the cost of carrying on trade, and raise prices in Germany at the very time when the financial situation was pressing for a reduction." Should the diplomatic situation permit, furthermore, Britain might curtail this evasion by applying the legal doctrine of "continuous voyage" and thereby lawfully seize contraband bound indirectly for Germany, transported to contiguous neutral territory in neutral ships. In 1905 Ottley was "strongly of opinion" that the "value to us of the right to invoke Continuous Voyage was, in a war with Germany, very great indeed"—though later he would modify this opinion.[120] The point to note is that, once again, the DNI was adamant that systematic attack upon German seaborne commerce would seriously damage the German economy.[121] Only at the very end of the document did Ottley concede, with considerable qualification, that perhaps economic pressure might work too slowly to satisfy the French government and consequently, for essentially political reasons, the Royal Navy might have to adopt a more aggressive strategic posture:

> And here it may be said at once that the overwhelming extent of our maritime supremacy would permit us to undertake operations of a nature which in ordinary maritime warfare would be unjustifiable, such

> as close approaches to hostile ports and attacks on defended positions. It would rest with our War Office authorities to decide whether advantage could be taken of this fact to undertake a military expedition on a considerable scale to any part of North German territory, and if so, at what point it would be likely to produce the best results.[122]

In portraying Ottley as an enthusiast for amphibious warfare, historians have long thought that such strategic ideas were representative of current Admiralty strategic thinking. Yet as the passage cited above clearly shows, this inference is mistaken: the DNI was decidedly equivocal as to their merit. As already shown, he began to contemplate mounting amphibious operations against German coastal territory only after Admiral Wilson had insisted such plans be considered and even then only in the context of overwhelming allied naval supremacy, a circumstance which he regarded as exceptional and temporary. When commenting upon such plans, Ottley took pains to emphasize that "close approaches to hostile ports and attacks on defended positions" were ordinarily "unjustifiable." Furthermore, the Admiralty should not propose any combined operations: he stated that all responsibility for any attack on Germany territory must "rest with our War Office authorities" and that if they proposed such an operation, the Admiralty would cooperate. The distinction between War Office and Admiralty initiative is vital. Ottley closed his memorandum with a recommendation that a joint services committee sit to study the feasibility of various amphibious operations. This document confirms that Ottley (and by implication Fisher also) viewed the possible launching of amphibious attacks against German territory only as a subsidiary to—not as the basis of—Admiralty strategic policy.[123]

A few days later, about 9 or 10 July 1905, Captain Ottley circulated a second paper expanding on the proposal for a joint services study "on overseas operations," now suggesting that the inquiry be conducted under the auspices of the CID. Sir George Clarke, the CID permanent secretary, clearly had been involved in the preparation of this document because several drafts he annotated survive.[124] Here yet again, Ottley stressed that "no countenance had ever been given to operations which would endanger H.M. ships," and that the Admiralty were now prepared to contemplate such risks only in light of the exceptional diplomatic circumstances of the moment.[125] Furthermore, where he referred to the possibility that the Navy might transport "60,000 British troops through the labyrinth of sandbanks and shoals shielding the German seaboard to a landing in Schleswig-Holstein," he made very clear that he was not proposing such an operation but rather that "the idea is merely thrown out as an indication of the kind of problem that the 'Sub-Committee on Over-sea Expeditions' might perhaps be called upon to confront."[126] But the real significance of the paper lies elsewhere. What previous historians have failed to notice is that Ottley was calling not for the creation of any new plans (against Germany or anyone else) but rather for the better preparation of existing ones; "amplifying" was the word he used. This is a point of fundamental importance and loaded with implications.

For at least twenty years, it turns out, the Admiralty and War Office had been quietly sketching various possible combined operations to capture specific enemy overseas bases and colonies. In his memorandum, Ottley referenced extant plans for the capture of the German naval base at Kiao-Chau (Tsingtao, China); French bases at Diego Suarez (Madagascar), Bizerte (Tunisia), and Dakar (Senegal); and Spanish Tenerife (in the Canary Islands). A separate paper written by the head of the Army's planning department at about this time confirms that "much money and labour has been expended in preparing schemes to capture Martinique, Berserta [*sic*], Diego Suarez, Noumea [New Caledonia], Dakar and Saigon."[127] One of these schemes, in fact, survives.[128] This file corroborates Ottley's allegation that to date preparations had been "only of a general character" and consequently that "if a sudden order were received from the government to prepare for a *coup de main* against any specific foreign possession, a great deal of elaboration would still be needed involving considerable delay."[129]

To the modern eye, the failure by the services' planning departments to complete these contingency plans to seize various foreign naval bases seems extraordinarily slipshod.[130] But as Ottley's July 1905 paper goes on to explain, the failure to complete the requisite preparations was symptomatic not of military myopia but rather of political distrustfulness: the cabinet had prohibited the Admiralty and War Office from making "offensive" plans—though evidentially the injunction did not preclude them from preparing sketches and keeping relevant intelligence on file.[131] Ottley went on to argue that such a haphazard approach to national war planning was dangerously out of date. Even the smallest combined operation, he argued, must be an "arduous" undertaking requiring "careful study and high organization."[132] The importance of extensive prior preparation had been underlined after joint maneuvers held the previous September involving the landing of 12,000 soldiers plus cavalry and artillery on an open beach at the resort town of Clacton-on-Sea.[133] The landings, which had been witnessed by foreign dignitaries and attachés, had been a fiasco, taking twenty-seven hours to complete. "After the Clacton maneuvers," Ottley later recalled, "the War Office and Admiralty jointly came to the conclusion that the operation of landing an army on an open beach in the face of a determined enemy was out of the question."[134]

Sir George Clarke, the permanent secretary to the CID, wasting no time in bringing Ottley's call for a joint services committee to the prime minister's attention. On Tuesday, 11 July, he wrote Balfour that "the need for such a body becomes more and more pressing."[135] He pleaded for Ottley's paper to be placed atop the agenda for the next CID meeting. "The object of the subcommittee," he explained, "is to arrive at certain definite plans for combined naval and military action in certain contingencies, and to work out these plans to the actual stage of giving effect to them."[136] Clarke further stressed there were already "many plans in existence both at Admiralty and War Office which require to be coordinated."[137] The topic was discussed at the seventy-fifth meeting of the CID (13 July) and the details thrashed out at the subsequent meeting held on 20 July.[138] On 24 July, Clarke advised the prime minister he had drafted a "charter" for the proposed standing subcommittee, and that both "Sir John Fisher and [General] Sir Neville Lyttelton [chief of the General Staff] have agreed to it."[139] For various reasons, however, the new committee proved stillborn.[140]

Most historians have interpreted Ottley's promotion and Fisher's endorsement of the standing subcommittee for combined naval and military action as critical evidence of Admiralty support for amphibious operations. But there are good reasons for doubting this interpretation. Many in the defense establishment at that time knew Fisher was following a hidden agenda and wanted the subcommittee "for certain purposes."[141] We shall look at what these were a little later. We have also seen that Ottley, who formally proposed the CID subcommittee, was at best lukewarm over the whole idea of combined operations strategy. Had the DNI undergone a change of heart? Buried in the Admiralty archives is a long-forgotten file that speaks to this subject. The documents therein, four memoranda written between February and July 1905, record a protracted and lively exchange of views on the subject of amphibious operations between Ottley, as DNI, and his opposite number at the War Office, Major General Sir James Grierson, the director of military operations (DMO). Previous historians have ignored this file, probably because it contained papers discussing British preparations for war *against* France, which does not fit the prevailing historiographical conviction that by this time the Navy was focused on war against Germany in support of France.[142] To ignore these lengthy and tightly reasoned papers is a mistake, however, for not only do they show that during early 1905 (i.e., after the Anglo-French entente) the Admiralty and War Office were still actively preparing for war against France, but also they shed considerable light on Ottley's strategic views—his preference for a strategy based upon economic pressure, and his skepticism about amphibious operations.

The first paper, written by Grierson around February 1905 and entitled "Military Policy in the Event of War with France," expressed the War Office's desire to "come to some general understanding as to the policy to be adopted in the event of war."[143] Essentially the DMO sought agreement from the Admiralty as to which of the various amphibious projects already on file should be developed. "Much money and labour have been expended in the preparations of various schemes of offensive operations, and before any new schemes are prepared or old ones revised it is indispensible [*sic*] that a clear expression of the views of the Admiralty should be obtained," he wrote.[144] Readers should note two points: first, that the initiative for amphibious operations came from the War Office; and second, that the Army advocated an invasion of French Indochina. In reply, Ottley advised Grierson that the Admiralty had always viewed these projects "more in the light of possibilities rather than of probabilities."[145] While agreeing with the necessity of prior planning for small-scale operations—perhaps to destroy naval units sheltering inside an overseas French port, for instance—the DNI questioned "whether an invasion of the larger French Colonies in force is likely to prove either necessary or desirable in the event of war."[146] To Ottley, the high risk of failure far exceeded any possible advantage. He thought it unlikely that Great Britain would wish to annex any French colonies, because none appeared worth keeping. In similar vein, Ottley questioned whether the capture of French colonies would provide Britain with much leverage at a peace conference.

Ottley argued that the application of economic pressure against France would provide much greater leverage.

> We must calculate with the fact that the burden of war would be already pressing more heavily upon France than ourselves, in view of the inevitable disappearance of French sea trade during the continuance of hostilities while our own was remaining relatively intact. Moreover, the longer the War lasts the greater will be the aggregate cost thereof.

And:

> The daily war losses of France would probably be greater than our own as already indicated, through the loss of all sea trade, and the financial distress would consequently force them to surrender before it would us.[147]

From these papers we may reasonably surmise that Ottley shared Fisher's preference for limited war. In time of war, the Royal Navy's primary mission should be to insulate the British economy from serious damage while simultaneously attacking that of the enemy. In the fullness of time the enemy would come to realize the futility of continuing the war and sue for peace. Believing that economic pressure would prove sufficient to bring France to terms, Ottley advised the War Office that "operations against French oversea possessions generally should not hold a place in our recognized War policy as being quite unjustified from the standpoint of academic strategy, and improbable as a matter of practical expediency."[148]

Grierson was taken aback by Ottley's reply and derided his comments on paramount importance of economic pressure as "almost unintelligible." "The General Staff," he rejoined, "emphatically dissents from the view that operations against French over-sea possessions generally should not hold a place in our recognized war policy."[149] Punctuating his arguments with "teachings from history," the general proceeded to dismiss as preposterous Ottley's "suggestion" that naval action alone could bring the enemy to the peace table, scoffing at the idea the French could be brought to terms by such "invertebrate measures of offence as the destruction of the overseas trade of a country like France which depends upon it mercantile marine in only very secondary degree for its wealth and prosperity."[150] "It is by no means certain," Grierson artfully asserted, that "the burden of War would press more heavily upon France than ourselves [Britain]." The general's view may be summed up by his forceful declaration that "there is a very grave divergence of opinion between the NID and the General Staff, not so much on the general question of strategy as upon the whole question of war policy, if not indeed upon the question of what war means."[151] Ottley's terse surrejoinder essentially acknowledged that the two departments held diametrically opposite views and challenged the general's presentation of history.[152]

This exchange of correspondence provides a wholly different context for viewing the strategic debate at the time of the 1905 Moroccan Crisis. Besides highlighting the danger of viewing the available evidence through the lens of a supposed anti-German imperative, the correspondence underscores both Ottley's faith in economic pressure as a decisive strategy and his skepticism about combined operations except, perhaps, as an adjunct to naval operations in distant waters. More significant still, they also show that the initial impetus for a review of combined operations strategy came not from the Admiralty but from the War Office and, that this debate predated the Moroccan Crisis. The Admiralty proposal for the creation of the CID subcommittee, therefore, cannot be seen as evidence of naval enthusiasm for an amphibious strategy but was put forward, rather, as a counterproposal to the War Office request for joint planning—the objective being to remove an ongoing and already contentious interdepartmental debate to the supervision of the Committee of Imperial Defence.[153] The Admiralty's action, in other words, was nothing more than one move in a much larger bureaucratic game that had little if anything to do with the immediate preparations of war plans against Germany. To interpret it otherwise is to impose later strategic developments on the context actually existing in 1905.

It must also be kept in mind that the CID at this time was still newly established.[154] Acting on the recommendation of Lord Esher's War Office Reconstitution Committee, in the spring of 1904 Prime Minister Arthur Balfour authorized the establishment of a small permanent secretariat (under Sir George Clarke) to record the renamed committee's deliberations and decisions. It is true that some (especially Lord Esher) conceived the CID as a first step toward the creation of a "joint staff," the fusion of the naval, military, diplomatic, and political leadership into a single body capable of formulating and administering imperial grand strategic policy. But the prime minister did not subscribe to this ambition: in 1904 his overriding objective was to achieve better coordination in defense matters with a view to finding significant cuts in military expenditures.[155] The minutes of the CID meetings held throughout Balfour's premiership (in 1904 and 1905) as well as the private correspondence of the principal players show unequivocally that he employed the CID as a tool of bureaucratic coercion to bludgeon the War Office into cutting the military budget, which had remained inflated long after the end of the Boer War. As the national fiscal forecast darkened and the government concomitantly became more desperate to find savings in the defense budget, the debates within the CID became increasingly acrimonious as the service departments fought tooth and nail for the largest share of the diminishing budget. In short, in 1905 the CID was *not* a professional planning staff or an executive organ.

Fisher's true objectives in proposing the CID combined operations subcommittee emerged in October 1905. Shortly before he returned from his customary six-week summer vacation, the First Sea Lord learned that during his absence no further progress had been made. On 10 October he begged the prime minister to force the Army into cooperating. "I am hot on this committee," he explained to Jack Sandars, Balfour's private secretary, because the War Office "will be *forced* to be ready, *forced* to get on, *forced* to cooperate and finally *forced* to be efficient."[156] Several days later Fisher prodded Balfour with another memorandum on the subject, urging him to tackle War Office intransigence head-on by demanding that it supply a digest of "the various existing schemes, stating the extent to which they had been already elaborated."[157] Fisher claimed "the main point to be borne in mind—often emphasized by the Prime Minister himself—[was] that under no circumstances was it contemplated that Great Britain could or would undertake single-handed a great military continental war, and that every project of offensive hostilities was to be subsidiary to the action of the fleet."[158] The whole tenor of Fisher's memorandum indicates that he was concerned less with the finalization of specific plans than with seeing the War Office firmly lashed to the CID, whose political members during recent months had shown increasing sympathy for a blue-water British defense policy. Again, Fisher's seeming encouragement of amphibious warfare planning was little more than another exercise in service politics connected to the ongoing battle over the defense budget.

The generals were no less devious in defending their institutional corner by exploiting the domestic political situation. Lord Esher complained it was common knowledge that the War Office was stonewalling in making defense cuts in the hope that Balfour's Conservative-Unionist government, fractured from top to bottom over the issue of tariff reform, would soon fall. The Liberal leadership was known to view the CID as a dangerously unconstitutional experiment that infringed upon the supreme authority of the cabinet, and many wanted it abolished.[159] In the event, Balfour defied the pundits and clung to power until the end of the year, but the fact remained that throughout the summer of 1905, most informed political commentators believed that the Liberals would take power any day. With Balfour preoccupied with holding his government together and anxious to avoid all controversy, the time was not propitious for the First Sea Lord to be asking the prime minister to compel War Office cooperation with the CID.[160] Balfour desperately wished to "leave things as they are."[161]

Before finally leaving the subject of alleged Admiralty support for combined operations against Germany, we must address one more block of evidence cited by those who have argued that amphibious warfare was the keystone of Admiralty strategic plans for war against Germany. Between August and October 1905, officers in the Navy and Army planning departments conducted a brief correspondence as to the feasibility of conducting amphibious operations against German territory. It began when Colonel Charles Callwell (an assistant DMO) sent Captain George Ballard at the NID a paper entitled "British Military Action in the Case of War with Germany," in which he optimistically asserted that a British amphibious attack in the area of Schleswig-Holstein might distract as many as 400,000 German regulars, reducing in turn their availability for an invasion of France.[162] The colonel asked for help working out the details for such an attack; the naval captain promptly wrote back for further details as to the objective and the number of troops envisaged, only to be told by (Army) Captain Adrian Grant-Duff that his boss had gone on leave.[163] As the weeks passed, Ballard grew increasingly frustrated with the continuing delay and was perplexed by the conflicting signals emanating from the War Office. On 3 October 1905, Callwell at last contacted Ballard again, only to tell him that the General Staff now considered any combined operations against German territory to be dangerously impractical and had concluded that Britain might provide more effective military assistance to France by sending troops to work directly alongside the French and possibly Belgian armies.[164]

In considering this evidence, it is essential to be clear on several points. First, the discussion was always strictly unofficial and carried on between relatively junior staff officers. When, moreover, the senior staff at the War Office learned of Callwell's initiative, they were most unhappy and ordered him not to send the Admiralty any further memoranda unless first cleared by the chief of the General Staff.[165] Similarly, Admiral Sir John Fisher could not possibly have seen the correspondence because he was on vacation outside the country for the entire period.[166] Second, as the file makes clear, the initiative came from the War Office, not the Admiralty (most historians have asserted the opposite).[167] In this context it will be recalled that the Ottley memorandum distributed to the CID in July stated categorically that responsibility for proposing such operations belonged to the War Office. Lastly, the unofficial Callwell-Ballard conversations were not directly connected with the abortive CID combined operations committee (which had been tasked to complete existing plans, not to frame new ones). When the Moroccan Crisis flared up again in

December 1905, Sir George Clarke knew nothing about these low-level conversations. The Callwell-Ballard discussions on amphibious attack against Germany, in other words, ran parallel to—not sequentially with—the contemporaneous debate over the coordination of combined operations.

Perhaps the most powerful and tangible indicator that Admiralty planners were not deeply committed to amphibious warfare strategies was their simultaneous preparation of other, fundamentally contradictory war plans. Fisher and Ottley exhibited markedly greater enthusiasm (and observed far greater secrecy) for their scheme to sow mines off the German coast immediately upon outbreak of war. As we shall see, this subject touched upon economic warfare strategy. The Royal Navy first perfected reliable automatic contact mines during the early 1890s, and for many years both Fisher and especially Ottley had been intimately involved in their early development. The latter, for instance, was responsible for the invention of the automatic "Ottley" sinker for mines (a device that allowed a mine to be dropped from a ship and moor itself at a preselected depth below the surface—still used today). But since 1894, Admiralty policy had been to suppress this weapon system and suspend further experimentation in the hope that if they did so (and noisily voiced their skepticism of its utility), rival powers perhaps would not realize its full potential. For more than a decade the Admiralty maintained their ostrich impression.

One of Captain Ottley's first acts upon becoming DNI, in February 1905, had been to draw attention to the "startling success achieved by automatic mines during the present [Russo-Japanese] war [that] inculcates a lesson which is likely to be only too readily accepted by foreign Naval Powers."[168] Ottley thought the Admiralty's policy of feigned ignorance ridiculous and argued that in light of recent events in the Far East "it would be sheer madness to delude ourselves with the idea that we alone have taken cognizance of them." The time had come for the Admiralty to exploit contact mines in its war planning even at the risk of tipping its hand to foreign powers.[169] Fisher connived to appoint Ottley chairman of a small committee to consider the question. In May 1905, the Admiralty duly accepted Ottley's recommendations to lift the edict and begin accumulating a stockpile of 10,000 mines; despite the bleak financial situation, the Admiralty placed a large order.[170]

On 14 October 1905, Ottley identified for Fisher "the most pressing" question to be dealt with upon his return from vacation as "the perfecting of our organization for the instant employment of the large number of offensive mines which we shall shortly possess, on the outbreak of war."[171] Ottley's letter indicates that the First Sea Lord had already signaled his approval for using mines to tighten the naval and commercial blockade of enemy ports. This document also sheds unexpected light on the sophistication of Ottley's war planning, and in particular his appreciation for the political and diplomatic ramifications of maritime warfare.

> You will remember that both Japan and Russia employed them [contact mines] freely in positions far outside the three-mile limit [to territorial waters]. Following upon the precedent thus created we shall under present arrangements do likewise, off the estuaries of large rivers in certain contingencies.
>
> But what I am anxious to bring to your notice is that such action on our part, resulting as it easily might in the wholesale sinking of neutral and non-combatant ships, would probably bring down upon us a storm of indignation from the rest of Europe, and would probably be very unfavorably viewed by a considerable section of our own people.
>
> This would not be the case if we laid these mines only in the territorial waters of our enemy, and clearly no rational being could object to their being laid in the narrow waters of approach to the naval arsenals of our enemy.
>
> We are now coming to the stage when the material for the purpose is fully available and the elaboration of our plans in full detail for carrying out certain specific operations with offensive mines is now being worked out.

Because the employment of the mines touched on important questions of national policy and international law, before finalizing the details Ottley wanted guidance from someone in executive authority, ideally the prime minister, whether "from the international law standpoint the operation for which we are now preparing is permissible." Additionally:

> We must not forget that if it be permitted to block the estuary of the Danube [Elbe][172] or any other great European river with mines, a similar prerogative cannot be denied to an enemy to block the entrance to the Mersey [Liverpool] and Thames [London]. Great as would be the losses we might inflict upon an enemy, the losses we ourselves might suffer would also be very great, and in view of our dependence upon sea trade for our very existence, it is open to question whether it will be to our interest to lead the way in this wholesale resort to offensive mines.

Ottley confessed he was the "originator of the offensive mine idea" but admitted doubts as to the course of action proposed and acknowledged powerful countervailing arguments.

> The use made by the Russians and the Japanese of this contrivance far oversteps the limits I had ever contemplated for it, and I do not believe that any such wholesale employment is likely to be sanctioned by the public opinion of Europe. Our action in providing a supply of these mines during the last few months has been strictly correct and logical. The dictates of prudence demand that whatever happens we shall be ready.

In this and subsequent documents, Ottley demonstrated his comprehension that naval war planning was intimately connected with questions of international law likely to have unpredictable diplomatic ramifications, and therefore was bound to require input from the highest reaches of government. In feeling his way forward, however, the DNI was frustrated to find that international opinion was badly fragmented on numerous questions of maritime law, and consequently there were precious few modern rulings upon which he could rely for planning purposes. The ongoing Russo-Japanese War was a powerful and daily reminder of this reality. Ottley was especially interested in obtaining guidance on the use of contact mines in international waters, and requested the subject be raised at the forthcoming Hague Peace conference scheduled to sit the following year.[173] Fisher, by contrast, exhibited few such qualms. Forwarding Ottley's letter to the prime minister, he indicated his enthusiasm for the plan and stressed, "It is most desirable NOT to bring it before the Defence Committee [CID]—only 2 or 3 people know that we shall soon have 10,000 of these mines ready!"[174]

Morocco Revisited and Sir George Clarke's Preparations for War, 1906

At the end of 1905 there was renewed concern within diplomatic circles that France and Germany might come to blows over Morocco and that Britain might be dragged into the war. Just how seriously Britain's political leadership took the situation is difficult to gauge. On 4 December 1905, Balfour resigned the premiership, and over the next few weeks politicians of all stripes were much too distracted by preparations for the general election to give much attention to foreign affairs. At the Admiralty, Fisher believed conflict was unlikely but nevertheless assured everyone that the Navy was ready for anything.[175] At the War Office there was scarcely greater interest—at least initially. The only official within the defense establishment to exhibit any real concern was Sir George Clarke, the secretary of the CID. Believing until then that the Admiralty had in hand specific plans, Clarke was dismayed to learn from Ottley, on 16 December, that "the Admiralty studies go no further than the mobilization of the reserve fleet."[176] He wrote to Esher lambasting both services for failing to take what he considered elementary precautions.[177] Among the questions he wanted answered were "whether our Channel Fleet should go to the Baltic early in the war," "whether a landing in Schleswig Holstein is practicable," "whether a landing in Denmark could be made," and "whether we should proceed at once to lay blockade mines at the mouth of the Elbe." Finding himself in a political vacuum, concerned that the Admiralty had not "thought out at all" their strategy, and perhaps eager to expand his bureaucratic empire, Clarke resolved to remedy these deficiencies and hammer out a definite war plan to present to the cabinet should the need arise.[178]

Beginning on 19 December 1905, Clarke chaired a series of unofficial meetings between himself, Captain Ottley, Lieutenant General Sir John French, plus the enigmatic Lord Esher, who recently had been appointed a permanent member of the CID. The unusual composition of the group should be noted. In no way can it be described as some sort of CID committee. No member of the political executive was present, nor was there any representative from the diplomatic corps. In his capacity as DNI, Ottley may be described as a CID regular, but Esher and certainly General French were not. Indeed, French was not even a member of the General Staff and thus was not in a position to speak for the War Office. (General James Grierson was still DMO.) French commanded the Aldershot garrison, which made him nominally responsible for the 50,000 troops of the hypothetical First Corps, intended to serve as a nucleus for any expeditionary force. He attended probably because he was known to be sympathetic to the sort of combined operations that Clarke was seeking to promote. Clarke's "preparedness group," as it was labeled, quickly reached the conclusion that any amphibious attack on German territory must be made at least 200,000 strong. The biggest drawback was that the British Army would struggle to find half this number of troops. Discussions therefore proceeded upon the implausible assumption that the French army would consent to divert 100,000 regular troops from their threatened frontiers to the proposed force. The absurdity of this assumption quickly became self-evident, and the idea was abandoned as "impractical."[179] Believing in the urgency of the diplomatic situation and determined to come up with some sort of workable strategy, even if only as a stopgap, Clarke turned next to consider the possibility of sending British troops across the Channel to help the French army stem the tide of a German invasion. He went so far as to open "unofficial" discussions with the French army staff as to where they might land.[180] As yet he was unaware that General Grierson had already taken steps in this direction.[181]

On 13 January 1906, Ottley wrote to Fisher informing him that General Grierson had joined Clarke's forum and revealing that it had been "settled between the military officers" that Britain would deploy approximately 100,000 troops to the Continent to stand beside the French army in resisting any German invasion.[182] What is more, the General Staff had secured qualified approval for its "talks" from Sir Edward Grey, the incoming Liberal foreign secretary.[183] This constituted not a promise to support France in the event of war but merely tacit approval for members of the General Staff to talk with their French counterparts in a noncommittal way.[184] Upon receipt of this news Fisher immediately strode across Whitehall to tell Clarke "he would never be party to military cooperation with the French on French territory."[185] On 18 January, the First Sea Lord forbade the DNI to attend any more meetings.[186]

It goes beyond the scope of this work to consider the full ramifications of the military conversations between Britain and France initiated during this period of crisis, which in any case have been examined exhaustively elsewhere. Yet before moving on, it is worth pointing out a couple of less well-known details omitted from some narratives. First, neither Clarke nor Esher was ever comfortable with sending a British army to the Continent, believing such a move "was unlikely to confer any real advantage upon our allies" and was certain to prove unpopular at home.[187] Second, as the diplomatic tensions subsided and calm returned, the logistical drawbacks to the General Staff plans became increasingly obvious and Clarke's opposition concomitantly hardened. Before the end of January 1906, he had reverted to his favored theme of amphibious operations.[188]

Some historians have taken Fisher's initial acquiescence to Ottley's membership in the preparedness group as evidence of the Admiralty's determination to make amphibious warfare—not the Continental commitment—the core of national strategy in the event of war.[189] If so, then the Admiralty certainly went about it in a very odd way. As early as 2 January 1906, Clarke complained to Esher about Fisher's uncooperativeness (which he attributed to

Fisher's belief that there would be no war) and lack of any plan save to "smash" the German navy.[190] The minutes of the meetings show that Ottley contributed remarkably little to the debates; whereas General French and later General Grierson advocated particular plans and distributed papers, the DNI contributed nothing in writing.[191] Whenever Ottley did intervene, moreover, it was invariably toward the end of a discussion and to point out some practical obstacle the others had overlooked. At the second meeting, held on 6 January 1906, for instance, Ottley raised the difficulties of operating a fleet in the Baltic during winter. Similarly, on 12 January, he pointed out the difficulties of entering the Baltic and operating a war fleet so close to neutral (Danish) territorial waters. To a cynic, the obvious conclusion was that the DNI was surreptitiously trying to sabotage the proceedings.

The uncharacteristically naive Clarke remained perplexed at the Admiralty's lack of cooperation in developing any amphibious operation, remarking to Esher that it should have taken Ottley no more than a couple of days to put together a concrete plan for "seizing Borkum as an advanced base."[192] Clarke drew the wrong conclusion from the Admiralty's obstructionist tactics. He believed that they possessed no plans and had been caught unprepared, when in fact the Admiralty simply did not wish to give Clarke what he wanted—which is not at all the same thing. As will be shown in the next chapter, the Admiralty had recently learned that the CID secretary was privately contemptuous of economic warfare: if so, then there was no point in presenting him with such a strategy.

By the beginning of 1906, any enthusiasm Fisher had for joint planning of combined operations—which, again, was not sincere but most likely bait to lure the War Office into the budget-slashing environs of the CID—had all but evaporated. None of his subordinates had come up with a definite scheme for operations against continental Germany, let alone devise something sufficiently credible to persuade the Army General Staff to participate. At the same time, Fisher was becoming increasingly wary of Sir George Clarke's ambition for the CID to play an even greater role in defense planning—a suspicion undoubtedly fueled by Clarke's energetic initiative during the recent crisis. In recent months, moreover, Clarke had begun to question aspects of Fisher's naval revolution, particularly the building of so many submarines (which he regarded as of little military use) and the building of the "monster" battleship and cruisers (HMS *Dreadnought* and the *Indomitable* class) then under construction.[193] Worse, he had begun voicing his thoughts to politicians. Such meddling had potentially serious implications for Admiralty policy and especially their construction budget.

* * *

Given that so many historians have erroneously asserted that before 1914 combined operations warfare formed the basis of Admiralty strategic thinking for a war against Germany, we cannot leave this subject without some final reinforcing comments.

While Fisher and Ottley publicly exhibited interest in amphibious warfare schemes, it is wrong to say they actively promoted them. Such operations were always considered to be secondary, not the basis of Admiralty strategy; the primary preference was always for economic pressure. Those historians who have argued otherwise have confused the icing for the cake.[194] The various discussions by Admiralty officials in 1905 as to the practicability of combined operations, either official or unofficial, imply neither a fundamental reorientation in British defense posture nor a radical departure from previous practice. For at least twenty years the War Office and Admiralty planning departments (such as they were at that time) had routinely updated and discussed schemes to capture various overseas bases in the event of war.[195]

Against the slender evidence that amphibious warfare "was prominent in Fisher's strategic views," and accordingly was the keystone of Admiralty policy during his term as First Sea Lord (1904–1910), we must consider his more considerable thinking (and actions) pointing in the opposite direction.[196] There is abundant evidence, for instance, that Fisher had thought deeply on the conduct of operations in "narrow seas" infested with torpedo-armed flotilla craft and come to the conclusion that it was just too dangerous. This had led him to develop and implement his theory of flotilla defense, the strategy of mutual sea denial in European waters. Ottley too had reached the same conclusions, albeit via a different path. Ottley's expertise in mine warfare gave him an acute appreciation of the dangers of operating a fleet in shallow waters off the European coast, a sensibility that was reinforced by his daily scrutiny during 1905 of intelligence reports on the devastatingly effective use of mines by the navies of Japan and Russia.[197] With these pieces of evidence taken together, it defies credibility to suggest that the Admiralty were ignorant of the dangers from torpedoes, submarines, and mines. It may be that in charting new strategic waters the Admiralty considered some outlandish ideas, but surely the point is, first, as Ottley so frequently pointed out, that the exceptional strategic circumstances of the moment permitted them to do so, and second, that the initiative for many of these outlandish ideas came from the War Office.

It must be admitted, however, that the Admiralty's negative appraisal of large-scale amphibious warfare against German territory was not sufficient to extinguish all naval interest in the idea. So long as he remained commander in chief, Admiral Sir Arthur Wilson continued to press for further studies.[198] Another proponent was Captain Edmond Slade, the president of the Royal Naval War College.[199] In fact, nearly every paper on the topic subsequently considered by the Admiralty during Fisher's administration originated from these two officers. Besides these two, advocates for amphibious strategy tended to be relatively junior in rank, holding unimportant positions—officers such as Colonel George Aston of the Royal Marines.[200] While the First Sea Lord did not suppress further investigations, it seems significant that until Slade moved from the Naval War College to become DNI in succession to Ottley (in November 1907), the Naval Intelligence Department expended few resources in this direction. Surely if Fisher was so keen on amphibious warfare, this topic would have been given a higher priority. During this period Fisher raised no objection to students at the Naval War College studying the problem, but this step was not as significant as some might think. Not until 1908 were direct links established between the NID and the college.[201] Ottley, meanwhile, made no secret of his contempt for papers sent him from the college.[202] During his brief term as DNI, Slade tried hard to resurrect Fisher's interest in amphibious schemes, but without any success—a fact he freely admitted in his diary. His subordinates in the NID, meanwhile, mocked such operations as "councils of desperation, which are entertained solely because no others are feasible."[203] Even Slade admitted that "the dangers and difficulties are very obvious," but he added that "the question to be decided is whether it is more dangerous to let the war drag on rather than end it as soon as possible, even if we do have to run great risks by doing so."[204]

2

The Envisioning of Economic Warfare

> The question to what extent you are to allow your belligerent rights to be curtailed in favor of the general progress of amity between nations, is a very difficult one to decide. I have always been disposed to hold the extreme view that we should stand fast on every belligerent right we have ever possessed or asserted, regardless of the fact that the necessary concessions of the same rights to other belligerents hit us very hard in the numerous cases when we are neutral.
>
> EYRE CROWE, 1907

In the aftermath of the 1905 Moroccan Crisis, Captain Charles Ottley resolved that the Admiralty would not again be caught trying to improvise a makeshift strategy when the next diplomatic crisis struck. As we have seen, the Admiralty had encountered considerable resistance to their suggestion that interdiction of German seaborne trade must inflict severe damage upon their economy, possibly sufficient to induce Germany to sue for peace. Opposition to this novel idea had come from within the service as well as outside. Undeniably, the Admiralty had based their proposals less upon calculation than upon an intuitive understanding of how the global trading system functioned and a few hasty estimates as to Germany's actual vulnerability. Ottley was the first to admit that his understanding of key elements in the proposed strategy was incomplete. Considerable research was required to obtain information about a wide range of topics, of which the most important was the true extent of Germany's dependence upon overseas trade. Scarcely less important was the need to consider the legal and diplomatic ramifications of the proposed action.

Remedying these shortcomings could not be accomplished overnight. The chief obstacle to an intensive study of these issues was shortage of administrative manpower. Already the NID was badly understaffed and overworked. Recently, moreover, the Treasury had declined an Admiralty request for a staffing increase.[1] But even if the money had been available, there remained a difficulty in finding men suitable to perform such work. Most rising officers continued to see a junior position at the Admiralty as detrimental to their long-term career prospects and injurious to their immediate personal finances.[2] Many simply could not afford to forfeit the additional pay that came with sea service and the command of a warship. One possible option might have been to tap the CID's budget, but after the falling-out between Fisher and Sir George Clarke—not to mention the latter's skepticism of economic warfare, detailed below—this was not feasible. As a result of these difficulties, the pace of research was certain to be slow.

The shortage of capable staff notwithstanding, in March 1906, Ottley urged Fisher to make the creation of concrete plans for the conduct of war (campaign plans) a high priority, if for no better reason than to head off anticipated criticism from the querulous Admiral Lord Charles Beresford. Currently serving as commander in chief in the Mediterranean, "Charlie B." was already slated to take over the Channel Fleet and succeed Sir Arthur Wilson the following year as the senior admiral afloat. Since his selection, however, Beresford had unexpectedly emerged as a leader of the so-called syndicate of discontent, a loose coalition of senior officers who were opposed to Fisher's administration but who could not agree among themselves precisely which of his reforms were objectionable.[3] Ottley reminded Fisher that war planning was Beresford's favorite hobbyhorse: for almost twenty years he had ridden it to attack previous naval administrations. Most recently, when Beresford had taken command of the Mediterranean Fleet, he had made a great fuss at not finding any war plans among the papers left him by his predecessor.[4] Ottley feared that if the Admiralty failed to provide Beresford with something suitable before he took command of the Channel Fleet, he would use this lapse to mount a potentially dangerous attack upon the current administration. Fisher was slow to react to this threat, probably too busy with more pressing concerns.[5] In May 1906, he mooted the idea of creating "a special campaign branch" at the War College in order to evade Treasury restrictions upon hiring additional staff at Whitehall. He was mindful that Ottley did not think much of the idea, however, and in any case, the entire subject was shelved the following month and remained so until the end of October.[6]

During the interim the Admiralty administrative staff was fully occupied gathering material to ward off an attack on the naval construction budget by the Treasury. The chancellor of the exchequer, H. H. Asquith, who succeeded to the premiership in 1908, had been given copies of internal Admiralty papers supplied to him by Sir George Clarke indicating that the Royal Navy was well above two-power strength.[7] Asquith used these papers to demand no less than a complete cessation in the construction of large armored warships. His aim was to find savings in the budget in order to permit the Liberals to deliver on their election pledges on social welfare projects. In making this call, he received strong support from the large radical element within the Liberal backbenches anxious to see Britain take the lead in promoting global disarmament. In order to "emphasize at the Hague Conference the good faith and desire of the British Government to bring about a reduction in armaments," in July 1906 the prime minister, Sir Henry Campbell-Bannerman, instructed the Admiralty to delete one battle cruiser from the annual program and delay the laying down of one of the three planned battleships pending the results of the upcoming peace conference.[8] In vain the First Sea Lord pleaded that "international alliances and, much more, international Ententes can be made and broken with far greater rapidity and ease than that with which battleships can be built."[9]

The idea of an international peace conference at The Hague had been in the air since late 1904, though it was not until April 1906 that formal invitations were issued for the following year.[10] The main topic of the second Hague conference was to be maritime law and the clarification of the rights of belligerents and neutrals in time of war. The need for legal codification had long been seen as overdue, and the British Foreign Office strongly supported the conference and its intent. Even the Admiralty could see merit in reform of the laws governing war at sea. Accordingly, Campbell-Bannerman instructed Sir John L. Walton, the attorney general, to form an interdepartmental committee comprising representatives from the Foreign Office, the Admiralty, and the Board of Trade (to present the commercial perspective). The Walton Committee was charged with deliberating upon "the subjects that might arise" and issues at stake for Great Britain, and assembling the essential facts so the cabinet could arrive at a policy and draw up the instructions for the British delegates to The Hague.[11]

Before proceeding, some knowledge of international maritime law at the turn of twentieth century is necessary. First, it should be understood that in diplomatic usage the phrase "international maritime law" was no more than a term of convenience to describe certain common principles traditionally incorporated into various bilateral (and nonbinding) treaties dating back to the sixteenth and seventeenth centuries, negotiated between European states to regulate and legitimate certain practices in connection with maritime warfare. Invariably, however, these agreements between states were vaguely defined and thus had been violated by belligerents with the strength (or permission) to ignore collective neutral opinion. In the aftermath of the Crimean War, an international committee met in Paris in 1856 to try to codify international maritime law, especially limits on how a belligerent might lawfully interfere with neutral trade that benefited its enemy. Although Britain had agreed to some restrictions on its claimed belligerent rights, enough loopholes remained in the resulting treaty to permit the Royal Navy to flex its muscles against enemy and neutral shipping. In any case, the interpretation of the Declaration of Paris remained the prerogative of national judiciaries. No statutory international court existed to regulate interpretive disputes, and no power had legal competence beyond its own territorial waters, which then extended only three miles from its shores.

At the beginning of the twentieth century, all the Great Powers recognized that belligerents could legitimately capture enemy property on the sea. Depending upon circumstances, it was also permissible to seize cargoes carried in neutral ships from neutral countries. If a belligerent was strong enough, it might declare an enemy port under blockade, closed to all traffic. All ships, enemy or neutral, that subsequently defied the blockade by trying to enter or leave could lawfully be seized if caught. International opinion accepted that blockade was a legitimate means of warfare, but it was hopelessly divided on many matters of detail. For instance, all agreed that a naval power could not simply announce an enemy's ports under blockade (this was sometimes known as a paper blockade), as the Union government did against the Confederacy at the beginning of the American Civil War. This was enshrined as the fourth clause of the 1856 Declaration of Paris, which stated, "Blockades, in order to be binding, must be effective, that is to say, maintained by a force sufficient really to prevent access to the coast of the enemy." But opinion differed as to how many warships were required, how close inshore they had to stand, or what happened if they were forced off station by bad weather.

Even greater confusion surrounded the meaning of the term "contraband." It was beyond dispute that a belligerent possessed the right to stop, visit, and search neutral ships on the high seas bound for enemy ports (even those not under blockade), and that if such a ship was found to be carrying contraband, the goods and sometimes the ship itself might be forfeit. In the abstract, contraband was property that was by its nature capable of being used by enemy forces for naval or military purposes. But there was no consensus as to what goods could legitimately be declared contraband, or under precisely what circumstances neutral ships could be legally condemned. By custom a handful of items, such as foodstuffs, were regarded as immune, but there had always been exceptions even to this general principle—for instance, if food was consigned directly to military forces or active theaters of operations.[12] In such instances food was deemed "conditional contraband," a term recognized under the Declaration of Paris, as distinct from "absolute contraband." In wars following the 1856 treaty, however, most of the Great Powers (including France, Britain, the United States, and most recently Russia) had stretched this to the point where in practice food was treated as absolute contraband.

Technological developments created further problems, which we shall examine more fully below. For instance, the hitherto widespread consensus that goods on board a neutral vessel exported from an enemy country could never be classed as contraband, since they had been purchased and thus had become neutral property, was endangered by changes in the global communications and financial system. The same changes also threatened the doctrine of continuous voyage (also known as ultimate destination), which held that if the ultimate destination of a contraband cargo was the enemy, the voyage of the vessel carrying it could be treated as continuous even if the vessel interrupted its voyage by stopping at neutral ports. Ducking these issues, the signatories to the Declaration of Paris had acknowledged the law of contraband but left the term "contraband" undefined. Belligerents remained free to define contraband according to circumstances. As Captain Prince Louis of Battenberg had dryly observed in 1903 to the Royal Commission of Food Supply in Time of War, "I suppose contraband of war is whatever the strongest party chooses to make it."[13] Or, more accurately, what neutral major powers would tolerate.

Admiral Sir John Fisher reacted to the establishment of the Walton Committee with a mixture of disdain and apprehension. On the one hand, he doubted that the conference would achieve any tangible results. As a plenipotentiary at the previous 1899 peace conference, he had seen at first hand how legal principles tended to shrivel whenever they conflicted with national self-interest. On the other hand, he was disturbed by the new Liberal government's declared support for the idea of global disarmament, which had worrying implications for current naval policy.[14] In April 1906, Fisher voiced his concerns to an old friend, making clear his conviction that the power to interdict international commerce (and finance) was a vital national weapon.

> We have a disquieting subject ahead in the new Hague Conference. All the world will be banded against us. Our great special anti-German weapon of smashing an enemy's commerce will be wrested from us. It is so very peculiar that Providence has arranged England as a sort of huge breakwater against German commerce, which must all come either one side of the breakwater through the Straits of Dover, or the other side of the breakwater the north of Scotland. It's a unique position of advantage that we possess, and such is our naval superiority that on the day of war we "mop up" 800 German merchant steamers. Fancy the "knock-down" blow to German trade and finance! Worth Paris![15]

Fisher's professed disquiet was a reference to a resolution by the U.S. government calling for "freedom of the seas." This term has been used in various senses, but it may be said generally to mean complete freedom of passage to neutral trade in time of war; extreme advocates also demand the immunity of all enemy private property at sea (merchantmen and cargoes). Freedom of the seas and immunity were the opposites of belligerent rights to enforce blockades and seize contraband. Through his political friends, Fisher knew that the new Liberal cabinet contained a group of radical Liberals (most notably Lord Loreburn) strongly in favor of the proposal to extend immunity to all shipping at sea in time of war, and that no fewer than 168 out of 397 Liberal Members of Parliament had signed a petition supporting the proposal.[16] Outwardly Fisher professed contempt: "These Hague Conferences want trade and commerce all to go on just as usual, only the Fleet to fight! ROT!!!"[17] Yet Fisher also recognized the political interest behind these utopian ideals was too strong to ignore, especially after Prime Minister Campbell Bannerman signaled his determination to make the conference a success. It was clear enough that the government intended to make concessions with or without the Admiralty's blessing.

Fisher appointed Captain Ottley, the chief proponent of economic warfare, as the naval representative on the Walton Committee. Ottley's main job was to persuade the others to recommend against endorsing the proposals for immunity of enemy and neutral property and for arms limitations. Otherwise the First Sea Lord gave the DNI a free hand to manage his unenviable mission. Ottley, appreciating that the slightest hint of hostility to the idea of a peace conference would likely prove counterproductive, professed sympathy with the government's general aim and agreed that every "endeavour should be made to limit as far as possible and to carefully define what are, and what are *not* a belligerent's rights in respect to contraband."[18] At the same time, he remained careful not to say anything that might somehow be exploited by the government to justify cuts in naval expenditures.

In endeavoring to thwart the proposal of immunity, Ottley faced an uphill struggle. From the naval perspective, Britain possessed the largest and most powerful fleet in the world and thus obviously stood to benefit the most from claiming wide-ranging belligerent rights. But the prevailing political sentiment of the day strongly favored greater codification of international maritime law and strengthening neutral rights even at the price of making substantial concessions on belligerent rights.[19] In almost a hundred years, Britain had clashed just once with a rival Great Power—against Russia during the Crimean War (1853–1856). Even then, the British government had allowed trade with Russia (the enemy) to continue almost unimpeded rather than enforcing an embargo. Conversely, whenever and wherever foreign nations fought at sea, it seemed that British merchants were the first to suffer. Given that British shipping companies controlled well over 50 percent of global oceanic tonnage, it was only a matter of time before belligerents seized a British-registered merchant ship or confiscated its cargo as contraband destined for their enemy. Invariably the result was a diplomatic tussle. From both the diplomatic and commercial perspectives, therefore, codification of maritime law (and especially agreement upon what could not be declared contraband) seemed highly desirable. As Sir Edward Grey (foreign secretary, 1905–1916) reminded the delegates chosen to represent Britain at an international conference on maritime law:

> It should be borne in mind that what the commerce of the world above all desires is *certainty*. The object of all rules on this subject should be to ensure that a trader anxious to infringe in no way the accepted rights of belligerents, could make sure of not being, unwittingly, engaged in the carriage of contraband.[20]

The idea that certainty in time of war was attainable and that merchants could rely upon due process today appears almost comically naive, yet at the beginning of the twentieth century it appealed strongly as a way out of the differences of interpretation over maritime law that had caused so much international friction and so many diplomatic headaches in the nineteenth century.[21]

In preparing the Admiralty's case for the Walton Committee, Ottley also had to fight a perception within government circles that traditional belligerent rights had become substantially unenforceable. During the recent Boer War (1899–1902), for example, the Royal Navy encountered practical difficulties in exercising the long-accepted belligerent right of stop and search on the high seas. There was a vast difference between trying to ascertain the cargo of an eighteenth-century merchantman carrying perhaps a few hundred tons and that of a twentieth-century tramp steamer carrying a mixed cargo of several thousand tons. Modern merchant vessels were simply too large for stop and search to be done safely at sea. Insisting that the conditions of warfare had changed, the Admiralty had directed their patrolling cruisers to divert vessels suspected of running contraband to the closest friendly port, where their cargo could be discharged and thoroughly inspected.[22] This departure from customary practice provoked howls of protest from neutral shippers at the disruption and expense thereby caused. Led by Germany, the neutral powers forced Great Britain to renounce the practice. The difficulties that Britain experienced during the Boer War in asserting belligerent rights left a deep impression upon many within the government and especially inside the Foreign Office.[23]

Doubts over the utility and applicability of current international law were reinforced by British experience during the Russo-Japanese War (February 1904–September 1905), this time as a neutral.[24] Russian attempts to claim certain belligerent rights to interfere with neutral merchantmen and their cargoes had run into fierce (and largely successful) resistance from the neutral powers, led by Britain and the United States.[25] Taking a leaf from the British book, the Russians unsuccessfully tried to claim that "changed circumstances" justified new measures, such as scuttling of neutral ships seized on the high seas and accused of carrying contraband. Similarly, when the Russians declared food and coal shipments to Japan to be contraband, the British government countered that food had never been treated as absolute contraband—although as one senior clerk in the Foreign Office pointed out, "International law is in such an unsatisfactory state that it cannot be said that the Russian contention is wrong."[26] Seeing potential future advantage in allowing the precedent to stand, the British government quietly acquiesced in the Russian categorizing coal as contraband, much to the consternation of their own senior diplomats.[27] The Russo-Japanese War also highlighted certain aspects of modern naval warfare that existing law simply did not contemplate. Throughout the war, for instance, both sides had resorted to laying autonomous contact mines outside of territorial waters, thereby creating a hazard to shipping on the high seas; this was a practice on which the Admiralty were keen for guidance.

All in all, recent experience suggested that in future wars neutrals would vigorously assert their rights to continue trading with whomsoever they chose, and that aggressive assertions of belligerent rights by warring powers risked provoking a violent backlash. In choosing a position, Sir George Clarke of the CID wrote in November 1904, the crux of the problem was

> whether the possible amount of injury we, as belligerent, could hope to inflict upon an enemy from the exercise of the right to search neutral merchant craft for contraband would be sufficiently important to counterbalance the resentment we should arouse amongst neutrals, and to compensate us for the inconvenience and loss which might be inflicted upon us as neutrals, is the question at issue.[28]

Clarke's advice was that under modern conditions the right to seize contraband in neutral ships seemed to be of little practical utility because the damage to the enemy could never be fatal. Furthermore, the proliferation of international trade over the previous thirty years and its increased complexity had rendered global trade effectively impossible to control. By imputation,

> sea pressure that can be brought to bear upon a Continental Power appears, therefore, to be far less effective now than formerly. If this is admitted, the advantage a belligerent State possesses from the right to capture contraband on the high seas, on the plea of "continuous voyage," must seem to be illusory.[29]

Consequently, he concluded that Britain should renounce the right to capture neutral vessels carrying contraband.

It must be stressed that in issuing this statement, Clarke was no more than voicing his opinion, unsupported by evidence or research, and viewing the subject from a narrowly mercantilist perspective, analyzing the problem in terms of monetary cost as opposed to strategic opportunity cost.[30] Nevertheless, historians have made much of this memorandum discounting the strategic value to Great Britain of attacking an enemy's trade, and have suggested it carried considerable weight with many leading politicians of the day and even with some Admiralty strategists.[31] While it is true that Clarke was widely recognized as a strategic expert, his reputation was never so great that ministers ever followed his recommendations in defiance of official War Office or Admiralty opinion.[32] More important, Clarke subsequently modified his views on this subject. After consulting several leading economists, Clarke by 1906 had accepted that the importance and vulnerability of German overseas trade was greater than he had previously allowed. He wrote privately to one expert in April 1906:

> I do not the least believe in the large captures which some people (such as Sir J Fisher) seem to expect. On the other hand I am inclined to think that the stoppage of all trade in German bottoms even for 6 months would very seriously affect Germany though not of course sufficiently to end a war.[33]

From this statement we might infer that Fisher and his supporters were claiming it could!

In May 1906, at the request of the prime minister, Clarke supplied to the Walton Committee a paper outlining his latest thinking on maritime pressure. He now advised that "it is impossible to estimate the degree of economic stress which would thus be imposed upon Germany, but clearly such stress would be severely felt throughout the whole commercial and industrial structure, and all the elements of the population depending thereon."[34] In the same document he went so far as to concede that "in the case of Germany, the stress would be exceedingly severe, while British trade would unquestionably benefit."[35] This amounted to a near total reversal of his previous position. On the issue of right of capture (immunity) Clarke fully supported the Admiralty position by stating that "we have nothing to gain and much to lose by abandoning the right in question."[36] Several months later he reiterated to the prime minister his conviction that "we cannot expect to capture on a large scale. By the *menace* of capture, however, we can drive an enemy's flag off the seas, and . . . [this] is our reply to the great military forces of the European Powers."[37] Unwittingly or not, Clarke's statement articulated one of the key tenets of the Admiralty's developing theory of economic warfare.

The 1907 War Plans

Despite Ottley's keenness for the Admiralty to formulate concrete plans for war, no progress had been made in 1906 before Fisher departed for his customary summer vacation. While abroad, Fisher convinced himself that writing war plans should be given a higher priority—if for no better reason, as Ottley had pointed out, than to deflect potential criticism of his administration for not having done so. There remained, however, the recurrent difficulty in finding personnel to do the work. Since March, precious NID resources had been further eroded by the necessity to respond to the Walton Committee and prepare for the coming Hague peace conference. On 16 October, Fisher wrote a revealing letter on the subject to the new First Lord of the Admiralty, Lord Tweedmouth:

> I only have one thing much on my mind, and that is the development of the War College at Portsmouth, which is a pressing matter—*a very pressing matter,* but I am going to talk to you at length about this on return. *Private.* Ottley and all his crew [the NID] look askance at it as they think they will be belittled by it—but no such thing! It's a real weapon against the Admiralty and I do feel personally guilty in not having pushed it. However, no one has seen the weapon lying about and so we have completely escaped criticism so far.[38]

After his return from vacation, sometime in early December 1906, the First Sea Lord summoned Captain George Ballard to his office and instructed him to form a secret committee to formulate detailed plans for war against Germany.[39] Ballard was the obvious choice given his contribution to the NID's studies since 1902, and in particular his intimate involvement with naval war planning during the 1905 crisis. He immediately requested the services of Captain Maurice Hankey (Royal Marine Artillery), who had shared an office with him at the NID and more recently served with him on a panel charged with reviewing coastal defenses at various bases around the world.[40] Ballard knew Hankey to be an excellent writer and a tireless assistant. Both were nominally assigned to cruisers in the reserve fleet at Portsmouth, thereby allowing them to work onshore while drawing sea pay and qualifying for promotion.[41]

Ballard assembled his committee at Portsmouth in January 1907. Besides Hankey, he had the assistance of two other junior officers about whom nothing is known except that one was "a mine expert" and the other "a gunnery expert" and that both "held appointments or commands away from Portsmouth and could only attend occasionally."[42] Contrary to frequent suggestion, Captain Edmond Slade (president of the Naval War College) was not a member; he was shown the drafts but "advised a few minor amendments only."[43] In mid-April 1907 (i.e., within four months) Ballard handed Fisher some sixty pages of typescript.[44] The speed with which the report was produced is significant: it provided barely enough time for two men to produce more than sketch plans, and it suggests that the committee probably worked from material supplied to them by the NID, rather than coming up with wholly original ideas. Indeed, on both counts, Ballard admitted as much. In a letter dated May 1909 reminding the First Sea Lord of his work, he described his report as consisting of eight alternative plans intended to meet varying contingencies for war with Germany. "Of these however only three would be elaborated in detail, as the others were based upon the co-operation of France, or assumed that Germany had taken certain initial steps which would only be roughly summarized."[45] Two of the three, moreover, had been "founded to a large extent on papers already in the NID which had been drawn up on previous occasions extending back over several years."[46] A couple of years later he wrote to Ottley in a similar vein.[47]

These details are important because the Ballard report has survived only in modified form, as part of a larger and later document known to historians as the 1907 War Plans.[48] Though often assumed to be the same, the Ballard report and the 1907 War Plans are in fact quite different documents. In November 1911, for instance, Ottley recalled that the Ballard report had evaluated and emphatically rejected the idea of capturing the German island of Heligoland, yet its rejection was omitted from the printed War Plans version (probably in deference to Admiral Sir Arthur Wilson).[49] Another letter from Hankey to Ballard mentions the deletion of references to sensitive intelligence material.[50]

The 1907 War Plans document has been the font of much scholarly confusion. Most differences of historical opinion arise from the mistaken assumption that it was solely the product of the Ballard Committee.[51] In fact, strong evidence exists that several of the plans were devised by a different group of officers known as the Whitehall Committee. In May 1909, the First Lord of the Admiralty told the prime minister that they had been compiled by a "Committee at Whitehall and [also] you had four specially selected officers at Portsmouth; the plans of 1907 were drawn up mainly at Portsmouth, at the War College, but partly also at Whitehall."[52] Thus the 1907 War Plans were really a compilation of prints and reports, authored by various groups or individuals, written at different times, conceived for different purposes, and intended for different audiences. Small wonder, therefore, that so many readers have remarked upon the serious inconsistencies contained within.[53] Nor does it help that there exist several editions of the 1907 War Plans, with varying content and pagination. Moreover, because all copies were printed at the Foreign Office and not at the Admiralty (in itself an intriguing fact), there are no printer's marks at the foot of the page to indicate edition or date.[54] The "standard" edition most commonly cited is that reproduced by the Naval Records Society in 1964.[55] It consists of five parts. Part I, the preface, titled "Some Principles of Naval Warfare," was written by the prominent naval historian Julian Corbett. Recently, however, it has been shown that Fisher had a hand in its composition and may even have sketched the first draft or at the very least provided Corbett with an outline of what he wanted.[56] Part II, the preamble, titled "General Remarks on War with Germany," contemplated various politico-diplomatic scenarios that might have led to war. This was nothing more than an updated version of an old memorandum composed by Captain Edmond Slade, the president of the War College.[57] The earlier versions of Part II also contain a miscellany of documents including a summary of various war games run by the War College. Part III contains the modified Ballard Committee report. The Naval Records Society copy identifies Slade's miscellany as part IV. Part V is a commentary on the other sections by Admiral of the Fleet Sir Arthur Wilson essentially supporting the key premise that close blockade was dangerously impractical.[58]

Let us review the plans themselves (Part III) in more detail. This section includes an introductory essay followed by four specific plans of campaign, identified as A, B, C, and D, each of which is further subdivided into two scenarios (A and A1, etc.) depending on whether France was allied to Britain or not. Plan A recommended what the committee termed a "distant" blockade strategy and was "based on the assumption that the loss to German commercial interests though the destruction or enforced idleness of German shipping will be so great that popular outcry will put a stop to further operations."[59] In other words, economic pressure would prove a strategically decisive weapon. Plan B was "based on the supposition that the destruction or enforced idleness of shipping under German flag is not in itself sufficient to bring Germany to terms," and reviewed the practicality of imposing a close commercial blockade that complied with the existing legal provisions governing capture and effective blockade (as defined under the 1856 Declaration of Paris). Plan B also entailed the sinking of blockships to obstruct the Elbe (a speculative plan considered by the NID in 1904 to hinder the debouche of the German fleet into the North Sea, as the Japanese had done to the Russian fleet at Port Arthur) together with the capture of Borkum (a then undefended resort island just off the mouth of the river Ems) to serve as an advance fueling base for short-range flotilla craft.[60] Plan C was an extension of plan B assuming that "still further pressure is necessary" and evaluated Admiral

Wilson's 1905 idea of a "reckless" offensive (i.e., amphibious operations on the German coast). Finally, plan D considered the possibility of operating a fleet inside the Baltic. Judging from deprecatory remarks made by Ballard in his introductory memorandum, Plan D (and D1) probably originated from the Whitehall Committee.[61]

Probably no Admiralty document has provoked such an astonishing diversity of opinion—or so many outlandish interpretations—as the 1907 War Plans.[62] Before attempting to interpret them, it is necessary to consider why they were written and how they were used. We know part III was mainly the product of the Ballard Committee, which was set up by Admiral Sir John Fisher and "worked under Fisher's immediate inspiration"; Ballard met with the First Sea Lord "once or twice a week in London."[63] No record has survived of what was said at these meetings, but it seems reasonable to suppose that the final product said what Fisher wanted it to say.[64] We also know that Fisher was instrumental in recruiting Julian Corbett to write part I as a preface to the Ballard report. Here, thanks to the survival of much of their correspondence, we have a much clearer idea of the timeline and objectives.

Fisher first broached the subject with Corbett on Sunday, 9 March 1907, and arranged to meet the following Tuesday.[65] Evidently they met, but Corbett did not immediately accept the commission. On Sunday, 17 March, Fisher wrote again, imploring, "You will be doing the Navy a lasting service by giving us the proposed preface an Epitome of the Art of Naval War."[66] Corbett relented and, with remarkable speed, submitted his first draft on 2 April. Two days later the First Sea Lord returned it to the historian with his handwritten corrections and a very telling request that Corbett redirect his focus. "It is more than kind of you to undertake the task and I'm very grateful to you," Fisher added. "*Please do not hurry as the sole object I have in view is to make it appeal to the non-professional* and you're the only one I know who can do this."[67] In other words, the intended readership of this supposedly secret document lay outside the Royal Navy.[68] Over the next three weeks Fisher remained in close touch with Corbett, until the final version was printed during the first week of May 1907.[69] Parts II and IV, a compilation of old papers and reports, originated from Captain Slade and the Naval War College. Incidentally, we know Ottley did not think much of Slade or his ideas; it was probably these that provoked him a couple of years later to remark that "preposterous notions were at the time abroad regarding the function of the Naval War College! People solemnly suggested that the educational establishment was to prepare war plans!"[70]

What did Fisher do with these plans? On 29 April 1907, he verbally briefed Admiral Lord Charles Beresford, the new fleet commander in chief, on his War Orders and personally handed him a copy of part III (the modified Ballard report). They were not given to him as executive orders.[71] "The eight different ideas in the print I gave you," Fisher wrote to Beresford the following day, "furnish (I think) a sufficient basis for all the present purposes."[72] In other words, they were intended to define the parameters of strategic discussion, not to function as concrete plans. On one surviving copy of the plans, indeed, is a prefatory statement that "the opinions and plans herein (to which others will be added from time to time) are not in any way to be considered as those definitely adopted, but are valuable and instructive of the variety of considerations governing the formation of War Schemes."[73]

Admiral Beresford was unimpressed with the eight plans given him and quickly saw them for what they probably were: a device to steer him into endorsing Fisher's preference for economic warfare. Ten days later, he stated in an official letter to the Admiralty that "it appears to me that Plan (A) is radically unsound" as well as "altogether impossible"; he correctly divined that "the object appears to be merely destruction of German merchant ships."[74] This "is certainly not the way to go to war with a great country like Germany."[75] The vehemence of Beresford's objections, and the fact that he said nothing about the other three plans, suggests that Fisher had intimated during their meeting on 29 April that the Admiralty's strategic preference was for economic warfare and a scheme of naval operations based upon distant blockade and flotilla defense. From other sources, we know Beresford violently objected to the inglorious role assigned his battle fleet, which was to provide cover for the flotilla operating in the North Sea.[76]

Over the next six weeks Beresford issued a series of quite extraordinary letters, questioning the competence of the Admiralty, his predecessor, the authors of the "war plans," and ultimately claiming sole responsibility for the conduct of war at sea. After denouncing everyone else's plans as "impracticable," moreover, Beresford proposed a strategy that required more warships than the Royal Navy actually possessed.[77] By June 1907, Fisher realized that compromise with Beresford over their differences in strategic outlook was impossible and tried to have him dismissed for insubordination.[78] Lord Tweedmouth, however, the First Lord of the Admiralty, shrank from such controversy. "I am the last person in the world to abrogate one iota of the supremacy of the Board of Admiralty," Tweedmouth wrote Fisher, "but I do think we sometimes are inclined to consider our own views infallible and are not ready enough to give consideration to the views of others who may disagree with us but who give us ideas and information which can be turned to great use."[79] On 14 June, Fisher changed tack and informed Lord Charles that the orders granting him the authority to command all warships in home waters was cancelled, and ordered all cruiser squadrons and flotilla craft to be transferred to a different command with immediate effect.[80] This was a massive blow to Beresford's prestige. Although Tweedmouth continued to wring his hands and seek a compromise between them, Fisher afterward avoided all debate of the subject, and it is notorious that the two admirals were thereafter at daggers drawn.[81]

During the spring of 1907, Fisher widely distributed copies of Corbett's introduction to the 1907 War Plans to "non-professional" readers. Among the first to receive copies were King Edward VII; Reginald McKenna, president of the Board of Education; Lewis "Lou-Lou" Harcourt, first commissioner of works (and public buildings); also James L. Garvin, a leading naval journalist.[82] It served, as the military correspondent for the *Times* once quipped, as "one of Sir John's semi-confidential manifestos printed for the advantage of the press."[83] Fisher's manipulation of Fleet Street was notorious, and Corbett's willingness to provide him with propaganda is well documented.[84] One recent scholar, Christopher Martin, convincingly argues that the production of the 1907 war plans, and Corbett's paper in particular, can best be understood in the context of the contemporaneous public debate over the Hague peace conference. He suggests they were written mainly to counteract the Liberal government's support for the immunity from capture of all private property at sea, by explaining "the fundamental problem that an extension of immunity would bring to the Royal Navy."[85] That Fisher handed a copy of this supposedly secret preface to current war plans to Augustus Choate, the chief U.S. delegate to the Hague Conference, strongly supports this interpretation.[86]

Further evidence exists that Fisher viewed the 1907 war plans as a device rather than as genuine plans. In January 1908, for instance, he had the 1907 war plans reprinted (and repaginated) for distribution to senior government ministers as a rebuttal to allegations made by Admiral Beresford that the Admiralty had no plans.[87] They were again distributed in 1909 fronted with a new preface written by Fisher stating: "The 780 pages herewith of print and manuscript are sufficient evidence of the close thought and study given to war planning during the last four years."[88] "I never told anyone my real plan of war," Fisher told one confidante in 1911, "but A.K.W. [Admiral Wilson, his successor as First Sea Lord], not being a Machiavelli, wouldn't tell the Cabinet anything. I, on the contrary, told them so much that they thought me perfect. I gave them 600 pages of print of war plans!"[89] Indeed, as Fisher claimed, it is difficult to see how the 1907 war plans could have been his "real plan for war," since they lacked details relating to the use of offensive mines, the theory of flotilla defense, the role of wireless, and war room control.[90]

The influence of political considerations on this document, however, does not mean that it contained no genuine strands of Admiralty strategic thinking. The difficulty is distinguishing the strategic signals from the political noise. Most of these signals can be found in part III, plan A, which hewed most closely to the original Ballard Committee report. In his memoirs, Hankey stated explicitly that the recommendation of the Ballard committee was to attack Germany through "economic pressure."[91] The committee, he went on to explain, was "greatly impressed" as to "the susceptibility of Germany to economic pressure, though we could not judge whether it would be possible to squeeze her into submission, or how long it would take, particularly in view of the assistance she could obtain from her continental neighbours."[92] In a letter to Fisher dated 1909, Ballard said more or less the same thing. He reminded the First Sea Lord:

> The first plan—known as Plan A—followed on its general outline the idea which underlay our operations in certain of the Dutch Wars of the 17th Century. By intercepting the Dutch trade as it passed up the Channel we forced the Dutch fleets to come out and defend it, and so brought on fleet actions near our own coast. This strategy, if applied under modern conditions, would cripple German oversea trade at a minimum risk and difficulty to ourselves. Possibly it might cause such loss to the enemy that the pressure of commercial influence—increasing in Germany—would end the war without further measures on our part as it did with the Dutch.[93]

From this passage it is clear that Ballard envisaged his "plans" as entailing a systematic attack upon enemy overseas trade with the object of causing extensive commercial dislocation within Germany. Although Ballard mentioned the possibility of fleet action, his final sentence made clear his belief that economic pressure might suffice to win the war without recourse to battle.

Linguistic imprecision obscures the radical nature of this strategy. In the 1907 Ballard Committee report, Ballard and Hankey described their preferred strategy of economic pressure as a "distant blockade," but they acknowledged that their usage of the term did not conform to the proper legal definition of "blockade," which contemplated only a "close blockade." Ballard and Hankey used ill-fitting old words because accurate new ones had yet to be invented. Existing legal language simply could not describe their strategy, and it took several more years to develop a new vocabulary. In the meantime, contemporary readers nevertheless recognized the novelty of the Ballard Committee's ideas through the linguistic haze. As one NID officer remarked after reading the Ballard report:

> It is a historical fact that no war has hitherto been brought to an end by such means as it is here proposed to employ. But on the other hand it must be remembered that the *modern industrial situation is unprecedented* and the effect of *such a blockade* as here proposed defies calculation.[94]

Like Ballard and Hankey, the officer who wrote these words understood the "unprecedented" nature of the strategy proposed but described it in terms of a familiar precedent. To resort to cliché, language and law lagged behind the strategic paradigm shift. The distinction between economic warfare and blockade will be explored further in the next chapter.

In the introduction to part III, Ballard went to considerable trouble to make clear the assumptions that had underpinned his committee's work, giving the distinct impression that he was trying to convince his reader that plan A (the distant blockade) was the only sensible option. He stated that in the event of war with Germany "our best reply would be to put Plan (A) in force."[95] As explained, plan A called for the Royal Navy to rely upon economic attack by positioning cruiser cordons at the entrances to the North Sea to interdict all trade carried in German merchant ships and assumed that this would be sufficient to generate strategically decisive results. "This assumption may be correct or otherwise," Ballard noted, "but it does at any rate represent the view of a considerable section of those well qualified to judge, and therefore is bound to be taken into account."[96] Admittedly, others were less sure. As another NID officer remarked:

> The fundamental question, on which as has been pointed out, authorities are divided, is whether any pressure of this kind which we can apply will be sufficient. This "master problem" is being examined as far

> as possible by the trade Division of the NID. But, on a point of such transcendent import it is considered that the highest financial and commercial experts might well also be called into secret council. For plainly, if indeed it should appear that such action cannot have the desired effect it is imperatively necessary that we should know it at once, so as not to build on insecure foundations.[97]

The meaning of this comment is open to two interpretations. Was the Admiralty trade division trying to calculate whether the Royal Navy could apply sufficient pressure to cripple German overseas trade? Or were they investigating the more fundamental question of whether the crippling of overseas trade would generate decisive economic pressure? Regardless, both questions required answers, and Ballard answered both in the affirmative. Economic pressure, he noted, "has the advantage of exposing our own ships to the minimum of risk, for it can be carried out beyond the ordinary radius of action of the enemy's torpedo craft, and without entering waters where hostile mines may reasonably be expected to lie."[98] At the same time—and this is highly significant—Ballard made clear his favored plan was predicated upon *not* complying with the legal definition of "effective" blockade. He especially emphasized that "the arrangement would not have the direct effect of a commercial blockade" because the Royal Navy could not legally stop neutral merchantmen carrying goods directly to German ports.[99] But for reasons explained below, he believed such leakage would not be as serious as it might appear.

Despite his clear preference for plan A, Ballard needed to address Admiral Wilson's point during the Moroccan Crisis that if Britain was allied to France, then "it is possible that Plan (A) might not be sufficiently aggressive to suit French ideas." In exploring the more aggressive campaigns (plans B, C, and D), Ballard and Hankey made little effort to hide their doubts as to their feasibility.[100] They explicitly admitted that plan B (the close blockade strategy) had been included as a straw man. "As the idea of a commercial blockade of German ports has been advanced," they wrote, "a plan has been drawn up for carrying out the same, but more to demonstrate the difficulties as compared with Plans (A and A1) than as an approved plan of operations."[101] They further stated that the adoption of a close blockade "would not add greatly to the punishment which Germany would suffer under Plans (A and A1), but it would much increase the risks we should incur ourselves." For a close blockade to have any hope of success, they insisted, the Royal

Navy must block the western end of the Kiel Canal (with blockships) and capture an island (Borkum) off the German coast to serve as an advance refueling base for flotilla craft. Both these operations, they predicted, would be extremely hazardous and costly undertakings.[102]

If such concerns were valid for plan B, then they applied even more forcefully to plan C, the "reckless offensive." Again, since explicit repudiation of Wilson's pet scheme for amphibious operations would have been grossly impolitic, they instead dwelled at length upon the "formidable" strength of German defenses in the western Baltic and invoked Ottley's favorite injunction that "attacks of this nature are not now considered as proper employment for vessels of war, unless under quite exceptional circumstances."[103] Perhaps the most telling measure of how seriously (or not) Ballard regarded operations in the Baltic was his recommendation that the French fleet carry out the operation.[104]

We turn now to some overlaps between the Ballard plans and current Admiralty thinking. In January 1907, just as the Ballard Committee was beginning its labors, a report arrived at Whitehall from Captain Philip Dumas, the newly appointed British naval attaché in Berlin.[105] Dumas' message was that Germany was daily becoming more vulnerable to economic attack, and consequently the Admiralty should look more closely at "starving Germany into submission by destroying her sea-borne trade." This idea did not spring fully formed from Dumas' mind. He knew that the Naval Intelligence Division was considering this strategy, as it was standard procedure for attachés to serve some months in the NID prior to being posted abroad. Except for some statistical information contained therein, the NID was not much impressed with Dumas' report. It was riddled with syllogisms and doubtful assumptions. The true importance of the Dumas report was that it prompted Ottley to write a critique pointing out its many shortcomings. In so doing, the DNI not only demonstrated his command of the subject but, more significant, touched on the findings of studies already carried out by the Admiralty (but no longer extant), which together suggest that the NID studies on economic warfare against Germany were by this date, January 1907, far more advanced than previously thought.

The DNI opened his comments by boldly asserting that "the effect of our preponderate sea power will be to drive the German flag off the seas and thus to inflict a tremendous blow on German trade, even though a certain proportion of that trade continues on through neutral ports, and in neutral bottoms."[106] Ottley went on to explain why he believed this "certain proportion" would be small and therefore not a significant problem. The NID had calculated (probably with the help of Lloyd's) that British shipping companies controlled approximately 55 percent of the world's oceangoing steam tonnage and Germany a mere 10 percent. (As discussed in Chapter 6, in actuality these figures underestimated the British monopoly.) In time of war, Germany therefore would be forced to rely upon neutral ships to carry her imports and exports. Yet after calculating the total oceanic carriage capacity of Norway, Sweden, France, Denmark, Italy, and the United States, Ottley explained, "It will at once be seen that the above-mentioned six neutral nations are absolutely unable to carry for Germany without starving their own national needs, indeed it seems doubtful if under any circumstances they could do so."[107]

Put more simply, Ottley argued that the combined neutral merchant fleets lacked sufficient capacity to service their own trading requirements, let alone spare anything extra for Germany. Going on to concede that the lure of high profits would likely induce some British merchantmen to turn a blind eye and carry goods for Germany through "adjoining neutral ports," Ottley proposed the government could—and should—take steps to outlaw this. In other words, he envisaged some degree of state control over the British merchant fleet. Ottley further speculated that networks of "secret agents" could be established in neutral countries tasked with tracking suspicious cargoes and gathering evidence for goods seized under the doctrine of continuous voyage. The DNI closed his analysis by reiterating his long-standing conviction that "it is difficult to avoid the conclusion that, in such a war the strangulation of her [Germany's] commerce would be a deadly blow to her."[108]

Thus the Admiralty plan for economic warfare against Germany depended upon exploiting Britain's effective monopoly in merchant ships to control the flow of material into Europe. If the German merchant navy could be swept from the seas and kept off them for the duration of the war, and British merchantmen prevented from carrying for Germany, then she must of necessity be cut off from the global trading system given the limited capacity of neutral shippers. Intriguingly, if we look closely, we find this same idea surreptitiously embedded within the Ballard plans.[109]

Assuming economic warfare would indeed produce strategic results, the question was whether Britain could apply sufficient pressure to throttle the German economy. This was primarily a naval operational matter complicated by legal considerations. Under international law, the complete interdiction of German seaborne commerce could be accomplished only by declaring her ports and coastline under blockade. But because of the dangers from mines and the enemy's own highly efficient torpedo-armed flotilla in the North Sea, as well as the legal and logistical difficulties of operating a fleet in the Baltic, Admiralty planners were unwilling to enter enemy territorial waters and therefore unable to mount a legal blockade of German ports. As the DNI declared in January 1907, "we shall probably have quite enough on our hands at the opening of war with the North Sea operations without looking for trouble in the Baltic."[110] Five months later he reiterated that close blockade was "virtually impossible" in the face of submarines and torpedo craft.[111] How, then, did the Admiralty still think they could isolate Germany commercially without resort to a legal blockade?

The problem with a distant blockade (i.e., the stationing of cruisers at a distance from the enemy coast, as Ballard prescribed in plan A) was twofold. First, it did not constitute a lawful blockade under existing international law. While a legal blockade would have empowered British cruisers to seize any vessel attempting to break the blockade regardless of its flag or cargo, the absence of a legal blockade would have meant that British cruisers could seize only German-flagged merchantmen and neutral vessels carrying contraband cargo. Nor could they stop neutral vessels from proceeding to German ports, loading German goods for export, and carrying them home (a critical point overlooked by most historians). Invoking the doctrine of contraband, moreover, was a move fraught with legal and diplomatic difficulties. As previously explained, there was no universally agreed definition of what could—and could not—be classed as contraband, and all recent experience showed that whenever belligerents tried to assert broad definitions of contraband, the result was friction and repudiation by neutrals.

Second, instead of carrying cargo directly to Germany, neutral merchantmen might just as easily discharge at the neutral ports of Antwerp (Belgium) or Rotterdam (Holland). Both ports were tightly integrated into the north European transport system and linked to Germany by canals and railways. The Royal Navy might check indirect German trade only by resort to the still more controversial doctrine of continuous voyage. Although such a step was not to be taken lightly, it must be emphasized that it was not impossible. Many historians and contemporaries have incorrectly assumed that German overseas trade could easily avoid the Royal Navy's grip by rerouting neutral merchantmen through neutral ports and therefore that the

Admiralty plans were totally infeasible. Such "breezy generalizations," Julian Corbett scoffed in June 1907, ignored "a nexus of practical considerations, complex and indeterminate to the last degree, and entirely beyond even approximate measurement. They seem airily to neglect the fact that the capacity of neutral shipping and of inland communications is not unlimited."[112] Carriage capacity was not perfectly elastic: Germany would encounter serious friction in attempting to transfer its requirements from overseas to neutral ports.

Even if Britain could not legally prevent indirect German trade though neutral ports, moreover, Germany would confront the enormous practical obstacle of insufficient neutral merchant shipping. The Ballard Committee insisted that "it is practically certain" that "the steam tonnage available to carry on the total trade required would be insufficient for the purpose."[113] When in 1905 General Sir James Grierson had rejected economic warfare as a decisive weapon by arguing that Britain would suffer more than France, Captain Charles Ottley had retorted, "The assertion is made that there is a risk of much of our maritime trade falling into the hands of neutrals, but nothing is said as to how the neutrals would find the requisite shipping to carry it, which at present they certainly do not possess."[114] Indeed, back in 1898, Ballard had examined this very question and concluded that neutrals could not possibly expand their merchant fleets rapidly enough to fill a wartime surge in demand for cargo space without staving their own needs: "To attempt to build the requisite number of ships would be the work of years, even with all the appliances of command of other countries, entailing besides an immense financial outlay on what would certainly be a very speculative investment."[115] They would also struggle to find enough neutral crewmen. Finally, European maritime law ruled out the possibility that belligerent vessels might be reflagged.

Britain could also potentially benefit from another shortcoming in international maritime law. The law relating to blockade, contraband, and continuous voyage applied mainly to cargoes, not ships. International law said nothing about belligerents forbidding their merchant ships from trading with the enemy or for enemy benefit. Such steps remained matters of municipal law and state regulations, over which international opinion had no control. In other words, there was nothing in international law to stop Britain from prohibiting all vessels flying the red ensign from carrying goods ultimately destined for or originating from enemy territory. Of course, there was no precedent or provision in British law for the state to impose such draconian legislation and so grossly interfere in the business affairs of the king's subjects. But that was another matter entirely.

There were other advantages to exerting economic pressure through control of ships rather than cargoes. In 1907, Rear Admiral Edward Inglefield, the former head of the NID Trade division and now CEO at Lloyd's of London, sent a letter to Captain Henry Campbell, the new head of the trade division, clarifying the intent behind certain procedures. He stressed the fundamental point of fixing on ships and not cargoes.

> I made some investigations with a view to determining the nationality of cargoes, and I made enquiries with a view to getting a weekly return from the Custom House Authorities of the cargoes of all ships arriving at, or sailing from, the United Kingdom. It was quickly apparent that such a return would be a gigantic task, requiring a staff of probably a hundred clerks to keep it going; and the fact that the ownership of goods in transit is often so indefinable, and the nationality of the owners when discovered are so mixed, that it was obviously futile to attempt any general classification of the nationality of the owners of cargoes. It was therefore soon apparent that the protection of trade must be based on the nationality of vessels.[116]

Besides providing further evidence that the NID was deliberating this matter in detail, that Inglefield should himself offer comments is of itself highly significant. Having served five years as head of the NID trade division, not only was Inglefield thoroughly conversant with the subject, but he had been closely involved in coordinating the Navy's investment in communications and intelligence infrastructure in order to develop a global shipping plot at the Admiralty. As chief executive of the largest maritime insurer in the world, moreover, which for insurance purposes maintained its own global tracking plot built upon its network of signal stations around the world, Inglefield knew better than anyone how much easier it was to maintain surveillance of merchant ships (especially when the majority were insured by Lloyd's and flew the British flag) rather than watching cargoes. His point about the inherent difficulty in establishing nationality and ownership of cargoes was fundamental; the legal complications associated with trying to capture cargoes were immense. Controlling merchant ships was an altogether easier undertaking.

International Law and Economic War

The Liberal government, it will be recalled, sought to achieve a meaningful codification of international maritime law and had set up an interdepartmental committee under Sir John Walton, the attorney general, to consider the official British position for the 1907 Hague peace conference. Captain Charles Ottley, the Admiralty representative, made no secret of his belief that throttling an enemy's trade would produce decisive results. However, when pressed to justify his faith, he steadfastly declined to reveal any details, keeping secret from the civilian committee members the Admiralty's interest in the international transport system. All he would say was that of all potential enemies, Germany appeared the most vulnerable to economic pressure.[117] Despite his reticence, Ottley accomplished his primary objective as a member of the Walton Committee, namely, to prevent endorsement of the idea to make private property immune from capture. In March 1907, the committee reported to the cabinet that Britain should oppose immunity, but at the same time advised that "it was in the interest of Great Britain that the policy of the Declaration of Paris should be extended to its logical end, and that a neutral's trade should be subject to no other restraint than the exercise of the right of visit and of effective blockade."[118] Fisher's response was to commission Julian Corbett to write yet another article pointing out the fallacy of such a recommendation. Corbett's "The Capture of Private Property at Sea" appeared in the June 1907 number of *The Nineteenth Century*.

Although the cabinet ultimately adopted Sir John Walton's recommendations as the basis of the instructions given to the British delegation, the British position was not yet finally settled. At the eleventh hour Lord Loreburn, a senior cabinet minister and leading proponent of immunity, petitioned the cabinet to reconsider the question of immunity, and the issue was still under discussion the week before the opening of the conference.[119] Hence the private instructions issued to the plenipotentiaries were as uncertain as they were ambiguous.[120] As one bemused delegate, Sir Ernest Satow, noted in his diary, "The Cabinet has decided not to abandon the right of capturing ships and cargoes, but do not want to shut the door completely."[121] Shortly before departing for the conference, Satow discussed the subject with H. H. Asquith, the chancellor of the exchequer. "On immunity of private property at sea," Satow recorded, "he [Asquith] said that he had read both sides of the controversy, and at the end of each paper perused he found himself agreeing with the writer."[122] Sir Henry Campbell Bannerman, meanwhile, continued to proclaim his platitudinous hope that the conference would advance the cause of world peace.[123]

Historians have subjected the Admiralty to much criticism for failing to prevent the Liberal government from weakening belligerent rights or explaining sufficiently clearly the basis of their war plans.[124] Indeed, not once during the Walton Committee's deliberations did Ottley challenge the government's willingness to offer concessions with the argument that Britain must retain the broadest possible belligerent rights in order to strangle Germany's economy.[125] To some, the failure to protest louder has seemed inexplicable and is attributed to a certain confusion of thought.[126] But to condemn the Fisher administration for acquiescing in the surrender of vital belligerent rights is to forget that governments and not admirals make national policy. It was permissible for the Admiralty to present their views in an effort to influence the formulation of policy, and Fisher certainly pressed this prerogative to the limit. Cabinet ministers were lobbied, propaganda material printed and circulated, and outside "experts" such as Julian Corbett recruited to publish articles presenting the navalist viewpoint.[127] Once the cabinet had settled upon a policy, however, the First Sea Lord was left with the alternatives of resigning or loyally following the government's instructions. For a variety of reasons, Fisher never contemplated resignation over this issue. Instead, he created a third course by simply declaring himself too busy with other matters and thereafter delegating the entire matter to Vice Admiral Sir William May, the Second Sea Lord. Admiral May, who was not an intellectual heavyweight, looked for guidance to W. Graham Greene, the civilian assistant Admiralty secretary (and uncle of the novelist), and to Captain Edmond Slade, the president of the Naval War College, who had gone into the subject in some detail.

Fisher assured a concerned Lord Esher that "the orders given to the Admiralty delegates are so stringent that they would leave by the next train if our fighting interests are tampered with."[128] These orders have not survived, but preconference minutes and memoranda suggest that they probably ran something like this: first and foremost, kill the immunity proposal; second, allow no discussion of the laws of blockade (the Admiralty believed British and Continental interpretations to be irreconcilable); third, promote regulation on converting merchantmen into warships; fourth, obtain guidance on the use of mines outside territorial waters; and fifth, if possible, tighten the rules governing the reflagging of merchantmen belonging to belligerents. At the same time, the Admiralty were prepared to go along with stricter definitions of contraband, though they quietly doubted whether any other nation would support such a transparently self-serving change. Otherwise, Ottley was entrusted with safeguarding the Admiralty's interests as best he could, and with keeping them informed of developments.

The second Hague peace conference opened on 15 June 1907. The British delegation was led by Sir Edward Fry, an octogenarian appeals court judge and devout Quaker. In order of seniority, the other plenipotentiaries were Sir Ernest Satow, a diplomat and oriental scholar; Lord Reay (Donald Mackay), a Scottish peer and politician who during the 1890s had served briefly as undersecretary for the India Office in the Liberal administration of Lord Rosebery; and Sir Henry Howard, diplomat and British minister to the Netherlands. They were accompanied by Captain Charles Ottley, the DNI; Lieutenant General Sir Edmond Ellis, representing the War Office; and Mr. Eyre Crowe and Mr. Cecil Hurst (departmental deputy legate) of the Foreign Office. The last four lacked plenipotentiary status.[129]

Eyre Crowe's letters to his wife describe in great detail the disharmony within the British team.[130] Fry and Reay in particular held the mere technical advisors in low esteem, excluding them from key meetings and ignoring their counsel.[131] That Satow was friendlier may be owed to the fact that he and Ottley had served together at the Tokyo embassy. After a fortnight, Crowe became so fed up with the petty wrangling and generally overbearing attitude displayed by the four plenipotentiaries that he told his wife, "I have given up all attempts to smooth matters and hope rather for an explosion."[132] Crowe had no respect whatever for the "stupid" Lord Reay, who "wants to override everyone, and busies himself with giving everything away in private talks with foreign officers. He will end by seriously compromising either himself or our whole mission."[133] Several times Crowe mentioned that he had been pressured by "our chiefs" to "write a dispatch home to say that they recommended a particular proposal which the military and naval delegates thought should not be agreed to."[134] On one occasion he prevented Lord Reay from sending home a cable "drafted by himself in which he made certain recommendations" that he claimed had been "approved by Ottley."[135] Crowe knew for a fact that Ottley "held diametrically opposite views to those attributed to him."[136] None of these details appear in the British official record of negotiations.

Captain Ottley maintained close telegraphic contact with the Admiralty and made frequent trips back to London. His early reports caused Lord

Tweedmouth, the ineffectual First Lord of the Admiralty, to write a number of letters to Sir Edward Grey, the Foreign Secretary, expressing dismay at the direction in which negotiations were proceeding.[137] Most alarming were the concessions made by the British plenipotentiaries to achieve agreement on the creation of an international prize court with appellate jurisdiction over national courts. None too politely, Lord Tweedmouth told Grey that the delegation had gone far beyond what had been envisaged prior to the conference (or what the Admiralty had agreed) and that the concessions offered appeared to constitute an unauthorized surrender of sovereignty that placed vital British interests at the mercy of foreigners. He subsequently told Grey that unless the unauthorized concessions were retracted, he must bring the matter before the cabinet. But after Grey called his bluff, Tweedmouth withdrew this threat.[138] As the weeks passed and it increasingly seemed the conference would disintegrate without tangible result, the Admiralty relaxed. As Fisher had predicted, the British proposal to abolish the right of capture with respect to contraband received short shrift. Conversely, the British refusal to be drawn into discussions on blockade law precluded exploration in that direction.[139] By late July, there was nearly total deadlock. In despair, Lord Reay wrote directly to the prime minister begging permission to make more concessions, warning that otherwise "our attitude at the conference will be severely criticized in the House of Commons on our own side."[140]

A surprising opportunity for concessions appeared in August. For reasons explained, the British delegation at The Hague had strict instructions not to enter discussions over blockade law.[141] Legal opinion held that British and Continental practices governing effective blockade (as described under the 1856 Treaty of Paris) were irreconcilable. Under British law, a merchantman lawfully could be seized at any time after leaving her home port if intent to run a lawful blockade could be proven. Continental lawyers, by contrast, insisted that a merchantman could be taken only if caught in the act of breaking a blockade—in other words, within the immediate vicinity of a blockaded port. On 2 August 1907, the Italian delegation introduced a novel compromise, suggesting that merchantmen might be condemned if found within a certain distance—*rayon d'action*—of a blockaded port. They arbitrarily set this distance at 100 miles. Initially, the British tried to suppress discussion (5 August) by pointing out a procedural violation; when that failed, they refused to participate in the debate (16 August) claiming they "had no instructions."[142] Then, a fortnight later, and to general astonishment, the British abruptly reversed their position and began actively promoting a modified version of the Italian plan. Even more extraordinarily, it was the Admiralty that took the initiative. The evidence for this is beyond dispute. Among Tweedmouth's private papers is the draft of a letter he sent Grey on 24 August, requesting that the delegation pursue the Italian proposal.[143] Sir Edward Satow recorded in his diary: "Admiralty asks us to take up blockade."[144]

Someone connected with the Admiralty—it is not clear whether it was Captain Ottley or Captain Slade—recognized an opportunity in the Italian proposal. If the Continental powers could be persuaded to accept a greater *rayon d'action* of at least 800 miles, then the new definition of "effective blockade" would prove highly advantageous to the Royal Navy's preparations for economic warfare. Essentially, it would permit the Admiralty to claim that a distant blockade met the legal criteria of an effective blockade. After unofficial conversations with various delegates, Ottley reported that an agreement was in reach if Britain was prepared to give a little more ground on the definition of contraband.[145] After reading this telegram, Vice-Admiral William May (the Second Sea Lord) recalled Ottley for discussions. Slade and Greene were also summoned to council. The resulting meeting agreed that the scheme should be formally presented to the conference.[146] "Looking at the matter from the strategic requirements of Great Britain," the Admiralty subsequently informed the Foreign Office, "their Lordships are disposed to think that 800 miles is the minimum limit which could be accepted. Any line drawn nearer to the blockaded coast than this, would take away the advantages which the geographical position of the United Kingdom confers"—a most revealing statement when viewed in the context of economic warfare.[147] There is no evidence, it may be noted, that Fisher was consulted over this initiative (he was out of the country), and a minute written several years later by Greene states that he had no involvement.[148]

The conference logjam broken, in less than a week a workable compromise appeared in sight. On 15 September, Ottley wrote "privately *at once*" to the Second Sea Lord reporting the latest progress. The German delegation had indicated they would agree to British demands "*never* under any circumstances to seize as Contraband the following raw materials—(1) Cotton, (2) Wool, (3) Metallic Ores, (4) Oil-seeds and Oils, (5) Mails, (6) Textiles."[149] This "free list," which appeared to protect key German (and British) industries from disruption in wartime whether Germany (or Britain) was a belligerent or not, was in fact no concession: if the British could get their desired redefinition of "effective blockade," which would allow them to seize all vessels attempting to run the blockade regardless of whether they were carrying contraband, then a narrowed list of contraband would not help Germany at all. In return for securing the desired new definition of "effective blockade," Britain would be required "to renounce once and for all (in common with all other powers) the intention to invoke the doctrine of Continuous Voyage for Contraband goods."[150] Ottley's letter reveals that the German delegates had initially demanded that Britain also surrender the right to apply continuous voyage with respect to blockade—an important distinction often missed—but he persuaded them (he thought) that this was asking too much.[151]

To understand the British reaction to this compromise formula, the meaning of the term "continuous voyage" in this context must be clear. Under the doctrine of continuous voyage, a development of the so-called Rule of 1756, belligerents claimed the right to stop vessels belonging to a neutral bound for the port of another neutral and to seize any goods intended for transshipment to enemy territory under blockade. Essentially, cargo was considered to be on a single continuous voyage from the port of lading to the port of delivery even if different portions of the voyage were in different ships. Implicitly, the law assumed that the destination of cargo and merchantman must be the same. If the shipowner could be shown to have been aware of the "unlawful" ultimate destination, moreover, then the intercepted ship too was liable to seizure.[152] In immediate and practical terms, therefore, the Admiralty's surrender of the right to invoke the doctrine of continuous voyage meant giving up all legal justification for stopping neutral merchantmen carrying goods for Germany to Antwerp and Rotterdam.

Sir Edward Fry, the head of the British delegation at The Hague, thought this "a good bargain" and urged acceptance.[153] He further claimed that Captain Ottley "concurs"—but this may not have been true. In a letter to the Second Sea Lord dated 15 September, Ottley said he had told Fry that the bargain *appeared* worth considering, "so far as any Paper guarantee can be effective," but had insisted upon the necessity of studying several important related questions.[154] In choosing whom to believe, one must take into consideration Crowe's earlier complaints that the plenipotentiaries tended, often willfully, to misrepresent the advice given them by the technical delegates. Readers will also recall that Ottley had a reputation for prevaricating on controversial matters; for him to have unequivocally concurred would have been out of character. Regardless, in his letter to Admiral May the DNI reviewed the arguments for and against acceptance. There could be no doubt, he reasoned, that any Admiralty attempt to apply the doctrine of continuous voyage on a large scale must lead to "dangerous disputes with powerful neutrals." In addition, given the enormous volume of trade that regularly passed through Rotterdam and Antwerp into the European hinterland, the British authorities must encounter formidable problems in differentiating between "legitimate" Dutch-Belgian trade and "abnormal" indirect German trade.[155] Furthermore, with the free list, the delegation had already signaled to the conference Britain's willingness to agree that food and bulk commodities should never be classed as contraband.

In view of these three considerations, retention of the doctrine of continuous voyage seemed to make little sense. "What Germany wants," Ottley reasoned, "and what (industrially) she as well as we may almost die for the want of are raw materials and foodstuffs (including bread-stuffs)." But if these were all immune from capture, "what then can we seize"? Against this argument, however, the principle of continuous voyage was still internationally recognized and therefore could be lawfully invoked even if any large-scale application of it must lead to diplomatic complications. If Britain chose to employ this in a war with Germany, "how far then will it be possible to injure Germany by invoking the doctrine of continuous voyage so as to seize German goods in neutral bottoms filtering into Germany"? Was it necessity to "cork the bottles" at Antwerp and Rotterdam? Could this be done effectively and at an affordable political-diplomatic price? In short, would the game be worth the candle? These were fundamental questions, and Ottley insisted they must be answered before any decision was taken to surrender the right of continuous voyage. He did not presume to know the answers.

By contrast, Captain Slade back in London felt no doubts that "under modern conditions" continuous voyage was effectively worthless. Though this doctrine might be invoked to seize a neutral merchantman and its cargo, he averred that it remained necessary to submit the action for judicial approval. He reminded everyone that a prize court would demand tangible proofs that cargoes were intended for an enemy destination before handing down a condemnation. The problem, Slade explained, touching on the same theme as Ottley, was that

> the Dutch and Belgian ports are the feeders of such a vast region, a great deal of which would be neutral, that it would be practically impossible to prove anything against the vessel. Suspicion and presumption are not sufficient grounds to go on when dealing with a court of

> law, and it would be obviously impossible to check half the trade of northern Europe because we considered that a small portion of it might be going to our enemy.[156]

Slade was adamant that gathering sufficient legal proof would be virtually impossible (and he was substantially correct). Whereas in the past, proof of destination and ownership usually could be found among papers on board the captured ship, by the beginning of the twentieth century this no longer held true because of changes in the way commerce was transacted following the development of the global cable communications network. These changes were what Ottley and Slade meant by the phrase "under modern conditions." The significance of this point cannot be overstated. It will, however, be much more convenient to explain these changes, their importance and implications, in the next chapter.

Admiralty discussion of whether to accept the proffered compromise slammed to a halt on the morning of 17 September 1907 after Captain Ottley woke up with second thoughts. He urgently cabled the Admiralty recommending the termination of negotiations.

> In view of great importance of question of Continuous Voyage as regards blockade I am strongly of opinion that unless you are clearly in favour of giving up the doctrine it is very essential that more time should be available for its consideration (stop) I am therefore suggesting that subject to your approval we should drop the question of blockade at this Conference (stop).[157]

He then boarded the first ship back to England to reaffirm his message in person. Once back in London, Ottley quickly persuaded Admiral Sir William May "to defer decision with regard to continuous voyage of blockade until a more convenient opportunity."[158] The Second Sea Lord promptly informed Lord Tweedmouth that "the questions are difficult ones and I concur with Capt Ottley the more you go into them the more difficult they seem."[159] Only Slade demurred; he continued to insist continuous voyage was practically worthless and accordingly that the bargain should be struck. He offered an additional reason in support of his contention, now arguing that Rotterdam and Antwerp lacked the port infrastructure to handle any significant increase in traffic and "the difficulties that would ensue in these ports will be quite sufficient to bring great pressure to bear on Germany."[160] May, however, was unconvinced, while Greene agreed that the Admiralty perhaps had been too hasty.[161]

The Admiralty's subsequent refusal to discuss the matter without further study proved sufficient to kill negotiations at The Hague. An irritated Eyre Crowe reported to his wife that the "arrangement I thought I had made with the Admiralty about contraband was upset by the subsequent proposals respecting blockade. Now I don't think anything will come out of it all for present."[162] On 24 September, Sir Edward Fry informed London that he now deemed it impossible "to bring to a satisfactory conclusion the negotiations for a special agreement respecting contraband and blockade on the proposed lines with Germany and France, and possibly other powers."[163] The Foreign Office was deeply disappointed. "The net result" of the conference, Crowe declared, "is practically nothing except the prize court convention. Whether that will be ratified by us, is another question."[164]

Admiral Sir John Fisher, by contrast, was well satisfied. As he had predicted, squabbles between the various powers, each trying to press for "rules" favorable to their own interests, had prevented the formation of any consensus on substantive issues. Writing from Carlsbad, where he had been vacationing since August, Fisher was delighted to report to King Edward VII the Russian foreign minister's agreement that "these war restrictions come to nothing when the time arrives."[165] In a letter to Lord Tweedmouth he positively gloated at the lack of tangible results.[166]

The First Sea Lord's elation was short-lived. Just three months later, on 14 January 1908, Sir Edward Grey informed the Admiralty of his intention to proceed with the establishment of an international prize court. Shortly after, he invited the ten leading maritime powers to a new conference to be convened in London before the end of the year.[167] The purpose of the new conference was subtly different from the last one. Whereas nations had assembled at The Hague to contemplate what maritime law ought to be, the purpose of the London Naval Conference was to discuss the principles of existing law. The aim was to harmonize conflicting interpretations in order to provide the proposed international court with agreed doctrines upon which to base its judgments.

The government set up another special interdepartmental naval conference committee to develop the British case, this time under Lord Desart, the Treasury solicitor, along with two representatives each from the Foreign Office (Eyre Crowe and Cecil Hurst) and the Admiralty (the DNI and a Captain Hickley).[168] Captain (now Sir Charles) Ottley also attended in his capacity as

CID secretary. In pressing for the international court, historians mostly agree that Grey optimistically believed he could negotiate a legal consensus so favorable to British interests as to overcome Admiralty objections.[169] Others, less impressed with Grey, have pointed out that while he may have expressed this hope, he was clearly willing to sacrifice whatever was necessary to achieve the desired legal codification.[170] Most new evidence tends to support the latter interpretation.

Before reviewing the deliberations of the naval conference committee, it is necessary to mention several important changes in personnel at the Admiralty. In May 1908, Reginald McKenna, the former education minister, replaced the ailing Lord Tweedmouth as First Lord of the Admiralty. A lawyer by profession, and a good one, McKenna quickly came to grips with his new portfolio. Over the course of the year, furthermore, he increasingly came to adopt the views of Admiral Sir John Fisher, whose attitudes on the subject of international law remained unchanged.

The second major change was the resignation of Captain Ottley on 12 August. Facing imminent compulsory retirement, midway through the Hague conference Ottley accepted an offer to become secretary to the Committee of Imperial Defence in succession to Sir George Clarke.[171] After a long delay suggestive of reluctance, on 28 October 1907 the First Sea Lord offered the post of DNI to the "clever" Captain Edmond Slade.[172] Although Slade's opinions differed materially from Ottley's on many issues, he was undeniably familiar with the complexities surrounding economic warfare, and this almost certainly was the reason for his selection. Yet it is significant that in giving Slade the position of DNI, Fisher did not also appoint him to several important Admiralty committees to which his predecessor had belonged. As Slade's personal diary makes clear, moreover, no sooner had he arrived at the Admiralty than he and the First Sea Lord began to bicker over questions of policy. Fisher belatedly realized that Slade's understanding of economic warfare was shallow and too academic.[173] After less than a year in the job, Slade was promoted and offered the command of the East Indies Station. Within the Admiralty it was an open secret that the First Sea Lord wanted him gone.[174]

Yet Captain Slade's short tenure as DNI produced some positive results. During the course of 1908 the NID made huge strides in the development of its plans for economic warfare against Germany. More crucially still, midway through the year naval planners made a quantum leap in understanding the distinction between traditional blockades and their new economic warfare strategy. This caused the Admiralty to regret having made any concessions during the run-up to The Hague. As Sir W. Graham Greene recounted seven years later, "The Admiralty acted subsequently only to the extent to which they felt themselves committed, and . . . throughout the discussion at the London Conference and subsequently their views on the subject gradually reverted to the previously accepted naval policy."[175] Of course, this intellectual breakthrough did not occur overnight, and for many months thereafter important details remained hazy. This lingering confusion was probably one reason why the advice the Admiralty gave to the naval conference committee, which sat between February and September 1908, did not reflect or conform to their latest thinking. Another reason was that Slade and Ottley had a major falling-out over the official advice given the naval conference committee and thereafter the latter declared himself as only "an interested outsider" (he was, after all, now CID secretary), complaining that "at every step Slade engineered the Admiralty policy."[176] Fisher too was very unhappy with Slade and, indeed, about October 1908 made arrangements to have him replaced as DNI. Even more suggestively, the First Sea Lord unsuccessfully tried to remove Slade as naval representative for the naval conference in favor of Ottley, though the latter was technically retired from naval service.[177]

The newly promoted Rear Admiral Edmond Slade, however, somehow survived Fisher's displeasure and retained his position a few months longer. In September 1908 he drafted the memorandum presented by the Naval Conference Committee to the Cabinet, recommending the stance Britain should adopt at the upcoming London Naval Conference scheduled to begin in December.[178] The cabinet approved with surprisingly little fuss, ministers confirming at the same meeting that the members of the Naval Conference Committee should become the official delegates to the London conference. Although Fisher and McKenna signed off on the memorandum, Slade's diary makes clear they were far from happy with its content.[179] That the Admiralty "generally approved" Slade's memorandum, furthermore, does not signify their endorsement—implicit or explicit—of the Declaration of London.[180] Indeed, the final text of the declaration, signed in March 1909, contained very significant departures from the document seen by Fisher and McKenna, and it incorporated major concessions to which the Admiralty had strongly objected. For instance, prior to the conference the Admiralty had been assured that the doctrine of continuous voyage for blockade would be retained. This assurance was "explicitly" noted on the file by Greene.[181] Both the draft report and the final instructions issued to the delegates on the eve of the conference also make clear that Britain entered the conference focused upon achieving ratification of the "Italian" definition of blockade tentatively agreed to the year before at The Hague.[182] Small wonder, therefore, that the Admiralty had endorsed the draft report: it promised a definition of blockade that would have legitimized their strategy of distant blockade while retaining the right to invoke the doctrine of continuous voyage against goods attempting to evade the blockade in neutral merchantmen bound for Antwerp and Rotterdam.[183] This interpretation was supported by Lord Desart, the Treasury solicitor, who was chairman of the conference committee.[184]

There are other reasons why general Admiralty approval did not constitute total approval. If control over the oceanic transport system formed the core of Admiralty plans for economic warfare, then, as Ballard had remarked with regard to the 1907 war plans, it was obviously essential that Britain

> take up an uncompromising attitude with regard to the transfer of German shipping to neutral flags or neutral owners after the outbreak of war to avoid capture. Plan (A) is dependent for its effect upon German shipping remaining under its own flag, and any large transfer to others would render it futile and deprive us of our chief means of injuring the enemy.[185]

In 1908, international legal opinion was divided over the legitimacy of belligerents reregistering their merchantmen under neutral flags of convenience.[186] Whereas under Russian, French, and German law it was illegal, under British and American law it was permissible under certain circumstances.[187] In this instance the Admiralty was keen to see customary British law replaced by Continental practice. The problem, as the naval conference committee noted, was that shipbuilding was one of Britain's largest industries and a key source of export revenue; shipbuilders possessed enormous political influence, and they were certain to fight tooth and nail any attempt by the British government to endorse the Continental interpretation of this law. As Slade noted, approval "would necessitate legislation on our part in order to give effect to the ruling. This would undoubtedly meet with great opposition in Parliament, and it is probable that we should fail to carry it out."[188]

When the conference on international maritime law opened in London on 4 December 1908, Eyre Crowe predicted swift and successful results.[189] After ten days his optimism had evaporated.[190] On 14 December, Slade confirmed that an impasse had been reached. Germany was threatening to break up the conference unless Britain agreed to renounce the right to invoke continuous voyage under all circumstances.[191] The Germans (along with the Dutch) also insisted upon the insertion of several clauses relating to the proposed new laws of blockade unfavorable to Royal Navy operational requirements.[192] Even Slade thought the German demands were excessive. He told the senior British plenipotentiary, Lord Desart, "We are not so keen on having this prize court that we must agree to it at all costs and that I would far rather see the whole thing abandoned rather than assent to the German contentions."[193] Watching events from the Admiralty, Greene worried that any concession on this point "means that Germany when a belligerent will be able to maintain a practically uninterrupted entry for a portion of her trade, whether contraband or not, through Belgian and Dutch ports."[194]

On 15 December 1908, the five conference delegates met with Sir Edward Grey, the Foreign Secretary, and Reginald McKenna, First Lord of the Admiralty, to discuss the pros and cons of bowing to the German demands.[195] Greene was also present. Speaking for the Admiralty, McKenna urged no surrender. While acknowledging that the difficulties in finding sufficient proof of destination and ownership rendered the doctrine of continuous voyage "of limited practical use," he argued that it nevertheless remained an important (and lawful) tool against neutrals. "Even if the detention did not result in the condemnation of the goods or ship," he reasoned, "the cost of freights and insurance would at once rise against the belligerent affected and assist in causing a financial crisis."[196] As he continued:

> It might be true that there would be a difficulty in proving the "continuous" carriage of a contraband against a vessel, and that it might not be possible to ignore the protests of a strong neutral; but a serious hindrance to this part of Germany's trade, coupled with a blockade of her own ports, could not fail to be of the first importance to us in war.

It is worth noting that McKenna apparently mentioned at this meeting the Admiralty's belief, hitherto kept secret, that British dominance of transatlantic carrying capacity was the key to strangling Germany. He alluded to this when discussing the importance of preventing the wartime reflagging of German merchantmen. Greene records: "It was agreed that by the existing rules of International Law this could not be done except to a very small extent and it was impossible that a neutral mercantile marine already fully engaged in its own trade could deal with such an enormous volume of additional trade."[197]

Failing perhaps to recognize the significance of this point, the Foreign Office never asked the Admiralty to dilate on the matter.

McKenna walked away from the meeting believing that he had won his case and that continuous voyage would not be surrendered unless Germany offered additional and tangible (albeit undefined) concessions. He was therefore distressed, several days later, to learn that Grey had authorized the conference delegates to renounce continuous voyage in return for definite lists as to what was and was not to be considered contraband—more or less the same free list the Admiralty had balked at twelve months earlier at The Hague. McKenna thought Grey was selling the Admiralty short, and a row ensued.[198] Initially the Foreign Office insisted it was "for Sir E. Grey to decide whether the British delegates are or are not authorized to continue negotiating with Germany on the subject of continuous voyage."[199] But McKenna refused to be put off on a point of such obvious relevance to the Admiralty and hounded Grey for an explanation of his reversal.

On 26 December 1908, the Foreign Secretary denied he had given McKenna any such promise. Explaining himself, Grey "expressed the view strongly that it would not do to break up the Prize Court Convention on the point of continuous voyage." He also made much of earlier Admiralty admissions (by Slade) that continuous voyage was not deemed vital.[200] "I admit," Grey went on, "we might find in it some pretext for creating a scare about freights and insurance," but to him this seemed insufficient justification for breaking up the conference over a seemingly trivial technicality.[201] Grey closed by threatening McKenna to accept his decision or else "I can see nothing for it except a Cabinet before the conference reassembles." The Foreign Secretary knew perfectly well that the majority of ministers would resent the disruption of their holidays and almost certainly back him. Recognizing inevitable defeat on a seemingly minor technical point unlikely to be appreciated by very many, McKenna yielded.[202] Alternatively, he may have wanted to keep his powder dry in anticipation of the looming larger battle over the number of large armored warships to be laid down the next financial year—the Admiralty's request for six vessels had met with a chilly reception when discussed in the cabinet during back-to-back meetings on 18 and 19 December.[203]

McKenna had another reason for not protesting Grey's action. Within official circles it was an open secret that, privately, the First Sea Lord objected strongly to the London Naval Conference, yet his objections had left the government unmoved. Across the top of one official paper Fisher irreverently scrawled that the "inevitable result of Conference and Arbitrations is that we always give up something. It's like a rich man entering into a Conference with a gang of burglars!"[204] On 5 November 1908, the admiral reported to a trusted friend that the previous day he had expressed strong dissent at an unofficial meeting on the subject with several senior cabinet ministers. Never before cited, the letter merits lengthy quotation, for it reveals a great deal about Fisher's thoughts on the enforcement of economic warfare and his idea of minimizing the attendant difficulties by making generous compensation payments. In essence, Fisher believed that it would prove cost-effective for Britain cynically to disregard the law and accept the financial penalty afterward. As he wrote:

> We were discussing yesterday for the international conference on Dec 1st the laws of blockade as desired to be altered by every one except England (as all are weaker on the sea!). They asked what should be the decision. I replied "make all the infernal fuss you can to get something elsewhere out of them quid pro quo but it don't signify a 'tinkers damn' what laws of blockade you make. *'MIGHT IS RIGHT'* & when war comes we shall do just as we jolly well like! *No matter what your laws are!* We've got to win and we ain't going to be such idiots as to keep one fist tied behind our back! There's a law against sinking neutral merchant ships but we should sink them—every one! We can pay two or three millions indemnity afterwards if willing but we shall have saved about 800 millions in getting victory & getting it *speedily* & so on." But these worms don't understand it & and looked at me as a wild lunatic.[205]

The Foreign Office, the chief sponsor of the London Naval Conference, was well aware of Fisher's private views. Eyre Crowe, who privately sympathized with the admiral, told Grey:

> Sir J[ohn] Fisher told me personally 3 days ago that in the next big war, our commanders would sink every ship they came across, hostile or neutral, if it happened to suit them. He added, with characteristic vehemence, that we should most certainly violate the declaration of Paris and every other treaty that might prove inconvenient.[206]

Crowe could have dismissed the admiral's remarks, as many in the Foreign Office had done before, as merely one of his "characteristic effusions," but, surprising as it may seem, his minute to Grey shows that he took Fisher's opinion seriously and was far from outraged by his disrespect for international law or hostility to the new treaty. In a separate paper written a couple of months later, Crowe acknowledged that "for a considerable period (about the early 'eighties [i.e., 1880s]) British Governments seriously contemplated denouncing the Declaration of Paris whenever England might find herself involved in a big war."[207]

Of course, in reality Fisher never could have issued such orders without the government of the day approving. Better than most admirals of that time, he understood the constitutional limitations of his office.[208] At the same time he possessed little faith in the dependability of international agreements and was convinced that in the event of a major war all treaties would disintegrate or be torn up on one pretext or another. Reginald McKenna, his political master, would in time come round to this same cynical view.[209] This is not the only evidence of the Admiralty's cavalier attitude toward the sanctity of international agreements. In a minute dated 1907, one official observed:

> It may be expedient for Great Britain, in the interests of her particular commerce, to try to limit the right of seizing contraband as much as possible, but, seeing that everything must come into this country by sea, and that we are not, in any sense of the term, a self-contained country, it is quite obvious that any nation at war with us would not view this proposal with any degree of satisfaction, and, judging by the fate of all previous treaties which have endeavoured to limit this fundamental right of nations in a sense which must be more favorable to one or other of the belligerents, it is hardly likely that any agreement which may be come to now with regard to this question of contraband can hope to have any greater measure of permanence. It is, therefore, far better policy on our part boldly to accept the law as it stands, and to endeavor to produce a workable formula which will exclude arbitrary enlargements of this belligerent right, designed principally to attack British trade when Great Britain is neutral. When Great Britain is belligerent, she can be safely trusted to look after her own interests, but the dangerous time for her is when she is neutral and does not wish to take such a strong line as to render herself liable to be drawn into war.[210]

Alas, we cannot say with certainty who wrote this minute, which had been detached from the original file. We know it dates from the time of the Hague Conference in 1907. Given that the dockets on this sensitive topic had such a limited circulation, we may confidently assert it must have been written by

Greene, Ottley, one of the assistant directors in the NID, or just possibly Slade. The most likely candidate is Greene, for it closely resembles his writing style, and Greene expressed a nearly identical viewpoint in a private letter to Lord Tweedmouth dated 20 September 1907. "So long as the [Royal] Navy is predominant," the assistant secretary wrote, "there is no need to fear that the ultimate result of a naval war would be modified by the concessions, while the risk of friction with neutrals would be much diminished."[211]

To properly grasp the Admiralty's position and their apparent lack of interest in the outcome of the London Naval Conference, we need to understand a great deal more of their latest thinking on economic warfare. This is the subject of the next chapter.

3

The Exposition of Economic Warfare

What I desire to bring before you is something different: the difficulty that may and must arise among leading States should they become engaged in war with each other in a measure that jeopardizes the mechanism of credit in the States affected, and throughout the commercial world generally. It appears to me that this is a formidable possibility of the international credit system that has never been adequately considered. And it has not been considered for the simple reason that as a matter of fact since this system became developed in its modern proportions there has been no war in which the leading nations most important to the system have been mutually involved.

SIR ROBERT GIFFEN, 28 March 1908

When Captain Charles Ottley, the director of naval intelligence, arrived at The Hague in mid-June 1907, he was confident in his understanding of economic warfare, based upon nearly two years of study. He believed that in time of war Great Britain could effectively isolate Germany from the global trading system, achieving strategically decisive results. He envisaged the Royal Navy sweeping the German mercantile flag from the high seas and containing her battle fleet within the North Sea; British merchantmen would be induced not to carry, or explicitly prohibited from carrying German trade indirectly via neutral ports. Meanwhile, neutral merchantmen—insufficient in number to be of much significance—could be deterred from carrying for Germany by the threat of confiscation under the doctrine of continuous voyage. In conjunction with several other measures (which we have not yet mentioned), Ottley felt sure the effect upon the German economy would be devastating. By the end of the conference, however, around mid-September 1907, Ottley had come to realize both that the world economic system was more complex and that the ramifications of some of the Admiralty's intended measures were likely a good deal more unpredictable than he had allowed. Four months of intensive thought and debate at The Hague prompted him to question some of his underlying assumptions.

For example, Ottley departed The Hague less certain that the doctrine of continuous voyage would prove sufficient to deter neutrals from carrying goods and supplies for Germany through neutral ports such as Rotterdam. He confessed to Second Sea Lord Vice-Admiral Sir William May in September 1907:

> I was strongly of opinion that the prima facie value to us of the right to invoke continuous voyage was, in a war with Germany, very great indeed. A more careful and detailed consideration of that right has led me to think however that it is easy to exaggerate the value of that right.[1]

Unlike Captain Edmond Slade, the president of the War College, Ottley did not regard the doctrine of continuous voyage as practically worthless; he maintained, rather, that its value could be gauged only after more study. Slade then tried to argue that their disagreement did not matter because the ports of Rotterdam and Antwerp lacked the capacity to handle any large increase in traffic consequent to the closure of Hamburg. If this was correct, then leakage through to Germany could never be serious. But Slade's supposition had not been established as fact. Backed by Graham Greene, the Admiralty assistant secretary, Admiral May agreed that the "questions are difficult ones and I concur with Capt. Ottley the more you go into them the more difficult they seem."[2] The Admiralty's unwillingness to be pushed into making hasty decisions caused the peace conference to break up.

On 1 November 1907, Captain Edmond Slade became the director of naval intelligence in succession to Captain Ottley. Pressure of other business, however, prevented him from launching an immediate investigation into the questions thrown up at The Hague. The First Sea Lord was much more concerned with managing the naval budgetary crisis and, so that he might concentrate on this, immediately delegated to Slade the task of framing the Admiralty's case for a major CID investigation into the possibility of serious invasion.[3] The intensifying row between Admiral Sir John Fisher and fleet commander Admiral Lord Charles Beresford became a further drain upon Slade's time.[4] Faced with so many distractions, therefore, it was not until May 1908—six months into his appointment—that he at last found time to conduct a reevaluation of economic warfare strategy.

Slade's first move was to circulate within the NID a memorandum demanding an assessment of the information upon which the Admiralty's view of the German economy was based. In this, he questioned whether the empirical evidence was strong enough to support the weight of policy placed upon it. With "the vulnerability of Germany through her overseas supplies being nowadays an accepted fact," he commented,

> it is considered desirable to obtain answers to the enclosed questions in order to gauge her actual dependence on these overseas supplies. The answers to these questions may indicate in a useful manner how far Germany does depend on overseas supplies, and to what extent these overseas supplies can be deviated from their normal to new channels in time of war.[5]

In other words, Slade demanded that Germany's dependence upon trade be quantified and, in light of the questionable value of the doctrine of continuous voyage, her capability to import raw materials and food through neutral Rotterdam and Antwerp be evaluated.

The investigation of these questions was primarily the responsibility of the NID Trade Division, now under the direction of Captain Henry H. Campbell. Since taking over from Captain Robert F. Scott (of Antarctic fame) in August 1906, Campbell had immersed himself in the subject of economic warfare.[6] While perhaps not as gifted as Rear-Admiral Edward Inglefield, who had established the department and run it for five years, Campbell was an indefatigable worker and made at least one important contribution to the development of the strategy. Campbell became interested in the theories of Major Stewart Murray, a retired Army officer who promoted the idea that modern British society was inherently fragile and if in wartime the nation's food supply was endangered, the resulting domestic unrest might well distract the government from its strategic objectives.

Campbell took Murray's ideas on the brittleness of modern industrial society and projected them onto Germany. He argued that Germany was equally dependent upon overseas supplies for food and commercial prosperity and equally riven with class conflict, and that her society must therefore be equally vulnerable to dislocation in time of war.[7] If the Royal Navy's systematic attack upon German trade failed to produce rapid economic collapse, he argued, it would at least germinate the seeds of social discord lying dormant within German society.[8] And if life for the average German worker could be made intolerable, the resultant social disharmony must act as pressure upon the German government to sue for peace. Murray's ideas were taken seriously by a great number of influential people. Thanks substantially to his activism, indeed, back in 1903 Prime Minister Arthur Balfour bowed to popular pressure and appointed a royal commission to investigate the security of British food supply in time of war.[9] In 1911, the government preemptively mobilized 30,000 soldiers to safeguard the national food distribution network from being disrupted as a consequence of large-scale industrial action.[10] Ultimately in August 1914, fear of social disorder induced the cabinet to release only four of the available six infantry divisions to France.[11]

Responding to Slade's memorandum of May 1908, Campbell assured the new DNI that his section had already examined many of the questions posed and had assembled a wealth of raw data detailing German dependence upon overseas trade and the inner workings of her economy. The Trade Division had investigated Germany's "oversea requirements, the economic effects of stopping the same, the origins of supplies, the quantities and values of the supplies and the movements of the tonnage carrying the same at various periods."[12] However, the precise workings of the northern European transport system linking Germany with ports in the Low Countries constituted a gap in their knowledge base.

On 28 May 1908, accordingly, the Admiralty sent the Foreign Office a questionnaire drawn up by Campbell and asked that it be distributed to senior British consular officers serving in northern Europe. The briefest glance at these questions indicates the Admiralty's desire to establish whether it would be practical for Germany to draw sufficient overseas supplies through neutral Antwerp and Rotterdam in the event of her own ports being closed.[13] Although the Admiralty had stressed the need for utmost secrecy, the Foreign Office inadvertently forwarded at least one copy of this top-secret document through the German postal system, known to be monitored by German intelligence; when this was discovered, the Foreign Office adjudged it "unnecessary" to notify the Admiralty of the slip—and never did.[14] We can only speculate whether German intransigence at the December 1908 London Naval Conference was motivated by the findings of their intelligence services. It is pertinent to note that in 1908 the German army chief of staff, General Helmuth von Moltke, observed that "for us, it will be of the utmost importance to have in Holland a country whose neutrality will assure imports and exports. It will have to be our windpipe that enables us to breathe."[15]

Over the course of the summer, the completed questionnaires trickled from the Continent back to London. Protocol demanded they first be sent to the Foreign Office, where they were received with smug satisfaction. The replies from consular officials in Antwerp and Rotterdam indicated that the local port facilities could handle "any amount" of additional shipping; furthermore, ample spare capacity existed on the railways and waterways connecting the ports with Germany—contradicting Captain Slade's claims to the contrary.[16] The Foreign Office was particular impressed with the reply from William Ward, the British consul in Hamburg, who claimed that "Germany, as regards the importation of foodstuffs, would not be embarrassed to any great extent by the blockade of her ports," though he conceded that German "industries would, however, be considerably impeded."[17] The Admiralty, though, disputed these assessments and rejected the various consular reports as virtually worthless. They had wanted statistics, not uninformed speculations. None of the reports contained much in the way of hard data to support the opinions proffered therein. As Captain Campbell remarked on the file, "the asserted ease" with which goods might be moved—for instance, from Rotterdam to Germany—neglected to factor in that "transference from sea carriage to overland transport must add enormously to the cost for the consumer; it is this additional cost that we must produce and reduce the German workman to a state which he feels intolerable" (and thus aggravate social unrest).[18] Campbell further reminded that surplus handling capacity at Rotterdam and Antwerp did not much matter anyway because the "neutral powers have very little [merchant] tonnage to spare to carry for Germany without starving their own national needs, and it is doubtful if they could spare any at all."[19] In a separate paper he emphasized, "In all questions of trade the number, nationality, net tonnage and value of shipping come very largely into the problem."[20]

Much less easy to dismiss, however, was the magnum opus submitted by Francis Oppenheimer, the honorary consul in Frankfurt. All the senior Foreign Office officials who read it felt that in scope and detail the Oppenheimer report was in a class apart. Indeed, it was so highly valued that it earned him a promotion.[21] It is therefore ironic that the Foreign Office had sent him the Admiralty questionnaire by mistake. The Oppenheimer report is frequently (though mistakenly) cited by historians as a decisive rebuttal of the Admiralty viewpoint, providing "a more realistic assessment of the likely economic effects of a blockade on Germany."[22] It concluded that blockade alone was not likely to bring Germany to her knees.[23] In terms of its influence upon the contemporary debate, however, Oppenheimer's report was of tangential significance. It did not reach London until October 1909, more than a year after the other replies and eighteen months after the circulation of the original questionnaire. As we shall see below, by this time the Foreign Office had already decided that the Admiralty's economic warfare plans would never work. At best, therefore, Oppenheimer's report may be said to have cemented their conjectural conclusions.

At first glance Oppenheimer's report seems impressive. It contained a wealth of information—and statistics—detailing the transport infrastructure linking Germany with not just Belgium and Holland but all contiguous countries. Oppenheimer's data cannot be faulted—his research effort was extraordinary. Scrutiny of his conclusions, however, reveals his employment of several questionable assumptions, beginning with the rather crucial supposition (which informed his entire analysis) that Britain and Germany would be facing off without allies. It seemingly never occurred to him that Britain might be fighting as part of a coalition, which leads one to wonder whether other government officials assumed along similar lines. Oppenheimer argued that measuring Germany's ability to import during time of war was not "solely" a function of transport communications but also must be "subject to modifications in accordance with the conditions prevailing on the world's markets."[24] His key assumption that only Britain and Germany would be involved in hostilities led him to believe that the world commodities markets would continue to function more or less normally, allowing Germany to draw necessary supplies (particularly grain) from Russia and other countries in the European hinterland. Of course, his conclusions fell apart if one believed that conflict would be on a far larger scale and embroil most of Europe including Russia. This point aside, as Captain Campbell at the Admiralty was quick to point out, though it was true that Germany imported grain from Russia (the world's largest food exporter prior to the First World War), most actually reached Germany by sea from Odessa via the Mediterranean and up the English Channel. With the Royal Navy firmly in control of this sea route, he deemed it unlikely that the Russian rail system (or the German one, for that matter) could cope with such a volume of freight—an assessment with which the German General Staff more or less agreed.[25]

Another questionable assumption underpinning Oppenheimer's conclusions was that, with respect to food, necessity would override all normal economic price constraints. He argued that because "foodstuffs form a part of the requirement which a people must satisfy," the "increased cost owing to an increased expenditure for carriage, would not be decisive as long as the import remains at all possible." In other words, German workmen could simply pay higher prices to obtain sufficient food, uncomplainingly spending their entire income if necessary. On its face this seems doubtful.

Turning to the importation of industrial raw materials, Oppenheimer conceded that German business might find it difficult to pay for all their requirements and acknowledged that any serious interruption in supply "would be little short of a national calamity." Yet simultaneously he insisted that that the Royal Navy could never achieve decisive results unless the "blockade of the German ports could at the same time be extended to the [neutral] Dutch and Belgian ports, which, for the international exchange of goods, are quasi-German ports."[26] This evaluation was predicated upon several further unspoken assumptions: that serious derangement of the German economy necessitated the stoppage of all trade, not just some trade; that the Low Countries would be able to both preserve their neutrality and be free to import on Germany's behalf; and, most important, that British merchantmen would be free to carry their additional trade.

Senior officials at the Foreign Office, however, could see none of these defects and hailed Oppenheimer's report as the final nail in the coffin of the Admiralty's strategic plans. "The conclusion to be drawn," Sir Eyre Crowe commented in October 1909,

> is that in a war between England and Germany the pressure which could be put on the latter's resources as regards imported food supplies and raw materials is very slight, and can never amount to a strain sufficient to induce Germany to sue for peace. There will be a certain amount of extra expenditure and a radical diversion of traffic, but these are not sacrifices that a nation will not readily bear in pursuit of a national war.[27]

Sir Charles Hardinge, the permanent secretary, agreed after reading the Oppenheimer report that it seemed "doubtful whether the blockade would in the long run prove really effective."[28] The Admiralty, by contrast, though appreciative of the raw data, rejected Oppenheimer's conclusions. As the DNI observed in a minute addressed to the Board of Admiralty, "Owing to certain factors having been overlooked, a somewhat too favourable case has been made out for Germany. The immense difficulties and dislocation, resulting from the diversion of commerce from the North Sea ports to other channel of ingress, do not seem to have been quite fully realised."[29] The

DNI's opinion was initialed without comment by Reginald McKenna, the First Lord, and three of the four sea lords. The Admiralty's rejection of Foreign Office "expert" opinion was not a case of sour grapes. For some time the naval planners had been in possession of another study, not taken into consideration by previous historians, prepared by a much more eminent authority and based upon a much more sophisticated understanding of how the world trading system functioned.

Enter Sir Robert Giffen

Captain Campbell's request to the DNI in May 1908 for his questionnaire to be circulated was accompanied by a suggestion that outside experts be called "into secret council." The head of the trade division mentioned that for some time he had wanted to forge still closer links with Lloyd's but had hesitated from fear that to do so must inevitably divulge the Admiralty's secret strategic intentions. Campbell offered another very good reason for consulting outside experts. "In the past," he wrote, "the difficulty has not been so much to obtain statistics, as to secure correct deductions from the figures which have been available."[30] In other words, Campbell's unit did not need additional economic data so much as expert assistance in deciphering the material already gathered. Further down the page he suggested approaching the Board of Trade for help. Rather than reach out to another government department, the Admiralty instead recruited "Professor" Sir Robert Giffen, KCB, FRS. Until his death in 1910, Giffen was an internationally recognized political economist (with an expertise in international trade) and regarded by many in government as Britain's "ablest" authority on statistical methods.[31]

Sir Robert Giffen was born in Glasgow in 1837, the son of a successful village grocer. After being trained in the law, he moved to London and in 1868 became assistant editor of the *Economist* under the celebrated Victorian political economist Walter Bagehot. The same year he assisted George Goschen (1831–1907), president of the Poor Law Board in William Gladstone's first cabinet, prepare a scheme for local taxation reform. This proved to be an important connection. Goschen's political career blossomed; he served twice as First Lord of the Admiralty (1871–1874 and 1895–1900) and once as Chancellor of the Exchequer (1886–1888). Giffen maintained close links with other leading political figures of the age, most notably Joseph "Joe" Chamberlain, and is credited with having helped him to frame the new bankruptcy laws introduced during Gladstone's second administration. Although their views on free trade differed, Giffen remained tightly within Chamberlain's orbit until the latter's death.[32] Through the patronage of such powerful friends, in 1876 Giffen joined the Board of Trade as head of its newly formed statistics branch. He evidently proved a most able civil servant and rose to the rank of controller general (effectively number three in the hierarchy). Concurrently, Giffen became a founding member of the International Statistical Institute, the Royal Economics Society, and the *Economic Journal*. In 1882 he was elected president of the (Royal) Statistical Society. Giffen wrote numerous books and articles on economic affairs and economic theory, and to this day, first-year economics undergraduates are introduced in their textbooks to the concept of "Giffen goods."[33] Robert Giffen is also reputed to have coined the phrase "lies, damned lies, and statistics."[34] In 1897, at the age of sixty, he retired from the civil service but continued to advise various government departments and leading politicians on economic subjects.[35] In 1903, for example, he was called upon as an expert witness by the Royal Commission on Supply of Food and Raw Materials in Time of War.[36]

Around 1905, Giffen began discreetly advising the Committee of Imperial Defence on economic and trade issues. Surviving fragments of private correspondence between Giffen and Sir George Clarke reveal that he helped the CID grapple with the economic dimensions of maritime law during preparations for the 1907 Hague Peace Conference. As shown in the last chapter, Giffen was instrumental in persuading Clarke that the importance of maritime trade to national economies was far greater than the CID had previously allowed.[37] Clarke's change in stance was reflected in the memorandum he wrote in May 1906 for the Walton Committee (the interdepartmental body charged with defining the government's position at the Hague peace conference). Reflecting the new advice given him, Clarke now advised:

> Since the period of great naval wars, the conditions of the British Empire have become sharply differentiated from those of other Powers, while the conditions of maritime trade and of naval war have undergone radical change. Our economic dependence upon trade is now absolute; even a temporary interruption of our maritime communications would involve consequences of the most serious nature; a prolonged severance would entail disaster.[38]

It is difficult to say when, precisely, the Naval Intelligence Department recruited Sir Robert Giffen to assist their preparations for economic warfare.

Thanks to George Goschen, he had been known to Admiralty officials since the 1890s. It seems Captain Charles Ottley met Giffen while serving as naval assistant secretary to the CID. In a paper dated 1905, Ottley indicated both his acquaintance with the economist and general approval of his ideas on the necessity for state insurance of merchant ships in time of war.[39] Captain George Ballard too was familiar with Giffen's work. The very latest date Giffen established his connections with the NID was 25 March 1908, the day on which Giffen delivered an exceptional paper to the Royal United Services Institute (RUSI) on the subject of war and finance.[40] Located in Whitehall, the RUSI was (and is) practically adjacent to the Admiralty building. Its evening lectures were normally well attended by naval officers. The title of Giffen's talk that day was "The Necessity of a War Chest in the Country, or a Greatly Increased Gold Reserve." (It should be noted that this paper is not listed in any bibliography of Giffen's work.) But in his opening remarks he acknowledged that the title of his paper was somewhat misleading and bore little relationship to his subject that day. Instead he would discuss "the difficulty that may and must arise among leading States should they become engaged in a war with each other in a measure that jeopardizes the mechanism of credit in the States affected, and throughout the commercial world generally."[41]

Giffen explained to his audience that he had been induced to pursue this line of enquiry by the "recent" (late 1907) financial storm that had swept the globe. Scarcely a single industry in the developed world had escaped the effects of the collapse of confidence in American credit and the consequent paralysis of U.S. internal and external trade.[42] Giffen argued that the crisis had not only demonstrated the economic interdependence of nations but also exposed serious weaknesses in the foundations of modern finance. Before proceeding further, it is imperative that readers understand that, unlike most contemporary commentators (and historians), Giffen was concerned *not* with credit in the context of the state borrowing to pay for wars, but rather with the credit issued by banks in the City of London that served to finance the global trading system.[43] This is a complex but necessary subject, for it subsequently (post-1908) became the heart of the Admiralty's plans for economic warfare.

The Importance and Operation of the London Credit Market

At the turn of the twentieth century Great Britain stood firmly at the center of the financial and commercial worlds. Historians often argue that London owed its position to its adherence to a strict gold standard, which acted as the fulcrum for international trade. But the link between gold and the global trading system was only indirect; merchants did not pay for goods with gold. On the day-to-day level the vast majority of international commercial transactions were conducted by means of credit drawn on a London bank. There was no direct connection between the issuance of credit and the gold standard. Furthermore, no direct correlation existed between the volume of issued credit and the stock of gold held at the Bank of England. Individuals, corporations, and even governments operated accounts in London and seldom held or supplied gold; banks advanced credit to anyone they deemed creditworthy.

Credit allowed far greater flexibility in the conduct of business. International confidence in the City of London, and in sterling generally, rested upon confidence that sterling could be converted at any time into gold without restriction or cost (though in practice conversions were rarely made). International opinion accepted that the Bank of England would do all that was necessary to maintain convertibility at the official rate and resist domestic political pressure to ignore this rule or allow sterling to depreciate.[44] Sterling became "as good as gold," and a credit with a London bank was viewed by most creditors as an acceptable currency (in the broadest meaning of the word) for settlement of debts.[45] To reiterate, inherent confidence in the stability of the system meant that gold flowed very little. It was the London credit market that served as the primary mechanism for international exchange. Yet this reality was neither reflected in classical economic theory nor, more important for our story, recognized in international maritime law. This point is critical.

The huge explosion in international trade after 1870 was made possible largely by the development of the London credit market—in addition to steep declines in transport costs consequent to the adoption of steam technology, and the development of instantaneous intercontinental communication facilitated by cable technology. The main form of commercial credit transaction was the bill of exchange.[46] A bill of exchange is an unconditional demand for payment of a specified sum on a specified date that has been drawn by one party on another and accepted by an acceptance house; in effect, an acceptance house is any bank, merchant, or financial institution that undertakes to pay the face amount of the bill on the date of maturity, thereby conferring that house's credit standing to the bill of exchange. Before the First World War, most bills of exchange were denominated in sterling, normally for a three-month term.

Let us take a hypothetical example to illustrate the operation of the system. A textile manufacturer in Lancashire (the purchaser) wants to buy cotton from a grower in Mississippi (the vendor). It is safe to assume that the average grower will not hand over his crop until he has been paid—yet his crop has to pass through several stages of production before the purchaser can make the money to pay him. The cotton must be shipped to England, graded in Manchester, spun into yarn, woven into textiles, and manufactured into a product that can be sold (say, shirts) for cash. Thus a period of time—months—must elapse between the initial purchase of the cotton and its ultimate sale after processing. Until then, the purchaser likely will not be in a position to pay for the cotton—but the vendor is not prepared to wait that long for payment. They compromise by conducting the exchange through a bank.

How does the exchange work? The purchaser opens a line of credit with an accepting house in London and draws up a bill of exchange in favor of the vendor, which is then accepted (i.e., the legitimacy of the bill is acknowledged) by the acceptance house. The bill of exchange is then express-mailed to the vendor, who upon receipt dispatches his cotton to England. Probably wanting to be paid in U.S. dollars as soon as possible, the vendor then takes his bill of exchange accompanied by the bill of lading (as proof the cotton has been shipped) to his local bank in Mississippi. The local bank buys the bill of exchange from him, at a nominal discount, in confidence that the bill will be paid by the London accepting house on the appointed date. The vendor is thus paid and his part in the transaction is complete. The local U.S. bank forwards the bill of exchange (together with the bill of lading, which now in effect serves as the legal title to the consignment of cotton) to its London branch or agent for eventual payment by the acceptance house upon maturity of the bill. The local bank's part in the transaction is now complete. Finally, when the accepting house receives payment from the purchaser, it hands over the bill of lading so that the client may collect the cotton from the docks.

This is not quite the end of the story, however. More often than not, the vendor's bank will not wish to hold the bill until maturity but instead will rediscount it to another party (most usually to a bill broker or joint-stock bank) through the London discount market. Here was another powerful incentive for international merchants to conduct their business through the City; only in London did there operate a discount market for bills of exchange, allowing merchants to cash bills before maturity. Bills drawn on London were consequently seen as liquid financial instruments. Through this market the same bill could be sold and resold many times before it finally matured. To give an idea of the scale of this operation, it is estimated that at any one time the London acceptance houses had between £300 and £400 million tied up in bills of exchange, of which more than half was tied up in multilateral (i.e., non-British) transactions, much of it American and German business.[47] In 1911, leading bankers estimated that three-sevenths of this sum financed British trade; the remainder financed foreign trade. To help put these numbers in perspective, during the ten-year period 1902–1911, annual British (visible) exports and reexports averaged £450 million; imports, £560 million.[48] Balance of payments was achieved through the export of services (i.e., invisibles—mainly banking, insurance, and shipping), which annually earned Britain about £100 million (half of which was earned by shipping); for the sake of completeness we should mention net property income from abroad (dividends and rents), which contributed another £140 million.[49]

From about 1870 on, subsequent to the surge in global trade, London accepting houses increasingly financed their operations by borrowing cheap credit advanced by the larger British joint-stock banks (such as the London City and Midland, London County and Westminster, or Barclays and Co.). Hitherto they had relied upon money advanced by the Bank of England.[50] The joint-stock banks—so-called high-street banks—possessed a huge client base and enormous sums in deposits and were chiefly responsible, through the practice of fractional banking, for the enormous inflation of credit before the First World War. It is well known that much of the wealth accumulated by these banks was invested overseas to finance large-scale infrastructure projects such as the building of Argentine railroads. Overseas investments proved to be highly profitable, far more so than domestic investments. It is sometimes forgotten, however, that the joint-stock banks could not tie up all their assets in long-term ventures, whether at home or overseas.[51] They needed to keep considerable sums liquid to service their depositors' day-to-day needs, which might fluctuate considerably.[52] As one contemporary banker rather elegantly put it, the "art of banking is to speculate with success on the chance that only a small proportion of creditors [depositors] will ask for their money in gold at the same moment."[53] Rather than simply store cash in their vaults, banks preferred to earn something by loaning it at nominal (market) rates to other city institutions or by purchasing short-life bills of exchange.[54] Joint Stock Banks regarded these commercial bills of exchange as especially desirable because they could readily be converted back into cash through the discount market: in other words, bills of exchange drawn on London acceptance houses were seen as safe, profitable, and above all liquid financial instruments.[55] So desirable did they seem that, before 1914, approximately 25 percent of joint-stock bank assets were held in short-term "London bills," with a further 10 to 15 percent of assets held on call (i.e., liable to be demanded at any minute) with bill brokers, stockbrokers, and other institutions—often also with large speculative holdings of bills of exchange.[56]

Given the interrelationships between the international credit markets, the operation of the global trading system, and the central importance of the City of London in facilitating trade by supplying liquidity to the world economy, Sir Robert Giffen did not exaggerate the significance of his subject when he stood before the Royal United Services Institute in March 1908. Giffen was fully justified in claiming that no one before had ever considered the implications of the global trading system if Britain and other leading industrial powers became involved in a major war. Giffen was certain that the consequences must be severe. "Such a war, it seems to me," he said, "would bring upon us, as well as upon the whole community of civilized States to which the system of international credit extends, quite unprecedented calamities and dangers. This would result from the breakdown of the credit system itself and the interruption of international commerce."[57] In plain English, Giffen feared that a major war would deliver a shock to the world credit system of such dimensions as to cause paralysis of the London credit market, which in turn would inevitably bring most if not all international trade to a dead stop, with devastating consequences for global economic activity.

In Giffen's estimation, all previous discussion on the subject had seriously underestimated the probable scale of such a crisis.[58] History, he warned, offered no lessons as to what to expect. Over the previous quarter century, profound changes had occurred in the international economy, the constitution of modern national economies, their relative dependence upon global trade, and the structure of international trade.[59] The experience of the last great Napoleonic war offered few insights into the financial problems likely to be faced in any future world war. Since then, Giffen reminded his audience, the global trading system had undergone a transformation; furthermore, during this period Britain had not herself been involved in a major war. Therefore, the modern system of credit-financed trade had never been subjected to the test of war. "There have doubtless been some most serious wars which disturbed credit more or less," he reasoned, "but in none of these was the working of the international credit system substantially endangered, while our own country—the citadel of the credit system—was fortunately not engaged."[60] "Nowadays," Giffen predicted, in an age of instant global communication, interlocking national financial systems, and general economic interdependence especially, war must unleash "vast indirect as well as direct effects." At the level of national economies, the effects of any disruption in trade would not be confined mainly—as in the past—to those sectors directly involved in overseas commerce; a shock wave would reverberate throughout the economy and possibly result in "civil tumult" on a scale not seen since the 1840s.[61] At the beginning of a major war, in other words, advanced economies would be exceptionally vulnerable to dislocation and possibly even collapse. The Admiralty had found their messiah.

The Admiralty's recruitment of Sir Robert Giffen proved to be a milestone, providing Britain's naval planners with the theoretical foundations upon which to build the strategy of economic warfare. The many passing references in planning documents to financial derangement, as distinct from destruction of commerce, now take on a wholly new significance for historians. Essentially, Giffen confirmed or rather clarified what Ottley, Ballard, and Slade all had intuitively sensed—that economic warfare was a strategy distinct from an orthodox naval blockade, with a different ultimate aim and targeting different economic mechanisms. We know Giffen confidentially supplied the NID with at least one paper amplifying his thoughts on the likely consequences of a major war and its economic impact upon Germany.[62] By autumn 1908, his ideas were having a discernible impact upon naval planners. In September, Edmond Slade, the DNI and now a rear-admiral, wrote a memorandum on the principles of trade defense (for internal Admiralty use only) referencing Giffen's key idea of interdependency and his prediction that the effects of dislocation to a nation's overseas trade would not be confined just to its maritime industries but likely would reverberate throughout its entire economy.[63]

The inherent complexity of Giffen's ideas demanded attentive consideration over many months. Probably for this reason, neither Slade not Ottley apparently gave any hint of this new thinking to the committee charged with preparing for the London Naval Conference on maritime law. Not until the end of 1908 did the Admiralty finally reveal to outsiders—prematurely, as we shall see below—their reforged strategy of economic warfare.

At the end of 1908, the prime minister unexpectedly called on the Board of Admiralty to review the strategic options open to the government in the event of war with Germany. Acute tensions in Franco-German relations over the so-called Casablanca affair, heightened by the recent Austrian annexation of the

Balkan province of Bosnia-Herzegovina, prompted one of the most serious discussions on grand strategy held by the Asquith government before the First World War. So grave appeared the international situation that on 5 November Asquith warned the opposition party leader that war with Germany appeared imminent.[64] The same day Foreign Secretary Sir Edward Grey alerted the Admiralty "to make preparations in case Germany sent France an ultimatum and the Cabinet decided that we must assist France."[65] Anxious not to be left behind, the War Office begged the prime minister to apprise the General Staff as to whether the government would sanction the dispatch of British troops to the Continent in support of France in the event of war.[66]

On previous occasions when war had loomed, the government of the day had tended to shy from discussing specific details of military plans in anticipation of war.[67] It was a significant departure from previous practice, therefore, when Asquith agreed to hear the War Office request. He directed Ottley to arrange a plenary CID subcommittee (chaired by himself) to review "the employment of a British military force on the Continent of Europe, as would enable the General Staff to concentrate their attention only on such plans as they may be called upon to put into operation."[68] Membership was limited to Asquith (prime minister), McKenna (First Lord of the Admiralty), Richard Haldane (war minister), and Lord Crewe (colonial secretary). These men effectively represented the nucleus of a war cabinet. In the absence of Sir Edward Grey, who was busy preparing for the London Naval Conference, the Foreign Office was represented by Sir Charles Hardinge, the department permanent secretary. Also present were three admirals and three generals plus the apolitical Lord Esher in his capacity as permanent member of the CID. This misleadingly named Military Needs of the Empire subcommittee (historians agree the subterfuge was deliberate) met three times: twice in December 1908 (at the height of the crisis) with another brief discussion held on 23 March 1909 at which several tepid conclusions were agreed. The final report, completed almost as an afterthought, was dated 24 July 1909.

The First Sea Lord, Admiral Sir John Fisher, was not at all pleased with Asquith's new committee. Skeptical of the chance of war, he was fully occupied in preparing the naval estimates for fiscal year 1909–1910. He viewed the entire proceeding as another Army ruse, merely another chapter in the ongoing battle between the Admiralty and the War Office to wrest the greatest share of the national defense budget.[69] That the Army General Staff subsequently made little progress toward completing its plans after the special CID committee wound up lends credence to his suspicions. Fisher participated in the committee intending not to divulge anything of the Navy's own plans. On the eve of the first meeting, he explicitly told Slade "that we had better not say anything at all about it."[70] This was less a symptom of Fisher's refusal to cooperate with the CID than a tried-and-true bureaucratic ploy. Fisher, a master at committee infighting, had employed this trick before at previous CID enquiries. The aim was to focus political attention upon any internal inconsistencies in the General Staff's plans, point to schisms within the military ranks, and generally allow the soldiers to discredit themselves. Quite likely, as some historians have argued, Fisher also pushed for "a general Cabinet discussion in which to hammer out the relative merits of direct European involvement"—knowing full well the majority of ministers would never sanction sending the British Expeditionary Force (BEF) to fight on the Continent.[71]

The First Sea Lord's disinclination to say anything about Admiralty plans was reinforced by his nearly complete estrangement from Rear-Admiral Slade, the DNI, and lingering distrust of Reginald McKenna, the new First Lord of the Admiralty.[72] The cordial friendship between Fisher and McKenna had not yet been formed.[73] The trust between Fisher and Slade, never good, recently had been irrevocably damaged by the latter's mishandling of the Admiralty's case during the 1908 invasion inquiry.[74] Fisher regretted having allowed Slade to revive studies into the practicability of amphibious operations against the German coast. Slade, it transpired, had communicated his ideas to the Army, which had gleefully encouraged his naiveté. These plans were frankly an embarrassment: even Slade's subordinates admitted they were little more than "a mass of verbiage."[75] Throughout the Military Needs of the Empire subcommittee meetings, Fisher steadfastly refused to discuss these amphibious schemes, deflecting repeated attempts by the War Office to bring them to the official notice of the CID.[76]

On Thursday, 3 December 1908, the Military Needs of the Empire subcommittee convened to discuss a General Staff memorandum laying out various schemes for committing the BEF to the continent of Europe in the event of war. At this meeting, Major-General J. S. Ewart, the DMO, declared the General Staff's preference for at once sending all available troops in the British Isles (now calculated to be four infantry divisions and one of cavalry, for a total of 110,000 men) across the Channel to support the French army in stemming the German invasion.[77] Historians of the First World War have long regarded this series of three meetings as a historic event, one of the main stepping-stones on the road toward the 1914 British Continental commitment.

Leaving aside the thorny questions as to whether in hindsight this proved the right decision and whether the decision makers fully understood the implications of what the General Staff proposed, there is nearly universal scholarly consensus that the political executive walked away from this series of meetings believing the Admiralty were unable to offer an alternative strategy. From the official minutes of the meetings (which were unusually abbreviated) historians have deduced that Fisher realized the Admiralty's amphibious warfare schemes would never withstand close scrutiny and accordingly displayed bureaucratic wisdom in remaining silent—albeit at the price of revealing the bankruptcy of his strategic thought. As Fisher's most recent biographer wrote, "The only alternative to Ewart's plan offered by the Navy—this at the second meeting—was reliance on an economic blockade of Germany."[78] Most scholars have broadly accepted the view expressed by General Sir William Nicholson, the chief of the General Staff, that "no success that we might have against Germany at sea would be of assistance to the French army at the moment when it was most required."[79]

There are two problems with the conventional interpretation of events. First, it is based mainly upon the official minutes printed by the CID, which most scholars recognize to be an incomplete record of what was said and discussed. Second, even when other sources have been used to supplement the official minutes, historians have not been aware of the Admiralty's strategy of economic warfare, which provides crucial context for interpreting them.

Taken together, both the official minutes and other sources demonstrate that the Admiralty's new plan for economic warfare was indeed discussed by the Military Needs of the Empire subcommittee. It was an alternative both to Fisher's silence about amphibious operations and to the traditional strategy of (legal) blockade. At the first meeting of the committee, Fisher launched an extempore exposition of economic warfare that does not appear in the printed minutes.[80] Fisher's autobiographical account of the event, written some ten years later, when he was 79 years old and in poor health, contains several obvious inaccuracies but nevertheless furnishes the plausible gist of his declaratory cascade:

> I am now going to relate one of the most dramatic incidents of my career. . . . There was what was called a Plenary meeting of the Committee of Imperial Defence long, long before the war. Our Generals . . . with white wands and splendiferous maps pointed out to their enthralled listeners the disposition for war on the French frontier and

> seemingly all were swept off their legs! I suppose I looked glum—The Prime Minister said, "Sir John, we've not heard you say anything." I said "no! It's purely a military matter!" "But you've something on your mind," said he, "say it." I steadfastly looked at the Field Marshal [General Nicholson] and his wand and said "if I were the German emperor I should tell my millions to *fight neither with small nor great* but fight only with the 160,000 [110,000] English and decimate them and massacre them." . . . The Prime Minister adjourned the investigation without a conclusion, and as I walked away with Esher I asked him unanswered if we weren't all d——d fools?[81]

There are indications, however, that Fisher's tirade at this first subcommittee meeting went a good deal further than just attacking the Army's Continental plans. In August 1911, Captain Maurice Hankey had occasion to remind Reginald McKenna of what had been said. Perhaps quoting from the original notes taken at the December 1908 meeting, or perhaps having been briefed by Ottley (who had been present as note taker) as to what actually had transpired, Hankey wrote:

> You will remember that at that time there existed a considerable difference of opinion between the naval and military members. The latter were strongly in favour of military action in support of France. The former, and especially Lord Fisher, held that to send troops would be a great mistake, *and that we ought to rely on commercial pressure alone.* Lord Fisher held the view that our relatively small army could not make the difference between success and failure in France; to send it would give Germany the opportunity (which she at present lacks owing to our preponderant sea-power) to strike a blow at us; Germany would, he contended, spare no effort to "contain" the French army, and hurl an overwhelming force on to the British wing, utterly defeating it and marching the remnant to Berlin; in fact to send an army at all would, he maintained, be to put our head into the lion's mouth. The Admiralty held, in fact, that in view of our maritime ascendancy our proper way of rendering assistance to France was to put such severe economic pressure on Germany that she could not continue the war.[82]

The details aside, such a radical conception of how war should be fought, suggesting that the outcome of a war might not depend upon victory in combat (whether on land or at sea), was, to say the least, a highly unconventional strategic view. What on earth must the politicians have made of such a novel and complex idea? Fisher apparently said enough, however, to pique the interest of at least one minister present. Even the incomplete official minutes record that Richard Haldane, secretary of state for war, "asked that the committee might be supplied with information as to Germany's power to hold out against [Britain and France] when she is deprived of her imports."[83] A striking statement! Rear-Admiral Slade promised to supply "some figures on this question" and "undertook to furnish a paper giving the information required."[84]

Two days after the first meeting of the subcommittee, Sir Charles Ottley sent McKenna a reminder that the prime minister expected a detailed statement from the Admiralty as to "the financial and economic pressure that would result to Germany." In the same letter (often cited but never in the correct context), Ottley assured McKenna that economic warfare was a perfectly credible strategy.

> The intelligence department have all the facts at their finger ends, the problem was constantly under investigation during the whole 3 years I was DNI, and Admiral Slade tells me he has given particular attention to it since he succeeded me. I do not know whether the Board have recently changed or modified their views from a year ago, but throughout the whole period that I was DNI the Admiralty claimed that the geographical position of this country and her preponderant seapower combined to give us a certain and simple means of strangling Germany at sea. They held that (in a protracted war) the mills of our seapower (though they would ground the German population slowly perhaps) would ground them "exceedingly small"—grass would sooner or later grow in the streets of Hamburg and widespread dearth would be inflicted.[85]

The Economic Warfare Paper

During the second week of December 1908, the Admiralty circulated to the members of the Military Needs of the Empire subcommittee the promised paper, titled "The Economic Effect of War on German Trade" (CID paper E-4). The economic warfare paper, as we shall hereafter refer to it, was discussed and reviewed on Thursday, 17 December 1908, at the second meeting of the CID subcommittee. Authorship of the paper traditionally has been attributed to Rear-Admiral Edmond Slade.[86] Yet the style therein differs so greatly from all Slade's previous memoranda that it seems likely it was the product of more than one author. That the paper was unsigned gives credence to this suspicion: Slade signed all of his other documents prepared for the CID.[87] The paper was most likely produced in cooperation with one of his assistants, or possibly his nominated successor, Rear-Admiral Alexander Bethell.[88] The exact authorship matters little, however. Its distribution meant it must have been approved by the First Lord (Reginald McKenna) and First Sea Lord as embodying the views of the Board of Admiralty.

In style and structure, the Admiralty's economic warfare paper was an unpolished document. It bore all the hallmarks of having been written in a hurry, its arguments disjointed and incomplete. Toward the end especially, it resembled more a list of points for discussion than a state paper. The imprecision is not surprising, however, as the economic warfare paper represented an early attempt to come to terms with a highly complex and difficult subject. True, it did not contain the sort of specific plans that the Military Needs of the Empire subcommittee had been formed to review. But manifestly it could not. Economic warfare necessarily entailed large-scale state intervention in the workings of both the domestic and international economy, starkly challenging traditional ideas about the role of government. In so doing, moreover, it far exceeded established boundaries of what constituted grand strategy and indeed the very nature of war. Economic warfare thus involved issues that were beyond the Admiralty's competence. The purpose of the paper was to highlight the necessity for government consideration of these issues, not to explain the strategy in detail. Nevertheless, a remarkable new strategic conception is evident.

In substance, the economic warfare paper consisted of thirty-eight paragraphs plus a number of tables and statistical appendixes, many of which addressed specific questions posed by Haldane at the previous meeting. The first sixteen offered little that was new.[89] They reiterated the Admiralty's long-standing contention that the modern German industrial economy was exceptionally vulnerable to economic attack. Statistics were deployed crudely to show that Germany was essentially an industrial and commercial power with thirty-three million German workers reliant upon industry and commerce for their livelihood, which in turn were heavily dependent upon overseas trade: "Two-thirds of her total trade is oversea and in some respects she is entirely dependent on countries separated from her by the sea for the raw materials with which to carry on her manufactures."[90] The obvious implication here was that separating German industry from its suppliers must lead to significant economic dislocation. Where this paper departed from previous Admiralty statements was its frank admission that total stoppage of all overseas trade would be unattainable.[91] The Admiralty went on to insist, however, that this impossibility did not invalidate their essential strategic argument, namely, that at the beginning of a major war the German economy was vulnerable to collapse.[92]

Quoting from a paper (since lost) that Sir Robert Giffen confidentially supplied to them, the Admiralty began with the contention that "the outbreak of a great naval war would be accompanied by a banking panic of unexampled dimensions."[93] There would be a general paralysis of the credit markets. In consequence, international trade would be severely curtailed. The paper emphasized that the "reason that trade is so sensitive is due to the uncertain basis on which it rests, namely credit. International exchange [i.e., trade] depends on credit and exchange [i.e., foreign currency balances]."[94] The inevitable dislocation to trade and financial systems consequent to the outbreak of war would place enormous strain upon all industrial economies. At the very least, disruption to businesses would be considerable: certain commodities would be in short supply, costs would rise, and relative prices would be deranged. Those nations engaged in military mobilization would face still greater disruptions caused by large withdrawals of manpower from the labor market and disruption to rail networks.[95]

Germany, the paper argued, was unusually susceptible to dislocation. Far more than any other country, German overseas commerce depended upon credit both to facilitate transactions and to attract customers. The interdependence of German banks and businesses for working capital, moreover, meant that upheaval would be transmitted rapidly throughout the entire system.[96] All these problems would manifest themselves immediately upon the outbreak of war, without any action on the part of the Royal Navy. Naval pressure would, of course, make German problems worse:

> It seems, then, that we must do all in our power to check German industrial output, or if possible stop it at its source (i.e., prevent the import of raw material). The effect of this proceeding would be to "discredit" her [undermine the creditworthiness of her financial institutions] and deprive her of the power of obtaining outside monetary assistance.[97]

In other words, the Admiralty argued that British action should not be limited to seizing German merchantmen and placing obstacles in the path of indirect trade through neutrals, though these actions would be important. Such an approach would amount to no more than a traditional blockade strategy. Economic warfare strategy entailed doing "all in our power" to disrupt the already strained enemy economy, recognizing that significant additional pressure could be exerted upon the German economy by systematically denying access to the largely British-controlled infrastructure of international trade—British banks, insurance companies, and communications networks. In essence, the Admiralty argued that the beginning of a major war would find the German economy teetering on the edge of a precipice and that British strategy should seek to push it over the edge and down into "unemployment, distress, &c., and eventually in bankruptcy."[98]

Here, then, was the theoretical foundation of economic warfare. But how could this aim be translated into practical policy? Though in this paper the Admiralty stopped short of making specific policy recommendations, clues abounded as to what they wished. The somewhat cryptic final paragraph stressed that Germany in wartime "*must* continue to draw supplies of foodstuffs and raw materials from overseas," and that "to supply these wants" merchant ships "*must* be supplied from outside sources."[99] The final sentences read as follows: "The only country likely to have suitable tonnage is Great Britain. The attraction of the high freight might cause British shipping to be diverted for this purpose to the detriment of our own trade." Clearly, the Admiralty was hinting at the need for the government to prohibit British shipping, insurance, banking, and communications interests from assisting Germany during wartime—a step that would entail unprecedented state intervention in the workings of the national and international economies. These steps were well beyond the competence of the Admiralty and required input from multiple government departments. As we shall see in Chapter 4, Ottley soon drove home the point in case the politicians failed to take the hint.

Two memoranda distributed subsequently to the committee also alluded to economic warfare. On 17 December 1908, Lord Esher circulated a paper with his thoughts on the discussion held at the first meeting. Essentially, it queried the logic behind the General Staff's Continental plan and suggested that the value of naval pressure was being underestimated. Significantly, Esher argued that "naval pressure upon German trade, German commerce, and German food supply, would be certain to influence the result of prolonged military conflict ashore."[100] He went on to argue that Britain's ability to inflict "deadly injury" upon German commerce and "the fear of raids" ought to be held "to be a sufficient fulfillment of our share in the partnership between us and the French nation."[101] Esher closed his paper by suggesting that if France demanded more of Great Britain, then perhaps a token force of cavalry might be dispatched to the Continent—an idea summarily dismissed by the soldiers.[102] In a memorandum challenging Esher's proposals, the General Staff deprecated the value of naval assistance to France: "It seems to the General Staff by no means certain that the naval predominance of the allies would affect the issue of the decisive struggle on land, especially if Germany continued to respect the neutrality of Holland and Belgium and we were consequently unable to blockade their ports."[103]

Finally, a letter from Ottley to Esher in October 1909, three months after the winding up of the Military Needs of the Empire subcommittee, strongly suggests that the subcommittee (or its members) discussed in detail the Admiralty's plan for economic warfare. On a list of subjects that Ottley believed required closer consideration by the CID, he included:

> the question of the *offensive* action to be taken by this country in the event of war with Germany or any other potential enemy. E.g. in the event of the war with Germany, there would appear to be two or even three directions in which we can act with vigor on the offensive. We can (A) attack Germany's oversea trade and communications: and (B) we can seize Germany's colonies, and/or (C) we can? *possibly??* turn against Germany the weapon which alarmists tell us she will turn against us, namely financial pressure and "cornering" of national resources.[104]

This is an extraordinarily important letter. Ottley identified three, not two, competing strategic ideas. Ottley clearly assumed, furthermore, that Esher was familiar with his differentiation between option A, which was a comparatively orthodox naval campaign against German seaborne commerce, and option C, which was the more complex strategy of economic warfare. His reference to "alarmists" implies that it had been discussed by the CID—yet, according to the official record, there had been no such debate.

Although the meetings of the CID subcommittee in December 1908 marked the first occasions on which members of the political executive heard the Admiralty lay out their plans for economic warfare, many of the Admiralty's (and Giffen's) ideas about the functioning of the national and international economies undoubtedly were familiar to them. Recognition of the recent transformation of the global trading system was fairly widespread by 1908; indeed, a major figure brought the issue directly to Asquith's attention between the second and third meetings of the CID subcommittee. In February 1909, Sir Frederic Bolton, shipping magnate and former chairman of Lloyd's, wrote to the prime minister drawing attention to (what he thought were) some overlooked implications of Giffen's published thoughts.[105] Bolton advised Asquith that Giffen's predictions that a major war must provoke a catastrophic dislocation of the "intricate trade system" suggested the danger of disruption of supply to Great Britain.[106] But Bolton also realized that similar disruptions would affect Germany:

> It is clear that any interference with overseas supplies will result in high prices and scarcity, and will bring severe pressure to the people generally. The financial and commercial distress will follow lines similar to those described by Sir Robert Giffen in reference to this country. There is no doubt that the industrial classes have far less power in Germany than in England, and without in any way attempting to forecast the development of the political situation, it can safely be said that it is impossible to increase beyond a certain point the burdens of an unwilling people.[107]

How much (if anything) Bolton may have heard unofficially about economic warfare is impossible to say, but it is clear he accepted Giffen's analysis as valid. Interestingly, Bolton's letter resulted in Asquith allocating CID funds to subsidize his continuing study and ultimately, in February 1910, to appoint a CID subcommittee to appraise his findings.

Readers familiar with the writings of Norman Angell may recognize much of the reasoning contained within the Admiralty's economic warfare paper. Angell, a journalist by profession, was the most prominent contemporary theorist before the First World War to discuss the geostrategic implications of mutual economic interdependence.[108] The relatively recent transformation of the global economy was a key theme in his 1910 classic, *The Great Illusion,* which sold more than two million copies before the war.[109] Angell attributed the "profound change" in methods of global trade to the expanded reach of European (largely British) banking systems, made possible by the development of "instantaneous dissemination of financial and commercial information by means of [cable] telegraphy, and the generally incredible progress of rapidity in communication."[110] The establishment of the global cable network during the mid-1880s allowed European merchant banks to lend money across the globe, in turn enabling capital-poor nations to finance their imports using short-term credit. This pattern was quite distinct from the simultaneous flow of money to facilitate long-term capital infrastructure projects (such as railways) that enabled hitherto inaccessible markets and raw materials to participate in the global trading system.[111]

Like Giffen, Norman Angell was concerned that one of the consequences of this interdependence meant that the global trading system had become a hazardously "delicate" organism and that the effects of a problem in one part of the world would rapidly be transmitted to all the others. Similarly, he also predicted that any major European conflict likely would cause catastrophic damage to the global financial system. According to his biographer, Angell acquired his insights not from Giffen but instead from a book by Hartley Withers, the financial editor of the *Times,* entitled *The Meaning of Money*—further evidence, incidentally, that the understanding of economic interdependence was widespread.[112] Compared to Giffen, Angell drew very different conclusions from this phenomenon. Assuming rational decision making, he argued that greater financial and trade interdependence between the major powers must diminish the likelihood of conflicts between them. The economic cost of war had become so great as to outweigh any possible advantage that might accrue from victory, making any decision for war a profoundly irrational choice. But as Angell's biographer stressed, this idea "was expressed in such loose and alarmist language as to create a widespread belief 'that the bankers would stop it [war] or the money would run out.' "[113]

Even though Angell's conclusions were fundamentally at odds with those of Giffen as circulated by the Admiralty, his book apparently was seen by members of the government as echoing the broad thrust of Giffen's theories. This might have encouraged them to engage the Admiralty's ideas more seriously than they otherwise might have done, though not, it must be emphasized, until more than a year later. Perhaps it might be better to say that Angell encouraged the politicians to give the economic warfare theory another closer look. Norman Angell's book made a particular impression upon Lord Esher, who subsequently became his patron and most ardent publicist.[114] Esher discovered Angell's book over Christmas 1909. On New Year's Eve he sent a copy to Arthur Balfour, the former Conservative prime minister. He sent additional copies to other senior figures within the government establishment, including Sir Charles Hardinge, the Foreign Office permanent undersecretary, another former member of the Military Needs of the

Empire subcommittee. During 1910, Sir Edward Grey publicly cited Angell's work at least twice. The *Daily Mail* described it as the "most discussed book in years."[115]

There is further evidence of widespread acknowledgment of Giffen's ideas. In April 1910, Edgar Crammond, secretary to the Liverpool Stock Exchange and a widely respected financial columnist, read a paper before the Institute of Bankers titled "The Finance of War" and predicated largely upon Giffen's ideas. In his closing remarks, the speaker granted:

> The general impression obtained from a study of the question of supply of credit in time of war is one of utter hopelessness as to the possibility of conducting our vast business in times of peace on such lines as would ensure avoidance of a commercial catastrophe on the outbreak of a great war.[116]

Perhaps keen to end his talk on a more optimistic note, the speaker ventured to remind his audience that the consequences of war were so "tremendous" that "financial considerations constitute a safeguard for the preservation of peace, the importance of which it is impossible to exaggerate." Furthermore, "if our own credit system were threatened with collapse, it is certain that the credit systems of all countries dependent upon it, that is to say, of all the great nations of the world, would be more or less involved."[117] All very true, agreed the president of the Institute of Bankers, Mr. Frederick Huth Jackson, a well-known merchant banker and director of the Bank of England: "Unfortunately the decision as to war does not rest with the mercantile community—it rests with the governments of the various countries."[118] This paper was brought to the attention of the prime minister and the CID.

Having reviewed the Admiralty's economic warfare paper on 17 December 1908, the Military Needs of the Empire subcommittee did not reassemble until 23 March 1909. A fortnight prior to the third meeting, Fisher complained to Lord Esher that since the threat of imminent war had subsided, the prime minister seemed determined to evade "the big questions." Further discussion of British grand strategy appeared pointless, he ventured, "until the Cabinet have decided the great big question raised in your E.5 [i.e., Esher's paper of 14 December 1908]: '*Are we or are we not going to send a British Army to fight on the Continent as quite distinct and apart*' from a naval strategy?"[119]

But of course, as Fisher knew perfectly well, Asquith would never pose so blunt a question to Liberal ministers unless faced by the threat of imminent war. When the CID subcommittee finally reassembled in March, after a brief desultory conversation the prime minister indeed dodged the key issue by announcing that "in the event of an attack on France by Germany, the expediency of sending a military force abroad, *or of relying on naval means alone,* is a matter of policy which can only be determined, when the occasion arises, by the government of the day." He added:

> In view, however, of the possibility of a decision by the Cabinet to use military force, the Committee have examined the plans of the General Staff, and are of opinion that . . . the plan to which preference is given by the General Staff is a valuable one, and the General Staff should accordingly work out all the necessary details.[120]

These conclusions were incorporated into and formed the basis of the committee's final report printed in July 1909.

Although neither Admiral Fisher nor General Nicholson succeeded in convincing the politicians that theirs was indisputably the better strategy, Asquith's decision nevertheless represented a victory for the War Office. For internal party political reasons Asquith had no intention of pronouncing in favor of one or the other strategy. Privately, he detested the General Staff's strategy (far more so than Fisher realized), but it would have been politically suicidal for him either to squash the Army General Staff or to insist upon better harmonization between the Navy and Army plans.[121] At the very least, these steps would have reopened the troublesome question of military reform (and the politically perilous matter of conscription)—which in recent years had been a graveyard for political careers and which the Liberal party was loath to discuss—and very likely also would have been seen as a rebuke of Richard Haldane, the secretary of state for war, an important political ally within the party.[122] Haldane might well have felt compelled to resign at such an indication of no confidence. We must consider also what possible advantage could have accrued to Asquith in expending so much political capital. Far safer, surely, for the prime minister to do as he did: to agree that the Royal Navy should apply some degree of economic pressure upon Germany, while at the same time allowing the General Staff to develop its "valuable" plan to deploy the BEF to France to help check the anticipated German military onslaught, however inadequate the force provided for this mission.[123]

For all this sophistry, there is no denying that Asquith's conclusions represented a bureaucratic victory for the War Office.[124] The General Staff plan for Continental intervention was not summarily ruled out of court and would be evaluated on its merits when the time came.[125]

Accordingly, most historians have agreed that the final report by the Military Needs of the Empire subcommittee strongly favored the Army to the detriment of the Navy. In the words of one, "Official recognition was given to the belief that the first battles in France would be decisive and that therefore a [naval] blockade strategy was of no importance."[126] Suggesting that the Admiralty strategy was ruled "of no importance," however, overstates the case. The committee's final report (drafted by Ottley) acknowledged that "a Power possessing command of the sea against Germany can by blockading her ports bring great economic pressure to bear against her." Ottley further wrote:

> [The committee] are of opinion that a serious situation would be created in Germany owing to the blockade of her ports, and that the longer the duration of the war the more serious the situation would become. We do not, however, consider that such pressure as could be exerted by means of naval force alone would be felt sufficiently soon to save France in the event of that country being attacked in overwhelming force.[127]

The operative phrase in this carefully worded paragraph is "naval force alone." In a letter Ottley wrote to Bethell some eighteen months later referring to this report, we find a reference—this time emphasized—noting that "the likelihood of action *by naval means alone* was distinctly contemplated."[128] The wording is both curious and obviously deliberate, as is the emphasis. As we shall see in the next chapter, Ottley was in fact drawing a vital distinction between a strategy of economic blockade based upon naval force alone and another based upon economic warfare. The former was limited and politically safer; the latter was a far more radical strategy that envisaged harnessing not only Britain's naval power but also her monopolistic control over world shipping, finance, and communications. The problem with endorsing the latter strategy was that it entailed imposing state controls over these service industries, steps that were unprecedented and certain to be politically costly. Certainly Asquith would not have considered incurring such costs without studying the matter in far greater detail.

Besides his reluctance to take politically expensive actions, another possible explanation for the prime minister's hesitation to endorse the Admiralty's radical economic warfare strategy might have been his discovery that the Navy leadership was not of one voice on this subject. In May 1909, Asquith called upon retired Admiral of the Fleet Sir Arthur Wilson to appraise various criticisms of Admiralty policy leveled by Admiral Lord Charles Beresford shortly after his dismissal from command of the battle fleet. For the preceding two years, Beresford had been steadfastly opposed to the radical aspects of Admiralty strategy, urging instead a strictly orthodox close blockade. Testifying before Asquith and a small committee of ministers, Wilson declared his support for the Admiralty in rejecting Beresford's counterstrategy as unworkable, agreeing that "a continuous close watch off all German ports, in sufficient strength to prevent anything from coming out, would be very difficult and costly to maintain" and therefore impractical. When questioned about his views on the Admiralty's strategic plans, however, Wilson became evasive. He thought that the Royal Navy ought to target the German battle fleet rather than her economy.[129] When pressed, he admitted that he did not think driving the German mercantile flag from the sea would produce sufficiently decisive results. Looking at the subject from a strictly orthodox perspective, he observed that "there would be an outcry from German ship-owners, but the rest of the community would suffer nothing more than a slight increase in prices"; he further predicted that "their trade would go on overland with other nations" and that more than likely "our own ships will supply them."[130] Perhaps realizing his political gaffe, Wilson quickly added that perhaps economic warfare might be useful in enticing the German fleet out of harbor to meet its doom—though his preferred form of bait was to use the Army to launch amphibious raids on the German coast.

Those who attended the meetings of the Beresford Committee all agreed that Wilson's "clear and straightforward manner" greatly impressed all and especially Asquith.[131] Lord Morley, secretary of state for the India Office, thought that while Admirals Fisher and Beresford each had his good qualities, "Sir A. Wilson strikes me, and I think the others of us, as much the best balanced sort of man, to say nothing of his having proved himself as a first rate commander."[132] When, three months later, Fisher announced his resignation (his authority within the service had been irrevocably damaged by the findings of the same Beresford committee), for a variety of complex political reasons that have been described elsewhere, he was persuaded that Sir Arthur Wilson was the admiral least likely to reverse his policies and accordingly should become his successor.[133] The prime minister, having developed a favorable impression of Wilson, voiced no objections to recalling a 68-year-old officer who had been retired from the service for almost three years. It was nevertheless a most unusual and desperate step to take.

Sir Arthur Wilson as First Sea Lord

Admiral of the Fleet Sir Arthur Wilson formally succeeded Lord Fisher as First Sea Lord on 25 January 1910. In agreeing to Wilson's nomination, Fisher had known that their ideas were not perfectly synchronized and that in many ways he was far from an ideal choice. "I wasn't sweet on it at first as Wilson is such a stonewall," Fisher confessed to McKenna after his candidacy was first mooted, "however you make a good point which converted me in saying that for two years a stone wall was desirable."[134] Fisher's initial instincts were right on the mark. Wilson's qualifications for the post of First Sea Lord were questionable. Known within the service as "Old 'ard 'eart," Wilson possessed a notoriously overbearing, even autocratic personality, and had a terrible record as an administrator. In 1901, while serving as controller, he had created such a bureaucratic tangle within the department that he was dismissed. "I never did a better day's work in my life than when I removed him from the Admiralty where he was an utter failure and a mischievous failure too," Lord Selborne later reminded Arthur Balfour.[135] Within the service, admiration for Sir Arthur Wilson's abilities as a fleet commander were tempered by wariness of his reputation for ignoring and even bullying subordinates. "I dare say *under the circumstances* Wilson is the best solution," sighed Vice-Admiral Sir Francis Bridgeman, the Second Sea Lord, "dull and uncompromising, as you know. He will never consult anyone and is impatient in argument, even to being impossible."[136] This view was widely shared.[137]

Thus Wilson was selected as First Sea Lord not for his abilities but because the alternative candidates were obviously so much worse. Furthermore, he had explicitly promised the First Lord he would maintain the current direction of Admiralty policy and not to deviate from the path ahead mapped out by his predecessor.[138] Indeed, McKenna apparently deceived himself into thinking Wilson was content to serve as no more than a figurehead, allowing the First Lord to direct Admiralty policy himself with the help of three reliable members of the "Fish-pond," Admirals Sir Francis Bridgeman and John Jellicoe (respectively, Second and Third Sea Lords) and Sir Alexander Bethell (DNI), with whom the First Lord enjoyed a particularly close working relationship. McKenna very quickly learned he had been mistaken in thinking Wilson was anyone's puppet. As his naval secretary pithily noted in his diary after the first meeting of the new Board of Admiralty: "Wilson is autocratic." Pamela McKenna was equally dismayed to find that "the dreadful Sir Arthur Wilson" did not shy from bullying her husband in the same way he did junior officers.[139]

What was the impact of Wilson's appointment upon the Admiralty's development of economic warfare strategy? Six months before becoming First Sea Lord, Wilson let slip to the prime minister his scant interest in the subject. It might be supposed, as some have mistakenly done, that under Wilson the Admiralty virtually abandoned the idea of using naval power to exert economic pressure.[140] In fact, the new First Sea Lord raised remarkably few obstacles to the further development of economic warfare strategy. The lack of tangible forward movement during his administration was due mainly to the government's delay in making up its mind whether to consider the more contentious aspects of economic warfare—most notably the need for large-scale wartime government intervention in economic life. Despite repeated pleas from Ottley, McKenna, Esher, and even Haldane, not until 1910 was the prime minister organizationally and mentally ready to contemplate such questions so obviously fraught with political dangers.

Wilson's disinterest in the economic aspects of warfare extended also to the Declaration of London. He looked the other way while Rear-Admiral Alexander Bethell, the DNI, who was fervently opposed to the treaty, mounted a guerilla campaign against ratification. Bethell's less-than-covert activities provoked an irate Eyre Crowe to complain to Slade (exiled to a command in the East Indies) that "your successor [Bethell] is trying to lead us a nice dance in regard to the international prize court and the Declaration of London." Furthermore, "a number of admirals are proclaiming everywhere that they have it 'on good authority' that these treaties were wrung from a reluctant Admiralty by an incompetent Foreign Office!"[141] The Admiralty bureaucracy also processed the relevant files at an unusually slow pace. In December 1910, for instance, the director of naval mobilization (DNM), tasked to redraft the war orders to conform to the provisions in the Declaration of London, complained that he did not understand the meaning of a certain clause in the treaty and asked for clarification. The Admiralty took six weeks to decide that the matter must be referred to the Foreign Office. A further five months passed before a partial answer (which was subsequently amended) arrived, and not until 7 July 1911 was the DNM able to move forward.[142] Not until Wilson had left the Admiralty (in November 1911) was the committee reformed; the revised manual was not ready before August 1914.[143]

This foot-dragging aside, the Admiralty as a whole could not ignore the Declaration of London. Their response has been the subject of close scholarly investigation, yet a satisfactory consensus is still lacking.[144] As was explained in the previous chapter, one reason is that historians have not, until recently, understood precisely what the Admiralty hoped to achieve at the London Naval Conference, or the significance of changes in the definition of several key principles of maritime law, in particular what constituted an "effective" (i.e., legal) blockade. Lacking comprehension of the relevant legal changes and unable to evaluate the Admiralty's success or failure in terms of their goals, historians have instead invariably characterized the Admiralty's position as incomprehensible or criticized them for meekly acquiescing in the Foreign Office surrender of the doctrine of continuous voyage.[145] Further obstacles to untangling the story exist in the form of contradictory statements made by the principal actors. In July 1911, for instance, Reginald McKenna, still the First Lord of the Admiralty, apparently misled Parliament when asked if the Board of Admiralty was consulted about the Declaration. "Yes, Sir," McKenna unequivocally replied; "the Board of Admiralty decided in support of the Declaration of London."[146] In fact, the Board never once formally considered the subject, as is evident from a perusal of the Admiralty minute books.[147]

However, neither the failure of the Board to discuss the matter nor Wilson's apathy mean that the Admiralty omitted to formulate a coherent response. The key figure in these efforts was Rear-Admiral Alexander Bethell. The DNI astutely saw that regardless of whether Britain ratified the Declaration of London, in wartime neutrals would press the Royal Navy to observe its main principles.[148] He adjudged, however, the declaration contained so many loopholes that the Royal Navy could successfully resist such pressure. Crucially, he saw the new definition of effective blockade, which theoretically legalized distant blockades, as a gain worth the sacrifice of applying continuous voyage to conditional contraband. This was of critical significance because a blockade permitted the Royal Navy to interdict German *exports* as well as imports and thereby intensify pressure upon her economy, whereas the laws of contraband did not permit the capture of exports from a belligerent country. Although the German (and Dutch) delegations to the London Naval Conference had inserted clauses into the treaty calculated to prevent the Royal Navy from declaring Germany under distant blockade (articles 18 and 19), Bethell contended that these had been so poorly drafted and were so ambiguous that the Admiralty might plausibly ignore them and plead before the international court—after the war—that their mistake (if it was ultimately ruled a mistake) had been made in good faith.

It is true that the surrender of continuous voyage now prevented the Royal Navy from lawfully stopping neutral merchantmen carrying all Germany's requirements to contiguous neutral ports, but the Admiralty had thought through the disadvantages and did not consider them as serious as historians have since made them out to be. First, the Declaration of London considerably tightened the rules governing the reflagging of merchant ships, making it effectively impossible for German merchantmen to sail under a neutral flag and avoid capture. Second, there was insufficient neutral shipping to carry German trade. Third, few neutral merchantmen were expected to ply the Baltic in time of war because of anticipated difficulties in obtaining insurance.[149] Fourth, nothing in the Declaration of London prevented Britain from prohibiting her merchantmen from carrying neutral goods for Germany's benefit. Arguably this method would shut the door on German trade much more effectively than invoking the doctrine of continuous voyage.

Based upon Bethell's analysis, the Admiralty drew up plans to impose a "distant" watch of German ports to conform to the new laws of blockade.[150] In the archives is a file containing the (unissued) operational orders for the fleet prescribing how the Navy would blockade the German North Sea coast according to the rules laid down under the Declaration of London, which included working papers on the legal aspects, endorsed by every senior official in the department connected with strategic planning.[151] In a memorandum therein dated October 1911, Bethell recorded the Admiralty's intention (which he recognized would prove contentious) that a distant blockade constituted an effective (legal) blockade and therefore British cruisers would have every right to stop and search all neutral vessels entering the North Sea to determine their cargoes and ultimate destinations. If discovered to be inbound for a German port or carrying contraband destined for Germany, they would be seized for violation of blockade. Those bound for neutral ports would be released. Bethell wrote:

> The area of operations [*rayon d'action*] may be considered to be the whole of the North Sea & the blockading force as all the vessels in that area including any cordon across from Scotland to Norway & across the straits of Dover.
>
> It is fairly certain that should we be in war [*sic*] with Germany we shall consider the above to be the correct interpretation of the Declaration of London & act on it. There may possibly be protests from some

> of the neutrals but I doubt their being able to sustain them before the International Court at The Hague.[152]

He further reasoned:

> There is no limit to the number of vessels which may be employed to fix the limits to blockade, nor any restriction placed as to their disposition or distance to the blockaded coast—provided they constitute an effective force to maintain the blockade. The cordons across the North Sea (Scotland to Norway) & the Straits of Dover are the outer limits of the blockading force & guard the northern and southern limits of the area of operations of the warships detailed to render the blockade effective.[153]

Graham Greene endorsed Bethell's analysis (hereafter referred to as the "Bethell interpretation") and agreed that under the Declaration of London the Royal Navy lawfully could cordon off the North Sea and declare Germany under blockade.[154] Even the First Sea Lord, Wilson, believed this interpretation correct and affirmed that the Royal Navy would aggressively enforce such a blockade. He decreed that if British cruisers encountered any merchant ships that purportedly were bound for neutral destinations but that had strayed from a direct path to their declared destination, the merchant vessels would be seized under presumption of blockade running.[155] The Admiralty also envisaged exploiting Article 20 of the Declaration, permitting the capture of outward-bound vessels, which the DNM reckoned would net the Royal Navy a large number of captures.[156] In other words, if naval intelligence discovered that a neutral ship had discharged its cargo at a German port, it was then permissible under the Declaration of London to capture it on its return (outbound) voyage, thereby reducing the already limited supply of neutral shipping for Germany.

True, several important issues were not addressed by the Admiralty in these papers, such as Germany's ability to continue some trade through Rotterdam. Considering that this had been their top concern for the previous five years, not to mention the DNI's demonstrable familiarity with the problem, this silence might seem odd. Yet, as we have seen, at the time when Bethell was writing, the Admiralty were still awaiting government authorization to prohibit British-flagged merchantmen from carrying for Germany. As we shall see in the next chapter, the Admiralty had neither forgotten nor abandoned their intention to exploit Britain's monopolistic position in transatlantic carriage and indeed were eagerly awaiting resolution. When Bethell penned the above appraisal in October 1911, he was aware (as were his intended readers) that the government was actively considering the more controversial aspects of economic warfare strategy. In fact, Bethell was the Admiralty's representative to the CID subcommittee that was examining this very question.

Thus the contradiction between the Admiralty's supposed commitment to economic warfare and reconciliation to the laws set down under the Declaration of London was more apparent than real. Although the Admiralty's plan for economic warfare differed fundamentally from the type of warfare contemplated by the declaration, the Admiralty believed that they could adapt it to their needs. The men who negotiated the Declaration of London were concerned with adapting eighteenth-century rules of maritime warfare to reflect "modern" conditions. War planners at the Admiralty, by contrast, framed their recommendations based upon an understanding of how the transformed world economic system actually functioned in the twentieth century. The Admiralty learned from Sir Robert Giffen that the growing dependence of national and international economic systems upon credit, communications, and shipping over the previous fifty years left them vulnerable to an unprecedented degree of disruption. The aim of economic warfare was not the mere interdiction of enemy seaborne trade (a blockade) but rather the maximization of pressure upon the economic systems underpinning the enemy's economy. To exploit German vulnerability, the Admiralty had to do both less and more than it had once done: it no longer had to interdict enemy trade completely, as in a traditional close blockade, but it now had to isolate the enemy from the global trading system by denying access to shipping, communications, and financial services. The Admiralty could afford to play along with the Declaration of London's obsession with "legitimate" actions to interdict cargos under the laws of contraband, so long as they preserved their freedom to target the infrastructure of the global trading system. The Admiralty realized that their plan for economic warfare redefined the boundaries of strategy to encompass normal economic activities and demanded large-scale government intervention into the workings of the free market economy. These dimensions of economic warfare were beyond the Admiralty's competence, and even beyond those of the Committee of Imperial Defence as then constituted.

4

The Endorsement of Economic Warfare

That war is no longer carried on solely by the Admiralty and War Office, and that every branch of the Public Service is concerned, are truths which have become more and more clear in consequence of the investigations of the C.I.D.

ARTHUR J. BALFOUR, 9 January 1912

The conditions of trade with the interwoven interests of nations and individuals have created conditions under which no great European war has yet been waged, and history does not afford very much material for our guidance.

LORD DESART, 21 February 1912

After the Committee of Imperial Defence (CID) voted to approve the final report of the Military Needs of the Empire subcommittee at the end of July 1909, the prime minister did not reconvene the forum until the following February. Sir Charles Ottley, the CID secretary, understood this "policy of inactivity" was due to the domestic political situation.[1] Asquith was preoccupied with the developing constitutional crisis consequent to the House of Lords' refusal to pass David Lloyd George's radical "people's budget." This story has been told too many times elsewhere to require reiteration here.[2] After the House of Lords finally voted to reject the budget on 30 November 1909, Asquith called a general election. In late January 1910, the Liberal party was returned to power, albeit with a greatly reduced majority.

Formal approval of the report by the Military Needs of the Empire subcommittee did not mean the political executive considered as closed the subject of British grand strategy in the event of war with Germany. Lord Esher in particular was most unhappy with the verdict, and even Richard Haldane, the secretary of state for war, agreed with him (and Ottley) that the final report had glossed over too much. Its shortcomings, all thought, were symptomatic of the limitations of current national defense arrangements.[3] Still hankering for the creation of a unified joint staff with executive responsibility for imperial defense, Esher campaigned for the CID to become more focused upon questions of high (grand) strategy and leave the mundane details to be worked out by the service departments. This plan necessarily implied a subordination of the Admiralty and War Office to a new strategic executive committee, an arrangement that was certain to lead to confrontation with the service chiefs. Thinking along parallel though different lines, Haldane saw himself as the ideal candidate to become, in effect, minister of defense.

Ottley, while agreeing with the necessity for reform, urged caution in trying to extend the CID's boundaries of responsibility at the expense of the established departments. In October 1909, he reminded Esher that

> until twelve month ago the committee [CID] was still on its trial, and a large section of the political intelligence of the Empire regarded us with grave suspicion. Even now, although we are at last out of the wood, and are *"bien-vu"* by both the great political parties, the position of this little office is ill-defined and amorphous.[4]

Warning that both the War Office and Admiralty would fight any attempt to usurp their traditional prerogatives to make policy, Ottley counseled aiming for a more modest goal. He suggested that the CID's efforts over the previous five years to map the outlines of a national policy for war demonstrated the necessity for much better coordination of departmental action, both civilian and military, prior to the outbreak of war. With this Haldane agreed, telling Asquith "there were a number of technical questions which affected various Departments . . . that ought not to be left for decision until after the outbreak of the war."[5]

Haldane might well have been alarmed to discover Ottley's ulterior motive for recommending reform of the CID: forcing it to tackle the Admiralty's plan for economic warfare. In October 1909, three months after he penned the final report of the Military Needs of the Empire subcommittee, Ottley began a lengthy correspondence with Lord Esher to discuss the future of the CID and the paramount necessity for more intensive investigation of certain "technical" subjects.[6] On his list of issues that he believed required closer examination was "the question of the *offensive* action to be taken by this country in the event of war with Germany or any other potential enemy," including the use of economic warfare involving the application of "financial pressure and 'cornering' of national resources."[7] It is quite astonishing—and this cannot be overstated—that the CID secretary should so soon be calling for another investigation into "*offensive* action" to be taken against Germany. Clearly he was unhappy with the final verdict, and determined to make the political executive confront the implications of the economic warfare strategy that the Admiralty had begun to unveil in the meetings of the Military Needs of the Empire subcommittee.

The CID reorganization and governmental rearrangements that would be necessary for effective cooperation both on economic warfare and on strategy more generally, however, posed serious political headaches for Asquith. As Ottley rightly insisted, to provide the necessary competence for evaluating complex strategies, specially appointed "technical" subcommittees consisting of outside experts and overseen by perhaps one or two political members from the CID executive committee would be necessary.[8] These would not become standing committees, but rather would be merely scaffolding to permit the development of necessary administrative infrastructure for coordinating service and civilian departments of government in time of war.[9]

Several times during late 1909, the prime minister put off making a decision over Ottley's proposal to create technical subcommittees.[10] He offered no written explanation for his dithering, compelling us to speculate. Asquith's preoccupation with the constitutional crisis must have been a major factor in explaining his reticence—but it was probably not the only reason. As has been repeatedly stressed, the CID was a relatively new institution. It had been created as a forum for the political executive to meet with senior naval and military planners to discuss and oversee issues of strategy. Acceding to the creation of technical subcommittees, however, would require Asquith to extend CID membership to senior civil servants working in civilian agencies such as the Board of Trade, and thus allow them a voice in defense preparations. While the committee had utilized such experts before, they had been called upon as witnesses only; quite simply, there was no precedent for civil service experts being included in the defense community. There were political implications to be weighed before approving such a significant innovation in the defense organization.

The second political problem posed by CID and government reorganization concerned military and naval infringements of the traditional prerogatives of civilian departments. Haldane, for instance, pointed to the necessity for agreed-upon procedures in the enforcement of wartime censorship over the press and the mails, which arguably was just as much a matter for the civilian Post Office and the Home Office as it was for the War Office.[11] The adoption of economic warfare would necessarily entail even greater trespass on civilian territory. To take just one example, the Admiralty plan would require the government to regulate the movements and cargoes of British-flagged merchantmen in time of war, to prevent them from carrying goods to Germany through neutral ports. Since regulation of the merchant shipping industry had long been the preserve of the Board of Trade, which possessed the expert staff, organization, and statutory authority, the simplest way for the government to meet Admiralty needs would be to task the existing Board of Trade organization with overseeing and ensuring compliance. The Board of Trade, however, was a bastion of free trade ideals and laissez-faire economics and might therefore be disposed to resist such interference in the free market. The government would have to confront powerful financial and commercial interests in order to implement the Admiralty plan for economic warfare.

At the top of the agenda for the 105th meeting of the CID, held on 24 February 1910, was a paper exploring the "future work of the CID."[12] After a short discussion, Ottley's recommendation to form technical subcommittees to tackle specific questions was approved. It was agreed, in the first instance, to launch two. The first subcommittee, under the chairmanship of Lord Esher, brought together representatives from the Board of Trade, Treasury, Customs, and the War Office to examine concerns over domestic transportation and distribution of food in time of war.[13] The second, of more immediate relevance to our story, was appointed to devise a set of protocols to govern the treatment of foreign merchant vessels caught in British waters upon outbreak of war.[14] This committee comprised officials drawn from the Admiralty and War Office plus no fewer than six different civilian departments of state. According to Captain Maurice Hankey (since the fall of 1908 the naval representative to the CID secretariat), the intended scope of this inquiry initially had been much wider. But, he reported to Esher, Admiral Sir Arthur Wilson (now First Sea Lord) "sees no object in an inquiry re the seizure of the merchant ships flying the enemy's flag on outbreak of war. In his view this is one of the questions which will have to be decided by the Government when war comes!"[15] Hankey complained that Wilson was willfully obstructing the CID;

Esher agreed this was indicative of the new attitude prevailing at the Admiralty.[16] Furthermore, retired Admiral Fisher originally had been the first choice for the chairmanship but had declined the position upon learning that the Foreign Office had balked at his nomination, insisting the committee be run by one of its men.[17] The position was ultimately given to Sir Charles Hardinge, the Foreign Office permanent secretary and a member of the former Military Needs of the Empire subcommittee.

On its face, the Hardinge Committee's task seemed simple. But as the membership quickly discovered, it involved a range of complex subjects, each with its own strategic and legal ramifications, and consequently the committee took more than six months to complete its studies and make its recommendations.[18] Throughout the proceedings, Rear-Admiral Sir Alexander Bethell, the DNI, repeatedly argued that the subject needed to be considered from a much broader perspective.[19] In so doing, he received subtle support from the secretariat, Sir Charles Ottley, and Captain Hankey.[20] Hardinge, perhaps a tad anxious to wind up the proceedings in order to assume his new position as viceroy of India, steadfastly refused to allow the committee to venture beyond its boundaries as originally defined. Remarkably, however, he accepted Bethell's argument. In the final report he advised that before the protocols offered by his committee were accepted, the CID ought to make a much broader inquiry into the whole subject of economic warfare. Hardinge thought it especially important that "the policy regarding the treatment to be accorded to British vessels trading with the enemy should be definitely and authoritatively laid down."[21] This question, as Ottley observed to Esher, was "a very great *legal* conundrum."[22] What powers did the state possess to regulate the wartime movements of British-flagged merchantmen or the cargoes they might carry?

With uncharacteristic zeal, the prime minister immediately approved this recommendation and at the 108th meeting of the CID, held on 26 January 1911, directed the formation of another technical subcommittee to consider "the whole question of Trade with the Enemy in Time of War."[23] Every single department of government with an interest in economic matters was allowed to send a representative. To chair the committee, Asquith handpicked an outsider to the defense community, a retired government lawyer with no previous connection to the Committee of Imperial Defence. A surprised Hankey told Esher, who had missed the meeting, "The P.M. personally nominated Lord Desart as Chairman of the sub-ctee on Trading with the Enemy."[24] One cannot help wondering at this point whether Asquith was shaping the committee with a particular result already in mind, or whether he actually favored having the subject properly investigated. There is, alas, no firm evidence on this.

The name of Hamilton "Ham" Cuffe, fifth Earl of Desart, has been all but forgotten by history. Lord Desart was born in 1848, the second of three sons, to the 3rd Earl of Desart, an Irish peer from County Kilkenny. Interestingly, in light of subsequent events, Desart was originally intended for a career in the Royal Navy. Between 1860 and 1863, he served as a midshipman on board an old wooden frigate stationed in Canadian waters. Naval service did not agree with him, however, and upon returning to England he quit the service, resumed formal academic studies, and in 1869 graduated from Trinity College, Cambridge. After a brief flirtation with a career in the diplomatic service, Desart settled upon the law and trained as a barrister, being called to the bar in 1872.[25] In 1878, through the patronage of Benjamin Disraeli, he became assistant solicitor to the Treasury. Desart was evidently highly competent at his job. By the age of forty-six he had risen to the top of his department, simultaneously holding the posts of Treasury solicitor, queen's proctor, and director of public prosecutions (in which capacity he represented the crown in the famous 1895 Oscar Wilde case). In 1898, after the death of his elder brother, Desart succeeded to the family title and estates but opted to remain in public service.

Lord Desart was well versed in international maritime law and, as Hankey admitted to Esher, possessed "rather unique qualifications for this particular sub-ctee."[26] In 1904, he had represented Britain before the international commission appointed to investigate the Dogger Bank incident. In 1906, he had been a member of the Walton Committee, charged with defining the British position at the second Hague conference. In January 1908, Sir Edward Grey had chosen him to chair the interdepartmental naval conference committee appointed to prepare the British case for the upcoming conference on maritime law. In December of that year, Desart was appointed senior British plenipotentiary to the London Naval Conference, which made him one of the chief architects of the Declaration of London. For his services he was awarded an English peerage, taking his seat in the House of Lords as Baron Desart of Desart. Asquith likely picked Desart for the job for his extensive experience in international maritime law and especially his familiarity with the Declaration of London. Yet it should not be forgotten that Asquith knew Lord Desart professionally (both were lawyers and had served in the Treasury) and thus would have been familiar with his qualities.

Lord Desart's Trading with the Enemy CID subcommittee (hereafter the Desart Committee) first convened on 13 March 1911 and did not complete its report until late September 1912. According to Hankey, the Desart Committee

> thoroughly explored every branch of the subject of Trading with the Enemy, including besides ordinary import and export trade such matters as financial dealings of all kinds, insurance, warlike stores, shipping services, etc. A great deal of evidence was heard, including that of bankers, insurance authorities, and consular authorities. In addition many enquiries were undertaken by the Treasury, Board of Trade and Board of Customs and Excise.[27]

In his memoirs, Hankey described the committee's final report (which he composed) as a milestone in the development of the CID. "Its recommendations," he wrote, "were incorporated into the War Book [a]nd when war broke out in 1914 the arrangements were carried out without a hitch and according to plan"—which, as will become apparent in later chapters, was a monumental exaggeration.[28] Hankey's précis in his memoirs of the Desart Committee's work omitted several vital details. He neglected to mention that one of the committee's primary purposes was to consider measures designed to prevent British merchant ships from trading between neutral ports to the benefit of the enemy. He made no reference either to the Desart Committee's consideration of similar state controls over banks. Given that most historians seeking to understand the development of British strategic planning before the First World War have drawn very heavily from Lord Hankey's two-volume memoirs, it behooves us to consider the implications of these discrepancies before turning to examine the work of the Desart Committee.

Like all memoirs, Hankey's recollections require careful handling. Samuel Williamson, the first of the few scholars who examined nearly all the documentary archives for the prewar period (and who actually met Hankey), observed, "That the CID's actual achievements were considerably more modest than admirers thought or Hankey claimed becomes progressively clearer with each new study on pre-1914 British defense policy."[29] Even Hankey's biographer, Captain Stephan Roskill, was driven to admit that "with all the official and private records open to historical scrutiny the truth seems considerably different."[30] It is important to bear in mind that although Hankey completed both volumes of his memoirs sometime in the late 1930s, official permission to publish was withheld owing to the sensitive nature of their content. In 1961, after indemnifying himself against prosecution for breach of official secrets, Hankey defied the government and published them, albeit in abridged form.[31]

It is also important to note that when Hankey wrote his memoirs, he was heavily engaged, from his position as cabinet secretary, in promoting economic warfare to become again the basis of British national strategy—meaning that the text about the past had a subtext about contemporary policy. During the interwar period, moreover, Hankey attracted controversy when he attributed the Allied victory in the First World War to Britain's successful economic strangulation of Germany. More controversial still was his claim that victory would have been swifter and losses concomitantly smaller if only the British government had sanctioned ruthless economic warfare from the outset.[32] In his memoirs he implied that placing an immediate chokehold upon the German economy would have been perfectly possible because before 1914 the CID had already examined "every aspect" of economic warfare.[33]

On paper, Maurice Hankey appears uniquely well qualified to illuminate the prewar contribution by the CID in shaping plans for economic warfare. Judging from the papers he wrote between the wars, moreover, he indisputably was an expert in the subject. And his involvement in preparations made before the First World War cannot be denied. Yet although Hankey joined the CID secretariat as naval representative in mid-1908, not until January 1911 did he become directly involved in economic warfare planning. That month, Ottley detailed Hankey to conduct some background research for the Desart Committee. He subsequently attended every meeting. In April 1912, Hankey's status changed after receiving an unexpected promotion to become CID permanent secretary after Sir Charles Ottley quit the post for the financial security offered by a directorship at the armament giant Armstrong-Whitworth.[34] Hankey remained head of the CID secretariat throughout the war, during which time the prime minister increasingly looked to him as his aide in strategic matters, and in this quasi-official capacity Hankey attended most wartime government meetings on grand strategy. At the end of 1916, Hankey became the very first secretary to the cabinet. That Hankey was involved with the prewar development of economic warfare is not disputed; there is, however, a question mark over the level of influence he exercised before 1914.

In his memoirs, Hankey portrayed himself as an ignored visionary and conveyed the impression that before the war he had been chiefly responsible for making prewar preparations for the economic pressure. Although he praised Admiral Fisher for pioneering the concept, he allowed virtually no credit to anyone else at the Admiralty; indeed, he implied they had been more a hindrance than a help.[35] Though Hankey acknowledged Ottley as his mentor, he downplayed the magnitude of his debt to him, neglecting to mention that the former DNI had been among the leading advocates for economic pressure. Another old boss, Captain George Ballard, scarcely rated a mention. In postwar interviews, Hankey managed to convince the author of the official history of the blockade that only "certain members of the [CID] staff, Captain MPA Hankey in particular," perceived the "complexities and potential" of economic pressure after the investigations by the Desart Committee.[36]

Hankey was undeniably a man of exceptional ability, but is it really plausible that a 32-year-old captain in the Royal Marines (equivalent to a Navy lieutenant) nearly single-handedly guided the British establishment down the path toward the adoption of economic warfare? Some historians believe it is and accordingly have afforded him the lion's share of the credit in the perceived "success" of the wartime blockade.[37] But from where, from whom, and when did Hankey obtain such revolutionary ideas, not to mention the requisite grasp of complex economic issues? No one before has ever posed these questions. His career prior to the CID secretariat suggests few opportunities for him to have acquired the requisite skills and knowledge.

In late 1898, upon gaining his commission, the 21-year-old Maurice Hankey was assigned to a battleship attached to the Mediterranean Fleet and served as an assistant to the fleet intelligence officer. His next assignment, in 1902, was to the coastal defense section of the Naval Intelligence Department. Although at this stage he was not involved in war planning, he had shared an office with Captain Ballard. Hankey remained in London until the end of 1905. He spent most of 1906 accompanying Ballard as a member of the Owens Commission on an inspection tour of overseas base defenses. He did not return to England until December of that year, whereupon Ballard invited him to join the infamous war plans committee. In April 1907, with the project completed, Hankey returned to the Mediterranean Fleet as chief intelligence officer and remained at Malta until mid-1908. While Hankey likely heard something of economic warfare from Ottley and Ballard, therefore, except for his brief stint as secretary to the 1907 Ballard Committee, he was never in a position to see the relevant Admiralty files or participate in discussions. At all other times he was either too junior in rank, in the wrong department, or simply out of the country.

During 1909, as assistant secretary to the CID, Hankey wrote several papers that touched lightly upon economic warfare, but they display only minimal understanding of the Admiralty's latest thinking.[38] The most conclusive evidence for his limited contribution to prewar economic warfare planning comes from a file dated 1911. On 16 February 1911, just one week after his assignment to the Desart Committee, Hankey wrote to Ottley brimming with excitement at having just stumbled across the Admiralty's 1908 economic warfare paper (discussed at length in Chapter 3). It is highly significant that he had never seen it before this date.[39] Hankey was "so arrested" by what he read that he immediately composed a seven-page memorandum drawing attention to what he regarded as transparent inconsistencies between "our national war policy," as prescribed in the Admiralty's 1908 economic warfare paper, and the current parliamentary debate over whether to ratify the Declaration of London. Hankey protested that ratification would be a catastrophe, "diminishing the power" of the Royal Navy to interdict raw materials for German industry.[40] He maintained that the German economy could be effectively choked only by rigorously enforcing all of Britain's "ancient" belligerent rights, including the doctrine of continuous voyage and the unfettered power to define contraband—when in fact the Admiralty planned to choke the German economy by restricting its access to neutral shipping and the other infrastructure of international trade.[41] This paper makes clear that Hankey had little conception of the distinction between (legal) blockade and the Admiralty's strategy of economic warfare. While the memorandum clearly brimmed with his enthusiasm for the subject, in and of itself it exhibited no special insight or originality of thought, and it seriously misunderstood the mechanisms by which the Admiralty proposed to target the German economy.

Hankey's memorandum left Sir Charles Ottley singularly unimpressed, especially with Hankey's naive understanding of "the political and international difficulties which stand in the way" of prosecuting economic warfare.[42] "Captain Hankey's Extreme Contraband proposals," the CID secretary commented two days later, "quite transcend in rigor the British Order-in-Council issued in the Napoleonic Wars" and amounted to "the destruction of the whole edifice of international maritime law built up since the days of Armed Neutrality [1780s] and consecrated by the Declaration of Paris in 1856." Besides thereby risking neutral indignation, Ottley went on, they further ran "counter to the policy to which we have ourselves consistently adhered for the last hundred years, and it is I fear quite hopeless to imagine that any British Government could be induced to contemplate a reversal of that policy."[43]

Nevertheless, Ottley confessed he was not averse to parts of what he dubbed Hankey's "rather drastic policy," but merely thought it unwise to broadcast the fact in time of peace. If the Royal Navy was strong enough and the diplomatic stars properly aligned, Ottley thought, Britain could ignore treaty constraints and afterward pay compensation to neutrals; buying off criticism would prove most "politic and would rob the neutrals of a very large part of their grounds for complaint."[44] (Readers may recall that Jacky Fisher had made exactly these same points to justify his silence during the negotiation of the Declaration of London.)[45] Notwithstanding his poor opinion of Hankey's reasoning and arguments, Ottley felt that the subject of the Declaration of London was "of such importance" as to merit reconsideration by the Admiralty and Foreign Office, and he promptly forwarded Hankey's memorandum (plus his response) to both for comment.[46] This seemingly contradictory move requires explanation.

Though Sir Charles Ottley officially supported ratification, he had always had his doubts and in recent months these had grown. As recently as 25 January 1911, he had spoken to the prime minister on the subject and "ventured to suggest the idea of referring the 'Declaration of London' to the CID," suggesting a strong subcommittee chaired by either Asquith or possibly A. J. Balfour "to thoroughly sift the whole thing to the bottom." He reasoned that "unless the Declaration can stand in the light, it must go into the waste paper basket."[47] Asquith had "promised to think it over" but swiftly rejected the idea.[48] Esher afterward explained to Ottley that since the issue had become politicized, with the Conservative party determined to oppose ratification, any inquiry was now out of the question. The government's credibility was at stake. Moreover, the Foreign Office was vehemently opposed.[49] In forwarding Hankey's paper and his own comments on it to the Admiralty and Foreign Office, therefore, most likely Ottley was taking a different path toward a fresh enquiry.

In seeking this goal, Ottley received no help from the Admiralty, which in fact greeted the arrival of the file with dismay. Reginald McKenna, the First Lord of the Admiralty, immediately summoned Ottley and Hankey to his office, whereupon he told both, in no uncertain terms, that he wanted the matter dropped. Explaining why, McKenna substantially restated Ottley's objections to Hankey's memorandum but added his belief that "although the action of the Navy might appear theoretically to be hampered, he did not anticipate this result in practice; he pointed our that international treaties are easily evaded . . . [and] some pretext would be found for our acting contrary to all the provisions of the Declaration of Paris and the Declaration of London."[50] McKenna further told them the Admiralty did not want to put their position in writing lest such a document fall into Foreign Office hands. Probably to ensure Hankey's silence, McKenna arranged for him to see retired Admiral Lord Fisher—who, Hankey afterward recorded, assured him that he "need not worry about these matters any more because it was absolutely certain that all these arrangements would tumble down as soon as the guns went off."[51] Despite having been doubly impressed with the vital need for secrecy and the necessity of letting the matter drop, Hankey returned to his office and blurted out all he had learned to a CID colleague, Major Adrian Grant-Duff of the Army General Staff. On 22 February, Grant-Duff wrote in his diary:

> The "worry" over the declaration of London still goes on and Hankey has now turned against it and denounced it as equivalent to tying up our right arm in a war with Germany. Fisher apparently allowed it to be negotiated with the deliberate intention of tearing it up in the event of war. Characteristic!

And two days later:

> McKenna's standpoint seems much the same. The Germans are sure to infringe it in the early days of the war, then with great regret we tear it up. If they don't infringe it we must invent an infringement![52]

The Foreign Office gave Hankey's paper even shorter shrift.[53] In a memorandum dated 27 February 1911, Cecil Hurst, the Foreign Office assistant legal advisor, dismissed Hankey's proposals as a foolish pursuit of "the will-o'-the-wisp."[54] Even if such extreme measures were adopted, he observed, they would fail to accomplish the annihilation of German trade "and therefore would not bring Germany to her knees." Hankey was so incensed by the Foreign Office's derogatory critique that on 8 March 1911 he composed a rebuttal.[55] And this is where the plot thickens. Not only is this document missing from both the CID and Admiralty copies of the file, retained only by the Foreign Office, but in this rejoinder Hankey displayed a vastly better understanding of the subject—so much better that we must suspect he had recently received coaching from Ottley.

In this paper Hankey's arguments adhered closely to the central tenets of the economic warfare plan—for instance, pointing out that it was not necessary to annihilate German trade in order to achieve decisive results (a complete reversal of the argument employed in his previous paper) and emphasizing the importance of regulating merchant shipping. His most significant remark was that economic warfare might work more quickly than many imagined. "The self dependence which enabled France a century ago to stand the strain for many years is absent in the case of modern Germany," he argued, "and consequently it should be possible to produce the same result as our ancestors produced in France a century ago, only in far shorter time."[56] Although various Admiralty officers had hinted at this possibility, Hankey's statement is the earliest surviving example of an explicit link between economic warfare and a short war rather than a protracted conflict.

The Foreign Office, however, remained unimpressed. On 8 March 1911, Grant-Duff recorded in his diary a conversation earlier that day with Sir Eyre Crowe: "And I find he shares my view that the 'sea pressure' on Germany in the event of war is not going to prove the effective weapon of war our sailors fondly imagine."[57]

For historians, the "proof" that the Admiralty must have lost interest in and even abandoned its hopes for economic pressure lies in the failure by either Reginald McKenna (First Lord) or Admiral Sir Arthur Wilson (First Sea Lord) to mention the strategy at the celebrated 114th meeting of the CID on 23 August 1911.[58] This meeting, long regarded by many historians as one of the pivotal events in British strategic planning before the First World War, was the only other occasion (after the landmark 1908 Military Needs of the Empire subcommittee inquiry) when Asquith and his senior ministers methodically contemplated national strategy in the event of war with Germany. In many respects the circumstances surrounding this meeting were very similar to those that had led to the 1908 meetings.[59] At the height of a war scare, during the Second Moroccan Crisis (1911), the War Office petitioned the prime minister for a special meeting of the CID to review and approve General Staff plans to send the BEF to the Continent in the event of a general European war.[60]

In a memorandum circulated prior to the meeting, the new director of military operations, Brigadier-General Henry Wilson, employed arbitrary and dubious arithmetic to plead that the immediate dispatch of Britain's entire available force of six infantry divisions would be crucial to the survival of France. He glibly argued that geographical constraints would prevent the Germans from bringing their superior numbers at once to bear and that the six British divisions would be sufficient to "tip the balance" of forces at the decisive point on the French northeast frontier.[61] Even if recent scholarship has tended "to de-emphasise the place of the 114th meeting of CID in Britain's preparations for the First World War," no one has yet denied that major political consequences followed.[62]

On 15 August 1911, Hankey (with Ottley's approval) wrote to the Admiralty warning that the War Office intended to exploit the current diplomatic crisis to stampede the government into endorsing its scheme. He darkly told McKenna that, at Haldane's insistence, both Fisher and Esher had not been invited to the CID meeting; back in 1908 both had been vocal in opposing the Continental strategy. Lords Crewe and Morley, both known opponents of the General Staff plan of sending the Army to France, also had been excluded.[63] "It is of course notorious that the DMO, [Brigadier] General [Henry] Wilson, who has brought this question to the front, has a perfect obsession for military operations on the Continent," Hankey explained. "If he can get a decision at this juncture in favor of military action he will endeavor to commit us up to the hilt: and in a few months time he will prove that with our existing forces we could not have rendered France proper assistance, and will seek to show that without conscription we cannot fulfill our obligations."[64] Writing from Italy a few days later, having just heard from Hankey, Fisher told McKenna that the upcoming meeting was clearly a sham and the "whole single object is compulsory service and an increase of the Army Estimates and military influence."[65] The Board of Admiralty agreed and prepared accordingly—meaning that they treated the upcoming meeting not as a serious debate of national grand strategy but as yet another round of bureaucratic squabbling with the War Office.[66]

The Admiralty position paper, which was cobbled together by Admiral Sir Arthur Wilson because the DNI was on leave, focused upon the inconsistencies in the General Staff plan.[67] Though the writing was stylistically dreadful, the Admiralty's opposition to the War Office strategy came across loud and clear: the paper stressed the inadequacy of the military forces available for such a mission and presciently forecast the political dangers attending such a strategy, warning it was "certain that if a British force is landed on French soil to assist the French Army it cannot be withdrawn . . . and the tendency will be to make increasing sacrifice in men and material to support it."[68] Admiral Wilson ventured that Britain's little army might better be employed helping the Royal Navy obtain uncontested command of the sea.[69] On this he did not elaborate, but almost certainly he was alluding to his pet scheme of using amphibious raids to draw the German High Seas Fleet into battle. He said nothing about economic warfare.

One more reason for the Admiralty remaining silent on this was to avoid a suspected bureaucratic ambush. "I think I ought to warn you," Hankey had added in a postscript to McKenna,

> that since the 1909 inquiry the War Office (DMO) have attempted to collect evidence to prove that the power of the Navy to put economic pressure on Germany is non-existent. They addressed a cunningly devised set of questions to the Board of Trade some time ago, which they may attempt to bring up if the Admiralty still maintain that naval means are sufficient.[70]

Hankey further reported that the Board of Trade's response insisted that the strategy of economic pressure was bound to fail because Germany could easily reroute her trade through the neutral Low Countries.[71] While hardly a conclusive refutation of economic warfare, this was sufficient bureaucratic reason to avoid being drawn into a debate on this issue within a forum that had been packed with members of the government sympathetic to War Office views, especially while the Desart Committee was still sitting.

Despite thus being forewarned and forearmed, the Admiralty ran headlong into disaster at the 114th meeting of the CID. A superlative presentation by the charismatic Brigadier-General Henry Wilson contrasted sharply with a particularly incoherent performance by Admiral Sir Arthur Wilson, and conspired to discredit the Admiralty in the eyes of the politicians and, no less important, blind them to the logical flaws of the Army's plan. In the morning session, Sir Arthur badly fumbled the Admiralty's cross-examination of the Brigadier's presentation, and his blunt refusal to assist the Army in making its preparations was viewed as absurd and even childish. According to Major Grant-Duff, who took the minutes,

> Asquith remarked with some asperity that the Admiralty had not answered either of the two questions asked by the G[eneral]S[taff] namely whether they would guarantee:
>
> A. Safe passage [of the Army to France]
>
> B. UK against invasion.

> This brought up the 1SL [First Sea Lord] who after a good deal of shuffling gave the first assurance, but the Admiralty's representatives in chorus said that they could not find the transports if the fleet was mobilizing at the same time.[72]

This evasion was nonsensical: the Admiralty transport department was responsible for the hiring and supply of all shipping required for all government purposes. In other words, it was their job to find the requisite transport, and given that well over half the world's merchant tonnage sailed under the British flag, to argue that ships could not be found was ridiculous. Admiral Wilson's discomfort at being chastised publicly by the prime minister was rubbed in by the energetic Winston Churchill, then home secretary, who had arrived at the meeting believing it to be a serious discussion of grand strategy and posed challenging questions to both sides.

During the afternoon session the situation for the Admiralty went from bad to worse. When the prime minister asked the Admiralty to expand upon their position paper, Wilson allowed himself to be drawn into unfolding his "half baked" idea of an amphibious assault against the German coast—his old 1905 'reckless offensive' plan. As Hankey afterward remarked, it rather "savored of having been cocked-up [*sic*] in the dinner-hour."[73] Haldane labeled it "puerile."[74] While McKenna listened in horror, Sir Arthur argued that instead of sending British troops to the Continent they ought to be employed for home defense and mounting amphibious operations to capture objectives on the German littoral, such as the island of Heligoland. All witnesses agree that Admiral Wilson's sketch presentation left his audience stunned.[75] It was not his patently unworkable ideas that shocked the politicians so much as his admission that, because of the need for secrecy, the plan of operations "was not even known to the fleet."[76] CID Secretary Sir Charles Ottley, who since his retirement had maintained very close links with Admiralty planners, afterward insisted no one in the NID had before heard of this "lunatic" plan. A couple of weeks later he recalled in a letter to Winston Churchill:

> When I was DNI (in 1906)—a special committee of officers of which Captain Ballard was one, of which Captain Hankey was secretary, sat, by Sir John Fisher's orders to investigate the plan of campaign for a war with Germany. We then came to the conclusion that—much as we should have liked to take Heligoland—the scheme was utterly impractical. It

> could not be done. . . . Now, I don't say we were right or wrong. But I will wager any money that the committee's work was never considered by Sir AK Wilson when he decided, off his own bat, in a contrary sense.[77]

One point needs to be stressed: the ideas Wilson expressed at the 114th CID meeting were very much his own and most certainly did *not* reflect current Admiralty policy. Shortly afterward, when news of his presentation leaked to the fleet leadership, the three most senior officers in the Home Fleets objected to the instructions Wilson subsequently drew up and issued to them.[78] But by then it was too late. The Admiralty's reputation had suffered irreparable political damage.

After the meeting Haldane skillfully exploited the Admiralty's refusal to transport the BEF to dramatize the lack of cooperation between the two service departments over strategic planning. Haldane intimated to the prime minister that unless McKenna was replaced, he would resign—putting himself forward as the ideal successor. By 10 October 1911, Asquith was persuaded that McKenna had lost control of the Admiralty, but instead of obliging Haldane, he instructed McKenna to swap offices with Winston Churchill. Upon being appointed First Lord of the Admiralty, Churchill promptly dismissed the First, Second, and Fourth Sea Lords—respectively, Admirals Sir Arthur Wilson, Sir George Egerton, and Charles Madden. Also ejected were Rear-Admiral Bethell, the DNI, and Captain Herbert King-Hall, the head of mobilization. In place of Sir Arthur Wilson, Churchill initially toyed with the idea of recalling to service Jacky Fisher before settling upon Admiral Sir Francis Bridgeman, the current fleet commander in chief. Prince Louis of Battenberg, now a vice-admiral, became Second Sea Lord. For the post of DNI, Churchill chose the highly regarded Captain George Ballard but quickly found they did not see eye to eye, and arranged for him to be superseded in a bureaucratic reshuffling of responsibilities. In Ballard's place he tried to recall Sir Charles Ottley, but Asquith refused to allow his departure from the CID. Ultimately the First Lord picked the colorless Rear-Admiral Ernest Troubridge.[79] It may be remarked that this near clean sweep of the Navy leadership did not result in any change in the Admiralty's strategic direction.

Though Hankey was correct in assessing the result as a "severe defeat" for the Admiralty, he was well wide of the mark when he claimed in his memoirs: "From that time onwards there was never any doubt what would be the Grand Strategy in the event of our being drawn into a continental war in support of France. [That the Army] would have been sent to France as it actually was in 1914."[80] In 1911, there existed insuperable difficulties standing in the way of political sanction for sending the Army to France upon outbreak of war.[81] More than half the ministers then serving in the cabinet remained deeply hostile to the whole concept of any military involvement on the Continent, and professed horror upon belatedly learning that during the recent crisis the British General Staff had been talking to their French opposite numbers and making arrangements for concerted action.[82]

Led by Lords Morley and Crewe, the ministers deliberately excluded from the recent CID meeting, opponents of a Continental commitment forced a wide-ranging cabinet review of Britain's commitments and foreign policy generally, some of the revelations from which threatened to split the government.[83] The prime minister was compelled to promise the cabinet that henceforth "no communication should take place between the General Staff here & the staffs of other countries which can, directly or indirectly, commit this country to military or naval intervention."[84] Esher did not exaggerate when he remarked in his journal: "There has been a serious crisis."[85] When they next met, moreover, Esher explicitly

> asked the PM whether he thought that it would be possible to have an English force concentrated in France within 7 days of the outbreak of war, in view of the fact that the Cabinet (the majority of them) have never heard of the plan. He thinks it *impossible!* How this would astound the [Army] General Staff.[86]

Esher was much relieved to find that even Asquith was privately skeptical of the General Staff plan to land the Army in France.[87] Why should he have been surprised? Better than anyone, Esher knew from firsthand observation that before the First World War, politicians consistently had declined to take any final, irrevocable decisions and, as a result, ended up maintaining multiple contradictory positions.

Trading with the Enemy

We turn now to consider the deliberations and report of Lord Desart's Trading with the Enemy subcommittee, whose work began to pick up just as the cabinet crisis over the Continental commitment unfolded. Readers will recall that the appointment of this CID subcommittee, in early 1911, sprang from

Hardinge's recommendation to the government to take a broader look at economic warfare. In particular, "the policy regarding the treatment to be accorded to British vessels trading with the enemy should be definitely and authoritatively laid down."[88]

The Desart Committee consisted mainly of high-ranking civil servants belonging to the various departments of state with an interest in what might loosely be termed "economic affairs," backed by a cohort of senior government lawyers. No fewer than three departments were represented by permanent secretaries: the Treasury by Sir Robert Chalmers, the Board of Trade by Sir Hubert Llewellyn-Smith, and the Board of Customs and Excise by Nathaniel J. Highmore. The participation of such senior officials is noteworthy. Also appointed were General Sir Beauchamp Duff (military secretary to the India Office) and Lawrence Abrahams (undersecretary for the India Office). The lawyers included James S. Risley (Colonial Office), A. H. Dennis (Treasury), and, particularly important, John Paget Mellor (1862–1929), also of the Treasury. During the war, Mellor would act as procurator general, meaning that he represented the crown before the prize court and was responsible for securing legal condemnation of merchantmen and cargoes seized by the Royal Navy. Another worthy of special mention was Cecil J. B. Hurst (1870–1963), the assistant legate at the Foreign Office (best remembered as the senior judge at the 1945 Nuremberg war trials). In 1911, Hurst, then 41 years old, was already a veteran of the economic warfare debate, having served as technical advisor at the peace conference in The Hague, as a member of the naval conference committee, and as the junior plenipotentiary at the London Naval Conference. During the First World War he became a key figure in framing British blockade policy. The only CID regulars assigned to the Desart Committee, besides Ottley and Hankey, were Lord Esher and Rear-Admiral Alexander Bethell (DNI). In December 1911, the latter was replaced by Rear-Admiral Ernest Troubridge (the chief of the newly created naval War Staff) and Captain George Ballard, recently returned to the Admiralty after more than four years at sea. The War Office detailed two midgrade officers from the General Staff.

The Desart Committee first assembled in March 1911, but the pressure of work upon many members prevented serious deliberation for more than six months, and not until November 1911 were the first witnesses called.[89] It is important to note that the Desart Committee was not assigned to explore every aspect of economic warfare. The prime minister appointed several technical subcommittees to work in parallel, of which the most important was Sir Mathew Nathan's Submarine Cable Communications in Time of War subcommittee, which was tasked to consider how best Britain might exploit her position at the center of the world communications network.[90] The state's ability to control the flow of information was, of course, not only important in the propaganda war but more critically (and less obviously) a vital aspect of economic warfare: banks and merchants communicated with each other and conducted their transactions mainly via cable telegrams. The subject merited its own committee because, unlike with the movement of goods and ships on the high seas, there were no neutral rights or preexisting international laws governing or restricting a belligerent's control over the movement of information. The significance of this cannot be stressed too much. Additional CID subcommittees investigated Press and Postal Censorship in Time of War, the Internal Distribution of Supplies in Time of War, the Maintenance of Overseas Commerce in Time of War, the Insurance of British Shipping in Time of War, Supplies in Time of War, and Emergency Powers in War.[91] All, to a lesser or greater degree, contributed to the study and preparation of economic warfare.

The Desart Committee completed its inquiries in May 1912, but it was not until December that the chairman handed the prime minister the final report.[92] This 475-page volume was the single most comprehensive document produced by the CID before the First World War.[93] It ranged widely over the global economic landscape, constrained only by lack of reliable economic data—and by political considerations. The final report is not a straightforward document and must be approached with a firm understanding of the context in which it was produced. First, it is important to appreciate that all the early working papers assumed a war between the British Empire and Germany without allies.[94] Midway through the inquiry, Desart ruled this scenario "hardly conceivable" and directed that henceforth members should base their analysis upon the assumption that the next war would be a Europe-wide conflagration.[95] In other words, the earlier papers submitted to the committee by various government departments were based upon a totally different set of assumptions than were later documents. This shift in underlying assumptions strongly favored the Admiralty, for, obviously, the greater the number of combatant nations, the smaller the number of neutral avenues left open through which overseas supplies could reach Germany.[96]

A second point to note is that, following standard CID practice, members and witnesses were allowed to edit their statements prior to the final printing.[97] It is quite clear that several subjects discussed during meetings were expunged from the printed record. Most likely for reasons of security, much of the testimony given by Admiralty representatives was deleted. The evidence for these deletions is contained within the report itself. As an example, the official minutes contain no reference to any discussion of state control over the British shipping industry, yet several annexed memoranda and even the final report make clear that discussion of this vital component of the Admiralty's plans did in fact take place.

Another point to keep in mind when reading the final report is that Lord Desart managed only with the greatest of difficulty to persuade all members of the committee to sign. Certain officials, most notably Sir Robert Chalmers of the Treasury and Sir Hubert Llewellyn Smith for the Board of Trade (who fifteen years earlier had worked directly under Sir Robert Giffen), found repugnant the idea of greater state intervention in the economy.[98] The opinions of these two senior civil servants mattered greatly, for both were widely respected and influential. Llewellyn Smith, known to posterity for his contributions to Edwardian social reform, was a particularly formidable character, and for so long as he remained at its helm, until May 1915, the Board of Trade remained steadfast in defending the interests of British businessmen ahead of national strategic imperatives. Robert Chalmers was no less stubborn in sheltering the City of London.[99] It took four months and many revisions before he was persuaded to append his signature to the final report.[100] As a result of his intransigence, large tracts of the economic landscape mapped by the committee, especially in the fields of banking and international finance, were deleted from the final report. "I think considering the difficulties," Lord Esher commented dryly to Hankey upon seeing the final copy, "the report is rather a remarkable one."[101]

Lastly, though it was not generally realized by most members, the Desart Committee was the victim of deliberate Admiralty subterfuge designed to slant the final recommendations. Initially, during the earliest meetings, the Admiralty declined to divulge anything of their "secret" operational plans. The chairman rightly saw their refusal as ridiculous. On 14 November 1911, Sir Charles Ottley advised Rear-Admiral Bethell, the DNI, that Lord Desart demanded the Admiralty provide at least an outline of their operational intentions in the North Sea because "the practicability of efficient blockade appears largely to affect the general question of Trading with the Enemy."[102] Taking the point, the Admiralty feigned cooperation—but, still not wishing to reveal their intention to mount a distant blockade (which, as we have seen, was legally controversial), misled the Desart Committee into thinking that in the event of war with Germany the Royal Navy intended to establish a traditional close blockade.[103] Ottley had a hand in this subterfuge. On the eve of the third committee meeting, he wrote Bethell "to warn you of the course the discussion may take on Wednesday next."[104] Ottley whispered to the DNI not to admit that the Admiralty believed close blockade impossible because to do so might jeopardize the outcome of the entire enquiry. He explained:

> Supposing a blockade of the enemy's coast was deemed impossible, it might very much modify the restrictions to be imposed on trade with the enemy. But if on the other hand the Admiralty hope to institute a blockade of the German coast it is obvious that the restrictions on trade through neutrals should be tightened up as much as possible.[105]

To be clear, the Admiralty did not want to admit their plan for distant blockade, lest they be drawn into a debate over its legality. Ottley apparently encouraged this deception because he was fearful that winning the committee's approval for economic warfare was going to prove a much tougher battle than originally hoped. Already Sir Hubert Llewellyn Smith had set up his stall in determined opposition to the whole strategy, and several other committee members appeared to have been swayed by his arguments.

From beginning to end, the redoubtable Sir Hubert vehemently opposed large-scale state intervention into the workings of the British or international economy. He insisted that the Admiralty's proposals violated every principle of economic theory and, if implemented, very likely would backfire upon Great Britain. His opposition extended even to imposing restrictions on British exports to Germany. Llewellyn Smith's opening position paper (which was based upon an earlier memorandum he had written at the behest of the War Office specifically to refute the practicability of economic warfare) insisted that "in the event of war with Germany, there would be little advantage in maintaining the legal prohibition against exporting merchandise to an enemy county." Economic theory taught that such a policy would be futile.

> There could not in time of war be any *direct* trade between the ports of the two countries carried on in the vessels of either, but there is little doubt that, even if trading with the enemy were nominally prohibited, a large amount of exports which were really destined for Germany would still be carried in British bottoms through the ports of Holland and Belgium.[106]

Llewellyn Smith allowed that a prohibition on indirect trading with the enemy "might for a time cause considerable distress in Germany. As time went on, however, trade would find an outlet through new channels, and the effect would grow less."[107] In other words, denying the enemy access to British trade would prove no more than a short-term inconvenience and was hardly likely to produce decisive strategic results. He uncompromisingly dismissed counterarguments put forward by the Admiralty (based upon Giffen's theories) that large-scale disruption to enemy trade, if achievable, would prove sufficient to "shock" the German economy.[108] To illustrate his point, Llewellyn Smith supplied statistics showing that two-thirds of British exports, by value, came from selling Germany coal, fish, textiles, woolen yarns, machinery, and iron and steel products.[109] If Germany was unable to obtain these from Great Britain, substitutes—albeit of inferior quality—might easily be acquired from rival foreign suppliers. The only commodities over which the British Empire possessed an effective monopoly were wool (from Australia), jute (from India), and palm nuts (from West Africa). This list prompted the alarmed Colonial Office representative to remark that the self-governing dominions and colonies would not long tolerate a British embargo on trade in their most lucrative exports.[110]

As the inquiry continued into 1912, Llewellyn Smith became increasingly shrill in denouncing economic warfare. "It would be impossible," he thundered at the meeting on 29 January, "even if we desire it, to prevent the export of British goods through neutral countries to Germany." Not true, interjected Nathaniel Highmore, chief of the Customs and Excise. Under English law the prohibition of exports was both lawful and simple to enforce. Despite finding himself contradicted on this key point of fact, Llewellyn Smith refused to admit that his assessment had been rendered invalid, and defiantly remarked that he "still felt grave doubts as to whether it could be done." Even if the state imposed a prohibition on exports to a certain neutral country, what was to stop merchants from shipping goods to another neutral country, then back to the original neutral for resale to Germany? Did the British authorities intend to track the ultimate destination for every cargo that left the shores of England?[111] Llewellyn Smith spluttered that it would be "out of the question to attempt to subject the whole of our carrying trade between neutral countries to the rigorous conditions which alone could make prohibition effective, without intolerable interference not only with our own carrying trade but also with neutral commerce."[112] Such interference, he predicted, would be construed by neutrals "as a monstrous attempt to stop them altogether from trading with our enemy."[113] Subsequent events showed his prediction about neutral reaction to be prescient, probably more so than Llewellyn Smith realized, but it was not adequately considered at this time.

During the last week of January 1912, Sir Charles Ottley circulated a memorandum ostensibly summarizing the discussion so far and indicating directions for further enquiry.[114] In actual fact it was a thinly disguised counterblast directed against Llewellyn Smith. For the committee secretary to thus intrude into deliberations midway through an inquiry (even if he was also the secretary of the CID) was quite unprecedented and powerfully suggests that Ottley feared the Desart Committee was on the point of rejecting economic warfare. The procedural anomaly aside, Ottley's memorandum is a critical document. It informed committee members that "the policy of using the weapon of economic pressure against the enemy is one which has been recognized by the Committee of the Imperial Defence as of great importance." To demonstrate the point, Ottley attached extracts from the final report of the 1909 Military Needs of the Empire subcommittee and the Admiralty's 1908 economic warfare paper.[115] Ottley explained that the CID understood that the means by which economic pressure could be brought to bear were, "first, by direct naval action, such as the capture of the enemy's shipping and the blockade of his sea ports, and, secondly, by legislative enactment, forbidding or restricting trade between British subjects and the enemy."[116] The phrase "legislative enactment" was highly significant: here was an explicit statement indicating that the political executive understood the necessity of countenancing state intervention in the economy. Ottley bluntly reminded the committee members that it was not their job to endorse or repudiate agreed-upon national strategy. Moreover, he concluded, "whether resort is had to legislative enactment in order to prohibit trade with enemy or not, naval measures of the most stringent character will be resorted to [in order] to bring economic pressure to bear."[117]

The Desart Committee discussed Ottley's memorandum at length at its meeting of 29 January 1912. Lord Desart corroborated that the committee was not being asked to evaluate economic warfare strategy, merely to identify the measures most likely to prove effective against Germany and gauge how vigorously they might be enforced commensurate with British interests.[118] Llewellyn Smith was having none of it. Hereafter he no longer bothered to cloak his contrary views in finely spun economic arguments but resorted instead to naked intransigence, as became apparent during subsequent discussions over restricting the export of "War-like Stores."[119] When presented with a provisional list drawn up by the military representatives, the Board of Trade brusquely "pointed out that such a course of procedure might prove highly detrimental to the trade of the country, as some of the articles included in this category figure for large amounts in the statistics of export trade."[120] Specifically, the Board of Trade objected to inclusion of nickel, chrome, manganese, tungsten, as well as iron, copper, zinc, aluminum, and tin, plus railway material, timber, steel, and cement. Every one of these items was indisputably a vital strategic raw material; it was absurd to object to restrictions on their export in wartime.[121] Robert Chalmers of the Treasury also, though less belligerently, turned a deaf ear to the chairman's message. He agreed with Llewellyn Smith that fettering British merchants and City traders in time of war seemed unwise and likely to inflict more damage upon Britain than upon her enemies.[122] The representatives of the Foreign Office and the Colonial Office seemed to concur.

At this point Lord Esher, the only permanent member of the CID present, moved to reinforce the chairman's message. On 12 February 1912, he circulated a paper reiterating that it was not the business of either the Board of Trade or the Treasury to challenge national defense policy. "We are not specifically concerned with the naval and military steps which have to be taken," he lectured. "It is our main function to consider what *additional* pressure we should be able to put upon Germany by adopting every means in our power to cripple her financially, and by the starving out of her people."[123]

Esher further pointed out that many of the Board of Trade's arguments asserting the ineffectiveness of economic warfare were based upon the mistaken assumption that war between Britain and Germany would be a "gladiatorial" affair. The "most probable kind of war we have to face," Esher corrected, would involve "Great Britain, France and Russia ranged on one side, with Germany, Austria, and possibly Italy on the other." In consequence, Germany would find herself "for purposes of supply, hemmed in on all sides"—deprived, contra Llewellyn Smith, of easy access to neutral carriage and ports. Esher demanded steps should be taken to ensure German isolation: "It is obvious that Great Britain could not venture to hesitate, whatever the political cost might be, to include Rotterdam and Antwerp in the area of blockaded ports"—a point that we shall return to later. Most important, Esher emphasized that economic warfare possessed enormous deterrent value and the potential to bring the war to a rapid close. Three times in his paper he stressed the importance of time in strategic calculations; this is the second instance, after Hankey's memo of March 1911, in which we find economic warfare explicitly described as a short-war strategy rather than a long-war one. In his summary, Esher remarked that if Britain "possesses the alliance of France and Russia, she undoubtedly possesses the means of exercising such enormous and fatal pressure upon Germany"; "so fatal would the pressure be, that I for my part can hardly conceive that Germany, except by an act of madness, would embark upon a war under such conditions."[124]

Steeled by these memoranda from Ottley and Esher, on 23 February 1912, Lord Desart asserted his authority as chairman and informed his colleagues that, like it or not, the inquiry would henceforth proceed upon the assumptions that the next war would embroil most of Europe and that the British government of the day would employ some form of economic pressure. The questions before the committee, therefore, were "how far could it be applied effectively, and how much should we suffer by its use?"[125] Llewellyn Smith muttered mutinously, "It would not be practical, even if it were expedient to stop all trade between the British Empire and Germany in time of war, and it would be a mistake to attempt what was impossible."[126] Chalmers was more restrained but equally unmoved. "As I understand it," Hankey wrote to Chalmers several months later while drafting the final report,

> your view is that, regarding the question from the standpoint of expediency, and disregarding sentimental considerations, our best policy would be to permit all trade with the enemy, except what is carried direct from British ports to enemy ports by British or enemy vessels. . . . You yourself proposed that at the outset of a war our policy should be to proclaim the law that all Trading with the Enemy is illegal—but my impression was that you would not attempt to enforce the law, unless very flagrant cases of breach were disclosed. At any rate you would not attempt to stop the trade through neutral countries.[127]

Esher and Chalmers crossed swords over the issue at the meeting of 23 February 1912. Chalmers tried to argue that military opinion was unanimous that the next war would be of short duration—in which case "it would not be worth while for us to exercise the weapon of economic pressure, which must necessarily require time to produce effect." In keeping with his paper circulated on the same date, Esher disputed both assumptions—that the war must be short and that economic warfare would be slow to take effect and should not be relied upon. "It was vital, therefore, that from the very outset of the war we should endeavor to bring the strongest possible economic pressure to bear," he wrote.[128]

The complexity and interconnectedness of the subjects explored by the Desart Committee render it effectively impossible to detail every aspect of their deliberations. Instead, we shall focus upon their investigation of the three most central—and contentious—issues. First we shall look at the committee's discussion on how best to check imports into Germany through contiguous neutral countries; second, the desirability of regulating the British merchant fleet; and third, to what extent it might be necessary or possible to impose controls over the British financial services industry and the City of London.

British defense planners were unanimous that Germany's ability to trade through contiguous neutral countries was an important and possibly critical factor in determining the viability of economic warfare. The Admiralty, the War Office, the Board of Trade, and the Foreign Office all had studied this question, and because each employed different underlying assumptions, each came up with a different answer. About the only point on which all were agreed was that the problem boiled down to the Low Countries. By accident of history and geography, two of Germany's most important seaports were located in foreign countries, Rotterdam in the Netherlands and Antwerp in Belgium. Before the First World War, Rotterdam was second only to Hamburg as Germany's gateway to the world.[129] Approximately 20 percent of Germany's total seaborne trade passed up the Rhine through Rotterdam, including two-thirds of her iron ore imports and one-half of her imported grain. Ports in other potentially neutral countries were adjudged to lack the infrastructure to cope with any substantial additional traffic.[130] Only Rotterdam and Antwerp were deemed to matter. As the Board of Trade put it, "The enormous importance to Germany herself of keeping one or both ports open can hardly be overstated."[131]

By the beginning of 1912, even the Admiralty admitted that the potential for leakage through the Low Countries could not safely be disregarded and steps to check the flow would have to be taken. They concluded there was just one solution. Because Rotterdam and Antwerp were so tightly integrated into the north German transport and distribution networks, to all intents and purposes they were German ports and ought to be treated as such. Rear-

Admiral Bethell told the Desart Committee in November 1911 that the Admiralty would leap at the slightest pretext to close these ports, neutral or not, to transoceanic traffic.[132] After the War Office pointed out that it was practically certain Germany would strike at France by infringing Belgian neutrality, supplying ample justification for the Admiralty to shut Antwerp, the issue narrowed to Rotterdam. In February 1912, after Captain Ballard was added to the Desart Committee, the Admiralty stated that ideally Rotterdam should be blockaded immediately upon outbreak of war. When the Foreign Office pointed out that such action was tantamount to a declaration of war, and that it "considered it to be in the interest of Great Britain to respect the neutrality of Holland," Ballard bluntly "demurred to the assumption that it was necessary to our interests to keep Holland neutral."[133] If the government would not permit the Admiralty to ignore Dutch neutrality, Rear-Admiral Troubridge thought, the Royal Navy would employ every imaginable trick to molest German trade consigned through contiguous neutral countries: "Large numbers of ships laden with grain call at Falmouth, for example, for orders [instructions], and it might be necessary to requisition the supplies on board these ships, either for our own use or to prevent them from reaching the enemy."[134] Similarly with tongue in cheek, Captain Ballard added: "Naval operations in the North Sea might not unlikely render peaceful navigation east of the Straits of Dover dangerous, and cause insurance premiums to and from ports in these countries [Holland and Belgium] to rise very high."[135] He reiterated that "many of the principal naval difficulties in the conduct of an Anglo-German war would disappear if Holland could be treated either as an ally or belligerent."[136] The Admiralty had concluded, as had the German General Staff, that war was interested in the Low Countries even if the Low Countries were uninterested in war.

During these discussions, Lord Esher supported the Admiralty's view that Rotterdam must be blocked "whatever the political costs."[137] When asked what pretext Britain might employ, he responded: "Our justification for violating the neutrality of Holland would be similar to Germany's justification for infringing the neutrality of Belgium."[138] Not surprisingly, the majority of committee members were uncomfortable with so flagrant a disregard of Dutch neutrality—yet at the same time they accepted the necessity of some sort of action. At Lord Desart's request, in February 1912, the prime minister directed the War Office and the Foreign Office independently to provide the Desart Committee with some guidance on this issue. Both quickly confirmed that a German "violation of Belgian neutrality is so probable that

Antwerp is not likely to be open to German trade."[139] On 25 April 1912, the subject was broached at a full meeting of the CID attended by Asquith and five other cabinet ministers, at which several intimated they were not opposed in principle to the idea of forcing Holland into belligerency.[140] Thereafter, the matter having been effectively kicked upstairs, the Desart Committee abandoned this line of enquiry.[141] Yet in his final report, Desart could not resist reminding the prime minister that regulating trade through Rotterdam was "of the utmost importance" not just to check the flow of supplies into Germany but also "to prevent evasions on the prohibitions on trading with the enemy" by British merchants.[142]

The second major issue addressed by the Desart Committee concerned the desirability of government controls over the movements of British merchant shipping in time of war and the possibility of regulating what cargoes they might carry between neutral ports. As noted, the Admiralty regarded these steps as especially critical to the viability of their strategy. No one present disputed the essential facts or logic underpinning the Admiralty's argument. The Board of Trade endorsed their calculations that neutral merchant fleets lacked the capacity to carry for Germany in addition to their own national needs, and therefore Germany could not possibly maintain her overseas trade without recourse to the British merchant fleet.[143] Llewellyn Smith nevertheless opposed the call for the drafting of legislation to prohibit British merchantmen in wartime from trading with ports in Belgium, Holland, or Denmark.[144] The Foreign Office representative to the committee, Cecil Hurst, loudly concurred. He did not doubt that the Admiralty's plan would work; his concern was that it would work all too well and thereby infuriate neutrals.

That said, the Foreign Office admitted there was nothing in international law to prevent Great Britain from regulating its merchant fleet. But, Hurst insisted, there "is no precedent for a belligerent Power taking this step in time of war" and that the "world at large would regard it as a wanton interference with commerce between two neutral States, and as an abuse of the power which the ownership of a large mercantile marine gave us." Neutrals, he warned, would bitterly resent seeing their trade "strangled by new and unheard-of remedies" and protest such a "violent departure from the established mode of conducting warfare."[145] Expected to protest loudest was the United States of America. American cotton growers, for instance, were totally dependent upon the British merchant marine to carry their product to foreign markets. "The policy of placing obstacles in the way of transport of American cotton to neutral ports in proximity to Germany involves the risk of creating bitter resentment in the United States of America," Hurst presciently cautioned.[146] If the committee deemed it essential to prevent U.S. cotton from reaching Germany, he postulated, could not Britain instead purchase the American crop through payments of special subsidies to domestic importers? The question was not (yet) pursued. Finally, Hurst predicted, if the government tried to impose such "a fetter on the shipping trade," British ship owners would likely seek to evade the ban by transferring their vessels to a foreign flag.[147]

In challenging the idea of controlling the wartime movements of merchantmen, Hurst found surprisingly few supporters within the Desart Committee. Doubtless to general amazement, the Admiralty representatives managed to identify several errors in the Foreign Office paper. For one thing, the wholesale reflagging of the British merchant fleet was not as simple as Hurst had made out. Captain Ballard was something of an expert on this subject, having fourteen years previously written a paper demonstrating why, in time of war, this would be practicably impossible.[148] The committee agreed with Ballard's logic and that anyway Britain could simply pass legislation prohibiting "the transfer of British ships to neutral flags during war."[149] Ballard scored a further point off Hurst by showing the error in his assertion that Britain lacked a precedent for regulating the British merchant fleet in wartime: "We ourselves prohibited British ships from carrying goods destined to the enemy country during the [Boer] war in South Africa."[150] But the critical argument explaining why majority opinion sided with the Admiralty on this issue was that "the British Government has a perfect right at any time to place such restrictions as it thinks fit on British shipping, and that neutral countries have no legitimate right to object to such restrictions."[151]

In its final report, accordingly, the Desart Committee recommended in favor of legislation "prohibiting British merchant ships from carrying specified articles of Warlike Store, of whatever origin and ownership" and certain strategic raw materials "such as raw cotton, raw wool, crude rubber and gutta-percha [an organic material harvested in Malaysia and used to insulate undersea cables—cables were classed as munitions of war]."[152] The committee hesitated only over whether Parliament should be asked at once (i.e., in peacetime) to enact suitable legislation or whether the government should wait until wartime. Ultimately, fearful of the political clamor such measures must raise, the majority thought "it would be undesirable to attract attention to measures we propose to adopt in time of war"; much better "to pass an emergency act on the outbreak of war."[153]

This irresolution infuriated Lord Esher. On 20 April 1912 he exclaimed to Admiral Lord Fisher that his colleagues on the Desart Committee possessed only "the narrowest conception" of what war meant.[154] "It is astounding," Fisher agreed five days later, "how even very great men don't understand WAR!"[155] Fisher went on to spell out his thoughts on the interrelationship between deterrence, trade, and economic warfare. Excerpts from this letter have been often quoted, but it is seldom read in its entirety or evaluated in its proper context, which is essential to deciphering its full meaning. Fisher wrote:

> When I was a Delegate at the Hague Conference of 1899—the first Conference—I had very animated conversations, which, however, to my lasting regret it was deemed inexpedient to place on record (on account of their violence, I believe!), regarding *"trading with the enemy."* I stated the primordial fact that *"the essence of war is violence; moderation in war is imbecility."* And then in my remarks I went on to observe, as is stated by Mr. Norman Angell in *The Great Illusion,* where he holds me up as a terror! And misguided! Perhaps I went a little too far when I said I would boil the prisoners in oil and murder the innocent in cold blood, etc., etc., etc. But it is quite silly not to make war damnable to the whole mass of your enemy's population, which of course is the secret of maintaining the right of capture of private property at sea. As you say, it must now be proclaimed in the most public and most authoritative manner that direct and indirect trade between Great Britain, *including every part of the British Empire,* and Germany must cease in time of war.[156]

It is hardly necessary to point out that this passage takes Fisher's most famous declaration on the meaning and character of war and relates it directly to economic war.

On 9 May, Esher duly completed (with Fisher's help) another memorandum in which he chided his colleagues that

> the subject [of trading with the enemy] is not one that can be approached in an academic spirit. On the outbreak of war the question is one of the first that the Government of the day would have to face. British traders all over the world will expect to be informed whether they were permitted or forbidden to trade with the enemy. It is impossible to strip the consideration of this subject from its political aspects.[157]

Esher further anticipated that British public opinion and allies would demand that "the maximum amount of pressure" be brought to bear upon the enemy. He also condemned the committee's preference to regulate only of certain selected commodities (listed above). Half measures, he felt, were doomed to failure.

> If public opinion would never tolerate for a moment trading by a British subject with the enemy, still less would it tolerate differentiation between one trade and another, for, in addition to the aroma of treason about trading of any kind with the enemy, it would unquestionably be thought extremely unfair that one man should be allowed to make a profit by selling supplies to the enemy and that another man should be precluded from doing so.

In vain Esher urged the committee to recommend that the government at once proclaim its intention in any future war to prohibit *all* direct and indirect trade with the enemy. He believed that such a threat would act as a powerful deterrent against war. Again, Fisher agreed: "It is a most serious drawback not making public to the world beforehand what we mean by war!"[158]

The third and most contentious issue contemplated by the Desart Committee was the possibility of manipulating the global financial markets to hasten the collapse of the German financial system.[159] To assist them, the Desart Committee summoned a coterie of experts from the City of London. Those consulted included Alfred C. Cole (1854–1920), chairman of the Bank of England; Frederick Huth Jackson (1863–1921), of the eponymous banking firm and president of the Institute of Bankers; Sir Felix Schuster (1854–1936), doyen of the London bankers, former president of the Institute of Bankers, and chairman of the gigantic Union of London and Smith's Bank (created by merger in 1902); and Lord Revelstoke (1863–1929), chairman of Barings Bank. Jackson and Revelstoke served also as directors of the Bank of England.[160]

Comparatively little survives of the Desart Committee's deliberations on the bankers' testimony: papers used by the banking subcommittee were excluded from the appendixes to the final report. Transcriptions of the testimonies of the expert witnesses were included, however, and from these we may infer the Desart Committee had three main areas of concern. First, what would be the consequences for the City of London if upon outbreak of war Germany declared a moratorium on all payments to British financial institutions? Second, might Germany be able to undertake any other actions to undermine the City of London, and if so, what steps might the government then take to counter them? Third, what measures might the British government take beforehand to insulate the City of London from the worst ravages of war? Was the solution to restrict the gold or perhaps ensure beforehand that the central bank maintained larger reserves of gold? Readers will note that all these were defensive measures, not offensive ones.

The bankers agreed that regardless of any calculated German acts of sabotage, "the financial situation in this country at the outset of war would be extremely grave."[161] Mr. Huth Jackson, perhaps the most brilliant of the group, predicted war would herald at best severe financial depression and, at worst, a total financial collapse that would bring the global trading system to a halt.[162] Lord Revelstoke similarly advised that "should a European war take place, the chaos in the commercial and industrial world would be stupendous, and would result in the ruin of most people engaged in business."[163] Sir Felix Schuster concurred that a war between the six European powers "might lead to a general stoppage of European credit altogether."[164] Alfred Cole's forecast was somewhat less grim, though still disconcerting. The bankers found the thought of a German moratorium on top of this disruption to be chilling. London banks held immense German obligations. A significant proportion of German overseas trade had always been financed in London.[165] British acceptance houses financed the overwhelming majority of "trade between Germany and the British Empire, and a good deal of the trade between Germany and other countries." Every day, London acceptance houses typically accepted about £7 million in bills of exchange. Estimates of the total amount of money tied up in sterling bills of exchange at any one time ranged from £300 million to £400 million, with the majority favoring the higher number.[166] Of this, according to Huth Jackson, more than £1 million a day was loaned to German firms.[167]

> From these figures it was possible to form some idea of the disastrous results which would ensue if Germany were to stop all remittances to this country. Even a temporary cessation of German remittances would probably be followed by the inability of the accepting houses to meet their obligations.[168]

The failure of the acceptance houses would paralyze the credit markets and result in a full-scale banking crisis.

The bankers further agreed that the size of Britain's stock of gold would be of marginal significance.[169] As Sir Robert Giffen had first suggested back in 1908, the City of London's Achilles' heel actually lay in its dependence on the international credit system, not gold. If a financial panic occurred, no amount of gold that could possibly be accumulated by Great Britain would prove sufficient to prevent a collapse. Frederick Huth Jackson confirmed this:

> The financial effects of a war between two Great Powers such as England and Germany did not depend solely upon considerations of banking and the export of bullion. Within the last fifty years a gigantic system of credit had grown up and had now become the basis of all international commercial transactions. Any interference with international financial relations could only be attended by disastrous consequences to the credit system.[170]

Perhaps the most alarming revelation was the degree to which British high street banks, which underpinned the entire British banking system, were exposed to a collapse in the international credit markets. Huth Jackson revealed:

> The amount of their acceptances [bills of exchange] held by the Joint Stock Banks was very large, and these institutions would probably find that from 50 per cent to 60 per cent of their portfolios were useless. As the numerous accepting houses and Joint Stock Banks are to a great extent mutually dependent[,] the whole financial system of London would be affected.[171]

Alfred Cole explained to his incredulous audience that this dangerous interdependency was the consequence of the way in which the London acceptance houses, in taking advantage of the quarter-century boom in international trade, had extended their balance sheets without raising additional capital in proportion. Instead of taking a loan from the Bank of England at the official rate, they funded their business growth by borrowing "cheap" money from the joint-stock banks and putting up their existing holdings of bills of exchange as collateral. The pyramid had been built on credit. In short, the acceptance houses were overleveraged and especially overexposed in German bills, leaving them vulnerable to collapse in the event of a major market panic.[172] In Cole's opinion, the joint-stock banks were equally to blame, having willingly—even recklessly—lent such enormous sums to the acceptance houses in the belief that bills of exchange were a safe and, more important, highly liquid short-term investment.[173] Cole may have exaggerated—there was serious antagonism between the Bank of England and the joint-stock banks over the latter's capture of the lucrative business of loaning money to bill brokers—but if he did, it was only slightly.[174] The banks' exposure in the credit market was real. Indeed, they themselves were major players in the discount market, holding many bills of exchange on their own account. It was self-evident that if the joint-stock banks simultaneously tried to recall their loans, the effect would be to suck the liquidity out of the international credit system, collapse the discount market, bankrupt many acceptance houses, and bring international trade to a standstill. This, as we shall see in the next chapter, is more or less exactly what happened in August 1914.

Lord Desart and the other members of his committee were persuaded "that a collapse of credit might occur immediately on the outbreak of war, or conceivably before the outbreak of war owing to the apprehension that the war was imminent."[175] While listening to Lord Revelstoke's testimony, Desart was moved to remark: "Does it not come to this, which governs the whole question we have got to consider—that both [Germany and the British Empire] must suffer stupendously; and then comes the question that underlies the whole of this enquiry, which can hold out longest?"[176] It is important to note that in asking "which can hold out longest," Desart was thinking in terms not of a war measured in years but rather of one measured in a matter of months. So bleak appeared the financial forecasts that Desart perhaps inadvertently but nevertheless discernibly shifted the committee's line of inquiry away from finding ways to intensify the economic attack upon Germany toward "the expediency of their considering the measures to be adopted for maintaining [British] credit."[177] In other words, he became more interested in devising defensive measures to insulate the British financial system from the consequences of an inevitable collapse in the credit markets and global trade than in finding ways to intensify the attack on Germany. Desart rejected objections from Sir Robert Chalmers, who protested that these matters were "outside the competence of the subcommittee."[178]

Yet in trying to come up with a plan to defend the banking system, Lord Desart received surprisingly little encouragement from the bankers he was trying to help. Under cross-examination, all refused to be drawn into recommending any specific preventative measures the government might contemplate to mitigate the scale of disaster. When pressed, Huth Jackson responded that the "general conclusion of the whole matter was that our policy should be to interfere as little as possible with international finance, and the business of acceptances, even if the enemy should adopt a policy of restrictions."[179] His advice, which amounted to a plea that government not fetter the City in any way, trust in market forces, and allow the bankers themselves to correct the situation, was loudly cheered by his fellows. The only state intervention the bankers were prepared to sanction—indeed, all agreed that such a step probably would be essential—would be for the Bank of England to declare a moratorium on payment of bills for a short period of time to enable the banks and discount houses to realize assets, raise fresh capital, and generally sort out their finances.[180] Other measures touched upon, but not discussed in any detail, included suspending the 1844 Bank Act (which would allow the Bank of England to print more paper money than warranted by its holding of gold), allowing banks to pool their financial resources in paying creditors, and requesting the Bank of England to fulfill its duty as lender of last resort by entering the discount market to buy up "surplus" bills of exchange.[181] We shall ignore the inconsistencies in the bankers' position.

The bankers also stressed the paramount importance of maintaining foreign and domestic confidence in the city by keeping sterling fully convertible into gold.[182] "To suspend the export of gold even for twenty-four hours," they warned, "might be to jeopardize our position as the principal bankers for the world, and the results might be so disastrous in the long run that it cannot be contemplated." Besides which, Sir Felix Schuster reminded his listeners:

> If we were engaged in a great war, we should have a vast expenditure of all kinds to meet, which, under existing conditions, we could only meet by means of credit instruments of one sort and another, and from that point of view it is desirable to keep our credit position as good as possible. If we abandon the attempt to pay our way by means of credit, and rely on the gold reserve of the Bank of England to pay our way, that reserve is so trivial that we should be embarking on a very foolish undertaking.[183]

This was an excellent and unanswerable point.

The testimony of London's leading bankers persuaded the majority of the Desart Committee that, as Sir Robert Giffen had predicted back in 1908 and as the Admiralty had subsequently argued, the outbreak of a major European war would be accompanied by a "financial catastrophe" of biblical proportions caused by inescapable and massive disruption to the credit system connected with global trade.[184] Only Sir Robert Chalmers questioned whether the crisis would be so severe, but his views were swept aside by the force of majority opinion.[185] The Desart Committee concluded that a general European war was certain to have a "grave" impact upon British financial institutions and likely "damage the whole fabric of British credit."[186] In reporting his findings to the prime minister, Desart apologized that his committee had been "unable to devise any protective or retaliatory measure to meet this danger."[187] In view of the City's importance and the general complexity of the issues, he advised that the City of London be exempted from the government's economic warfare campaign against Germany.

Parenthetically, barely a month after the committee finished taking evidence from the bankers, an article entitled "Lombard Street and War" appeared in the March 1912 issue of the *Round Table*.[188] This was a quarterly journal that served as the mouthpiece for a very influential political lobby led by Lord Alfred Milner, a celebrated colonial administrator, civil servant, and chairman of the Rio Tinto Zinc mining company; Milner was dedicated to promoting the ideas of free trade, imperial federation, and the union of all English-speaking peoples. Another article of faith within the *Round Table* movement was that the British Empire should stand aloof from Europe. What makes this article noteworthy is that the arguments therein were suspiciously similar to those employed by Lord Esher before the Desart Committee just weeks earlier. Lord Esher was closely associated with the *Round Table* movement, as was the author of the article, Robert H. Brand (1878–1963). In 1912, Brand was partner and managing director of the London branch of the merchant bankers Lazard Brothers. He was a fellow of All Souls, Oxford, and possessed many friends inside the Foreign Office and especially the Admiralty.[189] His younger brother, Captain Hubert Brand, was a rising star in the Royal Navy and in 1912 had just been appointed British naval attaché in Tokyo.[190] During the war, Robert H. Brand would become highly influential in blockade and economic matters.

Financial circles heralded Brand's article as an exceptionally fine analysis.[191] It eloquently explained why a failure of the credit system would have such a paralyzing effect upon industry and trade, making clear just how vital the credit system was for both national and global prosperity. Brand's declared object in writing his paper was "to sketch, in broad lines, what may be called London's place in the world of finance and Lombard Street's capacity to meet the shock of war." The opening sentence reads thus:

> A British Government ought to know what effect the outbreak of war is likely to produce in Lombard and Throgmorton Streets and what measures it may have to enforce to forestall a financial crisis, just as much as it should have plans for the strategic disposition of its naval and military forces.[192]

Brand's advice flatly contradicted that given the Desart Committee by Huth Jackson and the other bankers that the government should trust market forces (and the bankers) to reestablish financial stability. Brand implied that most bankers would welcome government plans intended to prevent a credit meltdown in the event of war. In this context he echoed warnings that many acceptance houses were overexposed and needed either to reduce their loans or to increase their capital reserves. Although Brand's article cannot be said to have had any measurable impact upon the deliberations of the Desart Committee, it confirms (with striking clarity of expression) just how widespread were concerns within the banking community over the impact of war upon the financial system.

The final report of the Desart Committee recommended "that the general policy at the outset of war with Germany should be to prohibit all trade with the enemy in goods, wares, and merchandise."[193] In so doing, they prophetically warned that, "judging from the experience of previous wars, it is almost certain that whatever policy is adopted by the Government it will be subjected to keen criticism from those who favour either a policy of prohibiting trade with the enemy altogether, or one of permitting all such trade."[194] Merchants, both British and foreign, they predicted, would protest loudly at any restraint on their trade.[195] The committee further warned that the burden of such a prohibition would fall "specially heavily" on the dominions and the colonies, which produced most of the Empire's primary commodities and whose support for British war policy was regarded as being by no means certain. Lastly, the committee forewarned that "some particular neutrals" (i.e., the United States) were certain to howl at any legislative ban on British ships carrying their goods, leading to diplomatic problems. They concluded, nevertheless, that on balance Great Britain would suffer less than Germany:

> By prohibiting trade with the enemy we should no doubt be augmenting the inconvenience and loss sustained by our own people, but inasmuch as the British empire is assumed to be able to preserve its communications with the rest of the world uninterrupted, we should feel the loss and inconvenience less acutely than Germany, whose communications with the outside world would be largely diverted to indirect routes.[196]

In using the word "communications," Desart of course was referring to sea transportation of goods, but he might just as well have been talking about information flowing through cables.

On 6 December 1912, the prime minister invited Lord Desart to attend the 120th meeting of the Committee of Imperial Defence, "to give an outline of the policy recommended by the sub-committee." Present to hear what he had to say were no fewer than nine cabinet-rank ministers—an unprecedented number. These were Asquith, Churchill (First Lord of the Admiralty), Haldane (lord chancellor from June 1912), David Lloyd George (chancellor of the exchequer), John Seely (secretary of state for war), Sydney Buxton (president, Board of Trade), Sir John Simon (solicitor general), Loulou Harcourt (secretary for the colonies), and the Marquess of Crewe (India Office).[197] Sir Arthur Nicolson, the new permanent undersecretary at the Foreign Office, deputized for the Foreign Secretary. Also attending were Lord Esher plus the usual complement of naval and military officers. Special invitations were extended to Sir Hubert Llewellyn Smith and Sir Robert Chalmers.

In his opening remarks, Lord Desart stressed the complexity of the subject (especially in financial matters) and how history was no guide to evaluating what was contemplated. Although he began his presentation by faithfully summarizing his committee's final report, as he continued his executive summary he deviated increasingly from the printed script to present a much stronger and more favorable case for economic warfare, demonstrating his deep command of the material. Desart emphasized two points in particular. First, he noted the necessity for the British government to take decisive steps to check transit trade through Belgium and Holland; he stressed that "commercial pressure could only be completely effective if these two countries were either our allies or foes." Second, he stressed the importance of prohibiting British merchant vessels from freely transporting key strategic commodities such as cotton, wool, oil, rubber, jute, and coal. Readers may notice that the items on this list had been classed as free goods under the Declaration of London, which meant that all were supposedly immune from capture as contraband. No one knew this better than Lord Desart—he had been the senior British plenipotentiary at the London Naval Conference. In emphasizing the importance of controlling what British merchant ships could transport between neutral ports, Desart left his audience under no illusion as to the likely consequences:

> We should have to face loud protests from some neutrals; for example, the United States of America would very likely object strongly to British ships being prohibited from carrying American cotton to neutral ports because of its supposed destination. They might maintain that, under the Declaration of London, raw cotton was free. But our position would be strong and logical. We did not propose to make cotton contraband, but merely to prohibit British vessels from carrying it when consigned to the enemy of their country, and this would be clearly within our rights.[198]

Listeners can have been left in no doubt that Lord Desart favored the vigorous prosecution of economic warfare.

Asquith and his ministers reacted positively to Desart's address. Though some concerns were expressed at the consequences of some of the proposed measures, these were mild and directed at the predicted level of collateral damage to the British and especially colonial economies. The minutes show that no one disputed the credibility of economic warfare as a strategy, and the consensus of the meeting was that Desart's recommendations should be implemented in full.[199] This is corroborated by Major Adrian Grant-Duff of the CID secretariat, who was present as note taker.[200] The official minutes further show that the ensuing discussions focused on the question of how to "cork the bottle" at Rotterdam. "Rather unexpectedly," Grant-Duff noted in his diary, David "Lloyd George took a strong view on the subject."[201] The chancellor of the exchequer said:

> The geographical position of the Netherlands and Belgium made their attitude in a war between the British Empire in alliance with France and Russia against the Triple Alliance one of immense importance. If they were neutral, and accorded the full rights of neutrals, we should be unable to bring any effective economic pressure upon Germany. It was essential that we should be able to do so.[202]

Lloyd George further opined "this question must be faced and settled now," as they "could not afford to lose a moment when war broke out."[203] Winston Churchill, First Lord of the Admiralty, agreed that "their neutrality [Holland and Belgium] was out of the question. They must be [treated as] either friends or foes."[204] While Asquith did not explicitly approve this line, he nevertheless conceded that "if they were belligerent the question would be much simplified."[205] The CID spent considerable time discussing an option apparently overlooked by the Desart Committee. Lloyd George suggested that Britain might "allow the Netherlands and Belgium to import what they required for their own consumption on the average with a reasonable margin added"—in other words, their imports should be rationed. Haldane and Seely both agreed. At the end of the CID meeting, the ministers present voted in favor of this resolution, personally drafted by Asquith in the midst of the meeting:

> In order to bring the greatest possible economic pressure upon Germany, it is essential that the Netherlands and Belgium should either be entirely friendly to this country, in which case we should limit their oversea trade, or that they should be definitely hostile, in which case we should extend the blockade to their ports.[206]

The significance of this conclusion cannot be overstated. It demonstrates beyond any doubt that the Admiralty's economic warfare strategy was not contemplated in an academic spirit within a forum of technical experts, but was discussed and agreed upon by the prime minister and his senior cabinet ministers. Furthermore, the Admiralty were fully justified in walking away from this meeting believing that their economic warfare strategy had been endorsed by the country's political leaders—something that the War Office, despite more than ten years of effort, had singularly failed to achieve with respect to its Continental strategy.

Predelegation

After nearly two years of study, the Desart Committee reached the conclusion that economic warfare, if implemented in full, would devastate the German economy, wreck her financial system, and in short order compel her to sue for peace. Their report outlined the various measures the British state might take to achieve this object as well as the attendant risks and costs. At the end of 1912, these findings were presented to the political executive and accepted without reservation. Thereafter, a widespread conviction grew up within British defense circles that a major European war "may be expected to have the effect of restricting very severely the commerce of the world" and very likely would result in a "general collapse of credit."[207] The question for the political executive was not whether the strategy should be implemented but rather, in light of the attendant high levels of collateral damage, how vigorously. This was not easy to evaluate. One thing was certain, however: it was a question for the government, not the Admiralty, to answer. Implementation of economic warfare would have ramifications that were just too important to be left in the hands of admirals. Economic warfare, in other words, was no longer a component of naval strategy but rather had become the foundation of national grand strategy, within which naval strategy had become a subset.

To the Treasury's undoubted relief, the prime minister agreed that the inherent fragility of the international banking system—not to mention its importance to the economic well-being of the country—meant that imposing controls over financial services was simply too dangerous.

> He was very doubtful if it was possible to do anything useful in the matter at all. Modern conditions were so extremely complicated that it was as often as not impossible to ascertain where any transaction began or ended. Any proposals to interfere with financial dealings must be treated with very great reserve.[208]

The members of the cabinet exhibited no such anxieties, however, when they agreed to controls over the merchant shipping industry. Moreover, they seem to have agreed with the Admiralty that this mechanism alone would prove sufficient to bring the German economy to its knees.

The residue of problems with no obvious solutions notwithstanding, the leading politicians of the day found economic warfare sufficiently attractive and gave their endorsement. Their approval was reflected not just in the conclusions approved by the CID but in action subsequently authorized by the prime minister to give effect to the policy. As Lloyd George had pointed out, there would be no time at the beginning of a war for the cabinet to debate every step outlined in the Desart Report.[209] Accordingly, the prime minister authorized certain departments of state to claim and exercise certain temporary powers immediately upon outbreak of war. In modern parlance, he arranged for the predelegation of executive authority. These powers and the actions they authorized were defined in a secret volume compiled and circulated by the CID titled *Coordination of Departmental Action on the Outbreak of War,* often referred to as the "War Book."[210] The Admiralty, for instance, was empowered in the name of the Privy Council to issue a royal proclamation forbidding the export from the United Kingdom of any items classed as "warlike stores," and to make amendments to the provisional list drafted by the Desart Committee as they saw fit.[211] The Privy Council possessed the statutory authority to issue such a prohibition under the Customs and Inland Revenue Act, 1879.[212] The same act provided for the Board of Customs and Excise to demand from exporters a bond triple the value of the goods they wished to sell, as surety against the goods reaching enemy hands. A draft bill was also prepared (and kept on file) intended to secure retroactive authority from Parliament for government actions taken in the name of the Privy Council designed to prohibit trading with the enemy at the outset of war.[213] Asquith was being very careful to operate within the boundaries of constitutional authority.

Unfortunately, few papers have survived detailing subsequent British preparations for waging economic warfare against Germany. The CID files for 1913 and 1914 are almost empty, compelling us to infer their content from the fragments that survive. The CID's preparation, in early 1914, of an edited version of the Desart Report for distribution to Dominion governments indicates that preparations in the direction of economic warfare continued.[214] It also seems that soon after the December 1912 meeting, the CID conducted studies into the practicality of Lloyd George's idea of rationing the imports of neutral countries that bordered Germany. This effort apparently foundered for lack of sufficiently detailed statistics on foreign imports and exports. Among the miscellaneous papers retained by the CID is a memorandum dated February 1913 by the Board of Trade that explained the shortcomings of contemporary trade statistics.[215] This and many later wartime documents confirm that foreign trade statistics (and even figures for Britain) were notoriously riddled with error. In addition, the data they contained were understood to be fragile, meaning that statistics were produced for specific purposes or to identify particular trends and could not easily be recollated for uses for which they had not been intended.[216]

It is probably no coincidence that several weeks after the idea of limiting Dutch imports was set aside, Captain Ballard at the Admiralty mooted an alternative method of checking the flow of imports into the Low Countries. Ballard assumed that the Admiralty would not be permitted to adopt the

Bethell interpretation of the Declaration of London. He further reasoned, "It is true that the doctrine of 'continuous voyage' was designed to prevent evasions of this nature, but its application is always attended with difficulties, and, when attempted on the scale required for the case under consideration, these difficulties would in practice probably prove enormous."[217] Ballard's solution was simple enough. He proposed to exploit a legal loophole in the Hague Treaty to lay a huge minefield off the Scheldt estuary, just outside of Dutch territorial waters, and another at the entrance to the Baltic. Ballard expected these minefields would produce "a paralyzing moral effect on trade in the east part of the North Sea including the approaches to Dutch and Belgian ports" and "would probably put insurance premiums up to a very high figure and create a difficulty in getting crews for ships intending to pass through."[218] The Board of Admiralty subsequently approved the idea. The only problem was a shortage of suitable mines. At the end of 1913, comparative trials were ordered for new mines, but for financial reasons the new mines were not ordered before the outbreak of war, causing serious consequences, as we shall see in Chapter 6.[219] Before the war sufficient funds were found, however, to print 50,000 leaflets warning mariners that such a minefield had been placed.[220]

By the eve of the First World War, economic warfare had become the cornerstone of British grand strategy in the event of a war with Germany. This is not to say that the government possessed a plan that had been worked out in every respect. The precise means to achieve the agreed ends were not yet settled. In practical terms, too many politically awkward questions had been sidestepped and nothing had been done to achieve harmony between the departments or to compel their cooperation. Within government circles powerful interest groups remained violently opposed to economic warfare, especially the Treasury and Board of Trade, which could expect the support of business interests as well as the City of London. As we shall see in the next chapter, when war came in August 1914 the deep-rooted antagonisms between the departments resurfaced, causing enormous problems for the British government in the implementation of policy. Yet when war came on 4 August, the Admiralty and the prime minister thought a national strategy had been agreed upon and was in place.

THE SHORT WAR
1914–1915

5

"Incidentally, Armageddon Begins"

The government has the whole situation well in hand—naval and military, financial, commercial and social—at least it thinks it has!

HERBERT SAMUEL, 4 August 1914

Widespread expectation of imminent war between the European powers during the last week of July 1914 generated a financial crisis of unparalleled severity. Though such a shock to the global economic system had been widely anticipated, not least by the Desart Committee, everyone was surprised by the scale of the panic, the speed with which global confidence collapsed, and the magnitude of financial devastation. Historians of the First World War have scrutinized the intricate diplomatic maneuvers in the weeks leading up to hostilities, as well as the political turmoil attending and generated by the decisions to set prewar military preparations in motion and, later, to declare war, but they have generally neglected to exercise the same level of thoroughness in dealing with the concurrent financial and economic aspects of the crisis. Few military histories detailing the beginning of the First World War reference the economic crisis or its severity.[1] Though a considerable, albeit dated, body of scholarship does exist detailing the meltdown of the world financial system.[2] In reviewing here the so-called July Crisis, we shall not concern ourselves with mobilization timetables or the diplomatic maneuverings subsequent to 28 June 1914, the date on which Serbian nationalists assassinated Archduke Franz Ferdinand, the heir to the Austrian throne.[3] We shall focus, rather, upon the unfolding financial-economic crisis and how concerns over commerce and trade influenced key members of the British political executive as they deliberated the possibility of war and contemplated national strategy.

The immediate trigger for global financial panic was the demarche Austria handed to the Serbian government at 6:00 p.m. local time on Thursday, 23 July 1914.[4] As one recent scholar has noted, the text "impressed every Foreign Ministry in Europe by its forty-eight-hour time limit and its drastic demands."[5] "I had never before seen one State address to another independent State a document so formidable in character," remarked the British foreign secretary, Sir Edward Grey, to his ambassador in Vienna.[6] The next morning, Friday, 24 July, the Austro-Serbian situation was discussed for the first time by the British cabinet, which hitherto had been transfixed by the troubles in Ireland. Directly afterward, Prime Minister H. H. Asquith reported to Venetia Stanley, his 26-year-old confidante, "The situation is about as bad as it can be." Grey did not think Serbia could possibly comply with Austria's "bullying and humiliating Ultimatum." "This means, almost inevitably," Asquith spelled out, "that Russia will come on the scene in defence of Servia [*sic*] & in defiance of Austria; and if so, it is difficult both for Germany & France to refrain from lending a hand to one side or the other."[7] Most European statesmen appear to have agreed with this assessment.[8] Having thus mapped out the road to European Armageddon, the prime minister proceeded "happily" to observe, "There seems to be no reason why we should be anything more than spectators."[9]

That weekend, as ministers pondered the increasing likelihood of a general European war, several began to perceive a danger that Great Britain might be sucked into the conflagration. After confirmation that Austria had rejected the Serbian reply, on Sunday, 26 July, Lewis Harcourt, the colonial secretary, motored over to the prime minister's weekend retreat to tell him "that under no circs. could I be a party to *our* participation in a European War," and to beg him to keep Winston Churchill on a tight leash in order to minimize the risk of inadvertent confrontation.[10] Lou-Lou Harcourt (1863–1922) was the scion of Sir William Harcourt (1827–1904), a radical Liberal politician who served as William Gladstone's right hand during the latter's third and fourth administrations. A shadow of his father, Lou-Lou nevertheless viewed himself as a senior member of the party and something of an expert in foreign policy. In the cabinet, he occupied the prized seat at Asquith's right hand.[11] During meetings he seldom asserted his opinions openly. Charles Hobhouse, the postmaster general, described Harcourt as "subtle, secretive, adroit, and not very reliable or *au fond* courageous," noting that he seldom interjected in ministerial discussions, preferring instead to converse in undertones with the prime minister.[12] Harcourt derived much of his influence through his links with the radical wing of the party, which was suspicious of Sir Edward Grey and the recent trend in British foreign policy, especially toward Russia. He was also one of the few senior ministers with a large enough house and establishment of servants to host a sizable number of colleagues. In short, Harcourt enjoyed sufficient stature within the party that the prime minister could not ignore his views. When, on Monday evening, 27 July, the cabinet reassembled to discuss the European situation—a meeting that left Winston Churchill convinced that "at least three-quarters" of the cabinet "were determined not to be drawn into a European quarrel"—Harcourt emerged as the "shepherd" of ministerial opinion in favor of neutrality, afterward asserting that eleven of twenty ministers would resign rather than consent to war.[13]

Though the majority of cabinet members opposed British participation in a general European war, it became rapidly apparent that ministerial wishes could not insulate Great Britain from the consequences of a Continental conflagration. When the European stock markets opened on Monday morning, 27 July, prices dropped across the board as panicked investors sought to liquidate their holdings. Within hours trading in Vienna was suspended.[14] That afternoon the shock wave reached New York. American brokers arrived at their desks to be greeted with a flood of sell instructions from European investors desperate to repatriate their wealth.[15] The next day and the next, the torrent of global selling intensified. Before the end of the week every stock exchange in every major country (including Wall Street) had been forced to close its doors. With so much asset wealth thereby effectively frozen and liquidity already in short supply, the prospect of numerous bank failures loomed large. Around the globe, firms began laying off workers; sharecropping cotton growers in Alabama and debt-laden wheat farmers on the Canadian prairies stared bankruptcy in the face.[16] In the City of London, meanwhile, the most disturbing feature of the panic was a slide in bond prices, even in gilt-edged securities such as consols (British government bonds).[17] Investors wanted cash. About midday on Tuesday, 28 July, Lord Rothschild, chairman of the eponymous banking house, desperately sought out Asquith to warn him that the French government intended to liquidate its sterling balances in London. The prime minister viewed the news as "ominous."[18] To stem the anticipated outflow of gold from Britain, the Bank of England began raising the discount rate in successive steps from 3 percent to 8 percent and ultimately 10 percent. Then and since, this action was much criticized for exacerbating the liquidity crisis, but according to orthodox economic theory it was the correct response, stabilizing the external situation before responding to the domestic panic.[19]

Contemporary commentators and economic historians have accused the joint-stock banks of aggravating the situation.[20] On the pretext that their domestic depositors wanted gold (though as yet there was no sign of a run), the London banks began recalling their short-term loans to various City institutions, including stockbrokers, bill brokers, and acceptance houses, and disengaging from the discount markets by jettisoning their own vast holdings of bills of exchange.[21] The London discount market choked on the surfeit of bills and the markets froze. The acceptance houses, which essentially financed most international trade, found themselves unable to renew loans to their customers (as the joint-stock banks were refusing to lend them the money), unable to retrieve their loans to European customers (because of moratoriums announced in most countries), and unable even to meet their obligations by realizing assets through selling bills of exchange (because there were no buyers). Because of the simultaneous jump in interest rates, moreover, many acceptance houses faced huge losses and possible bankruptcy, even in the event of no war. Without access to financing, the flow of international trade dried up to almost nothing.[22]

In New York, meanwhile, European investors continued to dump American securities and demand payment in gold or preferably sterling. Over the course of the week, the official sterling-dollar exchange rate climbed from $4.86 to $4.98; in gray markets it rose still higher, peaking around $6. Never before had the sterling-dollar exchange rate exceeded $4.91. By Thursday, 29 July, sterling (and gold) had become effectively unavailable in New York at any price, and the world foreign exchange system effectively shut down.[23] Normally, such a currency spike would have triggered a flow of gold from the United States to London as arbitrage companies exploited the different prices of gold in New York and London to earn fabulous profits.[24] But fear of war had pushed maritime insurance rates to prohibitive levels and effectively blocked the shipment of gold across the Atlantic.[25] The United States government surreptitiously ensured that this door stayed temporarily shut. The U.S. Treasury secretary, William Gibbs McAdoo, feared that if the Europeans were allowed to liquidate their American holdings unfettered, the United States might be forced off the gold standard, leading to severe domestic economic consequences—at the very least, a banking crisis and a wave of bankruptcies caused by U.S. corporations and civic authorities defaulting on their loans to British banks.[26] Because the U.S. Federal Reserve Bank was not yet fully operational, Congress conferred upon McAdoo extraordinary emergency powers to avert the cataclysm feared in U.S. political and banking circles.[27]

On 31 July 1914, no one yet knew for sure if the approaching war would remain localized to the Balkans or engulf all Europe, but it was already a certainty that the world economy must plunge into recession because of the severe damage to the global financial system. One contemporary commentator, Robert H. Brand, managing director of Lazard Brothers, noted that within the space of five business days,

> before a single shot had been fired, and before any destruction of wealth, the whole world-fabric of credit had dissolved. The Stock Exchange was closed; the discount market dead; the accepting houses unable to obtain any remittances as cover for bills falling due; the liquid assets of the joint stock banks, i.e., their Stock Exchange and Money Market loans, and their very large holdings of bills immobilized at the moment when their depositors were becoming restive; commerce at a standstill throughout the world; currency scarce; the Bank of England's resources highly strained. Such was the effect of a universal destruction of confidence.[28]

Just how close the global monetary system—based upon the gold standard—came to total collapse may be gauged from a letter Asquith wrote Venetia Stanley. On the afternoon of 31 July, he reported that "the Governor of the Bank [of England] is now waiting here to get our consent to the suspension of gold payments!—a thing that has not happened for nearly 100 years."[29] Given that the credibility of the entire world financial system rested upon the overriding commitment of central banks to maintain convertibility into gold, the consequences of such a decision were monumental.[30]

The prime minister, however, refused to sanction the suspension of gold payments.[31] Later that evening, he and several handpicked senior advisors sat down with the directors of the Bank of England and talked late into the night, mulling over their options. It was eventually agreed that the government must pledge the state's credit to bail out the City of London in order to restore confidence. The working out of the details was delegated to an improvised cabinet Treasury or banking subcommittee comprising seven senior ministers appointed the following morning, Saturday, 1 August.[32] The first step, taken on 2 August, was to proclaim the rest of the week a bank holiday.

Between 4 and 6 August, David Lloyd George, the chancellor of the exchequer, assembled politicians, industrialists, merchants, and bankers to discuss the best way forward.[33] In his memoirs, Lloyd George notoriously devoted a full chapter to "how we saved the city" and cast himself in the lead heroic role.[34] It emerges, however, that initially he favored suspending the convertibility of gold, making him a villain; allegedly, he changed his mind only at the eleventh hour after reading a memorandum by the young Cambridge economist J. M. Keynes explaining just why the prospect of a foreign drain of gold was so remote.[35] On 7 August, the government announced a one-month moratorium on settlement of all bills of exchange (later extended for a further month).[36] The same day interest rates were reduced from 10 percent to 5 percent, and the Treasury began circulating large numbers of hastily printed small-denomination banknotes, thereby injecting a massive dose of liquidity into the national economy. This helped, but the City and the exchanges still remained nearly comatose as the joint-stock banks continued to hoard their assets.[37]

Only after the Bank of England announced, on 13 August, that it would discount any and all bills of exchange drawn up prior to the declaration of war did the wheels of international commerce began to turn again—very slowly.[38] Ultimately the bank (indemnified against all losses by the government) ended up underwriting the entire stock of outstanding London bills of exchange, estimated to total between £350 million and £500 million. The bank ended up purchasing more than a third.[39] But even after taking this extreme step, money, as Lloyd George eloquently put it, remained "a timid and frightened creature."[40] Its courage returned only several weeks later after the British cabinet consented "to pledging British credit to the Bank of England to enable it to discount commercial bills all over the world to start business going again."[41] It was this action that seems to have proved decisive. In November 1914, Lloyd George confirmed to the House of Commons that to date "the total amount of bills discounted on the Government guarantee has been £120,000,000."[42] It provides some sense of the necessary scale of government intervention to know that at that time the British national debt stood at £625 million.

The British government's efforts to crank the world economic engine continued well into August and September and showed few immediate results beyond some success in preventing the crisis from deepening. For many months thereafter, there were few signs of recovery. And although importers still demanded goods, and exporters were available to supply them, the mechanisms for exchanging ownership (either by cash or by credit) remained effectively broken. Unable to sell their goods to overseas clients, exporters slowed production and laid off workers. Even firms that were able to find overseas buyers were unable to ship their goods. A precipitous drop in the number of available cargoes, a steep rise in maritime insurance, and general uncertainty caused by the threat of war encouraged owners of merchant ships to confine most of their fleets to port.[43] Not until late December 1914 did the United States begin shipping her cotton crop to Europe—at considerably reduced prices—and sales did not fully recover until the spring. But the important point to note is that the consequences of the financial-economic panic did not dissipate as rapidly as they had appeared. When in early August the cabinet sat to decide whether Britain would participate in the European conflict, the economic world was still crashing down around ministerial ears. Is it really plausible that the cabinet was oblivious or unconcerned?

Tiptoeing toward the Abyss

On Friday, 31 July, most intelligent observers believed there was little prospect of British intervention in the Continental war.[44] At the cabinet meeting that morning, the financial crisis dominated. Harcourt noted that Lloyd George reported "mercantile & business opinion" to be unanimously "aghast at any possibility" of British participation in war, as were the directors of the Bank of England and "all city opinion."[45] Business leaders were predicting massive factory closures and "wholesale unemployment." Harcourt wrote: "One man s[ai]d to him [Lloyd George] 'they won't be able to *buy* food but they will *get* it & England will be in revolution in a week.'"[46] The chancellor, he thought, had been "very eloquent ag[ain]st our participation & impressed [the] Cabinet."[47] Lord Morley thought so too. In his famous "Memorandum on Resignation," published posthumously after the war (1928), he stressed how Lloyd George had impressed upon the cabinet that British participation in war might propel the economic chaos to a socially inflammable level.

> He informed us that he had been consulting the Governor and Deputy Governor of the Bank of England, other men of light and leading in the City, also cotton men, and steel and coal men, etc., in the North of England, in Glasgow, etc., and they were all *aghast* at the base idea of our plunging into the European conflict; how it would break down the whole system of credit with London at its centre, how it would cut up

> commerce and manufacture—they told him—how it would hit labour and wages and prices, and when the winter came, would inevitably produce violence and tumult.[48]

In Lloyd George's own words, it seemed that "the delicate financial cobweb was likely to be torn to shreds by the rude hand of war."[49] Though it is true that several days later "the Chancellor of the Exchequer said rather tartly that he had never said he believed it [i.e., the possibility of financial catastrophe]," Lord Morley remonstrated that he and others had been left with the contrary impression.[50] Harcourt agreed, and the discovery that Lloyd George's initial desire was to suspend convertibility adds credence to this construal. Or had they heard only what they wanted to hear? In any case, Morley and others remained convinced that the virtual collapse of the international trading system was ample justification for nonintervention in the European war and continued to press this view in the cabinet. "In the present temper of labour," Morley felt sure, "this tremendous dislocation of industrial life must be fraught with public danger. The atmosphere of war cannot be friendly to order, in a democratic system that is verging on the humour of [18]48."[51]

Though ministers ultimately rejected Lord Morley's plea to avoid actual war, they did not necessarily repudiate his picture of the world teetering on the brink of economic abyss. Such concerns weighed far more heavily upon the cabinet than many historians have allowed. Perhaps scholars have tended to discount Morley's views because his memorandum was a thematic rather than chronological narrative of events. On this, however, it is good to recall the words of Winston Churchill:

> Yet it is, none the less, as true and living a presentment of the War crisis within the British Cabinet as has ever been, or probably will ever be given. All is there, and these fragments so shrewdly selected, so gracefully marshaled, are a better guide to the true facts than the meticulously exact, voluminously complete accounts which have appeared from numerous quarters.[52]

In separate conversations with the Austrian and Russian ambassadors, Sir Edward Grey also drew parallels with 1848, "the year of revolution," and alluded to the possibility that a general collapse of credit and industry might result in social collapse.[53] Meeting with French ambassador Paul Cambon after lunch on 31 July, Grey told him the cabinet felt at "present Engl[ish] opinion wd. not support our participation."[54] Cambon's official account of the meeting amplifies that Grey stressed the cabinet was deeply concerned that "Britain was facing an economic and financial crisis without precedent."[55] That evening, Asquith too noted that "the general opinion at present—particularly strong in the city—is to keep out at almost all costs."[56] Winston Churchill seemed equally pessimistic on this score. "The city has simply broken into chaos," he wrote his wife. "The world's credit system is virtually suspended. You cannot sell stocks and shares. You cannot borrow. Quite soon it will not perhaps be possible to cash a check. Prices of goods are rising to panic levels."[57] This last concern prompted Harcourt, on his own authority, to arrange for diversion to Britain of cargoes of food en route from the dominions and colonies to various European destinations.[58]

Others ministers thinking along similar lines included Sir John Simon, the attorney general. During the afternoon session of the cabinet on 31 July, he passed a note across the table to Harcourt pointing out that another reason for Great Britain to stay out of the war was "to reestablish European finance."[59] "I think our abstention is vital," Harcourt scrawled in reply.[60] The point was duly raised and discussed. That evening, Sir Edward Grey wrote to the British ambassador in Paris:

> The commercial and financial situation was exceedingly serious; there was a danger of a complete collapse that would involve us and everyone else in ruin; and it was possible that our standing aside might be the only means of preventing a complete collapse of European credit, in which we should be involved. This might be a paramount consideration in deciding our attitude.[61]

It might be argued that the foreign secretary cited financial reasons as a relatively inoffensive way to justify the cabinet's unwillingness to declare support for France, but such an argument does not explain why he expressed identical sentiments to his senior staff. On 31 July, Sir Arthur Nicolson, the permanent secretary at the Foreign Office, and Sir Eyre Crowe, the senior assistant secretary, virtually demanded that the British government declare unequivocal support for France.[62] Grey, they afterward told their friends, justified British nonintervention by reference to the financial panic in the city and the need to avoid "the ruin of commerce etc."[63] "Some of us thought that economic disaster would make itself felt more quickly after the outbreak of war; that it would rapidly become so acute as to bring war to an end," Grey recorded in his memoirs. "In that we were wrong, but we were wrong only in our estimate of the time and in the manner in which economic disaster would make itself felt."[64]

On 31 July 1914, Crowe recorded that the foreign secretary went so far as to speculate that Britain, because of her position at the center of the global economic system, might never again be able to participate in a major war. Crowe, who had worked closely under Grey since 1905, did not doubt that Grey meant what he said. After this conversation Crowe returned to his desk and put pen to paper.[65] The resulting memorandum dismissed concerns over the economy as exaggerated and attributed the panic in the City to agitation by German bankers. In a separate paper, attached to a recently arrived dispatch from Sir Francis Oppenheimer (a close friend) reporting that the global panic was not so severe in Berlin, Crowe gave further proof of his disregard for the economic crisis. "Germany is organized and the Government gives guidance and help. I am convinced everything here would similarly fall into its right place if the same guidance were given."[66] Such remarks suggest that Crowe, fixated upon the diplomatic situation, had no comprehension of the unfolding economic events and the attendant political implications. In Crowe's defense, however, it must be said that Oppenheimer's report was at least two days old and the financial situation had deteriorated very significantly since then. In one important respect, nevertheless, Crowe had a point: throughout the crisis, leadership by the British Treasury had been singularly lacking.

In the previous chapter we saw how the Treasury had been given ample prior warning that the mere prospect of war would be sufficient to provoke a financial cataclysm.[67] For at least six years, since Sir Robert Giffen's lecture at RUSI, the Admiralty had been anticipating that the prospect of conflict would herald an economic panic of proportions possibly sufficient to threaten social stability. For more than five years, the probability of panic—and the implications—had been widely discussed in official circles. In December 1912, the Desart Committee officially confirmed the Admiralty's assessment that the scale of panic would likely result in partial collapse of the financial system, with economic and social repercussions in turn. At the CID, Lord Desart had urged the government to adopt measures to insulate the London markets from such a catastrophe. But nothing had been done. In his memoirs Lord Hankey acerbically remarked that "no definite action was prepared in time of peace by the Treasury, who were less enthusiastic in war preparation than the other Government Departments concerned."[68] Through his work with the Desart Committee, Hankey knew that Sir Robert Chalmers, the Treasury permanent secretary until the beginning of

1914, had scoffed at the likelihood of serious panic and furthermore insisted that the Treasury alone must remain responsible for giving the government advice on such matters. Lloyd George, who as chancellor of the exchequer had been responsible for Treasury policy, disingenuously claimed in his memoirs that although "something of the kind had been foreseen" by the CID, "I do not think that the actual course of events had been generally anticipated."[69] This statement simply was not true.

At 1:00 a.m. on 2 August, the prime minister's late-night game of bridge was interrupted by news that Germany had declared war on Russia. Seeing general European war as now inevitable, Asquith grudgingly authorized Churchill, who was partnering him in the game, to bring the Royal Navy to the highest state of readiness. Later that morning, a Sunday, the prime minister convened an emergency cabinet meeting to discuss the growing crisis. In fact, there were two cabinet meetings held that day, which Asquith would later recall as an "infinite kaleidoscopic chaos of opinions & characters."[70] The first lasted from 11:00 a.m. to 1:55 p.m., the second from 6:30 p.m. to 8:00 p.m. The story of how majority opinion within the cabinet shifted that day from determined opposition to tacit support for British intervention has been exhaustively documented.[71]

Harcourt confirms that about half the ministers who walked into the morning meeting that Sunday were determined to keep out of the European conflict, not even to uphold Belgian neutrality.[72] Despite the urgent situation on the Continent, the first order of business was actually to approve various measures formulated by the banking subcommittee to alleviate the financial crisis.[73] Only afterward did the foreign secretary brief his colleagues on the European situation. Sir Edward Grey, having been prodded mercilessly for days by his staff at the Foreign Office, bluntly told the cabinet they could procrastinate no longer. The German army had invaded Luxembourg and was still marching westward. The foreign secretary demanded of his colleagues an immediate broadcast of the British government's unambiguous support for France and Belgium in the event of German invasion.[74] Herbert Samuel, president of the Local Government Board, told his wife: "The morning Cabinet almost resulted in a political crisis to be super-imposed on the international and the financial crises. Grey expressed a view which was unacceptable to most of us."[75] The majority demurred, and Grey's response was to threaten resignation.

At this point, in a most uncharacteristic act, Asquith spoke out against the majority by voicing his opinion that "it is against Britain's interest that France sh[oul]d be wiped out as a Great Power." After Asquith indicated he was prepared to form a coalition government or even resign, the whole tenor of the meeting was transformed and the cabinet found itself on "the brink of a split."[76] With difficulty, Asquith steered his ministers away from the precipice and successfully brokered a makeshift compromise, acceptable to fifteen out of nineteen ministers, whereby Britain would assure the French and warn Germany that Britain would not tolerate German naval operations in the Channel. This warning would be backed by the full mobilization of the Royal Navy. This fell short of Grey's requested public avowal of support for France, yet several ministers viewed it as tantamount to a declaration of war. Asquith then adjourned the meeting in order to allow tempers to cool. "Had matters come to an issue," Herbert Samuel reflected, "Asquith would have stood by Grey in any event, and three others would have remained. I think all the rest of us would have resigned."[77]

During the adjournment Grey motored off to the zoo to meditate among the birds before returning to his office to receive the French ambassador at 2:30 p.m. He informed Cambon of the cabinet's decision "that if the German fleet comes into the Channel or through the North Sea to undertake hostile operations against French coasts *or shipping,* the British fleet will give all the protection in its power."[78] But, he cautioned, the cabinet was not yet prepared to issue an unconditional promise to support the Entente in the event of war. Furthermore, not even a token component of the British Expeditionary Force would be released for service on the Continent.[79] Churchill took the prime minister to meet with Field Marshal Lord Kitchener, home on leave from Egypt. The latter counseled Asquith that the French would never forgive Britain for standing aside while their country was invaded.[80] Harcourt, meanwhile, joined eight other ministers at lunch, where they "agreed to refuse to go to war merely on a violation of Belg[ian] *neutrality* by a traverse for invasion purposes of territory but to regard any permanent danger or threat to Belg[ian] *independence* (such as occupation) as a vital Brit[ish] interest."[81] In other words, the antiwar party had shifted its stance and was now prepared to accept that German occupation of Belgium was incompatible with British interests but that a German invasion for the purpose of transit would be acceptable.

After the cabinet reassembled that evening, Grey relayed his conversations with the French ambassador and several other foreign diplomats he had chanced to meet. The prime minister then passed around a letter just received from the Conservative party leadership (masterminded by Major-General Henry Wilson) signaling its unconditional willingness for war. Asquith and Grey exploited this to make clear their determination to support France against Germany, even if it meant seeking a coalition government. Midway through the ensuing discussions, the cabinet learned that German troops had crossed the French frontier.[82] To those dozen or so ministers who, like Harcourt, had intended that morning to break the government rather than subscribe to war, it had become patently clear that their threat of mass resignation would not prevent Britain from joining the conflict. Although four ministers proclaimed their intent to resign, ultimately only John Burns and Lord Morley followed through. The remainder found various excuses for abandoning their professed principles. For several, the prospect of losing their ministerial salaries concentrated the mind wonderfully. When Jack Pease mentioned to his wife that he was thinking of abandoning the cabinet, she at once wrote back: "What do you mean by 'sticking to the ship'—did you intend resigning? You could not do it now in a moment of difficulty and no business prospects to look forward to."[83] The rest of the evening session was spent crafting a statement (which was completed the next morning) for Grey to deliver the following day to the House of Commons, requesting parliamentary approval for the government to issue France the proposed "naval guarantee" and warning Germany not to infringe Belgian neutrality.[84]

But what of the cabinet's concern for the economic situation? Just three days earlier ministers had argued that the implications of the financial crisis were so grave as to render British participation in a major war impossible. Had this been mere rhetoric? Although the prospect of imminent war had pushed geopolitical concerns to the forefront, economic concerns had not evaporated. It will be recalled that the first cabinet meeting of 2 August opened not with a discussion of war but with a review of measures proposed by the finance subcommittee on how best to contain the financial and economic problems. When Herbert Samuel wrote to his wife at the end of that long and emotionally charged day, he clearly had not forgotten the ongoing "international and financial crises." Harcourt's notes too show that while ministers went back and forth over whether to support France, their discussion was punctuated with talk about the economic situation and the authorization of additional countermeasures. Perhaps the best clue as to the cabinet's collective state of mind at this time is contained within the statement that ministers began drafting on the evening of 2 August and which was delivered to Parliament by Sir Edward Grey the next day.

Shortly before 4:00 p.m. on 3 August, the foreign secretary delivered to Parliament a speech regarded by many historians as the most brilliant of his career.[85] Grey stood before the House to request parliamentary endorsement of the cabinet's naval guarantee to France and public warning to Germany not to infringe Belgian neutrality. Although the foreign secretary was supposedly following a script provided by the cabinet, in several places Grey punctuated the message with what might be described as emotional outbursts.[86] Listeners soon forgot they were listening to a meticulously crafted statement issued by the cabinet. But, of course, that is exactly what they were listening to. Grey was not issuing a personal appeal to support France but delivering an official government statement (the product of two sessions of the cabinet) "intended to represent the mind of the Cabinet."[87] It therefore merits close examination.

Even to the casual eye, Grey's speech contained an unusual number of references to the Empire's dependence upon the Royal Navy. Grey cautioned his audience, however, that British naval supremacy could not insulate the national economy from the effects of a major European conflict. "For us, with a powerful Fleet, which we believe able to protect our commerce, to protect our shores, and to protect our interests, if we are engaged in war, we shall suffer but little more than we shall suffer even if we stand aside." Herein lay the central message of the cabinet's statement and likely also its viewpoint.[88] Grey explained:

> We are going to suffer, I am afraid, terribly in this war whether we are in it or whether we stand aside. Foreign trade is going to stop, not because the trade routes are closed, but because there is no trade at the other end. Continental nations engaged in war—[with] all their populations, all their energies, all their wealth, engaged in a desperate struggle—they cannot carry on the trade with us that they are carrying on in times of peace, whether we are parties to the war or whether we are not.[89]

He added that this was a war that

> no country in Europe will escape and from which no abdication or neutrality will save us. The amount of harm that can be done by an enemy ship to our trade is infinitesimal, compared with the amount of harm that must be done by the economic condition that is caused on the continent.[90]

This statement strongly indicates that the cabinet members viewed economic considerations as a major factor in their deliberations for war and had given considerable thought to the economic implications of participation. The attention to economic factors should have appealed to most Liberals, but large sections of Grey's party rejected his claim that Britain would suffer as much economically by standing aside as by participating, and continued instead to believe in the economic wisdom of neutrality.[91]

Privately, several cabinet ministers still apparently adhered to this view, which continued to play a major role in shaping opinions and policies. "The chief fear that haunts ministers," Lord Esher noted in his journal on 3 August, "appears to be not the naval or the military situation, but the inevitable pressure of want of employment and starvation upon the operatives in the North and Midlands; this may lead to a highly dangerous condition of affairs."[92] Harcourt, for one, remained consumed with worry over fear of "revolution in the north."[93] On 4 August he demanded cabinet approval for setting up a committee "at once to deal with food distribution." He arranged for large purchases of Australian meat and approached the Canadian government with a view to acquiring their entire new crop of wheat.[94] Herbert Samuel too remained apprehensive. As president of the Local Government Board, he was chiefly responsible for unemployment. "My task," he wrote to his wife on 4 August 1914, "is the organization of relief, for distress will come upon us very swiftly."[95] "In a fortnight's time," he immodestly anticipated, "mine will be the heaviest task of all, except the Admiralty's."[96] Samuel went on to tell his wife that "the government has the whole situation well in hand—naval and military, financial, commercial and social—at least it thinks it has!"[97] Perhaps better than any other, this remark captures the essence of the cabinet's mind-set: ministers saw themselves confronted by a monstrous hydra—and none of its multiple heads could be safely ignored without risking disaster.

War

Confirmation that German troops had violated Belgian neutrality permitted Asquith to rally his cabinet around the icon of Britain as the champion of small nations. In doing so, the prime minister received unexpected assistance from the king of Belgium, who personally pleaded with King George V for British military assistance. "This simplifies matters," the prime minister told Venetia Stanley, "so we sent the Germans an ultimatum to expire at midnight."[98] No reply being received from Berlin, at 11:00 p.m. GMT on 4 August the British and German Empires were at war. "Now we have our war," Winston Churchill was overheard remarking the next morning. "The next thing to decide is how to carry it on!"[99] In fact, thanks substantially to his efforts, the cabinet had already agreed—before war had been declared—that if Great Britain must fight, then she must limit her liability by following a maritime strategy. On 29 July, well before any decision had been taken as to whether or not Britain should participate in the coming conflict, the cabinet had examined the available strategic options. That same morning, Asquith had reminded his ministers that Britain was bound by treaty to protect Belgium's integrity and that to strike at France the German army must invade Belgium.[100] Harcourt was emphatic: "Everyone agreed we should not land troops *in* Belgium," although there was some discussion of the possibility of landing the BEF "on the French side of [the] Belgian frontier."[101] Talk of landing troops stirred Reginald McKenna, the home secretary and former First Lord of the Admiralty, to opine that Britain could "more effectively deal with German ag[g]ression on Belgium by our fleet sealing up German ocean traffic" to intensify the economic derangement, in anticipation that during the "first few weeks of war all German railways wd. be in use for troops & not available for ordinary food supplies."[102] The reaction to this thinly veiled first reference to economic warfare is not known.

Two days later, on 1 August, the cabinet held another more serious discussion of grand strategy. The idea of sending the army to France was again raised and rejected.[103] This definite decision was reaffirmed the next day and the next.[104] Writing privately to Venetia Stanley, Asquith professed to be "clear in his own mind" that the "despatch of the Expeditionary force to help France at this moment is out of the question & wd. serve no object."[105] During the discussion on 1 August, Harcourt asked the prime minister explicitly if he contemplated sending the BEF to France. "No, certainly not," Asquith replied.[106] This left the floor open to Winston Churchill, who reportedly dominated the second half of the meeting. In begging to mobilize the Royal Navy, he explained to his colleagues how Britain's naval supremacy would allow the government simultaneously to safeguard the nation and prosecute a war of limited liability.[107] "The naval war will be cheap," the First Lord of the Admiralty assured Lloyd George on a scrap of paper passed across the table, "not more than 25 millions a year." To this note he later added, "You *alone* can take the measures wh[ich] will assure food being kept abundant & cheap to the people."[108] Although ministers ultimately denied Churchill permission to mobilize the fleet, they walked away from the discussion believing that if Britain opted to stand by France, assistance could be limited to naval and economic support. As Cameron Hazlehurst put it, the cabinet had agreed—and could agree—that "blockade and the protection of commerce would be a cheap and honorable discharge of the nation's obligations."[109] This informal consensus notwithstanding, it must be pointed out that except for Reginald McKenna, the former First Lord, and of course Churchill, the cabinet possessed only the haziest understanding of what such a maritime strategy entailed.[110] Herbert Samuel was probably speaking for everyone when he affirmed on 5 August: "We [the cabinet] all have absolute confidence in the navy."[111] As we shall see, this combination of executive indifference and blind faith had immense consequences, which would become apparent within little more than a week.

In the meantime, the General Staff bridled at the Army's relegation to the strategic sidelines. The soldiers were furious at the cabinet's repeated refusals to permit Army mobilization. Since the cabinet's decision on 29 July not to commit the Army to the Continent, Major-General Henry Wilson had been prowling the corridors of Whitehall drumming up support for a reconsideration of the decision.[112] Senior ministers found themselves badgered over this question by confused backbenchers, eager newspapermen, indignant Foreign Office mandarins, and anxious French diplomats. At 4:00 p.m. on Tuesday, 4 August, Asquith finally allowed the War Office to begin calling reservists to the colors, but he denied permission for units to move to south coast ports for embarkation to France.[113] On Wednesday morning, 5 August, the soldiers' agitation showed signs of bearing fruit. Asquith relented and asked Haldane, the lord chancellor, to arrange that day what he termed, tongue-in-cheek, a "council of war" to discuss "the strategic situation, and what to do with the [Army] expeditionary force," which consisted of six infantry divisions and one cavalry division.[114] Asquith took care to inform the cabinet beforehand of his intention to hold a "council of war" and of its agenda.[115]

About four o'clock that afternoon, Asquith, Haldane, and Churchill met in the cabinet room at 10 Downing Street with the assembled constellation of senior generals (plus one admiral).[116] Also present was Field Marshal Lord Kitchener, whom the previous evening Asquith had prevailed upon to take temporary charge at the War Office.[117] Asquith's motives in choosing a soldier for the post of secretary of state for war ahead of the vastly more experienced Haldane apparently were "to shield the War Office from a lot of ill-informed and irksome criticism" in the conduct of the war, while at the same time to insulate the government in case of a military catastrophe.[118] In the eyes of the general public, "the unattackable K," as one cabinet minister dubbed him, provided the government with a cover of universally recognized military competence.[119]

In summoning this "council of war" the prime minister's intention had not been to "decide Britain's wartime strategy."[120] His objective had been merely to convene a forum for reviewing possible schemes for the employment of the Army. In seeking professional advice from this ad hoc committee of generals, moreover, the prime minister exhibited his long-standing distrust of the Imperial General Staff and their plan to commit the BEF immediately to operations in France.[121] Significantly, he did not invite the General Staff representatives to open the discussion but instead turned to Field Marshal Sir John French, who had been selected to command the field army and who he knew shared his reservations about the commitment of troops to France.[122] The latter required no prompting to voice his long-standing opposition to the staff's "with France" plan, which he claimed "was no longer possible" because of the delay in British mobilization.[123] He went on to advise following the old "with Belgium" option, which he had always preferred and which envisaged landing the BEF at Antwerp to fight alongside the armies of the Low Countries. This proposal foundered upon logistical considerations, however. Ironically, it was the Admiralty that delivered the coup de grâce by refusing to convoy troop transports past the Straits of Dover to Antwerp.[124]

If Sir John French failed to get his alternative plan endorsed, he nevertheless prevented the General Staff strategy from being adopted at once by default. His presentation emboldened several other soldiers to break ranks with the General Staff and for the first time in many years openly to voice their dissent with prewar plans. The minutes record that Field Marshals Kitchener and Roberts as well as Lieutenant General Sir Douglas Haig, commanding the BEF I Corps, proceeded to point out various weaknesses and suggest the plans be set aside.[125] The day before, in fact, Haig had written to Haldane (believing rumors that Haldane was about to be reinstated as war minister) advising: "This war will last many months, possibly years, so I venture to hope that our only bolt (and that not a very big one) may not suddenly be shot on a project of which the success seems to me quite doubtful—I mean the checking of the German advance into France." Haig preferred to see Britain wait "three months," building and training "so that when we do take the field we can act decisively and dictate terms."[126] Others, including Haldane, Churchill, and Hankey, harbored similar doubts at the wisdom of committing the BEF so soon to battle and said so at the meeting.[127] Small wonder, therefore, that Henry Wilson stormed out of the council condemning it as "an historic meeting of men, mostly ignorant of their subject," who had discussed strategy "like idiots." (Wilson habitually labeled anyone who disagreed with him as ignorant or stupid.) Yet the Army dissenters were unable to come up with any credible alternative to the General Staff plan of sending everything to France. At this point, without reaching any conclusions beyond agreement to discuss the matter with the French authorities, Asquith brought the meeting to a premature close, recognizing that it was pointless to proceed any further in this direction without explicit cabinet sanction to send the BEF out of the country—hence his statement at the end of the meeting that it would be "inadvisable to commit themselves to any more definite plan of operations."[128]

At the cabinet meeting the following morning, 6 August, the prime minister cautiously raised the subject of allowing the BEF to proceed to the Continent. Although Grey's 3 August speech to the House of Commons had committed Great Britain to the conflict in one form or another, Asquith knew that ministerial opinion regarded the commitment as brittle. "With much less demur than I expected," he afterward wrote to Venetia Stanley, ministers agreed "to sanction the despatch of an Expeditionary Force of four divisions."[129] The cabinet insisted upon retaining the other two divisions to meet anticipated civil disorder—surely the most tangible indicator yet of the cabinet's abiding concern over the economic situation and refusal to allow policy to be driven solely by military or strategic considerations. Harcourt in particular still fretted about social disorder and urged his colleagues to think carefully before agreeing to deploy the Army.[130] The prime minister, in fact, went considerably further than simply asking for approval to begin ferrying regiments across the Channel. According to Jack Pease, president of the Board of Education, Asquith and Kitchener together briefed the cabinet in considerable detail on the intended strategy.[131] The prime minister told the assembly that General French preferred to land at Antwerp—suggesting that the Belgian option was not yet completely dead.[132] Asquith and Kitchener both stressed that the BEF would be "kept on our right hand of naval force—not on the left of [the] French force" and would "stay within reach of the sea"; in other words, the British Army would operate independently of the French (in defiance of the General Staff plan) and deploy to "harass and delay" the German advance.[133] The commitment of the BEF to France was not yet certain, nor had the Continental commitment effaced other concerns.

Armed now with a cabinet mandate, Asquith reassembled his "war council" on the evening of 6 August, and they swiftly agreed that France was the only possible theater of operations for the BEF.[134] Military historians regard this as "the most significant single strategic decision taken by Britain in the war."[135] Why this should be so is not clear. It assumes that in August 1914, British national strategy and British military strategy were synonymous—which they most certainly were not. It also overlooks the vital fact that the war council was a nonexecutive body and thus theirs was a recommendation and not a decision. As Hankey had earlier remarked to Lord Esher, "The great question as to whether we shall do what our War Office friends want or not is, I believe, quite undecided and it must be settled at the Cabinet," not at the CID or even less by the so-called war council.[136] The consensus on landing the BEF in France notwithstanding, the war council remained divided on precisely where the four infantry divisions plus one of cavalry should be deployed. Only comparatively recently have historians appreciated just how strongly, and for how long, Lord Kitchener, the new secretary of state for war, resisted committing the BEF at once to the front line.[137] Although the war council agreed to begin ferrying men and equipment across the Channel, it was not until 12 August, after Asquith ruled it would be politically unwise to defy the professional opinions of both French and British general staffs, that Kitchener agreed to fall in with French wishes and deploy the BEF forward at Maubeuge on the Franco-Belgian border.[138]

Directly after sanctioning the release of four divisions for service on the Continent, the cabinet eagerly turned its attention to considering "a number of smaller [maritime] schemes for taking German ports & wireless stations in E & W Africa & the China Seas" submitted by the Admiralty.[139] Asquith exclaimed to Venetia Stanley these operations were "discussed with some gusto: indeed I had to remark that we looked more like a gang of Elizabethan buccaneers than a meek collection of black-coated Liberal ministers."[140] This statement was more than a colorful commentary; it reflected the relative importance ministers attached to the military and maritime dimensions of their official strategy, and emphasized that the Royal Navy remained the cabinet's weapon of choice. It may well be that ministers had (inadvertently) opened the door to a Continental commitment, but this most certainly had not been their intention, nor was it recognized at the time. A letter written by one minister, Jack Pease, to his brother at the end of August 1914 explains the prevailing mood: "We decided that we could win through by holding the sea, maintaining our credit, keeping our people employed & our own industries going—by economic pressure, destroying Germany's trade cutting off her supplies—we would gradually secure victory." He added, "Our Navy, finance & trade was our life's blood, & we must see to it that these are maintained."[141] Except for failing to define the word "gradually," there can be no clearer statement of cabinet intent.

Further insight into ministerial perceptions of British strategy may be gleaned from the abortive attempt to engineer a coalition of European powers in the tradition of their grandfathers during the French revolutionary wars. The grand coalitions of that era represented the apogee of maritime strategy, in which Britain concentrated her resources on naval power while relying on Continental allies and her own relatively small expeditionary force to provide a land complement, and they were the product of successfully melding diplomatic, naval, military, and economic power. Events during the Napoleonic era provided the lens through which many members of Asquith's cabinet viewed the making of war. The story of the abortive grand coalition of 1914, first raised in the cabinet on 3 August, is a curious and little-known episode.[142] The essential idea was to forge the minor European powers—including Belgium, Holland, Norway, Portugal, Spain, and Greece, plus maybe some Balkan countries—into an alliance against German aggression for the duration of the war.[143] From the military perspective, these small European powers could have contributed little to the allied cause, but from an economic warfare perspective, they were formidable.

The original impulse for this diplomatic initiative came from the Admiralty as part of their plan for economic warfare. On 3 August, Winston Churchill forwarded to Sir Edward Grey a memorandum endorsed by the First Sea Lord and chief of Naval Staff stating:

> We regard the part to be played in a naval war with Germany by the three small states bordering on the N[orth] S[ea], viz: Norway, Holland and Belgium, as of serious importance. The advantages wh[ich] their alliance w[oul]d offer us in blockading Germany & in controlling his naval movements cannot be over-estimated. Their decision appears now to be trembling in the balance, & strong action by England may rally them to our cause.[144]

That afternoon the cabinet mooted the idea but reached no decisions. That night, shortly before midnight, a number of senior ministers held an impromptu meeting to discuss an Admiralty request to place Rotterdam immediately under blockade, which naturally raised the question of Britain's relations with small Continental powers more generally. Present were Asquith, Grey, Churchill, Lloyd George, McKenna, and Harcourt. They rejected the Admiralty's request. Harcourt and Grey protested it was diplomatically and politically vital that the government not undermine their claim that Britain had been driven to war in "defence of small nationalities" by infringing Dutch neutrality.[145] The next morning Churchill begged the foreign secretary to rethink his opposition, pleading that the Navy would find itself "at grave disadvantages" if forced to respect Dutch neutrality.[146] Grey's reply has not survived, but it appears he counterproposed that Holland might be recruited to the alliance. Over the next couple of days the cabinet enthusiastically awaited the enlistment of Holland and the minor powers of Europe in a crusade against German militarism. Herbert Samuel noted with approval that "Grey is doing his best to get the rest of Europe on our side."[147]

Grey's effort to "get the rest of Europe on our side" has passed almost unnoticed by scholars.[148] His memoirs contain no mention of the diplomatic effort made in this direction—perhaps because, contrary to what Samuel thought, Grey was not "doing his best." At that time the foreign secretary was much more interested in the idea of creating a Balkan confederation than in winning over the unaligned northern European countries.[149] He also increasingly believed British interests would be better served by limiting the spread of the conflict instead of widening it, as he was being asked to do—hence his desire not to invoke the Anglo-Japanese alliance.[150] As for the proposed alliance of northern European neutrals, the original file containing the relevant correspondence shows that at 10:30 a.m. on 4 August, the Foreign Office dispatched a telegram addressed to various embassies and legations advising:

> HMG are informing Norwegian, Netherlands and Belgian governments that if pressure is applied to them by Germany to induce them to depart from neutrality HMG expect they will resist by any means in their power, and HMG will support them in offering such resistance and that HMG in this event are preparing to join Russia and France if desired in offering to Norway Netherlands and Belgian governments at once *an alliance* for the purpose of resisting use of force by German government against them and a guarantee to maintain their independence and integrity in future years. (Emphasis added)

Sir Eyre Crowe was delighted. "I presume there can be no doubt," he enthused, "that it would be to our advantage to obtain the active cooperation of as many states as possible."[151] But Grey dithered. Two hours later he ordered the text of the demarche just sent to be amended by substituting "common action" for "an alliance."[152] After luncheon, the foreign secretary ordered the demarche suspended even though it had already been delivered to the governments of Norway and Holland (presumably they were asked in the afternoon to forget what they had been told that morning).[153] No reasons were given; not even the senior department civil servants were offered an explanation. Crowe, who had spent much of his day further contemplating "the question of endeavouring to bring into a system of fighting alliances a ring of Powers surrounding the enemies," was left fuming.[154] Writing to his wife that night, Crowe reflected:

> It is a blessing one is kept so busy, otherwise one would be in a continuous state of despair at the hopelessly ineffective way the government does everything. They never seem to know their own mind for hours together. We had a very bad time here all last night. Orders were given, altered, countermanded, and restored at a blinding rate and all our carefully organized arrangements upset and made ineffective by the successive vagaries of the cabinet. It is a wonder the office worked at all.[155]

The precise reason for the retraction remains a mystery. One plausible inference is that Grey acted in deference to the sensibilities of Britain's Entente partners. The need to coordinate with allies was strong, yet within twenty-four hours of war the French government was already voicing to London its irritation at having not being consulted on a range of British diplomatic initiatives.[156] An early reply to the above telegram from Manfred Findlay, the British minister in Christiania (Norway), appeared to justify Grey's hesitation. Findlay reminded London of the basic dynamics of Nordic politics. There was no question that if pushed into war Sweden would side with Germany, but the assumption that Norway (which had obtained independence from Sweden only ten years before) would automatically side with the Entente was by no means certain. Both distrusted Russia more than anything, and if Russia threatened Sweden, Norwegian public opinion might well demand battle against the ancient foe.[157]

By 6 August, what little enthusiasm Grey had ever possessed for the idea of a grand alliance had evaporated. Crowe complained to his wife, "I am working him [Grey] up as well as I can to get alliances made with Spain, Portugal Italy and Greece, if not also Holland. But the waste of effort involved is great."[158] On 7 August, the foreign secretary finally met with the Dutch ambassador and raised officially the possibility of Holland joining the allies. Upon being told the Dutch intended to remain neutral, Grey declined to press the matter and even declared his sympathy for their position. He requested of the ambassador only that "Holland must not become a base of supplies for Germany."[159] Churchill demurred, "proposing to take the Dutch govt. by the throat" and force them to choose sides, an idea he pressed repeatedly in the cabinet over the next four weeks.[160] Grey also cold-shouldered a Portuguese offer to join the war against Germany.[161] Just as Grey was poised to hammer the final nail into the coffin of the grand coalition, however, a cable from the minister in Christiania arrived at the Foreign Office more optimistic at the prospect of recruiting Norway to the alliance and asking for permission to reopen negotiations.[162] But no sooner had the opportunity reappeared than it was gone again. The Foreign Office was told by the British minister in Stockholm that Norway and Sweden had just signed a secret pact to remain neutral throughout the conflict.[163] To the mystification and "perplexity" of his senior staff, Grey concluded that this (unconfirmed) report destroyed all hope of recruiting Norway, and he promptly closed the file.[164]

What was Grey thinking? The account above lends powerful support to Zara Steiner's judgment that Sir Edward Grey generally "failed to recognize the integral connection between strategy and diplomacy and never understood how one could assist the other if properly coordinated."[165] It also tends to corroborate her assessment that Grey had been mentally exhausted by the July crisis, possibly suffered some sort of breakdown, and had not yet recovered his mental equilibrium. At the time, it was common knowledge that the foreign secretary had been deeply affected by the outbreak of war.

Much less well known was that Grey's (arrogant) self-perception of failure in preventing the outbreak of war combined with his deteriorating health to produce bouts of deep depression. On 6 August 1914, Eyre Crowe complained to his wife, "I have the greatest difficulty in getting some energy into Grey."[166] Several weeks later Crowe reported, "I have just spent a quarter of an hour with Grey in order to cheer him up as far as possible. An utterly despondent leader is not inspiring."[167] Lloyd George and McKenna (who rarely agreed about anything) declared to Sir George Riddell they were fed up with Grey's imitations of Cassandra.[168] Asquith too expressed concern over his foreign secretary's tendency to acute pessimism.[169]

Although historical opinion is virtually unanimous on this point, the portrayal of Sir Edward Grey as a man caught in a downward spiral of depression is misleading and tends to conceal another side to his character. There is clear evidence that during the opening months of the war, Grey's demeanor oscillated violently: often he displayed acute pessimism, which manifested itself in lethargy and indecisiveness, but sometimes he advocated policies so spirited they bordered upon recklessness. The prime minister noted the foreign secretary's mood swings and more than once passed comment to Venetia Stanley. In October 1914, for instance, Asquith held up Lord Kitchener as a model for emulation: "K—with all his drawbacks—has the supreme merit of taking everything calmly, never either exalted or depressed. A great contrast to E. Grey: who is always up & down."[170] Grey, Asquith complained, lacked a "sense of proportion and perspective."[171] Grey "is curiously up & down—mostly down," he observed again several months later.[172]

The most explicit description of Grey's hitherto unsuspected displays of hawkish behavior at the beginning of the war is found in the recollections of Laurence Collier, one of six high-flying elite clerks assigned to the Foreign Office's "War Department." According to Collier, the night Grey announced his resignation, Sir Eyre Crowe walked into his office and "held forth" to him and two other colleagues:

> He proceeded to describe how naïf, ill-informed and unrealistic Grey had often been and how difficult to "keep on the rails." I wish I could remember half of what he said then: as it is, I can only remember the beginning of it and one further passage, where he said that, after war had broken out, Grey supposed that, because we were at war, we could do anything we liked and he (Crowe) had had to explain to him what was meant by international law. I was, in truth, too astonished at the spectacle of a man in Crowe's position expatiating to three Junior Clerks on his difficulties with the Secretary of State to pay much attention to the details of what he said; and indeed the scene is so astonishing that I may not now be believed when I record it.[173]

Further evidence will be provided below that tends to corroborate this extraordinary story. It should be noted also that even before 1914, others had remarked upon Grey's seemingly "reckless attitude" toward war.[174]

It is vital to understand Grey's mind-set, since during the early months of the war he retained almost unfettered control over the formulation of British foreign policy. With the full support of his staff, he was tenacious and uncompromising that the Foreign Office must remain solely responsible for all negotiations and arrangements with, or appertaining to, Britain's relations with foreign countries. As we shall see, whenever the foreign secretary's views clashed with those of another government department—for instance, the Admiralty—invariably Grey asserted his prerogative in diplomatic matters and proceeded to act (often unilaterally) as he saw best. He consistently refused to tailor his diplomacy to conform to British strategy as prescribed by the cabinet. In other words, Grey's private beliefs and attitudes seriously impacted the conduct of war policy, and especially the prosecution of economic warfare.

Playing by Whose Rules?

Before 1914, Admiralty planners consistently emphasized the need for speedy action at the outbreak of war. The catchphrase "instant readiness for war" punctuates numerous official and unofficial papers. In no area was this more important than in implementing economic warfare. Predicting that war would be accompanied by economic crisis, but unable to estimate its duration or precise severity, the naval planners wanted to turn the various screws at their command as quickly as possible in order to maximize the chances of quickly pushing the German economic system over the precipice. Prewar, broad political acceptance of the importance of rapid action at the opening of hostilities had led the prime minister to authorize the predelegation of executive authority, one of the most significant innovations in British defense policy before the First World War. It meant that immediately upon a declaration of war, the Admiralty and other departments were empowered to take a number of actions without further reference to the cabinet.[175] All these various emergency powers were set down in the "War Book," compiled and issued by the CID secretariat.[176]

The morning following Britain's declaration of war, Wednesday, 5 August, the government enacted a series of royal proclamations making it treason for any British subject to trade with any person or organization inside Germany. A royal proclamation was a legally binding edict or executive order issued by the state in the name of King George V and his Privy Council. Drafted before hostilities and kept on file, these were published in the *London Gazette,* the government newspaper for disseminating official information.[177] Specifically, owners of British merchant ships were warned, upon penalty of forfeiture, against "carrying contraband from one foreign port to any other foreign port" "unless the ship-owner shall have first satisfied himself that the articles are not intended ultimately for use in the enemy country." Exporters, meanwhile, were enjoined not to sell "contraband" or "war-like stores" to foreign buyers, whether enemy, allied, or neutral.[178] Inclusion of an item or commodity on the prohibited list did not constitute an exportation ban; merchants could apply to a Privy Council committee (another body foreshadowed before the war by the Desart Committee) for a license granting exemption. The application, however, had to be accompanied by a bond triple the value of the goods to be exported; the surety bond would be forfeit if the goods were subsequently found to have reached an enemy destination.[179] In other words, the state intended to regulate rather than prohibit exports.

Although some interdepartmental squabbles over which agency should be given the authority to compile the list of warlike stores had preceded the war, as of August 1914 the "War Book" assigned sole responsibility to the Admiralty.[180] This the Admiralty exploited to the full, causing eyebrows to rise at the Foreign Office.[181] For instance, the Admiralty imposed a total ban on the exportation of "forage and food of all kinds for animals, and also provisions and victual of all sorts which may be used as food for men."[182] The wording was unambiguous and allowed for no exceptions. Atop the list of prohibited industrial commodities on the list was coal, which of course formed the chief source of energy for industry and transportation everywhere. Given, however, that more than a million men in Great Britain earned their living as miners, more than in any other occupation, and that coal accounted for 10 percent of total British exports (by value), it is unsurprising that some thought the Admiralty had gone too far.[183] Walter Runciman, the president of the Board of Trade, and Sir Edward Grey at the Foreign Office quickly agreed—though for different reasons—that the exportation of coal ought not to be regulated; the Board of Trade was anxious to relieve serious unemployment among miners in the north of England, while the Foreign Office was keen to earn diplomatic credit with neutral coal-hungry South American countries.[184]

The central plank of economic warfare remained Admiralty control over the oceanic transportation system. On 1 August 1914, seventy-two hours before hostilities commenced, Churchill ordered the "war room" to be fully activated. The core of this organization was the oceanic shipping plot, very secretly developed some seven or eight years previously, which tracked on gigantic wall-mounted charts the movements of every warship in the world plus merchantmen of special interest such as colliers and large, fast merchant vessels with the potential to be converted into commerce raiders.[185] The system represented a huge investment in intelligence and communications technology (not to mention a sizable subsidy paid to Lloyd's of London for its assistance). In peacetime, the plot was updated every eight hours. After mobilization, the number of merchantmen tracked was increased and their positions plotted with greater frequently. On 1 August 1914, Captain Philip Dumas, an officer then serving at the Admiralty, noted in his diary that "everyone" with clearance to enter the war room was "watching the great wall maps with interest to see the positions of the German ships."[186] By this means observers could see that "within a week of the outbreak of the war the German mercantile flag had been driven from the high seas."[187] Of the 1,500-odd merchant vessels greater than 100 gross register tons belonging to the German merchant marine, 245 were captured, 221 were confined to operating in the Baltic, and 1,059 (representing 3.9 million gross register tons of shipping) were laid up in neutral ports.[188] Incidentally, the biggest and best German vessels ended up in the United States, which, as we shall later see, would have major consequences. The Admiralty was slightly annoyed at the magnitude of the last number, which was blamed upon U.S. commercial wireless stations relaying the German government's instructions to run for port. It had not occurred to Americans that this constituted an unneutral act.[189] British annoyance with the Americans was muted, however, by the belief that these vessels had been effectively removed from the board.

In exerting control over the British merchant fleet, the Admiralty received considerable unofficial assistance from Lloyd's of London. Several hours before the formal outbreak of hostilities, Lloyd's transmitted at the Admiralty's behest a signal to "all ships" advising that war was imminent and instructing them to stop at a British port for further orders.[190] Simultaneously, the director of the Admiralty's Trade Division, Captain Richard Webb, "issued 'suggestions' to ship owners whose vessels are bound to the North Sea or Baltic ports that in the public interest they should divert these vessels to U.K. ports."[191] Once the vessels were secured alongside, British customs officials (interpreting the new prohibition on the export of foodstuffs literally) denied clearance to leave for any eastward-bound vessel, British or neutral, that was carrying foodstuffs.[192] The enthusiastic cooperation of customs officials was ensured by allowing them to claim naval prize money for the capture of enemy property. Indeed, the very first prize case of the war was brought by Richard King, the collector of customs at the Cardiff docks, for "capturing" a

German commercial sailing vessel.[193] Most British and dominion shipping companies also cooperated. The Canadian Pacific Railway Company, for instance, which owned a sizable fleet of bulk cargo vessels normally engaged in carrying grain across the Atlantic, urged the Admiralty "to get in touch with the Port of London Authority as to the necessary storage of all these cargoes," so there would be no delay in converting their vessels into troopships.[194] The Admiralty acted upon this practical suggestion.[195] But clearly a significant number of British shippers chose to ignore the Admiralty's "suggestions," because the following week Captain Webb advised his superiors that "more drastic steps now appear necessary." From 16 August on, Royal Navy cruisers were instructed to divert—and if necessary escort—all British-flagged ships bound east of Dover back to port.[196]

Another, more subtle tool for keeping British merchantmen in port was that once the vessel was alongside, then technically her voyage was over and insurance on the ship (though not cargo) was terminated. Vessels wanting to put back to sea were therefore obliged to obtain new insurance or proceed without. Because of the war, however, commercial maritime insurance rates had shot up to a nearly prohibitive level of 20 percent.[197] Alternatively, owners of British registered vessels could apply for a government-underwritten war risks policy (approved by the cabinet banking subcommittee), available at a much lower premium. The catch was that a government policy mandated captains of merchant vessels to comply with all Admiralty sailing instructions and directions given by Royal Navy officers—with orders to stop all British vessels entering the North Sea.[198] Here again Lloyd's provided active assistance by passing on to the Admiralty Trade Division details of all "suspicious" applications for commercial insurance. Lloyd's notified the Admiralty of any cargoes that had cleared foreign ports (such as New York) and which they suspected of being intended for Germany.[199] From such intelligence the Royal Navy intercepted quantities of U.S. grain and copper purchased in early August for delivery to Rotterdam.[200]

As much as they could get away with it, the Admiralty also placed obstacles in the path of foreign merchantmen wishing to proceed east through the Straits of Dover. Naval officials colluded in playing dirty tricks to prevent merchantmen from leaving British ports. In the case of one collier, for instance, the Cardiff Railway Company deliberately "put coal in the fore part of the hold in such proportions as to give her a very uneven keel," thereby rendering her unstable and unable to put to sea.[201] At the outbreak of war some 128 neutral steamers in British ports were denied clearance to leave under the new regulations prohibiting the exportation of food, and ultimately were compelled to discharge from their holds an estimated half a million tons of grain.

Such legally questionable—though not indefensible—actions involved considerations of international law and quickly drew protests from various foreign governments.[202] One of the first to demand an explanation for the diversions of shipping and apparent confiscations of neutral property was Walter Hines Page, the United States ambassador to Great Britain. This, of course, was exactly the sort of problem that the Foreign Office had feared would arise. In the first instance, the Foreign Office claimed (quite genuinely) ignorance of the seizures and passed the American enquiry across to the Admiralty, which effectively ignored it.[203] "As the only anxiety is as to suitable compensation," Captain Webb disdainfully noted in the file, "this might be promised but this is a question for the Treasury Committee. Meanwhile it is not proposed to modify instructions in any way as to diversion of shipping."[204] A fortnight later, faced with mounting neutral anger, the British government agreed to buy all cargoes at London market rates and release the ships.[205] The diplomatic fallout from this Admiralty action was less severe than it might have been since German port authorities had obligingly behaved in a similarly arbitrary manner.

Yet British diplomats remained nervous. Because the Declaration of London remained unratified, disputes between belligerent and neutral powers remained governed by customary international law. For reasons already explained, this was seen as a sure recipe for diplomatic misunderstandings and legal headaches. Sir Eyre Crowe so dreaded the prospect that several days before Britain declared war he unofficially approached the Admiralty and begged them to endorse publically and adopt the Naval Prize Bill (i.e., the Declaration of London). His appeal was met with a flat refusal.[206] While the Admiralty had been reluctant to grasp the thorny issue of defining and codifying the rules of maritime warfare before the war, once hostilities appeared imminent it was the last subject they wished to contemplate. But it was only a matter of time before circumstances compelled the British government to address the issue. On the evening of 6 August, Sir Francis Bertie, the British ambassador in Paris, telegraphed London that the French were anxious to know if the Royal Navy intended to abide by the unratified Declaration of London.[207] A few hours later, the U.S. secretary of state, William Jennings Bryan, instructed Ambassador Page to make similar enquiries at the Foreign Office. Sir Edward Grey's first reaction was: "Ask what the Admiralty wish:

I should be disposed to have [*sic*] our naval authorities as free a hand as possible."[208] The next morning Grey met Ambassador Page and told him he thought it unlikely Britain would abide by the declaration, since Germany had already demonstrated her contempt for international law by sowing unanchored mines in the North Sea (in violation of the Hague Treaty); earlier that day a mine had claimed the new light cruiser HMS *Amphion*.[209]

Grey's senior departmental advisors, however, had different ideas and strove to subvert his willingness to let the Admiralty dictate policy.[210] Crowe felt strongly the government ought to comply with the Declaration of London, insisting that Great Britain was "deeply committed in the matter, not only by the negotiations with Germany but also by the categorical assurances given to Parliament in the course of the debates on the naval prize bill."[211] In fact, he had already told one shipping company that the Declaration of London "probably will be observed by the belligerents in the present war"—in direct contradiction to the view Grey had just expressed to Ambassador Page.[212] Cecil Hurst, the assistant legal advisor and the Foreign Office's expert on maritime law, agreed that the Admiralty could not be allowed a free rein. He also worried that differences in departmental opinions over the law would soon lead to trouble. He impressed upon the foreign secretary that, at the very least, "some pronouncement is necessary as to the rules which the naval officers are going to enforce as regards neutral ships and the property on board" and that "such a pronouncement is required for the guidance of our own Prize Courts and also for the information of neutral governments and the trading community in neutral countries."[213] Unlike Crowe, however, Hurst was mindful of the political unfeasibility in simply decreeing that Great Britain would abide by the Declaration of London. The treaty had been rejected by Parliament, the opposition Conservative party remained bitterly opposed to its ratification, and public opinion believed that the Admiralty was also opposed.[214] Cecil Hurst advised that the Foreign Office might sidestep the problem by issuing "a short statement, saying that the Declaration of London will be adopted during the present war except as to the following points, and then give a list of them. This plan seems to me to be the simplest and shortest." Sir John Simon, the attorney general, and Sir Edward Grey concurred.[215]

Across Horse Guards Parade, meanwhile, the Admiralty were still scrambling to find a position that would allow them to dodge the entire question of treaty ratification. Greene, the Admiralty secretary, who had been intimately involved in prewar negotiations over maritime law and who had always viewed the Declaration of London with a jaundiced eye, suggested "it might be sufficient" simply to give the French and U.S. governments each a copy of the latest naval prize manual "to satisfy them as to the line we are taking without committing ourselves definitely to ratification."[216] Vice Admiral Edmond Slade, the Admiralty representative at the 1909 London Naval Conference, was recalled to active duty and asked for his thoughts. "The differences are so small," he agreed, "that it would be sufficient to act on the [British] prize manual and not say anything about the Declaration of London or The Hague conference."[217] Prince Louis of Battenberg (First Sea Lord) and Churchill concurred in taking this passive line of least resistance.[218] But the Foreign Office rejected this evasion and wrote back insisting the government must issue a statement on the Declaration of London and, furthermore, "this announcement must indicate the rules by which HMG will abide during the war now in progress."[219] The attorney general and the Treasury solicitor's department, equally uncomfortable with the arbitrary appearance of recent policy, agreed that the preferred vehicle for such a statement was an order-in-council, a government edict issued in the name of the Privy Council (similar to a royal proclamation). No edict could be issued, however, until policy had been agreed upon—which, given the serious divergences in departmental opinion already evident, would not happen overnight.[220]

The Cabinet Appeal

How aggressively Great Britain should prosecute its economic warfare strategy—for this was the crux of the matter and determined even the legal position to be adopted—was not a question that could be decided at a departmental level. On Wednesday, 12 August, accordingly, Sir Edward Grey and Winston Churchill brought the matter before the cabinet for adjudication. David Lloyd George underlined the urgency of a decision by informing his colleagues of financial intelligence indicating that abnormally large consignments of wheat had been purchased in New York for delivery to Rotterdam, "undoubtedly having as their ulterior destination the German market."[221] "We want to stop this [trade]," Harcourt agreed, under the impression this could be easily accomplished.[222] Owing to the pressure of other business, discussion did not begin until the following day.

The ensuing cabinet debate, which ran from 13 August till 21 August, was one of the most important (and probably among the most bitterly fought) discussions of strategic policy of the entire war. It may seem surprising that any argument should have taken place, let alone lasted for so long. After all, the prime minister and his senior ministers had long enough known of the Admiralty's intention to wage economic war against Germany.[223] No fewer than seven members of the current cabinet (the most senior ministers) had been present at the 120th meeting of the CID, just twenty months previously, and therefore heard Lord Desart's summary of the "Trading with the Enemy" report.[224] None, at that time, had voiced objections.

Equally surprising is that this critically significant debate on strategy should have escaped historical notice. True, cabinet ministers tried to conceal their differences. As far as can be determined, only Lord Esher caught wind of their internal strife. "The blockade must be made effective as soon as possible," he recorded in his journal on 14 August. "Churchill is anxious to do this at once, but so far his colleagues do not agree with him."[225] Asquith's letters to the king, the official record of cabinet proceedings, were unusually (even for him) long in summary and short on details.[226] On 13 August, for example, the prime minister merely wrote:

> The main question discussed was as to the best means of cutting off the import of food supplies for Germany. Sir E Grey suggested a blockade of the North Sea German ports, and the treatment of food sent in by way of Rotterdam as conditional contraband i.e. liable to seizure when it was destined, directly or indirectly, for the German armies. This raises a number of difficult questions both of law and policy, which will be promptly considered by a cabinet committee.[227]

From this abridged account readers would be forgiven for assuming (as many have) that Grey's suggestion for "a blockade of the North Sea German ports, and the treatment of food sent in by way of Rotterdam as conditional contraband," amounted to a call for a close blockade.[228] But other documents prove this a mistaken interpretation. A memorandum composed later that day by the attorney general, Sir John Simon, makes clear that the scheme proposed was, in fact, "to institute a line of blockade across the North Sea and the Channel"—in other words, a distant blockade.[229] That the attorney general, an avowed pacifist, should have gone to the trouble to contribute a paper on this esoteric subject is intriguing—yet closer scrutiny of Simon's paper makes clear why he did so. It shows that Grey and Churchill presented the cabinet with the controversial Bethell interpretation of the laws of blockade, first articulated back in 1910–1911 by the director of naval intelligence at the time,

Rear-Admiral Sir Alexander Bethell. As explained in Chapter 4, Bethell had argued that ambiguities in the text of the Declaration of London permitted a distant blockade to be defined as "effective" in the legal sense—though he conceded that many international lawyers would disagree. Simon's memorandum advised strongly against such legal acrobatics, but because he did not—could not—show the Bethell interpretation to be wrong, it remained a possible option.[230] Sir Charles Hobhouse, the postmaster general, who took detailed notes of what was said at this meeting, recorded that a lengthy debate then occurred between the various members of the cabinet who were lawyers by profession. Hobhouse's notes further confirm that Grey presented the idea of treating "certain foodstuffs going to Rotterdam as conditional contraband" as a separate—albeit complementary—policy recommendation that entailed "rationing" Dutch imports to their prewar levels.[231] Harcourt agreed Grey had emphasized that "we cannot make contraband of food for the *civil* population of the enemy, but we can make *excessive* food beyond past average, conditional contraband as being intended for the German army."[232] Of course, the idea of restricting Dutch imports had been considered before the war; it is pertinent to note that shortcomings in trade statistics, upon which the rationing idea had foundered in 1913, had not been overcome by August 1914.

From the various unofficial cabinet diaries and private correspondence of the ministers present, it is clear that the debate over economic warfare was exceptionally bad-tempered and punctuated by frequent threats of resignation. Given that it came so soon after the near breakup of the government over the decision to participate in the war at all, it is small wonder that Asquith should have minimized the acrimony in his official record of cabinet proceedings. After Grey and Churchill explained to the other ministers how the Admiralty proposed to throttle the German economy, at least six of the nineteen present—mostly those holding junior portfolios (the "Beagles and Bobtails," as Asquith derisively labeled them)—expressed outrage at the proposed strategy.[233] That Sir Edward Grey was foremost among those pressing for aggressive economic warfare and willing to damn the diplomatic consequences came as a shock to many, including Hobhouse, Pease, and Lord Emmott, the commissioner for works. Emmott in particular, who had only just been admitted to the cabinet, was taken aback at seeing Grey (whom he admired and considered a friend) standing shoulder to shoulder with Churchill (whom he loathed) in pressing this "rather drastic" policy.[234] Hobhouse provides the clearest account of what happened next:

> Then we got onto the subject of Rotterdam as a depot for provisioning Germany. Grey who has never forgiven Germany for attempting to play him is the fiercest of us all to destroy her once and for all. He looks on her as the reckless author of war and its attendant miseries, and wishes to prevent her ever again indulging in the same cruel game. He proposed to institute conditional contraband i.e. that Holland should be entitled to unrestricted entry of the same quantity of supplies as she took from year to year, but that everything over that should be held to be for Germany and should be captured. Haldane thought a case for doing this could be sustained before our prize courts, the PM [Asquith] and [Attorney General Sir John] Simon thought contrary.[235]

Besides Grey, Churchill, and Haldane, the only other minister to show unqualified support for economic warfare was Reginald McKenna, the former First Lord of the Admiralty, currently serving as home secretary. According to Harcourt, the prime minister was nervous that "we may get into trouble with U.S.A. & Holland."[236] David Lloyd George was notably silent.

What, then, did the cabinet decide? As indicated in Asquith's letter to the king dated 13 August, the first step taken was to form an ad hoc cabinet contraband subcommittee to put forward specific recommendations.[237] The committee tactic, as Asquith employed it, was a favored device for siphoning controversy out of the cabinet. Grey, Churchill, McKenna, Lloyd George, and Runciman—though not Simon—met that evening directly after the cabinet session.[238] It may be noted that this list of names almost exactly parallels that given by Asquith several days later to Venetia Stanley as "the men who are really useful in these discussions."[239] Alas, no formal record of the contraband subcommittee's deliberations has survived. But some clues to the direction in which members were thinking may be gleaned from the memorandum they circulated that evening (13 August) directing the formation of a standing interdepartmental committee. This body was known by various names, most commonly the Enemy Supplies Restrictions Committee (ESRC for short), but it was sometimes referred to as the Restrictions of Enemy Supplies Committee, on occasions as the Restrictions Committee, or sometimes just as the Hopwood Committee after its chairman, Sir Francis Hopwood, a senior career civil servant with a superlative reputation, currently assigned to the Admiralty as Additional Civil Lord.

Besides Hopwood, the membership of the ESRC included Captain Richard Webb (head of the Admiralty Trade Division), Cecil Hurst (the Foreign

Office legate), and Paul Ashley (of the Board of Trade). Also appointed were Vice Admiral Edmond Slade (retired) plus two Members of Parliament—Leo Chiozza Money (a financial expert and friend of Lloyd George's) and Alan Burgoyne (best known as the editor of the Naval League annual).[240] Both the MPs were well-known big-navy men. Given the composition of the committee and the fact it sat at the Admiralty (borrowing their clerical staff), it is difficult to avoid the conclusion that the cabinet contraband subcommittee had firmly stacked the deck in favor of the Navy. Although the ESRC possessed no executive powers, within the government it was recognized as the "principal permanent body engaged in considering, from the point of view of policy, the measures adopted to prevent supplies from reaching the enemy."[241] Hopwood's instructions were:

> To examine and watch continually all means or routes by which supplies of food or raw material may reach Germany and Austria; to report weekly all importations or exportations to and from these countries coming to their knowledge; and to recommend by what methods, financial, commercial, diplomatic and military, they may be hampered, restricted, and if possible stopped.[242]

Additionally, the ESRC was specifically charged to prevent "the neutral port of Rotterdam to serve as a base of supplies for the enemy." To achieve these tasks, it had access to the considerable resources of the naval intelligence service. Where specific data were lacking, members were authorized to take whatever measures necessary to obtain it; for instance, on 15 August the ESRC subpoenaed the services of Sir Francis Oppenheimer, the Foreign Office's trade expert (who back in 1909 had written a comprehensive report on German trade), and dispatched him to Rotterdam "for the purpose of watching trade operations there" and gathering statistics.[243] In short, given the powers with which they endowed the ESRC, it seems that the five cabinet ministers on the contraband subcommittee intended to prosecute economic warfare aggressively.

Discussion of economic warfare policy and of the contraband subcommittee's recommendations dominated cabinet proceedings on Friday and Saturday, 14 and 15 August. On Saturday evening, Asquith told the king:

> The principal topic of discussion was again the best means of bringing economic pressure to bear upon Germany by cutting off her supplies of

> imported food. The main difficulty arises from the fact that her principal base of supply is the port of Rotterdam in neutral territory. The whole subject (which had been fully considered by the CID as far back as December 1912) was carefully reviewed both from a legal and strategic point of view.[244]

Thus, according to Asquith, there was no disagreement as to the goal of bringing economic pressure to bear against Germany; the only question concerned the "best means" for doing so. Harcourt's jotted notes supply further details of some of the means considered on the Friday. "The neutral scare about mines in the North Sea is passing away. Sh[oul]d we lay mines ourselves and blow up some neutral ships to deter others [?] or make food to Rotterdam conditional contraband on grounds of greater quantities imported than formerly."[245] Churchill, meanwhile, again proposed simply to declare Rotterdam a base of enemy supplies and impose a blockade. Powerful political and diplomatic objections attended all of these proposed means. Ultimately the cabinet devised a formula whereby the Royal Navy would "establish a blockade, but allow certain ships through our blockade to Rotterdam."[246] Unfortunately, Harcourt apparently missed the next day's meeting. The only detailed record of what was said on 15 August is Asquith's letter to the king, which states that the cabinet "resolved as a first step to invite the Dutch government to come to an agreement to prohibit the export eastward of imported foodstuffs, we on our side allowing the export from GB to Holland of the coal which she needs for her own industries."[247] In other words, in return for access to British coal and other vital goods, the Dutch would be pressed to limit their German trade.

On 17 August, a Monday, the cabinet reassembled at noon. In a letter to Venetia that day, Asquith laconically remarked, "We then resumed the topic (so familiar to you) of the 'strangulation' of Germany."[248] In reporting the latest developments, the prime minister employed an uncharacteristically abbreviated and disjointed style, perhaps reflecting his growing frustration with the failure to settle upon a policy. He wrote:

> The American protest, in the interest of neutral shipping, against our following the German example & laying down mines in the North Sea. As you know, I am all against this provocative & rather barbarous mode of procedure, and I strongly urged the development of the Runciman plan of taking up all the carrying ships we can get, and so diverting the

> trade from Rotterdam. There was a lot of talk about international law & its niceties (in wh. "The Impeccable" [Simon] took quite a good part) and Runciman is going to present us to-morrow with the flesh and blood on his skeleton.[249]

Asquith's apparently cryptic summary in fact contains a great deal of useful information. The first sentence alludes to the ongoing discussion about whether the Royal Navy should lay mines off the Dutch coast "and blow up some neutral ships to deter others."[250] Although "contrary to usage of war," the scheme was technically legal. A week before the Admiralty had distributed pamphlets warning mariners of their intention to lay "secret" minefields.[251] Harcourt understood: "We should warn all *foreign* shipping not to enter [our] minefield. This will make an effective blockade of Rotterdam. We want to keep Norwegian neutral flag from going to Rotterdam."[252] Asquith's letter to Venetia Stanley indicates there were two main objections to the mining plan: first, that several ministers (including the prime minister) thought the plan "barbarous," and second, that the American government had responded to the Admiralty's recent notice to mariners warning of mines with a diplomatic shot across the bow.[253] As an alternative to the mining plan, there was also the "Runciman plan": for the British government to dig deep into its pockets and purchase or charter as many neutral merchantmen as possible in a play to corner the market. Given that so many merchantmen remained idle because of the continuing hiatus in the global trading system (reflected in depressed global freight rates), the idea was not as far-fetched as it might sound. Runciman estimated the gross cost would run to £3 million a month.[254] For diplomatic reasons detailed in the next chapter, this elegant solution turned out to be a policy dead end.

After the cabinet adjourned, Harcourt cornered Asquith and alerted him to mounting unhappiness among the junior members of the government with the embryonic plan for aggressive economic warfare. Over the weekend, several had contacted him to voice their concern at Grey's "truculence" and the intended policy.[255] Besides Harcourt, the especially disaffected included Simon (attorney general), Emmott (commissioner of works), Hobhouse (postmaster general), and several others. These economic warfare moderates were more sensitive than some of their colleagues to moral issues and more punctilious about legalities, believing it "undesirable on general grounds to think of taking steps to starve Germany by preventing neutrals from carrying goods to Holland."[256] The idea that Great Britain should strong-arm a small neutral country such as Holland for "strategic reasons" reeked of hypocrisy. Implementing the proposed action plan, they further argued, seemed "madness" in light of the recent warning from the U.S. government.[257] It must be clearly understood, however, that the anxiety not to provoke America fueled rather than ignited ministerial apprehensions. Over the past few days, moreover, the moderates had already lent their full support to Walter Runciman, the president of the Board of Trade, who was complaining that the Admiralty's proclamation on warlike stores had embargoed practically everything and was seriously hurting British business.

Despite "voluble opposition from Churchill," on 14 August the cabinet authorized the immediate resumption of trade with Norway, Denmark, and Holland.[258] "We must release more commercial goods & materials for export," Harcourt concurred.[259] The next day, Runciman scored a further point off Churchill by obtaining cabinet sanction for the removal of coal and several other items from the controlled warlike exports list.[260] Thus aggressive implementation of economic warfare—whether one dates it from the Admiralty's activation of the war room system on 1 August, the issuing of royal proclamations on 5 August, or the establishment of the ESRC on 13 August—had lasted for a grand total of one day at least or two weeks at most. The government's decision, in effect, to allow the free exportation of coal was remarkable and caused questions to be asked in the House of Commons.[261]

Over the next few days the restrictions on British traders (and hence the effectiveness of economic warfare) were further diluted—showing, incidentally, that the moderate faction must have been considerably larger than the four or five names listed above. On 18 August, Harcourt proudly recorded that he had obtained cabinet sanction "to release practically all Dominion & Colonial exports for resumption of trade with neutrals."[262] A day later, the Board of Trade announced that the government had withdrawn the onerous requirement that applications for permits to export items on the prohibited list must be accompanied by a triple-value bond.[263] On 19 August the cabinet authorized yet further concessions.[264] Whereas the royal proclamation issued on the first day of the war had prohibited the exportation of "victual of all sorts which may be used as food for men,"[265] the cabinet decreed that henceforth "the proclamation permitting the capture of foodstuffs should be amended so as to include only wheat, flour, sugar, condensed milk, live animals intended for food, dairy produce, fodder and oats."[266] Even these reduced restrictions, however, were more than some ministers could stomach. That night an unhappy Alfred Emmott drafted a memorandum questioning the necessity for any interference with neutral trade when "the actual number of ships per Diem going in to Rotterdam now is (I am told) 7 against an average of 40 before the war."[267] These numbers, incidentally, were accurate.[268] Emmott dreaded "losing the sympathy of neutral nations which has hitherto been with us because we have gone into this war in defence of a small nation unfairly attacked."[269]

Emmott's lingering misgivings aside, by the end of the cabinet meeting on 19 August ministerial opinion had at last begun to coalesce. There was broad albeit subdued agreement that Rotterdam must be closed to German trade. With policy at last established, the contraband subcommittee met later that afternoon to hammer out the text of the long-awaited order-in-council to be issued for the benefit of the prize court and foreign governments.[270] It is important to understand that an order-in-council was not, as some historians have assumed, a statement of government policy; rather, it was a legal document supposed to reflect government policy.[271] The meeting was presented with a working draft composed by Sir John Simon, Crowe, and Hurst. This was actually the second or possibly third redaction. The original, submitted five days earlier, had been more or less a reiteration of the Declaration of London and had been summarily rejected by the Admiralty because it barred them from employing the doctrine of continuous voyage to interdict neutral shipping bound for neutral Rotterdam. Cecil Hurst had subsequently advised that the only way to give the Admiralty this sanction while allowing the British government to remain at least within sight of international law was either to reclassify food as absolute contraband or to repudiate those articles in the Declaration of London that limited the application of the doctrine of continuous voyage. After W. E. Davidson, the senior legate at the Foreign Office, counseled that declaring food as absolute contraband was out of the question, Hurst duly amended the order-in-council "so as not to tie the hands of the Admiralty over continuous voyage for conditional contraband."[272] This was the pedigree of the document presented to the cabinet subcommittee.

Minutes appended to the order-in-council by various lawyers make abundantly clear that the document's primary function was to afford the British government a legal rationalization—a pretext—to justify the Royal Navy's interdiction of German supplies through Rotterdam. Not everyone at the Admiralty was happy with this legal legerdemain. After reading the draft, Admiral Slade commented, "This appears to be satisfactory but practically it is almost impossible to apply it [continuous voyage] as the courts will never condemn, except on the clearest evidence, which is always very difficult to obtain."[273] Vice Admiral Doveton Sturdee, the new chief of the naval War Staff, echoed Slade's doubts "as to the political expediency of adopting an attitude the practical efficacy of which is in my opinion very doubtful, and which I think is just as sure to raise trouble with neutrals."[274] Although these objections had some validity, they missed the point. Churchill chided the two admirals for failing to see the big picture: "The vital importance of preventing Rotterdam from becoming effectually a base for the enemies supplies must not be overlooked."[275] The Foreign Office proposal to invoke the doctrine of continuous voyage offered the best way through the legal minefield ahead—though the path indicated was by no means safe.

The minutes of the meeting of the cabinet contraband subcommittee on 19 August confirm that the essential policy intention was that "all possible steps should be taken to prevent foodstuffs in particular from being imported into Germany in neutral vessels whether directly or through Dutch ports."[276] When it was belatedly pointed out that food remained classed as "conditional contraband" and that the "doctrine of continuous voyage" could only be invoked against items consigned to an enemy government or their armed forces (i.e., not necessarily against food), Reginald McKenna interjected with the assertion that "reliable reports" indicated the German government had assumed control over the distribution of food, and therefore the differentiation between military and civilian cargoes need not apply.[277] It is impossible not to be suspicious of McKenna's claim when one remembers his prewar remark to Hankey that "some pretext would be found for our acting contrary to all the provisions of the Declaration of Paris and the Declaration of London."[278] Yet no one present demanded evidence for this assertion—lending further credence to the view that the objective of the meeting was to devise a convenient pretext.[279] Article 5 of the draft order-in-council was duly amended. So confident were the ministerial members of the subcommittee that their cabinet colleagues would approve their draft document in the morning that they commanded that "H.M. Ships should be *at once* instructed to act in accordance with Article 5."[280] That evening, the Admiralty signaled their cruisers to stop and seize all German-consigned foodstuffs bound for Rotterdam "on the presumption they are destined for the use of the armed forces or of a Government department of the enemy state."[281]

In fact, belying the subcommittee's expectation of easy victory, the cabinet approved publication of the document only after "a protracted discussion" and further revisions to the text.[282] On 20 August, the prime minister informed the king that the cabinet agreed "to treat as conditional contraband,

and liable to seizure, food consigned through Dutch ports to a German destination."[283] The order-in-council was duly published in a special supplement to the *London Gazette*.[284] What Asquith neglected to mention, however, was that in order to assuage Liberal consciences, his cabinet had considerably narrowed the definition of what constituted "food."[285] He also avoided reference to the decision to placate British businessmen by relaxing controls over British exports. Together these two steps marked a further retreat from economic warfare. Churchill protested mightily, but to no avail. "The last 3 or 4 meetings have been occupied by consideration of the position of neutrals," Hobhouse noted in his diary on 21 August 1914, "Churchill jumping about from consideration to consideration, 'backing and filling' without rhyme or reason, but with incessant talk."[286] Pease agreed that the First Lord was "voluble and assertive but not convincing or clear."[287] Perhaps, however, ministers simply did not want to hear. The cabinet remained inherently fragile and worries over the economy remained strong. "When the government expressed their desire not to starve the civil population" of Germany, Hankey pointedly reminded Asquith several months later, after the consequences of the cabinet's decision to dilute economic warfare had become glaringly apparent, "it was hoped that the war would not be prolonged."[288]

"Such Like Technicalities"

Though Asquith succeeded in preserving the unity of his cabinet, he achieved less success in terms of practical policy. Although the cabinet had undertaken the whole series of meetings beginning on 13 August for the express purpose of clarifying the government's policy on economic warfare, the order-in-council approved on 20 August still did not clearly explain the government's intentions. For some reason, the prime minister neglected to issue clarifying instructions to the various departments assigned a role in the implementation of economic warfare. Each minister and each department were left free to draw their own conclusions as to what should be done and act accordingly. Officials at the Foreign Office, for instance, interpreted the order-in-council as a victory for moderation. They chose to believe the cabinet had compelled the Admiralty to abide by the Declaration of London, attaching little importance to the exceptions that had been sanctioned.[289] The Admiralty drew exactly the opposite conclusion, believing that the exceptions eviscerated the treaty. The resultant confusion is illustrated in a complaint from Crowe to Grey dated 21 August:

> We are receiving complaints and representations all round as to our arbitrary interference with the trade to Rotterdam. Our difficulty is dealing with these complaints is that we really do not know what the decisions of the gov't in this matter are and on what ground any such decisions are based or should be defended. Nor do we exactly know what action is being actually taken and by what authorities, whether in pursuance to a gov't decision or of some recommendation of one of the numerous committees, or without any reference to any superior authority at all. I am afraid the situation is getting rather chaotic for want of some clear indications of our policy and authorized line of action.[290]

The previous morning the Dutch ambassador had stormed in to see Crowe and "expressed himself with great indignation at the attitude adopted by HM Gov't on the question of foodstuffs. He said we had absolutely no right to hold up consignments of foodstuffs destined for Rotterdam."[291] He further claimed that in consequence his country stood on the brink of famine. "It is not to be wondered at that the Dutch gov are getting very anxious," Cecil Hurst sympathized. Other minutes appended to the file leave no doubt that most Foreign Office staff disapproved of what came to be termed the "Rotterdam policy."

Twenty-four hours later, however, the Foreign Office received an urgent telegram from the British minister in Holland that presented a very different picture of the Dutch situation. Sir Alan Johnstone reported that large quantities of Dutch-grown food were passing from Rotterdam up the Rhine in flagrant breach of the promise to prohibit the export of food. He had already confronted the local authorities about this, only to be told that the prohibition did not apply to goods "in transit."[292] While the Dutch were prepared to embargo items on the British list of prohibited exports, such as grain, they were unwilling to restrict foodstuffs that were not, such as potatoes. This news had significant implications because the policy hammered out within the cabinet over the previous eight days had been predicated upon Grey's assurances that in return for the resumption of British coal exports, the Dutch had already pledged to ban the reexport of all food to Germany. In issuing this assurance, it emerges, Grey had disregarded several warnings from embassy staff in Holland that the local situation was not as the Dutch ambassador in London represented.[293] As early as 12 August, the British naval attaché at The Hague had sent home a reminder that under the terms of the 1831 Rhine Convention, cargoes could be declared "in transit" for Germany after being discharged at Rotterdam.[294] He intended to warn the Royal Navy that cargo allowed to pass through the cruiser cordon might not necessarily be destined for Dutch consumption. The Foreign Office neglected to pass this dispatch on to the Admiralty until 20 August. "If they [the rules of capture] stand in the present form," whereupon exclaimed Greene, "food stuffs for Germany may slip through Holland, because they may be consigned to Rotterdam and THERE declared in transit."[295] It is hard to believe that the Dutch ambassador to Great Britain was not aware of this loophole. Holland's ambassador in Germany certainly knew of it, for on the eve of war he had assured the German foreign minister that Holland would honor the terms of the Rhine Convention and place no restrictions on German transit trade.[296]

The Foreign Office response to this first test of British determination to uphold the Rotterdam policy was, predictably, to seek a negotiated solution with the Dutch government. By contrast, the Admiralty (and the French authorities) demanded a more forceful and immediate reaction to what they regarded as unmistakable bad faith. "It is difficult to understand why they [the Dutch] are [so] short of grain," Churchill archly commented to Grey on 23 August. "The harvest has just been gathered, and judging by other countries it should be a good one. They ought, therefore, to be in possession of the whole home-grown supply for the year. If they are not it can only be because they have sold their harvest to the Germans."[297] Churchill's shrewd supposition was largely correct.[298] Forty-eight hours later, having still heard nothing from Grey as to how the diplomats intended to stem the leakage up the Rhine from Rotterdam, the Admiralty summarily informed the Foreign Office that they had instructed their cruisers to treat all contraband and conditional contraband items consigned to Dutch ports as intended for Germany. Their Lordships "presume[d] that the Dutch government will, in due course, become aware of this change in procedure."[299] New war orders were at once distributed to flag officers: "Destination to Germany may be presumed in the case of all foodstuffs consigned to Rotterdam, unless they are covered by a guarantee from the Dutch government that neither they nor their equivalent will be exported from the country."[300] In the space of one week the Royal Navy took fifty-two neutral steamers.[301]

Sir Edward Grey initially acquiesced to the wishes of the Admiralty. Overruling his advisors, who almost to a man were appalled at the illegality of the Admiralty action (and evidently less appalled at Holland's flagrant betrayal of its promises to Britain), he notified the Dutch government that until all food exports to Germany were stopped, "we must treat as suspect and capture all foodstuffs consigned to Rotterdam."[302] The next day, however, 26 August, Grey seemingly had a change of heart and appended his signature to a letter drafted by Crowe informing the Admiralty that the Foreign Office wished to adhere more closely to the principles enshrined in the Declaration of London.[303] Independent confirmation from Sir Francis Oppenheimer that the Dutch food prohibition was indeed largely ineffective arrived too late to change Grey's volte-face.[304] With both departments refusing to back down, the issue was referred to the prime minister for adjudication.

Precisely what the prime minister thought about this departmental squabble is difficult to ascertain because for once he did not confide the details to Venetia Stanley. Several days before, he had told her that he was tired of discussing "coal & contraband & continuous voyages & such like technicalities."[305] So too, apparently, were the rest of the cabinet ministers.[306] For want of evidence, therefore, we are compelled to infer the prime minister's opinions from his subsequent actions. This is not easy to do, for the picture is contradictory and confusing.

Asquith's first move, on 26 August, was to establish a blockade steering committee to be headed by Reginald McKenna and assisted by Walter Runciman.[307] The supposed function of the Coordinating Committee on Trade and Supplies, to give it its correct title, was to oversee "the various committees which are dealing with food supplies, diversion of ships and cargoes, and cognate topics."[308] That evening, McKenna produced a memorandum intended for circulation to everyone in official circles that spelled out government policy and proper department action. This document stated in unequivocal language that the foundation of government policy was to prevent "the transport of foodstuffs to Germany through neutral ports."[309] In quoting directly from the new instructions recently issued to naval officers, furthermore, he effectively expressed official approval for the Admiralty's action. This act also served to clarify for the other departments exactly what the Royal Navy hoped to achieve.

> The conditions prevailing at Rotterdam necessitate a different rule for vessels on their way for that port. Destination to Germany may be presumed in case of all foodstuffs consigned to Rotterdam, unless they are covered by a guarantee from the Dutch government that *neither they nor their equivalent will be exported from the country.* Where no such guarantee is found on board, the vessel should be detained and the circumstances reported without delay.[310]

The McKenna memorandum went on to define the procedures then to be followed. Once the ship reached an English port, customs officers would examine its cargo and send a report to London. Next, the Foreign Office would contact the Dutch government to ascertain if the cargo was guaranteed or if it wished to issue a guarantee, in which case the ship and her cargo would be released. If not, the ship and her cargo would be placed in prize court and responsibility for obtaining condemnation handed over to the procurator general (the Treasury lawyer responsible for prosecutions before the prize court). Nothing could have been clearer. So impressed was the Board of Customs and Excise with this model of precision and lucidity that it suggested copies be handed to foreign governments in order that they too might better understand British policy, but when presented with this sensible idea the Foreign Office unsurprisingly demurred; after all, Asquith and the cabinet had deliberately avoided precision and lucidity in the order-in-council of 20 August because their disagreements over policy ran too deep to achieve such goals, and McKenna's memorandum was effectively an end run around the cabinet's agreement to disagree.[311] The procurator general, John Paget Mellor, who had been a member of the prewar Desart Committee, hinted at deeper concerns. He warned that detaining neutral merchantmen for carrying conditional contraband was all very well, but still each case would have to be taken before the prize court. To obtain condemnation, he reminded them, "the Crown must prove its case as to the [German] government control of foodstuffs."[312]

Asquith's decision to hand control of the Coordinating Committee on Trade and Supplies to McKenna, one of the cabinet's strongest supporters of economic warfare, suggests that he was leaning in the direction of aggressive economic warfare, but two days later, he appointed Sir John Simon, one of the cabinet's fiercest critics of economic warfare, as chairman of the Privy Council's Trading with the Enemy committee, which was charged with issuing special exemption licenses to merchants who wished to export prohibited goods or contraband items. This was another committee that had been anticipated before the war by Lord Desart. By Treasury minute dated 28 August 1914, the prime minister conferred upon Simon's committee the unreserved authority to modify the list of prohibited exports, grant special exemption licenses, and issue or refuse licenses to firms manufacturing items made from strategic commodities. In effect, Asquith handed to Simon control of the regulatory apparatus set up to ensure that British goods did not reach the enemy.[313] Perhaps he adjudged this necessary to counterbalance the influence of McKenna.

In establishing two separate committees to oversee the enforcement of economic warfare policy and appointing two different chairmen with totally different outlooks, Asquith certainly appears to have been less interested in setting up an effective system of administration than he was in maintaining peace within his cabinet. Once again, Asquith may have preserved the delicate balance of cabinet-tolerated tension, but in terms of practical policy he had failed to tackle the diametrically different viewpoints held by the Admiralty and the Foreign Office, as reflected in their disagreement over how to resolve the problem of Dutch reexports via the Rhine. The conflicting viewpoints, the tendency to act unilaterally and without consultation, and the habit of treating the cabinet as a court of appeal set the pattern of departmental relationships on economic warfare issues for at least the next twelve months. Over the next few weeks, further complicating factors would emerge. These will be the subject of the next chapter.

6

The Problem with Americans

[Sir Eyre] Crowe tells me [the] Americans have been most disappointing: while they were neutral they prevented our effective blockade; now they talk & promise & *do* much less. [The] Americans were so angry at our blockade that they nearly came in against us. If they had left us a free hand the war might be over by now.

SIR FRANCIS OPPENHEIMER, March 1918

On 24 August 1914, confused reports began trickling across the Channel suggesting that the British Expeditionary Force advancing into Belgium had encountered a vastly stronger German army near the town of Mons and was now in headlong retreat.[1] Since midnight nothing had been heard, and catastrophe was feared. Harcourt noted it was "a grim cabinet" that day.[2] Confirmation the following morning that the French army was also falling back in disorder prompted Asquith to remark acerbicly that "the French plan of campaign has been badly bungled."[3] In the cabinet, Kitchener ominously forecast that "unless the situation improves greatly in 24 hours it will be very serious: we are going through 1870 again."[4] There was some discussion of evacuating the BEF through the port of Dunkirk, but lack of information inhibited decision making.[5] "At the moment we are in impenetrable fog as to what is happening," Emmott recorded in his diary.[6] Over the next several days, under siege from anxious friends and relatives demanding news of loved ones, cabinet ministers became frustrated at the lack of information, and concerned that Field Marshal Sir John French, commanding the BEF, "has lost his nerve."[7] Proclaiming himself "mystified and perturbed," on 1 September Asquith reprimanded the War Office for failing to keep the cabinet "properly informed."[8] The next day, Lord Kitchener, the Secretary of

State for War, crossed the Channel to British army headquarters on a fact-finding mission.[9] His report to ministers upon his return left them feeling little the wiser.

Traditional historical accounts argue that Britain's war policy was driven increasingly by concern for the military situation on the Continent. According to this interpretation, every step the German army advanced closer to Paris encouraged the cabinet to back away from its original maritime strategy and look for military solutions. According to the soldiers, victory depended upon just two conditions. First, France must survive Germany's attempt to deliver a knockout blow during the opening weeks of the war. Second, the French army must remain active on the western front in order to support the inexorable "Russian steamroller" rumbling in from the east. By mid-September the first condition apparently had been met. The French army halted the German advance at the Battle of the Marne (5–9 September) and then pushed them backward. Euphoria over the "Miracle of the Marne" was tempered, however, by concern for the Russians. After their ally suffered a pair of disastrous defeats at Tannenberg (25–30 August) and Masurian Lakes (9–14 September), members of the cabinet (along with everyone else) were disquieted to learn that "Russian steamrollers are designed to go quickly into reverse."[10] This setback notwithstanding, British confidence in the potential of the tsarist war machine to crush Germany remained intact. The cabinet accepted that the war would not be over by Christmas; for the next six months Britain must help buttress the French on the western front in order to buy the Russians time to refit before resuming their advance on Berlin. In his memoirs, Winston Churchill recalled that ministers accepted: "Such a conflict could not be ended on the sea or by sea power alone. It could be ended only by great battles on the continent."[11] But did this view accurately reflect majority cabinet opinion?

The recent trend in recent military scholarship has been to suggest that Britain's gravitation toward land operations in France was even more pronounced than previously allowed. Central to this argument is a revised historical assessment of Field Marshal Horatio Herbert Kitchener, who had been appointed secretary of state for war in August 1914 and remained in this post until his death in mid-1916. The earliest histories of the First World War, based largely upon the various postwar memoirs written by ministers who worked alongside him, were viciously critical of Kitchener's performance. While they conceded the field marshal's foresight in anticipating a long war, seen as "unlikely if not incredible" by the rest of the cabinet, he was condemned for botching Britain's military mobilization by failing to secure adequate munitions for his New Armies.[12] More recent scholars have modified this mostly negative appraisal of Kitchener's performance, crediting him with a broad strategic outlook focused upon the need to manage the Allied coalition.[13] To some extent a refurbishment of Kitchener's reputation is merited. Certainly the field marshal was quicker than most of his military and political contemporaries to grasp the reality of the situation in 1914.[14] But to portray Kitchener as a sage and visionary strategist, to suggest that he impressed his vision upon the bewildered cabinet—reflected in the building of the New Armies and thereby transforming the basis of British grand strategy—imposes a coherence upon events that is simply not supported by the documentary record.[15] In cabinet meetings Kitchener "never disclosed how or by what process of reasoning he made this forecast of the length of the war" or lucidly articulated his strategic vision.[16] Once asked by Hankey why he refused to enlighten the political executive, Kitchener reputedly quipped, "If they would only all divorce their wives I will tell them everything!"[17]

Yet Kitchener could hardly have formulated any definite strategic ideas until he possessed an accurate estimation of the resources at his disposal. At his first cabinet meeting, 6 August, he spoke of raising 100,000 extra troops.[18] On 24 August 1914, Asquith told Venetia Stanley that "Kitchener outlined at the Cabinet today his plans, which if they come off, will give us some 600,000 or 700,000 men by April in next year."[19] Several days later Kitchener asked permission to issue a second appeal for volunteers.[20] The prime minister was skeptical but acquiesced. Exceeding all expectations, during the first week of September alone 174,901 men enlisted in the army. On 1 September, an astounded Asquith remarked to Miss Stanley that the enthusiasm for military service was running so high that "it is becoming a question whether we should not try for the moment to damp it down."[21] Two days later the prime minister recounted that ministers had agreed to maintain recruitment "while the wave of enthusiasm is running high."[22] The cabinet's motives in doing so, however, were not necessarily to strengthen the Continental commitment: ministers, or some ministers, seem to have been as interested in addressing domestic economic and political concerns by alleviating unemployment and the attendant risk of civil unrest as in strategic deployments. The lack of design and purpose behind the military expansion is also reflected in the contradictory statements Kitchener made as to the eventual size of the force he was raising.[23] On 31 August, for instance, he talked about an army 750,000 strong (approximately thirty divisions). Eight days later the calculated number of divisions available "in 6 months time" had swelled to forty-six; days later the number stood at fifty.[24]

On 5 September 1914, the prime minister expressed doubts as to whether sufficient munitions of war could be procured from domestic sources to equip so many soldiers within the intended time frame.[25] He was not the only one. Even Kitchener, in rare moments of candor, was heard worrying about the "dearth of ammunition."[26] On 1 October 1914, Edwin Montagu, the financial secretary to the Treasury who had previously served as Asquith's parliamentary private secretary, was moved to warn, apparently not for the first time, that "you are, I think, running into a most awful morass with regard to the War Office."[27] Montagu was disturbed by the absence of direction over military procurement. The field marshal appeared to lack the slightest conception of the economic constraints or the financial consequences of his actions. "He believes that if he bangs the table and asks for anything from a blanket to a howitzer, it can be materialized out of thin air." But of even greater concern to Montagu was that "the Treasury has completely lost financial control of the War Office, and they state frankly that for many projects for which Treasury sanction is required, they have no time to get that sanction, and they refuse to organize any method by which they can get that sanction."[28]

In insisting the War Office was "falling wholly short of its enormous task" to equip the army being raised, Montagu clearly believed his own department was better suited to manage such vast expenditures.[29] He voiced no concern at the long-term fiscal and economic consequences of such a large increase in the size of the army.[30] Nor did he warn that Kitchener's military policy might be leading the country down a hazardous economic path. Montagu's objection was simply to waste caused by mismanagement and lax bureaucratic oversight.

Unmoved, the prime minister rejected Montagu's suggestion, a decision that Montagu attributed to Asquith's fear of being seen as fettering the service departments in the conduct of the war. He believed that Asquith had appointed Kitchener to the War Office for essentially political reasons, to shield the Liberal government from criticism in the event of military catastrophe.[31] This suspicion was likely correct; that said, Montagu was seemingly unaware (possibly having been misled by Lloyd George, who held a jaundiced view of the field marshal) that at this time the majority of the cabinet possessed great faith in Kitchener, believing him to be "generally right about the war."[32] "My own opinion of K's capacity increases daily," the prime minister told Venetia Stanley on 3 November 1914.[33]

As the weeks passed, economic confidence returned and fear of socioeconomic upheaval subsided, with the result that ministerial fiscal attitudes swung from pessimism to complacency. By the second week of September, the government was in possession of figures indicating that unemployment had risen far less than first feared, by just half a million, to about 6 percent of the insured workforce—though in the cotton industry this figure was estimated to be as high as 24 percent.[34] Continued belief in the likelihood of a relatively short war induced Lloyd George to reject expert advice to raise taxes to pay for the war, which was already costing the Treasury £1.5 million *per day*, opting instead to borrow through the issuance of Treasury bills.[35] In so doing the chancellor disregarded warnings that this method of finance was highly inflationary, believing that the war "could not possibly last beyond next autumn."[36]

Within the cabinet and government circles, the chimera of a relatively short war persisted. Ministers, probably the majority, clung to the belief that Kitchener was being unduly pessimistic in his warnings to the contrary. "I cannot even now believe that this war will be a matter of years," Alfred Emmott confided in his diary on 1 December 1914, "the waste is too heavy."[37] To a lesser or greater degree, the Treasury, the Foreign Office, the Board of Trade, and even the Admiralty still operated under the assumption of a short war. This was reflected not only in policy decisions but also in optimistic statements made by senior civil servants justifying inaction. Typical is the minute by the Foreign Office official arguing that iron ore intended for Germany should not be treated as contraband of war: "We may hope that the war will be over long before the iron ore can go through the various processes to convert it into an 'armament.' "[38] Despite acquiescence in the expansion of the army, there is no evidence—quite the contrary—that before the end of 1914 the British leadership adapted its strategic assumptions to the possibility that the war might last beyond one more campaigning season. Indeed, it would be more plausible—but facile—to argue that the cabinet possessed no coherent strategy. The War Office was recruiting as many soldiers as it could without regard for the financial or economic consequences; the Treasury was preoccupied by managing the ongoing financial crisis and trying to resurrect global trade; the Admiralty was still trying to implement its economic warfare policy over the mounting objections of the Foreign Office; increasingly the Board of Trade, Colonial Office, and Board of Agriculture asserted the necessity of allowing trade to reestablish itself and business to resume as usual. Each department myopically focused upon the problems immediately before it—precisely the situation that the Committee of Imperial Defence had been set up before the war to prevent.

The American Problem

As we saw in the last chapter, one of the cabinet's chief concerns during the acrimonious debate over how aggressively to prosecute economic warfare had been growing signs of hostility to the measures introduced from across the Atlantic. Sir Edward Grey insisted that the United States must be handled with care. Detained merchantmen were categorized under three heads: German vessels, those that had sailed from a U.S. port, and all others.[39] An Admiralty order to the fleet dated 17 August emphasized that "great care is to be taken in the diversion of neutral ships with neutral cargoes" because "it is of prime importance to keep the United States of America as a friendly neutral."[40] Furthermore, the day after the publication of the 20 August order-in-council, which authorized the Royal Navy to stop all cargoes bound for Rotterdam that were presumed to be intended for Germany, Grey instructed the British chargé d'affaires in Washington to assure the American authorities "we would see that they did not lose by the diversion."[41]

On 28 August, Grey met with the American ambassador, Walter Page, and expanded upon his promise, telling him that Great Britain would purchase rather than confiscate conditional contraband originating from the United States.[42] Recounting the meeting to his own officials, Grey explained, "In the case of what I called comparatively innocent contraband, such as foodstuffs, I thought it probable that we would be willing to let these cargoes be sold, and not confiscated, so that the exporters should not lose."[43] The foreign secretary was slow to inform the Admiralty of his promise to Page, and Admiral Sir John Jellicoe, the fleet commander, did not learn of it until four weeks later.[44] Whether Grey's failure to consult with the other interested parties (especially Reginald McKenna's Coordinating Committee on Trade and Supplies) was attributable to error, arrogance, or ignorance is impossible to say, but it was indicative of the prevailing Foreign Office attitude. Grey's concession was tantamount to guaranteeing American contraband cargoes against capture by the Royal Navy. This effectively placed American exporters in a win-win situation: either their goods reached Germany and were sold at premium prices, or, if the ships were stopped by the British, they would gain the consolation prize of being purchased at full London market value. But this was not all Grey promised.

As already explained, the keystone in the Admiralty's plan for economic warfare was to exploit Britain's dominance of merchant shipping. By royal proclamation issued on 5 August, the government had asserted its right to dictate the actions of merchantmen flying the red ensign. Historians have calculated that in 1914 Britain controlled approximately 45 percent of the world merchant fleet.[45] Though impressive, this percentage does not fully convey British strength. First, it is computed from figures based upon gross world tonnages, which include all steam vessels of 100 gross register tons (GRT) and upward. The vast majority of merchantmen engaged in the oceanic transportation of bulk commodities at this time were of 3,000 GRT and upward.[46] Although smaller vessels could engage in intercontinental trade, and some did, these were generally utilized in coastal trade or operated on inland waterways (such as the Rhine and the Mississippi). Second, in using gross tonnage figures scholars ought to set aside the 2.2 million GRT of shipping confined to the North American Great Lakes. The gross figures also include the merchant fleets of Austria and Germany, which had been essentially confined to port since the beginning of the war—indeed, many of these had been captured and thus ought be added to the British total, though to do so would be problematic (because of delays in prize court rulings) and anyway is not necessary for our purposes. A strong case can also be made for setting aside the tonnage normally confined to the Pacific—for instance, the Japanese merchant marine (1.7 million GRT), which in any case was Allied.[47] Taking these factors into consideration, the relative size of the Britain merchant marine in August 1914 was considerably greater than the generally quoted figures indicate. Instead of 45 percent, an estimate of 55 percent seems more realistic.

In fact, we can be still more precise. If we measure the relative strengths of the world's merchant fleet using numbers of oceangoing merchantmen (defined as vessels of 3,000 GRT and upward) rather than employing crude gross tonnages, then the British monopoly becomes even more pronounced. In 1914, there were approximately 4,800 merchantmen afloat of this size. Of these, about 600 were German or Austrian and thus unavailable. Of the remaining 4,000-odd, approximately three-quarters—3,000—were registered to British companies. Another couple of hundred flew the French flag. Contrary to popular impression, the United States was not "by far the largest neutral shipper" at the beginning of the First World War.[48] The French,

The World Oceangoing Merchant Fleet in 1915

Flag	10,000 GRT*	7,000–10,000 GRT	5,000–7,000 GRT	4,000–5,000 GRT	3,000–4,000 GRT	Total
British	140	280	558	933	1,152	3,063
American	14	23	104	67	97	305
French	16	19	86	48	59	228
Japanese	8	15	55	41	106	225
Italian	3	19	35	52	102	211
Dutch	8	19	61	30	71	189
Norwegian	2	5	20	47	42	116
German	42	71	159	150	122	544
Total	233	451	1,078	1,368	1,751	4,881

*Merchant vessels displacing more than 3,000 gross register tons (GRT).

Source: U.S. Department of Commerce, *Annual Report of the Commissioner of Navigation to the Secretary of Commerce for the Fiscal Year Ended June 30, 1915* (Washington, DC: Government Printing Office, 1915), 8.

Japanese and Italian fleets were larger. In June 1914, the U.S. merchant marine possessed just over 200 vessels displacing more than 3,000 GRT. Of these, just fifteen, aggregating 150,000 GRT, plied the Atlantic, and nine of those were passenger liners.[49] Other sources show that before the war, U.S.-flagged vessels carried fewer than one in ten cargoes originating from the United States; British vessels carried six in ten.[50] Official figures published by the U.S. Department of Commerce show that during the fiscal year ending June 1914, U.S.-registered merchantmen had transported just 11.4 percent of all U.S. imports (by value—most within the Caribbean) and 8.3 percent of her exports.[51] In August 1914, the four principal neutral nations bordering the Atlantic (United States, Holland, Sweden, and Norway) could together muster 600 oceangoing cargo vessels, as defined above—or roughly 15 percent of the world fleet.[52] Even this figure is obviously too high because it assumes that Holland abandoned her considerable colonial trade with Southeast Asia and that no U.S. vessels remained in the Pacific. But, for the sake of argument, let us use this inflated number.

Tallying the numbers above, we can see that Britain and the Allies controlled not 45 percent, nor 55 percent, but closer to 80 percent of the available transatlantic cargo vessels and thus were in a commensurately stronger position to exert control over the flow of goods across the Atlantic. Additionally, British dominated world shipbuilding. In 1914, British yards launched more than 60 percent of all new merchant vessels, and after the outbreak of war the sale of new merchantmen required a special export license.[53] In the last year of peace, Britain launched 1.9 million GRT of new merchant ships (the average size was 4,000 GRT).[54] Operating at full capacity in 1915, the U.S. shipbuilding industry turned out 200,000 GRT of new ships, barely one-ninth of British production. The other nations built even less. In sum, as the Admiralty had long maintained, neutral powers had no obvious and immediate alternative source of ships.

One of the key assumptions underpinning Admiralty war plans to control transatlantic traffic was that the German merchant fleet would be either captured or confined to port for the duration. In 1914, the German merchant register was the second-largest in the world; Germany possessed more vessels than the third- and fourth-ranked fleets combined. At the beginning of August 1914, when war appeared imminent, all German merchant vessels at sea ran for home or to the nearest neutral port in order to avoid capture. Approximately 350 vessels that might be termed first-class oceangoing bulk cargo vessels (representing 1.3 million GRT) ended up in U.S. ports, as did a number of passenger liners and smaller ships.[55] To make sure they remained bottled up, the Royal Navy maintained highly visible cruiser patrols hovering on the edge of U.S. territorial waters. German shipping lines with numerous vessels stuck in foreign ports were obliged to pay substantial sums (in foreign currency) for berthing space and maintenance in American ports. The estimated cost to Norddeutscher Lloyd alone was on the order of $50,000 per day. These fees were paid from loans issued by American banks using the vessels themselves as collateral.[56]

Unwilling to sustain this financial hemorrhage, German steamship companies tried to cut their losses by selling their vessels to anyone who wanted them. Before the war was one week old, both Norddeutscher Lloyd and Hamburg-Amerikanische Packetfahrt-Actien-Gesellschaft (HAPAG) opened negotiations with potential buyers in at least four different countries. This was a logical course of action—but it was also illegal. Under the Declaration of London, merchantmen of belligerents were prohibited from switching flags "in order to evade the consequences to which an enemy vessel, as such, is exposed." There existed an absolute presumption that such transfers were void if the transfer had been made during a voyage or in a blockaded port.[57] In fact, when the Declaration of London was being drafted back in 1909, the situation that occurred in 1914 had been considered and the conference had agreed the governing intention behind Article 56 was "to prohibit the otherwise bona fide transfer of a belligerent vessel to a neutral flag in a case where such vessel finds herself shut up in a neutral port from which she has no chance of escaping under the belligerent flag."[58] Throughout the war, the British Admiralty never tired of reminding everyone that Germany had subscribed to this interpretation, which was printed as clause 13 in the German naval prize manual.[59] Even if the Declaration of London was set aside, switching flags after the commencement of hostilities remained illegal under the customary law of several countries. French and Russian prize law refused to recognize such a switch under any circumstances. British and U.S. law was equivocal. Under certain circumstances reflagging was permissible—but those circumstances did not apply to the cases in 1914.[60]

The first indication received in London that German companies intended to sell rather than lay up their vessels was a discreet enquiry from the Chilean embassy, on 8 August 1914, for a clarification of Britain's attitude on this point of law.[61] As a potential buyer, the Chilean government, not surprisingly, was leery about paying cash to buy secondhand German merchantmen that apparently could be confiscated by any passing British cruiser. Without consulting either the Admiralty or the Board of Trade, and plainly without any thought of the consequences, Grey directed the Foreign Office to waive British rights and assure the Chilean government that the twenty or so German (HAPAG) vessels they wished to purchase would be immune from capture.[62] Four days later, the Foreign Office permitted three German vessels to be transferred to the Spanish flag.[63] More vessels switched to the Swedish registry. The Admiralty did not learn of these Foreign Office dealings until 13 August, after Grey happened to mention it to Churchill during a cabinet meeting. The Admiralty were formally notified the next day. Churchill begged Grey to rescind his instructions, but the damage had already been done.[64] Although Grey's concessions thus far involved just a handful of ships, he had set a precedent.[65] On 11 August 1914, the awful consequences became apparent: British intelligence intercepted a cable from the State Department in Washington (sent en clair) to the American legation in Denmark revealing clandestine negotiations to broker more than one million GRT of German ships presently confined in various U.S. ports between Boston and New Orleans.[66]

Since the beginning of the war, the U.S. government under President Woodrow Wilson had been quietly shepherding a bill through Congress to repeal a law that prevented foreign-built merchantmen from being added to the U.S. merchant marine register.[67] This had been enacted at the end of the Civil War, apparently as a reprisal against shipowners who had reflagged their vessels at the outbreak of that conflict.[68] The bill was formally sponsored by Representative Oscar Underwood of Alabama, the House majority leader. In seeking to drum up support for this initiative, President Wilson told a confidential gathering of congressional leaders that America must find ships or see her harvests "waste in the warehouses" if not "rot in the fields."[69] The president expended considerable political capital to force through the bill (hereafter referred to as the registry law). Administration spokesmen assured Congress there would be no diplomatic difficulties and encouraged investors to believe there was no serious obstacle to American firms and citizens purchasing German ships to carry American wares to Europe. Not all the president's advisors were so sanguine, however. "Colonel" Edward M. House, Wilson's de facto chief of staff and foreign policy advisor, warned Wilson from the outset, "There are all sorts of possible future troubles lurking in it."[70] "Your warning about the shipping bill is quite justified," Wilson dismissively replied two days later, "but I think the bill is so phrased that we could control action under it pretty carefully."[71]

London immediately recognized the connection between the change in American registry law and secret negotiations to buy the German mercantile fleet as the recipe for a first-class diplomatic row.[72] "No doubt the transaction would be neither legal nor beneficial to this country nor friendly on the part of the US Gov't," Crowe explained to Grey on 13 August, "but I am convinced that the transaction represents a deliberate policy which they will follow with or without our consent."[73] He advised officially ignoring the American initiative while issuing a "friendly reminder" of the relevant laws. Grey thought Crowe's suggestion sensible, but the cabinet demanded a stronger response.[74] Two days later, Walter Runciman, the president of the Board of Trade and a man of considerable practical experience in the maritime world (his father owned a shipping line), proposed another solution: given that the German merchant marine seemed to be available for sale, and the U.S. government was prepared to disregard Article 56 of the Declaration of London, then the British government should exploit its deeper pockets to outbid potential American purchasers. Since German companies obviously would not knowingly sell their ships to Britain, the approach would have to be made through an intermediary.

At the cabinet meeting on 17 August, Runciman recommended making the purchase part of a more comprehensive scheme for the government to buy or charter as many non-British merchantmen as possible with a view to cornering the market and thus reducing the number of available neutral vessels available to transport goods across the Atlantic.[75] Not only would this approach to restricting German trade through neutrals prove less confrontational than the alternatives then under consideration, he explained, but it allowed the government to remain within the boundaries of international law. It would be expensive, however: "Runciman thinks it might cost £3,000,000 per month," Harcourt recorded.[76] The inclusion of such details in several cabinet diaries, incidentally, confirms that the cabinet had been fully informed of the importance of controlling merchant shipping so as to regulate the flow of goods across the Atlantic.[77]

The moderates within the cabinet particularly welcomed the plan. Writing to Venetia Stanley on Monday 17 August, Asquith enthused, "I strongly urged the development of the Runciman plan of taking up all the carrying ships we can get, and so diverting the trade from Rotterdam."[78] Emmott and Harcourt were equally delighted with this clever solution.[79] Better yet, the plan seemed feasible. With the continued paralysis of the international trading system, the world's merchant fleets remained largely confined to port and were losing money.[80] To date, the Admiralty had been able to charter all the shipping they needed at well below prewar rates.[81] With the cabinet's blessing, Runciman duly asked Edward Grenfell of Morgan, Grenfell, and Co. in London to request Jack Morgan of J. P. Morgan and Co. in New York to approach the German bankers Kuhn Loeb, who were brokering the sale of German ships interned in U.S. ports.[82]

Two days later, however, the Runciman scheme turned to ashes when the Foreign Office discovered that "the US Government propose owning the ships themselves," with the intention of creating a state-owned and -run shipping line.[83] This was a new and most unexpected development.[84] The cabinet at once instructed that negotiations be terminated. Opinion was now unanimous that the German ships must not be sold to anyone. On 19 August, Jack Pease recorded that the cabinet "decided we should warn USA if they took over German liners we should hold ourselves free to take them."[85]

The few historians who have remarked upon this episode have erroneously concluded that the British must have been concerned that Germany would use the money it gained from the sales to purchase strategic goods.[86] The real concern was that these ships would be added to the U.S. registry and therefore become available to transport a flow of U.S. goods to Europe (and Germany).[87] The cabinet regarded this outcome not only as highly undesirable in itself, but much more as dramatically increasing the risk of Anglo-American confrontation. The Royal Navy would capture former German merchantmen flying the American flag lest they be used to transport goods to Germany—and it was quite lawful for the Royal Navy to do so. Jack Morgan quickly saw the implications and immediately warned President Wilson that he was piloting a collision course.[88] In London, Grey impressed upon Ambassador Page how greatly the British government was "apprehensive of these German ships being transferred to a neutral flag and engaged in conveying German trade and supplies during the war."[89]

The president of the United States was astounded at the British response. Writing to Robert Lansing, counselor to the U.S. State Department, Wilson asked if this "very unjustifiable and high handed [British] action" was at all defensible under international law.[90] But before Lansing had an opportunity to tell him it was, Josephus Daniels, U.S. secretary of the navy, interposed by sending the president an advance copy of the findings by the Joint State and Navy Neutrality Board, warning that the administration's proposed action unquestionably violated the letter and intent of Article 56 of the Declaration of London and therefore was sure to generate diplomatic friction.[91]

Back in London, meanwhile, after lunching with Churchill on 19 August, Asquith reported to Venetia Stanley that "the particular 'swine' at whom he [Winston] would now like to have a fling are his kinsmen in the United States."[92] (Churchill's mother, Jennie Jerome, was American.) The strength of Admiralty opposition to the proposed American purchase of the German merchant marine can be gauged from the memorandum Churchill afterward composed.[93] The First Lord of the Admiralty forcefully insisted that the foreign secretary protest recent unfriendly actions by the U.S. government. His "first point" called for the Foreign Office to press upon the U.S. government the distinction between "offensively" armed merchant auxiliary cruisers and "defensively" armed merchantmen. The U.S. government was considering banning all merchantmen fitted with guns from entering their ports.

> The second point that I hope you will be able to fight is: no transference after the declaration of war of enemy's ships to a neutral flag, as agreed upon in the Declaration of London. We cannot recognize such transferences, which are plainly, in the nature of things, designed to enable the transferred ship to obtain under the neutral flag an immunity from the conditions created by the war.
>
> I would earnestly ask that both these points should be pressed now in the most direct and formal manner on Powers concerned, and particularly upon the United States, and that very great pressure should be exerted.

> In this connection it may be pointed out that the United States have already allowed one or more ships, including the *Kronpriz Wilhelm,* to leave their ports armed, denuded of cargo, and cleared for action, and that to stop British ships of a self-defensive character is showing a partiality to one of the belligerents incompatible with fair and loyal neutrality.[94] If to this is to be added the attempt which Mr. [William Jennings] Bryan has made, by his personal intervention, to take over the Hamburg-American liners from Germany and run them under the American flag, it seems to me clear that a situation has arisen which, in the ultimate issues, ought, in some form or other, to be brought publically before the people of the United States. I am under no illusions as to their attitude, but the forces at work there in the present circumstances are such as to make it impossible for any Government to load the dice against England, or go openly one inch beyond an even neutrality.
>
> I venture to suggest to you that this position ought to be fought up to the point of full publicity, and that by every means and influence at our disposal, before we are forced to consider the various inferior alternatives which no doubt exist.[95]

The next day, 20 August, Colville Barclay, the chargé d'affaires at the British embassy in Washington, met with Secretary of State Bryan to discuss the matter.[96] During the meeting Bryan indicated his awareness of the British intention to exert control over all transatlantic carriage. He explicitly told the British diplomat that the U.S. government wanted the German ships precisely because British ships were refusing to carry cargoes to central Europe, and that the American government had no intention of standing by and watching Britain throttle U.S. exporters. At a White House meeting the previous day, the Treasury secretary, William Gibbs McAdoo, had told a gathering of congressional leaders that already fifty million bushels of wheat were piled up in elevators and freight cars, causing railroads to embargo the transportation of more to the ports of Galveston and New Orleans.[97] "Arguments were quite useless," Barclay weakly reported after his session with Bryan. "I can only repeat that any opposition on our part will be very badly received, and create a feeling of hostility, which must prove embarrassing and would probably destroy friendly relations now existing."[98] "It is quite clear that whatever we do the Americans intend to have those ships," agreed Victor Wellesley, head of the Foreign Office treaty department.[99]

Thenceforward the pace of events accelerated. On the afternoon of 20 August, news arrived in London that in record time the U.S. Congress had ratified the bill authorizing the addition of foreign-built merchantmen to the American register. Within hours a telegram arrived from the French foreign ministry demanding that their British counterparts join in issuing a stern warning to the U.S. government not to purchase the German merchantmen.[100] The Foreign Office declined to be rushed. Grey's advisors worried that Secretary Bryan's recent remarks to Colville Barclay indicated the strength of U.S. government feeling on the issue. "From the point of view of international law I do not think the US arguments could for a moment be maintained," Wellesley wrote. "The matter has, however, now developed into a question of high policy viz. whether or not it is of such vital importance to us to prevent the transaction taking place and thereby risking friction with the US at the critical juncture."[101] After further conversations with the U.S. ambassador, on 21 August Sir Edward Grey decided that formally protesting the American action would lead to serious trouble. In a move that would haunt the British government for the rest of the war, Grey later that afternoon telegraphed Washington that Britain would not protest the transfer on the condition that the U.S. government undertake not to allow the former German vessels to ply between European and U.S. ports.[102] In vain Churchill demanded a firmer stance, distributing to the cabinet several intercepted diplomatic telegrams showing how the U.S. State Department was allowing itself to be used as a conduit for communication between U.S. businesses and their customers in Germany. Even the pro-American Harcourt was driven to admit that this evidence was "a nasty indication of USA intentions."[103]

On the other side of the Atlantic, meanwhile, a relieved Robert Lansing at the State Department reported to President Wilson:

> There has been a very decided change of policy on the part of the British Government between the 18th and 21st [August]. From a general attitude of opposition on legal and technical grounds to our purchase of the German ships, they now do not oppose the purchase but seek only that this Government shall guarantee that the vessels purchased shall not trade to German ports or neutral ports easily accessible to German territory.[104]

Lansing was clearly uncomfortable telling the president what he did not want to hear: that the British government was more than justified in claiming that under international law the Royal Navy could lawfully seize any ex-German merchantmen caught on the high seas flying the American flag. There would exist, he admitted, "a strong presumption" that ex-German vessels had been transferred to the American flag to evade the consequences of war.[105] Fortunately, he hastened to adjoin, Sir Edward Grey's conditional promise not to challenge the transfers if the United States guaranteed that the ex-German vessels would not ply between America and Europe meant that the issue was no longer a question of law (and thus excused the counselor from submitting a formal opinion on the legality of switching flags). Ignoring the conditionality of the British promise, however, Lansing went on to advise strongly against making the pledge, for "to do so might invite protest from the German government."[106] The validity of Lansing's advice was thus itself conditional upon his obscuring the conditionality of the British position. Wilson nevertheless adopted Lansing's recommendations (the U.S. government never did issue a definite assurance that ex-German merchantmen would stay out of European waters) and set aside the aforementioned report of the Joint State and Navy Neutrality Board warning against the legal and diplomatic consequences of the sale.[107]

On 24 August 1914, accordingly, the president introduced a bill into Congress requesting an appropriation of $30 million to purchase merchantmen to be owned and operated by the federal government for a period of five years.[108] (This bill was distinct from the earlier successful registry law bill.) Sir Cecil Spring-Rice, the British ambassador, just returned to Washington, confirmed:

> The idea which is inspiring the President is that there is a great plethora of goods for export lying idle in American docks for want of the means for export and that it is a vital necessity for the farmers and other producers to bring their goods to the foreign market. Ships must be found and the German ships are at hand.[109]

Spring-Rice—who thought the American move good for defusing bilateral tensions, thereby demonstrating that he did not really appreciate the issue at stake—reiterated his deputy's earlier warning that the Wilson administration flatly refused to recognize British "rights" under Article 56 of the Declaration of London.[110] But in so doing, Spring-Rice neglected to inform Grey of significant congressional opposition to the Wilson initiative. Even Oscar Underwood, the House leader who had sponsored the registry bill, queried the wisdom of creating a fleet of government-owned former German merchantmen, rightly fearing this was sure to lead to confrontation with the warring powers, or, as one newspaper editor put it, create a "daily and deadly tinderbox for war."[111]

Even after London explained to Spring-Rice just how inimical to British interests the ship purchase bill really was, the ambassador still advised against direct confrontation with Washington. He now told London that powerful interests were determined the bill would never pass the Senate. The bill, he explained, was actually the brainchild of McAdoo, the Treasury secretary—who also happened to be the president's son-in-law. Spring-Rice claimed that the whisper in the Capitol was that McAdoo stood to gain financially through both his personal shareholdings and his connections with the German merchant bankers who were brokering the sale.[112] After these rumors had been corroborated from a French source, Grey authorized Spring-Rice to tell President Wilson of his son-in-law's nefarious dealings—but, afraid of a backlash, the ambassador did not.[113] Instead, Spring-Rice worked surreptitiously to bolster domestic opposition to McAdoo's ship purchase bill. Ultimately, as Spring-Rice had predicted, the bill encountered ferocious opposition in the Senate led by Henry Cabot Lodge, who happened to be an old friend of his. Another close friend of the ambassador, former president Theodore Roosevelt (Spring-Rice had been best man at Teddy's wedding), helped initiate a Senate investigation into the allegations of corruption. The bill consequently stalled and despite Wilson's urgent entreaties remained so until abandoned in February 1915. Another measure of how seriously the Wilson administration viewed the shortage of merchant shipping was the talk about employing U.S. Navy auxiliaries to carry U.S. exports to Europe.[114] In the estimation of Arthur Link, Wilson's most authoritative biographer, the president did not properly comprehend the legal aspects of the problem and "simply refused to face what were the almost certain perils of his program."[115]

Back in London, as details of the American ship purchase bill and the recent transfers of merchantmen from German to neutral flags became more widely known, Sir Edward Grey came in for considerable criticism. But as a disgusted Sir Eyre Crowe pointed out, Grey's earlier decision permitting the transfer of German merchantmen to Chile, Spain, and Sweden had undermined Britain's position. Since then, moreover, the situation had spun further out of control: the Mexicans, Brazilians, and Norwegians were also knocking at the door.[116] How could the British government now oppose transfers to the American flag? "I'm afraid," Crowe wrote, "we have tied our hands, and are now unable to support France in insisting on the US govt. respecting treaty rights."[117] (The French ambassador delivered his protest against "this flagrant breach of America's neutrality" on 27 August and again more forcibly on 3 September.)[118] "Let us hope the scheme will come to nothing," Victor Wellesley timidly chimed in.[119]

The Admiralty were less phlegmatic. Ten days later, his protests ignored, Churchill audaciously approved fresh orders instructing cruisers to seize any German merchantmen caught at sea flying the American flag.[120] The Board of Trade, hitherto the Foreign Office's staunchest ally against the Admiralty, was no happier. Walter Runciman complained personally to Grey upon learning of the transfer to the Chilean flag of twenty German (HAPAG) merchantmen. "However anxious we were to please Chile," he remonstrated,

> I am of opinion that with the object of restricting supplies for the enemy as well as helping British shipping we should have declined to recognize this transfer, on the ground that it was being made in order to avoid the consequences of vessels sailing under the flag of a belligerent.[121]

So many attacks from so many quarters sparked distress and recriminations within the Foreign Office. The foreign secretary asked his staff how this had happened. "We seem to have committed ourselves towards the Chilean Gov't to a policy which may be severely criticized as detrimental to important British shipping interests, and not in strict accordance with the rules of the Declaration of London which we have announced our intention to follow," Crowe dryly explained.[122] Incredibly, Grey proceeded to disclaim all responsibility, saying he knew nothing! The next day Crowe presented him with a paper detailing his responsibility for the entire mess—citing chapter and verse. The last entry in the file was an instruction from Grey to Crowe to come see him.[123] It may well have been this incident to which Sir Francis Bertie was referring when he wrote: "Crowe has completely lost his head. His Prussian blood came out and he was insubordinate & insolent to Grey, who has decided that his appointment to succeed Nicolson is impossible."[124] In October 1914, Crowe was removed as head of the War Department and sent into internal exile. His impending promotion was forgotten. Instead, Grey asked the ailing Sir Arthur Nicolson to postpone his retirement to remain on as permanent secretary.[125] Parenthetically, it was later learned that some of these ex-German Chilean steamers (still with German crews) had resupplied Admiral Maximilian von Spee's cruiser squadron prior to the Battle of the Coronel.[126]

The reflagging issue continued to reverberate.[127] On 16 September 1914, Grey pretended not to notice when Spring-Rice mistakenly told Secretary of State Bryan that the British government would not object to the transfer to the U.S. flag of German merchantmen purchased by U.S. corporations.[128] (Grey's earlier conditional promise—which the United States, with its failure to meet the relevant conditions, still had not technically triggered—had applied only to government-owned and -managed vessels.) Five days later the ambassador confirmed that twenty-four German vessels had recently switched to the American flag, and another twenty-seven applications were pending.[129] The most egregious case involved the Standard Oil Corporation and the transfer of twenty-five oil tankers. The corporation argued the vessels had belonged to its subsidiary (Deutsch-Amerikanische Petroleum Gesellschaft). But according to international law, the character of the vessel was defined solely by her flag, meaning that ownership per se was irrelevant. One of these tankers, the *Leda,* built and registered in Germany, under the command of a German master, crewed by Germans, and flying the German flag, had been captured on 8 August 1914 (i.e., before the change in the U.S. registry act) by the cruiser HMS *Suffolk* and lawfully condemned as a good prize. The Foreign Office, in "an act of grace," subsequently handed the vessel back to Standard Oil, which promptly renamed it the *Matinecock.*[130] In an amusing twist, the captain of HMS *Suffolk* sued the Foreign Office and after the war won his case (and the prize money).[131] More immediately, the Admiralty retaliated by instructing cruisers to stop all Standard Oil tankers on sight. Within seven days of these orders being transmitted, two were seized off Halifax, Nova Scotia, and another (the *Brindilla*) in the Mediterranean. After meeting with angry lawyers from Standard Oil, Sir Cecil Spring-Rice implored Grey to do something to stop these arrests: Standard Oil was applying massive pressure on the American government to secure their release.[132] Woodrow Wilson instructed the State Department to issue "an immediate and vigorous protest."[133] It did so, though even Lansing felt that, "stripped of sentimentality," U.S. action was nearly indefensible under international law.[134] Royal Navy harassment of Standard Oil's "German" tankers continued well into 1916.

There was yet another dimension to the reflagging issue. The continuing shortage of merchant shipping in the Americas prompted several large U.S. corporations to take advantage of the recent change in U.S. registry law to acquire their own merchant fleets to ensure transportation of their products to overseas markets. News that Americans and other foreign buyers were paying premium prices for older British steamers first reached the Foreign Office at the beginning of September 1914, and the Foreign Office made a halfhearted effort to discourage the practice.[135] But in this case the responsibility for action belonged to the Board of Trade, which had the power to block the transfer of merchantmen from British to foreign flag even in instances where the vessels were already U.S.-owned through a U.K. subsidiary—that is, it could block a change in registry even where there was no change in ownership. The (American) United Fruit Company, for instance, owned the British line Elders and Fyffe Ltd., which operated a fleet of twenty-four large (greater than 3,000 GRT) vessels. U.S. Steel owned ten more.[136] To general surprise, including that of the U.S. Department of Commerce, the Board of Trade approved the transfer of all thirty-four vessels even though the "British authorities would have been quite within the law to have declined to assent to the transfer to the American flag."[137] Again, the Admiralty did not learn of this move till the end of September 1914, by which time no fewer than fifty-one merchantmen had departed the British register.[138] The Admiralty protested that the damage to their economic warfare campaign was incalculable and unsuccessfully petitioned the cabinet to repudiate the legitimacy of the transfers already authorized.[139] But it was not until Christmas 1914 that the government finally published another royal proclamation banning further transfers.[140]

In early 1915, after the reflagging issue surfaced yet again, the Board of Trade shocked the cabinet by confessing to having sanctioned the reflagging of eighty-six British vessels.[141] Several months later, however, figures published in the United States revealed that transfers to the American registry alone totaled ninety-six.[142] In January 1916, after persistent questions in Parliament, the Board of Trade finally admitted that "the number of British ships transferred to foreign flags" during 1914 was in fact 210.[143] If we recall the absolute numbers of oceangoing merchantmen cited above, readers will appreciate that this was a significant number. Yet despite the royal proclamation prohibiting it, transfers of British merchantmen to foreign registries continued. Even the passage of the British Ships (Transfer Restriction) Act, in March 1915, did not entirely stem the flow.[144] Four months later, the Board of Trade admitted before an incredulous CID audience to permitting "older" vessels to be transferred to foreign flag in defiance of the law.[145]

During the first three months of the war, the Foreign Office remained perplexed as to why the United States government was so determined to secure the German merchant fleet and risk a breach in Anglo-American relations. Perhaps if the officials involved had possessed a better appreciation of the financial crisis still gripping the world economy, or if they had not allowed themselves to be titillated by the whiff of corruption surrounding the U.S. Treasury secretary, they might have realized that the U.S. economy, already fragile, was in trouble and British actions intended to isolate Germany from the global trading system were exacerbating the problem. As related in the previous chapter, in response to the global financial meltdown, McAdoo on 31 July had ordered the New York Stock Exchange shut in order to stop European investors from dumping their American securities and converting their dollars into gold for shipment to Europe. If such transactions were allowed to continue unchecked, he feared, the country would be drained of gold and the liquidity sucked right out of the U.S. financial system. The consequences would be calamitous.

Suspending convertibility was not an option since it would further discredit the already distrusted dollar. It is often forgotten that in 1914, the financial world viewed the United States as a debtor nation with a checkered financial past and its dollar as a second-class currency.[146] All the U.S. Treasury could do, therefore, was to make it as difficult as possible to ship gold out of the country in order to buy time for U.S. agricultural exporters to earn the foreign exchange vitally needed to stabilize the dollar and settle outstanding overseas debts.[147] Closing the New York Stock Exchange successfully prevented European investors from liquating their holdings in U.S. companies, but it did not completely eliminate the pressure on the U.S. currency. Various municipalities and corporations owed considerable sums to British financial institutions.[148] On 20 August 1914, Henry Lee Higginson, chairman of Boston-based Lee Higginson and Co., warned President Wilson that the amount of short-term debt owed to British institutions ran into the hundreds of millions and implored him to act fast to head off a crisis.[149] In fact, Secretary McAdoo was already aware of the problem and had taken steps to ascertain the exact size of the debt and, even more important, when it was expected to mature. It took several weeks for all the data to be gathered and calculations made. In early September, McAdoo's worst fears were confirmed: according to the New York Clearing House Committee, no less than $500 million would fall due before the end of the year—a sum that considerably exceeded current U.S. reserves of gold and foreign currency.[150] How could the shortfall be met?

The answer, under normal circumstances, was through the sale of primary goods and especially cotton. Though no longer king in 1914, cotton was still the United States' most important export.[151] Annual sales typically yielded $550 million in foreign exchange and represented one-quarter of total U.S. foreign earnings.[152] In comparison, iron and steel products earned $300 million (12 percent) and grains just $210 million (9 percent).[153] In 1914, cotton growers projected a bumper crop of nearly seventeen million bales of cotton, with each bale weighing approximately 500 pounds.[154] The majority (65 percent) of the U.S. cotton crop was normally exported overseas. Great Britain, Germany, and Austria between them usually took one-half (i.e., a third of the total U.S. crop).

As with all agricultural products, the revenue stream from cotton was seasonal. The first bales typically shipped toward the end of July, though picking continued till early September. From the cotton growers' standpoint, therefore, the European crisis broke at the worst possible time. At the beginning of July 1914, the spot price of cotton on the New Orleans exchange stood at 13¼¢ per pound. Mere rumor of war had been enough to cause a slip to 12¢. Several days later fears emerged of British participation in the conflict. When the New Orleans cotton exchange opened on the morning of Friday, 31 July (Wall Street remained shut), the expectation that the Royal Navy would blockade Germany caused prices to collapse.[155] In the space of just seventy-five minutes, cotton plummeted from 12¢ to 9¼¢, causing several brokers to declare bankruptcy and the exchange to close its doors. They remained closed until mid-November. The Americans' inability to ship their massive cotton crop to European markets created the expectation of a domestic glut.[156] Over the next several weeks, the price of cotton drifted downward, and by October it was selling below 6¢. The economy of the South had been dealt a crushing blow. A 50 percent drop in the price of cotton spelled bankruptcy for not just growers but all connected with the industry, including local banks. It is not too much to say that cotton was the very basis of life for the whole of the South. Eastern bankers refused to lend financial support, except at exorbitant interest rates, and southern business leaders loudly demanded a fiscally (and politically) costly federal bale-out.[157]

The threatened inability to move the cotton crop was devastating enough to the U.S. southern states, but the implications at the national level were hardly less serious. McAdoo's entire strategy for managing the ongoing financial crisis had been based upon the assumption that the United States would be able to earn foreign currency by selling its agricultural produce (at premium prices) to Europe.[158] He had further presupposed the availability of merchantmen to carry the American harvests to Europe, and British willingness not to treat those agricultural commodities as contraband. In August 1914 these assumptions seemed unlikely. Already the British government had (apparently) indicated its intention to treat food as contraband by permitting the Royal Navy to confiscate half a million tons of grain inbound for Germany. Pressured by the Admiralty, British shippers were declining to carry U.S. cotton to neutral ports contiguous to Germany, and Lloyd's of London was refusing to issue insurance. Cotton brokers complained that "European buyers of cotton in neutral countries will only pay for same when draft with bill of lading is accompanied by full war risk insurance."[159] And because Lloyd's was refusing also to reinsure cotton, U.S. insurance companies declined to write as well.[160] McAdoo's vaunted establishment of a new bureau within the Treasury to underwrite U.S. ships carrying U.S. cargoes against all "war risks" counted for little.[161] In 1914 the American ships to carry American exports simply did not exist—hence the desperation to acquire some.

Extension of Lists in September, the U.S. Protest, and the British Response

Until the end of August 1914, aside from the reflagging issue and the tiresome bickering with the Foreign Office, the Admiralty had cause to be reasonably happy with their economic warfare achievements. Though no blockade had been formally declared, the port of Hamburg had been closed to foreign trade. The Admiralty could further boast that Germany's second most important gateway, the port of Rotterdam, was also effectively shut. Except for two cargoes released by the Foreign Office on 20 August, not a grain of wheat had reached Holland by ship and none would do so until early October.[162] In detaining approximately fifty neutral merchantmen bound for Rotterdam during the last week of August, the Royal Navy had effectively discouraged more from trying.[163] This policy, moreover, had been retrospectively approved by the McKenna Cabinet Coordination Committee. On 28 August, however, Sir Edward Grey effectively destroyed the deterrence just established by promising Ambassador Page that Britain would purchase rather than confiscate all cargoes of American origin.[164]

The Admiralty endeavored to find another method to deter American firms from supplying Germany. The task was handed to the Enemy Supplies Restriction Committee, which, as readers will recall, had been established in mid-August under the direction of Sir Francis Hopwood of the Admiralty. On 9 September 1914, the ESRC proposed discouraging American indirect trade with Germany through a program of selective intimidation and harassment of neutral shipping. (British merchant vessels, at this point, were still prohibited from carrying contraband across the Atlantic and were *presumed* to be complying.) The committee advised:

> In view of the extreme importance of petrol to the enemy, we consider that immediate and drastic action should be taken to prevent such supplies from reaching him. We therefore recommend the seizure and diversion into British ports of one or more of the largest tank steamers now on the sea, bound for Rotterdam. The ship, or ships, should be captured on the ground that they are carrying conditional contraband, and should be dealt with by the Prize Court. We hope that this action may have the effect of deterring the charter of steamers for the trade at least temporarily. . . . Adjudication by the prize court will take two or three months, and we think the effect produced by one or two captures will be valuable even if the crown is mulcted in damages.[165]

Cecil Hurst, the Foreign Office representative to the ESRC, concurred. He told Sir Edward Grey, "Capture will be sure to lead to a certain amount of outcry in the United States of America, but we came to the conclusion that it would be worth it."[166] Twelve days later the Royal Navy detained the tanker *Chester,* plying Baton Rouge to Rotterdam.[167] In addition, the cabinet earmarked £130,000 to charter as many neutral tankers as possible.[168]

In recent days, the French had been growing increasingly annoyed with British vacillation over blockade policy and had been pressing for a much tougher line against the United States. On 12 September, Paris petitioned London to declare cotton contraband on the grounds that it was a key component in the manufacture of explosives. The Foreign Office was reluctant to do so because of the U.S. government's known sensitivity on this point. A committee appointed to consider the importance of cotton, moreover, had recently reported that Germany likely had ample supplies and that consequently there seemed to be no point in raising American ire by declaring it contraband. Several days later, the French submitted for Foreign Office consideration a extended contraband list that included iron ore and most metal-hardening agents.[169] "As we have declared our intention to adhere to the Declaration of London with certain modifications," Wellesley in the treaty department responded, "I do not see how we can possibly do this."[170] Unexpectedly, Grey demurred, and on 20 September 1914, the Foreign Office announced an extension of the definition of contraband to include copper, chrome, iron ore, leather, and rubber plus a broader range of foodstuffs—but not cotton.[171] Ten days later, however, several items were taken off the list once more after complaints by the Board of Trade and by the Board of Agriculture that British exporters were being unfairly hurt.[172]

In publishing the extended list of contraband on 20 September, the Foreign Office hoped the diplomatic status quo with the United States would remain undisturbed. Sir Cecil Spring-Rice and his British embassy staff in Washington encouraged London to believe the American government was content with the significant concessions already granted. Spring-Rice's "private" letters to Grey, which often were printed and circulated within the government, painted the comforting picture of America as a benevolent neutral. "I am sure we can at the right moment depend on an understanding heart here," he soothed.[173] At the beginning of September, Spring-Rice excitedly telegraphed London that President Woodrow Wilson had just confided in him: "Every thing that I love most in the world is at stake."[174] The interpretation the ambassador placed upon the president's remark was unmistakable: "Officially, he would do all that he could to maintain absolute neutrality and would bear in mind that a dispute between our two nations would be the crowning calamity." Spring-Rice's assessment was accepted. Even the prime minister professed his delight.[175] As a result, the Foreign Office interpreted the recent silence from the State Department as American acquiescence to British economic warfare policy. They could not have been more wrong.

For some time, Secretary Bryant had been quietly fuming at what he regarded as unwarranted and illegal British interference with American trade.[176] Since early September, moreover, Robert Lansing, the counselor at the State Department, had been consulting with prominent legal experts and was busy composing a formal protest.[177] It arrived like a bolt from the blue, therefore, when on 28 September Spring-Rice sent London an urgent telegram warning of an imminent U.S. demarche protesting British interference with American commercial rights and violations of international law.[178] The ambassador reported he had met that morning with Colonel House, who had shown him the draft.[179] Spring-Rice "was thoroughly alarmed," House wrote afterward in his diary.[180]

House rushed directly over to see President Wilson and prevailed upon him to replace the formal State Department demarche with a milder telegraphic protest and an offer to negotiate informally to find a mutually satisfactory "accommodation."[181] A former history professor, Wilson was quick to recall that barely a century earlier, Britain and the United States had gone to war over this very issue. "The circumstances of the War of 1812 and now run parallel," he grimly remarked to House, and it "was started in exactly the same way as this controversy is opening up."[182] By "eyes-only" telegram, Spring-Rice relayed to Grey the offer of private talks and urged acceptance, warning that the order-in-council of 20 August 1914 designed to achieve control over the transit trade through Rotterdam "as it stands cannot be accepted here and would certainly lead to violent agitation" and thereby "gravely affect the relations between U.S. and G.B."[183]

Over the next several days, Spring-Rice reiterated the importance of making concessions to the United States government. However anxious the president was to avoid conflict, he was facing midterm elections and, with the U.S. economy in trouble, could not afford to been seen as soft in defending perceived American rights. "The President is very much impressed by the gravity of the question because it touches the pockets and the prejudices of so many of the people. It happens to be just the sort of question which takes the popular fancy and also enlists the monied people as well."[184]

On its face, the U.S. protest appeared straightforward. The State Department objected to the novel measures introduced in the order-in-council of 20 August 1914.[185] Robert Lansing especially objected to the clause therein directing prize courts to "presume" enemy destination for "practically all goods consigned to neutral ports such as Rotterdam and Gothenburg as liable to seizure on the ground that they are for a person under control of authorities of the enemy state."[186] Quite correctly, he remonstrated that absolute "presumption of enemy destination" amounted to an unprecedented extension of belligerent rights. For Lansing, who was notorious for instinctively viewing all problems through a legalistic lens (he was often referred to as "the president's obedient law clerk"), the simplest solution would be for the British government to abide strictly by the rules of maritime warfare as prescribed in the Declaration of London without the "modifications and additions" inserted under its recent order-in-council.[187]

Because the original American demarche was framed in legal terms and included a demand to observe this draft treaty, furthermore, historians have tended to examine subsequent events from a predominantly legalistic perspective.[188] While mastery of the legal dimensions of the story is certainly important, placing them at center stage leads to a distorted view of subsequent events and, more important, a misreading of the underlying concerns and objectives of each government. Excepting maybe Robert Lansing, and even he not always, the other principal players were not thinking in narrowly legalistic terms. As an exasperated Spring-Rice remarked to Grey after one interview with Lansing: "You will see the difficulty of negotiating with a subordinate who has the lawyer's instinct to make good his case."[189] Walter Page too expressed irritation at Lansing's "fine-spun legal arguments (not all sound by any means) against the sections of the English proclamations that have been put forth."[190] Even President Wilson, who unquestionably defined the U.S. agenda, rejected Lansing's legalistic approach and instructed the State Department to find a better way to resolve Anglo-American differences. Fundamentally, Wilson's offer to find a private "accommodation" implied negotiations divorced from legal principles.

It is no less important to remember that although the United States Congress had ratified the Declaration of London, the British Parliament had not, nor had most other powers, which meant that by its own terms the treaty was not a valid expression of international law.[191] Accordingly, the Foreign Office regarded the State Department's attempts to pressure Britain to observe the declaration as dishonest and transparently self-serving. In demanding British adherence to this treaty, Cecil Hurst (the Foreign Office's legal expert) remarked, the Americans expected Britain to accept their dubious definitions of all clauses therein, and to disregard those manifestly inimical to U.S. business interests, such as that relating to the reflagging of merchantmen.[192]

Senior clerks in the Foreign Office treaty department pondered how in prosecuting economic warfare Britain might stay closer to the boundaries of customary international law. But where, exactly, did those boundaries fall? No one could say—which of course had been the original justification for adhering to the Declaration of London. "As regards continuous voyage & continuous transport we ought to be able to contend successfully on historical grounds against the U.S. complaints," Victor Wellesley speculated, but "the other question, presumption of hostile destination, is perhaps more ticklish."[193] Yet it was by no means impossible to rebut American complaints. During the U.S. Civil War (1861–1865), the northern states had invoked the time-honored plea that changed circumstances demanded changes in the application of generally recognized legal principles. American jurists had extended the "doctrine of continuous voyage," as applied to contraband law, into a canon whereby the "ultimate intended destination" of a particular cargo of contraband goods governed whether it could be legitimately seized; this interpretation became known to international jurists as the "American doctrine." Accordingly, northern courts had routinely condemned British merchantmen for contraband smuggling while plying between England and Nassau (a port in the British Bahamas).[194] Unfortunately, Hurst pointed out, in applying this new principle, American prize courts had still demanded tangible proof of intended destination for each cargo and upheld prosecutorial inference of ultimate destination only when the circumstantial evidence against the defendant was overwhelming (for instance, in a case involving cavalry sabers stamped with the motif of the Confederacy).[195] Hurst was of the opinion—rightly, as will be shown below—that under modern conditions of commerce, the prospect of obtaining similar proof against U.S. cargoes consigned ostensibly to neutral Holland was virtually zero. A far simpler and safer solution, he advised, would be to "come to an agreement with Holland which shall enable us to intercept goods for Germany without interfering with goods genuinely intended for Holland."[196]

Hurst's advice, combined with Spring-Rice's alarmist warnings of American "moral outrage" at Britain's embargo on food to Europe, induced Sir Edward Grey to promise Washington, on 30 September, that "any foodstuffs consigned to Holland and at present detained will be released and neutral ships will not be detained on the ground of containing foodstuffs."[197] That same day, Walter Runciman personally assured the Dutch ambassador in writing that "we shall not divert or detain your vessels which are carrying nothing else [but food]."[198]

Before the Admiralty had a chance to demand a retraction of the promises made by the Foreign Office and Board of Trade, which in effect unilaterally overturned cabinet policy, the U.S. State Department released the details to the press.[199] For obvious reasons this complicated matters. Even so, several cabinet ministers, including Churchill, McKenna, and Lloyd George, refused point-blank to honor Grey's and Runciman's pledges and steadfastly insisted that Britain must continue to interdict American food bound for Germany and occupied Belgium.[200]

In consequence, for almost a month the departments of the British government remained at loggerheads as the cabinet debated how best to mollify the United States and whether it was necessary to devise an alternative economic warfare policy. There was a nearly total breakdown in interdepartmental cooperation, and genial chaos reigned. Embarrassed Foreign Office officials were beside themselves. On 21 October 1914, Eyre Crowe angrily scrawled:

> The Netherlands minister made *another* violent protest today against what he described as our systematic disregard of solemn pledges given to him by Mr. Runciman and Sir E. Grey. He referred to the cases of two Dutch ships from New York to Rotterdam, carrying grain to Dutch

> consignees at Rotterdam, which, in spite of our undertaking, had been carried into Falmouth and were still detained there. . . . M. [Jonkheer Reneke de Marees] van Swinderen declared that neither our naval officers nor our customs officers paid any attention to FO assurances or directions, and openly said so.[201]

"It is no use giving assurances to foreign governments," Crowe fumed the next day in a separate paper, "unless we are sure that our naval officers will act up to them."[202] Until the cabinet agreed upon a new policy, the Admiralty steadfastly ignored the Foreign Office's protests and continued to detain all neutral ships that ran into their cruiser patrols.[203]

The prime minister's initial reaction to the news that the Americans were "making themselves disagreeable about the seizure and detention of cargos sent in their ships ostensibly to Holland" was concise and to the point. "We naturally don't want to have a row with them," he told Venetia Stanley on 29 September, "but we cannot allow the Germans to be provided for."[204] That morning he met briefly with Churchill, who left him with some policy options.[205] Over lunch, Asquith discussed these with Grey, Crewe, Runciman, McKenna, Simon, Haldane, and Lord Reading (the lord chief justice). The general mood of the group was one of intransigence.[206] Determination to resist American demands was reinforced by recent intelligence showing that U.S. companies were preparing to ship large quantities of refined ores, oils, and food to various neutral counties bordering Germany. Over the previous seven days, for example, copper exceeding the Dutch annual requirement by a factor of four had been cleared from American ports and was bound for Rotterdam. "Having regard to the figures of ordinary consumption," the ESRC concurred, "it obviously cannot really be intended for the neutral consignee."[207] This information was corroborated by insurance data supplied by Lloyd's.

Determined to stop indirect U.S. exports to Germany, but hoping to avoid being drawn into a debate over contraband law, the prime minister and his senior advisors decided to resurrect the prewar Admiralty plan to use mines to "produce a paralysing moral effect on trade in the east part of the North Sea including the approaches to Dutch and Belgian ports."[208] It will be remembered that at the beginning of the war, ministers had considered but ultimately rejected this "barbarous" plan.[209] While it was sharp practice, the proposed strategem offered several diplomatic advantages. Germany had been the first to scatter mines indiscriminately in the North Sea, and despite Foreign Office prodding, the U.S. State Department had refused to issue a demarche to the German government over the matter. In addition, at the second Hague conference in 1907, Great Britain had proposed restrictions on the localities where mines could be laid but had been voted down by no fewer than thirty-seven of the forty-four states attending—including the United States.[210]

After lunch on 29 September, the prime minister admitted he had been "reluctantly convinced" that "the only thing to be done is to sow the eastern part of the North Sea with mines—right down to between Rotterdam and Flushing."[211] That afternoon Asquith wrote Churchill:

> I have been thinking over our conversation this morning, and what you said about MINING has been reinforced by the conference a few of us had later as to the American attitude in regard to the Declaration of London etc. I am strongly of opinion that the time has come for you to start mining, and to do it without stinting, and if necessary on a Napoleonic scale. I don't know what supply you have in hand of the infernal machinery, but I feel sure you can't do better than make the most ample provision and use it freely and lavishly.[212]

The following day Asquith presented the plan to the full cabinet, and despite some misgivings it was "sanctioned (in principle)" pending the outcome of Grey's effort to reach an understanding with the United States through diplomatic channels.[213] "It is the only efficacious answer we can make," Asquith afterward explained to Miss Stanley, "but it will probably arouse a good deal of feeling in the American & the other neutral states."[214]

On 1 October 1914, Churchill duly instructed the Naval Staff to prepare a schedule for laying the proposed minefields.[215] The next day he abruptly departed London for a mission to persuade the Belgian government not to evacuate its hard-pressed army from the strategic fortress complex at Antwerp. Upon his return, six days later, he found that the cabinet had steeled itself to implement the mine-laying strategy. In his absence, furthermore, Asquith had already instructed the Admiralty to notify the maritime community of their renewed intention to lay secret minefields in the North Sea.[216] Ironically, the only significant remaining opposition to mine warfare now came from within—specifically from Vice-Admiral Doveton Sturdee, the new chief of the War Staff.[217] Sturdee, a self-proclaimed naval theorist of the Mahanian school, was notorious for his monochromatic view of sea power and his dogmatic insistence that the primary objective must remain decisive victory in a fleet engagement. "Every attempt to mine the enemy's coast he rejects out of hand," the assistant director of the operations division, Captain Herbert Richmond, vented in his diary. "He produced the old, stale claptrap that what we want to do is not to keep the enemy in but to get him out & fight."[218] While Churchill had been away, Sturdee had somehow managed to bend the First Sea Lord, Admiral Prince Louis of Battenberg, to his view. Captain Philip Dumas, the "director of mining," noted despairingly in his diary that Sturdee and Prince Louis had issued a joint statement (not found in the archives) "saying that it is not our policy to lay mines during this war."[219] The First Lord thus found his two most senior advisors standing shoulder to shoulder in demanding that he retract his recent advice to the cabinet. What was he to do?

At the Foreign Office, meanwhile, Sir Edward Grey had been meeting daily with Ambassador Page to work on the "accommodation." Also involved in these negotiations were Sir John Simon, the attorney general, and Chandler P. Anderson, the ambassador's legate, who had served as counselor to the State Department during the William Taft administration.[220] Grey kept the cabinet abreast of his progress throughout. Hobhouse recorded being told "the USA were getting very restive over contraband—foodstuffs they were bent on procuring freedom for [but] would make a bargain over oil, rubber, and even copper."[221] The use of the word "bargain" in conjunction with these commodities is important, for it implies that the Grey-Page negotiations were being conducted divorced from legal principles.

By 9 October, a formula had been provisionally agreed upon. In addition to lifting the effective interdiction of food to Europe, Grey promised to repeal the royal proclamations and issue a new order-in-council excluding "the most objectionable features" of the original. In the case of cargoes consigned to Rotterdam, no longer would the British government presume enemy destination. Goods consigned to a named Dutch trader would be allowed to pass unhindered.[222] In return, Grey requested two concessions of the United States. First, the Royal Navy must be permitted to seize cargoes "consigned in blank to a neutral country" (explained below).[223] Second, "we also want to reserve the right to apply the doctrine of continuous voyage where we can get no satisfactory agreement with a neutral country—that will prevent it from becoming a base of supplies for the enemy."[224] Grey and Page submitted the draft of the new order-in-council to Washington for approval.

This document described a fundamentally new British approach to achieving her objectives. Hitherto, British policy had been to limit the supply of American goods to Europe through control of transatlantic transport. Henceforward, the intent would be to limit demand for such goods from neutral countries bordering Germany. Page spelled out that the British government envisaged reaching agreements with the "Scandinavian states and Holland to guarantee non-exportation of supplies of military material to [an] enemy country."[225] In other words, the Foreign Office sought to choke demand for U.S. goods by inducing European neutrals to limit their reexport trade with Germany.[226] Page thought this accommodation acceptable and more than fair. In fact, one of his subordinates allegedly told an Admiralty official the "embassy were surprised at the readiness with which their requests in regard to contraband were met. There was a feeling that even more was conceded than was asked, much less expected."[227]

Washington, however, took a contrary view. Robert Lansing, who for most of October was acting secretary in Bryan's absence, believed that Page had been duped by a legal sleight of hand and that in many respects the proposed new British order-in-council was "far more obnoxious than the original."[228] Lansing promptly directed Page to suspend his negotiations with Grey pending further instructions.

The Admiralty were no more enthusiastic about the Foreign Office's blockade scheme, as we shall hereafter term it. Officers objected it implausibly presupposed that neutral powers undertaking to limit their transit trade would honestly enforce, or be able to enforce, their prohibitions.[229] Privately, several British diplomats shared this skepticism.[230] The Admiralty, to support their claim that this approach would never work, circulated a file of intercepted diplomatic telegrams (not found) purporting to "throw a lurid light" upon the activities of the Dutch government, and other documents implicating Dutch officials in the reexport of rubber.[231] Further intelligence incriminated Italian authorities in the reexport to Germany of grain, copper, and rubber.[232] Most explosively, naval intelligence possessed irrefutable proof, in the form of intercepted telegrams between the State Department and its various legations in Europe, some encrypted and all sent via circuitous routes, that high-ranking U.S. officials were colluding with German traders.[233] (British naval intelligence evidently was reading encrypted U.S. diplomatic traffic throughout the entire war rather than from the midpoint onward, as scholars have previously suspected.) One U.S. diplomatic telegram, for instance, read, "American Consul Bremen [Germany] advise Albrecht Weld Co. that Stephan M. Weld

Co. New York can probably arrange to ship 10–20,000 bales of cotton on American boat to Rotterdam." The last sentence, showing complete culpability, reads: "*Swiss banks think might be wiser to consign cotton to some American citizen Holland or citizen of Holland.*"[234] Allowing diplomatic channels to be used by private business interests was a flagrant breach of international telegraphic regulations and neutrality. The cable censor also intercepted communications between the offices of the Holland-America shipping line in New York and those in Rotterdam further detailing active assistance by the State Department to circumvent the British blockade.[235] The Admiralty forwarded all this information and more to the Foreign Office, but for many months thereafter the latter refused to act.[236]

On 12 October 1915, Spring-Rice cabled that Washington was unhappy with its ambassador's handling of the recent negotiations and would have "difficulty" accepting the proposed new order-in-council.[237] Fearing that negotiations had failed, the cabinet held "a long discussion" that afternoon as to "the expediency of further mining the North Sea, whether at the mouths of the Scheldt and Rhine, or at the entrance of the Bight of Heligoland"—until brought to a screeching halt by Churchill.[238] Hobhouse described what happened:

> P[rime] M[inister] and K[itchener] are very anxious to block the entrance to the Scheldt by mines on an extensive scale. WS C[hurchill] objected very strongly, nominally because he had only 2500 mines and couldn't, as he said, get any more, but really because he thought a minefield w[oul]d block in the German fleet and prevent or postpone the *réclame* of a naval victory.[239]

In fact, the Royal Navy's stock of mines was closer to double this number—the 2,500 figure applied to monthly production.[240] The postmaster general may have mistaken the numbers, but his representation of the First Lord of the Admiralty's opposition to the mining strategy was accurate. Several days later Churchill sent around a paper purporting to show that "the experience of the last three months seems to justify the partial and limited reliance put by the Admiralty upon mining as a method of warfare."[241] The Admiralty's unwillingness to implement the mining strategy effectively tied the government's hands. The cabinet had no other options but to instruct the Foreign Office to return to the negotiating table or, alternatively, ignore the U.S. protest.

On 16 October, Robert Lansing directed Page to break off further accommodation talks and to submit a demarche rejecting the British government's draft order-in-council and that repeated the original demand for Great Britain to abide by the Declaration of London "without any amendment whatsoever."[242] In so doing, the acting secretary of state persuaded the president that the avoidance of public controversy at home mandated that an accommodation with Great Britain be framed "in unimpeachable form."[243] By this he meant that the United States government should publicly acquiesce to new British blockade regulations only if they conformed to established legal principles (as interpreted by Lansing).[244] This advice amounted to a complete reversal in the U.S. position, forsaking the practical for the legalistic, and effectively subjugating the U.S. diplomatic position to domestic political considerations.

Lansing appreciated that Britain possessed legitimate practical reasons for not wanting to agree to abide by the Declaration of London. Indeed, he offered Spring-Rice some imaginative arguments that Britain might employ to evade the more onerous constraints imposed by the treaty, a gesture that left the Foreign Office simultaneously flabbergasted and distrustful.[245] But he seemingly overlooked that the British government too faced domestic political constraints that prevented it from committing to the declaration. All Lansing managed to do, therefore, was to cloud the issue and sow distrust. At the Foreign Office, Sir Eyre Crowe was not alone in thinking: "They [the U.S. government] were trying to get us to accept the Declaration of London in order to derive benefit from it."[246]

Arguably in a better position to judge than Lansing, Walter Page urged Washington to rethink the matter. Refusing to act upon Lansing's instructions to deliver what he regarded as an ill-conceived demarche, Page told Wilson:

> I cannot help fearing we are getting into deep water needlessly. The British government has yielded without question to all our requests and has shown a sincere desire to meet all our wishes short of admitting war materials into Germany. That it will not yield. We would not yield if we were in their place. Neither would the Germans. The English will risk a serious quarrel or even war with us rather than yield. This you may regard as final.[247]

There then followed a sharp exchange of telegrams between Page and Wilson.[248] The ambassador remained emphatic that the British government would never consent to adhere to the Declaration of London without modification. The president, however, complaining that the new British regulations "touch[ed] opinion on this side of the water on an exceedingly tender spot," begged Page "not [to] regard the position of this government as merely academic" before ordering him to deliver the demarche.[249] "Halfheartedly and plainly embarrassed," he did so on 17 October.[250] Afterward he reported that (as he had predicted) Grey had bluntly refused to adopt the Declaration of London or any treaty "that forbids the addition to the contraband list of articles such as rubber and iron ore, that are now necessary for the manufacture of war materials."[251] On 20 October, Spring-Rice visited the State Department seeking confirmation of Lansing's position, to find the latter stubbornly insisting "that the Declaration of London was the only common basis on which action would be taken."[252]

Then, abruptly, the acting U.S. secretary of state changed his mind. On the evening of 20 October, Lansing wrote to Woodrow Wilson now advising the administration to abandon its call for adherence to the Declaration of London and instead to "stand on the rules of international law which have been generally accepted"—adding, significantly, that "in the matter of the transfer of vessels there will be a decided advantage."[253] Had Lansing finally come to realize, as Page had repeatedly told him, that Britain would never accept the Declaration of London? Or did he perceive, as Colonel House's diary suggests, that the matter needed to be brought to a rapid close because the president had lost interest in the subject? From mid-October on, Wilson became increasingly preoccupied with the upcoming midterm elections, then just three weeks away.[254] It is idle to speculate further: we simply do not know what prompted Lansing's change of heart. What we do know, however, is that after a brief White House conference the following morning, Wilson approved the about-face and directly afterward Lansing told Spring-Rice the U.S. government offered no comment on the new British order-in-council but "reserves to itself the right to enter a protest or demand in each case," as it arose, in light of established principles of international law.[255] Relaying the news to London, Spring-Rice emphasized that the U.S. government now claimed to be free to reflag ex-German merchantmen.[256] But are historians right in assuming Lansing's message represented an end to the matter?[257]

It did not. In fact, London interpreted it as a veiled threat. "This will certainly help us as regards the doctrine of continuous voyage; but it remains to be seen whether the U.S.G. will not create difficulties for us in other directions by this complete volte face," warned Crowe.[258] The Foreign Office determined to make a major concession. On 23 October, Lansing and Spring-Rice met again.[259] Although no detailed record of this meeting appears to have survived, there are strong indications that the subject discussed was cotton. The very next morning, Lansing emphasized to Page the "increasing public irritation in this country" over Britain's failure to issue an "affirmative statement" that U.S. cotton would "not be subject to seizure and detention."[260] That same morning Spring-Rice and Wilson discussed this issue.[261] Across the Atlantic, meanwhile, Asquith attended what he described to Venetia Stanley as "a very trying meeting at the Foreign Office on the subject of contraband."[262] Again there is no record. Suggestively, however, on the morning of 26 October, Spring-Rice promised the State Department that Britain would not interfere with U.S. cotton exports to Europe.[263] Secretary McAdoo immediately released the news to the press, thereby causing a transformation in expectations.[264]

The next morning, the headline story in the *New York Times* read: "England Opens Seas to Cotton: Notifies the United States That the Staple Is Free of Contraband Seizure."[265] Demand for cotton rocketed causing prices to rise; in direct consequence, the sterling-dollar exchange rate adjusted sharply from $4.95 back to $4.89.[266] "The situation seems to be clearing up very happily," Woodrow Wilson wrote to Spring-Rice on 28 October. "I am particularly grateful that the way is opened so far as possible to the shipment of our cotton."[267] Thus Lansing's reversal of 20 October regarding the declaration was merely the prelude to a British concession on cotton, which proved decisive in appeasing the Wilson administration. Whether anyone expected the peace to last is unclear.[268]

Woodrow Wilson thus pacified, Sir Edward Grey pressed ahead with his plan to refocus British policy—henceforth to target European demand rather than U.S. supply—believing it would reduce the risk of future confrontations with the United States. Whether it would also prove effective in choking Germany was entirely another matter. Although the cabinet subsequently endorsed Grey's new policy, reflected in the promulgation of the second order-in-council, several cabinet ministers had misgivings.[269] Walter Runciman was one. He remarked:

> The PM is much more anxious to conciliate American opinion and to adhere to the principles of the Declaration of London than are many of his colleagues. I wonder what he would say in reply to the French delegates. My own wish would be to impede Germany in every way possible and EFFECTIVE short of a quarrel with American opinion.[270]

Winston Churchill agreed:

> I consider we ought not to give in on a vital matter as this, until it is certain that persistence will actually and immediately bring the United

> States into the field against us. I would not give way till the last minute. As for the smaller countries that are playing Germany's game, I would not consider them at all.[271]

To make the point, or perhaps merely a final gesture of defiance, Churchill directed the fleet to "bag" (i.e., seize) two Italian-registered steamers loaded with 2,000 tons of U.S.-mined copper.[272]

The net effect of the October 1914 order-in-council has been the subject of considerable debate. Opinion runs the gamut. According to some, it represented a major concession by Great Britain that "substantially weakened the economic campaign."[273] Others insist it masked "a general intensification of the economic campaign" and the imposition of even more stringent measures to restrict U.S. trade.[274] Some see little discernible difference.[275] Because Anglo-American squabbles intrude so frequently on the story of British blockade policy, it will be profitable to spend a little more time considering the issues and interests at stake, the factors involved, and the objectives each side sought.

It must be emphasized at the outset that the political executives on both sides of the Atlantic—not the diplomats or the international lawyers—remained firmly in charge of setting policy, and thus their concerns, which were primarily economic and political, deserve the closest scrutiny. Even when Lansing impressed upon Wilson the desirability that any agreements with Great Britain conform to legal principles, the justification he employed was essentially domestic political. When one appreciates the political and economic problems facing the United States, the Wilson administration seems to have been less concerned with the legal requirements of neutrality, less compliant with British demands, and far more assertive in defending immediate American interests (as opposed to abstract legal interests) than some scholars have supposed.[276]

The suggestion that the Wilson "administration was not particularly interested in whether American exporters were able to ship food to Germany" is simply incorrect.[277] The evidence indicates that Wilson's administration was deeply worried about the impact of the European war on the U.S. economy and the attendant political dangers. Livestock interests in the central states, the copper syndicate in the western mountains, and the Standard Oil Corporation (to name a few) were politically powerful, but the greatest interest was the cotton growers in the South.[278] "The thing that is giving us the greatest concern right now," President Wilson wrote on 15 October, "is the situation in the South in view of the tremendous curtailment of the market for her one marketable crop, the cotton. For a little while it looked liked bankruptcy, and that is among the disturbing possibilities yet."[279] As we have seen, implied British measures against cotton had wrought economic havoc in the Deep South.[280] Southern democrats, led by Senator Hoke Smith of Georgia, pressed Congress for massive—and politically impossible—federal aid ($500 million) to save the cotton industry and entire regional economy from implosion.[281] If the administration did not take decisive remedial steps, there appeared to be real danger of a political rebellion within the president's own party in the upcoming midterms.[282]

The political and economic importance of stabilizing the cotton industry was still broader, however. McAdoo, the Treasury secretary, was desperate to resume cotton exports in order to reduce the risk of default on the nation's overseas debts.[283] "I have spent more sleepless nights thinking about cotton than anything else with which I have had to deal since I took charge of the Treasury Department," he told Navy Secretary Josephus Daniels on 14 October 1914.[284] Other top figures in the administration were also worried. Lansing knew of McAdoo's concerns because he forwarded the request from McAdoo to the British government requesting that a delegation be sent to Washington (the Paish mission) to discuss the refinancing of American debt.[285] Despite his tendency toward narrow legalisms, Lansing was aware of the political and economic dimensions of the current crisis and understood the interconnection between cotton and national finances.[286] Colonel House, for his part, spent practically the whole of October desperately chivying New York bankers into financing the ill-fated and ultimately unnecessary rescue package for the cotton growers.[287]

Thanks to the British diplomatic staff in Washington, London was informed of the political and economic imperatives driving the Wilson administration. Spring-Rice's telegrams emphasized that "interest here centers on foodstuffs and cotton" and that "there is every sign that there will be a violent agitation set on foot in this country where exporting interests are very deeply affected."[288] Grey evidently paid close attention to these messages: when the Russian ambassador in London demanded to know why Britain was not exerting the utmost economic pressure upon Germany, Grey explained that the Americans were deeply worried about the fragility of their economy and that preserving their goodwill was a critical British interest.[289] The cabinet also understood the importance of cotton to the U.S. economy at this time, as evidenced by its serious consideration of the proposal that the British government purchase the entire U.S. crop; the idea was dropped only after it was suggested the Americans might misconstrue this action as a perfidious British attempt to take advantage of the prevailing low prices to corner the market.[290] Of all historians, Arthur Link understood the American position best. "It seems fairly obvious," he argued, that the president was driven by "political and economic necessity and the hope of averting conflict, rather than any principled conviction."[291] Even Link, however, did not grasp the entire picture.

Like many historians, Link interpreted the Anglo-American dispute primarily through a diplomatic and political lens, without fully grasping certain key changes in the infrastructure of global trade that bore on the negotiations. According to Link, the British position in these negotiations was simply to obtain American acquiescence in imposing the greatest possible restrictions on neutral trade, while being "careful not to offend the wrong American economic interests or too many of them all at once."[292] A number of practical commercial factors complicated the British position, however. In previous chapters we saw how since the 1880s, the scale and methods by which global trade was conducted had been transformed by the spread of the international cable telegraph network, the transport revolution consequent to the development of the steamship and the railroad, and the development of the international credit market. These changes were nowhere more apparent than in the bulk trading of commodities such as grains and ores, as reflected in the dramatic concomitant convergence of global commodity prices.[293] Between 1870 and 1914, the gap in average prices between wheat quoted on the Chicago and Liverpool exchanges dropped from 57.6 percent to 15.6 percent. Between Odessa and Liverpool, meanwhile, the difference in prices for the same commodity fell from 40 percent to almost zero. Similar trends are evident in data for cotton textiles, iron, copper, hides, wool, coal, tin, and coffee.[294]

By 1914, commodity trading was conducted by corporations through sophisticated mercantile exchanges. Already it was becoming commonplace for merchantmen simply to load a bulk commodity at a North American port and upon reaching European waters to radio or telegraph their corporate headquarters for instructions on where to discharge the cargo—perhaps London or Rotterdam or Hamburg—so as to make the greatest profit. This development had been alluded to by British naval officers during the Hague Peace Conference and emphasized by the Admiralty representatives to the

Desart Committee. In such cases, the cargoes were consigned "to order," as opposed to a named recipient—a point Sir Edward Grey emphasized to Walter Page during their negotiations in October 1914.[295] It meant that belligerents could no longer find unequivocal proof of a cargo's intended destination among the papers of the merchant ship transporting it because the ship had not begun its voyage with an ultimate intended destination.

In fact, the position was still more complicated. In the commercial world of 1914, the master of a tramp steamer typically knew nothing of his cargo except its general nature. Sometimes a copy of the bill of lading might be attached to the goods, but this rarely contained more than a description, the name of the supplier, the cost of shipment from the point of origin, and insurance information. More often than not, the bank financing the transaction was named as the consignee.[296] As we have seen, the bill of exchange (the contract between purchaser and supplier drawn up by the bank that was financing the transaction) as well as the original bill of lading (the de facto papers of ownership) never accompanied the cargo, but instead were sent by fast mail steamer to the accepting bank to act as security for payment. Additionally, nothing prevented the original purchaser from reselling his cargo while it was still crossing the ocean; he simply had to hand over the accepted bill of exchange in return for payment. The new owner could then reimburse the accepting bank for the bill of lading and collect the cargo. Possession of the original bill of lading conferred ownership.

From the commercial point of view, these developments in the operation of the global trading system made for much greater flexibility, which in turn improved efficiency—as reflected in the figures cited above showing price convergence. But the cost was reduced transparency. These normal practices rendered it all but impossible to determine ownership—which had major implications for a system of economic coercion based upon tracking cargoes. Quite simply, customary law contained no provision for the treatment of merchant ships loaded with cargoes that had no intended ultimate destination. The lawyers at the London Naval Conference of 1908 had assumed that the next port of call could be ascertained from her papers, and indeed this erroneous assumption had been enshrined as Article 32 in the Declaration of London.[297] Thus not only was the Declaration of London built upon legal principles dating from the eighteenth century but, much more fundamentally, those principles were predicated upon an eighteenth-century understanding of how the global trading system functioned. In 1914, no means or mechanism, municipal or international, existed anywhere to verify the ownership or destination of merchant ship cargoes; indeed, such controls would have been inimical to the pursuit of commercial efficiency. Clearly, in 1914 the immutable rights of neutrals under international law to maintain their legitimate trade had become fundamentally irreconcilable with the equally immutable rights of belligerents to prevent illegitimate contraband from reaching their enemies.[298] This was the problem confronting Britain and the United States.

The Open Back Door

In the midst of negotiating the second order-in-council with the Americans, it will be recalled, the Foreign Office had proposed a blockade scheme as an alternative to the Admiralty's plan of economic warfare. Whereas economic warfare focused on control of merchant shipping to achieve its ends, the Foreign Office scheme focused on limiting demand from neutral countries bordering on Germany. Aside from the manifest implausibility of expecting neutrals to cooperate, the most serious drawback to the Foreign Office plan was the amount of information required for it to work. While ships numbered in the thousands and the Admiralty possessed an infrastructure for tracking them, cargoes numbered in the millions and, because of the changes in the global trading system just described, there was no easy method of determining ownership. For precisely these reasons (as explained in Chapter 2), the Admiralty had before the war rejected the idea of tracking cargoes, and Asquith (as explained in Chapter 4) had shown his awareness of the problems when the CID discussed the report of the Desart Committee. In wartime, the problems would be even more acute, since greater financial rewards exponentially multiplied the incentive for fraud. Differentiating between legitimate end users and middlemen seeking quick profits required detailed knowledge of prewar business relationships between firms on both sides of the Atlantic. Yet no government institution at that time possessed even a fraction of this requisite body of information. Sir Edward Grey and the other architects of the new blockade system were undeterred, however: they believed that the quantity of trade that needed to be policed was small and thus administratively manageable.

The key assumption underpinning the Foreign Office's new blockade policy was that the goal of starving Germany could be accomplished by limiting the flow of goods through the port of Rotterdam. The supposition was derived from prewar studies by the Board of Trade indicating that no other ports in contiguous neutral countries possessed the dock or rail infrastructure necessary to handle a large expansion in transit trade for Germany.[299] This judgment had been incorporated into the conclusions of the Desart Committee; it had been assumed correct by the CID; and it had been at the core of the cabinet's Rotterdam policy, as reflected in the first (August) order-in-council. Even the Admiralty fixated on Holland, as indicated by their voluminous correspondence detailing various infractions by the Dutch authorities, and by Winston Churchill's repeated attempts to dragoon Holland into the war.

It came as a considerable shock, therefore, when naval intelligence alerted the blockade authorities to large quantities of supplies reaching Germany through a circuitous route via the Scandinavian countries. As "compared with the amounts [of contraband] going through Denmark and other Scandinavian countries," Captain Herbert Richmond noted on a staff appraisal at the end of 1914, "it appears that the amount going through Holland is infinitesimal."[300] Though he misjudged, the problem nevertheless existed.[301]

In fact, the first to suspect something might be amiss was Admiral Sir John Jellicoe. On 25 September, the fleet commander notified the Admiralty that in recent days the 10th Cruiser Squadron, patrolling the waters north of Scotland, had intercepted an unusually large number of ships bound for Norway.[302] The first indications of official recognition that Germany had discovered an unguarded back door appeared five days later in an ESRC report drawing attention to more intelligence showing abnormally large purchases of oil in Philadelphia for delivery to Norway.[303] On 4 October, after further investigations, the ESRC declared, "We have little doubt that the Germans are now endeavoring to use Scandinavia, and more especially Sweden, as the channel through which provisions of all sorts may be forwarded to the enemy."[304]

In early November, Captain William R. "Blinker" Hall, the newly appointed director of naval intelligence, invited comments from Captain Montagu Consett, the British naval attaché assigned to Scandinavia. Consett, as we shall see in later chapters, was an exceptionally diligent officer who was also regional chief of the secret intelligence service. Consett initially replied expressing skepticism and thought the quantity involved "has been grossly exaggerated."[305] He quickly learned he had been wrong. Suddenly there were signs everywhere. The Admiralty trade section calculated that during the second half of October alone, nearly fifty large steamers laden with U.S. grain had discharged their cargoes in Scandinavia. New York grain merchants were boasting of unusually large profits.[306] On 3 November, Sir Cecil Spring-Rice contributed a set of U.S. trade statistics showing that American "exports to Denmark are three times what they were last year . . . [and] the same may be said of Italy, Sweden and Norway, the backdoors of Germany."[307]

The discovery of the Scandinavian contraband trade meant that the Foreign Office, to implement its blockade scheme, would have to monitor all cargoes bound not just for the Dutch port of Rotterdam but additionally for all Norwegian, Swedish, and Danish ports. This exponentially increased the information requirement and the amount of work required to untangle the ultimate destination of each cargo. Furthermore, the Foreign Office's ability to establish these details was frustrated by the predicted refusal of neutral countries to supply the relevant data. At the end of October, for instance, the Scandinavian countries jointly announced that for the duration of the war their trade figures would be classified. In November, the Dutch government refused to supply statistics detailing the volume of trade passing along the Rhine River.

The new blockade system's dependence upon the cooperation of neutral governments in supplying economic data was really brought home to the Foreign Office after Robert Lansing persuaded the U.S. government to instruct U.S. port authorities to keep all ship manifests confidential for a period of thirty days after sailing.[308] "If this is carried out literally, practical sources of information will be closed to me," the worried British consul general in New York reported. "I have no doubt that you already recognise how seriously the order in question may affect our work."[309] The ESRC implored the Foreign Office to broaden its information-gathering efforts in neutral countries.[310]

Another problem the blockade authorities encountered was a growing number of false or deliberately incomplete ship manifests. Sometimes these cases merely involved subtle evasions—for instance, listing rubber as "gum," which in the United States was a perfectly legitimate description.[311] But in many others the deception was willful. "From the examination of intercepted telegrams," the Admiralty noticed, "efforts are being made to conceal the names of steamers, and any particulars regarding the nature and amounts of consignments which fall under our contraband lists."[312] Although under U.S. law the misrepresentation of cargo was illegal, the U.S. government consistently refused to prosecute the culprits even when presented with evidence by the Foreign Office.[313] In response, the British government instructed the Royal Navy to divert all merchantmen carrying goods of U.S. origin into British ports for detailed cargo inspection. The howls of protest from shippers at the resulting costs may be imagined. But the Foreign Office stood firm. "As long as we detain & inconvenience ships carrying potential contraband the trade in these articles will be hampered & restricted by exorbitant freight rates & insurance premiums," smirked one clerk.[314] In vain the State Department threatened to respond by imposing a trade embargo on exports to Britain. Foreign Office officials predicted, "The US trader won't want to cut off his nose to spite his face: besides we have luckily the means of [further] retaliations by preventing goods of which the allies have complete control from going to the US."[315] Crowe advised and Grey consented to warning the Americans unofficially that Britain was prepared to escalate if pressed.[316] London demanded the U.S. government rescind the restrictions on manifests or at least allow shippers voluntarily to supply the British with copies of their manifests.[317] Fearful of an all-out trade war, the diplomatic services on both sides of the Atlantic quickly set to work persuading shippers that cooperation was in their best interests.

All the while, supplies were now pouring into Germany. After the scarcities of the first three months of war, on 10 November 1914 grain in Holland was reported to be plentiful.[318] A couple of days earlier the Admiralty trade division had complained that five cargoes of Swedish iron ore had recently landed at Rotterdam and gone straight to Germany.[319] A Foreign Office clerk noticed that "although Holland is a county which largely *exports* meat both to England and Germany large quantities of meat have recently been *imported*" into Rotterdam. It was a source of much greater embarrassment, however, to discover that a large proportion of the foodstuffs entering Rotterdam were being supplied by British companies and carried there in British ships. On 17 December, it was noted there were "no less than 47 British vessels being actually en route for that port with such cargoes."[320] On 27 November 1914, less than four weeks after Robert Vansittart (then a junior Foreign Office clerk) had trumpeted the signing of the Anglo-Danish treaty banning reexports, the Foreign Office was obliged to admit that "enormous supplies have been pouring into Denmark of late" and that "the prohibitive system is unworkable in Denmark."[321] "We have proof that many German and American agents for Germany have established themselves in Denmark and no doubt elsewhere, and are importing enormous quantities of contraband into the neutral countries obviously for German use."[322]

The Danish government did not deny that it had failed to deliver on their promise. Instead it pleaded that the trade in contraband was being driven by wealthy U.S.-German business interests (such as the consortium of Chicago meatpackers) too powerful to resist.[323] Sources in Washington confirmed that "American and pseudo-American exporters are establishing agencies at Copenhagen, to whom shipments of contraband are consigned."[324] The Foreign Office at once expressed sympathy for the Danish position, agreeing that Denmark's government lacked the resources to enforce its edicts. Besides, as the British minister in Copenhagen pointed out, Danish "disinclination to take active measures" was reinforced by fear that to do so would provoke a German invasion.[325] The Admiralty, however, were less sympathetic. "We fully appreciate the delicate position in which Denmark is placed," Captain Richard Webb, head of the trade division, told the ESRC on 25 November, "but this is no reason why, as we pointed out in our last report, Denmark should become a constant and unfailing source of supply to the enemy of all sorts of commodities which in peace she does not even import."[326] The failure by the Danish authorities to stop this trade, the Navy felt, was a function more of unwillingness than of inability, and their intelligence bureau provided considerable evidence to back this assertion.

The Navy was right. Fear may have accelerated the flow of exports from the neutrals near Germany, but the underlying cause of the leakage was that supplying Germany with contraband was extremely lucrative. Practically every commodity could be sold in Germany for prices considerably higher than elsewhere.[327] In November 1914, the price of nickel in Berlin was double that quoted on the London metal exchange; aluminum was triple; copper and antimony were quadruple.[328] In December 1914 the same cargo of U.S. frozen meat could fetch more than twice the price (£2.9 million versus £1.3 million) in Copenhagen than in London.[329] Naval intelligence established that the leakage of copper through Denmark to Germany could be traced to a Danish minister with a "vested interest" in the metal trade who possessed "the authority to grant exemptions from regulations concerning the [re-] export of copper."[330] "It would seem," Sir Francis Hopwood, chairman of the ESRC, dryly commented, "that the Danes while no doubt cordially disliking their southern neighbours have subjugated their feelings to their commercial instincts."[331]

Even more problematic, however, was that Danish citizens were not the only ones succumbing to temptation. British businesses (and especially British banks) were facilitating the Danish import boom.[332] A particularly egregious example involved the sale of canned meat to the German army. Beef and lard from the United States entered Copenhagen to be processed and canned for sale directly to the German army.[333] "Millions of tins have been made for the [Danish] canning industry from English materials and sent to Germany in spite of the embargo in England," complained the head of the Admiralty trade division. "The average profit of manufactures on each kg of tinned meat," he added, was reportedly "high enough to tempt the most faint-hearted speculator."[334] The Board of Trade, however, insisted that such instances of indirect "trading with the enemy" were no more than isolated incidents, and for the moment the British government chose to believe those assurances.[335]

In his new capacity as head of the recently formed Foreign Office "Contraband Department" (which we shall examine in Chapter 9), on 27 November 1914 Eyre Crowe urged Sir Edward Grey to declare Denmark a "base of enemy supplies."[336] This step would allow the Royal Navy to invoke dormant articles in the second order-in-council and therefore to "apply the doctrine of continuous voyage to ships carrying to any Danish port goods on the list of conditional contraband."[337] Five days later the ESRC seconded the recommendation. But Sir Edward Grey insisted the Danish government be given one last chance and invited the Danes to send a delegation to London for talks. In an impossible position, the Danish representatives procrastinated for as long as they could. Admiralty officials became increasingly frustrated. Even Crowe was driven to agree that "I do not think we can postpone the decision until the agreement with Denmark is concluded."[338]

On 21 December, the Admiralty trade division formally asked that Denmark, and also Holland, be declared "bases of enemy supply."[339] Sir Francis Hopwood, who was in closer touch with Grey, advised the Naval Staff not to waste its time with the request. Officially the Foreign Office had not yet made a decision, yet according to Hopwood, Grey had already resolved to reject the idea and was deliberately tolerating the Danish procrastination only to buy himself time to find an excuse to justify his decision. "Had we seen any prospect whatsoever of our recommendation being accepted by Sir E Grey," he added, the ESRC would have joined the chorus. But "such a proposal would not have been entertained by him [Grey] then and his objections would be even stronger now."[340] Hopwood's prediction came to pass.

At the end of December, despite still having not yet found a justification, the foreign secretary declared he was satisfied with Danish promises to do better and accordingly Denmark would not be declared a base of enemy supplies. This was a triumph for Danish diplomacy.[341] Captain Webb could do no more than note sarcastically:

> Sir E Grey has now stated that he will not make Denmark a base of supplies because, while this would admittedly stop foodstuffs going

> through Denmark to Germany, it would also stop us getting supplies from Denmark. In other words, it seems that German troops must be fed rather than that the British population should go without such luxuries as bacon, butter etc.[342]

Even some Foreign Office officials found this decision difficult to swallow.[343]

As 1914 drew to a close, the British economic warfare campaign was in disarray. The various government departments involved in administration of policy continued to bicker. Officials complained of being swamped with data while simultaneously lacking the information they actually needed. Despite clear signs that their new blockade policy would not work, Sir Edward Grey and his subordinates insisted that additional resources and refinement of procedures were all that was required.

7

Admiralty Infighting

Winston and the Admiralty have not come up to expectations, and the PM in moments of private relaxation has been known to say that he believes that by the end of the war the reputation of the Admiralty will have suffered more than that of the War Office. As Charlie Hobhouse puts it: "this war will destroy the fame of the German army and the British Admiralty."

WALTER RUNCIMAN, February 1915

Two months after the signing of the armistice in November 1918, the new First Lord of the Admiralty, Walter Long, wrote to the head of the Naval Staff Trade Division, Captain Alan Hotham, asking him to clarify the Navy's opening moves in the economic campaign against Germany. Hotham replied he could not: "much of the work at that time was done verbally and in conference, and only the conclusions actually arrived at were noted and acted on."[1] He nevertheless ventured his opinion that, in hindsight, the Admiralty should have adopted "a very much stronger position than it did, or was able to do."[2] Having served two years in the post, working alongside men who had been in the Trade Division since 1914, Hotham undeniably possessed an informed opinion. Later in his career, while the official histories of the First World War were in the process of being written, he would express similar views much more forcibly, and they would come to define the official Admiralty position on the history of economic warfare.[3] Otherwise, the Admiralty archives contain few indications as to how the Royal Navy reacted to the cabinet's refusal, in 1914, to permit full-scale economic warfare against Germany. The private papers of the various officials serving within the naval administration at that time offer no more clues. The indications are, as Hotham implied, that the naval members of the Board of Admiralty made little fuss and lodged no protest. Why?

Much of the explanation lies with Winston Churchill's extraordinary power at the Admiralty and his ability to impose his strategic views. In August 1914, it was common knowledge that Churchill dominated the Board of Admiralty in all matters pertaining to strategy.[4] Vice-Admiral David Beatty, commanding the battle cruiser squadron, wrote to his wife on 19 August, "Winston I hear does practically everything and more besides."[5] Churchill admitted as much in his memoirs: "I exercised a close general supervision over everything that was done or proposed. Further, I claimed and exercised an unlimited power of suggestion and initiative over the whole field, subject only to the approval and agreement of the First Sea Lord on all operative orders."[6]

Churchill accrued this extraordinary control over the direction of strategy and operations in several ways. First, he brooked no discussion of what he deemed cabinet business, even with the First Sea Lord.[7] Second, he habitually banished officers who opposed or questioned him on any substantive issue.[8] The exception to this rule was Vice-Admiral Sir John Jellicoe, who was widely regarded as the outstanding officer of his generation, and whose approval the 39-year-old Churchill seemingly craved.[9] Finally, he appointed weak, malleable officers to the Board of Admiralty. In August 1914, the naval members of the Board of the Admiralty were Admiral Prince Louis of Battenberg, Vice-Admiral Sir Frederick Hamilton, Rear-Admiral Sir Archibald Moore, and Captain Cecil F. Lambert, respectively the First, Second, Third, and Fourth Sea Lords. Hamilton, who had held his seat for less than a month, was seen as a naval nonentity who owed his appointment largely to court influence and the popularity of his wife.[10] Moore, incumbent in the post for two years, had the reputation of being no more than a technocrat in charge of a technical department already scheduled to be replaced. Lambert, whose nicknames were "Wooly," for his lack of intellect, and sometimes "Black," because of his temper, was dismissed as a negligible force. In the eyes of the service only Battenberg possessed any real stature.[11] As First Sea Lord, moreover, he was constitutionally responsible for the direction of strategic policy. Yet the record shows he failed to exercise that authority.

For most of his naval career Battenberg was regarded as a competent but far from outstanding officer. Lord Esher, who before the war had been acquainted with most admirals, assessed him as "just above the average and that is all."[12] David Beatty similarly appraised Battenberg as better than many but still "lazy & has other disadvantages."[13] Battenberg had never exhibited a flair for strategy, and his technical knowledge was undeniably weak.[14] Though reputedly he was popular with his subordinates, his peers held him in low esteem and he was positively detested by the likes of Reginald Custance, Gerald Noel, and Charlie Beresford.[15] Rear-Admiral Hedworth Lambton, in 1904 very much the blue-eyed boy of the service and widely tipped to rise to the top of the profession, complained to Lord Selborne that Battenberg "hectors as if he were the German Emperor bullying a cringing Teuton. Does he suppose being at the Admiralty makes a man cleverer than he was before?"[16] During his early career Prince Louis had acquired the reputation of being a dilettante, a courtier officer who tended to avoid sea service in favor of shore appointments normally taken by retired officers. He gained an early promotion to the rank of commander because of his service on the royal yacht and elevation to captain at the relatively young age of 37 after becoming naval aide-de-camp to Queen Victoria (his cousin and also his wife's grandmother).[17] Battenberg's biographer tried to claim that his subject realized the damage such blatant favoritism did to his career and subsequently refused similar preferment.[18] In fact, Battenberg continued to exploit his royal connections and never shook off his reputation for backstairs palace intrigue.[19] This is not to say that he lacked merit or brains: in lesser commands he showed himself to be a fine seaman and a good officer. However, the accelerated promotions early in his career, thanks to his royal connections, deprived him of opportunities to develop the professional skills and instincts normally expected of a senior officer.

For much of his later career Battenberg was viewed as a follower of Jacky Fisher. In late 1902, with the latter's assistance and despite question marks over his lack of sea service, Battenberg was appointed DNI in succession to Rear-Admiral Reginald Custance—but only after the untimely death of the preferred choice and the unavailability of the alternative candidate.[20] Both Custance and Lord Walter Kerr, the first sea lord, had been against Battenberg being given the post, and his selection was made only at the last minute because no other had come forward.[21] Rather unexpectedly, however, Battenberg excelled in the position, thereby justifying Fisher's (and Selborne's) faith in him and in the process earning new respect from his contemporaries. But in October 1904, just days after Fisher became First Sea Lord, the two fell out. Apparently,

> on the occasion of the Dogger Bank affair [21–22 October 1904], the Czar [of Russia] sent a telegram on a Sunday [22 October] expressing his regret. The Foreign Office or whoever received the telegram hunted round everywhere for some one at Admiralty to deliver it to, Sir John Fisher being ill in bed. At last [Second Sea Lord Sir Charles] Drury was

> found at his flat. I believe that on the Monday or Tuesday [24 or 25 October], a Cabinet Council was held and Lord Selborne, First Lord [of the Admiralty], attended, taking Battenberg with him and mobilisation was to be ordered etc. Sir Charles [Drury] went to Sir John [Fisher] and said if he did not get up, war would be declared and that in the face of the Czar's telegram, it was a case for investigation etc. Sir John got up and went with the telegram to Cabinet and stopped all provocative measures and said to Lord S[elborne] in future he insisted on the First Sea Lord, not the DNI, being the advisor of the First Lord and J.F. determined not to let Battenberg ever come to the Admiralty again.[22]

Battenberg's version of events (written twenty years afterward) differs only in that he claimed Fisher had authorized him to advise Selborne, which seems unlikely.[23] Possibly Battenberg simply had been unable to contain the First Lord's thirst for action.[24] Whatever the truth, the fact remains that Battenberg departed the Admiralty earlier than scheduled and his requests for an extension to his term as DNI were refused.[25] He was given command of the 2nd Cruiser Squadron stationed in the Mediterranean. Fisher declined Battenberg's subsequent pleas to return to the Admiralty but continued to see him as a useful ally and gave him a series of secondary fleet appointments that allowed him to climb in rank.[26]

Seven years later, in late 1911, Battenberg was coming to the end of his term as commander of the reserve fleet and facing imminent retirement.[27] Then Winston Churchill was appointed First Lord of the Admiralty and, out of the blue, offered Prince Louis the position of Second Sea Lord. Though Fisher backed his candidacy, his support was qualified: he believed that Battenberg would serve as a competent paper pusher while he himself would provide Churchill with guidance on strategic and construction matters. Outside of Fisher's circle, Battenberg's eleventh-hour promotion was widely seen as having placed him "under substantial obligation to WSC for having given him a fresh lease of life."[28] In the event, Prince Louis served as Second Sea Lord for little over a year, loyally supporting Churchill's more controversial policies against all opponents, including the First Sea Lord, Admiral Sir Francis Bridgeman. In December 1912, Battenberg was elevated to the top slot after Churchill forced Bridgeman into early retirement on the pretext of ill health. Battenberg facilitated the purge by supplying Churchill with a number of private letters addressed to him by Bridgeman in which the latter stated he was not in the best of health.[29] This was not generally known.

Although at the outset of the war Churchill pressed dutifully in cabinet meetings for the full-scale implementation of economic warfare, his strategic interests rapidly shifted elsewhere. He became enamored with the idea of more aggressive naval offensives, including the old and discredited idea of amphibious operations along the German coast. His cabinet colleagues unwittingly encouraged his predilections by placing roadblocks in the way of economic warfare and ceaselessly pressuring him for the Navy to play a more active role. As a result, after three months Churchill no longer believed that economic warfare constituted an adequate offensive effort.

Churchill was particularly attentive to the ideas of his new chief of the War Staff, Vice-Admiral Sir Doveton Sturdee. A self-proclaimed naval intellectual, Sturdee was the disciple of Reginald Custance and former flag captain to Charlie Beresford. Sturdee's pomposity and arrogance combined with his close association with Beresford earned him the enmity of Fisher, who tried hard to sabotage his career. Even in retirement, Fisher had used his influence with McKenna to block Sturdee's appointment as Third Sea Lord.[30] Despite Fisher's efforts, however, Sturdee clung to both the service and the promotion ladder, aided by Beresford's friends and a large slice of good luck. Churchill's decision in late 1911 to pass over nearly twenty admirals in order to install Sir John Jellicoe as commander of the 2nd Battle Squadron (effectively deputy fleet commander) allowed those behind him on the flag list also to ascend several rungs in a single bound. By the end of 1913, Sturdee had risen to become a vice-admiral and thus was of sufficient rank to be considered by Churchill for the post of chief of the naval war staff in succession to Sir Henry Jackson. Even at the time questions were raised as to his suitability. Rough notes found among Churchill's papers suggest that Sturdee might in fact have been a substitute candidate: the First Lord had originally hoped to appoint Sir Reginald Custance to the post (Custance had been unemployed for six years) but had been compelled to back down in the face of uncharacteristically fierce resistance from Battenberg.[31] Ten years previously, Custance had been Battenberg's superior in the NID and had opposed the latter's candidacy to succeed him as director.[32]

During the opening months of the war the Royal Navy's operational performance was disappointing and on occasions downright poor. As Stephan Roskill has written, "There soon took place a whole series of blunders which greatly vitiated the confidence of the public in the Royal Navy and also, in the longer view, the authority and standing of the First Lord."[33] The failure by the Mediterranean Squadron to bring the German battle cruiser *Goeben* to action during the opening days of the war was just the first symptom of strategic mismanagement by the Admiralty.[34] In September, the Navy's failure to curtail the predations of German cruisers in the Indian Ocean and South Atlantic coupled with the loss to a single U-boat of three armored cruisers (*Hogue, Cressy,* and *Aboukir,* sardonically dubbed the "live-bait squadron") prompted Asquith to remark to Venetia Stanley, "I think (between you and me) that the Admiralty have not been clever in their outlying strategy."[35] Jacky Fisher too had thought that the cruisers were vulnerable to prowling torpedo craft, and had repeatedly said so before they were sunk.[36] During October, miscues accumulated while the Navy added nothing on the credit side of the ledger. Instead of basking in the limelight for which he longed, Churchill found himself attracting the lion's share of the blame for the Navy's embarrassingly lackluster performance.

Criticism of the Admiralty extended to the Fleet. Senior flag officers complained with increasing vehemence about the "present state of chaos in naval affairs."[37] Opinion was divided, however, as to who was chiefly responsible: Churchill or Sturdee? No one suggested the culprit might be Battenberg or the other sea lords, who appeared too weak to blame for anything. John Sandars, Balfour's political secretary, wrote that he had discovered from his numerous sources within the department that "the present Board is so weak that it never puts up a good fight against the 1st Lord" and that Battenberg "has no independent judgement and exercises no authority independently of Winston."[38] One naval officer had confided to Sandars that "the present [Board] is the feeblest and worst we have ever had. P[rince] L[ouis]s nickname is 'Quite Concur' owing to his frequent use of the phrase in his minutes."[39] "The whole point," as Fisher bluntly explained to Pamela McKenna, "is that Winston has surrounded himself with third-class sycophants."[40] Churchill chose pliable advisors so that he could shape policy without too much opposition yet execute his initiatives with at least a modicum of professional support.

Churchill's response to flagging confidence in his administration was to redouble his efforts to devise a formula for victory. His fertile imagination bred a litter of aggressive schemes for the war staff to evaluate. Over time, as the (comparatively) reasonable proposals were removed from the table, he generated increasingly wild and dangerous stratagems, thereby further undermining service confidence in his leadership. Churchill sought out officers within the Navy, both inside and outside Whitehall, who shared his desire for a naval offensive.[41] Throughout 1914 and into 1915, he especially favored the archaic plan to capture an island off the German or Dutch coast to serve as an advance base. The latest officer to champion the idea was Lewis Bayly, an admiral of the old school known for his exceptional "arrogance and combativeness."[42] Upon being presented with the Bayly scheme and asked to evaluate it, the naval war staff gave it short shrift. One officer labeled it a "desperate undertaking," another as "a gamble at best."[43] The senior staff bravely withstood Churchillian pressure to reconsider. In frustration, the First Lord tried to elicit the support of deputy department heads. Roaming the corridors of Whitehall one day, Winston chanced upon Captain Herbert Richmond, the assistant director of the Operations Division, and proceeded to try to convert him to his cause. "I did not argue," Richmond afterward wrote in his diary. "He was vehement in his desire to adopt an offensive attitude. I saw that no words could check his vivid imagination & that it was quite impossible to persuade him both of the strategical & tactical futility of such an operation."[44] Several weeks later, Churchill again cornered Richmond and tried to get him to back yet another wildcat scheme: Richmond confessed that he did not dare contradict the First Lord, "as I did not wish to oppose & be counted among the do-nothings."[45] Senior officers in the Grand Fleet were less reticent. At a conference of flag officers held in mid-September, a succession of admirals told Churchill that his latest "scheme if carried out would result in a national disaster."[46]

In Churchill's defense, it must be mentioned that throughout the early months of the war, he was under pressure from his cabinet colleagues for the Navy to contribute more to the war effort. The majority of naval officers at the Admiralty, however, counseled patience. "We have the game in our hands if we sit tight," Richmond surmised, "but this Churchill cannot see."[47] On this critical point even Sturdee agreed. "He tells me," a much relieved Richmond noted,

> Winston & the soldiers are at him because the Fleet is "doing nothing"—that he is making a "negative" use of the fleet. They seem to want him to parade around the coast. I was more glad than I can say to find how sound he [Sturdee] is on the subject. . . . I had been afraid that he was bitten with the idea that it should "do something," which, in the minds of these amiable amateurs, Winston & company, means fighting a battle with someone.[48]

Richmond's entry was doubly remarkable, since he departed from his usual practice of mercilessly criticizing Sturdee (and everyone else in authority).

One week later Richmond again quizzed his chief on this issue and again walked away satisfied: "He realises to the full that we may have to go through this war without a battle & yet the Fleet may have been the dominating factor all the time."[49] Churchill, meanwhile, grew increasingly annoyed at what he saw as the lack of aggressiveness of his professional advisors, a perception doubtless amplified by growing public criticism at the Royal Navy's generally disappointing performance.

Frustrated at "the impossibility of *doing* anything" with the fleet, Churchill turned his attention toward military operations on the Continent.[50] As the German army continued its advance through France toward the River Marne, he became increasingly restless at the opportunity being missed (for lack of troops) to strike at their open right flank. After extemporizing a shore bombardment force for service on the Belgian coast (the Dover Patrol), Churchill organized a brigade of Royal Marines and landed them at the Belgian port of Ostend, supported by various improvised auxiliary units officered by friends and relatives. He was particularly proud of his "mechanized brigade" (consisting of about 100 armored motorcars sporting naval-issue machine guns and between 200 and 300 motor buses).[51] Toward the end of September, Churchill strengthened his private army by ordering the creation of a "naval infantry division" composed of naval reservists; in so doing he brushed aside concerns expressed by the Second Sea Lord (Hamilton) about the implications of such a force for fleet manpower, and disregarded more vigorous opposition from the director of naval mobilization (Rear-Admiral Alexander Duff), who protested that the men could not be spared.[52] With mounting frequency, Churchill crossed the Channel to inspect his forces and formulate plans to employ them offensively, oblivious to the damage such excursions caused to his credibility.[53] In September, former prime minister Arthur Balfour smirked that "Winston for the moment, unfortunately, is much more anxious to rival Napoleon than Nelson, and thinks more of the Army than the Navy. One must hope for the best."[54] Commodore Charles de Bartolomé, from November 1914 Churchill's naval secretary, groaned that the First Lord seemed "bored with the Admiralty" and "could talk of nothing else but army operations."[55]

Churchill's opportunity for military glory came on 2 October 1914 with the arrival of a telegram from the British military attaché in Belgium to Lord Kitchener warning that his host government was on the verge of surrendering the strategically critical fortress complex at Antwerp. Seizing the moment, Churchill volunteered to cross the Channel and rally the Belgians for long enough to allow Britain and France to send reinforcements. With him he took his extemporized "naval infantry division" and the motley band of gentlemen volunteers driving their armored motorcars; the officers in this unit included Rupert Brooke, the poet, and Arthur Asquith, the prime minister's third son.[56] Upon arriving in Antwerp, Churchill tried to resign his Admiralty portfolio and have himself appointed commandant of all British forces in the city.[57] When the prime minister read out his request to the cabinet, ministers reacted "with roars of incredulous laughter." But as the days passed and Churchill continued to linger in Antwerp, holding theatrical ceremonies to give his friends battlefield promotions, the laughter faded, replaced by concern over his mental fitness.[58] Even Asquith, who thought very highly indeed of Churchill's talents, was shaken after learning from his son the magnitude of chaos at Antwerp.[59] "I trust Winston will learn by experience, and now hand over to the military authorities the little circus which he has been running," the prime minister confided to Miss Stanley.[60] Alas, Churchill did neither: upon his return from Antwerp he again requested that Asquith release him from the Admiralty and give him instead a military field command. "His mouth waters at the sight & thought of K's new armies," a bemused Asquith reported to Venetia. "For about ¼ of an hour he poured forth a ceaseless cataract of invective and appeal, & I much regretted that there was no short-hand writer within hearing—as some of his unpremeditated phrases were quite priceless."[61]

Three weeks later Asquith was far less amused after a delegation of senior cabinet ministers pressed him to strengthen the Admiralty leadership. Haldane and Lloyd George reportedly protested that "the Sea Lords are very weak and Prince Louis quite incompetent."[62] Asquith agreed with this evaluation: while Churchill had been in Antwerp, he had insisted upon personally taking charge at the Admiralty. On 6 October he confided to Venetia Stanley that "Winston persists in remaining there [Antwerp], which leaves the Admiralty here without a head, and I have had to tell him (not being, entre nous, very trustful of the capacity of Prince Louis and his Board) to submit all decisions to me."[63] Five days of supervising naval affairs left him contemptuous of "the gallant Prince Louis."[64] Asquith told Lou-Lou Harcourt he had "no confidence in the 1st Sea Lord or the whole board."[65] The story spread. On 10 October, Jacky Fisher confirmed to his old friend Lord Rosebery:

> There is profound dissatisfaction inside the Cabinet and out of it regarding Admiralty work in respect to the two points you mention—the

> explanation is quite simple—Winston like every genius *(and he really is a genius!)* will not brook criticism and idolizes power and so has surrounded himself with 3rd class sycophants—I have told him this to his face!—consequently there is an utter want of grasp in the naval administration. I believe the Prime Minister knows this best of all![66]

After Churchill returned from Antwerp, the prime minister counseled him to replace Battenberg with a more energetic naval personality.[67] On 19 October, Lord Haldane joined the chorus, suggesting the recall of either Fisher or A. K. Wilson. Churchill, however, remained deaf to these hints. Finally Asquith, pressed with increasing force by his senior ministers, put his foot down and insisted Prince Louis must go.[68] The press had got wind of Churchill's role in the Antwerp fiasco as well as his periodic excursions to the Continent, and on 22 October editorials appeared in the press stingingly critical of his performance as First Lord.

The problem with finding a replacement First Sea Lord was that there were no obvious candidates to fill the post with any real distinction—except one.[69] Yet although his name was on everyone's lips, Asquith hesitated to restore the mercurial Admiral of the Fleet Lord Fisher to the position of First Sea Lord.[70] At least six alternative candidates were considered and rejected before Fisher's selection was confirmed. The prime minister's vacillation did not stem, as some have argued, from any anxiety over the 73-year-old admiral's capacity for the job. Although events would subsequently demonstrate that Fisher was too old to withstand the rigors of administering the Navy in wartime while at the same time having to manage Winston Churchill, historians have overstated the level of prior concern about Fisher's mental powers and stamina. As the prime minister's eldest daughter (who knew and disliked the admiral) put it, "Although the shades of afternoon were approaching he was bubbling with vitality."[71] In his memoirs, Churchill insinuated that from the beginning Fisher had to "lead a careful life" and by evening was invariably "exhausted."[72] What he neglected to mention, however, was that Fisher habitually rose at 3:00 a.m. to begin work before dawn, and it is therefore hardly surprising that by evening he should have been exhausted. By contrast, the First Lord was a night owl who seldom awoke before 10:00 a.m. and then spent an hour or more sifting through office papers while eating his breakfast in bed.[73]

If the prime minister experienced concern over the union, then it was probably about whether Churchill was capable of keeping a sufficiently tight reign on Fisher. The admiral was notorious for possessing a strong and devious personality. Four years previously, he had nearly wrecked Asquith's government by engineering a Navy scare through his contacts in the press. "Fisher will exercise a very strong influence upon policy towards neutral shipping," Sandars predicted to Balfour. "Wisely or unwisely I don't say: but you know when Jacky is out on business *nice* considerations do not trouble him much."[74] This assessment was widely shared among naval officers.[75] David Beatty, who had served for two years as Churchill's naval secretary and therefore knew from firsthand observation his formidable character, backed Fisher to win any confrontation. He told his wife:

> The situation is curious: two very strong and clever men, one old, wily and of vast experience, one young, self assertive with great self satisfaction, but unstable. They cannot work together, they cannot both run the show. The old man can and will, the young man thinks he can and won't. Hence one must go and that will be Winston. I should not be surprised to see him removed at any time.[76]

Fisher claimed he was sounded out for the post of First Sea Lord around 20 October, "but there was a struggle to get me there which resulted in my not arriving till the 30th October."[77] Most prominent among Fisher's detractors was King George V, who provided Asquith with "an exhaustive & really eloquent catalogue of the old man's crimes & defects."[78] But most of the king's substitute candidates were transparently court favorites, totally unqualified for the position and unable to command the respect of the service.[79] As late as 26 October, Fisher despaired of his chances of being reinstated and was making preparations to leave the country to resume his residence abroad.[80] Despite harboring private misgivings as to whether Churchill and Fisher would work effectively in harness, Asquith overrode all opposition and insisted that the latter be returned to the Admiralty.[81]

In his memoirs Churchill claimed that he was instrumental in recalling Fisher to the Admiralty to fill the void left by Battenberg's voluntary departure. Historians have generally taken at face value Churchill's statement that after accepting Battenberg's resignation, "I sought the Prime Minister and submitted to him the arguments which led me to the conclusion that Fisher should return, and that I could work with no one else."[82] In actuality, as we have seen, the impetus for change originated in the cabinet, inspired more by the desire to remove the incompetent Battenberg than by a wish to recall Fisher.

Churchill's account is misleading in other important respects. First, far from orchestrating the switch so as to get Fisher, Churchill initially fought Battenberg's dismissal. Second, instead of Battenberg's retirement preceding Fisher's selection, only after Fisher's selection had been finally approved did Churchill notify Battenberg that he was expected to resign on the pretext that public outcry at a German-born officer in the Royal Navy was inhibiting his effectiveness.[83] Incidentally, the story deceived few.[84] Admiral Sir Francis Bridgeman (First Sea Lord, 1911–1912) reminded John Sandars that "Battenberg was subject to these attacks before he joined the Admiralty board."[85] Admiral Sir Stanley Colville (who was no friend to Fisher) concurred, adding that "from all one has heard and knows it is pretty well self-evident he [Battenberg] had become a non-entity and a simple tool in W.C.'s hand."[86] After conferring with various contacts inside the Admiralty, Sandars confirmed, "It is nonsense that the government have parted with P[rince] L[ouis] on the grounds of nationality"; rather he was deposed for "failing to standup [*sic*] against the First Lord's insane adventures."[87]

These details about the circumstances surrounding Fisher's appointment are significant, because the misreading of them has helped to fortify the mistaken belief that when Fisher joined Churchill at the Admiralty in October 1914, the two were in accord on most issues of naval policy. Historians have long insisted that until the inception of the Dardanelles campaign at the end of January 1915, they forged "an intimate and constructive partnership" that was "unique in the annals of the Admiralty."[88] Doubtless this notion has been fostered by the effusive expressions of friendship contained in their private correspondence, but it is a mistake to assume that their cordiality translated into agreement on most aspects of policy. Similarly, too much has been made of Fisher's gratitude to Churchill for recalling him to service. It was Admiral Bacon, his first biographer, who argued "it is impossible to overestimate the extent to which loyalty swayed Lord Fisher's actions."[89] He probably obtained this idea from Captain Thomas Crease, Fisher's devoted naval assistant.[90] While gratitude was undeniably a factor in the Fisher-Churchill working relationship, it was by no means the only one. Perhaps overly anxious to paint a sympathetic picture of his subject, Bacon neglected to qualify his observation by pointing out that Fisher's virtuous qualities shone only intermittently and were more normally eclipsed by his proclivities for intrigue and deviousness coupled with a thirst for power. Of course, the same might be said of Churchill. In this respect they were truly sparks from the same fire.

According to James L. Garvin, editor of the *Observer,* Fisher's gratitude toward Churchill was counterbalanced by resentment. Garvin's viewpoint merits consideration not just because he was a close friend and confidant of both men, but because he dined with each (separately) at least once a week throughout the winter of 1914. It was Garvin, moreover, who was responsible for brokering the reconciliation between them at the time of the Dardanelles inquiry during the summer of 1916. Several years after the war, Garvin undertook to review the first volume of Winston Churchill's memoirs. Although he declined to publish his thoughts after reading it, his notes nevertheless survive. In these, Garvin maintained that from the very beginning, "Fisher never forgave not being recalled at once [in August 1914] and the demonic genius of initiative chafed under Winston's direction."[91] He argued that Admiralty House, where Churchill lived, and Admiralty Arch, the First Sea Lord's residence, "became like two naval courts."[92] The idea that Jacky was quietly furious at Churchill for not having brought him back three months sooner is corroborated by a letter the admiral sent his son on 29 August 1914; hints of Fisher's resentment are also evident in another letter he wrote the same day to Jellicoe.[93] "My relations are a bit strained just now in *'the high regions'* [a reference to Churchill]," he reported to the fleet commander, and "I have to remember that *'I have had my hour'!*"[94] In fact, Bacon himself alluded to Fisher's smoldering antagonism when he wrote, "The shadow of impending trouble was always with him; a breach between him and the First Lord was bound, sooner or later, to occur. It started merely as a small rift, *immediately* after Lord Fisher's advent at the Admiralty, and widened almost daily."[95]

There is plenty of evidence of early friction between Churchill and Fisher. The most obvious was their tussle to gain the whip hand in the formulation and direction of strategic policy. Upon taking office, Fisher found that administrative procedures at the Admiralty had considerably changed since his departure four years earlier. As Bacon stated in his biography, Fisher was accustomed to the First Sea Lord being at the center of the Admiralty information web and so found the new staff arrangements, centered upon the office of the First Lord, to be inherently dissatisfactory and "productive of almost daily friction."[96] Bacon was referring to Winston Churchill's highly publicized (and politicized) reorganization in 1912 of the NID into the so-called naval war staff. For all the hype surrounding its creation, it performed more or less the same functions as its predecessor organization—to serve as a vital advisory (not executive) cog in the war-making machinery—with much the same personnel. There was but one change of importance: whereas previously the head (DNI) had been responsible to the First Sea Lord, there was now a flag officer in charge designated chief of the War Staff.[97] Significantly, Churchill had decreed that filling this new position was his prerogative and also that the incumbent should report directly to him.[98] Even before the war he had encouraged the chief of the War Staff to circumvent and contradict the professional opinion of the First Sea Lord.

Some historians have asserted that "if Fisher had better understood the need for a naval general staff, no doubt he could have reorganized Churchill's still-advisory Naval War Staff and placed it under his immediate leadership." Fisher might then, the reasoning follows, "have been able to moderate Churchill's eager pursuit of unsound projects without destroying his partnership with the First Lord."[99] Such opinions, however, presuppose that Churchill would willingly have relinquished his control over the War Staff.[100] They also overlook clear evidence that Fisher did in fact try surreptitiously to rechannel executive authority back to the office of the First Sea Lord but found it "a Herculean task to get back to the right procedure."[101] Given that a merger of the post of First Sea Lord with that of chief of the Naval Staff was out of the question, therefore, the only way Fisher could wrest back control of the decision-making machinery was to appoint his acolytes to key positions within the Admiralty organization. Indeed, it is notorious that one of Fisher's first acts as First Sea Lord was to try to eject several senior staff officers he considered unreliable.

The first to go was Vice-Admiral Sturdee. He departed the Admiralty on 4 November, but at Churchill's insistence was given command of the main task force being dispatched to the South Atlantic to avenge the defeat of Rear-Admiral Christopher Cradock's squadron at the Battle of the Coronel. A month later, Sturdee had the remarkable fortune to have his quarry stumble into his force refueling at the Falkland Islands and allow him to defeat them in battle. After Sturdee's departure for the South Atlantic, Fisher turned his attention to Rear-Admiral Arthur Leveson, the ineffectual director of the Operations Division. But not until the end of the year (after the Scarborough raid fiasco) did Fisher finally achieve his removal.[102] Fisher's anxiety to expel these two officers has been portrayed as irrational "headhunting" to get even with old enemies.[103] Yet it should be noted that within the service there existed widespread anticipation and even approval that these particular heads should roll. The day that Fisher returned, Captain Philip Dumas noted in his diary that "the great hope here is for Sturdee & Leveson to go."[104] Rather than being victims of Fisher's petty revenge, these two officers were casualties of an internecine battle to control the war staff machinery. Fisher made no secret of his wish to gather about him officers who could be relied upon—the unspoken subtext being that they should be loyal to him rather than Churchill.

The struggle to find replacements for these officers proved equally rancorous. Asserting his prerogative to appoint the new chief of the War Staff, Churchill (twice) offered the post to Admiral of the Fleet Sir Arthur Wilson. This was a transparent attempt to counterbalance the new First Sea Lord's influence.[105] Wilson's inability to delegate was legendary, as were his poor administrative skills, reluctance to communicate either in conference or writing, not to mention his generally abrasive personality. Indeed, Churchill himself had dismissed the irascible and dogmatic Wilson as First Sea Lord in 1911 for obstructing plans for administrative reform. For some reason, however, Wilson declined Churchill's offer to become chief of the War Staff, thereby opening the door for Fisher to advance Rear-Admiral Henry Oliver as a suitable compromise candidate. Oliver had previously served as Fisher's naval assistant and possessed the added merit of being already in the building, having recently been appointed naval secretary to the First Lord (the third in three months).[106] Churchill agreed, and the appointment was greeted with widespread approval.[107] In this instance both Fisher and Churchill had miscalculated. Significantly, for reasons that will become clear later, Oliver's deepest loyalty lay not with Fisher or Churchill but with his old mentor, Admiral of the Fleet Sir Arthur Wilson.

To fill Oliver's shoes as naval secretary, Fisher successfully inserted Commodore Charles de Bartolomé, another of his former naval assistants, and who was widely tipped as destined for great things.[108] Bartolomé was deemed an exceptional administrator and credited with possessing sound opinions. More remarkable still, he seems to have been trusted by all the various factions within the Navy—it is difficult to think of another officer of this rank of which this could be said. By the second week of November, Churchill refused to permit any further changes in administrative staffing. He protected Leveson from the Fisher's ire (unwisely, as it turned out) and also blocked the First Sea Lord's attempt to replace Roger Keyes with Sydney Hall as head of the submarine service. Temporarily thwarted, Fisher appointed Hall to his private office as "additional naval assistant," ostensibly to accelerate submarine construction, although internal documents make clear that his actual brief was far wider than indicated by the title of his office and that he was given access to intelligence and operational planning documents.[109] On 19 December 1914, Fisher grumbled to Jellicoe, "I have so much to uproot and such a lot of parasites to get rid of."[110] Next day he wrote:

> Winston has so monopolized all initiative in the Admiralty and fires off such a multitude of purely departmental memos *(his power of work is absolutely amazing!)* that my colleagues are no longer *"superintending Lords,"* but only *"the First Lord's Registry"*! I told Winston this yesterday and he did not like it at all, but *it is true!*[111]

Early in the New Year (17 January), Captain Hall finally replaced Keyes, and Leveson was ejected from the Operations Division and replaced by Captain Thomas Jackson, a veteran staff officer who had played a major part in creating the war room system before the war.

Churchill also undertook a more insidious initiative to undermine the authority of the First Sea Lord and check his ability to dictate Admiralty strategic policy to the full limits of his lawful authority, by creating an unofficial committee to advise him on strategic matters. This was known as the War Staff Group, or more simply the War Group. Originally, in August 1914, membership had included the First Lord, the First and Second Sea Lords, the chief of the War Staff, and the permanent secretary (all, except for the chief of staff, were members of the Board).[112] One week after Fisher's recall, however, Churchill dropped the Second Sea Lord (Hamilton) and permanent secretary (Greene) from the War Group and invited Admiral of the Fleet Sir Arthur Wilson and Admiral Sir Henry Jackson to take their places, despite neither holding official status or responsibilities.[113] Both were also added to the distribution lists for the most classified documents in the building and given free access to the war room, thereby conferring upon them the status of inner-circle decision makers.[114] Admittedly, there was something to be said for relieving officers of administrative duties by transferring those duties to "spare" admirals, who could concentrate their full attention on strategic problems, but the way it was done seriously undermined the authority of the Board of Admiralty. Besides, as Bacon complained, Churchill "did not merely consult these officers as a committee, but he also consulted them individually, and used their views as coincided with his own to argue with Lord Fisher when in disagreement with him—a procedure which could only result in friction and irritation."[115]

The squabble between Churchill and Fisher over control of strategic policy formulation cannot be attributed simply to a childish unwillingness to share power. In fact, their strategic outlooks were diametrically opposed—and not just over the Dardanelles, as historians have argued, but from the very beginning. Scholarly unawareness of this reality can be explained, in part, by the fragmentary nature of the Admiralty archives. But, remarkable as it may seem after the passage of nearly 100 years, the impact that Fisher's return had upon Admiralty strategic policy has never been subjected to scholarly analysis.[116] Arthur J. Marder, author of the highly regarded multivolume history of the Royal Navy during the First World War, accepted without question Churchill's vindictive claim that Fisher's

> genius was mainly that as a constructor, organizer and energizer. . . . To build warships of every kind, as many as possible and as fast as possible, was the message, and in my judgment the sole message, which he carried to the Admiralty in the shades of that grim critical winter of 1914. I, concerned with the war in general and with the need of making British naval supremacy play its full part in the struggle, was delighted to find in my chief naval colleague an impetus intense in its force but mainly confined to the material sphere.[117]

Marder agreed that Fisher had been recalled mainly to untangle administrative problems and that he willingly focused the balance of his efforts upon new construction.[118] He credited Fisher with having ordered "a vast armada" of 612 warships within four days after taking office.[119] (In fact, just twenty submarines were ordered, plus another twenty to be built in North America under the supervision of U.S. Steel magnate Charles Schwab.)[120] Marder's episodic narrative of the Fisher-Churchill administration (November 1914–May 1915) offered no analysis of the underlying Admiralty strategy during this period. Echoing the claims that Fisher and Churchill were practically of one accord until the initiation of the Dardanelles expedition, he held to the view that "both believed the ultimate object of the Navy was to obtain access to the Baltic, and turn the German flank in the west by landing a large military force for the occupation of Schleswig-Holstein . . . and landing a Russian army on the unprotected German coast of Pomerania."[121] This was to be the Admiralty's "strategic masterstroke"; everything else was subordinate to this vision.

Fisher's most recent biographer, Ruddock Mackay, more or less demolished Marder's representation of Admiralty strategy just described. Building upon evidence uncovered by Churchill's official biographer, Mackay established that "the contemporary evidence" supporting the assertion of Fisher's preoccupation with new construction and fixation upon the Baltic project was, to put it politely, "not very precise or reliable."[122] Mackay demonstrated beyond reasonable doubt that both contentions were built upon documents of highly questionable provenance. Several, indeed, can be shown to have been forgeries created by Fisher and Churchill after they learned, in mid-1916, they were to be called before a parliamentary commission appointed to investigate the fiasco at the Dardanelles. Perceiving they were being staked out for sacrifice by being denied access to official papers to allow them build their defense, Fisher and Churchill buried their differences and with the help of James Garvin and George Lambert, "concerted" their evidence to the extent of manufacturing purportedly official documents to support their presentations.[123] Recognizing the importance of minimizing how serious had been their differences on so many issues in order to present a united front to the commission, moreover, the two former antagonists agreed to argue that Fisher had not opposed the Dardanelles expedition per se but rather worried that it would divert too many resources from the Baltic project—which both agreed to plead had been the focus of their strategic policy.

As Mackay rightly assessed, the consequence of this deception was that although the admiral benefited in the short run by escaping the pillory for his erratic behavior during 1915, in the long run "Fisher's subsequent reputation has suffered from his decision to overstate, before the Dardanelles Commission, the extent to which his conduct as First Sea Lord was actuated by 'the Baltic plan.'"[124] Because Mackay was tentative in advancing his findings, however, their full implications were ignored by a generation of historians.[125] Moreover, Mackay obscured those implications by subscribing to Marder's judgment that Fisher possessed no special strategic intentions in 1914, being too preoccupied with day-to-day events to give serious thought to the subject. He advanced the rather unlikely hypothesis that Jacky's forays into the realm of strategy during this period were no more than acts of "sabotage" calculated to thwart Churchill's various harebrained schemes of the moment.[126]

Knowing how deeply the prewar Admiralty (and Fisher) were committed to economic warfare mandates a reconsideration of British naval strategy during the First World War. The long-standing view that the Admiralty wartime strategy was dictated by geography and simply involved the Grand Fleet supporting the blockade is no longer viable. In addition, given what has been already said about Fisher's strategic thoughts, and especially his part in sponsoring the development of economic warfare, it must be obvious that his views on naval strategy simply could not have mirrored those of Churchill.

Let us briefly review their positions. As we have seen, during the first three months of the war Winston Churchill hungered for a naval offensive. Fisher, by contrast, the architect of the "flotilla defense" sea denial strategy and chief sponsor for the development of economic warfare, consistently advised that the Royal Navy adopt a strategic defensive. On 16 August 1914, Fisher counseled Admiral Sir John Jellicoe, the newly appointed fleet commander, that "our policy should be that of the serpent, not the lion," and that "every day's delay is good for our fleet—that is my opinion—and every day strangles German commerce more and makes the German food dearer."[127] A fortnight later he again implored Jellicoe to remain patient: "The temptation for you to do something will always be exceedingly great, I know, but *'your strength is to sit still'* till *'the day'* arrives!"[128]

Contrary to popular impression, Fisher's first major act as First Sea Lord was not to convene a meeting of shipbuilders (that occurred on 3 November) nor to respond to the news that Rear-Admiral Cradock's squadron had been decimated at the Battle of the Coronel (this information did not reach London till 1:29 a.m. on 4 November).[129] On his first full day in office, 1 November, he requested an appointment with the prime minister and his senior ministers to discuss economic warfare. The following evening, directly after the cabinet meeting that day, there was a conclave at 10 Downing Street lasting about an hour. In attendance were Fisher, Churchill, Asquith, Kitchener, and Grey, plus Admiral Sir John Jellicoe, who had been summoned from Scotland especially for the meeting.[130] Although Churchill, as previously explained, had given up on the implementation of economic warfare, his attendance indicates he was prepared to allow Fisher the chance to change the government's mind.

At the meeting, Fisher asked permission to make three public announcements. First, the Admiralty desired to declare large areas of the waters around the British Isles off-limits to foreign fishing trawlers; second, they intended to lay several minefields in the North Sea at undisclosed locations; and third, the Admiralty wished at the same time to move all the navigation buoys in the North Sea and change the frequency with which they flashed warnings.[131] What did these actions—especially the last—have to do with economic warfare? A great deal. Besides being the principal highway to Germany, even today seamen regard the North Sea as one of the most difficult and dangerous stretches of water in the world. Altering the navigation markers significantly increased the hazards to shipping entering these waters and especially to foreign vessels without English pilots. Fisher's goal was to compel merchantmen headed for Rotterdam and other neutral ports east of Dover first to enter British territorial waters to collect sailing instructions charting a safe channel to their destination. Since the beginning of the war, he had wanted to "shut up the North Sea altogether to traffic of all sorts with the indirect advantage of blocking German supplies now freely passing through Holland & Sweden and the excuse would be these German mines being an utter peril to all navigation."[132]

Asquith perfectly understood and explained to Venetia Stanley that these measures would permit "the closing of the North Sea to all vessels, except those wh[ich] are willing to make their way along our carefully selected route."[133] The prime minister walked away from the meeting happy and even jocular. "One felt at once the difference made by the substitution of Fisher for poor L.B.," he afterward wrote: "élan, dash, initiative, a new spirit."[134] For weeks afterward he remained full of admiration—perhaps seasoned with a dash of apprehension—for the "unquenchable" old sea dog.[135] Apparently Fisher laid out the Admiralty's demands and presented the naval case so effectively that Sir Edward Grey was left floundering for a reply. Indeed, the admiral afterward penned Grey a note apologizing for his assertiveness.[136]

Directly after the conclave broke up, the Admiralty released a communiqué announcing that henceforth the Royal Navy would treat the entire North Sea as a "military area" and that in retaliation for indiscriminate German mining the Royal Navy would be laying secret minefields.[137] The Admiralty statement, undeniably the crudest blackmail, further warned that merchantmen entering the North Sea would be exposing themselves to grave dangers from mines—unless they first called for sailing instructions at the Downs. Merchantmen stopped inside British territorial waters could be searched for contraband much more thoroughly. Fisher relished the prospects. "This will humbug the Germans," he exclaimed to Admiral Beatty. "Also, as it will necessitate compulsory pilotage, we shall now be able to control effectively the neutral traffic now so remunerative to Dutch and Scandinavian pockets in feeding Germany!"[138] It took some time to coordinate with the French, but on 10 December the Admiralty executed their plan to move all buoys and lights.

When on 25 November 1914 officials at the Foreign Office—besides Grey, who already knew—belatedly learned of the Admiralty's "high-handed" design, they were predictably livid.[139] "This will probably produce an indignant protest from the Dutch who are I think chiefly interested," grumbled Victor Wellesley, of the treaty department.[140] Believing they had been presented with a neat Admiralty fait accompli, his subordinates initially saw no alternative but to comply. W. E. Davidson, the Foreign Office's senior legal advisor, agreed:

> It seems to me that we must assume that those who are directly responsible in such matters consider that it is absolutely necessary for the safety of the state to take these measures whether they are legally justifiable or not. In these circumstances I presume it must be done whatever the consequences.[141]

Sir Eyre Crowe, however, was less hasty, correctly divining that the Admiralty had not obtained cabinet approval for this policy. "And should the decision be that of the Admiralty I venture respectfully to suggest that it is of such far-reaching importance as to require some higher and more formal authority."[142] Grey, neglecting to mention his participation in the decision, agreed that the "matter should again be considered by HMG."[143] Accordingly, an interdepartmental conference was called, which did not sit until 1915 and did not manage to report before being overtaken by the German declaration in February 1915 of unrestricted submarine warfare.[144]

Fisher encountered further resistance to his plan from within. On the morning of 2 November, he ordered mines to be sown the following night off the Scheldt estuary (leading to Rotterdam), but the operation was cancelled after it was learned that German battle cruisers were at sea (covering the laying of their own minefield in the same vicinity).[145] About the same time Fisher learned about the Navy's low stock of mines. He immediately directed that telegrams be sent to the other Allies asking if they could spare any.[146] Nearly three weeks passed before Captain Philip Dumas, the head of mine warfare, finally submitted his revised calculations showing 7,500 mines on hand with another 15,000 under construction.[147] On 27 November, Acting Vice-Admiral Henry Oliver, the chief of the war staff, noted on the docket that in his opinion this number was more than adequate for present requirements; Fisher initialed the report next to the recommendation not to order more until the new year.[148] This did not necessary signify his concurrence that more mines were not needed: more likely it reflected his concern over rumors that the present model of mine was ineffective.

Opposition to Fisher's mining plan mounted within the Admiralty. Hankey reported that Churchill, backed by A. K. Wilson and Oliver, was employing a variety of pretexts for refusing to authorize large-scale mining off the German coast.[149] "I had twenty minutes talk with Lord Fisher this morning," he told Balfour on 19 December. "He is keen as ever on mining the enemy's coast, but he says that his Chief of Staff [Oliver] and the First Lord are so strongly opposed to it that he can do nothing."[150] Hankey, who agreed with Fisher's logic, went on to say that he personally had "more than once broached the matter to the First Lord, but he has each time brushed it aside as being out of the question."[151] The surviving fragments of evidence show that Churchill and Oliver claimed the strategy impossible because the Navy lacked sufficient mines—while at the same time blocking all attempts to procure more. They further claimed that the available minelayers were too old and too slow to risk sending into enemy waters. This was a much better excuse—but an excuse nevertheless.

Fisher countered by commissioning Julian Corbett to write a paper for him showing the strategic advantages of mines.[152] Circulation of this paper on 21 December led to a sharp exchange of correspondence between Fisher and Churchill. Fisher proposed laying minefields off the Amrum lighthouse, in the main channel west of Denmark leading to Hamburg and frequented by Swedish iron ore freighters. This was a hazardous operation that required the Royal Navy to penetrate deeply into German home waters. Acknowledging the risk that "those old minelayers of ours will be butchered if they go out," the First Sea Lord revised the plan to allow destroyers to place the mines. At least fifty were available.[153] But they were just a temporary solution: Fisher had already arranged for several merchant ships to be converted into fast auxiliary minelayers.[154] Churchill refused to approve the plan, however, dismissively comparing the laying of minefields to "having a few lottery tickets."[155] Churchill reiterated his belief that "the key to the naval situation is an oversea base" to permit a blockade of the Heligoland Bight.[156] (Of course, seizing an advance base off the German coast was fundamentally inconsistent with laying mines in the same area.) Other documents show that, since the beginning of December, the First Lord had returned to the idea of capturing an island off the German coast and had tasked A. K. Wilson with putting together a definite plan.[157] On 22 December he repeated to Admiral Fisher that "no scattering of mines will be any substitute for these alternatives."[158] There the matter rested until the first week of January 1915.

For most of the last fortnight of December 1914, Fisher was preoccupied with reviewing operational procedures and arranging a redistribution of the fleet in the aftermath of another disappointing naval performance during the Scarborough raid. On 16 December 1914, the German battle cruiser squadron raided the British east coast in an operation that involved laying mines and bombarding several fishing towns, which resulted in the killing or wounding of several hundred civilians. Alerted by their code-breaking unit, the Admiralty had ordered Vice-Admiral Sir George Warrender to intercept with his 2nd Battle Squadron, supported by Beatty's battle cruisers. For a combination of reasons Warrender failed in his mission. Bad weather, signaling errors, and inadequate sighting reports, coupled with a lack of initiative by subordinate officers and poor situational awareness—problems for the Royal Navy that would recur throughout the war—all conspired to make the scouts lose contact with the enemy and thereby prevent the capital ships from engaging.[159] Afterward, Fisher adjudged the performance of 16 December to have been "a fiasco" and "that all concerned made a mighty hash of it," and he accordingly demanded immediate and sweeping reform of procedures and personnel.[160]

Only Churchill's refusal to sack officers for a "single failure" and Jellicoe's plea that better replacements could not be found saved the admirals involved from dismissal.[161] But the after-action correspondence makes clear that what provoked Fisher's ire was not so much the failure to engage as the breakdown in basic procedures.[162] Most seriously, it was clear to all that Warrender and Beatty had been unable to maintain a clear picture of the tactical situation from the bridges of the respective flagships and thus effectively deploy their forces.[163] Warrender had spent much of the afternoon steaming in totally the wrong direction. From this experience the Admiralty inferred, as many before the war had argued, that the need to process contradictory information received by wireless while at the same time trying to coordinate the movements of dispersed squadrons to achieve an interception was beyond the capabilities of any admiral located on board a flagship at sea. In the official history, Julian Corbett pointedly remarked that "in all the war there is perhaps no action which gives deeper cause for reflection on the conduct of operations at sea."[164]

On 20 December, the Admiralty announced reform of the system of command and control for North Sea operations. The Admiralty informed Jellicoe that henceforth the Admiralty war room in London would direct fleet movements until the point when action became imminent.[165] This was a significant modification of the war orders given him at the beginning of the war. Fisher later explained the new approach thus: "*Admiralty work the strategy,*

Jellicoe works the tactics. That's a great principle and the justification for the wireless on the roof of the Admiralty."[166] On 21 December, the battle cruisers plus the First Light Cruiser Squadron were detached from the Grand Fleet based at Scapa Flow, moved south to Rosyth, and placed directly under Admiralty orders along with several flotillas of destroyers.[167] "At the first sign of another raid," summarized the official historian, Jellicoe would be ordered to sea "and assume the general direction, but as Whitehall was the center of intelligence the Admiralty would directly instruct Admiral Beatty what should be the rendezvous. For the same reason they also reserved to themselves the initial control of [the] flotillas."[168]

Much more contentious than overhauling the arrangements for command and control, however, was Fisher's insistence upon greater caution in the North Sea. He wanted the Grand Fleet to "stop these insane cruises" into the North Sea in the hope of catching the German fleet at sea. Mindful that Jellicoe favored this particular stratagem (as did A. K. Wilson), Fisher wrote to the former on the morning of 26 December, advising that he was no longer prepared to countenance the practice.

> For myself, I'm dead against your now being in the North Sea with your whole Fleet. I have said so over and over again, but the *mot d'ordre* is "trust Jellicoe, don't fetter him!" and it's somewhat hard for me to go against that cry, *but now I must!* and to-day I shall put in a formal written dissent for Board record![169]

"It is my decided opinion," the First Sea Lord advised a meeting of the War Group that afternoon, that "no big ship of the fighting fleet should go into the North Sea! When the German big fleet comes out THEN our big fleet will come out! WHEN the German battle cruisers come out THEN our battle cruisers will also come out."[170] "To this end an Admiralty order is necessary for our big ships not to fool about the North Sea doing [trade interdiction] work infinitely better done by armed trawlers properly supervised by big armed wireless yachts commanded by the elite of our officers and not with the 'leavings.'"[171] Despite objections from A. K. Wilson, who had long favored such offensive sweeps, Fisher's opinion prevailed (it is probable that he threatened resignation if he did not get his way), and Churchill unhappily approved the less aggressive stance.[172] On 29 December 1914, Fisher wrote to Pamela McKenna, wife of his close friend Reginald McKenna, brimming with confidence that his star was in the ascendancy.[173] Churchill, meanwhile, turned his attention to considering British grand strategy and the overall direction of the war.

Stalemate and the General Policy of the War

As was shown in previous chapters, throughout the opening months of the conflict the cabinet continued to regard itself as the ultimate political executive and insisted upon having the final say in all contentious strategic policy decisions, however complex or pressing. The problem was that the twenty or so ministers who made up the cabinet seldom agreed quickly, if at all, as to the best course of action. Ignorance of basic facts and the background to the particular question, inability to grasp complexities, and ideological prejudices frequently clouded sound decision making. Approval for action was achieved only at the price of compromise and delay. In order to avoid confrontation over difficult decisions and generally speed up the decision-making process, beginning in early November 1914 Asquith resorted to holding "secret" meetings (i.e., secret from his own cabinet) with preferred advisors. The net result was to disenfranchise the majority of the cabinet in order to speed up decision making and direct policy more firmly along lines preferred by the leadership. "These things are much better done so than in a huge unwieldy Cabinet," Asquith explained to Venetia Stanley.[174] Very quickly this council of war became known as the War Council and its members sarcastically dubbed the "war lords."[175]

On 24 November, Asquith invited former prime minister Arthur Balfour to join his conclave. "The only ministers summoned," Asquith confided in his letter of invitation, "are E[dward] Grey, Lord K[itchener], Winston [Churchill] & L[loyd] G[eorge]. They may bring with them one or two experts. Naturally, I don't wish this to be known."[176] "You realize, do you not," Balfour afterward explained to his secretary, "Asquith is anxious that the character and composition of this and future meetings of the sub-committee should be kept private, because he fears if they became known more of his colleagues will express a wish to attend, and the committee will become difficult and unwieldy." He added: "I entirely sympathize with him."[177] After the first few meetings Asquith moved to formalize proceedings by asking Hankey to attend to take notes. Despite the precautions taken, news of the meetings quickly leaked and senior ministers who resented their exclusion successfully forced their way back into the inner circle.[178] Within three months the original quintet had doubled and the capacity for rapid decision making was obviously lost.[179] "You do not get discussions in the War Council differing materially from those in the Cabinet," one minister quipped in March 1915, "you have the same protagonists in both, and all you do is to substitute a different set of spectators."[180]

By the end of 1914, the government faced growing public unhappiness with the prolongation of the war. The prime minister shared their frustration, privately admitting, "I am profoundly dissatisfied with the immediate prospect—an enormous waste of life & money day after day with no appreciable progress."[181] Historians agree that the early deliberations of the War Council were characterized by an increasing desperation to find a new formula for quicker victory. Churchill and Lloyd George returned from visits to the front lines convinced that the combination of mud and barbed wire in northern France prohibited success in that theater of operations, and they were disinclined to commit any more military resources there.[182] Balfour agreed: "The notion of driving the Germans back from the West of Belgium to the Rhine by successfully assaulting and capturing one line of trenches after another seems a very hopeless affair."[183] Even Kitchener exhibited sympathy.[184] On 30 December, the prime minister told Venetia he had just received "2 very interesting memoranda today on the war—one from Winston, the other from Hankey—written quite independently, but coming by different roads to very similar conclusions."[185] Both rejected the practicability of breaking the tactical deadlock on the western front and accordingly wished the government to reconsider "how ought we to apply our growing military power" and to find an alternative theater of operations for the new armies instead of sending them "to chew barbed wire in Flanders."[186] Lloyd George echoed their message in a third memorandum. Asquith responded to these papers by summoning "our little 'War Council' for Thursday, & Friday to review the whole situation."[187]

The similarities between these three memoranda, sometimes collectively referred to as the "Boxing Day memoranda," were more apparent than real. The strategic assumptions underpinning each were very different, as were the solutions recommended. All three agreed only that no more resources should be invested on the western front beyond what was necessary to hold current positions.[188] Also, they were in agreement that remaining on the defensive was not an option. As Hankey remarked to Balfour on 2 January, "I find that there is a very general feeling that we must find some new plan of hitting Germany."[189] Each author, however, had a different view on what that new offensive plan should be, and each took a different position regarding the importance of economic warfare within British grand strategy.

The Hankey memorandum opened with the supposition that the "remarkable deadlock" on the western front invited fresh consideration "for the employment of the surplus armies which will soon be available."[190] Although he devoted considerable space to considering possible technological means to overcoming the stalemate of the western front, his explorations in this direction were largely rhetorical speculations, and elsewhere in the paper he made clear his belief that the Prussian military machine could never be defeated if tackled head-on.[191] Instead, Hankey argued, "Germany can perhaps be struck most effectively and with the most lasting results on the peace of the world through her allies, and particularly through Turkey."[192] This statement has led many to argue that Hankey advocated an "eastern" or indirect approach to strategy. His advocacy of military operations in peripheral theaters such as Turkey notwithstanding, Hankey did not believe that such operations would prove decisive. Rather, he thought they would merely "supplement the tremendous asset of sea power and its resultant economic pressure, wherewith to ensure favorable terms of peace when the enemy has had enough of the war."[193]

Hankey's real concern was that the present economic campaign "seems to be breaking down to a certain extent owing to the enormous trade with Holland and Denmark." He nevertheless insisted that sea power remained "the greatest asset we have in the war."[194] In a separate (hitherto unknown) follow-up paper, Hankey reviewed the problems with applying economic warfare and advanced some remedies. The details of this second paper will be dealt with in the next chapter. Essentially, Hankey's Boxing Day memorandum needs to be seen primarily as a stricture against seeking victory using the Army and an attempt to refocus strategic attention back to maritime and economic methods.[195] That Hankey believed "economic pressure [w]as the main instrument by which the war could be won" is well documented in his memoirs and private correspondence.[196]

Lloyd George's memorandum shows that he was equally skeptical that the path to victory would be found on the western front.[197] He held a low opinion of Britain's generals, remarking privately to Asquith that he could "see no signs anywhere that our military leaders are considering any plans for extricating us from our present unsatisfactory position."[198] Like Hankey, Lloyd George too wished to see the half-million-man army that everyone assumed would become available in the spring of 1915 deployed in peripheral theaters, against Turkey and Austria-Hungary, with the "purpose of bringing Germany down by knocking out the props under her, and the further purpose of so compelling her to attenuate her line of defence as to make it more easily penetrable."[199] In contrast to Hankey, Lloyd George advocated a serious military commitment in the east, not as a mere supplement to maritime pressure, and he urged the government to recruit Romania and Greece to her side.[200] The Chancellor attached far less importance to economic warfare than Hankey, insisting that "no country has ever given in under such pressure."[201] Borrowing heavily from a recent article published in the *Round Table* by Robert Brand (whom readers may recall from Chapter 4), Lloyd George argued that "Germany is a country of enormous resources," and that if they husbanded their food stocks while continuing to pay high prices for contraband commodities smuggled through neutral countries, they could survive indefinitely. It should be understood that Lloyd George defined "indefinite" as "two or three years more."[202] Only toward the end of the war, he thought, with military operations having made Germany's defeat imminent, would economic warfare prove decisive by causing social collapse.[203] Unlike Hankey, therefore, Lloyd George believed that the path to victory lay in bolstering Russia with British munitions and in using the British Army to reinforce Balkan allies, not in economic warfare.

The real difference between Lloyd George's and Hankey's papers, however, was much more fundamental. For Lloyd George, the impetus for a new direction in British grand strategy was essentially domestic political, not grand strategic. Two political themes run through his paper. First, he warned his colleagues to consider the character of Kitchener's New Armies, which were

> a force of a totally different character from any which has hitherto left these shores. It has been drawn almost exclusively from the better class of artisan, the upper and the lower middle classes. In intelligence, education and character it is vastly superior to any army ever raised in the country, and as it has been drawn not from the ranks of those who have generally cut themselves off from home ties and about whose fate there is therefore not the same anxiety at home, the people of this country will take an intimate personal interest in its fate.

Lloyd George shuddered to imagine the political fallout "if this superb [new] army is thrown away upon futile enterprises such as those we have witnessed during the last few weeks" on the western front. He feared that "the country will be uncontrollably indignant at the lack of prevision and intelligence shown in our plans."[204] In other words, Lloyd George foresaw political danger in deploying Kitchener's volunteer armies on the western front, where they seemed certain to be slaughtered.

Lloyd George pointed to domestic political dangers from a second direction. The unexpected duration of the war coupled with the disappointing performance of Britain's armed forces to date had severely depleted the government's stock of political capital. Signs of unrest among the public and parliamentary backbenchers were growing. Public opinion, Lloyd George warned, has "ceased to be taken in by reports which exaggerate slight successes and suppress reverses." In consequence:

> A clear definite victory which has visibly materialized in guns and prisoners captured, in unmistakable retreats of the enemy's armies, and in large sections of enemy territory occupied, will alone satisfy the public that tangible results are being achieved by the great sacrifices they are making, and decide neutrals that it is at last safe for them to throw in their lot with us.[205]

When Lloyd George wrote of the "necessity of winning a definite victory somewhere," he struck a chord that resonated with everyone.[206]

Churchill's memorandum, which began life as one of his characteristically long letters, also opened with the premise that a success in France seemed unlikely.[207] In marked contrast to the others, his plan for victory envisaged Great Britain relying mainly upon her own devices to force a military decision against Germany. Quite simply, he called for "the power of the Navy [to] be brought more directly to bear upon the enemy." Whereas the other two memoranda were largely speculative exercises qualified by acknowledgments that further study was required, the First Lord's paper offered an instant solution. "The invasion of Schleswig-Holstein from the seas would at once threaten the Kiel Canal and enable Denmark to join us. The accession of Denmark would throw open the Baltic. British naval command of the Baltic would enable the Russian armies to be landed within 90 miles of Berlin." How seriously Churchill advanced this as a grand strategy is open to doubt. His real objective was probably much more limited: to persuade Asquith to force the Army to give him one division of veteran infantry to achieve his long-standing ambition to capture Borkum. "The capture of a German island for an oversea base," he insisted, "is the first indispensable step to all these possibilities."[208] In a transparent bid to induce Asquith to overrule the War Office and direct that troops be allocated for this task, he closed with the prayer that "without your direct guidance and initiative, none of these things will be done; and a succession of bloody checks in the West and in the East will leave the allies dashed in spirit and bankrupt in policy."[209] But perhaps the most remarkable aspect of Churchill's plan, considering that he was First Lord of the Admiralty, is that, alone among the three petitioners, he made no reference to economic warfare or factored it into his equation for victory.

After Asquith informed Churchill about Hankey's more comprehensive proposals, the First Lord hastily recast his letter into a paper intended for wider circulation.[210] In the resulting memorandum, Churchill was even more explicit than before in demanding "3 infantry brigades of the highest quality" to seize Borkum as an advance flotilla base.[211] He further assured the prime minister that "I have talked to Hankey [and] we are substantially in agreement and our conclusions are not incompatible."[212] Quite how he arrived at this understanding is hard to comprehend, since Churchill's and Hankey's views in fact diverged sharply. On 1 January 1915, Asquith penned Churchill a short note acknowledging receipt of his revised paper, asking him to draw up detailed plans, and promising that the War Council would deliberate within a week.[213]

At the Admiralty, Fisher was oblivious to these developments. He was busy tidying up various miscellaneous operational details. On 2 January 1915 he sent Churchill a list of outstanding problems connected with North Sea policy, together with a recommendation that most of these could be solved by resorting to a stategy of mining. "I think the whole North Sea ought to be cleared of everything and a mine blockade of the German ports established," he advised. "That will humbug the new American transport company three *of whose* have already passed through the merchant ship channel from Stylt to Hamburg with cotton and probably copper underneath!"[214] (Such stories were widely believed at the time.) The significance of this letter lies in the connection Fisher drew between mines and economic warfare; his explicit intent was "to blockade the German ports and stop this American traffic now so abundantly in progress," which would be the most important of the several advantages accruing from such a policy.[215] In his postscript, Fisher cheerfully acknowledged that on this issue "I am quite aware I'm in a minority of one! *(but I've often been in that same minority so don't much mind!).*"[216] Churchill's immediate reply, if he sent one, has not survived. It is certain, however, that the two men met that morning when Churchill handed him a copy of Hankey's Boxing Day memorandum and a discussion ensued.[217] That same day Fisher and Hankey lunched together.[218]

On 3 January 1915, Fisher learned from Hankey that the prime minister had summoned the War Council to sit four days hence to review British grand strategy for the coming year. But he did not take the news seriously. "I suppose it will be like a game of ninepins," he wrote facetiously to Churchill, "everyone will have a plan and one ninepin in falling will knock over its neighbour."[219] Fisher's letter also contained what many historians have argued was a fateful suggestion that planted the seed in Churchill's mind to initiate the Dardanelles campaign.[220] But it must be understood that Fisher's conception of the Turkey plan—if seriously intended, which, judging from the tone of his letter, it probably was not—was based upon the condition that troops were available. (Technically, three divisions of regulars just returned from India—the 27th, 28th, and 29th—were still available, having not yet by this date been fully fitted out or detailed for overseas service.)[221] If genuine, then this was conceptually different from the bastardized Navy-only plan later advocated by Churchill and ultimately approved by the War Council. But this anticipates our story.

Later that same morning, Sunday, 3 January 1915, Churchill summoned the Admiralty War Group to discuss and prioritize the various plans for the future currently on the table. The First Lord justifiably believed it to be essential that the Admiralty speak with one voice at the upcoming meeting of the Asquith War Council scheduled for the following Thursday. He wanted the War Group to consent to giving top priority to his plan to capture Borkum (as outlined above in his memorandum to the prime minister) as an advance base. Fisher and some of the others expressed strong objections. Frustrated, Churchill sought other alternatives; a couple of hours later, on his own initiative, he sent a private telegram to Vice-Admiral Sackville Carden, commanding a squadron in the eastern Mediterranean, enquiring if he thought "the forcing of the Dardanelles by ships alone a practicable operation."[222] Carden did not reply for several days and for the present no further steps were taken. The following morning, 4 January, Fisher arrived at the office and was stunned to find sitting on his desk an order cut by the First Lord (dated the previous day) directing that "all preparations should be made for the capture of Sylt" (the code name assigned to Borkum) two months hence.[223] The result was "a big explosion" from the admirals protesting the First Lord's dictatorial language and behavior in trying to impose his will upon Admiralty policy.[224]

Some hours later, after tempers had cooled, Churchill wrote to Fisher reemphasizing the importance of going into the War Council, now just three days hence, with a clear agenda and unified purpose. The First Lord reissued his demand that the First Sea Lord support his request for a regular division of infantry to capture Borkum. In the same letter, Churchill implicitly rejected Fisher's counterproposals, exhorting the First Sea Lord to forget the Mediterranean and to remember that "Germany is the foe, and it is bad war to seek cheaper victories and easier antagonists."[225] "With regard to mining," he closed in a peremptory tone, "you should put forward definite and practical proposals."[226] Perhaps stung by the patronizing note, Fisher retorted that Churchill's plans violated several key tenets of British naval policy, the most important of which was "to conserve our Naval Superiority over the Germans and in no wise jeopardize it by minor operations whose cumulative effect is to wear out our vessels and incur losses in ships and men."[227] In any case, Fisher added, amphibious operations in the North Sea were out of the question during the winter months, and therefore the most that could be accomplished at present was to prepare for such an operation in the spring.[228] "I agree that Borkum offers great possibilities," Fisher soothingly but disingenuously wrote, "but it's a purely military question whether it can be held"—knowing full well that the Army insisted it could not. That day, Captain Thomas Crease, Fisher's trusted assistant, told Captain Richmond, "They can go on getting out plans as much as they like, but Jacky is simply not going to do them in the end." The First Sea Lord, Crease declared, "didn't intend to have the Borkum business done."[229]

Fisher adhered to his different strategic vision. As a secondary move, he argued that a push in the Levant could be useful. He insightfully pointed out the substantial economic advantages that would accrue to the Entente by reopening the trade route to the Black Sea and thereby allowing Russian trade to flow. Significantly, such a rationale for opening a Turkish front was quite distinct from diverting German military resources—but alas, Fisher did not elaborate. Incidentally, it is important to be clear that Fisher, like Hankey, always regarded the Turkey plan as a subsidiary operation that would employ only surplus naval forces (i.e., old warships). He never wavered in his insistence that the North Sea must remain the primary theater of operations; he also believed that current arrangements were still unsatisfactory and a change in approach was necessary.

As we have seen, since his return to the Admiralty in November 1914, Fisher had been emphatic that mines were the best answer to the Navy's strategic and operational troubles. As per Churchill's request, he now attached two documents outlining "definite and practical proposals." The first, simply entitled "Mine-Laying," encapsulated the opinions Fisher had held "since the war began."[230] The second was a statement showing projected deliveries of new mines over the next several months.[231] Fisher laid out the multiple advantages that would result from "an offensive mine-laying policy," and the consequent necessity at once to order more mines and convert more fast liners into auxiliary minelayers.[232] These documents illustrate Fisher's desire to rely upon mining as the basis of North Sea strategy. Although he believed that the battle-fleet should stay on the defensive, his overall strategy was not defensive: he thought that economic warfare, aided by mining, constituted a powerful offensive tool.

In his memoirs, Fisher angrily insisted his "Policy of the Submarine Mine favored us, but our authorities couldn't see it. I printed in three kinds of type: (1) Huge capitals; (2) Italics; (3) big Roman block letters the following words, submitted to the authorities very early in the war:— 'Sow the North Sea with Mines on such a huge scale that Naval Operations in it become utterly impossible.'"[233] Fisher further emphasized "that British Mining Policy dished the neutrals. When the neutrals got blown up you swore it was a German mine—it was the Germans who began laying mines."[234] Fisher's demand for large-scale mine laying in the North Sea was a coherent subsidiary to economic warfare, with well-defined aims, and fully consistent with the strategic views he expressed both before and during the war. Furthermore, it demanded a major redirection in the current naval strategic policy away from commanding the North Sea for Britain toward simply denying it to Germany: the latter necessarily excluded the possibility of seizing islands off the German coast. Fisher's proposals were not just different from Churchill's vision, therefore, but totally antagonistic.

Already Fisher had started to drum up support for his coup.[235] Probably at his behest, Jellicoe had offered the Admiralty his "remarks on the question of a mining policy which it is submitted should be adopted," and this paper was steadily winding its way through the Admiralty labyrinth.[236] The commander in chief's letter, which was heavily marked by the First Sea Lord's green pencil, largely echoed the call for the laying of mines on both the German and British coasts (the latter as a deterrent against further raids) and, if necessary, using destroyers to plant them until the fast auxiliary minelayers became available. In appending their thoughts on the subject, Captain Dumas and the DNO confirmed that 5,000 mines were available. Both officers (probably wisely) refused to be drawn into "the questions of policy" entailed.[237] Fisher also received encouragement from the officer commanding the mine-laying squadron, who, while conceding that his present ships were dangerously inadequate, valiantly declared he would lead his squadron into the Bight if given a large escort.[238]

By the time that the file with Jellicoe's letter had completed its circuit of the Admiralty administration, however, resistance to Fisher's vision had solidified. Oliver, the chief of staff, adhered to his view that the mines would inconvenience the Navy more than solve its strategic problems.[239] A. K. Wilson was equally skeptical, insisting the plan "overlooks the fact that the mining policy of the powers that aim at keeping the sea open must necessarily be quite different from and much more difficult than the policy of powers whose main object is practically to close it to all comers."[240] This remark entirely missed the point, of course: Fisher *wanted* the North Sea closed to all traffic, believing this the most expeditious way of cutting off Germany from overseas supply. Despite this opposition, Fisher managed to carry the day, at least temporarily. On the night of 8–9 January, the Royal Navy sent four old minelayers deep into the Heligoland Bight, where they placed approximately 500 mines off the Elbe estuary.[241] It was an extremely hazardous operation and the force was lucky to escape undetected. Its achievement did not constitute total victory for Fisher's strategic vision, however; it merely won an early round.

To recap, during the first week of January 1915 the naval leadership were evaluating two sets of proposals embodying two incompatible strategic ideas. Churchill's plan envisaged the Royal Navy exerting command over the North Sea to capture a German island for use as an advance base for short-range flotilla craft so as to permit the main fleet to adopt a more aggressive stance. He called for the assembly of ships and equipment so that the operation could be launched in the spring of 1915 as soon as the weather moderated. Fisher's plan, based upon his concept of sea denial, called for the opposite: the Royal Navy would more or less evacuate the North Sea and sow large numbers of mines so as to disrupt the flow of trade across the North Sea and thereby increase the economic pressure on Germany.

While various middle-ranking officials deliberated, Churchill and Fisher vied for Jellicoe's support, both seemingly viewing the fleet commander's endorsement as critical. On 4 January 1915, the First Lord wrote to the commander in chief begging his endorsement of the plan to capture Borkum.[242]

Jellicoe wrote back rejecting all such "island operations" as impractical and successfully withstood repeated assaults by Churchill to change his mind.[243] Unbeknownst to Churchill, Jellicoe had already promised his support to the First Sea Lord. Fisher was delighted with Jellicoe's unequivocal rejection of the First Lord's initiative: "You say golden words when you protest *'against taking risks for which there is no compensating advantage.'*"[244] On 12 January, Fisher again wrote to Jellicoe, complaining that "AK Wilson and Oliver and all the small fry [junior staff officers]" were all opposed to mining, "of which no doubt the First Lord will take full advantage, as he is dead set against a mining policy."[245] A couple of days later he appealed to Jellicoe for support, begging him to tell Churchill "that a mining policy of the eastern end of the British [English] Channel against submarines is obligatory." On 15 January, Jellicoe did so in unequivocal language.[246] Three days later an irritated Churchill replied: "As to mines—you know my views. We have never laid one we have not afterwards regretted."[247] At the Admiralty, Churchill resorted to standard bureaucratic delaying tactics: requesting further consideration by the War Staff and certain practical experiments.[248] "My view is that the mines should be laid at once," Fisher scrawled angrily (and deeply) across the docket, "and I protest against these delays."[249]

Here is it worth reiterating that it is a mistake to view the Churchill-Fisher relationship and British policy making solely through the prism of the Dardanelles. In early January 1915, Fisher was not absolutely opposed to this operation. His objections were specific rather than general: he thought it foolhardy to attempt a solely naval assault, and he did not want the Dardanelles to distract from the more important theater in the North Sea. Nevertheless, so long as the naval commitment in the Mediterranean remained limited and the Army's commitment substantial, Fisher recognized that the Dardanelles operation might have some advantages, especially by providing economic relief for Russia. Thus, although their disagreement over the Dardanelles certainly did not help their relationship, Fisher was much more upset with Churchill over North Sea strategy than over hypothetical operations in the Mediterranean.

Their dispute over North Sea strategy provides the key context for understanding the Admiralty's stance at the meetings of the prime minister's War Council held on 7, 8, and 13 January 1915—the meetings at which Churchill had hoped to present a united Admiralty front. On these dates, Asquith and his colleagues reviewed the practicability of various plans for a strategic offensive, most of which involved joint naval and military cooperation, in addition to the plan submitted by the British Army commander to launch another frontal assault against the Germans in Flanders, which was quickly dismissed. The front-runners were Churchill's scheme to capture Borkum, and another put forward tentatively by Lord Kitchener to seize the port of Alexandretta. Under intense pressure from the French government to send more troops and matériel to the western front, however, and mindful of growing discontent among the Allied powers that Great Britain was not pulling her weight, Kitchener dithered as to when troops would be available to mount any new operation.[250]

In fact, both Kitchener and Fisher would have preferred to husband their resources for another several months before undertaking any new commitments, but the political members of the War Council made clear that delay was not an option. The unavailability of troops, or rather Kitchener's unwillingness to commit the few that remained in England, led the War Council to consider what the Navy alone might achieve. The notion that a proposed operation expedition to seize the Dardanelles would not involve a large landing force was an unexpected twist that Fisher afterward described to Kitchener as "damnable."[251] Ultimately, after three weary sessions, the War Council accomplished nothing beyond authorization to make preparations, which Asquith anticipated "will keep the Navy & Army busy till March."[252] Small wonder that Fisher later commented to Jellicoe that *"the way the war is conducted both ashore and afloat is chaotic! We have a new plan every week!"*[253]

Churchill interpreted the conclusions of the War Council as authorization to reinforce the naval squadron in the eastern Mediterranean in anticipation of final approval to launch an attack somewhere against Turkey. Between 14 and 21 January, Churchill began detailing large numbers of warships to join Vice-Admiral Sackville Carden (formerly dockyard superintendent at Malta) and his improvised squadron at the Dardanelles. As the list grew and grew, Fisher became increasingly uncomfortable. Given his focus on the North Sea problem, he did not mind elderly warships being sent, but he did object to the addition of so many modern warships—including three battle cruisers—*"all urgently required at the decisive theatre at home,"* he told Jellicoe on 19 January.[254] At lunch with Geoffrey Dawson, the editor of the *Times,* the day before, had Fisher railed against the disorganized conduct of the war by the War Council, complaining that Asquith "had no initiative, always voted with the majority in council, and cared most for keeping his party together."[255] In a reflection of Fisher's concern over the North Sea, he also lambasted Grey for "taking no action for fear of offending neutrals."[256]

Despite his focus on the North Sea, Fisher had as yet done nothing to impede Churchill's preparations. Aside from its implications for helping Russia, Fisher realized that the Dardanelles operation could be a useful "feint" to distract Turkish attention away from Alexandretta, whose capture he and others approved.[257] But as Churchill committed more and more ships to the Mediterranean at the expense of the North Sea, Fisher's opposition hardened. On 20 January, he took his complaints about Churchill to Hankey, who passed them along to Asquith. As the prime minister relayed to Venetia Stanley:

> He [Fisher] likes Winston personally, but complains that on purely technical naval matters he is frequently over-ruled ("he out-argues me"!) and he is not by any means at ease about either the present disposition of the fleets, or their future movements [i.e., to the eastern Mediterranean]. Of course he didn't want Winston, or indeed anyone to know this, but Hankey told him he sh[oul]d pass it on to me. Tho' I think the old man is rather unbalanced, I fear there is some truth in what he says; and I am revolving in my mind whether I can do anything, & if anything what?[258]

Two days later Asquith found a solution—which in fact Fisher had planted with Hankey. On 22 January, Asquith instructed Churchill to summon Jellicoe from Scotland to attend the next War Council scheduled six days hence. Appalled, the First Lord immediately went round to see Asquith to protest the fleet commander being summoned to sit in judgment over his policy.[259]

Here again, in Fisher's correspondence with Jellicoe, we see that Fisher regarded the North Sea rather than the Dardanelles as the key issue. In a letter to Jellicoe dated 20 January 1915, previously misdated by historians, the First Sea Lord prepped the commander in chief to expect a summons from the prime minister and in the process revealed much of his own thinking:

> I imagine you are going to be asked by Cabinet orders what is your opinion as to mining the German Fleet into its anchorages that it can't get out into the North Sea without giving the warning signal of clearing the approaches of mines—just precisely similar to Admiral Togo putting mines down off Port Arthur, which the Russians had to clear away before going out, and so giving Togo warning, whose base was

> many hundreds of miles away, as you know. As fast as the Russians cleared the channel, then Togo next night put fresh ones down and so kept the Russians busy! Togo thus laid down *many,* many thousands of mines.[260]

Fisher claimed that Kitchener supported this defensive stance "but that the majority of the Cabinet [War Council] are against it."[261] There is no question that Fisher had been recently lobbying the other members of the War Council on this. On 11 January 1915, for instance, he penned a short note to Lloyd George mentioning a discussion earlier that day and urging him to read a line in Julian Corbett's book *England in the Seven Years' War* between pages 373 and 374.[262] The line reads: "There is no clearer lesson in history how unwise and short-sighted it is to despise and ridicule a naval defensive."[263]

Asquith's invitation to Jellicoe worked just as Fisher had hoped—aided by a conveniently timed illness. On the morning of 22 January, Fisher wrote briefly to Churchill apologizing that he would not be in the office that day because he had a cold. "Please don't attempt to catch it by seeing me," he added, "as there is nothing on except those d——d mines which you are all quite determined shan't be put down"—a caustic remark that further underlines the relative importance he attached to this issue.[264] Perhaps suspecting that Fisher's chill was more hostile than physical, and fearing that the First Sea Lord and Jellicoe might unite against him in front of the War Council, Churchill abruptly withdrew his opposition to the First Sea Lord's plan to block the Channel with 5,000 mines and agreed "to proceed with a revised scheme."[265] That evening Fisher wrote Churchill from his sickbed: "When Bartolomé appeared last night with the mine chart my heart was glad and my glory rejoiced!" (a reference to Psalms 16). The next morning, 23 January, still too ill to return to his office, Fisher wrote Churchill an oblique thank-you letter: "I made no criticism—half a loaf is better than no bread, and we shall get on!"[266] Having thus prevailed over the First Lord on the matter he regarded as key, Fisher quickly scrawled a note to Jellicoe counseling him to refuse the proffered invitation from Asquith to come to London.[267] The mere threat of Jellicoe attending the War Council had proved sufficient for Fisher's purposes.

It seems that Fisher, still sick, did not actually return to his office until Monday, 25 January, although he may have put in a brief appearance Sunday afternoon during the Battle of Dogger Bank.[268] He spent most of the weekend recuperating, sending letters, and putting the finishing touches on a memorandum he had been preparing, with the assistance of Hankey and Julian Corbett, entitled "Memorandum by the First Sea Lord on the Position of the British Fleet and Its Policy of Steady Pressure."[269] According to conventional opinion, Fisher's aim in producing this document for the War Council was to combat Winston Churchill's plan to force the Dardanelles, and accordingly it is solely in this context that the message it contained has been interpreted.[270] While it is true that in drafting this memorandum Fisher had expressed a desire to squash Churchill's ambitions to force the Dardanelles, this was neither the sole intent nor the primary one. Reading this memorandum literally and without distortion through the lens of subsequent events, it is clear that the central message was that the First Sea Lord should be allowed unfettered authority over the direction of naval strategy, and that the primary focus of operations should remain the North Sea—both swipes at Churchill.

In the opening paragraph, Fisher declared his objective to provide the War Council with a statement "as to what our naval policy in this war is to be." His recommendations were simple and unambiguous: Fisher advised patience, that the government must "be content to remain in possession of our command of the sea, husbanding our strength until the gradual pressure of sea power compels the enemy's fleet to make an effort to attack us at a disadvantage." In other words, he advocated a strategic defensive, a strategy fundamentally at odds with that advanced by the First Lord. By "pressure of sea power," Fisher of course was referring to economic warfare, which, he warned, was "a slow process and requires great patience."[271]

An intensification of economic warfare was necessary, according to Fisher, because the current blockade policy appeared ineffectual. This policy would succeed or fail in the North Sea, which required more resources. In his words:

> To cut off the enemy's trade we ought to aim at a complete closing of the North Sea, and the declaration of a blockade. The machinery of a blockade is already established and maintained between Scilly and Ushant, and between Hebrides and Norway. It is remarkable and beyond all praise and admiration how our patrols have, in the furious gales that have continuously raged all this winter, so completely blocked the passages into the North Sea as to identify every steamer that has sailed from foreign ports for the North Sea. Difficulties with neutrals and adherence to an absolute international law based on the conditions of a century ago, and quite inapplicable to technical developments

> of modern warfare, have also prevented us from declaring an actual blockade.[272]

Elsewhere in the paper Fisher rejected "joint operations against continental Germany [as] impracticable in view of the enemy's strength in submarines," a reference to the Borkum operation. He also cautioned against all "coastal bombardments or the attack of fortified places without military cooperation," a reference to the Zeebrugge/Ostend operation but arguably also to the Dardanelles plan. In other words, his objections to bombardments and amphibious landings were general rather than specific to the Dardanelles plan. They also buttressed his case for authority over North Sea strategy, which was the main purpose of the paper.

Fisher submitted the finished paper to Churchill on 25 January, along with a request that the numbered copies he had prepared be distributed prior to the War Council scheduled three days hence.[273] Hankey claimed Churchill was furious.[274] The next day the First Lord drafted a counterblast to the First Sea Lord's memorandum but by private letter told Fisher he wanted to discuss the matter with the prime minister before either document was circulated.[275] That interview occurred on the afternoon of 27 January. Remarkably, Asquith ruled that the First Sea Lord's memorandum should not be circulated but that Churchill's reply to it should![276] The only conceivable explanation for the prime minister's action is that he had already decided the Dardanelles expedition should proceed and did not want the subject debated further. Upon receiving Asquith's verdict on the morning of 28 January, Fisher was justifiably affronted and intimated to Churchill and Asquith that he was contemplating resignation on the grounds of irreconcilable strategic viewpoints.[277] "I am not in accord with the First Lord and do not think it would be seemly to say so before the Council," he told the prime minister. "His reply to my memorandum does not meet my case."[278] To Churchill: "My position is quite clear:— I make no objection to either Zeebrugge or Dardanelles if accompanied by military cooperation on such a scale as will permanently hold the Belgian coast to the Dutch frontier and our permanent military occupation of the Dardanelles Forts *pari passu* with the Naval bombardment."[279]

No one took Fisher's threat that seriously, nor, it seems, did the admiral intend they do so. Rather, his threat was a shot across the bow. As Asquith remarked to Venetia Stanley that evening, "He [Fisher] is always threatening to resign & writes an almost daily letter to Winston, expressing his desire to return to the cultivation of his 'roses at Richmond.'"[280] Similarly Fisher characterized the proceedings as a series of "fierce rows" rather than a resignation issue.[281] Asquith nevertheless acknowledged "growing friction between Winston & Fisher" and admitted to Venetia that he had pressured the admiral that morning into "withdrawing his opposition to the operation against the Dardanelles."[282]

In the week before the meeting of the War Council scheduled for 28 January 1915, two events occurred that changed the context for debating the proposed Dardanelles operation and altered the dynamics of the squabble between Fisher and Churchill. One was diplomatic and well known; the other was domestic political and has never before been considered by historians. The two combined to hearten members of the political executive to look upon the proposed Dardanelles expedition with greater favor than before and, furthermore, to view it as a domestic political decision rather than a strategic one. Accordingly, what follows below (and in the next chapter) is a new account of the origins of the Dardanelles campaign.

As already related, the plan to bombard the forts at the Dardanelles to enable a fleet to force a passage up the straits had been intended to coincide with an amphibious operation to seize Alexandretta, an important railway junction in Syria which many viewed as the future gateway to the Levant and (via pipeline) to the oil fields of northern Persia.[283] In the event of a reverse at the Dardanelles, as Churchill told Kitchener, the British intended to claim that the fleet operation had been no more than a feint.[284] The problem was that shortly after the beginning of the war the French had claimed responsibility for all of Syria and the Foreign Office had already signaled its tacit acquiescence.

On 18 January, Churchill handed the French naval attaché in London a memorandum outlining Britain's strategic intentions in the Near East, which was duly forwarded to the Ministry of Marine in Paris. The French response was icy. On 21 January, Winston professed to being "bewildered and upset" upon learning that the French minister of marine, Victor Augagneur, a professor turned politician, objected strongly to any British operation in the eastern Mediterranean, jealously insisting that the British plan to seize Alexandretta infringed upon French interests.[285] On the afternoon of 26 January, the French minister arrived in London and met privately with Churchill. Before the meeting Sir Edward Grey urged Winston "to let the French have what they want in this memo: even about Alexandretta," warning that "if it is not agreed to I foresee very untoward consequences."[286] Churchill obligingly gave way, remarking that anyway "Lord Kitchener [now] informs me that he cannot now fix any date for the Alexandretta expedition."[287] Churchill and Augagneur duly agreed to postpone the planned expedition until such time as the French were ready to mount it themselves; in the meantime, the British operation to force the Dardanelles would proceed.[288] Thus by the evening of 26 January, the significance of the Dardanelles operation had materially changed for diplomatic reasons.

The second, hitherto unknown factor in the changing context for the Dardanelles was domestic political. Since the end of 1914, the British government had become increasingly alarmed over increases in the price of food and other necessities of life. On 12 and 13 January, the cabinet held back-to-back meetings to review the causes and possible solutions. Ministers agreed that food prices had already reached a politically sensitive level and worried that they might rise even higher, to perhaps a socially dangerous level. The Board of Trade and Board of Agriculture hurriedly undertook a survey of the situation, whose results were discussed at the cabinet meeting on 20 January. The forecasts were so dire and the political implications deemed so serious that Asquith formed a secret food prices committee and—remarkably—appointed himself chairman. The committee met for the first time two days later. For reasons that will be explained fully in the next chapter, within days both Asquith and Lord Crewe (secretary of state for India, member of the War Council, and the prime minister's right hand) came to believe that there were powerful domestic political reasons—namely, the hope that opening the route to Russian grain would reduce food prices at home—to reopening the Dardanelles.

According to the minutes of the War Council meeting held on 28 January, approval of the Dardanelles expedition was swift, with the politicians agreeing that the potential for huge political and diplomatic gains far outweighed the consequences of possible naval reverse. Asquith told Stanley that the plan was "warmly supported by Kitchener & Grey, & enthusiastically by A.J.B. [Balfour]."[289] Balfour appears to have been speaking for all when he pronounced that "it is difficult to imagine a more helpful operation."[290] Subsequent correspondence between those present at the meeting suggest that the politicians were seduced by the promise of an easy and much-needed victory that could be accomplished with the limited resources immediately to hand.[291] Military and diplomatic intelligence encouraged them to believe that the Gallipoli peninsula and even Constantinople were low-hanging fruit ripe for the plucking.[292] Contempt of risk and presumption of success led the politicians to disregard Fisher's reservations. They told themselves that in the event of a reverse the attack could simply be broken off.[293] Even several weeks later, after Asquith learned that the risks involved were a good deal greater than Churchill had described and that ultimate success required troops on the ground, the prime minister felt "strongly of opinion that the chance of forcing the Dardanelles, & occupying Constantinople, & cutting Turkey in half, and arousing on our side the whole Balkan peninsula, presents such a unique opportunity that we ought to hazard a lot elsewhere rather than forgo it."[294]

After the War Council of 28 January 1915, Fisher consistently maintained (until his testimony in October 1916 to the parliamentary commission) that the decision to attack the Dardanelles had been made for "political reasons" in defiance of professional naval opinion.[295] Directly after the meeting (i.e., on 28 January) Fisher told Sir Francis Hopwood that "he did not care what happened," claiming he had been absolved of responsibility.[296] In Fisher's own words: "The politicians took the bit between their teeth and decided it was a Cabinet and not 'expert' question."[297] For this reason, he claimed, he withdrew his threat to resign. "I protested from the very first," he explained for the umpteenth time to Jellicoe at the end of March 1915, "but the Cabinet were persuaded into it by Balfour and the First Lord, and it was made a purely political question."[298] In a letter written to Balfour in early February 1915, Hankey substantially corroborated Fisher's account, writing that from "Fisher downwards every naval officer in the Admiralty who is in the secret believes that the Navy cannot take the Dardanelles position without troops. The First Lord still professes to believe that they can do it."[299]

Throughout March and into April, Fisher (and Hankey) lobbied incessantly for an independent panel of experts to review the technical feasibility of the expedition, the latter warning, "It is conceivable that a serious disaster may occur."[300] Both Fisher and Hankey became even more concerned after Churchill issued a communiqué to the press announcing the British intentions. "There ought to have been no blatant press announcement at the outset, and the bombardment ought to have been announced merely as a demonstration," Hankey commented to Lord Esher on 15 March.[301] "Myself I think it utter folly to publish a word about the bombardment," Fisher agreed, "but it is all Foreign Office business and pressure from Russia and France. We are their facile dupes!"[302] When on 18 March 1915, the admiral commanding the fleet at the Dardanelles informed the War Council that the

Turks had inflicted serious losses upon his fleet and caused him to break off the attack, Hankey recorded in his diary that "Lord F[isher] and I [were] in the rather unenviable position of being able to say 'I told you so.'"[303]

Contrary to what most of the politicians involved in the decision to launch the attack later claimed, all knew of Fisher's "opposition to the operation against the Dardanelles."[304] Indeed, in November 1915, Asquith publicly told the House of Commons: "After full investigation and consultation with the naval experts, including the Admiral commanding in that part of the Aegean, and notwithstanding—I am betraying no secret in saying this—some doubts and hesitations, which undoubtedly there were in the mind of our principal naval advisor at that time, Lord Fisher, the government felt justified in sanctioning the attack."[305]

Fisher may have professed disinterest in the outcome at the Dardanelles, but he certainly did care about gaining approval for his preferred North Sea strategy. At a private luncheon given a few days later by the newspaper magnate George Riddell, attended also by several cabinet ministers, Fisher proclaimed: "Our proper plan is to blockade Germany *and the adjoining neutral countries.* That is the way to end the war."[306] On 11 February, Fisher met once more with Riddell and "again urged the necessity for a general blockade."[307] At the end of that month, the First Sea Lord was still complaining to Jellicoe at "our absence of a complete blockade" ostensibly because "we really are stupid in our funk of neutrals!"[308] There are signs he was becoming more frustrated—even fractious—at Winston Churchill's increasingly dictatorial behavior and continued opposition to laying mines off the German coast.[309] The only glimmer of encouragement was that the government was at last taking steps to tighten the blockade. This will be the subject of the next chapter.

THE LONG WAR
1915–1916

8

Vigorous Indecision

The war lords are sad at their stalemate, and Winston in particular sees no success for the Navy (+ himself) anywhere. But we go ahead all the time, sure that by doing our best we shall succeed if not in a dramatic coup then in a sturdy endurance that will outlast German, or rather Prussian, plunges.

WALTER RUNCIMAN, January 1915

Between Christmas 1914 and the New Year, the British government despaired over the strategic situation. "It is curious how opinion alters in this war," Lord Emmott, a cabinet minister outside of the inner circle, remarked in his diary on 4 January 1915. "At the moment people here are much more inclined to believe in a long war and to see the difficulties of moving forward in the west."[1] "The worst of it is," agreed U.S. ambassador Walter Page, that "no end is in sight. Everybody here expects a long war."[2] In the previous chapter, we saw how recognition of stalemate on the western front led to a reevaluation of national strategy. The prime minister and his War Council were desperate "to get at the enemy from some other direction, and to strike a blow that would end the war once and for all."[3] The "necessity of winning a definite victory somewhere," to borrow Lloyd George's phrase, coupled to a number of other domestic considerations, encouraged Asquith and his senior ministers to gamble on killing several birds with one stone by disregarding expert advice and endorsing Winston Churchill's hastily conceived plan to strike at the Dardanelles.[4] As Asquith confided to Venetia Stanley in early February: "It is of much importance that in the course of the next month we should carry through a *decisive* operation somewhere, and this one will do admirably for the purpose."[5] The "importance" was domestic, political, and economic.

The possibility that the duration of the war must be measured in years as opposed to months obviously had large economic and financial ramifications, yet the cabinet was slow to accept this possibility or factor it into its grand strategic calculations. David Lloyd George in particular presumed that the wealthiest nation on the planet need not worry about such matters. After all, Britain was the largest creditor nation in the world, possessing immense overseas holdings that—it was complacently assumed—might always be used as collateral against foreign loans or, if necessary, sold.[6] Since the beginning of the war, the chancellor had consistently rejected the advice of his Treasury advisors to raise taxes to meet government requirements.[7] The cabinet did not begin considering the fiscal implications of a long war before its meeting of 15 December 1914. Even then, it was Allied—not British—finances that commanded its attention.[8] Harcourt noted in his diary that there was a lengthy cabinet discussion on how to meet calls from various allied nations for financial assistance.[9] Although it is true that for several months already the British government had been providing money to the allies, these had been relatively small sums to help overcome cash flow problems, not the significant subsidies now being demanded. Failure to form a consensus prompted Asquith to summon the War Council.

Meeting the next day, Lloyd George reviewed for those present the list of applicants for British money. Standing at the front of the queue and knocking loudest were the Russians, requesting no less than £100 million to procure industrial plant and munitions from overseas. To put it in perspective, this sum exceeded Britain's entire annual peacetime defense budget and was equivalent to one-seventh her national debt. The Russians had tried to raise this sum privately on the London market only to be told that their credit (never solid anyway) was insufficient and that their only chance to raise any money was to have the British government guarantee the loan.[10] The closure of the Dardanelles, consequent to Turkey's entry into the war, had proved simply devastating to Russian trade, finances, and thus credit. The Belgian government in exile, meanwhile, had its hand out for £16 million.[11] To general bemusement, France, one of the richest countries in the world, asked to borrow £12 million.[12] Lastly, a commission of Romanian bankers had recently arrived in London on a quest to find £12 million, intimating that if Britain did not lend them the money, then Germany would.

Upon learning of the magnitude of the loans being requested, Arthur Balfour, the former Conservative prime minister who, as we saw in the last chapter, had recently joined the War Council, expressed dismay. If the government seriously intended to grant such immense sums, he advised, then "it was essential that our economic position be well maintained."[13] The problem, as he saw it, was that the government's policy of uncontrolled military recruitment appeared fundamentally inconsistent with this necessity, for clearly it was "essential that a large part of the population should continue in their normal employments" in order to generate sufficient revenues and foreign exchange to finance such loans. The logic was irrefutable and provoked silence. Such a complex topic required careful thought.

At Asquith's behest, accordingly, Balfour undertook "to write a paper on the question of 'recruiting and our economic position' "—"to ascertain how far, and in what trades, it was safe to continue recruiting, and when the point was reached beyond which our economic position would be weakened by continuing enlistment."[14] Perhaps the most intellectually powerful statesman of his generation, Balfour possessed a well-known predilection for analyzing complex, multifaceted economic problems. Moreover, though his scholarly attainments in philosophy are well known, it is not generally realized that in later life he became something of an economist. From 1907 until shortly before his death in 1930, Balfour was writing a treatise on economic theory.[15]

Balfour spent New Year's Day 1915 setting down on paper his thoughts on the relationship between military recruitment and economic policy in a memorandum titled "The Limits of Enlistment."[16] He concluded that, given the increasing likelihood of protracted conflict and the evident growing necessity to purchase munitions of war "not only for ourselves, but in part for our allies," the government must at once apply the brakes to military recruitment. In addition, steps must be taken to bolster the economy and rebuild British exports. Failure to do so, he warned, would damage Great Britain's long-term economic health and Britain's overseas credit, thereby risking London's position as banker to the world.[17]

In issuing this disconcerting forecast, Balfour pointed to various economic indicators already signaling problems. A fortnight earlier, almost unnoticed, the price of sterling on the New York exchange had dipped below its par value of $4.86. This was a direct consequence of the yawning deficit in the balance of trade between Britain and the United States. The problem, Balfour explained, was due not so much to surging British imports from the United States (mainly bulk commodities such as food) as to the continued weakness of British exports. Exports were down approximately 40 percent (by value) over the corresponding period the previous year.[18] In short, Balfour called upon the government to strike a better balance between military recruitment and industrial production in order to preserve confidence in British currency, credit, and the general long-term health of the economy. He reasoned thus:

> We must import food, raw material, probably gold, and probably munitions of war. We must therefore, although a creditor country, make immense foreign payments, and this can only be done either by borrowing abroad, or by exporting goods, or by selling securities. Of these three expedients the last is undesirable; the first undesirable, and perhaps impractical as well; only the second seems worthy of consideration.

It followed "that anything in the way of enlistment that cripples those industries which either produce commodities for our export trade, or produce commodities at home (such as foodstuffs), which, if not made by ourselves, must be purchased abroad, may, and indeed must, diminish our fighting efficiency."[19] With an eye to the postwar future, Balfour rejected paying for the war and shoring up the exchange rate through the liquidation of national wealth by selling overseas assets.

Although Balfour's central message was clear enough, the understated language and tone he employed made "The Limits of Enlistment" read more as a speculative essay than as a policy prescription. It was a typical Balfour perambulation on the head of a pin. Though seldom referred to by historians, in light of subsequent events this paper was as important and prescient—arguably more so—as the three celebrated Boxing Day memoranda. Not only were the complexities of Balfour's arguments greater, but he was the only one to recognize that the selection of Britain's optimal strategy really depended upon one's estimate of the war's likely duration. In other words, he surmised (correctly) that the impact of financial and economic considerations hinged upon the time factor, and that their significance would expand and intensify the longer the war progressed. This point is key.

Yet while it is easy to admire the intellectual qualities of Balfour's paper, it is important not to overstate its merits as a strategic assessment. As critics pointed out, in framing his arguments Balfour had employed several questionable assumptions and used incomplete evidence. While he certainly identified the interconnectedness and complexity of the problems confronting the government at the beginning of 1915, he clearly misread some elements in the equation, rendering many of his recommendations inappropriate.

Above all, Balfour had not appreciated that limiting Britain's war liabilities was transparently incompatible with the requirements and expectations of her allies.

Already France and Russia had sent clear signals that they were unhappy with the level of Britain's contribution to the allied war effort. In recent weeks, a worried Lord Kitchener had been imploring the cabinet to take steps to bolster the alliance.[20] Britannia may have been short of munitions and military manpower, but her pockets remained deep. In mid-January 1915, after meeting with a delegation of disgruntled Russian financiers, Lloyd George too was driven to admit that "there is a feeling that we are not doing enough, & are 'on the make' "—that is, seeking to profit from the war. The chancellor afterward reflected to his private secretary and mistress, Frances Stevenson, that "we did attempt to drive too much of a bargain with them [the Russians] over the financial transactions. Pals and partners do not lend each other money at 5%!"[21] Lloyd George's remarks clearly indicate he believed that the British government's parsimoniousness toward its allies was a mistake. Another problem in Balfour's assessment was his unrealistic vision of a massive export drive.[22] Nor did he take fully into consideration, as will be shown below, the fundamental incompatibility between policy of export-led growth and the Navy's economic warfare strategy.

Balfour's paper was printed on 5 January 1915 and distributed prior to the War Council meeting two days later. It made little impression upon the other members of the executive. For different reasons, none of the other participating ministers saw the necessity of subordinating strategic choice to economic considerations. Churchill gave the proposition particularly short shrift, blithely asserting that recruitment could safely continue without "unduly affecting the economic system."[23] Lloyd George steadfastly adhered to his belief that Britain's wealth was so great and her overseas credit so strong that such concerns were manifestly unwarranted. None of the ministers shown the paper were yet ready to abandon all hope of a rapid end to the war; of course different ministers held different assumptions as to what "rapid end" might mean.

Playing on this sentiment, Kitchener directed his staff to produce a paper calculated to mislead the War Council into believing the war would be over before the projected economic and financial consequences of unlimited military recruitment might come to fruition. The field marshal, it seems, was the only member of the War Council to view Balfour's paper as a serious—and unwelcome—contribution to the strategic debate. Major-General Charles

Callwell, the officer he tasked to write the paper, understood perfectly that it was intended for political consumption, "to prove that the Germans will run out of men within the next few months."[24] Callwell's paper seemingly produced upon its intended audience the desired effect. Asquith subsequently wrote to Venetia Stanley with renewed confidence that the war would be over before the "inevitable" economic problems highlighted in Balfour's paper would have time to become debilitating.[25] As late as March 1915, Asquith still half believed that the war could be over by the end of the summer.[26]

Mindful of unhappiness within official circles at the government's handling of the economy, however, the prime minister instructed the CID to circulate Balfour's memorandum to senior departmental civil servants.[27] Here it met a very different reception. "The Limits of Enlistment," it seems, articulated fears for the economic well-being of the country held by a large number of senior government officials. Within days, several departments of government had been sufficiently emboldened to approach the War Office with demands for a curb in recruitment. Uncontrolled military expansion, they complained, was causing labor shortages in several key industries, including shipbuilding, engineering and especially transportation. On Thursday, 7 January 1915, the War Office promised the Board of Trade that it would suspend enlistment of "armaments workers, railway employees and woolen workers."[28] The Board of Trade later came back asking for limits on the enlistment of coal miners (who were, incidentally, among the highest-paid workers in England).[29] The following Monday, the War Office agreed to consider an Admiralty request that recruitment in all shipbuilding towns be restricted.[30] The Board of Agriculture issued a similar appeal.[31]

On 11 January 1915, the Board of Trade submitted to the cabinet its considered thoughts on Balfour's paper. Written by our old friend Sir Hubert Llewellyn Smith, the departmental permanent secretary, this document gave voice to the clamor from employers up and down the country at the worsening labor scarcity and the attendant difficulties in conducting business.[32] It endorsed Balfour's call for the government to rein in the Army's expansion, supplying additional evidence to show that "the progress of recruiting is threatening to reduce the supply of labour below the irreducible minimum necessary to enable the war to be effectively carried on."[33]

In a related and accompanying paper Walter Runciman, the president of the Board of Trade, brought the cabinet's attention to the politically worrying recent increases in the price of imported food. This he attributed primarily to a recent sharp increase in freightage caused by the Admiralty Transport Department having requisitioned more than one thousand merchantmen for war service without any apparent regard for the impact upon civilian trade. The withdrawal of so many vessels from the shipping pool, in effect, had contracted world carrying capacity, resulting in increases in freight rates.[34] On the eve of war the normal price for chartering an ordinary tramp steamer had been 3s. per month on the dead weight (i.e. per ton); at the end of 1914 the rate had doubled.[35] On longer routes the increase had been even greater. The cost of shipping grain from Argentina to Britain, for instance, had more than tripled.[36]

The "serious rises in the prices of bread, meat, coal & other necessary commodities" were the principal subjects of discussion at back-to-back meetings of the cabinet held on 12 and 13 January 1915.[37] To rebut the charges of Admiralty mismanagement, Winston Churchill distributed a memorandum written by Graeme Thomson, the phenomenally talented 40-year-old head of the Transport Department, whom the First Lord heralded as the greatest transport man since Noah.[38] Thomson's paper convincingly demonstrated that Runciman's accusations were ill founded. There was currently no shortage of merchantmen available for charter. Although because of government requisitions there were fewer vessels available to carry trade overseas, the demand for shipping had fallen by an even greater amount as a result of the collapse in volume of global trade. The Admiralty had done no more than give employment to idle ships. Thomson nevertheless acknowledged that freightage had become more expensive, and this required explanation, which he proceeded to give.[39]

Thomson clarified that the increase in freight rates was due to several factors, but mainly was the consequence of severe congestion in civilian ports. This, he claimed, was directly attributable to Army recruiting. The resultant shortage of stevedores (the unskilled labor normally employed to load and unload cargoes) meant that merchantmen were now spending much longer in port. A lack of dockyard warehouse space and a deficiency of locomotives to haul imported goods swiftly away from the ports was compounding the problem. As a result of the delays in loading and unloading, merchantmen were compelled to sit idle for up to a fortnight incurring demurrage charges—obliging shipowners in turn to increase freightage.[40] In a subsequent report, Thomson would show that increases in freight rates were also attributable to the shortage of cargoes for export from the United Kingdom, obliging many ships to clear for overseas in ballast—which of course meant they could recoup their overhead only by charging more for inbound freight.[41] In his first paper, Thomson volunteered that he had "repeatedly" explained all this to the War Office but that its staff had refused to listen.[42] He added also that Admiralty officials had met with port employers and labor unions in an unsuccessful attempt to improve efficiency by negotiating the removal of restrictive labor practices.[43] Thomson's paper concluded with a dramatic warning: if military recruitment continued unfettered, the government would be compelled to adopt radical and politically difficult, not to say unpalatable, remedies, such as recruiting foreign stevedore labor to work in British ports or imposing state control over the entire merchant shipping industry.[44]

All eyes shifted to Kitchener, who responded with a point-blank refusal to suspend Army recruitment in sea ports. According to Asquith (and confirmed by Harcourt), the field marshal imperiously suggested that "women sh[oul]d be employed[,] and when it was pointed out that they are not suited or accustomed to load and unloading cargoes he replied that they were so employed at Zanzibar!"[45] The combination of Asquith's unwillingness to press an issue, which he did not seem to regard as serious or perhaps did not yet fully understand, and Kitchener's intransigence induced the cabinet to postpone making any decisions and seek further evidence before taking action.[46] Over the course of the following week, opinions were solicited and reports prepared.

On 20 January 1915, the cabinet gathered to review the new economic forecasts.[47] Further study had revealed a situation even worse than suspected. The Board of Trade reported that business and social organizations were unanimous: the recent "rise in prices of foodstuffs has been so great that the welfare of the masses of the people is seriously threatened."[48] Representatives of organized labor were clamoring that "the position is so grave that the Government should take control of food supplies."[49] No statement could be more calculated to make the cabinet sit up and take notice; it revived the dormant specter of civil disorder that had so concerned the politicians at the beginning of the war.[50] The Board of Trade further warned that its earlier prediction the price of wheat might double over its prewar price no longer seemed a distant possibility but "now appears a probability."[51] Llewellyn Smith bluntly summarized: "The government must decide what it wants to be the highest price that the country can afford to pay for bread."[52] The Board of Agriculture corroborated these assessments with detailed statistics confirming the growing scarcity of and the rising price of wheat on the world markets.[53]

The cabinet's response to this alarming assessment was to appoint two ad hoc cabinet committees, one to tackle the problem of rising food prices and the other to find a solution to the growing economic problems stemming from the shortage of labor. It is a measure of how seriously ministers regarded the first problem that they prevailed upon the prime minister himself to accept the chairmanship of the Rise in Food Prices Committee. A disconsolate Asquith informed Venetia that the work would entail wearisome study of intricate and technical questions such as "how far are the prices of commodities really influenced by questions of freight charges" and "if we can solve the freight question have we really, materially or substantially, affected the price of, say, bread."[54]

At once it must be stressed that the *food prices* committee was completely separate from the *food supply* committee, established at the beginning of the war and charged with ensuring "a constant supply of food for the people of this country at cheap, or at any rate, reasonable price."[55] The cabinet food supply committee, which consisted of Runciman (Board of Trade), McKenna (Home Office), Lord "Bron" Lucas (Board of Agriculture), and Edwin Montagu (financial secretary to the Treasury), had been most active in its mission. As early as October 1914, it had considered but rejected the idea of fixing the price of bread, largely because of the massive political implications of such action and also because it recognized that the state lacked the machinery for enforcement.[56] Anticipating significant price rises, nevertheless, the supply committee had implemented a plan to create a strategic wheat stockpile. Beginning on 12 December 1914, the British government began secretly purchasing two million quarters (a quarter was 480 pounds) of wheat futures. Responsibility for purchasing the contracts was entrusted to a secret committee chaired initially by R. Henry Rew, assistant secretary to the Board of Agriculture.[57] But the world price of wheat rose faster and higher than expected.

From Asquith's letters to Venetia Stanley, we discern that the cabinet food prices committee first met on Friday, 22 January 1915, and that there were a further four "dismal" meetings before it was wound up on the eve of a major parliamentary debate on the subject held on 11 February 1915.[58] Besides the prime minister, membership included Lord Crewe (secretary of state for India), Lucas, Runciman, and Montagu, plus two senior civil servants, Sir Francis Hopwood (Additional Civil Lord at the Admiralty and chairman of the ESRC) and Harold "Bluey" Baker (the financial secretary to the War Office, a trusted friend of the prime minister, and someone with a good head for numbers).[59] The merest glance at these names tells us that it was an unusually high-powered committee. Again, it cannot be stressed enough just how unusual it was for the prime minister to chair a cabinet committee.

Another unusual measure—almost unprecedented, in fact—was the enlistment of a secretary. Asquith described him as "a very clever young Cambridge don called Keynes"—none other than John Maynard Keynes, the celebrated economist, then 31 years old and just appointed to the Treasury as assistant special advisor to David Lloyd George.[60] On 22 January 1915, Keynes wrote to his father: "I am now very busy, having become secretary of a secret committee of the cabinet, presided over by the prime minister. First meeting this morning."[61]

The food prices committee assembled at 11:30 a.m. on Friday, 22 January. It quickly established that the rise in prices was a global problem rather than a national one, and was caused mainly by a contraction in the world food supply. Board of Trade statisticians confirmed that since the beginning of the war, the average price of food in Great Britain had already risen by 24 percent, but in some commodities the increase had been greater. Wheat, for instance, had risen by 72 percent chiefly because of Russia's inability to send her surplus to market.[62] There can be no better illustration of the global character of the world food supply or the severity of the disruption to the trading system caused by the war than to consider that although the wheat harvest in India had been bountiful, prices had risen so high and so fast that the Punjab faced imminent famine because so much grain was leaving the country. (The high world price for wheat made it profitable for Indian grain merchants to sell a far greater proportion of the national wheat crop for export.) At the end of 1914, the government of India prohibited the further exportation of wheat in order to defuse possible social disorder. This solution, while obviously beneficial to the grain-eating population of India, was greeted in London with dismay. This move was certain to exacerbate the general world shortage, further entrench the United States' position as the sole nation with a significant grain surplus, and lead to further price increases.[63]

Asquith's decision to take the chairmanship of the new food prices committee had major and hitherto unappreciated consequences for British strategy. At the very first meeting of the food price committee, Lord Lucas (Agriculture) advanced the idea of fixing a ceiling for the domestic price of bread. This proposal amounted to a call for direct state control over wheat prices and necessarily entailed a government subsidy to guarantee adequate supply. As mentioned, the food supply committee had already considered and rejected this idea several months earlier, mainly because the government lacked the administrative machinery to enforce fixed prices. Lucas's renewed scheme drew a fierce reaction from Asquith. Keynes's detailed handwritten minutes of the meeting (extending to six pages) record, "The Prime Minister would have none of it, declaring it would be easier to storm the Dardanelles than to carry such a measure—and much cheaper."[64] In his evening letter to Venetia Stanley, Asquith summarized the price committee's findings that afternoon in such a way as to suggest he had undergone an epiphany.

> There is no doubt that we are at last beginning to feel the pinch of war, mainly because all the German ships wh[ich] used to carry food are captured or interned, and the Admiralty has commandeered for transport &c over 1000 of our own. Further, the Australian crop has failed, & the Russian (wh[ich] is a very good one) is shut up, until we can get hold of Constantinople & open the Black Sea.[65]

These two documents cited above are of immense significance, for together they demonstrate that by this date, 22 January, Asquith had drawn a mental connection between the high price of wheat, the desirability of releasing the abundant Russian crop, and the (consequent) need to reopen the trade route to Russia by capturing Turkish Constantinople. The prime minister reiterated this assumed relationship in a subsequent letter he penned to his lady friend. "The only exciting thing in prospect (after seeing you on Friday) is what will happen in the Dardanelles," he wrote. "If successful, it will smash up the Turks, and, incidentally, let through all the Russian wheat wh[ich] is now locked up & so lower the price of bread."[66]

On 25 January 1915, Keynes produced a memorandum reviewing the preliminary findings of the food prices committee and offering some analysis. Here he emphasized the global nature of the problem. Doubtless to Runciman's chagrin, he reported that the "influence of the freight problem, though important in itself, on the wheat problem, is, I think, over-estimated."[67] Closer scrutiny of the Board of Trade's data had shown that increased freightage accounted for just 15 percent of the increase in the price of bread.[68] (Incidentally, this did not prevent the food prices committee from instructing the Admiralty, a fortnight later, to reduce the number of merchantmen under government charter.)[69] "There is much evidence," Keynes further explained, "that the recent rise in prices has been largely due to urgent purchases on account of various governments"—including the British War Office, for instance, which had instructed its agents to purchase forward contracts without regard for prices.[70] The French and Italian authorities had been equally heavy-handed, thereby creating a bidding war.

The most significant part of Keynes's paper lay in his "summary of proposals" for government action designed to achieve lower wheat prices. After reviewing all the options, Keynes advised that aside from "buying freely and selling, if necessary, at a loss" (in effect subsidizing bread prices—as had been done with sugar):

> The few definite proposals, made above, are all rather trifling. But there does not seem sufficient justification *yet* for a drastic policy on the lines of the sugar deal. In the realm of action the only thing really worth doing is to storm the Dardanelles. That done this particular problem would soon lower its crest.[71]

In retrospect, the timing of Keynes's paper (confirming Asquith's instinctive conclusions) could not have been more significant. So impressed was the prime minister that he ordered it circulated as a cabinet paper. Scrawled across the top of the official copy is a handwritten note stating, "Printed for use of the Cabinet 28th January 1915." But there was no cabinet meeting that day—only the sessions of the War Council, at which Asquith overruled the objections of Admiral Fisher and decreed, with otherwise unanimous support, that the Navy should attempt to force the reopening of the Dardanelles.

A closer reading of the War Council minutes reinforces the argument made here that the principal justification for the inception of the Dardanelles campaign was economics. Although there is no reference here to discussion of Keynes's paper, the benefits Keynes had listed that would accrue from resuming Russian exports of wheat to the West were discussed and emphasized.

> Mr. Balfour pointed out that a successful attack on the Dardanelles would achieve the following results:— It would cut the Turkish army in two; It would put Constantinople under our control; It would give us the advantage of having the Russian wheat; and enable Russia to resume exports; This would restore the Russian exchanges, which were falling owing to her inability to export, and causing great embarrassment; It would also open a passage to the Danube. It was difficult to imagine a more helpful operation.[72]

Writing to Hankey a couple of days later, Balfour again stressed that the main advantage in reopening the Dardanelles was that "Russian corn would be released from Odessa to the immense advantage both of the Russian seller and the British consumer."[73] On 2 February, Hankey supplied the prime minister with a more detailed summary of the tremendous "economic and political advantages" that would accrue.[74] "*Great Britain* would obtain the wheat she requires, and the considerable amount of shipping locked up in the Black Sea. Every expert agrees that all danger of a shortage of food supplies and excessive prices would disappear"; concurrently, "*Russia,* by selling her wheat, would re-establish her exchanges, and be able to pay for her supplies of war material, which, at present she can only do with great difficulty and embarrassment."[75]

The British government's concern during the winter of 1914–1915 over the price of wheat and other so-called necessities of life clearly merits much closer examination than it is possible to provide here.[76] Before moving on, however, it is noteworthy that during February 1915, prices continued to accelerate to the point where there appeared in Britain a very real danger of actual bread shortages. Henceforward, government purchasing was stepped up and the Rew Committee was reinforced, with the chairmanship passing to Sir Alfred Bateman, formerly of the Board of Trade and a member of the 1902 Royal Commission on Food Supply in Time of War.[77] Keynes was also appointed. Though the committee was careful not to attract notice by making large purchases, its activities were soon discovered, leading to yet further speculation. This unprecedented state intervention into the markets was technically illegal because it involved expenditure of public money without parliamentary sanction.[78]

The resulting outcry from Parliament and British wheat traders was so great that on 4 April 1915 the government halted purchasing.[79] Keynes remonstrated that the government was running a huge risk, as insufficient wheat had been contracted to tide the nation over the summer months.[80] Although British grain merchants had made adequate purchases, a scandalous proportion had been resold (for enormous profit) while in transit, ending up in the hands of European buyers.[81] As the weeks passed and the world stock of grain diminished, prices climbed. The severity of the situation is sufficiently illustrated by the following excerpt taken from a memorandum prepared by Keynes dated 1 May 1915:

> The most important figures are the following: Up to the end of the cereal year, 31 August 1915, the requirements of the importing countries of Europe, allied and neutral, are estimated at 21,500,000 quarters. The supplies

> to meet this demand are only 16,500,000 quarters. The situation is so well recognized that several governments have embarked on purchasing for themselves, in particular, the governments of France and Italy, who have been, and are, buying largely without much regard to prices. Those who do not get their supplies in good time will not get them at all.[82]

To provide for its population over the summer months before the next harvest, Great Britain needed to import 10 million quarters of wheat. Only about half of this had been secured before the activities of the secret purchasing committee were suspended. Space prevents us from exploring this fascinating and important subject any further.[83]

Equally complicated and politically threatening was the concurrent cabinet investigation into the impact of military recruitment on manpower resources. On 21 January 1915, Hankey circulated a CID memorandum summarizing the problems uncovered so far and concluding that it was vital, "from the naval and military as well as from the economic point of view, to take as soon as possible some steps to ensure ample supplies of labour without unduly interfering with recruiting."[84] Hankey promised another paper detailing the problems with trade unions, but this was either never completed or never distributed.[85] The latter explanation seems more likely: from the outset, Asquith exhibited a marked disinclination to probe deeply into questions appertaining to organized labor.

Lurking within the various papers circulated by the Admiralty and the Board of Trade during recent weeks had been ominous references to union intransigence over the adoption of measures designed to enhance labor productivity. Given the appalling state of prewar British industrial relations, any talk of compelling workers to accept changes in labor practices was guaranteed to make contemporary politicians blanch. Yet in 1915 what alternatives were open to the cabinet? All other options considered thus far appeared to be worse. As shown above, the Admiralty had already speculated on the possibility of bringing in cheap foreign labor to work on the British docks—a recommendation that carried a stratospheric political price tag. Scarcely less palatable was the suggestion by Kitchener (seconded by Edwin Montagu of the Treasury) to draw more women into the workforce.[86]

Pressed to take action, on 27 January 1915 Asquith convened a meeting at the CID, attended by no fewer than eighteen ministers and senior departmental civil servants, to discuss "The Limits of Enlistment."[87] It opened with an unsuccessful appeal from Balfour for a curb in military recruitment. "It would be a dreadful thing at this stage to put a limit on recruiting," Kitchener retorted; "it would be an end of all recruiting."[88] Three times that morning he reiterated this statement. Kitchener also revealed, for the first time, that he wanted an army of 3.8 million, that he had already enlisted 2 million, and that for the rest of the year he needed to recruit 30,000 men each week (or 1.5 million men total). With the exception of Haldane and Lloyd George, the majority thought these numbers fantastic. Balfour, McKenna, and Runciman were especially vigorous in denouncing the Army's insatiable demand for men, arguing that it threatened to strip manufacturing of labor and so destabilize the economy.[89] Though outnumbered, the field marshal remained steadfast, refusing to accept that his military mobilization endangered the economy. The "whole question," he countered, could be resolved if the government would just take a firm hand in directing the allocation of national labor resources; he was referring to the compulsory reform of labor practices and to utilizing more women in industry. The meeting closed in deadlock, with agreement only to make further study—a decision that amounted to a victory for the War Office.[90]

Asquith's disinterest in the entire proceedings was apparent in the letter he wrote afterward to Venetia Stanley.

> They had a long discussion in wh[ich] I took very little part on the "limits of Enlistment": the object being to devise some way in wh[ich] the necessary industries of the country can be carried on by men of non-military age, or disqualified for health &c, & by women. There was much cry & little wool, and in the end I formulated 2 or 3 rather platitudinous propositions, to which they all agreed.[91]

Kitchener's obstinate political obtuseness, coupled with Asquith's unwillingness either to compel a change in military policy or to invest in politically expensive solutions, barred further discussion of "the limits of enlistment" for another six months. During this period, the labor situation further deteriorated and the options diminished.[92] Yet in Asquith's defense it needs to be said that he was probably right in thinking that such radical solutions were as yet politically unattainable. Just days later, unhappy over rising food prices, the Scottish engineers union initiated an overtime ban in support of its demands for higher pay; this action swiftly became a fortnight-long all-out strike.[93]

Another explanation for Asquith's lethargy in mobilizing the economy for a long war was his half-held belief the war might be over before the end of the year. He was not the only one with this hope. In March, Sir Edward Grey, the foreign secretary, told a former cabinet colleague that he was "certain that the war cannot last more than a few months longer. England could go on for a long time, but the continent cannot; and particularly Germany cannot."[94] Asquith's optimism was fueled further by assurances from British diplomats in late March 1915 that their effort to recruit new allies, including Italy, Greece, Romania, and Bulgaria, would shortly bear fruit.[95] With the Russian and French armies also poised to launch counteroffensives, which their generals proclaimed had every chance of success, Asquith told Venetia Stanley he looked forward to April 1915 as "the really critical month of the war." He added: "So much depending upon whether the coin turns up Heads or Tails at the Dardanelles."[96]

Not all within the government accepted Asquith's assessment of the strategic situation and especially his contention that in the short run little more could be done to improve the organization of the economy for war. By the early spring of 1915, Kitchener's idea that the government should act to achieve a more efficient distribution of labor resources had taken root in the fertile brain of David Lloyd George. He was fast coming around to the view that it was necessary to "mobilize the whole of our manufacturing strength for the purpose of turning out at the earliest possible moment war material."[97] On 15 February 1915, Lloyd George affirmed in the House of Commons his conviction that Britain must make a greater sacrifice and commit more resources to the war effort.[98] The following week he openly demanded from the cabinet the imposition of state control over all production facilities capable of being adapted to produce munitions; this has been called his "manifesto for total war."[99] He wanted to organize the industrial resources of the county to produce enough munitions not only for the British New Armies but also to reequip the Russian army.

Yet Lloyd George's vision, however prescient it may appear in hindsight, ignored numerous economic and political realities. "I am glad to think that there are more factories available for the output of war material in this country," Kitchener sarcastically retorted on 25 February, "but the real crux of the situation is, in my opinion, the organization of the skilled labor required to work the machinery."[100] Churchill and Runciman concurred, adding that going down the road of centralized direction would mandate state control over more than just factories producing munitions; to be effective, it must encompass a far larger proportion of British industry and therefore must involve government intervention in the economy on a proportionally greater scale.[101]

There was also the necessity to obtain buy-in from the labor unions.[102] Asquith concurred that "the thorniest question" was persuading workers to accept more flexible working practices. The unions would never agree to concessions unless the government introduced controls against profiteering and compelled employers to settle outstanding demands for higher pay to offset rising food prices.[103] Notwithstanding these warnings of the difficulties ahead, the cabinet authorized Lloyd George to draft a bill to obtain the requisite legislative authority for the government to dictate industrial production, and the Defence of the Realm Act (1915) was ratified by Parliament on 16 March.[104] It marked only the beginning of the effort.

Economic Warfare Revisited and Reform of the Blockade Administration

Running closely parallel to but slightly behind the debate over the necessity for better economic management was a renewed discussion over economic warfare against Germany. For reasons that will become clear, these two issues had become different sides of the same coin in that the political and economic considerations underpinning policy decisions were virtually identical.

Since the beginning of the war, the prosecution of economic warfare was being increasingly hindered by flagging political willingness, both at home and among the allies, to countenance "offensive" measures that entailed collateral damage to their own economies. The point is well illustrated by the minutes of a meeting between British and French blockade officials held at the end of 1914 to discuss a further extension to the list of contraband; delegates spent far more time bickering over which strategic resources should be exempted on the grounds of special interest.

For instance, the French authorities declined to restrict aluminum (key in manufacture of zeppelins). The British could hardly object, as they were disinclined to impose restrictions upon the exportation of high-grade cotton fabric (used to make zeppelin skins—as was apparent after one shot down over London was found to have been constructed from fabric made in Lancashire).[105] The British delegates refused to embargo sales of tin or wool. Meanwhile, the Foreign Office begged that nitrates (key in manufacture of explosives and as fertilizer) be exempted for fear it "would produce a very bad impression in Chile." The French were similarly anxious not to offend their customers by restricting sales of silk or wine.[106] Outside the conference, the War Office, Board of Trade, Colonial Office, Foreign Office, and India Office all petitioned for certain items to be exempted. Lord Kitchener, for instance, who technically remained viceroy of Egypt, lobbied against restrictions on the export of Egyptian cotton.[107] The government of India opposed controls over the export of jute (used in sandbags); the Canadians were "most reluctant" to restrict the export of nickel (vital to the manufacture of military-grade steel).[108]

By the beginning of 1915 the cabinet recognized that dissatisfaction with the workings of the blockade, both at home and abroad, had reached levels that could no longer be ignored. British businessmen were becoming anxious at the failure of international trade to revive. Complaints were pouring into the Board of Trade that sales were being lost because of all the red tape now smothering the exportation of goods from the British Isles.[109] The new rules governing the export of prohibited goods were intolerably complicated, the forms poorly drafted, the procedures for obtaining the requisite licenses slow and cumbrous.[110] Exporters thought it especially ridiculous that they were required to fill out paperwork in order to obtain permits before selling their wares to allied nations and the dominions.[111] Merchants hated dealing with the new government bureaucracies, complaining they were staffed by men ignorant of business. "In fact," Walter Page reported to Washington on 28 December 1914, "this government has more protests from its own shippers and merchants than it has from all the neutral countries combined. . . . they even come to me to see if I can't find ways to help them."[112] Meanwhile, stories that some firms were systematically evading the British blockade to earn vast profits in Europe were circulating within the business community and press. "Economic pressure," Hankey summarized in his famous Boxing Day memorandum, "appears to be breaking down to a certain extent owing to the enormous trade with Holland and Denmark."[113]

Similarly aggravated American businessmen induced the Wilson administration at the end of 1914 to protest Britain's capricious interference with "legitimate" U.S. trade and, especially, the arbitrary enforcement of published British rules and procedures.[114] "The uncertainty of freedom of trade," the State Department note remonstrated, "is one of the chief, if not *the* chief, grounds of complaint."[115] In contravention to Grey's promises made the previous October, cargoes continued to be detained upon suspicion alone. "I fight Sir Edward about stopping cargoes," Walter Page assured President Wilson; Grey "yields and promises this or that. This or that doesn't happen or only half happens. I know why. The military ministers balk him. I inquire through the back door and hear that the Admiralty and the War Office of course value American good-will but they'll take their chances of a quarrel with the United States rather than let copper get to Germany."[116]

With considerable exaggeration, the State Department note protested that "many of the great industries of this country are suffering because their products are denied long-established markets in European countries," thereby "threatening them with financial disaster." With respect to U.S. copper exports, for instance, it was claimed that

> seizures are so numerous and delays so prolonged that exporters are afraid to send their copper to Italy, steamship lines decline to accept it, and insurers refuse to issue policies upon it. In a word, legitimate trade is being greatly impaired through uncertainty as to the treatment which it may expect at the hands of the British authorities.[117]

To a degree, of course, this had been quite deliberate: since October the Foreign Office had endorsed the deliberate harassment of strategically important cargoes to inhibit trade. But, without doubt, this had been multiplied by unintentional muddle and confusion in the application of rules.

The Wilson administration believed its note was "as unoffending and unthreatening as any American protest could have been in the circumstances."[118] But that was not how it was interpreted in London. Within the Foreign Office, the American note provoked hostility and even disdain. As Sir Edward Grey remonstrated to Ambassador Page, the claim that British action was destroying American business was palpably contradicted by figures published by the New York Port Authority (through which more than a third of U.S. exports passed) indicating that exports to Europe in November were at record levels.[119] This complaint appeared all the more unwarranted given also that the British government was purchasing rather than confiscating U.S.-owned cargoes seized as conditional contraband. After five months of war, just forty-five American-owned cargoes and eight ships had been placed in prize court, and one of those already had been released.[120] Within the British government there was a general feeling that the Americans were being unreasonable and driven by commercial greed. The recommendation of Sir Eyre Crowe, now in charge of contraband matters at the Foreign Office, was to adhere "resolutely" to current policy and even tighten the blockade where necessary:

> The State Department and I am afraid the President too, cannot be relied upon to deal fairly with us. They believe it pays them better to obstruct this country in the legitimate exercise of its belligerent rights than to obstruct the illegitimate practices of the German-American contraband traders because they have been accustomed to find the country giving way to them whenever they parade their alleged difficulties with public opinion.[121]

Commander Frederick Leverton Harris, MP, a senior Admiralty intelligence officer about whom more will be said later, insisted in a letter to Grey dated 5 January 1915 that it was "a matter of fact America is doing a roaring trade with neutral countries."[122] Sir Francis Hopwood, the chairman of the interdepartmental Enemy Supplies Restriction Committee, agreed that the American protest had been instigated by certain powerful U.S. interest groups.[123] Even the prime minister expressed himself indignant toward the United States, convinced that

> their merchants & ship owners have behaved & are behaving as fraudulently as they can, knowing perfectly well that most of the copper &c wh[ich] is shipped often under false papers for Holland & Denmark is really destined for Germany. But they have some technical points in their favor, and the President whose position becomes daily more precarious, dare not offend the powerful money interests. What a country![124]

The only member of the cabinet to voice discordance was Sir John Simon, the attorney general, who reminded everyone that, unfortunately, from a strict legal standpoint, the American complaints were largely justified.[125] Confronted with having to choose between either bowing to what was perceived to be unreasonable U.S. pressure or advancing novel interpretations of international law, it is hardly surprising that Asquith persuaded the cabinet to defer the matter until a later date.[126] Certainly it is wrong to suggest that British ministers felt intimidated by the U.S. protest or that their inaction reflected fear that their position was untenable.[127] As it happened, the cabinet decision to postpone making a formal reply suited the U.S. government as well.[128]

At the meeting of the War Council on 7 January 1915, problems with the machinery for administering blockade regulations were acknowledged and the necessity for reform agreed upon. The prime minister directed Colonel Hankey, who had highlighted the problem in his Boxing Day memorandum, to investigate and report. Six days later, Hankey supplied some practical ideas on how to buttress the faltering blockade.[129] His report, dated 13 January 1915, identified two main areas of concern: first, a shocking lack of coordination between the various departments responsible for the administration of blockade policy, and second, an embarrassing level of indirect British trade with the enemy.

Boiled down, Hankey's solution to both problems was better information management, especially in the exploitation of intelligence. London, he argued, was awash with commercial intelligence, which if properly exploited could be used by the blockade authorities to identify and plug the leaks. The problem was that this information lay scattered across several departments and agencies. The Admiralty, Foreign Office, Board of Trade, Board of Agriculture, and War Office each collected commercial intelligence. In addition, the various censorship bureaus (cable, wireless, and post) set up to manipulate the flow of information between Germany and the outside world were harvesting unexpectedly bountiful evidence of contraband smuggling by traders both at home and abroad. The problem was that each saw only part of the trade jigsaw puzzle.

Largely because of departmental jealousies and conflicting agendas, information sharing was haphazard, therefore rendering collation as well as systematic and timely analysis almost impossible. The obvious solution, Hankey proposed, was to create a central clearinghouse to receive, process, and distribute all commercial intelligence. Such a bureau, he further advised, should be headed by "a person of standing (e.g. a Cabinet Minister)" and staffed by a professional secretariat charged with keeping detailed records as well as generating much-needed statistical data to help quantify trade flows.[130] In advancing this proposal, Hankey had no fear of its rejection. On the contrary: all the departments recognized the merits of a central clearinghouse—and all wanted the task of winnowing the grains of commercial intelligence from the mountain of chaff. Hankey favored entrusting his parent department, the Admiralty, with the responsibility.

In advancing his second major concern, trading with the enemy, Hankey displayed much greater caution. Here he was entering a political minefield: for several months government officials had been trying to bury evidence of the severity of the problem. The minutes of the ESRC show that between September and December 1914, the Admiralty repeatedly complained that

British businesses were defying government proclamations banning them from trading indirectly with Germany through contiguous neutral countries.[131] But the government had chosen to accept Board of Trade assurances that the examples provided were no more than isolated incidents and therefore the magnitude of the problem was not great. Executive reluctance to address the problem of trading with the enemy was not entirely a function of political embarrassment. It reflected also the mixed message the government had sent the business community. On the one hand, trade in certain items was subject to unprecedented regulation under the "trading with the enemy" proclamations. On the other, the government propaganda machine was exhorting patriotic British businessmen to "capture" German trade in foreign markets.[132]

At the beginning of the war, merchants had been delighted at the thought that their government (read the Royal Navy) would be leading them in an economic crusade against their most dangerous commercial competitor.[133] By the end of 1914, however, this enthusiasm had wilted as it became clear that supplanting German trade with "British enterprise" was not so simple.[134] Replicating many German goods was found to be impractical, requiring substantial investment in plant, labor, and time. In addition, merchants were perturbed to discover that the government's crusade did not extend to attacking German firms located in neutral countries. German business concerns in South America were a case in point. Before the war, German houses had made large inroads into traditionally British-controlled interests in grain, tobacco, and coffee. In 1915, these German firms were not only still operating but prospering, their goods being carried to Europe—and indirectly on to Germany—in British ships and (still) being financed by British banks.[135]

Before we hasten to judge, it should be noted that several British banks and shipping companies had tried to decline business with Germans resident in South America but subsequently had been advised by the Treasury that such trade was *not* illegal.[136] There were cases, indeed, where British shipping companies not wishing to carry "enemy-owned" goods had tried to escape contractual obligations entered into before the war but were forced to comply by German overseas firms' threats of legal action in foreign courts. Appeals for assistance to the Foreign Office were rebuffed.[137] "However much we may regret it," Cecil Hurst of the Foreign Office wrote, "the Board of Trade do not wish these consignments to be interfered with."[138] Other British firms were less conscientious. As the chairman of the Harrison steamship line explained to a troubled Captain Richard Webb, head of the Admiralty

Trade Division, "British ships would have to abandon the whole of the Brazilian trade if they refused to carry for such German firms," and that "if it is abandoned, it will not be recovered."[139]

On 13 January 1915, therefore, in raising the issue of trading with the enemy, Hankey understood that he was touching on a sensitive spot and the Board of Trade especially was certain to resist any call for tightening of export regulations. His recommendations were thus cautious and modest. As a first step, he advised an overhaul of current arrangements for processing applications for special exemption export licenses. It will be recalled that back in August 1914, the prime minister had entrusted to a committee under Sir John Simon, the attorney general, the unenviable responsibility of differentiating between legitimate and illicit trade in the adjudication and issuance of special export licenses. Hankey found that the Simon committee was floundering in a sea of unprocessed paper. "The applications have now become so numerous," Hankey told the CID, "amounting to an average of over 900 a day, that it is impossible for the committee to consider every case separately, and it is understood that the majority are dealt with according to precedent and established principle."[140] That applications were not being properly scrutinized was a serious discovery, but Hankey's survey of procedures revealed still worse failings. Incredibly, he found that licenses were being issued "without due regard to the amounts of the different articles leaving the country" and "without full knowledge" of the end user's identity. Worse, the committee had kept no records. In consequence, no one had any idea of the total quantity of any commodity shipped to a particular agent or country. In effect, the licensing committee had assumed that each British exporter submitting an application was doing so in good faith and had itself established the legitimacy of the customer.

Hankey's accusations of serious laxity are corroborated by Foreign Office records. Independently of the CID, Sir Eyre Crowe of the newly created Contraband Department of the Foreign Office had been sufficiently disturbed by recent Admiralty accusations to initiate his own discreet enquiries into the export licensing process. Not unreasonably, he had assumed that no license could be issued until the Simon Committee was perfectly satisfied that the "consignment in question will not find its way to the enemy." But as Robert Vansittart, the Foreign Office liaison officer to the Simon Committee, admitted on 21 December 1914, this was not the sole criterion employed and decisions were almost always influenced by considerations "in connection with maintaining trade in this country."[141] "You are aware," Vansittart archly remarked, "that *absolute* certainty is unobtainable . . . otherwise everything to everywhere w[oul]d have to be stopped."[142] The justification ran thus: if British companies were prevented from supplying a certain item, then "Holland would purchase them from e.g. America, & then we should then either have to stop them as contraband [and deal with the ensuing diplomatic uproar] or let them go through. If we did not seize them as contraband, all we should have achieved by stopping the exportation from the UK would be loss of the trade to this country."[143]

From other sources too, Crowe learned just how badly the licensing system worked. A few weeks later, commenting on an enquiry from the Australian government as to whether it was permissible to export copper (absolute contraband) to the United States, Crowe acerbically noted, "I doubt whether we can properly insist on the colonies prohibiting the exportation of copper when we in the United Kingdom are freely giving licenses to export to practically all neutral countries."[144] Crowe's minute provoked a discussion within the Foreign Office as to what the policy really was and who was responsible. "I hear so many different statements as to what is happening that I am somewhat bewildered," confessed Cecil Hurst.

> I understood that Sir Edward Grey's direction, that no licenses should be issued for the export of copper without the sanction of a Cabinet Minister, still held good, but I am repeatedly told that licenses are being issued freely and yesterday I was informed that the Foreign Office had now decided that Switzerland was to have as much copper as she wanted.[145]

Who was to blame?[146] No one was really sure, and certainly no one was held accountable.

On the morning of 14 January 1915, the prime minister convened a special CID trade coordination committee to discuss Hankey's recommendations.[147] Although the speed with which Asquith summoned his advisors would suggest he recognized the importance of the subject, he evidently was not much interested in the proceedings; afterward he told Venetia Stanley, "I had a dullish Committee meeting, and then lunch."[148] The printed conclusions record that the committee essentially followed Hankey's recommendations. The participating ministers agreed to form under a cabinet minister a new government agency—complete with a statistical unit—to serve as "a Clearing House for all war commercial information."[149] This was called the Trade Clearing

House of the new War Trade Department.[150] But instead of placing this new agency under the supervision of the Admiralty, as Hankey (and Sir Francis Hopwood of the ESRC) advised, the prime minister organized it as an adjunct to the Treasury under his personal supervision.[151] Alas, nothing survives to account for Asquith's curious decision, but we may speculate he did not trust the Admiralty, Foreign Office, or Board of Trade (all firmly entrenched in their policy beliefs) to paint an undistorted picture.

Asquith further deviated from Hankey's blueprint. He assigned to the new War Trade Department full responsibility for evaluating and issuing all export licenses. This requires comment. To the modern eye, joining an agency charged with analyzing foreign commercial intelligence with an organization tasked with regulating domestic trade appears an unnatural union. Yet there was a crude logic behind the creation of this hybrid organization. To create an accurate picture of global movements in strategic commodities required the War Trade Department to monitor all cargoes, regardless of origin, ownership, or destination, in order to track changes in ownership through the complex web of exchanges and financial institutions. Given the importance of London in financing most international trade (and as an entrepôt), essentially the same information could be used to police the business activities of British companies.

At the same time, Asquith was anxious that the new agency not infringe upon the constitutional prerogatives of the established executive departments of state. He therefore established the War Trade Department as an administrative body, not an executive one. (Though, as we shall see, in practice it exercised a kind of executive authority in that it could choose which departmental policy to enforce). The War Trade Department, in other words, was intended as a purely administrative creation that could be superimposed over the existing executive structure. To oversee the new agency, furthermore, Asquith chose Lord Emmott, the scion of a cotton-spinning family from Lancashire who had recently joined the cabinet as first commissioner of works, and whom he regarded as among the weakest members of his cabinet.[152]

Hankey was essentially correct in believing that the effectiveness of the blockade could be significantly improved with—indeed, depended upon—better information management. There was no question that hitherto the existing exploitation of intelligence had been dissipated and haphazard. Yet, recognition of the potential notwithstanding, hindsight demonstrates that Hankey was not the best judge of what was actually possible and consequently was far too optimistic in believing he could easily bring order to chaos. He seriously underestimated the quantity and quality of data required to generate the information necessary to make blockade policy work effectively. Nor did he appreciate the weaknesses in many official statistics, or that the source data used to create them could not be easily adapted for use by the blockade authorities, or that much necessary data had not yet even been assembled. In short, Hankey failed to grasp the magnitude of the task ahead. Though to be fair, neither did anyone else—certainly not the Foreign Office architects of the current blockade policy. To understand why all in authority so badly underestimated the information requirement of their chosen policy, let us consider briefly the commercial intelligence resources then actually available.

The first thing to remember is that the prewar British intelligence system—such as it was—had been organized primarily to gather military and diplomatic rather than commercial information. The Foreign Office maintained a commercial department, which existed mainly to make trade treaties, process material generated by the commercial attachés, and generally service its chief customer, the Board of Trade. The latter department operated a trade intelligence unit and a statistical branch. These civilian bureaus never looked at commerce from a warfare perspective (except when posed questions by the CID—the results we have seen). The Admiralty possessed three sections within the Naval Staff experienced in considering economic warfare matters: the Intelligence Division, the Transport Division, and the Trade Division. Because prewar Admiralty plans for economic warfare had been focused on strangling Germany through interdiction of the transatlantic transport system, it is important to note, the existing machinery and staff expertise were geared primarily toward tracking merchant ships.[153]

Additionally, shortly after the outbreak of war, the cabinet established under Admiralty control the Enemy Supplies Restriction Committee, whose function was mainly to find ways to intensify the economic pressure on Germany, but also, using borrowed Admiralty clerks, to divine "the nature and magnitude of the consignments passing to Scandinavian counties and Holland" as well as "whither and whence was the main trend of trade."[154] Within the Admiralty there was another secret intelligence section tasked with monitoring cable and wireless traffic for evidence of clandestine business transactions between American and German firms. It was run by the mysterious Frederick Leverton Harris, MP, who during the war rose rapidly in importance and influence.[155]

Born in 1864, the eldest son of a wealthy Quaker businessman with interests in coal mining and shipbroking, Leverton Harris spent most of his adult life supervising the marine underwriting arm of the family business empire (Harris and Dixon Ltd.), operating under the umbrella of Lloyd's of London. He evidently prospered, for during his lifetime he assembled a large art collection, which after his death in 1926 was bequeathed to the Dulwich Picture Gallery in London.[156] Leverton Harris apparently kept very few friends, though he is known to have been close to Austen Chamberlain, the former Chancellor of the Exchequer in the Balfour administration and eldest son of Joseph Chamberlain, the tariff reformer.[157] In 1900, Leverton Harris entered politics and was duly elected Conservative Member of Parliament for Tynemouth, a seat he retained until 1918.[158] The mystery surrounding Leverton Harris begins with his commission as an honorary lieutenant in the Royal Navy Volunteer Reserve (at the age of 42) with seniority dated 29 May 1905.[159] This and other evidence suggests that before the war, Leverton Harris must have been one of the several private individuals who served the Admiralty in an undefined part-time capacity, most probably as an advisor to the naval intelligence department or possibly connected with the establishment of the global shipping plot.[160] Given his experience in maritime commercial matters, both make sense.

An internal Admiralty memorandum dated August 1914 lists Leverton Harris as head of the quaintly named Miscellaneous Duties section (T.11) of the Naval Staff's Trade Division. In early 1915, he was promoted to the rank of commander in the Royal Navy Reserve.[161] His responsibilities were never defined precisely in the official organization charts, but documents show he liaised with Lloyd's of London and was in charge of analyzing commercial intelligence.[162] In his memoirs, Rear Admiral Douglas Brownrigg, who ran the wireless censorship bureau out of Room 37.OB, recalled feeding Leverton Harris with intercepts and noted he "seldom left his office before 2 a.m. He had a passion for work, and no one handled it with more rapidity and accuracy."[163]

Leverton Harris's true status within the naval administration is suggested by the location of his office within the Admiralty building. The internal telephone directory shows he occupied room 61.OB, one of the most desirable rooms on the first floor, with a view of the courtyard and just yards from the Admiralty Board room. More tangibly, he was situated in the most restricted part of main building, in a completely different wing from the rest of the Trade Division (to which he was nominally attached). Leverton Harris was two doors down from Brownrigg and directly adjacent to room 40.OB, home of the Admiralty's most famous (and then completely secret) code-breaking unit.[164] Leverton Harris wrote numerous cabinet briefing papers on issues connected with economic warfare incorporating information gleaned from commercial intelligence. His opinions were highly respected. In 1916, Ambassador Walter Page described Leverton Harris to President Woodrow Wilson as "the man who really makes the blockade."[165] Such a remark could be dismissed as mere hyperbole, but Leverton Harris had just been appointed undersecretary (number two) to the Ministry of Blockade, where he remained until the end of the war. Leverton Harris declined all honors except for the rank of honorary captain in the Royal Navy.[166]

As related, in October 1914 the Foreign Office persuaded the cabinet to adopt a new approach to the economic coercion of Germany. Instead of interdicting ships to control (American) supply, the blockade aimed at restricting (European) demand. Treaties with all the contiguous neutrals were hastily negotiated whereby in return for continuing access to British trade (and coal) they agreed "voluntarily" to limit their transit trade with Germany. The Foreign Office further argued that less diplomatic friction would result if, instead of applying a blanket ban on trade between neutrals, which had been the net effect of the Admiralty control over shipping, Britain targeted contraband smugglers. In addition, when cargoes were seized, the blockade authorities felt it was preferable to provide foreign governments with specific evidence of wrongdoing by their misguided citizens trading in contraband (hence the blockade system sometimes being described as the evidentiary method).

The Foreign Office system was based on several dubious assumptions. One was that most German transit trade must pass though Rotterdam; another was that neutral governments would cooperate honestly and be willing to police their own trade; a third was that British traders would scrupulously avoid trading with the enemy; a fourth was that the British authorities would be able to find unequivocal evidence against contraband runners sufficient to persuade foreign governments and prize courts of illegality. All these assumptions, as the Admiralty had warned, were quickly demonstrated to be naive. By the end of 1914, the British government found itself committed to a strategy that required huge amounts of information to operate at all, let alone effectively. Expressed most simply, the information required to watch millions of cargoes of indeterminate ownership was several orders of magnitude greater than tracking just several thousand ships whose ownership was legally defined by their flag.[167] To this aim, the new Contraband Department of the Foreign Office, under the direction of Sir Eyre Crowe, swallowed ever greater quantities of intelligence resources in its quest to track the movement of practically every cargo passing between Europe and the Americas. We shall return to this in the next chapter.

A fortnight after Asquith's decision to establish the War Trade Department (the new agency did not become operational for six weeks), Reginald McKenna, a staunch supporter of economic attack, circulated the first in what became a series of memoranda discussing the problem of trading with the enemy. As home secretary, he had the responsibility for arranging the prosecution of infringements of licensing procedures. On 25 January 1915, McKenna alleged, "There is reason to believe that, in spite of the Trading with the Enemy Acts and Proclamations, a considerable volume of unlicensed trade is being carried on with Germany through neutral countries."[168] Echoing Hankey's findings, he averred that procedures for obtaining export exemption licenses were absurdly easy to circumvent. Striking a tone of incredulity, McKenna reported that to qualify for a license an exporter had only to submit an application and swear an oath before a justice of the peace that "to the best of his knowledge and belief" the goods were "not intended for consumption in enemy country." By profession a lawyer, and a good one, McKenna assessed the oath as so badly worded that even with tangible evidence of deception the courts would not hand down many convictions. The home secretary singled out two British companies for misbehavior: Messrs. Cadbury (purveyors of chocolate) and, astonishingly, the merchant bank Frederick Huth and Co. (whose senior partner was Frederick Huth Jackson, one of the financial experts consulted by the Desart Committee). Both firms, McKenna accused, had recently sold such huge quantities of cocoa and coffee, respectively, to European wholesalers that "it is impossible to doubt" that the cargoes were really destined for Germany.[169] He further implied that some British officials had been criminally lax in performing their duties. These remarks sparked a lively debate that extended till the end of February.

McKenna's memorandum prompted a counterbarrage of resentful denials, including a viperous response from the Board of Trade.[170] Without addressing the substance of McKenna's complaints, the other departments of state all rejected his accusations, dismissed his proposed remedies as unworkable, and insisted that he had exaggerated the volume of illicit trade. "We do not want to interfere with the ordinary course of legitimate trade," the Board of Trade thundered, and thus "a too elaborate system of precaution is simply not worth while, and must do more harm than good."[171] Readers will at once recognize this as the same argument employed before the war in opposition to adoption of the economic warfare strategy. Endeavoring to stand aloof from the squabble, the Foreign Office contented itself with a circulated reminder that diplomatic agreements with neutrals now served as the foundation of blockade policy. Runciman interpreted this to mean that "Sir Edward Grey has definitely stated that he wishes our policy for the present to be one of confidence in the effective operation of the prohibitions, and thus we are practically bound to grant licenses for the export of copper to neutrals, if the latter have prohibited its export."[172] Put another way, from the Foreign Office point of view, evidence of malfeasance was irrelevant: export licenses should be approved to all destinations where the responsible government had promised to prohibit reexport.

McKenna disagreed and persisted in his campaign. On 12 February, with the War Trade Department still not yet functioning,[173] the Home Secretary took it upon himself to summon the first in a series of high-level interdepartmental conferences to discuss irregularities in licensing procedures.[174] Yet after hours of discussion these meetings achieved nothing beyond a consensus that McKenna's suspicions were probably right and that prosecuting offenders under existing laws would be difficult.[175] Even when customs officers were convinced that goods leaving the country were probably bound for Germany, "they have no power to prevent the exportation of goods other than goods on the prohibited or restricted lists." During the first nine months of the war, ninety cases had been forwarded to the director of public prosecutions, of which twenty had ended in conviction. This might, or might not, sound impressive, but of greater significance was the trivial nature of the prosecutions. The vast majority of cases were brought against small firms involved in trading such critical war munitions as bicycle handles, pocketknives, and pickled eggs. They usually ended with the court issuing a warning or small fine.[176] It is interesting, to say the least, that throughout the war, formal charges were never brought against any large company—even though dozens were indicted in official departmental correspondence.

Because the case files detailing the allegations against the larger firms no longer survive, we can only speculate as to why no major prosecutions were launched. One scholar has suggested that the reluctance to act was due to a deeply rooted Edwardian aversion to interfering with business.[177] Another plausible explanation is that there existed an intangible conglomerate of people, including politicians, civil servants, and City magnates—often referred to as "the establishment"—who opposed such prosecutions. When the idea was first suggested in April 1915 that the British government publish a blacklist of firms engaged in trading with the enemy, it produced an internal outcry.[178] Alternatively, officials took no action because the scale of evasion was just too great. Yet whatever the actual reason, McKenna's committee came to the conclusion that prosecution of offenders was just not practical. Instead, the McKenna committee opted for a policy of deterrence. As recorded in the minutes, they could agree that "it is desirable to create the impression among traders that the Government are very vigilant in this matter."[179] To accomplish this, the Board of Trade circulated a reminder to the business community warning of the penalties of trading with the enemy. Yet the fact remains that for the remainder of the war, the number of prosecutions for trading with the enemy remained low, and charges were brought only against small businessmen committing relatively trivial offenses.[180]

There was of course another dimension to the problem of indirect British trade with Germany, and that was the facilitation of such trade by the financial services industry. In 1914, international transactions depended upon telegraph cables, banks, insurance companies, and shipping. The war did not cause any regression in the sophistication of the international trading system. Even after the outbreak of war, such services were not easily available elsewhere. British cable companies continued to control communications across the Atlantic; technological as well as financial factors prevented effective competition.[181] American banks had only just begun to compete with the British in the short-term credit market (i.e., bills of exchange), and because they were allowed to open foreign branches only after 1913, with the passage of the Federal Reserve Act, their connections with foreign banks in places such as Scandinavia were underdeveloped. The American merchant marine was not large enough to service the requirements of U.S. exporters, let alone foreign clients. Similarly, U.S. insurance companies declined to issue policies unless they could lay off risks on London. To say the least, therefore, it appears highly suspicious that during the winter of 1914 a huge trade grew up virtually overnight between Scandinavia and the United States. One might well argue that the greatest untold scandal of the First World War—though admittedly the case is largely circumstantial—was the degree to which contraband trade through neutral countries was financed by the City of London and carried across the Atlantic in British ships.

The earliest expression of official suspicion in this direction is found in a memorandum dated 7 December 1914 written by Robert H. Brand, formerly the managing director of the merchant bank Lazard. After being rejected by the Army for poor eyesight, Brand volunteered at the Admiralty (his brother was Captain Hubert Brand) and was assigned to work under Leverton Harris in the T.11 section.[182] Readers may recall that before the war, Brand had written an article exploring the impact of war upon the global trading system that had appeared in the *Round Table* about the same time as the Desart Committee had been deliberating what to do about banking controls in the event of war. Brand's status was further enhanced in January 1915 after he became secretary to the Cornhill Committee, the role of which will be explained below. During the First World War Brand would rise to prominence as a member of the Canadian Munitions Board (1915–1917), deputy chairman of the British mission in Washington (1917–1918), and financial advisor to Lord Robert Cecil, chairman of the Allies' Supreme Economic Council (1919). During the Second World War his achievements would be yet more impressive.[183]

In December 1914, Brand advised Sir Francis Hopwood, chairman of the ESRC, of his suspicions that much German contraband trade was "probably" being financed by the City.[184] He had discovered that "large credits are being opened for Holland, Denmark and other countries and it is probable that some at least of this trade finds its way through to Germany."[185] In a separate paper, also sent to Hopwood, Brand made the point that the existing intelligence arrangements were too diffuse, and he recommended consolidation of the various committees and agencies under either the Admiralty or the Board of Trade (but not the Foreign Office). Only then, he thought, might the government be able to gather sufficient evidence to stop the City from lending "too freely."[186] Apparently Brand persuaded Hopwood that his suspicions were well founded, for several days later Hopwood wrote to Sir Edward Grey: "I saw Mr. Lloyd George and the Lord Chief Justice [Reading] recently and pointed out to them that the Germans were financing most of their trade through London accepting houses. The Chancellor of the Exchequer thoroughly appreciated the point and convened a meeting at which the governor of the Bank of England was present."[187] For once action was swift. On 7 January 1915, the British government published a new royal proclamation intended to deny German businesses worldwide access to banking facilities in the City of London by making it an offense for banks to conduct business on behalf of enemy-owned firms even when such firms were located in neutral countries.[188]

These measures to restrict German access to the City of London met with limited success. Many years after the war, Lord Robert Cecil, who served as minister of blockade from 1916 to 1919, admitted to the historian Marion Siney that "the financial blockade was the least successful of any of the measures undertaken."[189] Though this is not a subject that has received much scholarly attention, one recent researcher has uncovered evidence of certain British banks willfully exploiting various loopholes to continue financing the operations of German companies in South America.[190] Again, however, the destruction of official records makes quantifying the magnitude of the problem virtually impossible. Even where the head of any particular organization wished to conform to government regulations, moreover, this was no guarantee of effective compliance. Take, for example, allegations that British maritime insurers continued to issue policies on U.S. cargoes bound indirectly for Germany. As the chairman of Lloyd's reminded the Admiralty, few corporate entities had striven harder to work with the authorities in choking German trade.[191] Yet the intelligence services uncovered evidence that not all the underwriters in his organization were so scrupulous. In April 1915, an official at the War Trade Department wrote to Brand:

> I know how difficult the question is and that your [Cornhill] committee has probably gone into it very thoroughly and under the best legal advice, but the fact remains that the enormously increased shipments to neutrals are still receiving assistance from Lloyd's insurance covers, though no doubt no individual Underwriter is willingly and knowingly lending such assistance and the hint may be of use to you.[192]

This brings us to the so-called Cornhill Committee. During the First World War, monitoring of the banking industry with respect to trading with the enemy was theoretically the responsibility of the Treasury. In actuality, the City was allowed to regulate itself under the eyes of the Cornhill Committee. First convened on Friday, 22 January 1915, this body consisted of prominent magnates and City men connected with banking, insurance, and shipping interests.[193] Until he joined the cabinet in May 1915, its chairman was Austen Chamberlain. He was succeeded by Lord Inchcape, a leading banker and later chairman of the P&O shipping line.[194] Other members included Walter Cunliffe, chairman of the Bank of England; Sir Raymond Beck, the chairman of Lloyd's; the ubiquitous Commander Frederick Leverton Harris, of the Admiralty Trade Division (close friends with Austen Chamberlain); and Leverton Harris's subordinate Robert Brand, who initially was appointed secretary but subsequently became a full member.[195]

Quite how the Cornhill Committee operated or precisely what it uncovered is difficult to discern because its official records were deliberately destroyed immediately after the war. Individual committee members kept few papers and, for the most part, remained tight-lipped about their wartime activities.[196] Only now and again did hints slip out. For instance, on 14 January 1915, Alwyn Parker, the deputy of the new Foreign Office Contraband Department (and yet another friend of Brand's), reported his conversation a couple of days earlier with Lord Inchcape concerning London's role in facilitating trading with the enemy.[197] Parker related to Crowe:

> He told me (and his opinion as director of a large bank is of value) that if the financing of contraband trade via Scandinavia by certain financial houses in London were discontinued the contraband trade would collapse. He mentioned in particular Messrs. Goschen and Fruhling as active, and it is obvious from the manifests of vessels sent up by the customs that the London County and Westminster Bank (which included Mr. Harry Goschen and Sir E. Barrington amongst its directors) and especially the London City and Midland Bank are taking a very prominent part in financing provisions going to Germany via Scandinavia. It is no doubt impossible to take legal action against these banks, but morally they are severely to blame, and I wonder if Sir E. Grey could not intimate to them how prejudicial it is to British interests. It is perfectly sickening to think that these banks are making profits at the expense of our soldiers' lives.[198]

Other major banks accused of facilitating enemy trade were the Hong Kong and Shanghai Bank and also Marcus Samuel and Co.—the merchant bank stepsister of the Shell Oil Company.[199] With the destruction of most relevant records, verifying these accusations is practically impossible. From the snippets that do exist, we know that in early 1915 the Cornhill Committee scrutinized the activities of British shipping lines carrying Argentine wool to the United States and Scandinavia.[200] Another large-scale investigation was conducted into the suspected manipulation of freight rates for wheat on the Baltic Exchange.[201]

Other fragments show that the Cornhill Committee cautioned the Treasury on 22 February 1915 that the acceptance houses would never submit to the vetting of all bills of exchange. In other words, banks would never allow the government to direct who could or could not be granted access to British credit. The best that could be aimed for might be to ask the banks to "supply to the Treasury, in confidence, fortnightly returns of business *already done*" for retrospective scrutiny.[202] The first formal report by the Cornhill Committee, submitted to the Treasury on 2 March 1915, exonerated the City of charges that it "willingly" provided direct financial assistance to the enemy.[203] But "the question, whether such assistance may in some cases be given indirectly," it went on to suggest, "is a more difficult one to determine."[204] Although the committee's first report leveled no specific accusations of impropriety, it certainly hinted at serious malfeasance. It noted, for instance, that certain big joint-stock banks had issued a suspiciously large number of documentary cash credits and finance bills (interbank loans) to previously obscure institutions in Scandinavia.[205] The committee hastened to add that such behavior was not necessarily indicative of willful misbehavior but rather—creatively, this—might simply reflect "ignorance" of the government's wishes and a general sense of detachment from the war. The Treasury, it advised, should address banks directly and take them into its confidence: the City generally knew who ought and ought not to be trading with whom in northern Europe.[206]

This was sound advice, yet the Treasury moved slowly to tap this source of information. Not until 1 April 1915 was this proposal evaluated at an interdepartmental meeting of government officials connected with war trade issues, at which it was agreed that for administrative reasons responsibility for "avoiding any financial assistance to enemy trade must remain with the banks and finance houses."[207] On 3 May 1915, the Treasury secretary, John Bradbury, issued a circular letter to some 190 City banks and financial institutions, "asking them to send to the War Trade Dep[ar]t[ment] Weekly Statements of the credits which they grant and which are utilized, for the purpose of financing trade between neutrals."[208] Banks were further requested to obtain from their prospective clients a guarantee that the goods being financed were not intended for an enemy destination.

These measures may sound impressive and in comparison to prewar laissez-faire practices must have been viewed by many bankers as tyrannical, but in reality they were neither onerous nor effective. First, it should be noted that banks were requested, not required, to submit to these tests. Second, not until 10 June 1915 were standardized forms printed and instructions issued on how to fill them out. Third, the shape or level of the required guarantee was not defined.[209] In theory, compliance was monitored by the Finance Section of the War Trade Department under Sir Adam Block—another agency whose official records were destroyed directly after the war.[210]

In reality, the blockade authorities had no way to verify if banks were complying or to detect malfeasance unless a bank made a slip and gave credit to an already identified enemy agent named on the War Trade Department consolidated blacklist. After just one month of operation, the Cornhill Committee advised that these measures were wholly insufficient.

Acting upon this advice, in August 1915 the Treasury tried to introduce more rigorous controls over advances of credit by City financial institutions to neutral-owned firms—but hastily withdrew them after just three days in the face of City outcry.[211] In April 1916, the Cornhill Committee considered a report by Lord Eustace Percy, a senior official at the Foreign Office (and a friend of Brand's from Oxford), drawing attention to the continuing weakness of the current system of City regulation and the prevalence of abuse.[212] This appears to be the only document on this subject that has survived, and only then because Brand kept his copy. The significance of this document speaks for itself and justifies the lengthy quotation that follows.

> For the bulk of goods which they import including those received from Germany, neutral countries are obliged to pay cash (3 and 6 months documentary acceptances having been greatly curtailed). If they cannot pay cash their imports are restricted, and in the same way they receive cash for their exports. These cash payments are effected by buying or selling, as the case may be, telegraphic transfers of money through neutral banks from or to the countries with which they are dealing, or through credits opened in London. It is safe to say that the bulk of these transactions are done or cleared in London. A cutting down of these facilities could be used to reduce the imports into any country and in effect ration that country.
>
> It is said that the transactions of the foreign exchanges have assumed vast proportions since the war began and the Dutch and Scandinavian banks are putting through business of incredible magnitude. Small banks, in places like Amsterdam, Rotterdam, Copenhagen, Cristiana, Bergen, Malmo, Trondheim, and Stockholm put through as much business in a day as they would in a month of normal times. There is no other basis possible for all this finance than trading with Germany.
>
> If half the time now taken in enquiring into suspicious shipments of merchandise were devoted to controlling the exchange market, much more effective results would be obtained. At present there is no effective check on transfers of credit from one neutral country to another.

> Declarations only appear to be asked where documentary credits are opened through London for the benefit of named third parties, but Scandinavian bankers can avoid even this precaution, for they can open such a credit direct in America and cover it by purchasing dollars in London or placing pounds sterling at the disposal of America without let or hindrance. In this way a neutral can open non-enemy credits through London and give the requisite declaration, and enemy credits direct covering the exchange in London and so avoid the declaration. Some banks do require declarations, but there is no uniformity of system, and if one bank insists, it does so at the peril of losing business.[213]

There can be no more damning statement of the ineffectiveness of British controls over the financial services industry. We cannot say just how important access to British financial resources was to the enemy, but there is no question that—at least in the minds of contemporary experts—it must have been substantial and even critical.

Unrestricted Submarine Warfare and the Third Order-in-Council

On 4 February 1915, the German government announced that fourteen days hence its U-boats would treat the waters surrounding the British Isles as a war zone and all vessels found therein would be liable to attack without warning. This declaration is generally taken as signaling the beginning of the first German campaign of unrestricted submarine warfare, though arguably it was no more than a formalization of existing German practice. For the British government, however, the official statement came as a godsend, providing the excuse ministers had been looking for to intensify their own economic warfare campaign.

At the end of January 1915, pressured by Admiral Fisher, Churchill had requested cabinet approval for tightening the blockade by interdicting "*all trade with & from Germany to neutrals*—to declare an effective blockade and let nothing in." Harcourt remarked that this proposal generated much discussion within the cabinet and "much difference of opinion."[214] The following week, Churchill again raised the subject of stopping "all enemy cargoes of food & to partially starve the neutrals bordering on Germany & supplying her," this time presenting it as a retaliatory measure.[215] On this occasion he found his audience more sympathetic.[216] Charlie Hobhouse, the postmaster general, spoke for the majority when he declared himself now in favor of vigorous blockade, stipulating only that "until Germany killed or allowed to perish some crew of a merchantman we could hardly stop enemy cargo on a neutral ship, but once a case of a merchant crew having been lost occurred we should stop everything going to Germany."[217] Only Asquith and Simon spoke out against the idea, doubting that the Germans would make good on their threat.[218]

The cabinet's greater willingness to countenance a more aggressive blockade posture had less to do with the real or imagined predations of German U-boats than a concurrent hardening of attitudes toward the United States. Several key ministers who had previously opposed stringent enforcement out of concern for American sensibilities had been incensed at the recent behavior of the U.S. government. Since the beginning of 1915, the feeling had grown within the British establishment that the Americans were becoming unreasonable in their protests. British eyes widened after the failure of the Wilson administration in early January to prevent a band of pro-German citizens from trying to inflame American and neutral opinion by exposing the contradictions between British blockade policy and international law.[219] Led by U.S. senator William J. Stone (D-Mo.), a group of German American citizens purchased two former German merchantmen, the *Wilhelmina* and the *Dacia,* reregistered them as U.S. vessels, loaded them with American grain and cotton, respectively, and dispatched them with great fanfare to Germany. The instigators dared the British government to stop them.

On 27 January 1915, the cabinet had been in an angry mood when it debated how best to respond to this provocation. Lord Lucas and Charlie Hobhouse, both of whom eight months earlier had been among those most opposed to economic warfare, now favored taking a hard line and were "for telling USA quite plainly that while we would pay a fair price for anything we stopped, we were not to be frightened or deterred from stopping anything or everything."[220] Ultimately the Royal Navy evaded the trap by asking the French navy to arrest both as reflagged German vessels, rightly calculating that the Americans would mute any outcry against the country that had helped them gain their independence.

Ministers therefore were well primed when Churchill formally proposed, on 6 February, that Britain should retaliate against Germany's blatantly illegal declaration of unrestricted submarine warfare by authorizing the Royal Navy to "seize and detain all ships containing cargo of a useful kind (particularly food) going to Germany, or presumed—wherever ostensibly going—to have a German destination." To support his claim of the seriousness of the situation, he circulated an appraisal by the Naval Staff asserting that the submarine blockade of the British Isles was "no idle threat" and required a response.[221] Although Churchill's proposal was not put to a formal vote (it was very rare indeed for a vote to be taken), the majority of ministers agreed that the German declaration offered a sufficient justification for British retaliation. Privately, even Sir Edward Grey admitted that the German decree alleviated many of his difficulties with the United States.[222] The prime minister, however, thought Churchill's formula a little rich for his tastes. "We shall get into the devil's own row with America if we seize all the cotton shipped from the Southern States," he predicted in his evening letter to Venetia Stanley.[223]

On the subject of cotton, we might mention that since the beginning of the year the British government had been assiduously ignoring the swelling stream of cotton flowing from the United States to central Europe.[224] Since the end of 1914, American cotton exports had recovered remarkably. It is estimated that during January 1915 alone, half a million bales of U.S. cotton reached Germany either directly or indirectly, equivalent to 25 percent of normal German imports. Climbing demand for cotton was reflected in the prices quoted on the New Orleans exchange. Readers will recall that upon the outbreak of war, fears of a glut collapsed the price of cotton to 6¢ per pound. By the beginning of January 1915, the price of a pound of cotton had risen to 8¢ and a month later was approaching 10¢.[225]

For most of February 1915, the cabinet argued back and forth over the wisdom of adopting a more aggressive blockade policy. Riding the new mood within the cabinet, Winston Churchill was relentless in pressing for escalation, bombarding his colleagues with ideas for intensifying the economic pressure against Germany. On 10 February, ministers provisionally approved his proposal to interdict all German trade, both inbound (to Germany) and for the first time also outbound (German exports). "We intend by way of retaliation," Asquith nervously told Venetia Stanley, "to seize & keep every ship & cargo, wherever found, which is German in origin, ownership, or destination, by whatever disguises its real character may be concealed."[226]

Asquith, nevertheless, remained uncomfortable with several aspects of the plan and continued to view with trepidation the reaction of the United States to these further departures from customary international law. Yet at the same time he recognized the necessity for action to prevent, for instance, the revival in German exports. During the first two months of the war German exports to the United States had been effectively throttled. By the end of 1914, they had recovered remarkably, to approximately 56 percent of their prewar levels.

During the first quarter of 1915, German exports had risen to nearly 60 percent of prewar levels, and the trend was still pointed upward.[227] This could not be allowed to continue if for no other reason than that exported goods earned foreign exchange that could be used to pay for imports. The difficulty, however, was in legally stopping enemy exports: under international law the only legitimate way of doing so was by declaring a formal blockade.

Unsure what to do, Asquith characteristically procrastinated. To Churchill's dismay (according to Harcourt), the prime minister insisted that before acting the government ought first to consult the French. Their government promptly sent across two representatives to discuss how best to increase "the stringency of economic pressure on Germany."[228] At the next cabinet meeting, Simon reported that the French were nervous about the plan, preferring to clothe the new policy in legal garb by formally declaring a blockade of Germany. This was rejected by the Foreign Office.[229] Undaunted, the Admiralty held their course. On 12 February, Churchill wrote to Runciman requesting that the Board of Trade begin allowing neutral ships to apply for government-subsidized maritime insurance policies. In part the First Lord hoped this might counteract Germany's attempt to deter merchantmen from plying British waters. But his main objective was to entice U.S.-flagged vessels into the war zone in the hope that some might be torpedoed by U-boats, thereby entangling the U.S. government in a diplomatic row with Germany. "For our part, we want the traffic," he explained, "the more the better; and if some of it gets into trouble, better still."[230] Initially Runciman was hesitant, but ultimately he complied.

On 15 February, Churchill endeavored to nudge policy further forward by revealing to Parliament that the cabinet was considering the repudiation of several established principles of international law in order to tighten the blockade against Germany.

> So far, however, we have not attempted to stop imports of food. We have not prevented neutral ships from trading direct with German ports. We have allowed German exports in neutral ships to pass unchallenged. The time has come when the enjoyment of these immunities by a State which has, as a matter of deliberate policy, placed herself outside all international obligations, must be reconsidered. A further declaration on the part of the allied Governments will promptly be made which will have the effect for the first time of applying the full force of naval pressure to the enemy.[231]

It is not clear whether Churchill had forewarned the prime minister—surely he did—but his speech certainly was well received in the press and in Parliament.

After the cabinet meeting on 16 February, the prime minister reported to King George V:

> Mr. Churchill and others strongly urged that we should announce our intention to seize and detain all cargoes, under any flag, or food or other useful commodities, as to which there is a presumption of German destination, and also all cargoes of German exported goods in neutral bottoms. This was the prevailing opinion in the Cabinet, but the PM, Sir E Grey and Lord Crewe urged very strongly the importance of not alienating and embittering neutral and particularly American opinion: the proposed reprisals being obviously much more injurious to neutral commerce and interests, than the more or less illusory German threat.[232]

Again, Hobhouse's diary largely corroborates Asquith's report and confirms that the general mood was one of belligerence, with little regard for Grey's concerns.[233] Still, however, the prime minister refused to authorize action. "This brings us into all sorts of possible troubles with the neutrals & especially America," the increasingly apprehensive Asquith explained to Venetia Stanley. "Winston, McKenna, Ll[oyd] George &c are full of blood and thunder, but they haven't thought out the thing & its consequences: and so I determined to have a second Cabinet this afternoon, and a War Council tomorrow morning."[234] But Asquith's plea for moderation went unheeded.[235] He was no more successful after two more cabinet meetings held on 18 February and 24 February. On each occasion he failed to shift the balance of opinion in favor of greater caution and accordingly closed each meeting without recording any conclusions.[236]

On 25 February, a fresh wrinkle emerged to give the cabinet pause. Ministers learned that for the past fortnight Sir Edward Grey had been in secret negotiations with President Woodrow Wilson's special envoy, Colonel E. M. House.[237] House had been charged with the mission to broker a peace between the belligerents. He carried with him yet another demarche from the U.S. government protesting the Royal Navy's interference with American trade, and also the threat that unless the British mended their ways the United States might retaliate with an embargo on the sale of all munitions to the allies.[238] Privately, Asquith found it hard to take Colonel House or his ideas seriously; the American had "a lot of rather chimerical ideas: one is that of a Union of all nations, including the United States, fight against any one of them that breaks the peace, and in the meantime the compulsory closing of all the great armament producing works," he wrote.[239] Less amusing, however, was a demand that the European powers immediately recognize the principle of "freedom of the seas." This term was used in various senses but in this instance translated to complete freedom of passage for neutral trade. A more extreme definition of the phrase demanded the immunity of all enemy private property at sea. Asquith saw it as necessity to play along for the sake of maintaining good relations.

During his unofficial discussions with House, Grey conveyed the impression that Britain might consider lifting the "food blockade" of Germany in return for stopping submarine attacks on merchantmen.[240] In expressing this view, Grey acted totally without authority, consulting only Sir Arthur Nicolson, the Foreign Office permanent undersecretary (who agreed that the possibility was worth exploring).[241] Only afterward did Grey tell the prime minister what he had done; Asquith immediately decided that it was best not to confuse the cabinet with the news. The only person in whom the prime minister confided was Hankey, who was appalled. He immediately replied urging no relaxation of the blockade, reminding Asquith that a food blockade "has always been contemplated as one of main means of warfare by the Committee of Imperial Defense."[242] While undoubtedly correct, this hardly reflected the realities of the current situation. Since late 1914 the "food blockade" of Germany existed largely on paper and nowhere else. Although the Royal Navy was still detaining ships carrying foodstuffs believed bound for Germany, the vast majority were being released on instructions from the Foreign Office. This is clear from an ESRC report dated 25 February 1915, protesting the latest Foreign Office edict that grain from the United States "should in no way be interfered with."[243]

Before the cabinet had finally settled upon the exact form of its intended reprisals policy, and while negotiations with the French were still ongoing, on 1 March the prime minister informed the House of Commons, during a debate on the vote of credit, of the government's intentions to retaliate against the German proclamation.[244] "The British and French Governments will, therefore, hold themselves free to detain and take into port ships carrying goods of presumed enemy destination, ownership, or origin."[245] Asquith's remarks, which were widely reported in the press, contained a confusing mixture of spicy remarks and dollops of ambiguity:

> The retaliatory measures we propose to adopt, the words "blockade" and "contraband," and other technical terms of international law, do not occur, and advisedly so. In dealing with an opponent who has openly repudiated all the restraints, both of law and of humanity, we are not going to allow our efforts to be strangled in a network of juridical niceties. We do not intend to put into operation any measures which we do not think to be effective, and I need not say we shall carefully avoid any measures which violate the rules either of humanity or of honesty. Subject to those two conditions I say to our enemy—I say it on behalf of the Government, and I hope on behalf of the House of Commons—that under existing conditions there is no form of economic pressure to which we do not consider ourselves entitled to resort. If, as a consequence, neutrals suffer inconvenience and loss of trade, we regret it, but we beg them to remember that this phase of the War was not initiated by us.[246]

While Asquith's government left everyone in no doubt that a change in blockade policy was imminent, the lack of specifics produced much uncertainly as to exactly what was intended.[247] The U.S. government was especially perplexed, and on 2 March Woodrow Wilson said so to the Washington press.[248] The president instructed Walter Page to seek clarification.[249]

Over the next several days the cabinet met several times in an effort to finalize its policy. "I must say," Lord Emmott, head of the newly created War Trade Department, recorded in his diary on 3 March, "there is a lack of any very clear idea of how we are going to deal with Germany's goods (through neutrals). No one seems to have thought it out."[250] At one extreme "Churchill wants to stop every ship to & from neutrals," Harcourt reported, and at the other was "Grey[,] anxious not to act excessively."[251] Apparently it was Charlie Hobhouse, the level-headed postmaster general, who devised the formula (ultimately adopted) whereby Britain should *claim* the right to stop all German trade but in practice be selective "so that the Yankees might be let down lightly."[252] In the words of Jack Pease, cabinet policy would be "to go quietly taking only picked cargoes least annoying to USA."[253] Still, Grey protested that this brew was too strong for the Americans to stomach, urging his colleagues to further dilute the retaliatory measures.[254]

However, the Foreign Secretary's assessment did not reflect the prevailing view within the Contraband Department of the Foreign Office. Crowe felt strongly that "Sir C Spring Rice has invariably shown himself more alarmed than subsequent events justified—we have had very bad experience in trying to negotiate 'amicable arrangements' with the U.S. government."[255] At the end of the day, the prime minister still inclined toward Grey's position, but he could count on support from just Crewe and maybe a handful of the others. Conversations with various ministers held on 3 and 4 March made clear to him that the majority of ministers would not weaken the brew any further; indeed, some were still demanding greater potency.

Two examples will suffice to demonstrate the confrontational mood that prevailed at this time within cabinet circles. On 5 March, the cabinet gave serious consideration to a memorandum circulated by Winston Churchill floating Admiral Fisher's preferred strategy of declaring a formal blockade of Germany. In so doing, the First Sea Lord wanted to employ the Bethell interpretation (see Chapter 4) to justify the seizure of all neutral ships trying to run the blockade, and also to sow large numbers of mines in the international waters off neutral ports in the North Sea.[256] The tone of this memo reflects Churchill's long-standing hostility to mine warfare and makes clear he presented this paper as a stalking horse. Indeed, he himself observed therein that the government should consider this alternative, "which strikes blindly at commerce, whether enemy or neutral, and endangers non-combatant life," only if neutral governments refused to accept his more reasonable retaliatory measures, which had been provisionally agreed upon.[257]

In fact, cabinet ministers were considering other, yet more draconian measures of retaliation. In late February, Hankey had forwarded the proposal that another way to enhance the effectiveness of the blockade would be to attack German grain production directly by using aircraft to sow "blight" on their field crops. Churchill was leery of resorting to biological warfare, but Lloyd George and several others liked the idea.[258] Several weeks later a modified version of the scheme, substituting incendiaries for biological agents, was presented to the cabinet, but for unspecified reasons it "did not meet with much favor."[259] On this occasion Churchill supported the scheme, but Grey and others denounced it as an illegitimate form of warfare.[260] Not until June, after French military authorities vetoed the idea for fear of German retaliation against their crops, was the idea finally dropped.[261]

More than a week after Asquith had warned of an imminent change in blockade policy, still no official statement had been issued. On 9 March, Eyre Crowe implored the government to "announce a definite line of action as soon as may be": "We are being inundated on all sides with enquiries as to what we are going to do under the reprisals declaration made by the Prime

Minister in Parliament. Neutral governments and merchants, as well as British firms are all feeling embarrassed by the prevailing uncertainty."[262]

Crowe's prodding finally spurred the government into motion, the result being a flurry of telegrams between Paris and London in an effort to harmonize French and British texts. These show there remained considerable differences between the allies as to the best way forward. Unwilling to wait any longer, on Friday, 12 March the British government printed in the *London Gazette* the new (third) order-in-council, in which it declared its intention to isolate Germany completely from the international trading system by imposing a complete interdiction, inbound and out, over all German overseas trade.[263] The "retaliation blockade," as it was known, was of course not a blockade in the legal sense but rather was justified as an act of reprisal against the illegal action of the German government in declaring the waters around the British Isles to be a "military area."[264] It was reasoned that because the new policy was an act of "retaliation," no justification in law was necessary.[265]

To summarize: on 1 March 1915, the prime minister asserted his government's intent to retaliate against the German submarine campaign by intensifying the British blockade against Germany. He told the House of Commons, "There is no form of economic pressure to which we do not consider ourselves entitled to resort."[266] Ten days later, on 11 March, the government formalized its new policy of interdicting all German overseas trade with the publication of a new order-in-council. This document, often referred to as the "retaliatory" order-in-council, explicitly warned neutral shippers against "carrying goods with an enemy destination, or which are enemy property"; vessels caught defying this edict would be detained and forcibly redirected to a British or other friendly port to discharge their cargoes. Such unequivocal statements created widespread public expectation, both at home and abroad, that the British government was determined to ruthlessly enforce economic warfare regardless of the diplomatic consequences or any disruption that might be caused to the world economic system. Indeed, Asquith had remarked explicitly in his aforementioned speech to the House of Commons: "If, as a consequence, neutrals suffer inconvenience and loss of trade, we regret it, but we beg them to remember that this phase of the War was not initiated by us."[267]

Asquith's bellicose public pronouncements, however, masked considerable private reservations and a fear that the new blockade policy would provoke "the devil's own row with America."[268] Sir Edward Grey shared this fear and in vain had pleaded with the cabinet that the proposed new measures were too heavy-handed, too great a departure from established international law, and therefore certain to inflame American opinion. The French foreign ministry reportedly shared these concerns as well.[269] True, the Conservative party leadership had promised the government its support in taking an aggressive stance—Andrew Bonar Law told Ambassador Page that his party had been consulted and was fully behind "our plan of blockade."[270] But not everyone concurred. Arthur Balfour, a member of Asquith's executive War Council, confessed to Hankey that he was "a little anxious about all this controversy about food-stuffs for Germany" and thought the government should "reserve violent action until the behavior of Germany (not its threats) give provocation which all reasonable opinions would regard as sufficient."[271] Balfour went on to state that, personally, he thought it "unlikely that we shall starve Germany into submission; and I am not sure that I would do it if I could."[272]

After nearly a month of debate, the majority of the cabinet refused to be deflected from retaliating vigorously against Germany. They did so, moreover, in full recognition that this highly provocative stance was sure to antagonize neutral opinion. It remained to be seen if the Americans and other neutrals ultimately acquiesced or resisted with threats of force.

9

A Management Problem

> The story of our so-called "blockade" during this period is too long and too technical to be told in these pages, except on the broadest lines. But in the story of the Supreme Command it cannot be wholly omitted—if only to illustrate how public business ought *not* to be conducted in such grave matters.
>
> LORD HANKEY, *The Supreme Command*

In this chapter we shall examine the administrative procedures and machinery put in place to collect, digest, and disseminate the information necessary for monitoring compliance and enforcing the blockade. In so doing we shall demonstrate how dependent the Foreign Office–designed blockade system was upon the injection of vast quantities of information for its operation. We shall see why much necessary information either was not immediately available to administrators or quite often simply did not exist. We shall review how various government departments took a hand in gathering and processing this requisite information. We shall explain why much of the data demanded by blockade administrators frequently tested and often exceeded the limits of what was bureaucratically or technologically possible during the early part of the twentieth century. We shall look also at the consequences of departmental rivalries, conflicting agendas, the sometimes arbitrary and capricious behavior of senior policy makers. Lastly, and above all, we shall review the consequences of the near absence of executive control over the implementation of cabinet defined blockade policy—or, rather, the lack of political willingness by the leadership to compel adherence. As a corollary to this, we will see how the political failure to impose discipline upon the departments was often excused by the lack of information or by the existence of conflicting information—thereby creating a vicious circle.

In previous chapters, we have presented the Foreign Office and the Admiralty as the principal protagonists. In this chapter and the next we shall see how actions by other departments, especially the Board of Trade and to some degree also the Treasury and the Board of Agriculture, became increasingly important.

Though the prime minister and the foreign secretary were unable to dissuade the cabinet from adopting a retaliatory blockade policy they believed too extreme, they nevertheless obtained several concessions "in deference to American sensibilities" so that—in the words of Postmaster General Charles Hobhouse—"the Yankees might be let down lightly."[1] A Foreign Office memorandum dated 10 March 1915 makes clear that initially

> the object aimed at in enforcing the Order in Council should be to secure that ships will not carry goods of German origin, destination, or ownership. Vessels should therefore be detained long enough to make them feel the inconvenience of carrying such goods, and the advantage of not doing so.[2]

The same memorandum went on to state that over time "treatment should gradually grow stronger," with the ultimate object of cutting off Germany completely from overseas trade.[3] Although no precise timetable was given, it would seem the cabinet envisaged full implementation within three months: the Foreign Office assured American cotton growers that all bales of the previous year's crop destined for Europe and contracted before 2 March would be allowed free passage or be purchased by the British government at the contract price.[4] As the typical bill of exchange on cotton extending to ninety days, this effectively meant the new rules of capture would not take effect until about June 1915. The other major concession Asquith and Grey extracted from the cabinet was an extension of the previous agreement not to confiscate American goods classed as conditional contraband, but instead compulsorily purchase them at fair market (London) prices.[5] (It should be remembered that the price of most strategic commodities was considerably higher in Continental Europe than in London—in some cases double or even triple.)

Judging by his subsequent actions, the foreign secretary clearly was far from satisfied with the sufficiency of these concessions. On previous such occasions, as we have seen, Grey had not shied from disregarding cabinet instructions whenever, in his opinion, they conflicted with what he perceived as broader diplomatic objectives. So it proved again in March 1915. It will not be necessary to weary the reader with the details of every instance. Suffice it to provide the most egregious example, which was the decision not to confiscate German products manufactured in neutral countries (such as China or Brazil) unless consigned directly for German territory. In the cabinet, Grey had opposed the inclusion of this clause, designed to bankrupt the overseas subsidiaries of many German companies, but he had been overruled and new orders to the fleet had been issued.[6] Undaunted, the foreign secretary approached Sir George Cave, chairman of the interdepartmental Contraband Committee, whose role was to adjudicate whether a specific cargo was contraband, and asked that he turn a blind eye to such cargoes. It is important to note that from the beginning of 1915, Cave's Contraband Committee sat in the same suite of offices occupied by Sir Eyre Crowe's Contraband Department of the Foreign Office.[7]

In arranging for goods produced by German overseas subsidiaries not to be captured, Grey neglected to inform the cabinet or any of the other agencies also involved in administering blockade policy. In fact, the naval members of the Contraband Committee did not discover this subterfuge until nine months later. "The result," one officer angrily remarked, "has been that goods of enemy property, if of neutral origin and carried in neutral or even British ships, are allowed to pass freely through blockading forces, and enemy firms overseas are thus enabled to continue trading."[8] "The orders to the fleet say that vessels carrying goods of suspected enemy ownership are to be detained and sent into port," but "when such vessels are sent in the Foreign Office orders their release."[9] The uncertain evidence makes it possible to disagree as to the consequences of Grey's action in willfully defying explicit cabinet instructions, but there is no denying his deceit.

Later in the war Sir Edward Grey came in for a great deal of criticism for his interferences with official cabinet-sanctioned blockade policy. In his postwar memoirs, he justified his behavior by claiming his conduct had been necessary to prevent the alienation of the United States. He argued (ex post facto), "The blockade of Germany was essential to the victory of the Allies, but the ill-will of the United States meant their certain defeat."[10] By this he meant that whereas Germany and Austria were self-sufficient in munitions, the Allies were "dependent for an adequate supply on the United States." "It was better," Grey thus reasoned, "to carry on the war without blockade, if need be, than to incur a break with the United States about contraband and thereby deprive the Allies of the resources necessary to carry on the war at all or with any chance of success. The object of diplomacy, therefore, was to secure the maximum of blockade that could be enforced without a rupture with the United States."[11] Though Grey's disingenuous chronicle is vague on dates and details, historians have generally taken it at face value, and to some extent this is understandable. The importance of American munitions (and money) to the ultimate Allied victory in 1918–1919 is indisputable, making Grey's rationale appear both legitimate and straightforward. His failure to explain how and when, precisely, he developed this apprehension was presumably thought not to matter.

Scrutiny of cabinet and Foreign Office files, however, shows that while Grey consistently believed in the importance of preserving U.S. goodwill and appeared always ready to appease the American government with concessions over the blockade, before the end of 1915 he did not rationalize his actions in the context of munitions dependence. And it would have made no sense to have done so, for, as we saw in the last chapter, the government was at this time looking to meet the Army's (and its allies') needs by expanding domestic munitions production. Another reason to doubt Grey's story is that it can be shown he still at this stage remained unconvinced that Britain must prepare for a long war—an essential prerequisite for any belief in Allied munitions dependence. Lastly, there is no evidence that anyone in the British government—even Grey—yet believed the Allies were dependent upon the United States. Indeed, when this was first suggested to the cabinet in late July 1915, the idea was rejected as alarmist and even ludicrous.[12]

For nearly 100 years, historians have failed to penetrate Sir Edward Grey's motives or accurately map the nebula that was British foreign policy during his stewardship of the Foreign Office.[13] Conclusive evidence simply does not exist. Consequently, it is futile to grapple with such questions as how or why Grey and the Foreign Office were able so successfully to defy the cabinet in the implementation of the March 1915 retaliatory order-in-council, for it is plain they did. In defying the cabinet's wishes, moreover, Grey relied upon the assistance of a small but sufficiently powerful faction within the government. This included Prime Minister Asquith, Lord Crewe, Lord Lucas, Runciman, Harcourt, and Emmott. As we shall see below, the last of these was a particularly useful ally. Although a political lightweight, Lord Emmott presided over the new War Trade Department, which meant he controlled the newly established statistical bureau established to collate the data and supply the political executive with critical information necessary to gauge the effectiveness—or otherwise—of blockade policy.

Before we turn to examine the role of the new War Trade Department in the blockade machinery, it important to be clear that although the March 1915 retaliatory order-in-council represented a shift in blockade policy *intentions,* the *means* employed to achieve the stated objectives remained essentially unchanged. The Foreign Office–devised blockade machinery remained firmly focused upon cargoes, not ships, and upon the containment of European demand rather than control of American supply. The British government also retained its commitment to differentiate between "legitimate" neutral trade and "illegitimate" contraband transshipment and so minimize the collateral damage to innocent neutral trade. Under the new rules of capture published in March 1915, furthermore, the government declared its willingness to purchase rather than seize American cargoes presumed ultimately destined for Germany. Even cargoes of absolute contraband were not placed in the prize court without absolute and unequivocal proof of enemy destination. In other words, the evidentiary method remained the cornerstone of blockade policy.

As explained in the previous chapter, in our review of Colonel Hankey's January 1915 report into the inadequacies of administrative procedures, "evidence" was a largely a function of information. Fundamentally, therefore, the effectiveness of the British blockade system depended critically upon the acquisition of adequate tangible evidence for presentation to the prize court or, more precisely, to aggrieved foreign governments to justify the detention of foreign-owned cargoes. The requisite evidence could be harvested from raw commercial data gathered from across the globe by various intelligence agencies. The "information problem" consisted not only of acquiring data in sufficient quantity and quality but also of its timely (and effective) processing into usable information.

Since the beginning of the war, both the Admiralty and the Foreign Office had invested ever-increasing quantities of bureaucratic resources to improve their information networks, reflected in the repeated jumps in the numbers of personnel allocated to the task.[14] In the unending quest to obtain better information, moreover, government agencies resorted to measures formerly believed unthinkable—in both senses of the word. Before the war the CID had considered reading every item of mail entering and leaving the country, but rejected such a policy on both ethical and practical grounds.[15] Official aversion to tampering with private mail is well illustrated in an apocryphal tale told in the unpublished autobiography of Captain Reginald "Blinker" Hall, the Admiralty's famous wartime director of naval intelligence. Hall claimed that shortly after taking office in November 1914, he used discretionary funds to establish an unofficial mail censorship bureau staffed by volunteers to glean information on German imports of contraband financed through British banks and other middlemen. He claimed that when the authorities discovered his operation, Runciman, of the Board of Trade, was so revolted that he tried to have Hall jailed for interfering with the mails. Only after Reginald McKenna pointed out the tremendous potential of the system was the prime minister persuaded to formalize it. This was swiftly done, though control was given to the War Office.[16] Whether the story is true or not, in early 1915 Hankey identified the mail censor as the single most valuable source of intelligence on contraband trading.[17]

Throughout 1915, there was a scramble to improvise data-gathering and -processing capabilities. The Foreign Office retasked its consulate staffs to collect shipping data, including original ship manifests. These were the essential raw material. They were used by London to identify cargoes of contraband and to look for patterns that might identify middlemen in neutral countries trading on behalf of Germany. They also represented the basis of statistical data allowing decision makers to ascertain the volume of trade in strategic commodities between the United States and Europe and thereby gauge the effectiveness of their policies. In a dispatch dated 13 March 1915, British Ambassador Sir Cecil Spring Rice reported that the Washington embassy had at last completed its arrangements for obtaining copies of practically every manifest for every ship clearing every major U.S. seaport for European destinations. These were gathered, by means fair and foul, by consular officers posted in chief U.S. ports including Baltimore, Philadelphia, Boston, New Orleans, Galveston, Savannah, San Francisco, and Portland (Oregon).[18] The operation in New York was so large (that port handled a full one-third of U.S. exports) that the consul general in New York organized its own shipping department, which reported directly to London. Also based here was an information-gathering organization (about which little is known) run by the capable Australian-born British naval attaché in Washington, Captain Guy Gaunt.[19]

Each day, British diplomats in North America dispatched sheaves of manifests to the Contraband Department of the Foreign Office in London. Copies were sent directly to the regional naval intelligence centers in Halifax, Nova Scotia, and in Bermuda.[20] As many as possible were telegraphed, but the limitations of the transatlantic cable meant that most (more than 90 percent) had to be sent by fast mail steamer.[21] These normally arrived in London several days ahead of the vessels carrying the actual cargoes to which they appertained. Upon reaching London, the manifests were sent first to Sir George Cave's interagency Contraband Committee. If the cargo description was deemed suspicious, the information was passed over to the Admiralty and a cruiser sent to intercept the vessel carrying the goods and escort it to a British port for detailed examination. The point to note is that responsibility for determining if a ship or cargo would be seized belonged to a bureaucratic machine in London, not to naval officers commanding cruisers at sea.

Initially, the British embassy staff in Washington tried to compile statistics to quantify the flow of selected strategic commodities across the Atlantic from the manifests they had gathered. The results were tabulated and forwarded once a week to London. The utility of these proved limited, however. The Admiralty Trade Division complained they were full of errors, there were frequent inconsistencies in the categorization of certain items, and they were generally insufficiently detailed.[22] Until late 1915, responsibility for quantifying the volume of strategic commodities entering Europe from across the Atlantic actually belonged to the Admiralty-based ESRC because of its ability to supplement manifests with insurance data supplied by Lloyd's and other information clandestinely acquired by Leverton Harris's T.11 intelligence unit. Even then the figures produced were fragile. First, not until late 1915 was the Foreign Office persuaded of the necessity to expand its organization for the gathering of ships' manifests to include merchantmen clearing South American ports for neutral destinations.[23] This improvement, incidentally, met with fierce objections from British shipping lines, who through the shipowners association and the Board of Trade protested that this would cause them excessive delays and expense.[24] Second, responsibility for monitoring flows of goods entering and leaving U.K. ports remained the Board of Trade's responsibility. Theoretically the War Trade Department collated both sets of information into a consolidated database, but an effective cross-referencing index was not available before late 1915.[25]

The adoption in March 1915 of the retaliatory order-in-council exponentially increased the magnitude and complexity of the information problem (not to mention the clerical workload). In fact, the timing of the change could not have been more unfortunate. The various departments and agencies responsible for administering policy already were struggling to set up the machinery for gathering and processing the requisite information to monitor contraband between North America and Europe. Now they were required to keep watch on practically all seaborne commerce, both inbound and outbound. The added workload, therefore, aggravated already severe difficulties.

Despite considerable prior preparation, the Admiralty and Foreign Office quickly found themselves overwhelmed by the sheer volume of data they now needed to process. For many months thereafter both struggled to catch up. In the desperation to do so, responsibilities were jettisoned. In May 1915, officials at the Contraband Department frankly admitted it was "wholly impossible for us to digest and act upon the reports of the ESRC" and so ended up simply ignoring them—which, it may be observed, they were inclined to do anyway, as the Foreign Office refused to admit that it was bound to act on the recommendations of what it regarded as a rival organization.[26]

At the end of July 1915, Sir Edward Grey admitted to the cabinet that the blockade machinery was still failing to cope with the volume of business.[27] Nearly a year later, in March 1916, at a meeting attended by midlevel bureaucrats from various agencies connected with the administration of blockade policy, the continuing problem of information overload was again discussed.[28] War Trade Department officials confessed that it was "almost a physical impossibility to get sufficiently full information on every item in the limited time available to help the Contraband Committee, all one could do was to pick out the most important items." In addition, there were continuing problems with information quality; for instance, "so much cargo is refused at the time of shipment that cabled information is frequently received of goods being booked for shipment which however is not shipped."[29] Throughout 1915 and well into 1916, systemic weaknesses in the administrative machinery as much as willful departmental obstruction blunted the effectiveness of the blockade.

At the Admiralty, meanwhile, before the new rules came into effect in March 1915, the Naval Staff Trade Division made a tremendous effort to reform internal administrative procedures to cope with the anticipated increase in caseload and to speed up processing. Yet Captain Richard Webb and his staff too found that they had seriously underestimated the increased effort that was required. An internal memorandum dated 1 March 1915 well illustrates the sort of information problems faced, and offers insight into the attendant technological constraints. The primary concern was how to sift the wheat from the chaff as quickly as possible; the consequences of failure were considerable.

> It is obvious that very great trouble is likely to arise unless adequate arrangements are immediately put in hand for the consideration of manifests before the vessels arrive at UK ports. Unless this is done, there is bound to be the most serious congestion, and at the same time vessels will be delayed for extended periods which will only result in serious lack of tonnage for the purposes of trade, and enormous claims for expenses and compensation against the Admiralty. The problem arises as to how to get every possible information about cargoes by a time about 3 or 4 days previous to the arrival of the vessel.[30]

In this instance, the issue was how to assemble all the relevant documentation in the short time available, including such details as "the insurance or destination of their cargo and the chartering and ownership of the vessel." The necessity to have all information on hand was emphasized: "An isolated telegram is very often of little interest unless it is shown together with all the other papers concerning the matter."[31] The chief obstacle to consolidating all this information was the mismatch between the card indexes to the various files held by different agencies. The necessity to cross-list had not been previously anticipated because it had been assumed the system would remain focused on tracking ships, not cargoes. The following remarks made by the assistant director of the (T.1 section) Trade Division on 3 March 1915 are illustrative:

> Unfortunately the index of the Restriction of Enemy Supplies Committee's file is of no practical value to us so far as concerns the vessels and their cargoes. Their telegrams are laboriously filed under the commodity and recipients and senders of telegrams, and if any information about a particular vessel is required it involves turning up a great many dockets and carefully extracting the papers that relate to the actual voyage of the vessel in question.[32]

In the short run there was no alternative. Clerks were obliged to search laboriously through masses of files looking for the relevant information, make copies (by hand), and return the original documents to their place. But it proved impossible to keep close tabs on more than twenty selected commodities because of the sheer quantity of information that needed to be collated. Everything else was simply ignored.

The director of the Trade Division, summarily rejected the option of reclassifying his department's index system by commodity instead of by ship to make it conform to that of the ESRC.[33] Although he appreciated the desirability of accurately monitoring the flows of more strategic commodities into and out of neutral countries, he was adverse to sacrifice ship tracking capability in order to achieve this.[34] Captain Webb justified his decision not to rebase his index by emphasizing the "remarkable manner in which Shipping lines of neutral countries and insurance systems are recognising our ability to carry out our intention as evinced by their anxiety to come to terms with us."[35] Instead he petitioned the Board of Admiralty for yet more bureaucratic resources to help construct and maintain an additional (parallel) card index integrating both his database and that belonging to the ESRC. This assistance was not forthcoming, and an additional year passed before another attempt was made to resolve this problem.

The immediate consequence of new and tighter blockade regulations was an increase in the information load. Because the machinery could not cope with the increased volume of data to be processed, the result was worsening congestion in British ports during the spring of 1915. The situation was exacerbated by merchants and shipowners not behaving as expected. The Foreign Office had hoped that offering owners generous prices for their confiscated cargoes would induce them to settle quickly and waive damages. This would have allowed the British authorities immediately to facilitate the purchase of the cargo by a third party and so release the merchant ship. It was with considerable dismay, therefore, that the Foreign Office found that neutral "claimants in practically every case are refusing to give any such undertaking."[36]

As a result, after all warehouse space was filled, cargoes had to remain on board merchant ships, and the ships in port, until the disputes were settled. The lengthier the delay, the greater the number of spoiled cargoes, the larger the demand for compensation, and of course the greater the port congestion.[37] At a gathering of blockade officials held on 13 April 1915, John Mellor, the procurator general, advised that more and more shippers were challenging compulsory purchase of their goods through the courts, and "there can be no doubt but that the claims of very large amounts are already piling up."[38]

Though the Foreign Office took the lead in gathering raw data, Admiralty personnel demonstrated a better understanding of how those data should be organized and exploited, as well as devising solutions as to how identified gaps could most easily be bridged. The Admiralty's surprisingly greater proficiency in manipulating commercial data may be explained by their early recruitment of outside expert assistance and the assimilation of these men of business into positions of trust within the Naval Staff organization. In March 1915, every member of the staff assigned to the Contraband Department of the Foreign Office was a career diplomat, men notoriously unsympathetic to trade interests before, during, and after the war.[39] By contrast, no fewer than thirteen of the twenty-one officers assigned to the Admiralty Trade Division belonged to the Royal Naval Volunteer Reserve. This particular brand of naval officer had received no naval training—except perhaps lessons in putting on a naval uniform—but all had strong City connections and collectively possessed enormous expertise in international business. Those identified include Frederick Leverton Harris (senior partner of Harris and Dixon, shipbrokers), Robert H. Brand (managing director of Lazard Brothers, bankers), and Sir Frederick Bolton (former chairman of Lloyd's). There were also the brothers Leander and Frederick H. McCormick-Goodhart, scions of an Anglo-American family possessing large mining interests in both Kent (in the United Kingdom) and Colorado (in the United States), not to mention a respectable slice of the equity in the International Harvester company of Illinois, founded by their maternal grandfather.

For instance, it was at the suggestion of the Admiralty Trade Division that in mid-March the Foreign Office began issuing its consular officers preprinted forms in order to help "systematize the statistics which we receive from the various neutral countries."[40] It was again the Admiralty that pointed out that correctly gauging the flow of trade between the United States and contiguous European neutral countries required the monitoring not just of U.S. exports but also of imports (of U.S. goods) into individual European countries.[41] The ease with which cargoes might legitimately be resold while in transit—never mind the opportunities for fraud lent by the commercial system—rendered the interpretation of U.S. export figures by themselves problematic. In April 1915, accordingly, the Foreign Office instructed consular officials in Scandinavia, Italy, and Holland to gather data on imports and exports through local ports, classify each cargo under one of forty-nine headings, tabulate the information, and submit it to London.[42] "It is proposed to collect and print every week the returns thus obtained."[43]

By mid-March 1915, the Foreign Office architects of the blockade system broadly accepted they had been overly optimistic in believing that neutral governments would be able to prevent their merchants from seeking to make huge profits by reexporting contraband items to Germany. They also conceded they had been wrong to believe foreign governments would readily assist them in identifying such breaches by providing accurate trade statistics.[44] In a paper dated 1 May 1915, Robert L. Craigie, a midlevel official in the Contraband Department, underlined this:

> Too great reliance cannot be placed on the statistics which are, somewhat tardily, issued by the countries concerned, since it is obviously in their interest to show as low an import as possible. A comparison of the huge United States export returns for last year with the much more modest returns of the importing European Powers is instructive and it does not require great ingenuity to devise methods by which the figures could be "cooked" with very little risk of detection.[45]

Of all the contiguous neutrals, Sweden was by far the worst offender. As Captain Montagu Consett, the British naval attaché in Scandinavia, emphasized to Blinker Hall, the head of British naval intelligence, "We have absolutely no means of obtaining information concerning Swedish imports and exports. No information is given by the Swedish government; on the contrary it is very carefully concealed."[46] Esme Howard, the minister in charge of the Stockholm legation (and a notorious apologist for the Swedish government), acknowledged that the official statistics published by the Swedes for the first quarter of 1915 were "not by any means complete and that the actual imports in that period were on the whole not improbably double the amounts represented."[47]

It proved equally difficult for blockade officials to establish the ultimate end user of cargoes arriving in Sweden. This task fell to Robert Vansittart, another middle-ranking Foreign Office official who would later rise to prominence. In an internal office memorandum dated 10 March 1915, Vansittart frankly admitted he had no reliable way of telling if the consignee named on a manifest was a consumer (i.e., an end user), a broker, a forwarding agent (i.e., a reseller), or simply fictitious.[48] His only source was a set of prewar commercial trade directories, and these he found to be of little use. The necessity to build a "Who's Who" database of European traders—or, more to the point, who traded with whom—had been recognized by the ESRC, which since October 1914 had endeavored to build what was called the Neutral and Enemy Trade Index. The project was short staffed—just two clerks could be spared to keep track of firms involved in trading twenty strategic commodities (somewhat arbitrarily defined)—and progress had been slow.[49] The ESRC continued to struggle with this responsibility until it was transferred to the War Trade Department toward the end of 1915.

To an extent, the uncooperativeness of foreign agencies and the unreliability of their data may be regarded as understandable. What was not expected, and far more embarrassing for the British authorities, were the difficulties encountered in establishing the level of British trade with contiguous European powers, especially in reexports. Theoretically, the volume of exports clearing British ports could be gauged from the data routinely collected by the Board of Customs and Excise from copies of ship manifests and the like. Customs officers, however, were habitually focused on raising revenue, and some were none too scrupulous in ensuring the proper completion of all paperwork. Provided the value of the goods being exported was listed, they often overlooked the frequent omission of cargo weight.[50] There were also inconsistencies in the format of data generated by different ports in the British Isles. For these reasons and others, Customs figures were found too unreliable to be of practical use. R. H. Harwood, the senior statistician assigned to the War Trade Department, explained why:

> The monthly returns of the customs house, even if they could have been produced with sufficient promptitude, were unsatisfactory for the purposes of the blockade, because they were classified on a system which was devised without any reference to war conditions, and which, moreover, corresponded to none of the systems employed by the northern neutrals.[51]

The new War Trade Department statistical bureau ultimately decided there was no alternative but to rebuild the database from scratch. The decision was approved in March 1915, and new forms based upon a new format were printed and distributed to customs officials; in May the data began to flow, but not until August 1915 was the statistical bureau able to supply the Contraband Department and other agencies with a set of provisional trade figures.[52] Even then Harwood admitted they were far from complete and contained serious errors.[53] He begged the Contraband Department of the Foreign Office to redouble its efforts to gather copies of ship manifests from all over the world, as many as possible. Robert Craigie clarified for the dull-witted within his department that trade statistics produced by the Trade Clearing House "are very largely based on manifests and the more manifests we can supply him [Harwood] with, the more complete will the figures be . . . The only way to get these is, as we have proposed, to make it obligatory to British Steam Ship companies to furnish them and to put pressure on foreign companies to do the same."[54]

The problems with the quality of British statistics were known by those at the top of the blockade organization. Lord Robert Cecil, who in 1916 would become minister responsible for the blockade, admitted to Admiral David Beatty that the War Trade Department statistics detailing imports into Scandinavia and Holland for 1915 incorporated perhaps just 75 percent of all inbound cargoes.[55] In 1916, Sir Ralph Paget (recently promoted to become minister to Copenhagen) had occasion to remind Eyre Crowe that much of the statistical data upon which British blockade policy was built was unreliable. Paget previously had been assistant undersecretary in charge of the American department, and thus he was intimately familiar with this problem. Paget told Crowe, "It is questionable whether we really have any idea of how much actually is going into Germany and whether the figures given us are correct. Some people maintain they are not but they cannot prove it so I think we must console ourselves by hoping that they are."[56]

The Blockade and the War Trade Department

The War Trade Department was created by Treasury minute dated 17 February 1915.[57] As previously related, for reasons that are not entirely clear the prime minister handed the new agency a dual mission. One branch, the Trade Clearing House (later renamed the War Trade Intelligence Department), served as the pivot for the collection and dissemination of commercial intelligence. Colonel Hankey's report of 13 January had emphasized that the efficient distribution and analysis of commercial intelligence was crucial to identifying leakage and therefore to the effectiveness of the blockade. Subordinate to this division was the new statistical bureau (later made separate and named the War Trade Statistical Department). The second main branch of the War Trade Department processed and adjudicated applications from merchants for special exemption licenses to export items on the prohibited list.

To head this new non-executive agency, the prime minister appointed Lord Emmott, a minister with strong pro-trade, anti-economic-warfare credentials. Sir Nathaniel Highmore, the retired permanent secretary of the Board of Customs and Excise who had been a member of the prewar Desart Committee and who theoretically was intimately familiar with the goals of economic warfare strategy, was recalled to public service and appointed permanent secretary.

The promulgation of the retaliatory order-in-council of 11 March 1915 nearly led to the crash of the fledgling War Trade Department. While the new bureaucratic machinery was still being set up, which was largely dictated by the speed at which Emmott and Highmore could pry experienced staff away from other government departments, there was a jump in the number of applications for export licenses. (Already since the beginning of the war, incidentally, in just four months, a staggering 66,000 approval notices had been issued.)[58] Instead of 900 applications per diem, which had been the average when the War Trade Department was first conceived, the daily number of applications surged past 1,600 and the new agency found itself swamped.[59] Emmott's first response was to instruct his handful of staff to give each application only the most cursory examination and stamp it approved. The result was a mini-boom in British exports to the Continent. This was a source of relief at the War Trade Department, delight at the Board of Trade, but headaches and consternation at the Admiralty and the Foreign Office, for there was no doubt that much had been passed on to Germany. More seriously, Emmott also suspended the setting up of the economic intelligence Trade Clearing House and temporarily reallocated its staff to help clear the backlog of export applications. As a result, no statistical data were processed, which meant that no one was really sure just how large the surge in exports had been.[60] The effect was to blind the entire government.

For his management decisions, Emmott came in for considerable criticism.[61] At the cabinet meeting on 30 March, Harcourt recorded, "Winston is furious about licenses to export from the country to neutrals" and had viciously attacked Emmott.[62] Thereafter, the War Trade Department was subjected to constant fire from the direction of the Admiralty. This antagonism, which lasted the duration of the war, was exacerbated by personal animosity between Winston Churchill and Lord Emmott. Since the two had first come together in the cabinet, the egotistical, brilliant, and eloquent Churchill had clashed frequently with the "honest, slow, laborious" Emmott, who was handicapped in debate by his "whining mechanical voice."[63] The two had long hated each other.[64] Defending himself, Emmott pleaded there had been no other way to prevent a total collapse of the licensing system, which would have produced chaos or the virtual cessation of British exports.[65] Clearly, Emmott believed he had done the right thing, and it must be admitted that according to his own standards he had done so. It must also be admitted that

Emmott had first tried to obtain from the prime minister "an authoritative pronouncement as to the policy the Contraband and Licensing Committee should adopt in reference to commodities going to neutral countries adjacent to Germany and Austria."[66] But no guidance had been forthcoming.

Directly after the cabinet meeting of 30 March, Reginald McKenna summoned the senior men from all departments and agencies connected with the administration of blockade policy to "lay down definite principles" for the guidance of the War Trade Department.[67] At the meeting, clearly still smarting from Churchill's attack earlier that day, Emmott reiterated the unfairness of the criticisms leveled against his department, pointing out that he was responsible neither for the administrative muddle he had inherited nor for the huge backlog of license applications. "It is clear," he further averred, "that 'Business as Usual' and crippling German trade are inconsistent." Economic policy and blockade policy had become intertwined, and the two aspects of policy needed to be approached as one. His personal preference was clear: like Runciman, Emmott was not against attacking German trade, simply opposed to measures likely to produce collateral damage to British trade. Mindful of the political implications, he warned that "to curtail very sharply the quantity of goods allowed to be exported [from the United Kingdom] will cause a good deal of trouble and dissatisfaction among our traders at home."[68]

Unable or unwilling to resolve this crucial contradiction in government policy, the assembly of officials set aside this issue and moved on to discuss the difficulties in obtaining a clear picture of international trade flows, and in particular an accurate measure of the volume of imports into European countries contiguous to Germany. Emmott records in his diary (although the minutes do not say so) that there ensued a lengthy discussion on how statistical evidence could be used to limit European contiguous neutral imports to their prewar levels, and it was agreed "we are to carry this out as soon as may be."[69] The first necessity, however, was to remedy the inadequacy of available statistical data; the British government could not very well limit European imports to their prewar levels until they first knew what those levels had been. Lord Emmott promised that his new statistical branch would compile the figures if the Board of Trade and the Admiralty could assist in assembling the necessary data.[70] But in the meantime, what else could be done? No suggestions were offered.

The importance of obtaining reliable statistical data was also discussed by the meeting in the context of the landmark *Kim* case. The *Kim* was a Swedish-owned merchantman seized in late 1914 along with three other Scandinavian-registered vessels laden with American meat and lard owned by a consortium of Chicago meatpackers. Although no direct evidence could be found showing the meat was ultimately destined for Germany, the circumstantial case was overwhelming. For instance, the end product (processed meat) was packaged into unusual-sized tins that happened to match the dimensions of the canteen boxes carried by German soldiers. Intelligence had uncovered that at least one member of the packers consortium had a contract to supply tinned meat to the German army.[71] (But could it be proven the meat actually on board the *Kim* was intended for the German army? That was the legal question.) The most decisive evidence was statistical. The combined cargoes of the four vessels contained more than 19 million pounds of lard, whereas the average annual Danish importation from all sources was less than 1.5 million pounds. So greatly did these cargoes exceed the normal level of Danish annual imports (by a factor of twenty-four) that the meatpackers' plea that it was all for domestic consumption was manifestly ridiculous. The procurator general, however, was nervous at trying to use this statistical evidence to establish a presumption of enemy destination, as there was no historical precedent for doing so.

The British government had tried to escape this dilemma by seeking an out-of-court settlement with the meatpackers, but talks had foundered on disagreement over the value of the cargoes. The meatpackers demanded £2.9 million (the amount they would have been paid upon delivery in Copenhagen); the British offered just £1.3 million (the fair market price in the United Kingdom).[72] The magnitude of this difference illustrates not only the level of disruption in the international trading system but also the magnitude of the incentive for American businessmen to trade indirectly with Germany. Within the British government there was reluctance to give way over the *Kim,* but at the same time all agreed it would be far better to reach an amicable understanding instead of referring the case to the prize court for adjudication. On the latter point even the Admiralty agreed.[73] The intransigence of the meatpackers, however, left the British government no option. The landmark *Kim* case was heard in July 1915, and two months later the verdict was handed down in favor of the crown. As we shall see in the next chapter, the court permitted the use of statistical evidence, though later it qualified its endorsement of the precedent.

After several hours of discussion on 30 March, during which the participants were unable to agree on the instructions to be given to the War Trade

Department, McKenna brought the meeting to a close. The picture was just too hazy: more information was required before firm decisions could be made. Such considerations, however, did not stop the Foreign Office, Board of Trade, and Admiralty—the big three departments in blockade policy—from issuing Emmott with their own (contradictory) instructions anyway. In early May 1915, Emmott caustically remarked to Grey that there were too many "cooks" involved in "stirring the same broth" and the net result was that all "waste time in criticizing each other."[74] In vain, Emmott looked again to the prime minister to reconcile the contradictions and impose some coherence upon the government's approach to the management of economic and blockade affairs. But Asquith declined to be drawn into the middle of what was becoming an increasingly acrimonious fight.

In the absence of a clear directive, Emmott proceeded as he thought best. This was valiant but unwise: in trying to forge coherence from the mass of contradictory departmental edicts, he moved himself into the center of the bureaucratic cross fire and became a convenient target for those wishing to shift blame for the increasingly visible disconnect between declared, agreed, and actual blockade policy. The emergence toward the end of April of irrefutable evidence that his department had been excessively liberal—that is, lax—in approving exemption export licenses compounded Emmott's problems. The Admiralty accused him of having undermined the effectiveness of the blockade, and the Foreign Office denounced him for having compromised diplomatic relations with neutrals. By 11 May 1915, Emmott had become so uncomfortable that he wrote to Asquith threatening resignation unless given "a measure of protection" from the other departments. "The work of the licensing committee is very difficult," he cried plaintively, "it cannot please everybody and I do ask that the best construction should be placed upon its efforts, and that it should not be condemned unheard."[75] Somehow the prime minister managed to smooth Emmott's ruffled feathers and he was persuaded to stay.

The following week, however, Emmott lost his cabinet seat in the reshuffle subsequent to the formation of the coalition government (detailed in the next chapter). His exclusion from the reconstituted executive was seen by some as a major blow. "It is a sorrow to me," Runciman consoled him, "you are no longer to be at No. 10 [Downing Street; i.e., a member of the cabinet] to act as one of the brakes on reckless gentlemen [Churchill] who wanted to seize all foreign property and fight every neutral."[76] Perhaps reflecting how little importance was attached to the post, Emmott nevertheless retained the chairmanship of the War Trade Department. This decision proved to have serious consequences, the most significant being that the head of the War Trade Department was no longer in a position to contribute his expertise, such as it was, to cabinet discussions of blockade policy. (Though it might be remarked this was likely advantageous to Asquith in that it prevented Emmott from divulging too much contentious information.)

Though subsequent to his exclusion from the cabinet Emmott was always informed promptly of its decisions, he did not always understand the reasoning behind the changes in policy, and predictably this led to misunderstandings—especially given the continuing poor working relationships between his bureau and the three principal blockade departments, the Foreign Office, Admiralty, and Board of Trade. The particular animosity between his agency and the Admiralty had already been noted. Although supposedly friends with Walter Runciman, Emmott complained behind his back that he and his staff at the Board of Trade were always "so difficult to deal with."[77] (The sentiment, incidentally, was reciprocated.)[78] Emmott's attempts to forge a better understanding with the Foreign Office through direct links with Sir Edward Grey proved fruitless. The foreign secretary declined to be drawn into discussion of such "nauseous" matters as "contraband & kindred subjects that don't exist in time of peace and are a disagreeable brood spawned by war."[79] As Grey's subordinates knew only too well, the foreign secretary was simply not interested in dealing with any subject involving statistical or technical arguments.[80]

Emmott viewed the Foreign Office staff as the worst to work with, tending to arrogate authority and take action unilaterally.[81] The matter "that is almost driving me to despair," he protested to Asquith,

> is the constant chopping and changing in the Foreign Office instructions and the ludicrous shortsightedness of some the requests we receive. This is not due to Grey or to anyone else who has acted for him during his absences from the Foreign Office. The instructions I speak of seem to come from much lower down in the organisation.[82]

Emmott was alluding here, of course, to Sir Eyre Crowe and his subordinates at the Contraband Department of the Foreign Office. Nevertheless, invariably Emmott chose "to carry out F[oreign] O[ffice] instructions implicitly"—and even zealously when they were substantially in accord with his own views on any particular subject.[83] For instance, he subscribed to Sir Edward

Grey's dictum that Britain must honor the terms of the treaties recently signed with the various contiguous neutrals, even if the other signatories did not.[84] Emmott shared the Board of Trade's view that "we are practically bound to grant export licenses for any commodity to any neutral countries that had prohibited its reexport."[85] But Emmott was much less enthusiastic about the Foreign Office's predilection for treating the issuance of export licenses as a tool of diplomatic coercion. In May 1915, he railed when the Foreign Office peremptorily instructed him to suspend all licenses for Sweden and Bulgaria, thereby causing considerable disruption to his department.[86] Though he ultimately complied—"I may say," he afterward confided in Lord Crewe, "that I think these instructions are often given without due consideration of the effect upon our trade and are much too rigid in character."[87]

However tempting it may be to dismiss Emmott's complaints and denials of responsibility as attempts to escape blame for weak internal management at the War Trade Department, beneath them lay a legitimate grievance, namely, the continuing ambiguities and contradictions within broader government policy. Emmott was perfectly correct in protesting that his department had never been given "any clear guidance as to how far the trade and national finances of the country are to be considered in reference to licensing [of exports]" and that no one else in the government had considered "war trade problems in relation not only to their effect on the enemy but also on our own trade as affecting our power to hold out in a long war."[88] There was no denying either, as Emmott constantly reminded everyone, that no effective mechanism existed for reconciling the myriad differences in departmental opinions on complex questions of policy. Smooth running of the blockade administrative machine demanded the highest level of cooperation between the various departments of government involved, yet department inclinations ran more to petulance and unilateralism. In theory, responsibility for departmental coordination belonged to Sir Francis Hopwood's standing interdepartmental committee, the ESRC. But as Emmott pointed out, the ESRC was a non-executive body consisting largely of civil servants, and anyway "its members do not agree among themselves on many questions of policy."[89] With this observation Colonel Hankey was in complete agreement.[90]

The only body involved in coordinating blockade policy that also had executive authority was the cabinet. At the beginning of the war, the cabinet had tried to adjudicate the policy differences between the Admiralty and the Foreign Office, but with limited success, as we have seen. By the beginning of 1915 the cabinet had become even less effective in reconciling departmental differences. Not only were the issues themselves highly complex but, more important, ministerial opinions had polarized and become entrenched. By now, asking the cabinet to adjudicate on a point of departmental difference connected with the blockade was as futile as infantry launching a daylight frontal assault on the western front. Even at the time it was argued that the prime minister should have compelled reconciliation between the conflicting departmental viewpoints and imposed discipline upon the recalcitrant. Hankey and Hopwood wanted him to confer executive authority upon a single minister in all matters pertaining to economics and war (provided, of course, "their" minister was given the job). But such a solution contained too many serious constitutional as well as political implications and consequently was not the kind of innovation that Prime Minister Asquith was ever likely to entertain.[91] And as long as the cabinet was so deeply divided over how ruthlessly to enforce the blockade, such a draconian approach remained politically out of the question.

Sweden and the Foreign Office

The prime minister's unwillingness to resolve the contradictions in government policy not only resulted in inconsistencies and inefficiency in the management of blockade policy but also created tremendous friction between the various interested departments. On 21 May 1915, Hankey privately warned Asquith that "dissatisfaction with the existing organization of the various War Trade Committees" was threatening to explode. "I have received constant complaints," he reported, "that the system as a whole does not work as smoothly as it ought to, owing mainly to the difficulty in coordinating the efforts of those bodies which are all working on different branches of the same subject."[92] Nowhere was this disconnect more apparent, nor the heat generated by bureaucratic friction greater, than in the interdepartmental squabble over how best to handle the Swedish problem.

By the beginning of March 1915, Foreign Office staff in London accepted that the Swedish government had no intention of honoring its treaty pledge not to reexport contraband items to Germany. Goods allowed through the blockade on the understanding they were for domestic consumption had been pouring into Germany. Officially the Foreign Office maintained there was no evidence to support accusations of systematic or widespread abuse. Some believed this was true. This included Sir Esme Howard, the minister at the Stockholm legation, who routinely dismissed evidence supplied by his commercial attaché, Oswald Phillpotts, that "a considerable part of the goods arriving at Gothenburg from America are really destined for German receivers."[93] Howard insisted that the quantities detected were comparatively insignificant and therefore hardly constituted evidence of systemic abuse by the Swedish authorities, as claimed.

Similarly, when the Contraband Department queried how then British-made goods delivered to Sweden had reached Germany, Howard retorted that the fault lay with the War Trade Department in London for having granted export licenses to "unreliable and second-rate" firms.[94] Howard's allegations of regulatory incompetence contained more than a grain of truth, but this in no way validated his broader argument that the Swedish government was innocent of misbehavior. "It is no use pretending," Crowe chided him in a letter dated 27 March 1915, "that our confidence has not been rudely shaken. Things have gone through, en masse, openly, under our noses and those of the Swedish authorities."[95] "At present Sweden gets all the benefits from her arrangements with us, she is doing a roaring trade at our expense, and our one object of keeping our stuff from passing to Germany via Sweden is altogether frustrated."[96]

Howard's refusal to accept he was being duped by his host government led to calls, echoed even within the Foreign Office, that he should be replaced.[97] Sir Francis Hopwood, chairman of the ESRC, was particularly critical of the minister, maintaining that Howard did not at all "appreciate the commercial side of all the troubles."[98] Though Grey acknowledged Howard's deficiencies, the latter remained Britain's representative in Sweden for the duration of the war. Of course Hopwood was not so naive as to think that stemming the leakage through Sweden could be accomplished simply by a change in personnel. The problems, he recognized, were deep-rooted and stemmed all the way back to the Anglo-Swedish trade treaty hastily drafted and signed the previous November (1914). Hopwood believed that the Foreign Office had blundered in negotiating the "unfortunate agreement with Sweden," and since then, "both sides have suffered from it."[99] The document had been so poorly drafted that various branches of the government had been under siege ever since from lawyers hired by various commercial interest groups demanding clarifications in the meaning of certain clauses.[100] At the same time, Hopwood was aware, or at least suspected, that Sir Edward Grey had secretly instructed the Contraband Committee to turn a blind eye toward much of the contraband bound for Sweden.[101] To what extent he understood the reasoning behind this decision, however, is a different matter.

The naval authorities were surprisingly quick to detect the Foreign Office's laxity in enforcing the blockade with respect to cargoes bound for Scandinavia. On 20 March 1915, Admiral Sir John Jellicoe, the fleet commander in chief, wrote officially to the Admiralty expressing outrage at discovering that out of ninety-six vessels arrested in northern waters for contraband smuggling by the 10th Cruiser Squadron during the first two months of 1915, just one ship had been sent forward to the prize court; all the others had been released.[102] Jellicoe professed equal bewilderment at the lack of action against former German oil tankers, taken over by the Standard Oil Corporation and now flying the American flag, caught carrying petroleum across the Atlantic.[103] However much officials at the Admiralty may have shared Jellicoe's frustration and however egregious the infractions, they could do nothing—and were reluctant to admit their impotence. Their official reply was curt and uninformative. "It is only to be expected," the Admiralty secretary wrote, that of the ships sent in, "only a small proportion will be subsequently be sent to the Prize Court"; as for the former German oil tankers, they had been allowed by the Government to pass "for political reasons."[104] Angered by what he justifiably regarded as the Admiralty's unhelpful reply to legitimate questions, Jellicoe took steps to find answers by other means; he formed his own private economic intelligence unit—more on which in a later chapter.[105] Jellicoe was no more successful eliciting answers through unofficial channels. The bickering between Fisher and Churchill over the Dardanelles and North Sea policy now consumed all their collective energies, leaving little time for consideration of other matters such as blockade policy.[106] On 4 April 1915, Admiral Fisher frankly admitted to Jellicoe, "I have little time for anything else but increasing anxiety over the Dardanelles situation."[107]

The foreign secretary's disinclination to adopt a firm stance against Sweden owed much to his growing concern over the weakness of Russia. Since Turkey had joined the war and closed the Dardanelles in November 1914, Russia had been more or less economically isolated from the global trading system. Her grain surplus, her chief source of foreign exchange, remained effectively locked up in the Ukraine. Just how damaging this was for the Entente can hardly be overstated. We have already seen how the ensuing contraction in world grain supply produced a significant rise in food prices across the globe during the winter of 1914–1915 and how the expectation of further increases was the source of much domestic political concern. For Russia, of course, the political and economic consequences were far more serious. Besides the obvious implications for Russian commerce and internal finances, the inability to earn foreign exchange complicated her attempts to purchase equipment from overseas.

Even when Russia obtained the money to pay for munitions and machine tools, getting them physically into the country was problematic. With her ports in the Black Sea and Baltic effectively closed, the only remaining direct gateway into western Russia was via the port of Archangel. Located within the Arctic Circle, however, Archangel was icebound for much of the year and additionally lacked the port infrastructure and, most important, the rail link needed to handle much traffic. Using thousands of reindeer-drawn sleds to haul goods to and from the port proved no substitute. To obtain vital supplies, therefore, Russia was forced to rely upon transshipment through Sweden.[108]

The Russian dependence upon the Swedish trade route provided the pro-German Swedish government with a powerful negotiating weapon to use against the Allies. Once Sweden recognized that the war would be a protracted affair, the government decided to exploit this to the fullest. From the beginning of 1915 Swedish diplomats became much more forceful in asserting their country's right to trade with Germany. Each time the British threatened to tighten up, the Swedes would gently squeeze the Russian lifeline.[109] In March, the Swedish government informed London that henceforward it would allow only as much material to be transshipped to Russia as Britain would allow Sweden to reexport to Germany. Although Foreign Office officials deeply resented being thus blackmailed (and so effectively), the Russians begged them to comply. Already, on 26 February 1915, Sir George Buchanan, the British ambassador in St. Petersburg, had told London the Russian government felt strongly that "absolute freedom of transit through Norway and Sweden is of vital importance to Russia both from a point of view of national defence and of its industrial interests."[110] The Russian foreign minister reinforced this message by personally telling Buchanan just how vital he thought the "transit-trade both of conditional and absolute contraband through Scandinavia to Russia and they are most anxious that nothing should be done which might prejudice it."[111] Such an explicit request from an ally, the Foreign Office felt, simply could not be disregarded even if, as naval officers and even some diplomats believed, the Russians exaggerated the importance of the Swedish transit trade. Despite frequent British requests to do so, the Russians proved unable to enumerate just how vital this route was to their war effort. Not until January 1917 did they finally provide some rudimentary trade statistics, which were immediately set aside as demonstrably inaccurate.[112]

Grey's unwillingness to press Sweden was reinforced by a warning from the Board of Trade that Britain too was reliant upon that country for important material, especially timber and iron ore. Within the Foreign Office there was considerable skepticism whether this claim was true. But although officials tried, lack of data (again) meant they were no more successful than the Russians in quantifying precisely how vital Swedish raw materials were to British production. In the absence of definitive proof either way, Grey opted to take no chances.

The unsuccessful enquires by the Contraband Department did turn up one interesting discovery, however. On 3 April 1915, Robert Vansittart, assigned to watch Sweden, reported to Crowe that

> the situation as regards goods in transit to Russia via Sweden is profoundly unsatisfactory. I have investigated a number of applications and found them to be fraudulent. I expect the same thing is happening in regard to rubber and tin, and very probably Germans are trying to get hold of consignments in this way i.e. by applications nominally for Russia but really for diversion en route across Sweden.[113]

Further investigations by Howard in Stockholm unearthed further evidence regarding the "deviation of goods to Germany which are ostensibly in transit from Great Britain to Russia." The Russians, it further transpired, were well aware. In fact, the Russian commercial attaché in Stockholm not only condoned the practice but mentioned that his government was buying certain items direct from Germany (probably in return for grain). He "did not seem to think that there was any particular harm in this trade," Howard incredulously reported.[114] These disclosures, not surprisingly, did not leave the Foreign Office.

In mid-April 1915, Foreign Office attitudes toward Sweden shifted. The scale of contraband trade between Sweden and Germany was becoming impossible to ignore and there were growing demands for retaliation. Sir Edward Grey's willingness to attempt a more forceful approach was encouraged by the anticipated reopening of the Dardanelles to Russian trade. Indeed, the mere announcement of Britain's intention to storm the Gallipoli peninsula caused a drop in wheat futures on the Chicago exchange. Optimism about the Dardanelles had significance elsewhere. On 12 April 1915, Grey summoned the nerve to take direct action designed to check the flow of Scandinavian iron ore into Germany, sanctioning the capture of Swedish-registered bulk ore carriers.

Two days later the Swedish government reacted angrily to the seizure of the freighter *Sir Ernest Cassel,* carrying iron ore bound for Rotterdam, by shutting off the flow of munitions through Sweden to Russia.[115] Viewing the Swedish move as mere posturing, and doubtless anticipating that Sweden's power of blackmail would soon be at an end with the reopening of the Dardanelles, Grey called their bluff. He did so, moreover, without first consulting the Russians or the legation in Sweden.[116] Much to Howard's consternation, Grey then further escalated the mini trade war by instructing the War Trade Department to suspend the issuance of export licenses for Sweden.[117]

For many within the blockade administration Grey's measures did not go nearly far enough. Sir Leo Chiozza Money, a Liberal MP, an important member of the ESRC, and known to be in the confidence of the increasingly influential Lloyd George, was not alone in denouncing the Foreign Office for its failure "to protect our interests as belligerents." He demanded that Sweden be declared "a base of supplies to the enemy"—which would have been tantamount to the complete interdiction of her seaborne trade.[118] On 4 May 1915, a delegation of conservative MPs from the Unionist Business Committee met with Grey to tell of their unhappiness with his timidity toward Sweden and other neutrals.[119]

Despite the Foreign Office's reticence in sharing knowledge of what was happening inside Sweden, the naval intelligence department had its own sources and kept the Admiralty well informed.[120] Captain Reginald "Blinker" Hall, the director of naval intelligence, maintained close contact with Captain Montagu Consett, the British naval attaché for Scandinavia. Their private correspondence indicates that, in addition to his naval duties, Consett acted as the regional head of the Secret Intelligence Service.[121] His letters contain frequent references to information obtained by clandestine means that was purposely not included in his official reports; protocol demanded that his official dispatches be routed through the Foreign Office, and experience taught that procedural muddles often led to lengthy delays and sometimes the disappearance of enclosed documents.[122] Instead Consett took to communicating directly with the Admiralty, a circumvention that constituted a breach of protocol and proved the source of much diplomatic irritation. Throughout the war Consett was a staunch advocate of economic warfare. He repeatedly tried to spur the Admiralty into more forcefully protesting the Foreign Office's inaction. He not only possessed a sharp pen—his attaché reports were usually mercilessly critical of Foreign Office diffidence—

but was endowed with a surprisingly sound grasp of economics and statistical methods. On one occasion the diplomats were left flabbergasted when Consett wrote a report on Danish agricultural production that exposed serious discrepancies in official Danish figures missed by the British commercial attaché.[123]

Captain Consett's unsuspected talent for economic analysis was more than counterbalanced by his stupendous lack of tact. He made no secret of his contempt for certain senior British diplomatic staff in both Copenhagen and Stockholm, accusing them of "whitewashing proclivities," incompetence, and even outright corruption.[124] Consett's effectiveness was further compromised by his flagrant—almost habitual—disregard for Foreign Office protocol and his willingness to indulge in petty squabbles and feuds with diplomatic staff, most infamously with Sir Esme Howard.[125] Such behavior discredited him in the eyes of officials sitting in London—or, rather, made it easy for diplomats such as Howard, who deeply resented the captain's interferences in matters outside his formal area of competence, to discredit him back home. "As regards the larger political issues involved," Howard once imparted to Crowe, "his [Consett's] judgment is in my opinion about as useful as that of a 42cm shell in a glass store."[126] "If he and such as he had guided the general policy of the war," Howard told writer, historian, and poet Hilaire Belloc after the war, "the result would have been indeed as the Russians said 'disastrous and incalculable.'"[127] Much more might be written about this—and about Esme Howard's displays of pique after each and every clash with his obstinate naval attaché. Suffice it to say here that other senior British diplomats who worked alongside Consett admired him and agreed with him; those who disliked him conceded he was usually proven right in his assessments.[128]

The level of detail contained in the Consett-Hall correspondence is impressive and important. At the end of April 1915, for instance, Consett asked Hall if he had yet seen the latest report from the commercial attaché in Sweden. (Hall had not.)

> From this you will see that goods of every sort, including copper, are pouring into Germany from the west coast of Sweden. This however, I believe, is nothing compared to what is going from the east coast ports, especially Oxelosund & Nykoping [serving the city of Stockholm].[129]

Hall wrote back to Consett thanking him for this intelligence and asking if he had "any idea what sort of traffic is being conducted between Sweden and

Russia." The DNI added he was particularly interested in learning if "the amount of goods sent to Russia [was] in excess of that sent to Germany."[130] In so doing, of course, Hall demonstrated that the naval war staff was well aware of the problems inside Sweden and was also looking—independently—at exactly the same issues as the Foreign Office. Consett replied, "It seems quite certain that a great deal of the goods that are supposed to be going to Russia are really going to Germany," and he added, "My own opinion is that a lot of nonsense is talked about this traffic to Russia." Such assessments, of course, were in direct contradiction to those submitted by the British diplomatic service, which insisted that the quantities of goods reaching Germany through Sweden were trifling and that the transit trade should be the defining factor in the framing of British policy toward Sweden. Consett was forced to admit, however, that he had little hard evidence to support this view because "we have absolutely no means of obtaining information concerning Swedish imports and exports." The best Consett could do was supply Blinker Hall with several more concrete examples of "goods that are supposed to be going to Russia [but] are really going to Germany."[131]

Another reason why the Foreign Office trod so softly around Sweden was the growing suspicion that Scandinavia had become the principal conduit for British firms illegally trading with the enemy.[132] By the late spring, firm evidence had emerged that the scale of this trade was larger than even the worst pessimist had feared, causing the Contraband Department of the Foreign Office to become increasingly uncomfortable with the hypocrisy of the British position.[133] An exasperated Eyre Crowe minuted on one such report, dated 19 May, "The whole policy of cutting off German supplies by means of the blockade established under the Order in Council of March 11 is being practically frustrated by the failure to prevent the export of certain important classes of goods, notably foodstuffs, from this country."[134] Cecil Hurst chimed that he had more than once raised the matter with the Board of Trade but found its staff always disinclined "to put an end to the present condition of things under which we are exporting large quantities of foodstuffs which go to Germany."[135] In a separate paper Hurst reported that the Foreign Office, Admiralty, and ESRC had "done their best to grapple with this subject" but the "obstacle that has to be overcome is the inertia of the Board of Trade, who are not yet satisfied that this further impediment in the way of British trade is necessary."[136] Although the Board of Customs and Excise had offered to assist by invoking its power to prohibit the export of food, this offer was made on condition that Grey provide the board with instructions to treat all Swedish consignees "as suspicious." The Foreign Office was unwilling to assume this responsibility, fearing that such a letter would too greatly offend neutral—and departmental—sensibilities.[137]

In mid-May 1915, realization within the political executive that the military assault at Gallipoli had failed in its objective caused a shock that reverberated throughout the British government. The political impact will be discussed in the next chapter. The most immediate diplomatic consequence was a realization that the Swedish blackmail would not be broken anytime soon; this caused Grey to sound a diplomatic retreat by directing the War Trade Department to resume the issuance of licenses for "Rubber, Tin, Nickel, Aluminum and Coal from this country to Sweden for the present."[138] As if to rub salt into the British wound, Sweden instantly resumed the reexport of British goods, including rubber, to Germany. "I suppose, under the circumstances, we cannot prevent this sort of thing," fumed one Foreign Office clerk, "as we are, I understand, dependent upon Sweden for certain highly important commodities connected with the manufacture of explosives, [and thus] not in a position to use any lever against them."[139] "If it were not for that," Crowe confirmed in a letter to Howard, "we should certainly not be putting up with their [Sweden's] gross impertinences from morning till night. All confidence in their goodwill is dead and gone."[140]

That said, Britain's alleged dependence on Sweden for war materials had not yet been established as fact. "I still feel far from convinced that the supply from Sweden is absolutely indispensable," Alwyn Parker, Crowe's deputy, remarked on 3 June.[141] The Foreign Office again pressed the Board of Trade for evidence to support its earlier assertion that this dependence was great, but was told in reply that the available statistics were so imperfect that quantification was presently impossible.[142] Here lay the crux of the matter. The lack of reliable statistical information meant that no one could say, even approximately, how dependent Britain truly was upon Sweden any more than it could be quantified how vital the Swedish land bridge was to Russia. "Until we are clear about the position," Crowe recorded, "it is practically impossible to determine the attitude which we ought to adopt towards the Swedish gov't generally."[143] In the meantime, accordingly, the Foreign Office (i.e., Grey) opted to remain on the safe path and assume that Britain's dependence upon Sweden was great. The inclination for caution was doubtless reinforced by the periodic peremptory Russian pleas not to add to their troubles by provoking Sweden to war.

The resumption of trade with Sweden incensed many within the government. On 15 June, Sir Francis Hopwood of the ESRC was moved to warn

Lord Crewe, the acting foreign secretary, "I have had difficulties with my committee. Its naval, military and parliamentary members seem to want to make her [Sweden] a belligerent."[144] Tempers were further inflamed after Members of Parliament pried figures from the Board of Trade showing that despite the supposed implementation of the retaliatory blockade, British re-exports of cotton to contiguous neutrals had soared.[145] The story was widely reported in the press. On 22 June, the government was forced to quell public outrage by introducing emergency legislation specifically to prohibit the re-exportation of this key commodity, used in the manufacture of explosives.

The next day, Lord Robert Cecil (the new undersecretary at the Foreign Office), aided by Cecil Hurst, met again with representatives of the parliamentary Unionist Business Committee, only to be told bluntly that although the new legislation was a step in the right direction, it was not nearly sufficient. Referring to Sweden, the delegation stated, "The time has passed for considering the feelings and wishes of the neutral contiguous counties and that they should be treated in a more summary manner in order to prevent them from sending things through to Germany."[146] Although the Foreign Office representatives "promised to enquire into the matter," internal departmental minutes show there was no intention to do so. Arthur Nicolson (permanent secretary to the Foreign Office) appended a note to the file explaining that it had been decided that the "policy advocated by the committee, if carried out, would embroil us with all neutral countries affected and would be, I imagine, of very serious disadvantage to our ally Russia."[147]

Instead, Grey sent Robert Vansittart, then serving in the Swedish section of the Contraband Department, to Stockholm to try to defuse tensions and broker a treaty more acceptable to both parties. "The primary concern of the mission," according to Vansittart's biographer, "though not explicitly stated, was to ensure Swedish neutrality."[148] Yet this evaluation is difficult to sustain. Upon his arrival Vansittart quickly assessed the situation as hopeless, because the Swedish delegation was packed with pro-German sympathizers disinclined to compromise. He requested that London revise his instructions to allow him to give ground and broker a makeshift agreement on the plea that it was better to reach some sort of settlement on minor issues than nothing at all.[149] Crowe seethed at his timidity. "It looks rather as if these proposals [from Sweden] were put forward in order to produce a rupture. We must certainly contemplate having to do without any agreement."[150] Alwyn Parker, his deputy, agreed the "radically vicious" terms could not possibly be accepted.[151] Vansittart was ordered to persevere.[152] But after the second British failure to seize the Gallipoli peninsula (in August 1915) irrevocably weakened his hand, Vansittart was permitted to break off negotiations and return home. Could the Foreign Office have adopted a stronger line? The Admiralty certainly thought so, and some in the Foreign Office were inclined to agree. But the majority thought the Russian situation too parlous to risk war with Sweden. The Russian army had been in retreat since May 1915, and six months later the eastern front had only just begun to stabilize. For most of the summer, moreover, Russian domestic politics had been in turmoil. What would have been the reaction in Petrograd if Britain had pushed Sweden to war?

Coal and the Board of Trade

Since the earliest days of the war, foreign access to British coal had been recognized as one of the most powerful bargaining levers in the British economic warfare armory. Shipowners especially prized the quality of Welsh coal above all others. The best "steam coal" could be transported halfway around the world and still find a market where locally mined coals were available at considerably less cost. Various European countries relied upon British coal to run their factories and railways. For trains operating on tracks built over steep gradients, such as in Italy or Scandinavia, quality British coal was essential for efficient running and in some cases for operation at all.

On the outbreak of war, coal had been declared a "war-like" store and its exportation subject to regulation. According to Harcourt, Winston Churchill had asked the cabinet to commandeer the entire output of the south Wales coal mines—only to be told he was mad![153] On 15 August 1914, the British government had presented Holland with an ultimatum inviting "the Dutch government to come to an agreement to prohibit the export eastwards of imported food-stuffs, we on our side allowing the export from Great Britain to Holland of the coal which she needs for her own industries."[154] The threat had worked and the agreement was obtained—after a fashion. But on 20 August, after some heavy lobbying by the coal industry and the Board of Trade, the cabinet voted to remove coal from the list of controlled exports, and this was done the very next day.

The export of coal remained unregulated until the early summer of 1915. During the interim, it is perplexing to note, the British authorities made no further attempt to coerce recalcitrant neutrals by wielding their coal supply weapon. In fact, exports to contiguous neutrals rose above prewar levels.[155]

The initiative for reregulating the exportation of coal originated, ironically, from the Board of Trade. On 23 March 1915, Runciman warned the cabinet he "thought it necessary to restrict the export of coal owing to shortage[s] for manufacturing purposes."[156] The past few months, as a result of so many miners enlisting, coal production had been in steep decline. Domestic supplies had become scarce and expensive.[157] The situation was further complicated by the threat of a national strike by coal miners, who were demanding a 20 percent pay rise "to meet the extra cost of living."[158] Coal, it should be remembered, was not only the chief source of energy for British industry and transportation but also the main source of heating in homes. This made it a "necessity of life" and thus its price of political interest.[159]

On 6 April 1915, the Board of Trade announced an enquiry into the coal supply problem, warning the industry to expect a measure of state control.[160] On 22 April, restrictions on exportation were announced.[161] "Restriction," it will be remembered, meant regulation, not prohibition. Exporters could supply their overseas customers provided they first obtained a special exemption license from the War Trade Department. But for coal, the Board of Trade insisted upon retaining full control and that adjudication must be done by its own special three-man "Coal Committee." The chairman was Russell Rea, a Liberal MP and colliery owner—as were both other members of the committee.[162] We know that the Coal Committee liaised with the War Trade Department, but their precise relationship was unclear.

Sir Edward Grey initially welcomed this innovation. He at once wrote to Runciman promising his full support, conditional only upon the Foreign Office being given a voice in decision making and the right to insist upon coal being supplied to certain countries "for political reasons."[163] On 27 April 1915, the newly appointed coal commissioners met briefly with Sir Eyre Crowe and his staff at the Foreign Office; after a general discussion on the perils and pitfalls of controlling exports, the coal commissioners asked the diplomats for a clear statement of what, specifically, they expected.[164] The latter proved incapable of providing an immediate answer to this straightforward question. In fact, the diplomats had nothing specific in mind other than an expectation that they would have the final say in determining which foreign countries would be given continued access to British coal and which would be cut off. The assumption, in effect, was that the Coal Committee would allow itself to be subordinated to the Foreign Office. The meeting closed with the Foreign Office promising shortly to furnish Russell Rea and his colleagues a written statement of its requirements.

Over the next several days Sir Eyre Crowe and his staff put considerable thought into the implications of restricting the supply of coal, what effects such a prohibition would have upon Britain's relations with certain countries, and the relations between those countries and Germany. Summarizing these discussions in an internal memorandum dated 28 April, Orme Sargent noted that while on its face the threat to withhold coal ought to be a powerful tool for coercion of recalcitrant neutrals, "the first thing to find out" was if these countries might be able to obtain their requirements from Germany. "If," he hypothesized, "it is found that Germany is in a position to export coal, I think we ought to be very careful about curtailing the supply to Scandinavia, Holland & Switzerland." Vansittart wholeheartedly concurred with the necessity for caution pending further study. Summing up, Crowe agreed that before a policy could be framed, "we must be very careful about driving Scandinavian countries in to reliance upon Germany for coal supply,"[165] because "if the Germans can supply it they will certainly stipulate that in return for coal they should receive copper or other prohibited articles."[166]

Instead of seeking expert counsel to help answer these technical questions, Crowe looked internally to the diplomatic staff assigned to the overseas embassies. Telegrams were sent out soliciting the opinions of senior diplomats posted in the countries most likely to be affected.[167] Judging from their replies, they simply asked their host governments for an approximation of how much British coal they wanted! It is hardly surprising that, with the exception of Stockholm, the ministers at each embassy or legation deplored the plan and insisted that depriving neutrals of British coal would serve only to strengthen Germany's diplomatic influence.[168] The opinions of the various ministers and ambassadors, incorporating recommended quantities of coal to be given to each neutral, formed the basis of a Foreign Office memorandum printed and forwarded to the Coal Committee. Before the Contraband Department had time to digest this information and formulate specific policy recommendations, however, it received a rude check.

When Robert Vansittart wrote to the secretary to the Coal Committee outlining his ideas on the best procedure for referring suspect cases to the Contraband Department for adjudication, the committee secretary, E. J. Elliot, a civil servant belonging to the Board of Trade, replied on 18 May that the Foreign Office was operating under a serious misapprehension. The Coal Committee was answerable to the Board of Trade, not the Foreign Office; furthermore, "I am afraid that in view of the absolute necessity of quick dispatch in dealing with applications for licenses to export coal and coke, it is out of the question to refer doubtful or suspect cases to the Foreign Office."[169] Judging from the minutes attached to the file and especially the acerbic remarks directed toward the competence and fidelity of the Coal Committee, there is no question that the diplomats took umbrage at being effectively told to mind their own business. They resolved to send a letter to the Board of Trade requesting Elliot be instructed to be more cooperative. Evidentially anticipating swift compliance, the Foreign Office proceeded to send across its thoughts on the rules that should govern the export of coal to countries adjacent to Germany.[170]

Three days later, on 21 May, the Coal Committee formally replied to the Contraband Department memorandum. The implacable Elliot told Crowe's staff their memorandum totally missed the point and provided his committee with "little assistance in performing the duty laid upon them of restricting the total exports in the interests of our own country and its most necessary industries."[171] He expanded:

> This Committee's investigations have already convinced them that the position in regard to the Coal supply at home is a very serious one, and exports must be reduced to a considerable extent, and this general overriding necessity, they think, has been scarcely realized by the writer of the Foreign Office Memorandum. For example, when it is suggested that licenses should be granted for shipments to Denmark to the extent of 267,000 tons per month, they would point out that this would be a greater export than that of either of the last two years.[172]

Elliot's sharp letter went on to point out other weaknesses in the Foreign Office assessment, the factors its staff had failed to take into account, and the experts it had not consulted, in so doing making clear to any impartial reader that the Coal Committee knew what it was about and furthermore, in this instance, the Contraband Department clearly did not. Afterward, only Vansittart was prepared to admit that perhaps the diplomats had been too hasty and should have studied the matter more closely before advancing their opinions.[173]

Blithely ignoring the clear signals that the Coal Committee fully intended to retain the whip hand in the formulation of policy, the Contraband Department pressed on regardless. A week later, the Foreign Office decreed an embargo on all coal to Sweden except for cargoes consigned for use by the Swedish state railways.[174] In addition, instructions were issued that no coal should be supplied to neutral colliers destined for ports inside the Baltic—effectively compelling colliers to discharge their cargoes at Goteborg on Sweden's Kattegat coast. The thinking behind this edict was to prevent Germany from seizing British colliers entering the Baltic.

The Coal Committee reacted to these "rather startling" decrees by reminding the Foreign Office, on 1 June, that Britain depended upon Sweden for timber and iron ore (parroting the Board of Trade) and politely suggesting again that the diplomats might like to give the subject more careful consideration.[175] In the meantime, it would continue to issue licenses for the export of coal as normal.[176] What could the Foreign Office in the face of such intransigence? Lacking the authority to intrude in the affairs of another department—no one disputed that the Coal Committee indeed fell within the orbit of the Board of Trade—there was nothing that could be done except put on a brave face.[177]

The Foreign Office climb down was admitted in a letter sent to the Admiralty dated 16 June. It stated, essentially, that the qualified embargo on coal to Sweden would remain in force, but all other restrictions would be cancelled. How real this embargo was in practice is open to considerable doubt, however. Captain Consett was able to demonstrate that large quantities of British coal continued to reach private Swedish companies.[178] Howard continued to moan that the Coal Commission was giving the coal to the "wrong" firms.[179]

The episode described above was unquestionably a serious bureaucratic defeat for the Foreign Office. But it was also much more than this. Since the introduction of the blockade system, Grey had striven to make his department the hub of the blockade machinery and assume responsibility for all key policy decisions. The altercation between the Board of Trade's Coal Committee and Foreign Office's Contraband Department demonstrated that the latter was not (yet) all-powerful in blockade matters. It shows there was in practice not one but at least two administrative hubs. As we shall see in later chapters, the Board of Trade's unwillingness to bend to Foreign Office demands was not limited to the exportation of coal. In short, the Foreign Office possessed the dominant voice in framing policy affecting the interception of foreign cargoes presumed intended for Germany, but the Board of Trade (and its satellite committees) maintained control over goods of British origin. The disconnect between the Foreign Office, the Board of Trade, and the Admiralty, proved a major handicap to the effective maintenance of the blockade against Germany.

We cannot leave the subject of coal for Sweden without mentioning the campaign waged during the summer of 1915 by Captain Montagu Consett, the naval attaché for Scandinavia, for a total ban. In a series of reports he argued that Britain's power to withhold coal for Sweden represented a decisive weapon, that Swedish aggressiveness over trade policy was a bluff, and accordingly that Britain could impose far tighter restrictions on Sweden without any real risk of war. In June 1915, Consett backed his claims with an impressively detailed report demonstrating that without access to British coal the Scandinavian economies would collapse.[180] "Not one of these countries can exist without our coal," he declared, and Sweden was the most vulnerable of all. In July, Consett reiterated: "Any hopes of these countries being able to obtain any large amount of coal from Germany was out of the question, and that the amounts actually received were so small when compared with the total requirements [5 million tons per year] that they were for all practical purposes a negligible quantity."[181] Consett maintained that Sweden's only conceivable option would be to obtain coal from the United States, but he calculated that distance and price (not to mention the problem of finding the estimated eighty large colliers needed to ferry it across the Atlantic) made this an impracticable proposition. Its controversial recommendations aside, Consett's report, which was the product of considerable research into both German production and the shipping constraints attached to its export, was the most comprehensive survey on the subject available to the British government. A third report submitted a fortnight later supplied further evidence that Germany could not possibly meet Sweden's requirements.[182]

Consett's reports brought him into collision with Esme Howard, the head of the Stockholm mission. He and other senior diplomatic staff airily rejected Consett's conclusions, though it is striking that none produced any contradictory evidence. "Everything possible has been done by Legation in order to bring discredit on my report and nothing whatever to support and prove my assertions," Consett fumed in a private letter to Blinker Hall.[183] Doubtless he would have been surprised to learn that the junior clerks in the Contraband Department who had seen his report saw its value and had been so impressed that they wished it to be forwarded to the obdurate Coal Committee to demonstrate just how important it was to restrict exports.[184] Hardly surprisingly, their seniors disapproved.[185] Crowe duly minuted on the file that the overriding concern was now "to keep Sweden out of war."[186] Given that several senior members of the Russian government had explicitly restated this to be their view as well, there was never any real chance that the Foreign Office was going to make the effort to fight the Board of Trade over the issue of coal for Sweden. As Sir Edward Grey told the cabinet, "We owe it to Russia, especially in view of the urgent representations made to us by the Russian Govt., to make to Sweden the maximum concessions compatible with our attainment of the supreme objects of the war."[187]

For reasons we can only guess at, Consett received no high-level support from the Admiralty in waging his campaign against Foreign Office diffidence. By this time, June 1915, Churchill and Fisher were no longer in charge, having been replaced respectively by Arthur Balfour as First Lord and Admiral Sir Henry Jackson as First Sea Lord. Astonishingly, the new naval leadership professed that economic warfare policy was no longer its responsibility and therefore declined to challenge the Foreign Office (and the Board of Trade) over the issue.[188] Officers lower down in the organization, it may be noted, saw differently. Hall assured Consett that "I am doing my best to press the coal question but the faint hearts at the shop over the way [a reference to the Contraband Department] appear to think that Stettin [a German port in the Baltic] is in a position to supply as much coal as Sweden requires, and there is the usual havering going on."[189] Captain Webb felt equally strongly that the coal question "is being scandalously handled."[190] In June 1915 he vainly submitted a note to the First Lord protesting, "Sweden is the principal offender, and the chief source of supply for Germany at present, and goods are flowing through her ports in enormous quantities."[191]

Lest it be assumed otherwise, Admiralty officials were fully alive to all the complexities of the situation. Webb fully understood that "cutting off German supplies through Sweden and Holland involves diplomatic and economic difficulties which cannot be surmounted so easily," because "to starve Germany in the larger sense of the word, would mean starving Sweden and Holland too."[192] He appreciated that for Britain to take a stronger line against Sweden meant risking the transit trade to Russia, the loss of "certain key commodities," and possibly even Sweden joining the war against Russia. Nevertheless, Webb felt that the Foreign Office was not doing enough, and "these difficulties should not be summarily dismissed as insurmountable."[193] The point here is that mid-level naval officers such as Webb and Hall, who favored more rigorous enforcement of the blockade, were not myopic or unaware of the various diplomatic and political aspects of the situation. The reason naval officers so frequently arrived at a different answer to any particular equation was not that they had overlooked some particular variables so much as that they attached different weights to each. Whether naval officers were entitled or properly qualified to make such judgments is another question.

Yet although the Admiralty refused to back Consett against the Foreign Office, they did nothing to silence him. It might be noted that the Admiralty Trade Division had already conducted its own studies into the potential of the coal coercion weapon and, moreover, had come up with another plan to wield it far more effectively (and with less risk of confrontation) than the two variations on embargo tactics proposed by the Foreign Office and Consett. Several weeks earlier, the Admiralty had suggested that the supply of British coal to neutrals could most easily be manipulated by regulating the movements of colliers, which the Admiralty already routinely tracked, and by controlling merchant ship access to British-owned bunkering (fueling) facilities across the globe. Merchants who failed to comply would be blacklisted—that is, denied access to these facilities.[194] Readers will appreciate that this transparently amounted to a reversion to prewar Admiralty methods of waging economic war by exercising control through regulation of the transport system. To his credit, Crowe immediately recognized the merit of this approach, though he correctly foresaw that the Board of Trade would object on various grounds.[195]

Sure enough, the Coal Committee duly submitted a variety of excuses why this should not be done, claiming, for example, that neutral shippers would refuse to carry Swedish goods to Britain unless given a return freight of British coal.[196] The Admiralty nevertheless went ahead and implemented the plan on its own authority, and by mid-June the "new unofficial scheme" (as Robert Vansittart dubbed it) was in place: owners of neutral ships wishing access to British bunker fuel were required to sign a guarantee that they would not trade with Germany, upon penalty of blacklisting. Not until October 1915 was a more comprehensive scheme put in place—albeit with certain foreign shipping lines being granted exemptions for various diplomatic or commercial reasons.[197]

10

The Summer of Discontent

It has been considered advisable up to the present to say as little as possible of the measures by which the Retaliatory Policy has been carried into effect. This prudent reticence coupled with the alarming figures of the imports of certain commodities by contiguous neutrals has undoubtedly given rise to very widespread uneasiness and sporadic expressions of jealousy.

OWEN ST. CLAIR O'MALLEY, Contraband Department, June 1915

Shortly after the outbreak of war, Andrew Bonar Law, leader of the opposition Conservative-Unionist party, had offered the Liberals a parliamentary truce for the remainder of the calendar year. Asquith had accepted with alacrity. This did not mean—as is sometimes supposed—that the government would not be subjected to parliamentary criticism; it was merely an agreement not to contest by-elections for the anticipated duration of the war. Yet, consciously or not, the truce does seem to have inhibited Bonar Law and his front bench team from pressing the government harder to disclose more details about national strategy instead of passively accepting from Asquith those crumbs of information he was willing to drop.[1] Doubtless too there existed a certain patriotic reticence to attack the government in time of war. But whatever the reason, until Christmas 1914 parliamentary criticism of government action was noticeably muted; from this Asquith unquestionably benefited in that it alleviated pressure upon him to resolve the major contradictions in national strategy, especially in connection with the blockade.

By the New Year, however, the prolongation of the war combined with the lackluster performance of Britain's armed forces strained Conservative forbearance.[2] Though the Conservative leadership agreed to extend the truce, there were audiable rumblings of discontent from the backbenches. In January 1915, twenty-five Conservative Members of Parliament broke from the ranks to form the Unionist Business Committee.[3] Over the next couple of months, this small but steadily growing band of backbenchers posed increasingly difficult questions of the government. W. A. S. Hewins, for instance, former director of the London School of Economics, questioned why the government was not adopting a more vigorous approach toward industrial mobilization. Ernest Pollock, meanwhile, the Unionist Business Committee's vice president, began probing inconsistencies in blockade policy and in so doing uncovered some disturbing facts.

Pollock correctly deduced that the contiguous neutrals were selling most of their homegrown food supplies and raw materials to Germany (at enormous profit), then turning around and replenishing stocks for domestic requirements from overseas. Rather than make an exposé, Pollock wrote to the foreign secretary asking for confirmation of his findings—and an explanation. Much to Sir Eyre Crowe's dismay, Sir Edward Grey felt compelled to meet with Pollock and his colleagues from the Unionist Business Committee.[4] He unhappily confirmed the truth of the allegations and explained he had allowed the practice so as not to alienate neutral opinion.[5]

Recognizing the mounting damage to his ministry's prestige, Prime Minister Asquith became increasingly anxious to find "a clear definite victory somewhere." Doubts this might be accomplished in northern France within reasonable cost or time frame spurred the executive War Council to look about for an alternative theater of operations. At the end of January 1915, the political members of the War Council settled upon Winston Churchill's stratagem for a quick and easy victory—by attacking the Dardanelles with the objective of knocking Turkey out of the war. Though it quickly became clear that Churchill's initial calculations had been absurdly optimistic and, to a considerable extent, he had misled his colleagues over the degree of support the plan enjoyed among professional naval officers, the ministers elected to redouble their bet instead of canceling the operation. Between March and April, they funneled all available military resources to the eastern Mediterranean in hopes that the meager army thus scraped together would prove sufficient to overcome Turkish resistance on the Gallipoli peninsula and thereby open the straits to a naval advance into the Sea of Marmora.[6] The politicians felt that the potential gains of a success still far outweighed the possible losses resulting from a defeat.[7]

Concurrently, Asquith rebuffed increasingly frantic attempts by Admiral Lord Fisher to have Churchill's Dardanelles operation reappraised.[8] On 6 April, Asquith, Churchill, and Kitchener (who had muzzled certain Army officers who shared the First Sea Lord's concerns) met and agreed the amphibious attack must go ahead. "None of them appeared to me in the least to realize the extreme difficulties of the operation," thought Hankey, who was present at the meeting to take notes. "[General Sir Ian] Hamilton's plan seems to me fraught with the possibility of appalling military disaster, if the Turks can fight at all."[9]

So it came to pass. On 25 April 1915, the Allied army at the Dardanelles attacked. Although the assault force achieved a bridgehead, strategic control and tactical creativity were woefully lacking, leading to far higher casualties than expected. As a result, insufficient reserves were on hand to exploit the local superiority purchased and advance inland. As Hankey had feared, instead of collapsing, the Osmanli army exhibited a fierce determination to fight. Within a fortnight all hope for a rapid and cheap victory had evaporated. By the beginning of May 1915, news of the failure had become public.

Politically, the failure to storm the Dardanelles was a catastrophe for the already weakened Asquith government. It extinguished lingering optimism about a quick end to the war, undermined resistance to increasingly shrill French demands for more British troops on the western front, and, most especially, intensified pressures upon the government to mobilize the economy. As explained, Asquith and his ministers were not blind to military and productive advantages that would accrue from centralized organization of industrial and manpower resources. In mid-March, the government had introduced legislation granting itself the enormous requisite powers to impose control over industry, but since then the impetus had been lost, owing mainly to the high political price tags attached to several measures that could not be skirted.[10] Within the government there existed serious differences in opinion over the best direction forward.

David Lloyd George, believing the War Office had demonstrated itself incompetent to manage its munitions requirements, had for several months been pressing for the creation of a new state-run organization to take charge of all industrial plant and military production. In deference to Lord Kitchener, however, the prime minister had refused to separate the military procurement arm from the main body of the War Office. Instead, he placed another coordination committee atop the existing coordination machinery; the upshot, as one leading scholar has put it, was to pile "confusion upon confusion."[11] Lloyd George grew increasingly outspoken. On Friday, 16 April, after a bitterly contested cabinet meeting, Kitchener "declared that he could no longer be responsible for the War Office under such conditions" and tendered his resignation.[12] After a weekend of cajoling, the prime minister persuaded Kitchener to resume his duties, and the status quo was temporarily reestablished.

Then on Tuesday, 4 May 1915, in a budget speech delivered to the House of Commons, Lloyd George obliquely attacked Kitchener's administrative competence. The chancellor spoke of deficiencies in munitions production and the growing shortage of labor, linking these twin problems to the War Office policy of uncontrolled military recruitment. The time had come, he suggested, for the government to exercise "discrimination" in accepting volunteers for the Army "so that that recruiting should interfere as little as possible with the output of those commodities which we export abroad, and which enable us to purchase munitions for ourselves and our allies."[13]

Perhaps coincidentally, perhaps not, Lloyd George's attack coincided with the opening of a fearsome press barrage against the government's slowness in mobilizing the economy. Lord Northcliffe, owner of the *Times* and the popular *Daily Mail,* charged the Asquith administration with gross mismanagement of the war effort.[14] On 6 May, the *Times* ran an editorial calling upon the Liberals to abandon their laissez-faire "voluntary" approach to the prosecution of the war and devise a comprehensive scheme of "national organization" to boost munitions production.[15] The term "national organization" was a euphemism for the "compulsion" of labor—that is, a demand that the state take responsibility for the allocation of industrial manpower. At the extreme, proponents envisaged the creation of "industrial battalions" with workers under virtually military discipline.[16] Asquith's lack of energy in this direction did not signify he was oblivious to the problem or the ideal solution. Rather, he and his senior ministers feared, quite genuinely, that state compulsion of labor risked unleashing a maelstrom of political, social, and economic unrest.[17]

On 17 May 1915, to the surprise of political commentators, the dismay of his party, and the general bewilderment of his ministerial colleagues, Asquith announced the formation of a coalition government. He took this decision apparently without consulting even his oldest political friends, Haldane and Grey.[18] The news was broken to ministers in a circular letter peremptorily instructing them to resign their portfolios.[19] Asquith told them:

> I have for some time past come, with increasing conviction, to the conclusion that the continued prosecution of the War requires what is called

> a "broad-based" Government. Under existing conditions, criticism, inspired by party motives and interests, has full reign, and is an asset of much value to the enemy.
>
> The resignation of Lord Fisher, which I have done my best to avert, and the more than plausible Parliamentary case in regard to the alleged deficiency of high-explosive shells, would, if duly exploited (as they would have been) in the House of Commons at this moment, have had the most disastrous effect on the general political and strategic situation.[20]

The events outlined in this statement are generally known. Three days earlier, on 14 May, the Northcliffe press had created a political uproar by publishing an article attributing the failure of the Army's recent offensive in France to a shortage of artillery shells. Although targeted at Lord Kitchener, the brunt of the subsequent criticism had fallen upon the prime minister after an enterprising journalist seized upon the contradiction between the Army's complaints and a speech Asquith had delivered in Newcastle several weeks earlier, in which he had assured his audience "there is not a word of truth" in stories that the Army was short of ammunition.[21] Shortly thereafter, rumors had begun to circulate that Admiral of the Fleet Lord Fisher had resigned the post of First Sea Lord over irreconcilable differences with Winston Churchill.

After learning of Fisher's resignation—and the admiral made sure he knew—Andrew Bonar Law spurned the opportunity to seize the reins of government. He instead approached Lloyd George and warned him he could not prevent Fisher's many parliamentary friends from creating a row. The implied threat was clear. Lloyd George at once took Bonar Law to meet with the prime minister. After a brief talk the two party leaders agreed it would be in the national interest to form a coalition government. In agreeing so readily to the formation of a coalition government, historians are not in complete agreement as to Asquith's precise motives.[22] However, there is general consensus that Asquith seized upon the excuses offered by Fisher's resignation and the coinciding shell crisis to disregard party opinion and enter into a coalition government.

While the causes and significance of the so-called shell crisis have been exhaustively discussed by military historians, Fisher's resignation has been less well understood, as have the implications for naval policy.[23] Because he quit the Admiralty before his successor was appointed, promoting accusations that he deserted his post in time of war, and because this was not the first time he had threatened resignation, historians have tended to pillory the admiral.[24] It is generally held—mistakenly, however—that Fisher's resignation was attributable to some combination of madness, mental fatigue, and megalomania. Tired and aged he certainly was; increasingly impatient and prone to intolerance also. There is no doubt the septuagenarian admiral was not the force he once had been, as six months spent administering the Admiralty in time of war while struggling to cope with Churchill had taken its toll. But to a lesser or greater degree this was true of many other members of the government.[25] Contemporary witnesses who actually met with Fisher on these critical days reported him relaxed and rational. Even Asquith told his daughter Violet that when delivering his ultimatum, "Fisher had been very friendly and mellow but complained that he found W[inston] impossible to work with."[26] Only in accounts written after the event were claims made to the contrary.[27] Jacky's private and official correspondence shows that if his stamina was failing, his mind remained sound and his phenomenal administrative talents unimpaired.

To portray Fisher's resignation as an act of petulance is equally insupportable.[28] The evidence would suggest, rather, that his action was a calculated and premeditated political ploy that misfired.[29] "I don't mean to explode my bomb without dead certainty it will act," he confided in Hankey just three days before it detonated.[30] Like Asquith and most other principal players on the strategic stage in mid-May 1915, Fisher aimed to exploit the prevailing atmosphere of political crisis—to oust Churchill and thereby wrest full control over Admiralty policy. It was "a trial of strength," as one Admiralty official termed it. On Saturday, 15 May, Fisher intercepted the prime minister as he was climbing into his car outside 10 Downing Street and declared he was unable to remain Churchill's colleague.[31] With the shell scandal just breaking, the admiral likely believed Asquith could not possibly refuse this implicit ultimatum at such a time.[32] Indeed, Asquith told Lloyd George he did not take Fisher's threat as seriously meant.[33] Two days later McKenna confirmed to Charlie Hobhouse that the admiral had not resigned as such, merely informed the prime minister "he could not continue at the Admiralty if WSC remained as First Lord."[34]

Although a proper account of the Fisher-Churchill "trial of strength" is long overdue, space prevents us from reviewing here all the myriad components of the saga.[35] For our immediate purposes it is sufficient to state (perhaps a little tendentiously) that Fisher underestimated the strength of Asquith's almost filial affection for Churchill and failed to anticipate that Andrew Bonar Law might spurn the proffered opportunity to oust the Liberal government and instead seek coalition.[36] Additionally, there is no question that after placing his high card on the table, Fisher played the rest of his hand poorly.[37] Partially because of bad advice, perhaps also because of tiredness, but mostly through misreading of the political undercurrents, on 19 May Fisher sent Asquith "a quite indefensible letter" stating his conditions for remaining. This caused the prime minister to discard his plans to retain Fisher in tandem with Balfour as First Lord and exclaim to friends that the admiral "had become a raving maniac who ought not to be at large."[38] So outrageous were the terms in the letter that even Fisher's closest friends found themselves, after being shown the document, unable to support him any longer.[39] The admiral afterward acknowledged his mistake, apologized, and resigned himself to a period of exile.[40] Three weeks later Asquith no longer thought Fisher "insane."[41]

In agreeing to a coalition government, Asquith stipulated that the Liberals must control the majority of the key offices of state, and inexplicably Bonar Law agreed.[42] The new Asquith coalition, formed on 26 May, left Grey entrenched at the Foreign Office and Runciman in control at the Board of Trade. Lloyd George shifted to the newly formed Ministry of Munitions, and McKenna took his place as chancellor; Sir John Simon became home secretary. Winston Churchill was retained as a member of the cabinet with the sinecure of chancellor of the Duchy of Lancaster. Lord Kitchener remained at the War Office. Except for the Admiralty, given to Balfour, the Conservatives received none of the key departments involved in the prosecution of the war. As Lord Crewe smugly remarked to Lloyd George, the distribution of offices "place[d] only one Unionist Minister in the inner circle [Balfour], and him not one of their inner circle as it now exists."[43] Asquith's success in persuading his former political enemies to accept relatively unimportant portfolios was aided by the hesitation several felt in stepping into the limelight. Until the last minute Lansdowne and Long shrank from joining the cabinet, though ultimately, along with Lord Curzon, they accepted honorific portfolios.[44] Bonar Law was given the Colonial Office and Austen Chamberlain the India Office, positions with "no real authority" in war policy.[45] Selborne took the Board of Agriculture and Sir Edward Carson became attorney general.

What has all this political chicanery got to do with British blockade policy? Quite simply it provides vital context for understanding subsequent events. One of the main arguments advanced in the present work is that to a degree far greater than previously thought, the cabinet retained control over the direction of British strategy. If so, then it follows that the advent of the coalition must have changed the dynamics of policy formulation. Although Asquith retained the premiership, at the most basic level he was no longer supreme in the cabinet because he always needed to consider the reaction of Bonar Law and the other Unionists.[46] It must be remembered, furthermore, that before the war the Liberals and Conservative leaders had been poles apart on a range of political issues: free trade versus tariff reform, home rule versus direct rule for Ireland, taxation policy, and constitutional reform, to name but a few. War or no war, such bitter ideological differences could not be forgotten overnight.[47] Both sides recognized that many of the policy decisions they took, ostensibly for military or strategic reasons, likely would produce serious, enduring domestic political consequences.[48] Both sides, therefore, looked for opportunities to further their prewar domestic agendas. In other words, political policy motives were conditioned by internal political considerations, which in turn were to some degree determined by the level of prewar agreement or disagreement within governing circles over various issues.

Following back-to-back meetings on 26 and 27 May 1915, the new coalition cabinet signaled its intent to conduct a thorough reassessment of national strategy, instructing the War Office, Admiralty, and Board of Trade to furnish memoranda detailing past, present, and future policy.[49] The inclusion of the Board of Trade is intriguing and possibly indicative of the direction in which some Conservatives had been pressing. Yet in a remarkable display of political dexterity, on 27 May Asquith obtained agreement that there could be no discussion of military or industrial compulsion before the government had completed a census of the workforce, a bureaucratic path that was certain to be lengthy, meandering, and filled with administrative pitfalls.[50] Lord Selborne accordingly withdrew his memorandum titled "Note on National Organisation" and calling for all men from the age of 17 upward to be subject to military law.[51] As doubtless Asquith had hoped, within a fortnight the ministers found themselves mired in detail well short of the point where discussions could begin.[52] It took a month for the cabinet to agree whether the national register should include female as well as male workers. And nearly three months passed before the survey was begun.

During the cabinet discussions of strategy over the next several weeks, there was no lack of ministerial imagination or initiative. On the contrary: the principal players had very clear ideas on how to win the war. Indeed, that was the problem. So intent were some ministers on securing endorsement (and the necessary resources) for their favored projects to win quick victory, they eschewed debate of long-term considerations. The most intractable were those who believed that the capture of the Dardanelles remained the foremost strategic objective. This faction included Arthur Balfour (Admiralty), Kitchener (War Office), Churchill, and Lord Crewe. The Conservative minister Lord Selborne was another "member of what he might call the 'utmost vigor party' as regards the Dardanelles."[53] In seeking to recruit Lord Curzon to the cause, Balfour insisted, "That the policy of retirement is impossible must be manifest to the meanest intelligence."[54] Together with Asquith, Bonar Law, and Lord Lansdowne, these nine constituted the Dardanelles Committee, the new name given to Asquith's old council of war.[55]

This group's desperation to obtain the requisite full cabinet sanction before dispatching military reinforcements to the Dardanelles caused discussion of other cabinet business to be either truncated (as on 4 June) or postponed entirely (as on 8 June).[56] On 9 June Churchill told his brother he and his colleagues were determined "to carry the Dardanelles through 'coûte que coûte'" (whatever the cost).[57] On 18 June, Asquith reported "a rather turbulent discussion over the Dardanelles" in the cabinet and noted that Sir Edward "Carson, Winston & Ll[oyd] George very nearly came to blows" over sending as many as six divisions of reinforcements.[58] The last-named opined that the government was "marching straight to disaster."[59] Yet at the same time, Lloyd George was behaving in an equally single-minded manner, demanding an independent ministry with full authority over War Office purchases. He reportedly "dominated" discussion at the cabinet meetings on 14, 16, and 18 June.[60]

During these first few weeks, the new cabinet devoted remarkably little attention to considering the blockade or the economy. As we have seen, by this stage of the war the political executive understood that these two issues had become so intertwined that neither could be discussed meaningfully without consideration of the other. This is not to say that no one believed that the economic aspects of grand strategy to be of relatively insufficient importance. In fact, a large number of cabinet memoranda were generated, as well as voluminous inter- and intradepartmental correspondence. But the fact remains that within the cabinet there was no serious discussion of these thorniest of issues. Indeed, it was avoided.

Complying with cabinet instructions to prepare a statement detailing past, present, and future policy, Walter Runciman, still president of the Board of Trade, distributed three memoranda intended for review at the meeting on

4 June. The first was entitled "Statistical Note on the Limits of Enlistment." As the title implies, essentially this was an updated version of Llewellyn Smith's paper circulated the previous January drawing attention to the detrimental economic effects of unfettered Army recruitment. In this updated version, Llewellyn Smith reviewed the latest statistical data basically showing that the War Office had reneged on all of its promises. Large numbers of skilled workers from vital industries continued to be enlisted into the Army in defiance of assurances given four months earlier. In the interval, the Army had recruited some 624,000 men; of these, no fewer than 92,000 had been "category A" workers.[61] The latter figure represented about 10 percent of the prewar skilled workforce in industries identified as vital to the war effort. Llewellyn Smith stopped short of claiming that continued War Office recruitment would wreck the economy, but he advised that "while it might not seriously cripple industry, [it] would greatly hamper it."[62]

In the second paper, "Effect of Diminished Exports on Foreign Exchanges," Runciman explained "the effect of withdrawing workmen from industries conducted mainly for export" and "what may be the effect of diminished exports on foreign exchanges."[63] Here the Board of Trade essentially argued there was a direct correlation between the level of British exports and the availability of labor; simply put, more soldiers meant fewer workers and therefore lower export revenues. Runciman drew attention to the widening gap in the British balance of trade, which since the beginning of the war had increased from an annualized deficit of £15 million to nearly £170 million.[64] At the same time, Britain had promised aid to the other Allies totaling £200 million per annum.[65] Very simply, Great Britain was running a massive external deficit, the financing of which was an open question. Yet Runciman, soon aided by McKenna, experienced the greatest difficulty in getting ministers to understand that the richest country in the world faced monetary constraints.

In the third memorandum, "Food Supplies of Germany," which previous historians have mistakenly attributed to the Foreign Office, the Board of Trade made an oblique attack on the continuation of the blockade.[66] This paper challenged claims that "Germany is about to be faced with a real shortage of food."[67] It argued, in fact, that the opposite was true. Citing data gleaned from the German press, the Board of Trade questioned whether Germany was experiencing any real shortage of food at all. Although prices had risen in Berlin on average by 56.5 percent, Runciman contended this could not automatically be taken as indicative of shortages. Normal market conditions did not apply because the German state was expropriating supplies and fixing prices. The memorandum concluded that there was little evidence of actual hardship inside Germany. In the accompanying covering note, Runciman bluntly stated, "There is no evidence that Germany has, in fact, ever been in sight of anything like a grave shortage, and there are some indications that the situation is now improving."[68] In short, the blockade was ineffective. Here he offered no comment, confident the facts he had presented would be sufficient for others to draw their own conclusions.

Asquith's letter to the king dated 4 June makes no mention of any cabinet discussion that day (or on any subsequent day) of the three Runciman memoranda.[69] Yet it is curious that on 5 June, Colonel Hankey wrote to the prime minister about "the recent debate" over the Board of Trade papers.[70] Hankey reported that he had already canvassed ministers on the subject (presumably overnight) and had found the majority "expressing the hope that there would be no relaxation of our efforts to put economic pressure on Germany."[71] This letter indicates that, in fact, some high-level discussion of the three Runciman papers had taken place, either inside or outside the cabinet. Possibly the prime minister had prevented official debate of their content because so many key ministers—Lloyd George, McKenna, Grey, and Carson—had been absent from the meeting that day.[72]

The speed with which Hankey reacted to the Board of Trade memoranda was important, and due largely to his having been forewarned of the attempt to undermine support for the continuation of the blockade. Several days earlier, while the coalition government was still being formed, Hankey wrote Captain Richard Webb at the Admiralty trade division asking if he had heard stories that certain ministers were discussing the idea of "giving up blockade in return for Germany agreeing to a cession of her submarine campaign."[73] Alas, Hankey's letter failed to elucidate, identify suspects, or, most important, suggest who appeared to be listening.

Webb's reply was unhelpful. He said only that he thought the news terrible, asserting that whereas the British food blockade was seriously hurting Germany, the U-boat campaign represented no more than an inconvenience to Great Britain.[74] When, however, Hankey wrote back on 28 May asking what evidence Webb could supply to support this assessment, the latter was compelled to admit, "I cannot give you any direct help in the matter of special information in this Dept. as regards the present and future states of food supplies in Germany."[75] "As a matter of fact," he added, "I several times raised the question in the restriction committee [ESRC] of getting some statistics on the subject, but was always given to understand that it was hopeless and [Sir Francis] Oppenheimer corroborated that."[76] The paucity of tangible evidence supporting Webb's assertion was evident in his summation. "To my mind, the best proof of the effect which our policy is having, lies in the efforts Germany is making to induce us to relax our attitude," he wrote to Hankey.

> This, you will say, doesn't answer your question of what evidence have we of shortage in Germany (now or in the future). I submit it is FOLLY to wait for proof. If proof does come it may, and probably will, be then too late. . . . EVERYTHING must be stopped. This is a war of extermination not one of platitudes about business as usual. The best way of protecting our trade is by beating the enemy. If we don't do that then there won't be any trade to protect.[77]

Militarily, Captain Webb was undoubtedly correct, but such arguments were never going to appeal to the political leadership.

Abandonment of Blockade

In the last chapter, we saw how Sir Edward Grey unsuccessfully tried in March 1915 to persuade his cabinet colleagues to moderate the terms of the retaliatory blockade. His failure induced the Foreign Office to take unilateral and covert action calculated to dilute its severity. In his memoirs, Grey defended himself against charges that he had undermined the blockade by claiming he recognized that retaining American friendship was paramount to ultimate victory because of the Entente's muntions dependency. Grey's policy was "to secure the maximum of blockade that could be enforced without a rupture with the United States."[78]

Yet the Foreign Office archives for this period contain no reference either to recognition of an Entente munitions dependence upon the United States or concern of an impending breach in Anglo-American diplomatic relations. On the contrary: minutes written by Sir Eyre Crowe and other senior officials in the Contraband Department of the Foreign Office generally exuded optimism, not pessimism. All had been pleasantly surprised at the mildness of the American response to the publication of the order-in-council outlining the retaliatory blockade. The State Department note of 30 March 1915, communicated to the Foreign Office on 2 April, contained no threats, implicit or explicit; it was framed in legalistic terms and had merely protested "for the record" that British actions lacked justification in international law.[79]

Just one diplomat forcast an imminent chill in Anglo-American relations: that was the overexcitable Sir Cecil Spring Rice, the British ambassador in Washington. Since the beginning of the war, it will be recalled, Spring Rice had been feeding Grey a steady stream of reports warning that Woodrow Wilson's sympathy for the Entente hung by a thread and reminding him that the president remained a hostage to domestic political considerations.[80] The ambassador was constantly urging London to buttress Wilson's support by making concessions over the blockade. By early 1915, however, most officials in London had come to discount the ambassador's views as overly pessimistic.[81] "Sir C. Spring Rice has invariably shown himself more alarmed that subsequent events justified," Eyre Crowe observed in March.[82] Crowe adhered to this opinion throughout 1915.[83] Lord Eustace Percy, who had served under Spring Rice at the Washington embassy before being posted back to London, shared this assessment.

> Throughout the war, as before it, we have been nervous about the US to the point of periodically considering revision of our attitude. I believe that this nervousness is quite unjustified. We have to face unpleasantness in the US, but they are wholly calculable and are none the more serious because they are shouted at us through a megaphone in our own language. We are fighting for our existence and one of the stakes we have to play is the friendship of the US. I am prepared to back that stake to the end, subject only to that respect for vital interests which one has to show in dealing with every nation.[84]

In Washington, President Wilson adopted a sensibly pragmatic stance to the publication of the British retaliatory blockade.[85] There is little evidence to support the view that he resisted calls from some of his advisors for a firmer response out of sympathy for the Allied cause.[86] In gauging the president's initial reaction, it must be remembered that the retaliatory order-in-council had merely announced Britain's future intentions in very general terms, and Prime Minister Asquith had issued a public assurance that the new measures would not impinge upon "innocent" and "legitimate" neutral trade. Because of the sunset clauses contained therein, moreover, the full effects of the new rules would not be felt for several months. If official American policy was to protest *specific* infractions of international law, as avowed the previous October, then as yet the United States had no grounds for complaint.

True, there exists evidence of some American sympathy for the British. Even Secretary Bryan accepted that the advent of the submarine presaged change in the traditional method of blockade and that technological circumstances permitted change in the application of legal principles. "If we recognise the submarine as a legitimate engine of war, we cannot ignore the change in the location of the blockade line made necessary by the use of the submarine," he told Wilson. "So far as the blockade[s] of enemy's ports are concerned, I believe the use of the submarine justified the withdrawing of the cordon to a sufficient distance to protect the blockading ships."[87] But as the weeks passed and it became evident that the British government was bent on regulating the flow of practically all European trade, Wilson's attitude hardened. Indeed, the president had been on the verge of approving strong diplomatic action when, on the afternoon of 7 May 1915, news reached Washington that a German U-boat had torpedoed the passenger liner *Lusitania,* resulting in more than a thousand dead, including 270 women, 94 children, and 124 American citizens.[88] The sinking had a profound effect on the Wilson administration and significantly changed the context of U.S. foreign relations. We shall return to this story a little later.

In London, meanwhile, Grey became increasingly despondent in cabinet meetings, rebuking his colleagues for their bellicosity over blockade policy, which he claimed had placed the Foreign Office in an impossible position. In mid-April, he warned that the "situation may at any moment become acute."[89] At the beginning of May, after Colonel Edward House returned to London, Grey's cries became increasingly shrill.[90] In a memorandum to cabinet dated 7 May, the foreign secretary warned that "a very serious change is coming over public sentiment in the US because of England's delay and many arbitrary interferences in dealing with American neutral cargoes."[91] In fact, the text of his memorandum had been copied practically verbatim from a private telegram Wilson sent to House two days before demanding British concessions and threatening a U.S. embargo on "the shipment of arms and war supplies."[92] Grey's ministerial colleagues did not take this threat too seriously. "I don't think that, in their present mood, they are likely to do anything of the kind," Asquith scoffed in one of his last letters to Venetia Stanley, "but in view of the possibilities K[itchener] has conceived the grandiose idea of transporting to Canada the 3 or 4 big works wh. are now making guns & shells for us in the States. Meanwhile that truly wonderful product called 'American opinion' is pursuing its usual mysterious & incalculable course."[93]

President Wilson's threat notwithstanding, throughout May and into June 1915, Sir Eyre Crowe remained confident that the Foreign Office could rebut any American protest. Scrutiny of American allegations of "many arbitrary interferences" with their trade had been found to translate, during April, into the detention of thirty-six cargoes, mostly cotton, which the government had purchased at (inflated) contract prices, and just one ship.[94] For Crowe, the only potential source of unease was that the United States might discover Britain's hypocrisy in failing to regulate her own exports to the contiguous neutrals.[95] But upon this possibility he did not dwell.

Crowe and his staff drew additional confidence from the knowledge that the "complaints as to the great injury suffered generally by American trade, in consequence of the interference due to British naval measures, derives little substance from the published American trade returns."[96] Figures recently published by the U.S. Department of Commerce showed American exports at record levels and that the U.S. monthly balance of trade was now running at a surplus of nearly $175 million (against just $25 million for the corresponding period the previous year).[97] Better yet, the American government was embarrassed by those figures, and the Foreign Office knew it.[98] On 28 May 1915, Spring Rice seemed to be in one of his more optimistic moods when he confirmed:

> I hear Secretary of State [Bryan] at cabinet said H[is] M[ajesty's] G[overnment] had cut off trade of US with neutrals. President [Wilson] asked [the] Min[ister] of Finance [*sic*—the Treasury secretary] to prepare memo which he did showing that up to end of March US trade with neutrals had increased 50% over trade of corresponding months in year before, which was hitherto the record.[99]

Generally speaking, although direct U.S. exports to Germany and Austria had suffered, overall exports to Europe were up sharply—by more than 400 percent over the previous corresponding period.[100] Most of these increases were presumed to be really intended for Germany.[101]

"What can one say about the American complaints[?]" Crowe rhetorically asked the Foreign Office permanent secretary, Arthur Nicolson, on 11 June 1915. "They really are a gross impertinence and one longs to tell Mr. Page [the U.S. ambassador] in so many words that these complaints are made by people who know that they are baseless and who are consequently acting with deliberate bad faith, with the obvious purpose of picking a quarrel with this country."[102]

In the United States, the sinking of the *Lusitania* on 7 May 1915 was widely regarded as an atrocity.[103] In the words of Arthur Link, the "sinking of the *Lusitania* had a more jolting effect upon American opinion than any other single event of the World War" and "represented an important turning point in American opinion in general."[104] This is not the place to explore all the political and diplomatic ramifications of the ensuing crisis. Suffice it to say that scholars broadly agree that although President Wilson was anxious to meet public demands for a vigorous American response, at the same time he remained determined to keep the United States out of the war. As we have seen, when news of the sinking arrived in Washington the president had been on the verge of issuing a strong protest against the British blockade (though what exactly he had in mind is unclear). Seeing it as foolish to pick an argument with the United Kingdom while the United States stood on the brink of war with Germany, Wilson directed the State Department to suspend its protest against the British blockade. He instead looked to Colonel House to induce the British government to make concessions.[105] British naval intelligence was listening.[106]

At their previous meetings back in February 1915, before the promulgation of the retaliatory order-in-council, Grey and House had discussed the idea of Britain lifting its food blockade of Germany in return for a cessation of submarine attacks on merchantmen.[107] Grey had told only the prime minister and Arthur Nicolson, the Foreign Office permanent secretary.[108] When House returned to England in May, discussion of this possibility resumed. On 14 May, House excitedly telegraphed Wilson that "Sir Edward Grey had just said he *thought* his government would be willing to lift its embargo of foodstuffs if the Germans would abandon their campaign against merchant shipping and agree to stop using asphyxiating gases and killing non-combatants."[109] Delighted, Wilson urged House to press for concrete agreement. Five days later House reported that Grey had agreed to present this modus vivendi to the cabinet "and he would support it personally."[110] On 21 May, House cabled Wilson that "Grey has talked with the present Cabinet ministers and with the opposition members that are to come in and he says in his opinion this government will now consider the suggestion you made to both Germany and

England in your note of February 22d [actually 20 February], provided some additions to cover poisonous gases."[111]

This is an extraordinarily significant document. Except for Hankey's letter to Captain Webb alluding to some rumors, there is no record anywhere in the British archives that discussion of this idea had progressed up to the cabinet. And there is no reason to doubt the authenticity of House's claims. According to other American documents, the bargain was offered to Germany and foundered only after the Germans replied they would consider such an understanding only if the lifting of the blockade was broadened to include "cotton, copper, rubber, and such other raw material as does not directly enter into manufacture of munitions of war."[112] This negative reply did not put an immediate end to the matter.[113] On 28 May, Wilson ordered the U.S. ambassador in Berlin to try again.[114] The following day, Wilson met personally with the German ambassador in Washington, intimating that if Germany agreed to "the complete cessation of submarine warfare," he could persuade the Allies to "end the blockade of foodstuffs."[115]

At the beginning of June 1915, Sir Cecil Spring Rice at last became aware of President Wilson's peace-mongering. (As yet he remained ignorant of the secret conversations between Grey and House.) On 6 June, he urgently telegraphed London that Wilson had revived his ambitions to persuade the belligerents to subscribe to the doctrine of "freedom of the seas," and requested instructions.[116] Spring Rice's information may not have been completely accurate, but it represented the gist. In sending this alert, Spring Rice again reminded London of the treacherous political crosscurrents in Washington. He restated his earlier warnings that "Americans will not acquiesce in the principle that foodstuffs destined for the use of a civil population can rightly be treated as contraband," and counseled that "it would be politic to be liberal in this matter."[117] He explained that "the price of farm products is rather low and the American farmer is attributing this to our action." The American farmer "is a dangerous person to offend and has very strong representation in the House [of Representatives]."[118] Robert Lansing told Spring Rice that the meat industry was "vital to the prosperity of some of the central states."[119] Spring Rice's fear was that pro-German interest groups might be able to forge an alliance with the farm interest, persuade the nation that the British food blockade was a "crime against civilization," and thereby force through Congress legislation prohibiting the export of munitions. The ambassador's constant message was that "our food blockade, as applied to the civilian part of the German nation, is what tells chiefly against us in the public opinion of the United States."[120]

Spring Rice's telegram of 6 June arrived in London hours after Sir Edward Grey left for a month of vacation. It was deciphered by Eric Drummond, his private secretary. Drummond, aware of his master's clandestine talks with House, deemed the ambassador's communication so sensitive that before giving it to Lord Crewe, who had been deputized as acting foreign secretary, couriered it to Grey along with a draft reply of his own composition.[121] Aside from some minor edits, Grey approved the reply, which acquainted Spring Rice with the substance of his talks with Colonel House over freedom of the seas, and returned it to Drummond. In an attached note, Grey explained he was taking the long view:

> If we cannot be secured against aggressive war being made upon us we should agree to forgo interference with commerce at sea in time of war. I believe also that in view of the future development of the submarine and our excessive dependence on overseas commerce it will be to our interest that the sea should be free in time of war.[122]

In this controversial opinion, Grey believed he had the qualified support of Sir Eyre Crowe, who recently had commented on another paper (albeit with undertones of sarcasm) that "we might well agree to allow foodstuffs to proceed to enemy countries if proved to be destined for the civil populations" on the condition that the U.S. government undertake to declare war on Germany in the event she broke her pledge not to resume unrestricted submarine warfare or "similar barbarous methods of warfare."[123] Drummond, in finally forwarding the by now sizable docket to Lord Crewe, took it upon himself to emphasize that

> Sir Edward Grey has already told Col. House [21 May] that his personal opinion was that the new Cabinet, when it was formed, would not refuse to consider such a proposal, but Col. House informed him a few days later [28 or 29 May] that the Germans had "turned down" the proposal that they should give up their submarine warfare if the importation of food into Germany was permitted; thought there were indications that they might consider a proposal, if it admitted the importation of raw material as well as of food, but they had plenty of food.[124]

On 14 June, Grey wrote directly to Lord Crewe stating he favored the bargain even at the price of abandoning the attack upon German exports. He explained that he favored freedom of the seas because "it is probable that the development of the submarine will a few years hence make it impossible for us ever again to close the sea to an enemy and keep it free for ourselves."[125]

Lord Crewe apparently concurred. He informed the cabinet on 18 June,

> Sir Edward Grey writes to me that he thinks the decision of the Cabinet is required as to "whether we should lose anything material by ceasing to prohibit the import of all foodstuffs into Germany through neutral ports and by falling back, as far as foodstuffs are concerned, upon the ordinary rules that apply to conditional contraband."[126]

Lord Crewe went on to explain:

> It seems probable, from Sir Cecil Spring Rice's recent telegrams, that the United States will again put forward some proposal that we should consent to forgo part of our blockade policy in return for a surrender by the Germans of their submarine warfare against merchant-ships.[127]

In floating this *ballon d'essai,* the acting foreign secretary made explicit, further down the page, that "to forgo part of our blockade policy" must necessitate relaxing restrictions on other commodities besides food and therefore was tantamount to the virtual abandonment of the blockade of Germany. He made no attempt to weigh the pros and cons or explore the political ramifications of such a dramatic shift in policy. Yet the way in which Crewe presented Grey's case and his choice of language in certain passages suggests he thought the idea worthy of consideration. He informed his readers that if, as seemed likely, Germany made concessions to appease American opinion over the *Lusitania,* then Britain would be compelled to reciprocate over the blockade. He closed by asking the members of the cabinet to decide what concessions they would be prepared to make in such an eventuality.

The message contained in Lord Crewe's memorandum was extraordinary enough. Yet still more astonishing was the reaction of the cabinet—or, rather, the lack thereof. After less than twelve months of war, one would have expected ministers to summarily reject any relaxation of the economic campaign, let alone a proposal tantamount to its effective abandonment. But they did not. There were no eruptions; not even the First Lord of the Admiralty protested. In fact, for almost a month the cabinet considered this question on its merits. Of course, there was never any question that such an enormous reversal of policy would have been admitted publicly. Most likely the blockade would have been maintained in name, but in practice the seams would have been further loosened to allow more neutral goods to reach Germany, thereby rendering the blockade almost completely ineffective.

For so long and apparently so seriously did the cabinet ponder the matter, in fact, that the French government caught wind of these deliberations and on the last day of July voiced its objection. Such a dramatic volte-face, their chargé d'affaires in London howled, "would be described all over the world as part of a general defeat of the allied cause."[128] Crowe, who reported this in the account of his conversation with the French diplomat, reminded his colleagues that

> the French government had been most reluctant at the time [March 1915] to accept our reprisals policy. They had pointed out the dangers of American opposition and warned us that if we did decide upon it we must stick to it, as it would never do to abandon it again under American threats. Yet this was now apparently going to be done, and again France was hardly given fair time or opportunity even to examine and discuss so grave a change of policy.[129]

For some months, the French government had been unhappy with Britain's handling of Allied blockade policy. As early as January 1915, French blockade officials had pointed out many of the drawbacks to the Foreign Office blockade system, particularly the difficulty in gauging the true levels of imports into contiguous neutral countries, and proposed a conference among the Allies to discuss the practicality of several alternative approaches. To French annoyance, the Foreign Office ignored the proffered invitation until 5 March.[130] For several more weeks the Contraband Department further procrastinated, and it was not until the third week in June that officials from Britain, France, and Italy finally sat down in Paris to discuss how best to stem the leakage of contraband into Germany. (Ironically, this was the same week that Crewe presented his memorandum to the cabinet suggesting a relaxation in blockade policy.)

The Paris conference opened with the hosts proposing that the Allies restrict their exports to contiguous neutral countries to "normal" (that is, prewar) levels.[131] None too politely, the French delegates pointed to the "immense increase which has taken place in the export from this country [Britain] to neutral countries contiguous to Germany."[132] In unofficial conversations, the Foreign Office representatives, Cecil Hurst, Robert Craigie, and Owen O'Malley, found that their French counterparts were livid at the recent surge in British exports to continental Europe. They were mortified to discover also that the French possessed an embarrassment of statistical evidence to substantiate their accusations, and were *au fait* with the weaknesses in British licensing procedures that had led to this situation.[133] The source of this damaging information remains unknown to this day. Upon their return from the Paris at the end of June, the British team unanimously impressed upon their superiors that "there is, unfortunately at the present moment, a widespread belief in France that the situation created by the war has been and is being exploited by merchants in England to the lasting detriment of their French rivals in the neutral markets of Europe."[134] "If we now refuse to meet them over the proposal," Craigie warned, "the 'Guerre Économique' would then degenerate into an unseemly scramble among the belligerents to increase their exports regardless of destination," and the blockade of Germany would collapse.[135]

Sir Edward Grey responded to this unwelcome development by laying the blame at the door of the Board of Trade. In a letter dated 6 July 1915, he intemperately berated Walter Runciman's department for placing him in such an "exceedingly embarrassing" position.[136] This was a little rich considering that only days before, Grey had been trying to coax the cabinet into virtually abandoning the blockade. Three days later, the Foreign Office sent the Board of Trade copies of the resolutions passed at the recent Paris conference, adding that they favored ratification of the French plan and expected it to be implemented forthwith.[137]

The idea of rationing the imports of neutral countries adjacent to Germany was not new. "If it were not for the difficulties we should have introduced it long ago," Cecil Hurst reminded his colleagues.[138] The chief obstacle to this apparently simple solution had always been the lack of reliable statistics on international trade flows. At the CID in 1912, readers will recall, and again in August 1914, the British government had considered but ultimately rejected the idea of imposing rationing on the imports of the Low Countries. In December 1914, the attempt had failed to ration copper bound for Switzerland.[139] In March 1915, the Admiralty had revived the idea once again. At an interdepartmental meeting held on 30 March, Lord Emmott of the War Trade Department asked the Board of Trade to help his newly formed statistical unit to calculate the "normal" levels of imports into contiguous neutrals for about two dozen strategic commodities. This prompted the Foreign Office to investigate the practicability of the measures proposed.

In May 1915, Robert Craigie of the Contraband Department submitted a paper exploring the necessary steps in adopting a rationing policy. His report confirmed what everyone knew: that the greatest hurdle remained "the absence of reliable and absolutely up-to-date statistics."[140] Craigie's report also shows, incidentally, that the Foreign Office was well aware of just how poor these were. Neutral European governments could not be trusted to report their trade figures, Craigie bluntly stated. Nevertheless he was cautiously optimistic that the British government might compile its own figures of inter-neutral trade utilizing their increasingly comprehensive database of ship manifests.[141] Quite whether Craigie appreciated the magnitude of the task he was proposing must be an open question—it was a formidable undertaking and would require additional large investments in information management. But the advantages of rationing appeared irresistible.

Under the current blockade system, the British authorities were compelled to differentiate between legitimate foreign trade and illegitimate contraband smuggling, which meant that before a cargo believed intended for Germany could be seized it was necessary to find proof of the fact sufficient to persuade a prize court. A contemporaneous memorandum written by Cecil Hurst confirms that Contraband Department policy was to "consider as suspect and detain only those particular consignments in respect of which some enemy destination happens to have been intercepted."[142] In other words, on a day-to-day level, the British authorities were stopping suspicious cargoes only when in possession of hard evidence, usually from intercepted cable traffic, that a specific cargo was really intended for an enemy.

The procedures in force are well illustrated in a separate paper by Robert Craigie detailing the treatement of cargoes of oil bound for Copenhagen. There was no question, he opined, that the quantity of oil recently imported into Denmark was manifestly far above the Danes' domestic requirements (the quantities involved allowed no other plausible interpretation than that much was being passed to Germany). Yet, much to the Admiralty's distress, Sir Eyre Crowe had insisted upon the release of all the oil tankers "in the absence of any evidence against the consignees."[143] This was the justification: under the evidentiary system, it was not sufficient to show that many cargoes consigned to a neutral were being passed to Germany; the law required *specific* evidence that a *specific* cargo was intended for Germany. For reasons explained by Lieutenant William Arnold Forster, RNVR, the junior Admiralty representative to the interdepartmental Contraband Committee, this was virtually unobtainable. "The consignor has only to be furnished with a list of names in a neutral country, names which are unfamiliar to the Contraband Committee and which may merely represent so many clerks in a forwarding agent's office, to make it impossible to detain the consignments."[144] Put simply, the administrative resources available to the committee rendered it impossible to track each and every cargo to its final end user.[145]

The chief advantage of neutral rationing was that it obviated the need to make such a distinction and therefore also the necessity for adequate legal proof. Quite simply, whenever a contiguous neutral tried to import more than its quarterly norm, the consignment would be considered as ipso facto suspect and detained.[146] Under the proposed rationing system, in other words, responsibility for rooting out fraud would be thrown back onto the neutrals. At least that was the theory. As Sir Eyre Crowe dryly commented upon Craigie's paper, "I foresee difficulties of a serious nature as regards the proposed warning to American shippers not to ship where *we* think the neutral country has had enough."[147] Here Crowe was alluding to the fact there was no precedent under international law for a prize court to condemn a cargo based upon a "statistical probability" it was intended for the enemy. (Hence the significance of the *Kim* case, discussed in the last chapter and further below.)

The legal objections to using statistically derived information to establish the probable destination of a specific neutral cargo applied equally to the imposition of quotas on neutral trade. This argument formed the basis of the Board of Trade's objections to rationing, sent to the Contraband Department on 19 July 1915.[148] Echoing Crowe's own doubts on this score, the Board of Trade felt that even if reliable statistics could be devised, it seemed highly unlikely that neutral governments, especially that of the United States, would consent to their trade being forcibly restricted to levels set by the Allies. Replying on behalf of the Foreign Office, Cecil Hurst acknowledged that the difficulties to be overcome were formidable but advised that the legal hurdles were not insurmountable.[149]

Understanding now the problems facing blockade administrators in early 1915, and indeed the problems with the entire blockade system, readers perhaps can see why the cabinet did not at once reject the Foreign Office proposal in June 1915 to relax the blockade. The fact is that by this time, there was widespread recognition within government circles that the current system, based upon the evidentiary method, was failing to prevent large quantities of supplies from reaching Germany. Moreover, it was by no means clear how much damage was being inflicted upon the German economy. The Board of Trade had made a persuasive case that Germany faced no serious shortages; if anything, her position appeared to be improving. Neutral rationing represented an alternative policy approach—but the administrative, legal, and diplomatic costs entailed were enormous and, furthermore, the various departments with a stake in economic matters were deeply divided as to the wisdom of its adoption.

Under the circumstances, therefore, could ministers really be faulted for wondering if the blockade was a war-winning weapon or even a vital component of their plans for victory? Indeed, if we go back and more closely examine the text of Crewe's 18 June memorandum to the cabinet, we find that this is precisely how he framed the case for relaxation of the blockade. The very first sentence asked "whether we should lose anything material." The question was not whether the cabinet agreed with Sir Edward Grey that retaining the friendship of the United States was Britain's most vital interest; the question, rather, was whether it made any sense to antagonize the Americans (and other neutrals) by wielding a weapon that did not seem to work anyway.

What did individual ministers say on this matter? As mentioned, it is a surprise that Arthur Balfour, the new First Lord of the Admiralty, did not at once challenge Lord Crewe's memorandum. Neither did Winston Churchill, his predecessor.[150] If anything, Churchill appeared to endorse Crewe's arguments: the same week he advised the cabinet, "We are not entitled to assume that any shortage in men, food, munitions, and money will prevent the Central Powers from maintaining the war at least until the year 1916 is far advanced."[151] Given Churchill's belief that the war could last no longer than this owing to financial exhaustion on all sides, the logical implication of this statement was that he no longer believed blockade was a decisive strategy. Most inexplicably of all, there is no indication that Admiral Sir Henry Jackson, the new First Sea Lord, demanded a rebuttal. The Admiralty's participation in the ensuing debate was limited in every sense of the word. Balfour permitted those members of the naval staff directly involved in blockade administration to express their views and even saw to it that their memoranda were circulated to the cabinet—albeit not until three weeks into the debate and with disclaimers that they did not represent the Admiralty position. Captain Richard Webb, Frederick Leverton Harris, and Sir Francis Hopwood were all emphatic in their opinions, yet especially the first two were far too junior to exert decisive influence on a cabinet-level debate.[152]

The fact is that not a single cabinet minister reacted (in writing) to the contentious Foreign Office proposal. It therefore fell to Colonel Hankey to issue a rebuttal.[153] On 23 June 1915, he submitted to the cabinet a rather tepid document that amounted to little more than a plea for the government to keep faith in the potency of economic warfare.[154] There is evidence this paper in fact was written by Julian Corbett, the naval historian, who was then working at the CID historical section.[155] Recognizing that the paper had failed to make an impression, the following day Hankey began composing a much longer memorandum that approached the problem from a completely different direction. Assisting him in marshaling his arguments was Edwin Montagu, the financial secretary to the Treasury, and several other mutual friends.[156] Hankey's new paper was entitled "The Future Policy of the War" and opened with the premise "that the present war must be prolonged into 1916, and perhaps into 1917." He then laid out the salient features of the current strategic situation: that the Russian forces were too badly damaged and ill-equipped to launch an offensive; that the French had exhausted their reserves; and that the new British Army would not be combat-ready until 1916. The only conceivable Allied strategy, he reasoned, was to fortify the western front to "German standards" and maintain a policy of attrition for at least a year, until the Allied armies were ready for an offensive. To this end it was critical that the Dardanelles be reopened so that supplies could once again flow to Russia.[157]

In framing his arguments, Hankey borrowed heavily from Lord Kitchener and from Arthur Balfour, in many respects no more than restating views he had overheard them express during meetings of the Dardanelles Committee, which he had attended as secretary. In recent months both ministers had arrived at the view that "this war has degenerated into one of attrition," that there must be no premature commitment of the Army to the western front, and that the only offensive action Britain should take in 1915 was to seize the Dardanelles.[158] Broadly speaking, the cabinet had accepted these recommendations as the basis of British strategy for the next twelve months. Lou-Lou Harcourt was left in no doubt (and accepted) that the Allied attrition "strategy in France in coming months [was] to be 'offensive defensive' & war of attrition to kill men not gain ground."[159]

Hankey's contribution to the strategic debate was to highlight the danger that before 1916 "the whole cause of the allies may collapse for lack of the sinews of war"—that is, money. His memorandum reviewed, line by line, the factors relevant to Britain's deteriorating financial position and in so doing painted a shameful picture of muddle and vacillation. In the process he touched upon Army recruitment, labor shortages, inefficiencies in industrial production, the decline in economic output, the fall in exports and the consequent yawning gap in the balance of payments, and the deterioration in the strength of sterling.

Hankey emphasized the growing financial strain upon the British state imposed by the building of the New Armies while at the same time trying to meet the growing demand for subsidies from the other Allies. "It must be admitted," he artfully commented midway through his paper, "that the attempt simultaneously to maintain an immense army, to supply it adequately with munitions, and to stimulate exports savors of the impossible."[160] Hankey insisted that the government must fix the size of the British Army at an affordable level; before this could be done, it would be necessary to ascertain the true magnitude of Britain's financial obligations in the United States (another indicator that no one really knew the answer to this question). In the meantime, Britain should seek to maximize the pressure upon the German economy so as to impede the country's war effort and ensure that her financial system would be the first to crumple. What Hankey sought to demonstrate, in other words, was that Grey's proposal to relax the blockade could not be considered without reference to the broader economic context. To put it another way, blockade policy was no more than a single facet of a much larger and more complex debate that the cabinet had scarcely begun to consider.

This, more or less, was also the opinion of Edwin Montagu, Asquith's highly respected former parliamentary private secretary and now financial secretary to the Treasury. The following week, on 3 July 1915, Montagu sent the prime minister a seventeen-page letter articulating his own arguments.[161] Montagu began by stating that the ineffectiveness of the blockade was self-evident. This he attributed to deficiencies in the machinery of government and the associated failure to coordinate departmental action. "If you would accept my suggestion of a new War Trade Department," he declared to the prime minister, alluding to his effort in early May to persuade the cabinet to consider the matter, "I am quite certain we should have more success than we have had hitherto because I fear there is evidence that the Board of Trade, in its anxiety to maintain as much trade as possible, has been too easy with the Germans."[162] The essential thrust of Montagu's argument was that the blockade remained an essential component of British strategy and that its potency could be vastly improved through a combination of administrative reform and imposing better departmental discipline.

Montagu intimated he had a great deal more to say on this subject, and three weeks later would do so, but for the moment his immediate focus—"what is really the burden of my prayer"—was the failure by the coalition cabinet to address the economic dimensions of national strategy. (And he was not the only middle-ranking politician expressing such concerns at this time.)[163] The cabinet needed to face up to the fact the nation's finances were in disarray. "I cannot understand how the government is content to go on recruiting and recruiting men of all ages and employments," he pleaded. "We must increase our export trade and we can only increase our export trade by the employment of many more men than at present, not only on munitions but on the normal avocations." Montagu went on to restate Hankey's argument that the combination of attempts to purchase munitions in the United States, the even greater expenditure on food and raw materials, and the subsidies to the other Allies were just not sustainable and must soon wreck Britain's credit abroad.[164]

This, of course, was not the first time Asquith had been reminded that Britain's financial strength was not in fact limitless. There are striking similarities between Montagu's letter of 3 July 1915 and Arthur Balfour's memorandum "The Limits of Enlistment" dated 1 January 1915. Both urged the government to keep one eye firmly fixed on the postwar world; both stressed the importance of retaining Britain's wealth and thereby maintaining her credit; and both argued that these considerations required the government to rein in the military expansion and strike a more considered balance in the distribution of the national factors of production. There was, however, one essential difference between the two. Whereas Balfour wrote in anticipation of a long war and had extrapolated trends to imagine the economic problems that would result if the government did not adjust policy, Montagu's paper, written six months later, claimed that the British economy was already crippled and the state teetering on the brink of a financial crisis.

On Monday evening, 5 July, Asquith put aside Montagu's letter to catch the boat train to Calais in order to attend an inter-Allied strategy conference. Upon his return, three days later, he found waiting on his desk yet another paper on the subject of blockade policy. Though no longer a member of the cabinet, Emmott evidently had heard of its recent deliberations and of the criticisms leveled against his department. The first half of his memorandum was nothing more than one of his lengthy diatribes on the difficulties faced by his War Trade Department. The second half of the paper was much more interesting, however. Here Emmott ventured his opinion that not only was the blockade not working and thus futile but its impact was very likely more "crippling" to British than German trade.[165] For good measure Emmott threw out his opinion that the contemplated "rationing [of] the neutral countries adjacent to Germany in accordance with their normal requirements for internal consumption in peace time" would not work. He echoed the position taken by Board of Trade that restricting British exports not only would damage the nation's already strained finances but also seemed pointless because "an ample supply can reach these countries direct from overseas"—that is, the United States. Emmott cited the supply of lubricating oil as a case in point: the result of limiting British exports of this product had been to hand the trade to Standard Oil Corporation.[166]

Unhappily for Emmott, although his memorandum was given only limited circulation, a copy fell into the hands of the Admiralty and was distributed for remarks. "It is unfortunate," spluttered Leverton Harris, "that in the twelfth month of the war, the Chairman of the War Trade Department fails so entirely to grasp the fact that this country is fighting for its existence."[167] In the summer of 1915, Leverton Harris's star was very much in the ascendancy; besides his position on the naval staff (he now held the rank of a full commander in the Royal Navy) and continuing role with the Cornhill Committee (the self-regulatory watchdog for the City of London), he was chairman of the Foreign Office committee responsible for monitoring German exports (the Enemy Exports Committee). This, incidentally, was the one bright spot in the recent picture. In March 1915 German exports to the United States had recovered to 60 percent of their prewar level, but by June they had plummeted to an estimated 13 percent—an impressive achievement that Leverton Harris could justifiably attribute substantially to his own labors.[168]

Effortlessly, Leverton Harris took Emmott's example and exposed the fallacious reasoning underpinning his entire argument. "Germany to-day is in the most urgent need of Lubricating Oil," he explained. So chronically short of lubricating oil was German industry that despite purchasing huge quantities of U.S. oil at inflated prices through neutrals, soap and lard were being used as substitutes. Citing recent trade figures showing that imports of this product into Scandinavia were currently four times prewar levels, Leverton Harris asserted that most of the U.S. oil imported into Holland and Scandinavia was obviously going straight to Germany. Even more outrageously, Board of Trade figures showed that British reexports of refined lubricating oil to Scandinavia and Holland had risen from 6,448 gallons in April and

May 1914 to 419,485 imperial gallons (approximately 12,000 U.S. barrels) for the corresponding two-month period in 1915.[169] "It will be seen from the above figures," he concluded, "that whilst the Oil exporters of the United Kingdom have every reason to be satisfied, the action of the Licensing Committee is certainly open to criticism."[170]

Robert Brand, meanwhile, took copies of each paper (almost certainly from Leverton Harris, as the two shared an office at the Admiralty) and circulated them to the Cornhill Committee. He arranged for them to be placed at the top of the agenda for discussion at the meeting set for 20 July. Alas, the minutes of that meeting have not survived, but given the character of the regular audience, we may safely assume that Emmott came in for further attack. Curiously, despite such overwhelming evidence that British oil companies were prospering, Emmott persisted in his belief that "we are killing the export trade in lubricating oil from this country to Scandinavia and Holland."[171]

In considering the government's options over blockade policy—whether it was practical to fix the problems and revitalize policy or simpler just to throw in the towel—Asquith and the cabinet also had to combat growing public suspicions that Germany's overseas trade was not quite so dead as the government boasted. In the press there were lurid stories of neutrals helping Germany evade the blockade, and in Parliament there were demands for explanations as to why the government was not plugging the leaks. After all, had not Asquith assured the House of Commons at the beginning of March 1915, "There is no form of economic pressure to which we do not consider ourselves entitled to resort"?[172] Since April, protesters had been agitating over why the government had failed to classify cotton as contraband.[173] Given that cotton (or rather cotton waste) was a vital component in the manufacture of explosives and aircraft, and that technically there was no legal obstacle to the British government declaring it contraband (the Declaration of London being unratified), public opinion viewed the government's inaction as inexcusable.[174] After the U.S. Department of Agriculture boasted of record sales of cotton to central Europe, public unhappiness in the United Kingdom reached levels that were politically impossible to ignore. "Every bale of cotton which reaches Germany," screamed the *Daily Mail,* "means either an allied cripple or a corpse."[175]

Because most cotton destined for Germany was routed indirectly through neutral countries, it is impossible to be sure just how much of the 1914 U.S.

cotton crop she acquired. Official American export statistics show that between November 1914 and March 1915 approximately 250,000 bales were shipped directly from the United States to German ports. Over the same period more than six times as much (1,657,000 bales) is known for certain to have been shipped there indirectly. The actual amount was likely far larger. Between January and July 1915 no fewer than 5,937,361 bales of U.S. cotton were shipped to central Europe—against just 3,713,234 bales during the corresponding prewar period.[176]

At the end of May 1915, naval intelligence circulated a deciphered U.S. diplomatic cable indicating that the American government was unhappy with British treatment of U.S. cotton.[177] The attempt to appease the United States by agreeing, in effect, to buy all cotton shipped across the Atlantic had been an expensive failure. In early July, Sir Edward Grey admitted that the "special and generous agreement has prevented neither the cotton interest nor the United States Government from keeping up continuous series of protests against our blockade policy."[178] A wave of panic and anti-British sentiment was already washing over the U.S. southern states in response to the increasingly loud calls in the London press to categorize cotton as contraband and pay nothing for cargoes seized.[179] According to Ambassador Spring Rice, most of the profits from recent cotton sales had gone to speculators, who had bought contracts at the beginning of the year when the price had been low, instead of directly into the hands of the cotton planters and consequently had failed to alleviate their debts or assuage their anger.[180] There was another, more practical objection to continuing this policy. The chairman of the Liverpool docks reported that warehouses between Liverpool and Manchester were filled to overflowing with more than a million bales, and there was simply no space to put any more.[181] On 12 July, Leverton Harris injected a sense of urgency into the debate by reminding Grey the 1915 cotton crop was about to come to market and that the British government must immediately make up its mind as to the policy it wished to follow.[182] Although the total acreage of American cotton sown in 1915 had been reduced by a good 10 percent, the crop yield was projected to be excellent and the total harvest larger.

On 14 July 1915, the cabinet devoted almost the entire session to discussing cotton in the context of blockade policy. The official record is meager in detail, but it is clear from other documents that this was a critical meeting.[183] From the beginning there existed majority consensus that cotton must be declared contraband. The military reasons for doing so were uncontestable; mounting public and parliamentary pressure made it a political imperative.

Yet at the same time all recognized that the U.S. government would see this as a provocative act. The previous fall, President Wilson had made very clear to the British government that the welfare of the U.S. cotton industry was crucial to the republic's economic well-being and, one might add, to the president's political comfort. Both governments, in other words, faced irresistible domestic political pressures propelling them to adopt courses of action that inevitably must lead to diplomatic confrontation.

Asquith's official record of this meeting states that Grey spoke strongly against the proposal.[184] Harcourt's record concurs and adds that he and Crewe "spoke strongly against the expediency of declaring cotton contraband" as well. The meeting was something of a historical occasion in that also attending was Sir Robert Borden, the Canadian premier, the first time any outsider was allowed to participate in the cabinet's deliberations. Borden too "was opposed to declaring cotton contraband because of probable American feeling in S[outhern] States."[185] The majority, however, rejected this cautionary advice and resolved to go ahead and declare cotton contraband.[186] This was a momentous decision. The cabinet had consciously voted to defy American sensibilities over an issue on which the United States was known to be highly sensitive.

Directly afterward, Asquith threw caution to the wind by writing to Edwin Montagu saying he was now ready to listen to his proposals for reforming the machinery for administering blockade policy. He asked him to provide a schema for "a new War Trade Department."[187] Five days later Montagu delivered his blueprint for reform. After the briefest perusal, Asquith directed that it be circulated to the cabinet. Printed across the top of the document of the official version was an endorsement with Asquith's initials that read: "Subject to any criticisms that may occur to my colleagues, I am disposed to agree with his main recommendations. The existing arrangements appear to me to be confused and even chaotic. The matter is urgent, and calls for prompt treatment by the Cabinet."[188] That Asquith should have issued such an unequivocally supportive statement is noteworthy enough. But it seems all the more remarkable after reading the "main recommendations," which were rather drastic.

Montagu's scheme called upon the prime minister to appoint a single minister to take responsibility for all executive decisions relating to blockade matters. He envisaged a kind of "ministry of blockade" (though he did not use the term) that would assume all the responsibilities currently dispersed between the various established and emergency departments. Montagu appreciated that, constitutionally speaking, this was a radical and even draconian proposal. He also knew that Asquith had rejected the idea twice before: in January and again in May 1915.[189] Montagu nevertheless insisted this was the only way conceivable to overcome the weakness of the current "embarrassing" system, and especially for reconciling conflicting departmental viewpoints. "One hears rumors of a good deal of friction," he sardonically wrote, and "it is pretty obvious that the conflicting forces are just left to work themselves out." Montagu attributed the resulting policy failures to the bureaucratic muddle caused by the multiplicity of executive and non-executive agencies, each focused upon its own agenda, and the failure by all to coordinate policy. The staff of the War Trade Department came in for particularly strong criticism, for having forgotten that their primary mission was to help restrict enemy supplies, not to assist the Board of Trade in promoting British exports. There was also implied criticism of the Foreign Office Contraband Department.[190]

Taken together, the cabinet decision to challenge the United States by classifying cotton as contraband, and the prime minister's endorsement of a major administrative shake-up in the blockade machinery to make it bite harder, amounted to a rejection of the foreign secretary's aim "to secure the maximum of blockade that could be enforced without a rupture with the United States."[191] That is to say, Asquith and the cabinet had decided that the risk of rupture was worth taking.[192] On 20 July, Hankey begged Asquith to stand firm, reminding him:

> Hitherto we have rather taken the line that we do not desire to starve out Germany, but that our Naval and economic policy be directed solely towards depriving the fighting forces of their armaments. Even the blockade policy was represented as being more a retaliation for the German threat of a submarine blockade rather than wh[at] it really is, namely, a drastic enforcement of the power given us by command of the sea. . . . Earlier in the war, when the government expressed their desire not to starve the civil population, it was hoped that the war would not be prolonged. The situation now, however, has entirely changed.[193]

To summarize: it seems that by the week of 20 July 1915, Asquith had connected sufficient economic dots to recognize that the blockade remained a potentially decisive strategic weapon in the Allied arsenal that was not being properly utilized. The idea that the prime minister's faith in economic warfare had revived is apparent also in a letter he wrote the following week to Lord Selborne, his new (Conservative) minister of agriculture. Asquith emphasized:

> There remains to be considered the result of economic and financial attrition. I do not think that we shall starve the Central Powers into submission. They are too self supporting to enable us to achieve our end that way; but the financial difficulties both of their Governments and of the commercial and industrial interests may bring them to their knees before the military force is exhausted. But if we are to wear the Central Powers down by economic and financial attrition we must be able ourselves to "stay the course" longer than they can, and that is why I believe that finance is going to settle the result of this war just as much as arms, and in the value of small economies as well as of big ones.[194]

The fascinating thing here is the prime minister's expression of greater confidence in the effects of financial pressure than in those of economic pressure.

Sir Edward Grey too acknowledged that the tide of strategic opinion within the cabinet had turned. "I understand that the Government are now proceeding on the assumption that this will be a long war, lasting for another year or more," he wrote to Asquith on 20 July.[195] "If this is so," he continued, "I feel strongly that we must husband our resources: our staying power is great, but it is not unlimited."[196] In the next paragraph, Grey (borrowing from Balfour and Montagu) laid out the main economic implications for a long war and concluded that it was now obviously necessary for the government to grasp the nettle and strike a better balance between the needs of the Army and the needs of the economy. "The matter is so important that I would ask to have it discussed at an early date at the Cabinet." He added: "It also has a bearing on Foreign Policy: for, without confidence that we are prepared for and ready to endure a long war, it is impossible to handle some foreign questions, particularly those with the US."[197]

In replying, the prime minister indicated his acceptance of the argument that the size of the Army's coat must be cut according to the available economic cloth: "The desirability and even necessity of laying down without delay a fixed limit of numbers, both for the Army and for munitions workers is a point upon which I have for some time been insisting. I have asked McKenna to put down the case in writing."[198]

A Rapid Retirement

No sooner had Asquith finally achieved cabinet consensus on blockade policy than with blinding rapidity everything began to unravel. When cabinet ministers had voted on 14 July to snap their fingers at the United States by reclassifying cotton as contraband, they knew the U.S. southern states would not be happy and would demand that the president seek redress. But they calculated there would be sufficient countervailing forces at work (too many American firms in the north were making too much money off the Allies to want an arms embargo) and consequently the inevitable diplomatic storm could be weathered. What they had not bargained on, however, was simultaneously antagonizing powerful American interests in the Midwest and in the East. It is difficult to be precise about the exact timing or sequence of events. Dates on letters indicate when they were written but not when they were sent or received. Minutes written on files are usually dated but seldom include any indication of whether they were penned in the morning or afternoon. As best as can be determined, events unfolded as follows.

Readers will recall that back in late 1914, the Royal Navy had seized four Scandinavian merchantmen bound for Denmark laden with American meat and lard owned by a consortium of Chicago meatpackers.[199] Although government lawyers tried several times to reach an out-of-court settlement, negotiations foundered upon the intransigence of the meatpackers and the dispute moved to the prize court for adjudication.[200] Through sheer bad luck the hearing of the *Kim* case opened on 12 July 1915. It was widely known beforehand that the procurator general planned to build his case upon statistical evidence to establish a presumption of ultimate destination (and thus guilt). Both the theory and the evidence were sound, but the argument had never before been judicially tested. At the behest of Robert Lansing, who had just succeeded William Jennings Bryan as U.S. secretary of state, Ambassador Page sent embassy staff to attend what was destined to be a landmark case.[201] No one—then or now—seriously doubted that the meatpackers were supplying the German army. The issue was, rather, whether the court would accept the sufficiency of statistical evidence to establish reasonable presumption that the particular meat found on board the *Kim* was intended for Germany.

Ultimately, the prize court accepted the admissibility of statistical evidence—thereby establishing a precedent—and ruled in favor of the crown. But Judge Samuel Evans gave the defendants leave to appeal, and in his later published ruling considerably qualified the verdict he had delivered from the bench.[202] In policy terms, the consequences of this ambiguity were dire. The procurator general subsequently advised that although the precedent had been established, he thought that until the appeal had been heard it was unwise to prosecute any more cases based upon statistical evidence. Before the hearing closed, the meatpackers realized they had lost the case and their property was going to be confiscated. On 17 July 1915 Sir Edward Carson, the attorney general, wrote to Sir Edward Grey warning that the meatpackers' furious representative had vowed to retaliate by marshaling their considerable political clout back home (including House minority leader James Mann) to rouse the Midwest against the British cause.[203]

The same week, a Royal Navy cruiser intercepted the *Neches,* a U.S.-flagged steamer carrying goods of German origin from Rotterdam to New York, and ordered her to discharge her cargo at the nearest British port. This was the first attempt by the British authorities to treat enemy exports as contraband, another legal innovation incorporated into the March 1915 retaliatory order-in-council. The laws of contraband had never hitherto been applied to enemy exports: exports to neutrals were deemed as sold and thus the property of the neutral.[204] Denouncing the British action as "indefensible and beyond belief," on 15 July Robert Lansing instructed Walter Page in London to protest the British action in the strongest possible terms.[205] Later that evening he summoned Sir Cecil Spring Rice to his office and lectured him upon "the necessity for more considerate and liberal treatment of American trade, particularly cotton, oil, and meat products."[206] The U.S. secretary of state warned that "unless some radical change is made, the situation will become so serious politically that it will be difficult, if not impossible, to find a solution."[207]

Before the Foreign Office had time to react to Lansing's ranging salvo, however, the situation escalated. When the secretary of state issued his message he was not yet aware of the British government's intention to declare cotton contraband. This information did not reach Washington until late on 18 July; given Lansing's already elevated temper, his reaction to the news may be imagined. On the morning of 19 July, Wilson wrote despairingly to House that if the British began seizing U.S. cotton, then congressional pressure for an embargo on the sale of all munitions to all belligerents would become irresistible.[208] Through unofficial channels, House relayed the president's grim warning to the British government.[209] In London Page visited Grey for "a long unofficial conversation" to discuss "the political dangers that have arisen and may arise about interference with the cotton trade."[210] The ambassador emphasized

> that the British government really must understand that there must be more considerate and liberal treatment of American trade, and must realize that the American Government considered as unjustifiable in law the general policy of the British government in seizing American shipments on the mere presumption of enemy destination, and in restraining American trade with neutral countries. There was widespread irritation and dissatisfaction in the United States, and, unless some radical change could be made, it was difficult to find a solution. The question was increasing in gravity and reaching a crisis.[211]

Grey immediately assured Page he would ask the cabinet to reconsider its decision over cotton and that, at the very least, the British government would resume purchasing "enough of the new crop to keep the price up to a reasonable figure."[212] The subject was discussed at the cabinet meeting that day, but without resolution.[213] Ministers were undecided whether to retract their decision to declare cotton contraband, which had not yet been announced. On one hand, the message from the American government was unequivocal; on the other, the public clamor at home for the trade to be stopped was overwhelming. They nevertheless agreed to open a precautionary channel to Washington. The cabinet directed Sir Richard Crawford, the British commercial attaché in Washington, to talk quietly with Chandler P. Anderson, formerly the counselor to the State Department and now chief counsel for the cotton growers association.[214]

If these events were not enough to elevate Grey's consternation to panic level, on 21 July Sir Cecil Spring Rice alerted the Foreign Office that the U.S. State Department had finally learned the magnitude of U.K. exports to the Continent and that Lansing reportedly was apoplectic. Two days later Spring Rice telegraphed news that the State Department was preparing a memorandum documenting Britain's hypocrisy and general perfidy.[215] This news was confirmed by British intelligence, which obtained a sneak peek at the report compiled by Robert P. Skinner, the U.S. consul general in London, just sent to Washington via cable.[216] The Skinner report painted a lurid picture of Britain exploiting the war "to stop the legitimate trade of the United States with neutral countries in order to capture the trade for the British Empire, and are therefore allowing goods to be exported from the United Kingdom which they have not allowed to be imported into the same countries from the United States."[217] Skinner claimed that while U.S. goods had been stopped, British trade in identical items to Scandinavia had soared. British exports of luxury food items such as coffee were up 328 percent, tea by 272 percent, and cocoa by 471 percent.

"I am much afraid," Eyre Crowe concluded on 23 July after leafing through the intercepted report, that "we have *no* answer to the United States in regard to the enormous quantities hitherto shipped from this country owing to the refusal of the Board of Trade to restrict the export."[218] Of course the Contraband Department had for some time known that the problem existed, but the Skinner report indicated that the situation was far, far worse than they had ever imaged. (What really hurt was that Skinner had used official British figures—supplied by the Foreign Office—to make his case.)[219] A distressed Spring Rice reported he had met with Secretary Lansing, who had waved Skinner's report in his face while giving vent to his views on the systematic detention of U.S. cargoes bound for neutral countries while Britain was selling identical goods in the same markets.[220]

In fact, although they did not know it yet, Crowe was too hasty in believing the British case untenable. As an afterthought, the Foreign Office forwarded the Skinner report to the Board of Trade for information. After examining it, Sir George Barnes, the department's number two, discovered that Skinner had slanted much of his statistical evidence. For instance, it was true that British exports of wheat to Europe during the first five months of 1915 were 428 percent higher than they had been the previous year and U.S. exports of wheat had risen by "only" 318 percent. But, the Board of Trade pointed out, Skinner's use of percentages was highly misleading. An examination of the actual quantities exported showed that British sales had increased from 14,339 hundredweight to 61,384 hundredweight. By contrast, U.S. wheat exports over the corresponding period had risen from 1.1 million hundredweight to 3.7 million hundredweight. This is not to say British traders were entirely innocent: reexport of cocoa had soared from 3 million pounds to nearly 14 million pounds (U.S. cocoa sales had leapt from 12,300 pounds to more than 16 million pounds). It transpired also that U.S. cargoes detained but subsequently released appeared in British export figures as a reexport.[221] Not surprisingly, the Foreign Office was delighted with the Board of Trade's analysis and felt it was sure to "take the wind out of Mr. Skinner's sails"—though, it admitted on reflection, "it is depressing reading from the point of view of enemy supplies."[222] But this would not be known to the British government until the next month. In July, the Foreign Office feared the worst.

Appearances notwithstanding, as Hankey had reminded Asquith just three days earlier, the question of whether the government should bow to American pressure was complicated by the lack of necessary information needed to make an informed decision. The Wilson administration threatened an arms embargo in retaliation, but just how serious were the implications for the Allied war effort? In truth, no one within the Supreme Command could quantify even approximately how dependent Britain and the other Allies were upon the United States with respect to munitions. As mentioned, there was a belief in some quarters that the position might not be so bad, that British-owned munitions plants in the United States might simply be shifted across the border to Canada and reassembled in friendly territory. Hankey accordingly urged the prime minister to take steps to "ascertain definitely and in terms of figures how far the Allies are dependent on the American resources for their supplies of munitions of war."[223] He further begged Asquith to remember that the position was far from hopeless, that the British Empire could retaliate with its own embargo and potentially inflict far more damage on the United States. Finally, he implored him to instruct the Foreign Office to remind the Americans that a trade war would prove mutually destructive.[224]

On Thursday, 22 July, Asquith blandly informed the king that the cabinet had held a lengthy discussion on cotton, but he merely recorded the fact and supplied no details beyond stating that "a definite decision was adjourned."[225] According to Harcourt, the meeting opened with an announcement from Grey that Anglo-American relations were "getting daily more serious."[226] To demonstrate his point, he then handed out copies of assorted noxious telegrams recently received from the State Department and despairingly asked his colleagues to tell him how the Foreign Office should respond.[227] Grey then tabled a memorandum reissuing his call for a general relaxation of the blockade.[228] "I think that we should lose very little by adopting this policy and we should undoubtedly gain by the diminution of friction with neutral countries," he advised. Simply doing nothing, he insisted, was not an option because "the attitude of the United States towards us will become increasingly disagreeable."[229] From other sources, we know that ministers agreed to give ground on the *Neches* case—though it is not clear if all members of the cabinet participated in this decision. All we know is that Balfour afterward issued secret orders "that in view of the situation between the United States and Great Britain, no American ships outward bound from Europe, although presumably carrying German goods, should be stopped by our cordon."[230] A decision was also taken to turn a blind eye toward the "traffic in contraband and enemy goods sent by parcel post."[231] These are hardly trivial concessions, yet it could be argued they did not denote any reversal in policy but represented practical steps calculated to buy time.

The very next day, however, 23 July, another bombshell landed on Asquith's desk. Readers will recall that several days beforehand the prime minister had asked Reginald McKenna, now chancellor of the exchequer, "to put down the case in writing" for fixing a limit on the growth of the Army and numbers of munitions workers.[232] This he had done. So alarming were the figures that McKenna initially showed them only to Asquith, Balfour, and Kitchener.[233] McKenna's memorandum declared that the financial position was worse than expected and that consequently the strategic options open to Great Britain were far more limited than had been assumed. Coincidentally, the previous evening (21 July) J. P. Morgan and Co. had been unable to raise sufficient foreign exchange to pay for a Russian munitions contract guaranteed by Great Britain. It is too much to say that the British government's credit in New York had failed, but it certainly presaged problems ahead. McKenna took immediate steps to rectify the deficiency by borrowing $50 million of U.S. securities from the Provincial Life Assurance Company to serve as collateral for a loan raised by Morgan.

In his confidential memorandum, McKenna warned that the event was a clear sign the government had financially overextended itself, which he pointedly attributed to uncontrolled military recruitment and the consequent damage to the nation's export industries. Thanks to the financial irresponsibility of Kitchener and Lloyd George, the Treasury lacked both control and precise knowledge of Allied munitions purchasing in the United States on credit. Furthermore:

> The numbers withdrawn at present from the labour market have already proved sufficient to embarrass us in meeting our financial obligations to our Allies, and further withdrawals on a large scale would render our financial task so difficult and burdensome as disastrously to impair our financial position and imperil the supply of food, raw materials, and munitions to this country and our Allies.[234]

McKenna concluded that spending in the United States must at once be curbed. He did not argue there was nothing else that could be done—merely that nothing else should be done before the British government put its financial house in order.

"I had a more or less tiresome day," Asquith wrote Sylvia Henley, his new friend (and Venetia Stanley's sister), on 23 July, beginning with "a long & rather weary interview in the morning between K[itchener] & McKenna—who alas!, thou[gh] generally right, was singularly rasping & unpersuasive in argument."[235] Also attending were Arthur Balfour and David Lloyd George. Because no record was kept, we don't know exactly what each protagonist said, but from memoranda subsequently distributed to the cabinet, we may reasonably infer that McKenna proposed a moratorium upon any new contracts with American firms, arguing that it made little difference anyway because the United States was already saturated with Allied munitions contracts.[236] Unwilling to cull his projected seventy-division-strong army, Kitchener responded with a number of suggestions as to how else the government might achieve the necessary economies in foreign exchange. These included the introduction of civilian rationing, extending the income tax to encompass the working classes, and encouraging women to join the workforce.[237] It is hard to conceive of a list better calculated to make any Edwardian politician shudder. Lloyd George similarly refused to accept McKenna's conclusions, dismissing the recent foreign exchange problem as a combination of mismanagement and aberration. Balfour remained characteristically silent. For a couple of days, Asquith pondered what this all meant and what to do.

On Sunday, 25 July, Asquith sought advice from the trusted Montagu and Lord Reading. Together they met with Walter Cunliffe, the governor of the Bank of England. Afterward Asquith responded to McKenna's warning of impending financial Armageddon, admitting it had caused him "a good deal of disquietude."[238] The prime minister instructed McKenna that "it is of primary importance to our credit that none of the American contracts should be dropped through inability to provide exchange for the moment."[239] The money must be found: he should redouble his efforts to raise collateral by borrowing American securities from British financial institutions "as quietly and unostentatiously as possible," and gather bullion from home and the other Allies. McKenna took the schoolmasterish tone of Asquith's letter to imply censure and resented that the prime minister had gone behind his back, especially in talking to Cunliffe, who had been putting it about that the chancellor was overreacting.[240] It should be noted, however, that others shared McKenna's concerns. Sir Edward Grey, reporting a conversation with Edward Grenfell of Morgan Grenfell, told Asquith:

> He spoke to me most seriously about the monetary situation as regards payments to America. I asked him what measures could be taken. He said that to avoid disaster it was essential to send some gold to the United States & that France & Russia should be made to do this: and that it was also essential NOW to take legislative powers to acquire

> United States Securities held in this country. These two steps he said were necessary now. He also urged on general grounds that blank tickets should be introduced to secure economy in imports. I am much concerned at the situation, but do not know enough to judge.[241]

In any case, the measures taken outlined above proved sufficient to alleviate the immediate crisis but did nothing to address McKenna's broader point that the current financial squall was indicative of major storms ahead. Nothing was done to curb British spending on the Army or its allies.

No sooner had the prime minister disposed of one problem—or thought he had—than another emerged. The following Monday morning Asquith's sponsorship of the Montagu plan for reform of the blockade machinery received a crippling blow. Senior administrative staff at the Board of Trade and the Foreign Office unanimously declared the scheme unworkable. Sir Hubert Llewellyn Smith spoke for all in contemptuously dismissing the idea of a new blockade ministry operating "independently of the existing great Departments of State which possess all the knowledge and experience [of] a chimera."[242] His two principal assistants submitted notes in chorus. From the Contraband Department of the Foreign Office, Sir Eyre Crowe also insisted the Montagu scheme was "quite unworkable," as "the interference with neutral ships and cargoes raises some of the most delicate problems of international relations. It would be impossible to handle the questions of prize, contraband, and blockade satisfactorily except in the closest touch with the executive branches of the Foreign Office."[243]

In rejecting Montagu's scheme, Crowe may have been right in asserting that its author had underestimated the complexities of blockade administration. It is hard to say if Crowe deliberately ignored Montagu's oblique criticisms of his own bureau or if they merely passed over his head. Crowe was not known to be an obtuse bureaucrat, but on this occasion he certainly gave a good impersonation by describing his Contraband Department as the model of efficiency and that "No other arrangements could secure the same rapidity of action."[244] After Grey decreed that this memorandum should be distributed to the cabinet, wiser heads within the Foreign Office recognized that Crowe's self-congratulatory remarks were both inflammatory and wide of the mark, and they were omitted from the printed version.[245] In the face of such determined and unanimous opposition to Montagu's proposals at the administrative level, there was no question of moving forward with his blueprint for reform without considerable modifications, and the plan was temporarily shelved. In August it was again reconsidered but ultimately was rejected in favor of a less ambitious scheme of reform.

After the cabinet meeting on Tuesday, 27 July 1915, Asquith wearily informed the king that his ministers had again reviewed the blockade policy, that again "much difference of opinion was exhibited," and that again a decision had been postponed.[246] According to Harcourt, Grey again circulated a draft reply to the U.S. government that proposed withdrawing the retaliatory order-in-council and promising that hereafter Britain would conduct her maritime war strictly according to established precedents of contraband law and continuous voyage.[247] This was tantamount to complete surrender. Revoking the retaliatory order-in-council would have required Britain to relinquish her grip, only just established, over German exports, which many believed was one area where the British blockade was really hurting Germany.[248] A plan to defuse diplomatic tensions (proposed by Sir Robert Crawford, the commercial attaché at the Washington embassy) through buying off the American cotton growers was also discussed, but ministers balked at the enormous cost.[249]

The decision to postpone the discussion over blockade policy and how far Britain should give ground to America over the blockade (not to mention McKenna's demands for fiscal retrenchment) was almost certainly conditioned by the hope of imminent victory at the Dardanelles.[250] Several weeks earlier the cabinet had approved General Ian Hamilton's request for three fresh divisions at Gallipoli—plus another three to make sure the job was done right, additional reinforcements to bring the divisions already on the peninsula up to full strength, and all available artillery shells. The executive Dardanelles Committee believed this ought to be more than sufficient to ensure that the new offensive, scheduled for early August, produced decisive results.[251] Indeed, the prime minister deemed success at Gallipoli so vital that he consented to send out Winston Churchill to impress upon the generals the vital importance of victory.[252] At the eleventh hour, however, this plan was scotched by the cabinet (apparently fearing that Churchill "was sure to commit us to follies and impose them on [General] Sir Ian Hamilton"—in other words, pressure him to launch a do-or-die attack regardless of casualties).[253] Instead, the cabinet sent Colonel Maurice Hankey to hand-carry the last-minute dispatches to Hamilton. He arrived at headquarters on 28 July 1915.[254]

11

The End of the Beginning

We are now on the eve of a most critical battle in the Gallipoli Peninsula. If we are successful, results will follow and the fall of Constantinople will dominate the whole character of the Great War and throw all other events into the shade. If we fail to obtain a decision and only make some progress, but not enough, then some of the gravest and most painful problems will arise.

WINSTON CHURCHILL, 15 July 1915

As the war entered its second year, expectations in London were running high for a victory at the Dardanelles. On 4 August 1915, the prime minister confided to Sylvia Henley that Kitchener had postponed a trip across the Channel to see the French army commander. "He doesn't like to leave sooner, as he wants to be here during the Dardanelles crisis, wh[ich] I gather ought to come to an end early in the week. (This is all *very secret*)."[1] Asquith's excitement intensified after a letter arrived from Hankey reporting he had reached Gallipoli and found the naval and military commanders "quite confident that they can put the thing through."[2] This letter, however, was ten days old. When Asquith read these words on 8 August, the "big attack" had been under way for nearly thirty-six hours and the army was floundering.[3]

The importance the prime minister attached to Hankey's news—he described it in a following letter to Mrs. Henley as "much the best account I have seen of things at the Dardanelles"—reflected the uncommunicativeness of General Sir Ian Hamilton, the theater commander, whose telegrams home were as infrequent as they were meager in detail. Subsequent letters Asquith wrote to Mrs. Henley contain further evidence of mounting frustration at the lack of news from General Hamilton. He was not the only one. On 11 August, Lord Stamfordham, the king's private secretary, expressed similar sentiments to Lord Esher when he remarked, "We are holding our breath as to the results of the last 5 or 6 days fighting. Ian Hamilton's communications are too metaphorical & poetic to give an exact idea of what has happened."[4]

Until the result of the big push at Gallipoli became known, the cabinet was not expected to make any firm decisions on the various outstanding issues relating to blockade policy. Anticipating a quiet few weeks, Sir Eyre Crowe made preparations to snatch a brief vacation during the traditional holiday month. Many of his staff had already departed for the country. Until then, he set to work helping to help mend fences with the French government. The previous week the foreign secretary had more or less ignored a complaint from the French chargé d'affaires that his government was unhappy at having recently discovered the British cabinet was contemplating a relaxation of the blockade. "He spoke with some evident feeling about what he called our systematic neglect to consult the French government in these important matters except in the most perfunctory way," Crowe relayed to Grey, and "thought that we were apt to act too precipitately and without proper deliberation."[5] In particular, the French objected to not having been consulted over the possible reclassification of cotton as contraband, rightly pointing out that such action must have a serious impact upon the Entente's relationship with the United States. They also reiterated their unhappiness with the level of British exports to the Continent.[6]

On 5 August, French embassy staff restated their government's discontent over trade and blockade policy. The same day Sir Francis Bertie, the British ambassador in Paris, telegraphed London urging immediate steps to conciliate the French. On 8 August, Sir Edward Grey conceded that the French grievances were valid and by telegram suggested a conference to discuss the next step.[7] The French interpreted this as an invitation and two days later informed the Foreign Office that a delegation was boarding the next boat train to London and would arrive the following day! Taken aback, Crowe felt compelled to cancel his planned family vacation. Apologizing to his wife, he explained that a "number of French delegates are coming over tomorrow evening to discuss contraband and blockade questions and American policy. I dare not leave Grey alone with them, and the offer that [Maurice de] Bunsen might take charge of the matter whilst I went away, is enough to make me stay at all costs."[8] (This was not unusual behavior for Crowe, who tended to be obsessive about keeping abreast of events.) He afterward scrawled a hasty invitation to the Board of Trade.[9]

At the top of the agenda for the Anglo-French conference on blockade policy, which ran from 12 to 14 August, was a list of specific articles and commodities that the Allies would seek to ration for importation by the contiguous neutrals.[10] This was agreed upon, though little else was. To French annoyance, no date was set for implementing neutral rationing after the Board of Trade pleaded for more time to assemble the necessary statistical data to calculate precise quotas for each country. Crowe agreed delay was unavoidable.[11] The other important topic discussed was how to manage the American problem; on this the French essentially acquiesced in the British decision to go ahead with the reclassification of cotton as contraband and the payment of danegeld through supporting the market price.[12]

As we saw in the previous chapter, in July 1915 the U.S. government had reacted sharply to being told the Allies intended to classify cotton as contraband. Through private and official channels, President Woodrow Wilson had threatened that such a move would provoke Congress to embargo the exportation of U.S. munitions and implied he would not squander his own political capital trying to resist such a call.[13] There was no question that if the British went ahead, the consequences for U.S. cotton growers would be severe. Though there was no longer any fear that a collapse in the cotton industry might trigger wider economic collapse, Wilson remained fearful that the impact upon the South must be severe and thus produce serious political consequences. Sir Richard Crawford explained to London that "the southerners were in a panic because they feared a second collapse of the cotton market more disastrous [for the South] than the one that had occurred the year before," when prices had fallen by more than 50 percent in a matter of weeks.[14] Many cotton growers were already carrying large debts as a result of being compelled to sell their 1914 crop below cost; a second poor year would push many into bankruptcy. Senator Hoke Smith, a Democrat from Georgia, had warned Wilson that if cotton became contraband, then southern congressmen would vote en bloc in support of demands by pro-German lobbyists to embargo the sale of munitions.[15] In other words, the Wilson administration was motivated less by concern for the economy or any legal principles than by domestic politics. This is not to say the president's concerns were exaggerated.[16]

The British response was to seek a compromise. The cabinet instructed Crawford to approach Chandler P. Anderson, the former counselor to the State Department and now chief counsel for the cotton growers association. Sir Cecil Spring Rice was initially skeptical that a settlement could be reached, telling Grey that the real stumbling block was not the cotton growers but Secretary of State Robert Lansing, who was fervently opposed to the classification of cotton as contraband.[17] On 31 July, however, the ambassador appeared more optimistic. That morning, Anderson had intimated to Crawford that both the administration and the cotton growers likely would acquiesce if the British government agreed to purchase as much as necessary to prevent another price collapse.[18] It remained only to agree upon the number. This was not as simple as it sounded because so much depended on the supply, which was a function of the success of the harvest and of course the level of demand from other buyers.[19]

Walter Runciman and the Board of Trade thought that instead of committing to upholding a specific price, it would be more reasonable for the British government simply to buy 3 million bales (the normal peacetime imports for the Central Powers).[20] The cotton growers, however, insisted upon a commitment to underwrite the market price at 10 cents per pound, which seemed a little cheeky considering that the current price was just 8½ cents. Charles H. Burr, another lawyer retained by the cotton growers, estimated that the British government might get away with buying just 2 million bales—though at a cost to the taxpayer of £20 million, or approximately $100 million.[21] By any standard, this was a staggering sum.

On 10 August 1915, nevertheless, Grey confirmed to Colonel House, "We are prepared to enter into any arrangement that will make the price of cotton stable and prevent its collapse."[22] Three days later, Spring Rice and Crawford met with Colonel House and Benjamin Strong, the governor of the Federal Reserve Bank of New York, and it was agreed the British government would buy cotton whenever the price stood below 10 cents.[23] Simultaneously, the U.S. Federal Reserve would supply southern banks with up to $30 million to entice growers to hold back their cotton (effectively limiting supply and thereby alleviating the downward pressure on price) by offering them cheap loans. The agreement took effect on Saturday, 21 August 1915, and the following Monday purchasing began.

During the quiet first week of August 1915, there was a brief revival of cabinet interest in the Montagu scheme for blockade reform. On Friday, 6 August, Lord Curzon of Kedleston, a Conservative peer who had joined the coalition cabinet (without departmental responsibilities), summoned Lord Emmott, the head of the War Trade Department, to a meeting. Whereupon an indignant Emmott wrote afterward to the prime minister, "He told me that the cabinet had accepted a scheme prepared by Edwin Montagu for a reconstructed War Trade Department of which you [Asquith] had asked him (Lord Curzon) to be the head."[24] Readers will recall that a fortnight before, the prime minister had endorsed Montagu's call for the myriad components of the blockade machinery to be consolidated into a single department under a single minister with full executive powers.[25] The idea had stalled, however, in the face of vociferous criticism from senior administrators within the established departments. Emmott reacted angrily to being thus notified he had, in effect, been dismissed, and insisted on a face-to-face meeting with the prime minister.

While he awaited a reply, Emmott composed a petulant rebuttal of the allegations leveled against him (which was distributed to the cabinet), reminding everyone he was not responsible for the policy mess. The blame, he insisted, belonged primarily to the Foreign Office for frequently issuing "ridiculous instructions," and to the Board of Trade for pressuring his department always to keep in mind "the necessity of keeping up our export trade in order to pay for our imports."[26] Interestingly, he leveled no accusations at the Admiralty. On 8 August, Asquith met with Emmott just before boarding a train for Scotland and assured him that Curzon had been mistaken and that the matter was not in fact settled yet; Asquith invited Emmott to submit his thoughts on the matter.[27]

Five days later, Emmott sent Asquith (and Curzon) his considered judgment on how best to achieve the "greater co-ordination [that] ought to exist between the various Committees dealing with War Trade problems."[28] This memorandum was more or less a restatement of the views he had expressed during the previous four months. Emmott was skeptical of achieving any positive results. In his opinion, friction with the bureaucratic machine was the inevitable consequence of the fundamentally irreconcilable differences between the various participating agencies, each bent on its own agenda despite knowing that other, "rival" departments held opposite views. This much was obvious. Emmott also agreed with the Board of Trade that a unified ministry with "plenary authority" was a chimerically impractical idea.[29] In his covering letter to Asquith, he opined that handing "ultimate authority" to a single minister would likely exacerbate departmental jealousies. Emmott specifically warned him against giving the job to the Contraband Department, providing several pages of recent examples to show why they were demonstrably incapable.[30]

Because the Foreign Office remained unwilling to adopt a firmer line against the United States, Emmott continued, and so restrict the flow of goods across the Atlantic to European contiguous neutrals, "the question arises whether we are to refuse licenses in regard to such commodities and so acquiesce in handing our trade over to our chief commercial rivals, or of granting licenses for moderate quantities to endeavor to retain some control of the trade and benefit British exporters."[31] Put another way, until Britain achieved effective restrictions on U.S. trade, limiting British exports was both futile and damaging to the national commercial interest. Emmott nevertheless accepted that "the time has come when policy ought to be dictated in its broad lines" by "some more powerful and authoritative body whose duty it would be to consider war trade problems in relation not only to their effect on the enemy but also on our own trade as affecting our power to hold out in a long war." If this system were adopted, he advised allowing the Contraband Department to act as lead agency—"in spite of my grumbles about the Foreign Office"—but recommended that policy to be set by a committee of three or four cabinet ministers, which would also serve as a "court of appeal" to settle collisions between department interests. Emmott acknowledged that this transparently timid reform was "the best that could be hoped for, rather than what really ought to be done."[32]

Unbeknownst to Emmott, Lord Curzon had independently reached more or less the same conclusions—that the political, personal, legal, and constitutional hurdles standing in the way of a unified "Department or Ministry for dealing with War Trade Problems" were just too great. On 10 August 1915, he sent the prime minister a detailed letter explaining why he now refused to lift the poisoned chalice.[33] This merits quoting at length. Curzon argued that "such a ministry could only be effective if (a) it was created in response to an admitted public demand, (b) it were, and continued to be, strongly supported by all the departments affected or concerned."[34] Neither condition was true.

> In the papers submitted to me there is no indication that the FO [Foreign Office] would welcome such a departure. On the contrary, the new Minister, if he were to exercise a really effective authority, could hardly fail to come into early collision with the FO. Not a word has been said in favour of the change by the President of the Board of Trade. All he does is to submit, without comment, and therefore presumably with assent, two notes by his leading subordinates, one by Sir H. Llewellyn Smith, which is almost contemptuously hostile, the other by Sir George Barnes, which is scarcely less favorable.[35]

Echoing Emmott's remarks, Curzon concluded that "the crux of the matter" lay in the allocation of final executive authority. If a new ministry was created,

> the new minister will be powerless to improve matters unless he has executive authority. Otherwise he will be the fifth wheel in innumerable coaches. But the possession, and still more the exercise of such power, will bring him into immediate collision with his colleagues. . . . In fact his life could hardly fail to be one of incessant warfare with his colleagues . . . and the result I fear will be not less friction but more.[36]

Asquith seems to have treated this emphatic rejection as putting an end to the Montagu scheme.[37] But the problems it had tried to address remained. The following week Emmott pressed Asquith at least twice over the "urgent necessity for the creation of a supreme body to define policy and arbitrate inter-departmental disputes."[38] Asquith's unresponsiveness prompted Emmott again to threaten resignation from the War Trade Department.[39] On 20 August the prime minister finally informed Emmott that the unification of all administrative machinery relating to war trade matters was impractical and that "we may find a way to attain the desired result by simpler and less ambitious methods."[40] But for the next few weeks Asquith was far too busy with other concerns to find such a way or even to articulate his thoughts for a better solution to the problems identified.

Failure at the Dardanelles: Finance, Conscription, and War Policy

We return now to the Dardanelles. The operational objective of the August offensive was to burst across the Gallipoli Peninsula from the direction of the beach at ANZAC Cove, the previously unnamed landing place of the Australian and New Zealand Army Corps (ANZAC), and seize the commanding heights along the Sari Bair ridge to threaten the enemy army's flank and rear. The main attack was to be delivered by Lieutenant-General William Birdwood's veteran ANZAC troops, supplemented by a brigade of regular Indian troops plus five brigades of New Army volunteers just arrived from England. A further five New Army brigades were tasked to capture Suvla Bay by amphibious assault so as to cover the ANZAC's northern flank as well as secure a better logistical base for future operations.[41] Despite phenomenal bravery, the ANZAC attack fell short of its objectives. In the north, meanwhile, the force of 20,000 green British troops under the command of General Sir Frederick Stopford landed almost unopposed at Suvla Bay. But instead of advancing 6,000 yards to occupy the ridge in front of them, they proceeded to consolidate their beachhead and dig in.[42] General Sir Ian

Hamilton, the commander in chief, failed to intervene until too late and the opportunity perhaps to salvage the ANZAC reverse was lost.

By 11 August, Hamilton's staff accepted that the operation had failed and advised the cancellation of further attacks. This was also the view of Hankey, who had been a witness to the fiasco at Suvla Bay. General Hamilton, however, unwilling to admit defeat, pleaded with London his operation had come within an ace of success and that one more push should prove sufficient. To say the least, this was an optimistic assessment of the tactical situation. That afternoon Kitchener informed the cabinet that "Ian Hamilton [was] making [an] advance but not rapidly + not very satisfactorily" but assured ministers he had "no doubt it will be done in the end."[43] How did the ministers receive the news? Walter Runciman wrote to his wife of "the haunting anxieties of the Dardanelles where we have ALMOST had a big success.[44] Asquith told Mrs. Henley he did not know what to make of the situation.[45]

On Saturday afternoon, 14 August, the prime minister departed London to spend the weekend at the coast. Late Sunday afternoon, he wrote Mrs. Henley with distressing news:

> While I was out in the afternoon K[itchener] arrived suddenly from Broome [Park] at our little villa. He was not able to find me, but left behind his news, wh[ich] was not good. Ian Hamilton wires bitter complaints of the incompetence of [General] Stopford (commanding 9th Corps) & his divisional generals, which had blocked his intended advance & compels further delay.[46]

Abruptly he broke off his narrative to motor back to London. The following morning, Monday, 16 August, Asquith resumed his communication:

> But the most sickening thing is the failure of the surprise landing then the incompetence of the generals. It might have transformed in a day the whole fortunes of the campaign. If only you were here, I could tell you a lot that I dare not put down on paper. As you know, I am not apt to be downhearted, but AJB [Balfour] (who has just been here) and I agree, that, in the whole 12 months of the war, nothing has happened comparable to this. Everything was perfectly conceived & admirably arranged: the Turks were wholly unprepared: and the presence of one man with any gift of leadership w[oul]d have ensured a brilliant & resounding success.[47]

Manifestly the prime minister was dismayed if not distraught by the news, which killed his last hope the war might soon be over. By nature Asquith was not a vindictive man, so it is perhaps a measure of his unhappiness that initially he urged Kitchener not just to relieve the generals responsible but to have them cashiered.[48] The failure to take the Dardanelles inflicted upon the government's self-confidence a blow that cannot be overestimated.

The fiasco of the August offensive also proved the last throw of the dice at the Dardanelles. Though over the next few months the executive War Committee periodically discussed launching yet another bid to capture the Straits, on each occasion priority in the allocation of increasingly scarce resources was found to lie elsewhere. Ultimately, at the end of the year, and with much recrimination, the cabinet endorsed the decision to cut its losses and evacuate the peninsula.[49] But this anticipates our story.

Concerned at the appearance of fractures within the alliance, on 20 August Kitchener blocked calls to insert another 100,000 troops into the mire at Gallipoli by insisting all available troops be sent to France to conduct an offensive "necessary to relieve pressure on Russia and keep the French Army and people steady."[50] A fortnight earlier, the Germans had captured Warsaw and afterward driven the Russian armies further back than expected. The French government had recently changed and there were hints the new ministry might seek a negotiated peace if the British refused to support their army's next offensive. The cabinet unhappily agreed there was no alternative. Accordingly, ministers gave their reluctant consent to allowing the BEF (now including New Army divisions) to launch an attack at Loos despite skepticism of any chance of success. As Lloyd George told his colleagues, "All our staff in Flanders are against the share given to us to do: we are in for certain disaster though it may help the French."[51] In approving the operation, it must be emphasized, the majority of ministers envisaged this reinforcement of the western front as a stopgap measure while they deliberated other strategic alternatives. It was one thing for the cabinet to agree on the necessity for a new policy direction but, as we shall see below, something else for twenty ministers to agree upon which was best.

When Asquith arrived back in London on 15 August, more bad news awaited him. "I have come back into a welter of trouble," he told Mrs. Henley, without mentioning what this second problem concerned.[52] There are two possibilities. Most likely Asquith was alluding to a precipitous drop in the value of sterling against the dollar.[53] Discussion of the exchange rate crisis dominated cabinet proceedings on Monday, 18 August, to the exclusion of all other subjects.[54] It will be recalled that a few weeks earlier McKenna had alerted the cabinet to the Treasury's fears that Britain had become financially overextended and must bring its spending in the United States under control, but his warning had gone unheeded. Since then, the British government had further extended its liabilities in the United States (for instance, the recent commitment to purchase $100 million of cotton).[55]

Forced now to confront financial realities, Balfour (Admiralty), Runciman (Board of Trade), and Grey (Foreign Office) came around to McKenna's view that Britain could not afford to sustain a large army—and continue to subsidize the Allies with money and equipment—without liquidating most of the national wealth and inflicting potentially irreparable long-term damage to the economy.[56] McKenna and his allies pleaded for retrenchment in the war effort and time to rebuild the economy. This was a controversial proposal. While these issues were under discussion, the cabinet agreed as a first step to send a team to the United States under the trusted Lord Reading, the lord chief justice and a former financier, with instructions to seek a loan of between $500 million and $1 billion from the New York banks.[57] Another mission under D. A. Thomas (later Lord Rhondda) was sent to inspect munitions plants in North America, which ultimately led to the establishment in Canada of the Imperial Munitions Board under W. Lionel Hichens and Robert H. Brand.[58]

Alternatively, in his letter to Mrs Henley the prime minister might have been referring to the recent eruption of the hitherto dormant conscription debate. Again, readers will recall that back in May 1915, Asquith had shunted discussion of compulsory service to a cabinet committee charged with surveying the manpower resources of the country. The necessary legislation had been passed on 15 July and the census taken exactly one month later. But even before the findings had been compiled, the pro-conscription lobby both outside and inside the government began anticipating the conclusions and demanding that preparations be made.[59] On 11 August, Runciman complained to his wife that the entire cabinet meeting that day had been wasted discussing the subject.[60] In order to defuse tensions Asquith was forced to give ground and appointed Lord Crewe, his most trusted lieutenant, to head a committee of six ministers "to ascertain and examine the resources of this country and of our allies for the prosecution of the War up to the end of the year 1916."[61] It is a matter of historical debate whether in forming this committee Asquith already recognized the necessity for conscription, remained opposed, or was simply trying to buy himself more time in the hope something would turn up that would allow him to dodge this politically costly issue.[62] In practical terms it mattered little.

The War Policy Committee, which met twelve times during the last weeks of August, formally delivered its report on 6 September.[63] The four pro-conscription members of the committee—Churchill, Curzon, Chamberlain, and Selborne—found Crewe's recommendations too insipid for their taste and submitted a separate report calling for the immediate introduction of compulsory service. The minutes of their meetings, indicate that the conscriptionists had dominated the proceedings and none too subtly twisted testimony and bent evidence to suit their agenda. For instance, they adjudged some of the figures supplied by the Board of Trade "too discouraging" and arbitrarily adjusted them. Equally unpalatable Treasury figures were ignored on the grounds the department had "taken a too abstract view of the position," that "in a war such as this, in which the passions and sentiments as well as the interests of mankind are involved, it is dangerous to rely too greatly on economic maxims."[64] Such blatant distortions incensed Reginald McKenna, the chancellor of the exchequer, who immediately challenged the findings of the War Policy Committee and reissued his warning to the cabinet that conscription of manpower on the scale proposed would wreck the economy.[65]

It lies beyond the scope of this book to detail the complex story of how during the fall of 1915, pressure mounted upon Asquith to disregard warnings of impending national bankruptcy and finally to agree, in January 1916, to the introduction of conscription.[66] But to comprehend subsequent events with respect to blockade policy, it is necessary to say something of the strategic debate that raged within the cabinet between August 1915 and January 1916.

It is not sufficient merely to state that during this period cabinet opinion became polarized between those who were willing to countenance conscription against those wanting to initiate financial retrenchment. Reginald McKenna's case against conscription was more sophisticated than many military historians have allowed, and commanded much more political support. Furthermore, McKenna was not ideologically opposed to conscription; rather, he favored a totally different strategic approach to the war. He contended that, if necessary, Britain could fight indefinitely provided action was taken immediately to organize the economy properly and cease the squandering of national treasure on the Army. "I had a long and confidential talk with McKenna about national service," Hankey recorded in early September. "His argument briefly is this—that if we take many more men we cannot hope to supply our allies, to whom we are committed to the tune of about £1 million a day—not in money but in goods and credit. His plan is limit our army, but to give our doles gratis as a gift and not as a loan. Balfour is in general agreement."[67]

McKenna's opponents insisted a long war of exhaustion would not work because ultimate victory depended upon the military might of France and Russia, which were already showing signs of war weariness. As Bonar Law said to Balfour, French manpower reserves had been almost exhausted already, and consequently their field army "can be kept at the present level only for a short time."[68] Yet it is important to understand that the proponents of conscription, with the exception of Lloyd George, who still refused to believe that the richest country in the world faced any kind of financial boundaries, broadly accepted McKenna's warnings that their preferred path indeed ultimately led to financial ruin. "It looks like bankruptcy next year & means that if Germany can last we can't," Harcourt gloomily noted.[69] Bonar Law and the other conscriptionists argued this meant that Britain should build the largest army possible that could be deployed for an offensive in the summer of 1916, in a bid to achieve victory before the money ran out.[70]

The real points of dispute between the pro- and anti-conscriptionists, therefore, were how quickly the financial end would be reached and whether the improvised British Army would prove sufficient for the task. Much, of course, depended upon the lengths to which the cabinet was prepared to go in the conscription of money. "Bonar Law wants a census of all American securities in this country—in order if necessary to seize them," Harcourt recorded with alarm during the cabinet meeting on 14 September, but "this was thought dangerous as liable to frighten people into transferring their stocks to America."[71] While the cabinet continued to debate strategy, the Ministry of Munitions spent lavishly abroad, quite often without Treasury approval, thereby further exacerbating the financial situation.[72]

For the remainder of 1915, ministerial bickering resulted in the near paralysis of decision making. Twenty men simply could not reach agreement over conscription, national finances, whether to persevere at the Dardanelles, whether to remove Kitchener as war minister (and if so, how), and a range of lesser questions. All the while, defeat followed defeat. Viewed through contemporary eyes, these months were a period of "everlasting drift"; as a despairing Edward Carson (attorney general) told a sympathetic Winston Churchill, "I feel every day more inclined to retire altogether, not because of any particular policy but because there is *none*—absolutely *none*."[73] The prime minister's unwillingness or inability to force a decision one way or the other led to mounting dissatisfaction with his leadership and a growing conviction that the political executive as presently constituted was too unwieldy for the conduct of wartime business.[74] Both Carson and Churchill subscribed to this view and both ultimately resigned. The former remained in London bent on bringing down the coalition government by becoming, in effect, the leader of the opposition in Parliament. Churchill rejoined the Army and took command of a battalion on the western front.[75]

The Blockade Again

At the beginning of September 1915, the cabinet briefly set aside the twin issues of national finances and conscription to venture briefly once again into the blockade policy quagmire. By now all thought of the Montagu plan for the creation of a centralized ministry of blockade had been abandoned. The prime minister had been persuaded to address the key problem of departmental coordination through "simpler and less ambitious methods."[76] There nevertheless remained several outstanding questions of policy that required decision. Most important was the imminent introduction of neutral rationing, a completely new approach to the management of the blockade, which proponents argued would significantly tighten the noose around Germany's economic neck. The previous month, the Foreign Office had prematurely assured the French that neutral rationing would be adopted as soon as the import quotas for each country had been worked out. But as yet executive approval had not been granted.[77] The cabinet also faced the need to address the midsummer discovery that indirect British trading with the enemy was taking place on a far greater scale than even the most pessimistic commentator had thought. The necessity for action was spurred by the knowledge that this embarrassing situation had become generally known.

On 1 September 1915, Grey proposed to the cabinet a way past this last problem. Harcourt records that the foreign secretary initiated "a long discussion as to whether we are wise in keeping so many goods out of Germany." Why not, he put forward, allow the Germans to squander their hard currency and "let in all objects of pure luxury"?[78] He ventured that "our indiscriminate prohibition of German imports may be found at end of the war to be our greatest blunder."[79] Grey asked the cabinet for an immediate decision as to "whether we shall let two big ships full of coffee from S America go into Sweden."[80]

The driving force behind this initiative was in fact the new (Conservative) undersecretary of state for the Foreign Office, Lord Robert Cecil (1864–1958), the third son of the Marquess of Salisbury, the former Conservative prime minister.[81] His reasoning ran as follows:

> By injuring Germany's financial and economic position, the difficulties put in the way of Germany supplying herself were enhanced. Germany had now come somewhere near the limit of her financial resources, and if she buys tea and coffee it is evident that she cannot afford to spend much on copper etc. He urged that it was really a question of concentrating our efforts. It was essential in his opinion that the Contraband Committee should direct their attention to keeping out from Germany commodities of vital importance for carrying on the war and not bother about the more ordinary things. He considered we should concentrate on such articles as oils and fats, meats, metals, rubber, cotton and wool. Subject to the policy of blockade he was inclined to encourage Germany to spend money on imports.[82]

The basic theory was not without merit and indeed harked back to prewar Admiralty studies.

The question of whether to restrict the reexport of coffee and similar products might seem a trivial matter, but it was fraught with implications.[83] Hitherto coffee had been regarded as a foodstuff and thus treated as conditional contraband. To permit its free export, therefore, contradicted declared British blockade policy. Worse, it implied official tolerance of indirect British trade with the enemy, which the Desart Committee had warned likely would prove corrosive to civilian morale. Another, more emotive argument for continuing to block the free import of coffee was that it was a stimulant. Soldiers insisted that "life in the trenches would be well nigh intolerable were it not for such comforts as tea, cocoa, spirits, tobacco, coffee and perhaps wine."[84] Many within the government believed (almost everyone felt qualified to express an opinion) that depriving Germany of "comfort foods" would cause far greater damage by sapping morale than could ever be inflicted upon her financial systems by allowing free import.[85] Lloyd George argued for making "the Germans as uncomfortable & irritable as possible so as to produce a pro-peace party there."[86] But it should also be noted that British sales to Europe of coffee, tea, cocoa, and tobacco had all featured prominently in Robert P. Skinner's report, which accused Britain of placing obstacles in the path of U.S. exporters while allowing her merchants to export the exact same commodities.[87] One might plausibly speculate that Grey, in putting forward the initiative, was less interested in exerting greater pressure upon the German economy than in finding an excuse not to plug an embarrassing hole in the blockade. It certainly looked that way.

"So evenly balanced" was cabinet opinion over Grey's proposal, Harcourt wrote, that Asquith took the unusual step of putting the question to a vote: eight ministers voted for stopping the coffee, and twelve were against.[88] It is remarkable that such a novel argument could have induced a major and far-reaching shift in cabinet policy after perhaps an hour of discussion by a group of men who knew nothing about the details—an interesting commentary indeed on the nature and caliber of cabinet decision making at this time.

Grey, nevertheless, had his mandate and duly instructed the Contraband Department to comb the list of prohibited exports to separate items "considered as of direct military value" from those not.[89] Crowe was skeptical of the proposed initiative, seeing it as amounting to "practically abandoning our blockade policy so far as imports into Germany are concerned."[90] Even Sir George Cave, chairman of the Contraband Committee, who seldom (if ever) spoke out on questions of policy, questioned the wisdom of such an abrupt change and begged the cabinet to reconsider. Two days later coffee was back on the restricted list pending further investigation.[91] After a further week of to-and-fro the cabinet failed to reach agreement whether trade in "luxury items" such as coffee should be controlled.[92] Throughout this period Hankey spent long hours talking to Julian Corbett, searching for arguments "to keep tender-hearted ministers up to blockade."[93] Every time the matter seemed settled, a new consideration emerged. On 11 September 1915, the prime minister lost patience with the subject, declaring such technical issues were more properly discussed by experts and announcing the formation—or more accurately reconstitution—of a war trade coordination committee.[94]

The new-look War Trade Advisory Committee (WTAC), established by Treasury minute dated 20 September 1915, supplanted the ineffective Admiralty-dominated Enemy Supplies Restriction Committee, set up at the beginning of the war under Sir Francis Hopwood. In function, the new committee was little different from the old one. It also inherited its administrative staff, its archival database, and most of its membership.[95] More than half of the original thirteen voting members of the WTAC (including Hopwood) had belonged to the predecessor committee.[96] These men undeniably brought to the new organization enormous experience and knowledge of war trade issues—but they also brought their entrenched opinions and history of antagonisms toward each other. Most of the supposedly new members also may be classed as the usual suspects. For instance, seats were given to Lord Emmott, Sir Nathaniel Highmore, and W. C. Bridgeman, all of the War Trade Department, as well as Sir George Cave, of the Foreign Office–controlled Contraband Committee. The most important difference between the old and new committees was the inclusion of a senior cabinet minister and three junior ministers. For the unenviable task of leading the WTAC, Asquith selected the ever-dependable Lord Crewe, one of the staunchest opponents of economic warfare, who still frequently stood in for the ailing Sir Edward Grey at the Foreign Office.[97] The three juniors were Lord Islington, the undersecretary at the India Office, who had been a member of the prewar Desart Committee (and thus was well acquainted with war trade issues) and who was the son of an admiral;[98] Lord Robert Cecil, the number two at the Foreign Office; and Arthur Steel-Maitland, undersecretary at the Colonial Office.[99]

At the first meeting of the WTAC, Lord Crewe explained to those assembled that their primary function was "to work out the details of various questions before they were submitted to the Cabinet."[100] The question immediately to hand was whether to relax controls over the reexport of comfort foods. Hopwood elaborated:

> The Prime Minister had said that there were various committees working in different directions . . . and that it was to be the duty of the War Trade Advisory committee to coordinate the work of these various bodies and to bring together the Chairmen and representatives of these committees into one committee. The scope of the Advisory Committee was not one of general inspection and initiation of policy; its business was to offer advice on matters submitted to it.[101]

The WTAC therefore cannot correctly be described as a "court of appeal" because it was a non-executive body and its advice was subject to ratification by the cabinet.[102] In practice, as the minutes amply demonstrate, the WTAC acted more as a conciliation service to mediate between warring departments and their satellite committees. In more ways than one it was a microcosm of the government. It adopted the same cabinet-style approach to problem solving, attempting to achieve departmental coordination through collective decision making. Like the cabinet, consideration was invariably slow, politicized, and characterized by a general lack of urgency. One important difference was that the chairman did not set the agenda. Any departmental representative could submit a topic for discussion or arbitration. Whenever necessary (and more often than not), a "non-interested" member would be tasked to form a subcommittee to investigate the issue and offer a supposedly impartial opinion.[103] The WTAC expended considerable resources (and time) generating phenomenally detailed reports on topics as diverse as the workings of the international nickel cartel and the coffee-drinking habits of Scandinavians.[104] In short, it lacked focus.

The difficulty in reaching rapid (or indeed any) consensus was exacerbated by a steady expansion in committee membership. Lloyd George insisted his Ministry of Munitions be given representation and nominated another former member of the old ESRC, Sir Leo Chiozza Money, a financial journalist with the reputation for being "especially competent" with figures.[105] In mid-November 1915, Ernest Pollock (formerly of the Unionist Business Committee) joined ex officio as the chairman of the Contraband Committee upon Sir George Cave's promotion to become solicitor general.[106] Yet Cave stayed on. Within three months membership swelled to twenty.

From the historian's perspective, the most useful result of the WTAC subsuming the ESRC was the keeping of much more detailed minutes as to precisely who argued what. Better than any other contemporary set of documents, the minutes of the WTAC record the arguments employed by the pro-trade lobby to justify their resistance to blockade policy—and well illustrate the level of sympathy for this view within the government. On no subject was this more evident than in the ensuing debate over the free export of comfort foods. Over the next five months or so, items such as coffee and cocoa were added, then removed, then readded, then finally removed again from the free list.[107] The issue of comfort foods became pivotal to the ultimate direction of blockade policy. Those in favor of treating them as free goods became increasingly impatient in demanding that the blockade of Germany be subordinated to domestic commercial interests. In November 1915, for instance, the Board of Trade pleaded that government vacillation had caused British coffee merchants to accumulate vast stocks—warehouses in London apparently contained enough coffee to provide for the population of the British Isles for the next two years—and that to suddenly prohibit its export seemed "unfair" and would result in bankruptcies.[108] The committee agreed and permission to export was granted. But no coffee was sold. It emerged there was a glut on the world market (due to overproduction in Brazil) and the Dutch were refusing to take British stock. This led to the rather ridiculous suggestion by Lord Crewe that the Foreign Office should, in effect, compel Holland to buy British coffee for clandestine reexport to Germany.[109] This leaked to the press, producing public outcry.[110]

The most important issue examined by the WTAC during the last quarter of 1915 was the idea of limiting the importation of strategic commodities by contiguous neutrals to "normal" prewar levels. In June 1915, at the Paris inter-Allied conference on blockade, the French government had demanded that rationing become the basis of Allied blockade policy. At their next meeting, in August, the Foreign Office delegates had signaled their general concurrence and assured their counterparts that rationing would be introduced as soon as the Board of Trade supplied the figures necessary to calculate the normal imports of various contiguous neutrals and so fix the size of their quotas.

It is most important to appreciate that at this stage the policy envisaged was the *forcible* rationing of European neutrals, very different from the policy actually introduced at the end of 1915 of "voluntary" or "negotiated" rationing. The official history of the blockade made no reference to this critical difference, and ever since it escaped scholarly notice.[111] That originally the Allies had planned forcible rationing is made very clear in a letter Crowe sent to the Board of Trade in August, in which he wrote: "As soon as the legitimate demand of a contiguous neutral state in regard to any particular rationed article has clearly and unmistakably been exceeded, the exports from all the Allies to those countries should be stopped and goods from neutral countries should be placed in the Prize Court."[112]

Forcible rationing promised major administrative advantages. Most important, no longer would the British authorities need to seek evidence to differentiate between legitimate and illegitimate neutral trade. The whole paraphernalia of end user certificates and neutral guarantees against reexportation, not to mention the enormous intelligence-gathering effort required to unmask enemy purchasing agents, could have been reduced. Each neutral would be allotted a fixed quota of controlled commodities, and it would be for neutral governments to police their trade and stop "dishonest action" by their traders to ensure their domestic requirements were met.

In assuring the French government that forcible rationing would soon be adopted, the Foreign Office had seriously underestimated both the administrative difficulties entailed and the strength of opposition within the British government. Ever since rationing had been first mooted, Walter Runciman had been lobbying furiously behind the scenes, arguing that further restrictions on British trade must cause irreparable damage to the economy. The Foreign Office had been aware of the Board of Trade's machinations—which included dragging its feet in supplying the statistics needed to implement neutral rationing—but seemingly did not take the challenge seriously.[113] Anticipating eventual cabinet approval, in early September Crowe asked Robert Craigie (author of the previous report on the nuts and bolts of rationing policy) to arrange an interdepartmental conference to finalize arrangements and prepare a discussion paper laying out a "definite programme."[114] On 14 September it was distributed.

A fortnight later, on 4 October, John Mellor, the procurator general, replied that the Contraband Department's proposed rationing scheme appeared to be based upon an overly optimistic interpretation of the recent *Kim* judgment. He explained it was all very well for the British government to decree that goods in excess of a neutral country's quota would be presumed intended for the enemy and therefore subject to seizure, but they must still be lawfully condemned. Mellor pointed out that although the prize court had recognized the admissibility of statistical evidence, the judge had gone on to indicate limits to the use of statistics in establishing a presumption of enemy destination. "While I think that evidence of excessive importation would be material on the question of the destination of the goods," Mellor counseled, "it would not, in my opinion, be safe to assume that such evidence would be accepted as sufficient *prima facie* proof of enemy destination."[115] There was no denying the charge: this mistaken assumption clearly underlay Robert Craigie's memorandum setting out a "definite programme," which, incidentally, had been endorsed by the departmental legate, Cecil Hurst.[116] The procurator general, in effect, had called into doubt the entire rationing policy and left the Foreign Office temporarily stunned.

A fortnight later, at the WTAC, the Contraband Department representatives still had not found an answer when, during an argument as to whether British oil companies should be allowed to export lubricating oil to Scandinavia, Lord Emmott turned and pointedly asked the Foreign Office representatives whether rationing was going to be implemented or not.[117] Lord Crewe directed the formation of a WTAC subcommittee to consider the question. Reporting to his superiors, Hurst begged that the "opportunity ought to be taken to try and arrange a definite plan of campaign on the subject of rationing policy."[118] "For months past we have talked about it and hankered after it," he reminded them, but "the real difficulty with which we are confronted is the objections that will be raised by neutral powers. I do not foresee any better opportunity arising for discussing these questions and getting the recommendations approved by the Cabinet."[119]

Hurst nevertheless cautioned that because the "subject bears so largely upon our relations with foreign powers that I think it is desirable that I should arrange for Sir Eyre Crowe to be invited to attend the [WTAC subcommittee] meetings and take part in the discussions."[120] This was done.[121] That Sir Eyre Crowe was not a member of that committee evidently did not matter. Clearly the Foreign Office recognized that its understanding of the issues was confused, and it did not want another department exploiting this vulnerability. More bluntly, there was no way the Foreign Office was going to allow a policy subcommittee with a direct channel to the cabinet to submit recommendations on a matter so intimately appertaining to foreign relations without having strong Foreign Office representation on that subcommittee.

Before the subcommittee convened, however, there occurred an important change in the policy context. For many months, the Wilson administration had been quietly growing increasingly vexed at British interferences with American trade to neutral Europe. Until the sinking of the *Lusitania* on 7 May 1915, the president had been on the verge of issuing a formal protest. For so long as there remained a chance of war with Germany, Wilson declined officially to press the matter and confined himself to expressing his displeasure unofficially through Colonel House. But since then "it had been a question of *when,* not *if*" the United States would contest the legality of Britain's retaliatory blockade.[122]

In August 1915, Spring Rice warned London that pressure upon the administration to take action against the "illegal" blockade was building.[123] When, therefore, U.S.-German relations began to thaw, in late September, Wilson and Robert Lansing returned to confronting the British over their "interferences with American ships and cargoes destined in good faith to neutral ports."[124] On 9 October, Lansing forwarded to Wilson the draft of a note "we have been working on for so long a time."[125] He reminded him of the "hundreds of letters from American importers and exporters asking what we are doing to relieve the situation in which they find themselves."[126] Wilson and Lansing finalized the text of their demarche on 21 October and then, at the president's insistence, transmitted it to London via diplomatic courier instead of cable.[127] When Walter Page presented it to the Foreign Office on Friday, 5 November, therefore, it hit like a bolt from the blue.[128] It was at once printed for distribution to the cabinet and discussed the following Monday.[129]

On all previous occasions when the United States formally protested British blockade policy, the president had allowed the two ambassadors—Walter Page in London and Spring Rice in Washington—first to review the draft and suggest amendments (inadvertently allowing British intelligence to see it too). Recently, however, Wilson had begun to discount Page's opinion, feeling he had become out of touch with American opinion and as a result had failed to represent the administration with sufficient vigor.[130] At the same time, administration officials had become distrustful of the British ambassador.[131] On 14 October, House's patience with Spring Rice snapped. The colonel had intended that day to discuss with him the draft demarche (albeit in outline, as he did not have an actual copy in hand). The ambassador arrived tired and in a bad mood, and angered House by responding to his opening remarks by affirming, "No matter how low our fortunes run, we will go to war [with the United States] before we will admit the principle of blockade as your government wishes to interpret it." Their conversation rapidly degenerated into a blazing row. "I lost my temper and told him I regarded his remarks as an insult," House recorded in his diary.[132] Evidently this outburst happened very early in the discussion—or Spring Rice was not paying attention to what House was saying—for after the ambassador returned to the embassy he sent Sir Edward Grey a telegram with the comment that the impending U.S. protest "was moderate and technical."[133] This was far from correct.

The American note, dated 21 October 1915 (or 5 November by British reckoning), represented a direct challenge to the new "maritime system"—as the Americans termed it—put in place the previous March by the British government. The United States government rejected Britain's right to "retaliate" against German infractions of international law by resorting to measures that also violated accepted legal principles (and which hurt American traders). As Sir Edward Grey explained to the cabinet, the United States "made it clear that they will not listen to any justification based on the ground of retaliation, and the use of this argument has no effect in the United States except to cause irritation and resentment."[134] It must be understood that the U.S. position was not an uncontestable expression of universally accepted legal principle. American legal theory (or interpretation thereof) did not automatically equate to international law.[135] So what was the actual significance of the American note? Arthur Link, the doyen of Wilson scholars, initially thought it "a powerful protest with a profoundly important immediate significance and menacing possibilities for the future," but later appeared to change his mind.[136] Most scholars have characterized it as a toothless "lawyer letter" devoid of any real significance and written mainly to appease disgruntled domestic businessmen. Ernest May correctly observed that "It did not demand that Britain give up her practices," nor did it threaten "measures of retaliation" if Britain remained obdurate.[137]

Did the note have any real impact upon British blockade policy? Scholars have given this question scant consideration. On 11 November 1915, Sir Edward Grey confidentially advised Colonel House, "I do not know what our [official] reply will be to your Note about Blockade & Contraband," but "my feeling in reading it was that, if we admitted all its contentions, we could not prevent Germany from trading, at any rate though neutral ports, as freely in time of war as in time of peace." He added: "The friction & trouble we have over this matter is so great I have often wished, in despair, to give it up: but that would go near to abdicating all chance of preventing Germany from being successful."[138] Grey's letter leaves its readers with little doubt that the British government would not now withdraw its retaliatory order-in-council.

Woodrow Wilson's reaction to this message is hard to gauge, for when House visited him to discuss the letter on the evening of 27 November 1915, he found the president much more interested in discussing the possibility of having Spring Rice recalled.[139] Sir Horace Plunkett, one of the unofficial conduits between Wilson and House, on one side, and Grey and Balfour, on the other, and who happened to be in Washington at that time, was told: "The chief trouble in the Anglo-American situation was the temperament of Sir Cecil Spring Rice."[140] In early December, Wilson decided that House should return to Europe for direct negotiations with the British leadership, confident that this way their differences over the blockade might be bridged. House was also tasked to arrange the recall of that "childish," "incompetent" "mischief-maker"—Sir Cecil Spring Rice.[141] The colonel arrived in England on 6 January 1916.[142]

As Grey had warned, the American note failed to induce any changes in current British blockade policy. The Foreign Office was not impressed with the arguments therein, or with Spring Rice's accompanying calls for immediate concessions to preserve Anglo-American relations. On 18 November, Crowe spoke for most when he remarked, "We constantly receive advice from Sir C Spring Rice that we must go on making further and further concessions to the US govt."[143] But experience had shown, he went on to add, that the more deference Britain paid to U.S. demands, the more the Americans appeared to expect. The subject was revisited several times over the next few weeks, yet on each occasion Crowe restated that concessions were pointless except to provide some temporary relief from Wilsonian complaints.[144]

In pressing this view, Crowe received support from the highly regarded Lord Eustace Percy. The former number three at the Washington embassy agreed that the "recent somewhat bellicose utterances" from across the Atlantic needed to be seen more as expressions of U.S. irritation at the "confusion and muddle" attending the implementation of British blockade policy.[145] The indispensable Eric Drummond (1876–1951), private secretary to Sir Edward Grey (and later Lord Perth, the first secretary-general of the League of Nations), agreed "that American opinion chiefly objects to our blockade policy on the grounds that it is not really effective in shortening the war."[146] Others agreed that the problem lay in the ineffectiveness of Spring Rice.[147] But Grey, backed by Nicolson, his permanent secretary, refused even to consider relieving his old friend.[148] Upon learning that Colonel House was en route back to London, the Foreign Office suspended further discussion until his arrival.

While the American protest had no discernible impact upon current blockade policy, it certainly made an impression upon contemplation of future policy. Buried in its middle was an explicit warning to the British government not to draw any more "conjectural conclusions" from trade statistics.[149] This, of course, was a reference to the recent *Kim* judgment against the Chicago meatpackers. This warning caused the WTAC to look much more closely at the legal aspects associated with the new policy of compulsory rationing for neutrals. To this end, Lord Crewe solicited an opinion from Dr. Alexander Pearce Higgins (1865–1935), deputy (though de facto) Whewell Professor of International Law at Cambridge University.[150] Replying on 19 November, Higgins confirmed Mellor's opinion that after "keeping in view in particular the points raised in the American note," there existed no justification under current international law for the prize court to condemn a cargo seized merely because it would have constituted an importation in excess of the figure shown by statistics to be the normal requirements for that country. At best, he counseled, the *Kim* case "will have the effect of creating an atmosphere of suspicion surrounding the goods, but this fact alone will not justify condemnation."[151] The burden of proof remained with the prosecution to demonstrate that each specific parcel of goods was intended for resale to the enemy. This gloomy assessment was reflected in a WTAC subcommittee report circulated the following month.[152] In a concise three-page report, the subcommittee, which Crowe was advising, warned that forcible rationing must inflame neutral opinion and therefore should not be adopted. Instead, the government might try to induce neutrals voluntarily to ration their own imports.[153]

In making this recommendation, the WTAC subcommittee (and Crowe) looked to recent modifications to the agreement with the Netherlands Overseas Trust (NOT). This organization, consisting of leading Dutch merchants and bankers, had been set up in early 1915 and was recognized by the Dutch government as being solely responsible for the importation of commodities that had been classed by the Allies as contraband. In return for unfettered importation, the NOT guaranteed not to reexport the goods consigned to it. In September 1915, the Foreign Office had induced the Dutch "voluntarily" to limit their import of raw cotton. The apparent success of this arrangement encouraged the Foreign Office, after the arrival of the American note, to apply this "voluntary rationing" principle to Denmark.[154] Accordingly, on 16 November the Foreign Office rapidly negotiated a treaty recognizing the Merchants' Guild of Copenhagen and the Industrial Association of Denmark as the *associations de négociants* solely responsible for the importation of contraband items into that country.[155] But upon whose authority? The WTAC subcommittee on neutral rationing had not yet reported (and would not until mid-December).

Two days later, on 18 November, at the next scheduled WTAC meeting, this question was put to Lord Robert Cecil, the undersecretary of state at the Foreign Office, whose responsibilities recently had been expanded to encompass the Contraband Department. He bluntly replied that the Foreign Office "did not ask the Committee to pass an opinion upon this matter as it was in reality a Foreign Office negotiation with certain Danish Delegates. He further stated that the [rationing] sub-Committee had been asked to deal with the broad principles only."[156] If this was true, then what was the purpose of the subcommittee? Or of the WTAC, for that matter?

Several members of the WTAC strongly disputed the Foreign Office contention that it was solely responsible for framing policy on neutral rationing. Ernest Pollock, the new chairman of the Contraband Committee, was particularly forceful in his objections, reminding everyone that in the past neutrals' promises to restrict their trade had been proven worthless. "Guarantees he said are taken, but the amounts which have gone in [imported] prove that the real destination can only be Germany." In fact, Holland was already violating her latest promise to ration her importation of food. "We allow the Dutch 225,000 tons of Maize per quarter," he explained, and while this amount had been reached already, still more cargoes were en route. Pollock wanted to apply the terms of the agreement with the NOT and seize these additional cargoes, but the Foreign Office demurred. With Lord Robert

Cecil's approval, "Mr. Hurst, in reply, pointed out that under our agreement with the NOT we had no power to ration Holland, we only desired to persuade the NOT to ration itself."[157]

By now well fired up, Pollock proceeded to denounce as "thoroughly unsatisfactory" the Foreign Office's tolerance of European neutrals selling their domestic produce to Germany and then being allowed freely to import replacements.[158] This surely, he argued, was an illegitimate practice and should be stopped. (A year earlier, Winston Churchill had made the same point.) Although precise figures were unavailable to the WTAC, it was obvious enough that the small neutral European states were supplying a significant percentage of the foodstuffs imported to Germany. During the first eleven months of 1915, sources show, Germany imported roughly a million tons of Dutch-produced food, and she brought in yet more in 1916.[159] But for these sources, the German chancellor reputedly told a gathering of Prussian politicians, Germany would have collapsed.[160] Of course the WTAC did not know this, but it did know that "Demark sells all her own Bacon, owing to the high prices offered by Germany, and revictuals herself with the cheaper material from the USA."[161] Leverton Harris agreed with Pollock and chimed in that it seemed equally ridiculous that Sweden should be allowed to sell all her domestically mined copper to Germany and then import 14,000 tons from the United States during the first nine months of the year.[162]

On 2 December 1915, Sir Leo Money of the Ministry of Munitions circulated a memorandum with the latest statistics showing the magnitude of re-exports to Scandinavia during the period January to September 1915. From these he inferred, "It is impossible to resist the conclusion that the United Kingdom herself, through her own traders, has played a part in supplying Germany with over-sea produce in this present year [1915]."[163] He pointedly "urged the Board of Trade to issue a further notice in the press warning British traders to exercise caution in their trade with neutral countries."[164] This was subsequently done, but in a way that Money disapproved of. Several weeks later he again harangued the WTAC over British exports to Europe. "Was not the UK acting as a base of supplies to the enemy? This raised the question urged by the United States of America, that while we restrict the trade of neutrals, when it suits our policy, we allow our own traders to continue to trade with the enemy."[165] Frustration at the ineffectiveness of the blockade and anger at the Foreign Office's unilateral behavior were threatening to boil over.

A New Twist: Enter Sir John Jellicoe

We need now to wind the narrative back a few months and examine recent events inside the Admiralty. After the departure of Winston Churchill and Admiral Lord Fisher in May 1915, in matters relating to the blockade the new naval leadership exhibited extraordinarily little energy. When, in June, Lord Crewe had advanced Sir Edward Grey's proposition that relaxation of the blockade might act to Britain's advantage, Arthur Balfour, the First Lord of the Admiralty, expressed no formal objection either verbal or written. Nor, it appears, did he come under any pressure to do so from Admiral Sir Henry Jackson, now First Sea Lord. As the debate rumbled on from June into July, the First Lord maintained his silence. Lord Curzon once characterized Balfour as "inscrutable" in the cabinet: "sitting silent and detached as though he were a spectator on Mars, observing through a powerful telescope a fight between the astral inhabitants of Saturn."[166] Was Balfour's silence during cabinet discussion of the blockade thus merely symptomatic of his normal attitude, or maybe some clever political ploy? Or did he just want to avoid provoking a confrontation?[167]

In August 1915, Balfour told Lord Emmott of the War Trade Department that the Admiralty no longer claimed responsibility for blockade policy. "As I conceive the matter," he wrote, "the Admiralty as such have no policy one way or the other as regards trade. No doubt, as a department, they may be interested in some special commodity of which they happen to be large users; but this is a different matter."[168] Balfour further stated that, as far as he understood the delineation of responsibilities, blockade policy and licensing procedures were the domain of the Foreign Office and Board of Trade, respectively—"and of course the government as a whole."[169] Emmott was astonished and at once replied:

> Your observation that the Adm[iralty], qua Admiralty, have no policy as regards trade; I can only assure you that is not my experience at the W[ar] T[rade] Department. With or without the knowledge of the 1st Lord [i.e., Balfour], the T[rade] D[ivision] of the Admiralty has expressed the strongest views on trade questions.[170]

Emmott went on to list the various trade committees on which the Admiralty was represented and the difficulties he daily encountered in dealing with their naval representatives.

Amusingly, the same day that Balfour disclaimed Admiralty responsibility for policy formulation, the Admiralty secretary formally requested that the Cornhill Committee instruct British insurers to refuse policies on all British-made goods exported to Holland and Scandinavia.[171] The Cornhill Committee, as readers will recall, was the body responsible for monitoring the City of London, and its leading lights included Leverton Harris and Brand of the Admiralty staff trade division. Possibly Balfour was ignorant of this letter being dispatched, but if so, this does not reflect well on his grip over his department. In any case, he apparently took action. Suggestively, the Admiralty representatives to the Cornhill Committee were absent from the meeting at which this request was discussed. In consequence, no one challenged the Foreign Office representative who told the Cornhill Committee, "There is no justification for interfering with the insurance of goods shipped from this country under license granted by the War Trade Department."[172] Britain had signed treaties with all four governments and also with trade associations in the same countries, and an embargo on maritime insurance would violate the spirit of those agreements.[173]

Balfour's lack of vigor incensed naval officers. None was more vocal than Admiral Sir John Jellicoe, the fleet commander. As early as March 1915, Jellicoe had voiced puzzlement at London's prosecution of blockade policy, especially the release of so many neutral merchantmen caught carrying contraband items to neutral European destinations. The captures had been lawful and the officers under his command had followed cabinet-approved fleet orders to the letter—so why, he enquired, were the majority of these vessels subsequently released without even examination?[174] There is no doubt that Jellicoe genuinely found the Admiralty's refusal to press for rigorous enforcement of declared policy inexplicable.[175]

After his requests for explanations were rebuffed, Jellicoe formed at his base in Scotland his own private economic intelligence unit. To head it, he recruited Edward Hilton Young (1879–1960), a socially prominent London barrister and Liberal MP with expertise in the financial aspects of corporate law. Young had published two books: *Foreign Companies and Other Corporations* (1912) and *The System of National Finance* (1915).[176] His superior credentials as a fiscal analyst are further underlined by his appointment, after the war, as financial secretary to the Treasury and his election, in 1936, as president of the Royal Statistical Society. In matters relating to finance and trade, in other words, the evaluations of Lieutenant Young, RNVR, were not the musings of a naval amateur.

It is obvious that the fleet's economic intelligence unit could not have possessed anything like the information resources available in London. This fact is so self-evident it raises questions about the purpose of this unit—or rather the purpose of the information it generated. From the various reports Young compiled, we can see he relied chiefly upon published data and official government reports. But Young, along with many other officers in the fleet, was well connected both politically and socially. Through such unofficial channels he obtained much additional information. On top of that, sensitive material came in from various middle-level naval officers working within the blockade bureaucracy who disagreed with official policy. Likely candidates include Montagu Consett, the outspoken naval attaché in Scandinavia; Guy Gaunt, the more tactful but similarly opinionated naval attaché in Washington, D.C.; and Charles Dormer and Horace Longden, the Admiralty liaison officers to the War Trade Department and the Contraband Committee, respectively. Captain Richard Webb and the rest of the Naval Staff Trade Division were also regarded as prime suspects.[177] To what extent Sir John Jellicoe and his staff encouraged officers to circumvent the chain of command cannot be determined. Nevertheless, it remains a fact that Jellicoe frequently displayed an uncanny knowledge of subjects unconnected with his main responsibilities.

During the second half of 1915, Jellicoe became increasingly outspoken in his correspondence with the Admiralty as Young uncovered more and more evidence of government laxity in enforcing published blockade procedures. The fleet commander protested that the Foreign Office system of blockade based upon promises by neutrals not to reexport contraband to Germany simply was not working, and he was among the first to advocate forcible rationing for contiguous neutrals.[178] In June 1915, barely a week after the Paris conference at which this possibility was first seriously raised, Jellicoe implored the Admiralty to support the change.

Throughout August, Jellicoe subjected the Admiralty to an intensive barrage of letters punctuated with snippets of annoyingly embarrassing information gathered by Young that suggested problems. On the third of that month, for instance, he cited statistics showing a recent rise in British reexports of cotton to contiguous neutrals and asked for an explanation.[179] The next day, he protested the systematic release of neutral vessels carrying contraband items to Europe and invited explanation for why the share prices of the sixteen leading Danish shipping companies had risen on average by 54.7 percent since the beginning of the war.[180] Of course, these factoids proved little, if anything, but they helped foster suspicions, and the Admiralty undoubtedly found them awkward and discomfiting—which is probably exactly what the admiral intended. On the twenty-seventh, Jellicoe leveled more specific charges, submitting statistics from which he inferred "that Great Britain has become a base for the supply to Germany via neutral countries of certain goods."[181] His reasoning may have been slightly wide of the mark, but his general complaint was by no means fanciful and therefore could not be ignored.

Jellicoe's attacks culminated on 1 September 1915 in a letter claiming the fleet had lost confidence in London's management of the blockade.

> I am strongly of opinion that the pressure of our sea power upon Germany as at present applied, cannot seriously inconvenience that country. It is in our power to cause her the greatest embarrassment, but instead we are only producing a situation of slight inconvenience. She is doing her best to stop our trade and I urge that we should let every other consideration give way to the one main issue, to crush her, both economically, and when the opportunity offers, by force of arms.[182]

Appended to the letter was a statistical report compiled by Hilton Young highlighting discrepancies in various official figures and showing how poorly the contiguous neutrals were living up to their guarantees not to reexport contraband to Germany.[183]

Such outspokenness by the fleet commander mandated an official response. But Balfour rapidly discovered that forging an appropriate reply was complicated by the sympathy the admiral's views enjoyed among the Admiralty middle-level staff. Captain Richard Webb, the head of the trade division, for instance, acerbically remarked that Jellicoe's figures probably underestimated the magnitude of the problem.[184] The officer assigned to dissect Young's statistical appendix pointed out a few trifling errors in his understanding of certain procedures, then told his chiefs, "I cordially concur with the entire memorandum."[185] The only member of the Admiralty to voice any sort of objection was Sir Francis Hopwood, the civil servant who, as head of the ESRC, knew more than most about blockade policy.[186] Yet even Hopwood hesitated to contradict the admiral: he merely ventured that perhaps the position was more complicated than the fleet commander had allowed, and perhaps he did not fully comprehend the diplomatic aspects.[187] Undeniably there was some truth here—but again, this did not invalidate the broad thrust of Jellicoe's criticisms that there existed serious inconsistencies between British policy and practice. Admiral Jackson, the First Sea Lord, cryptically concurred that Jellicoe should "be informed of the political difficulties involved: and also, if it can be done truthfully, that the distant blockade is more than of slight inconvenience to the enemy."[188] The use of the phrase "if it can be done truthfully" is as interesting as it is ambiguous. Did he mean the Admiralty had not been telling the truth to the fleet commander, or that someone had suggested deliberately misleading him? Or was this simply an off-the-cuff remark that merely reflected his own long-standing doubts over the efficacy of economic warfare?

Perhaps sensing there was, in fact, no way to respond to Jellicoe's complaints "truthfully" without antagonizing most of the Naval Staff, Balfour endeavored to sidestep. Ignoring the fleet commander's missive clearly was not an option, so instead he had it forwarded to the Foreign Office. However, anxious not to provoke a row with Grey, he deftly instructed it be sent unofficially to the interdepartmental Contraband Committee, which sat at the Foreign Office in the same office space as Crowe's Contraband Department. Balfour further mandated that the covering letter emphasize that the Admiralty did "*not* express agreement with the C-in-C's views."[189] In disposing of Jellicoe's letter in this acrobatic manner, Balfour managed to avoid tangling with the commander in chief and to acquaint the Foreign Office with the level of unhappiness in the fleet over its handling of blockade policy, while not giving offense by saying so officially.

This adroit maneuver might just have worked had not Sir George Cave, the chairman of the Contraband Committee, been so obtuse. In a patronizing tone, Cave replied to Jellicoe that vessels detained by the fleet were released only after the neutral country to which they were destined had provided Britain with a guarantee that their cargoes would not be reexported.[190] Jellicoe knew this! Had Cave bothered to do more than glance at the first page of the admiral's letter, he would have seen that Jellicoe's main complaint was that contiguous neutrals were demonstrably failing to live up to their promises.[191] This, moreover, had been the entire focus of the attached appendix, compiled by Hilton Young. Commenting upon the exchange, Captain Webb sighed that Jellicoe was wasting his time trying to debate blockade policy with the Foreign Office.[192]

There is another possible explanation for why the First Lord of the Admiralty treated the fleet commander's complaints in this unconventional manner. It is likely that Balfour realized that Jellicoe's letters were part of a much broader challenge to official blockade policy. Recently the fleet commander had circumvented the proper chain of command by writing on blockade policy to another senior cabinet minister. In a letter to Rear Admiral Dudley de Chair, commanding the 10th Cruiser Squadron patrolling the northern approaches, Jellicoe admitted, "I am still arguing with the Admiralty about contraband and I have started a private correspondence with McKenna on the subject of additions."[193] He reported that McKenna was doing his best to help but that "the government is in mortal dread of offending some of the neutral powers."[194] A further indication that Jellicoe was playing political games was his secret meetings with Admiral Lord Fisher, who at that time was agitating to be reinstated as First Sea Lord or at least gain a seat on the War Committee—the latest incarnation of the political-military executive responsible for the strategic direction of the war.[195] Writing to his wife from France, Winston Churchill acknowledged (with a trace of envy) that Fisher enjoyed a political following and that there existed a real possibility he might be recalled.[196]

On behalf of the Admiralty, the Second Sea Lord wrote unofficially to Jellicoe warning that he was playing with political fire and imploring him to desist.[197] Jellicoe ignored this request and well into 1916 continued to indulge in political activism, for such it was. In this context it is worth reflecting that in mid-1915, Jellicoe was the last nationally recognized British military leader with an unblemished reputation and who enjoyed massive popular approval. Indeed, until the disastrous Battle of Jutland, public confidence in the Navy remained high and there was widespread expectation the fleet would (somehow) deliver the decisive blow to win the war. This conferred upon Jellicoe tremendous latent political power. Given the fragility of the coalition government during the fall of 1915, the possibility that the admiral might publicly voice his dissatisfaction with official policy was a prospect ministers could not afford to ignore. His outspokenness appeared threatening.

Beginning in October 1915, Balfour changed his approach and began routinely forwarding Jellicoe's letters to the Foreign Office for comment—through official channels—and even consulted him on how best to reply to the latest American demarche.[198] What induced the First Lord to handle the fleet commander with more solicitousness cannot be ascertained from the records, but we do know that the Contraband Department became steadily more irritated at the resultant stream of "not very helpful criticism."[199] For the most part its staff dismissed Jellicoe's complaints as based upon "ignorance of what we have done."[200] Irritation induced officials to become less and less cooperative in supplying the Admiralty—especially Jellicoe—with any information.[201]

Even more annoying, from the Foreign Office perspective, was that the admiral's repeated jabs emboldened middle-level Admiralty staff officers to find the courage and voice their dissent with Foreign Office policy. "We here suffer daily from the lucubrations of Cmdr. Longden on the contraband committee," a clearly irked Crowe wrote to Walter Runciman on 19 November 1915; "I should very much like to hear from you a few words on these matters."[202] Crowe went on in this letter to vent his spleen against Captain Consett, the naval attaché for Scandinavia, and closed with a censure directed against all naval officers: "This office is beginning to feel exceedingly sore at the way the Admiralty are treading on everyone's toes, and I am experiencing the greatest difficulties in preventing actual rows and resignations. The present is only one of many instances of the overbearing attitude of our naval authorities."[203]

Toward the end of 1915, Jellicoe tightened his focus of attack upon the Foreign Office system of treaties with neutrals.[204] Somehow he had learned that the contiguous neutrals were being allowed to sell their domestic produce and "revictual" themselves from the United States (this was not yet generally known). "By means of the guarantees exacted," he scathingly wrote, "it is no doubt hoped to prevent these commodities from finding their way to the enemy. But provision is not made, apparently, to prevent the exportation to Germany of a like quantity of goods already in the neutral country concerned, on arrival of the consignments which we have passed."[205]

Perhaps not coincidentally, just nine days later Ernest Pollock voiced exactly the same complaint in a WTAC meeting.[206] Inadvertently or otherwise (and it is quite possible the two were in communication), Jellicoe had trespassed into a policy debate then under way over whether Britain should ration imports into contiguous neutrals, and if so, how. The Contraband Department of the Foreign Office resented the admiral's contemptuous rejection of "neutral guarantees." "I do not see how," wrote one official, "the Contraband Comm'te could be stricter towards cargoes than they are being."[207] Alwyn Parker, the deputy, agreed. "I think rationing is only possible by means of agreements such as that with Denmark, of which there is abundant evidence that the Admiralty disapprove" and "to which the Commander-in-Chief takes exception."[208]

On 18 December 1915, Admiral Sir John Jellicoe journeyed to London for talks with Lord Robert Cecil. This unprecedented meeting had been arranged by Arthur Balfour (Cecil's first cousin), who also attended along with Leverton Harris.[209] The minutes show Jellicoe was explicit in his criticisms: "He told us that the officers of the fleet were very uneasy and suggested that more drastic measures should be taken." In reply, Cecil restated the diplomatic and legal obstacles to more rigorous enforcement and why compulsory rationing was impracticable. He promised to send Jellicoe some papers on the subject and invited him to comment upon them. In effect, the political head of the Foreign Office Contraband Department feigned to ask the fleet commander for his endorsement of voluntary rationing.[210] Lord Robert Cecil's solicitude for Jellicoe's opinion was remarkable and must be seen as a reflection of his concern.

The plausibility of this interpretation seems greater when one appreciates that their meeting took place against the background of a major political storm, arguably the most serious attack upon the government since the formation of the coalition cabinet. The fleet's unhappiness with the management of the blockade had become the subject of society gossip, and it was widely known "that the Navy & Jellicoe in particular are in despair about the blockade."[211] "I do not expect any important concessions to our demands," Walter Page advised Woodrow Wilson on the last day of 1915. "The Navy party has public opinion squarely behind it."[212]

Public Protest and Parliamentary Scrutiny

Heightened public concern over the effectivness of the blockade owed much to recent stories in the press reporting government laxity and general unhappiness within the Navy.[213] On 2 November 1915, the prime minister delivered to Parliament a statement on the "naval and military situation"—the first in nearly a year—that left the House of Commons cold.[214] In the debate that followed, the government came in for much criticism from the backbenches. Historians have frequently commented upon remarks made by Edward Carson, recently resigned from the cabinet, who attributed British military ineffectiveness to Asquith's dithering and the general unwieldiness of government decision making, and who wanted the creation of a small "war cabinet" empowered to make all important decisions.[215] For our story, however, much more important was a later speech delivered by Admiral Lord Charles Beresford (Jacky Fisher's old nemesis and since 1910 Member of Parliament for Portsmouth). Never one to pull his punches, Charlie B. gave voice to public gossip that the Foreign Office had been "interfering with the actions of the fleet" in prosecuting the blockade of Germany. So inflammatory were his remarks that the usually taciturn Lord Robert Cecil was moved to rise in protest.[216] In defending his department, Cecil cited statistics to demonstrate the effectiveness of the blockade. Unluckily, the numbers he used contradicted those Sir Edward Grey had given to the U.S. secretary of state and which just recently had been published in the U.S. press. More unluckily still, Sir Alfred Markham (a friend of Lloyd George) had copies to hand and was thus able immediately to point out the discrepancy.[217] Discomfited, Cecil evaded all further questions before sitting down.[218] The following day the press gleefully seized upon the contradiction.

A few weeks later, news of the Foreign Office's secret trade deal with Denmark leaked to the *Morning Post,* causing a furor. The government's refusal to divulge any details to Parliament added fuel to the fire.[219] An attempt by the Foreign Office to dampen criticism by clandestinely showing the editor of that newspaper, Howell Gwynne, a copy of the Danish treaty backfired.[220] Afterward Gwynne wrote to Lady Bathurst, the owner of the *Morning Post:*

> While I cannot say that all our criticisms of the Agreement were absolutely justified, what I do say is, that my visit to the Foreign Office shows that they do not realise that the blockade could be ever so much stricter if only they put their hearts into it. The evil of the matter is, that the Admiralty and the Foreign Office do not pull together, and there are departmental quarrels.[221]

To Gwynne, this was a revelation.

The government's shuffling responses to parliamentary criticism of its blockade policy contributed greatly to its public image of muddle and irresolution. On 12 December 1915, Lord Robert Cecil predicted in a letter to his wife that the government soon must fall. "I doubt it will last over Christmas," he wrote. "But *what* is to take its place?"[222] Several days later, another (former) liberal junior minister tartly remarked in Parliament:

> It seems rather a curious thing that during the whole of the continual attacks in the House of Commons the Secretary of State for Foreign Affairs [Grey] has never himself dealt with the matter but has left it entirely to the Under-Secretary [Cecil]; and the Under-Secretary, it has been noticed, has constantly said that he does not know the position and will have to make inquiry.[223]

Attacks on blockade policy culminated, on 23 December, in a pre-recess adjournment debate. Successive Members of Parliament rose to demand that the government respond to public "dissatisfaction" and issue "a stronger statement than it has yet been able to do with regard to the work of the blockade."[224] Standing to reply, Cecil found the House of Commons in no mood to be lectured on the constraints of international law or the necessity of respecting neutral rights.[225] By this stage, perceptions of government incompetence had gathered so much momentum that the details and validity of the criticisms were beside the point. "There may be a good explanation," one backbencher remarked, "but so far as we can judge the Navy is practically rendered impotent in achieving that great stroke towards victory of which we all believe it capable."[226]

Alas, there is no record of how the prime minister or his cabinet reacted to this embarrassment; they were too busy dealing with other matters. That same week, the long-brewing storm over conscription finally broke, marking "the climax of 6 months of discontent & protest," as Asquith observed to Edwin Montagu.[227] The premier was far too busy trying to hold his government together in the midst of the ensuing political crisis to give serious thought to blockade matters. While the conscription story is too well known to require detailed recounting here, the gist was that Lloyd George and most of the Conservatives threatened to resign unless conscription was introduced, while McKenna, Runciman, Grey, Balfour, Simon, and Birrell warned they would resign if it was.[228] Ultimately, a compromise was found, and on 4 January 1916, the Military Service Bill was introduced before Parliament.[229] There remained, however, more than a month of bickering over the exact distribution of manpower between the Army and industry.[230]

Over the same period, the cabinet was also obliged to respond to a request from the new chief of the Imperial General Staff for a major summer offensive at the Somme. General Sir William "Wully" Robertson was uncompromising in his belief that the only path to victory was on the western front. Again the story is well known. Ministers were initially unenthusiastic, doubtful of success, and fearful of the human cost. Sir Edward Grey spoke for many when he wrote to the prime minister on 14 January 1916:

> I am much impressed by the arguments against the offensive, but I am still more impressed by the fact that all military opinion is united in favor of it and that nothing else is suggested as possible, except a prolonged defensive, to end in the exhaustion of Germany. I do not believe that a

> satisfactory peace can be secured only by the policy of exhausting Germany. I think that Germany will be exhausted before another year is over, and that the same is true of others; and, if things remain as they are, I think there will be a sort of general collapse and inconclusive peace before next winter. I believe that the only chance of victory is to hammer the Germans hard in the first 8 months of this year. If that is impossible, we had better make up our minds to an inconclusive peace.[231]

For the purposes of this study the significance of this document lies in the foreign secretary's de facto admission he possessed no confidence that the blockade would prove ultimately to be a decisive strategic weapon. Through in the past he had avowed similar sentiments, never before had he said so in such unequivocal language. The absence of sufficient evidence renders it difficult to gauge the extent to which his cabinet colleagues shared this view, that relying on the blockade to win the war was not a serious strategic option. The fact is that, one by one, the members of the political leadership were induced to withdraw their objections to the ill-fated Somme offensive. On 25 January 1916, Robertson's request was approved.

While the cabinet deliberated military matters for the year ahead, the wrangling over blockade policy refused to abate. Stung by the public criticism of his department, and convinced that naval officers were chiefly responsible, Sir Eyre Crowe composed a rebuttal intended "to give an account of the manner in which the sea power of the British Empire has been used during the present war for the purpose of intercepting Germany's imports and exports."[232] In fact, the document said almost nothing about sea power, providing its readers instead with a summation of Foreign Office blockade policy that emphasized the legal and technical obstacles in "distinguishing between goods with an enemy destination from those with a genuine neutral destination."[233] Yet it did contain a useful commentary on how the application of sea power was effectively hamstrung by the disconnect between international law and the actual functioning of the modern commercial system. It further explained:

> The conditions of modern commerce offer almost infinite opportunities of concealing the real nature of a transaction, and every device which the ingenuity of the persons concerned, or their lawyers, could suggest has been employed to give to shipments intended for Germany the appearance of genuine transactions with a neutral country.[234]

Interestingly, the Foreign Office printed two versions of this paper. The original, dated 28 December 1915, was distributed to cabinet—though it is not clear on precisely what date. A modified version was laid before the House of Commons on 4 January 1916 and published the next day as a parliamentary white paper entitled "Statement of the Measures Adopted to Intercept the Sea Borne Commerce of Germany."[235] The difference between the two may be found in the introduction; the cabinet version contained criticism of Royal Navy leadership and claimed the Admiralty were largely responsible for the unsatisfactory state of international law, insisting they had endorsed the stance taken by British delegates at the prewar international conferences on the laws of war at sea.[236] Otherwise, in function and substance, the two versions were identical. In both it was claimed that the blockade "is already successful to a degree which good judges both here and in Germany thought absolutely impossible, and its efficiency is growing day by day. It is right to add that these results have been obtained without any serious friction with any neutral country."[237] In actuality, as has been made abundantly clear, all this was far from the truth.

Far from defusing public criticism of the Foreign Office, the publication of the white paper caused an explosion. Sir W. Graham Greene, the Admiralty secretary, who had been intimately associated with the prewar debate on international maritime law, protested to Balfour that the document "seriously misrepresents the position of the Admiralty" and must not be allowed to go unchallenged.[238] Anxious not to be drawn into another row with the Foreign Office, the First Lord prevaricated and tried (unsuccessfully) to smother the subject. But Greene's anger was as nothing compared to that of Jellicoe, who took strong exception to the statement that the blockade was proving a good deal more effective than some (i.e., naval officers) were arguing.

Writing to the Admiralty on 10 January 1916, the fleet commander drew attention to inconsistencies contained in the white paper and contradictions therein with official War Trade Department figures.[239] Over the previous year, he pointed out, the importation of animal fodder into the four northern neutrals had been more than a million tons above their normal requirements; from this he inferred that "the greater part of this excess has gone to the enemy in the shape of live stock and meat."[240] Writing to Lord Cecil several days later, the admiral drew attention to figures showing large increases in the importation of meat, coffee, fruit, and mineral oils into the contiguous neutrals. "But according to the White Paper," Jellicoe remarked, "it would appear to be thought that little of it finds its way to the enemy."[241]

"I write letter after letter on the blockade questions, but the FO seems quite imbecile," Jellicoe simultaneously moaned to Admiral Lord Fisher. "They are afraid of their own shadows and imagine every neutral is anxious to go to war with use and can do us harm. I don't believe it and never shall till I see the declaration of the war."[242] Fisher agreed.[243]

Howell Gwynne, editor of the *Morning Post,* found the white paper equally unpersuasive, and throughout January 1916 his newspaper remained in full cry against blockade policy. That month he published a series of articles under the banner "The Blockade Farce" that made effective use of U.S. trade figures to illustrate increased American exports to contiguous neutrals.[244] "Had the Navy not been hampered by the Foreign Office," Gwynne thundered in one editorial, "it is probable that Germany before this would have been forced to sue of terms or to surrender, having been starved into submission."[245] Less sensational but far more impressive was the exposé on Danish trade by Basil Clarke of the *Daily Mail.* This intrepid war journalist had traveled to Denmark and somehow managed to obtain a set of Danish trade figures (which of course were highly confidential) that purported to show the development, since the beginning of the war, of an enormous transit trade from Britain and the United States to Germany. The *Times* too devoted considerable space to discussion of the blockade.[246]

Quickly these accusations were taken up in Parliament. Particularly damaging was a speech by Lord Sydenham (formerly Sir George Clarke), the prominent defense expert and former CID secretary. On 13 January 1916, he rose in the House of Lords to direct Parliament's attention to the "very remarkable and somewhat disturbing" increase in British exports to contiguous neutrals.[247] Offering the example of cocoa, he asked the government to explain why exports to Europe had increased fivefold since the beginning of the war. But his most significant remark was the statement "It was always certain that economic pressure must play a great part—perhaps the greatest part—in bringing this war to an end; and if we had acted as the Northern States did in the [American] civil war I am perfectly certain we should have had peace before this."[248]

Editorials, letters, and speeches such as those cited above induced Lord Robert Cecil to become more and more concerned that mismanagement of the blockade was becoming a rallying point for opponents of the government. Writing to one confidant, he confessed his fear

> that the rising war passion in this country may drive us into some blockade actions which it would not be easy to defend. There are all the

> signs of a great increase in public temperature, due mainly to the stress and strain of war and to the reckless irresponsibility of journalists.[249]

He went on to explain:

> I am not afraid of the existing House of Commons, but I am of some great popular movement which would sweep away all constitutional barriers. I am always telling the ministers of the northern neutrals [i.e., Scandinavia and Holland] what danger they are in, but they naturally only believe that I am talking diplomatically.[250]

Meeting later that week with Colonel House, recently arrived from the United States, Cecil contradicted Grey by affirming that the present public mood disallowed any possibility of British concessions to the United States over blockade policy.[251] Robert Skinner, the U.S. consul general, independently confirmed:

> The [British] Government is being taken to task with great violence for having permitted large quantities of goods to reach Germany, and public opinion is in such an angry frame of mind that it is extremely improbable that the blockade policy can be modified in the direction of greater liberality. The conviction prevails that Germany is suffering severely from economic pressure, and there appears to be a demand for the application of still greater pressure.[252]

On 12 January 1916, Cecil bluntly told Sir Edward Grey that the only way to defuse criticism of government blockade policy was to improve the policy's effectiveness by overhauling the administrative machinery for enforcement. Lord Crewe's War Trade Advisory Committee, he declared, set up after the rejection of the Montagu scheme, had failed to reconcile the departmental differences that were hobbling consistent and effective implementation.[253] "I venture to submit that our blockade policy has become so important and complex, that its direction demands the undivided attention of a cabinet minister," Cecil wrote. "What is wanted is unity of direction and responsibility."[254] It is not clear when, exactly, Grey passed this recommendation on to the prime minister, but it does not much matter.[255] The same week the same message reached the cabinet via a different route.

On 18 January 1916, Edwin Montagu returned to the cabinet as chancellor for the Duchy of Lancaster (while retaining his position as financial secretary to the Treasury) and at once resurrected his plan for a ministry of blockade.[256] Three days after the meeting, Winston Churchill received from his sister-in-law a satirical skit of what transpired. It runs as follows:

> *The Cabinet.*
> Sir E. Grey: "I think something ought to be done about the 3 committees (he forgot the other 15) & a minister appointed to control them."—sniffs—
> PM. "I thought something had been done, Grey."—
> Montagu: (his first Cabinet since he resigned eight months ago) "In May at my last Cabinet I drew your attentions to the fact that there ought to be a minister appointed to be responsible for the 18 (not 3) committees."
> Lord Curzon—"Yes indeed—and I now recall that it was me myself I offered as the said minister." Sniffs.
> PM: "Well I think we ought to appoint a committee to look in to this"—[257]

What gives this parody credibility is the allusion to Curzon's provisional appointment to become minister of blockade. Only a handful of people had known about this. Against this evocation of cabinet irresolution, we have Harcourt's cabinet journal noting only that blockade was one of the principal subjects discussed by the cabinet on both 18 and 25 January 1916.[258] This was not a subject that interested Lou-Lou, and so he provided no details.

In listening to Montagu's plea, the cabinet cannot have been unaware that criticism of the blockade had spread to inside the government. At the last meeting of the WTAC, held on 13 January 1916, Basil Clarke's aforementioned articles on the Danish trade with Germany had been discussed at length. Sir Leo Money of the Ministry of Munitions told those present "he believed the *Mail*'s statements to be substantially true." Ernest Pollock, chairman of the Contraband Committee, agreed that "there was no answer to the *Daily Mail* as he was convinced that we were feeding the Germans in the sense of allowing or being obliged to allow these imports."[259] How best to meet raging press criticism was the chief topic for discussion at the next meeting. Commenting upon the latest batch of statistics just published in the *Morning Post,* Leo Money opined that the inferences drawn were "substantially true." Brushing aside objections, he said that

> it was useless to reply to this article and those of the *Daily Mail* by pleas such as mistakes in details or that the goods in some cases were im-

> ported into Russia. The best answer, not a complete one, was the one on which he had laid stress last week, viz. the improvement which was apparent in the latter part of 1915 . . . [but] he cautioned the September figures shewed a revival of trade not altogether reassuring.[260]

If some members of the cabinet did not yet appreciate the magnitude of internal discontent over blockade policy, then their illusions must have been dispelled after an unprecedented attack upon the Foreign Office made during the WTAC meeting of 20 January 1916.[261] Truly remarkable was the number of departmental representatives who—perhaps emboldened by the absence that day of both Lord Crewe and Lord Robert Cecil—went on record to support the criticisms. It began with an attack on the current system of intelligence.

> Sir Leo Money was of opinion that we had not a sufficiently developed organization to report upon the course of trade, nor were we kept acquainted with the practical results of the decisions of the Committee. We had largely to depend upon individual efforts to obtain information. There was no Intelligence Department to watch trade as a whole, with the result that the Committee were only appraised tardily of matters which really needed immediate attention.[262]

As Sir Leo continued, it became clear he was targeting the Foreign Office. As we have seen, intelligence was the foundation of the blockade system, and since the beginning of the war the Contraband Department had worked assiduously to become the prime supplier of trade intelligence and, as far as possible, the hub for its gathering and distribution. Adding insult to injury, Money observed:

> How different it was with the Press in which articles appeared, which although perhaps not absolutely accurate in all detail, yet gave just the class of information required. What was needed was proper representation in each country. Pushful men of the type of the special commissioner of the *Daily Mail* were needed, who, had they had official assistance, would have rendered even greater services.

After the briefest silence, Sir Francis Hopwood confessed "he was in sympathy with Sir Leo Chiozza Money's desire for a better system of intelligence."[263] Then, in succession, Ernest Pollock and Leverton Harris, G. J. Stanley of the

Board of Trade, and Lord Islington of the India Office voiced concurrence that the Foreign Office was too slow in obtaining and passing on trade intelligence.[264] Admiral Ernest Slade was even more explicit in his criticism, asking, "If the *Daily Mail* had been able to send out a representative and obtain such figures from reliable sources why had not this been done officially[?]"[265] This prompted Money acerbically to recall "a special agent of the FO who had been sent over to Denmark in August 1914 to watch trade and commerce of that country and had not apparently been officially heard of since."[266]

"From the point of view of the fighting forces it would be difficult to find more dismal reading than that contained in the first 7 pages of this report," commented Captain Richard Webb after reading the minutes. "'Failure' is stamped all over it, and Mr. Pretyman's [Board of Trade] summing up of Sir L. Money's complaint 'that it was nobody's duty to look for leakages' seems to have gone uncontradicted for the simple reason that contradiction was impossible."[267]

In the days that followed this WTAC meeting, tempers became frayed at the Contraband Department. Reacting to Admiral Sir John Jellicoe's latest epistle condemning voluntary rationing as a waste of time, Crowe wrote angrily: "I cannot help feeling that if he [Jellicoe] wishes to criticize the Foreign Office—which in any case is not his business—he should lay his complaints before the Admiralty who can then deal with them."[268] He paid no heed to Robert Craigie's warning that much of the admiral's statistical evidence seemed valid.[269] Crowe was equally uninterested in his subordinate's opinion that the admiral's preference for rationing by compulsion contained a great deal of merit.[270] His sensitivity comes across clearly in the following extract:

> A great deal of the valuable time of our already overworked department is, as it is, taken up with the work involved in dealing with the newspaper attacks organized or encouraged by naval officers against the Foreign Office, and we ought not really to be called upon to answer these irresponsible charges week after week. What would the Admiralty say if members of the Foreign Office or say our legations at Athens & Bucharest were perpetually to accuse the navy of gross incompetence and carelessness, and attack them in the press for making the work of diplomacy impossible by the bungled naval attack in the Dardanelles, for example! . . . The officers of the fleet have evidently very little to do.[271]

Crowe was not the only senior blockade official to believe that naval officers were behind the recent attacks. "The fact is that a certain number of people seem to be anxious to ferment this newspaper agitation, fair or unfair," Emmott complained to Lord Crewe. His chief suspects were the officers of the Admiralty trade division.[272]

In dealing with the press, Crowe exhibited equal impatience. On 20 January 1916, he ordered the War Trade Department to scrutinize some of the figures being bandied about in the press. Within twenty-four hours, Mr. Harwood, the senior statistician, submitted his preliminary accounting.[273] Crowe seized upon it as a decisive rebuttal. "Even Mr. Harwood's entirely provisional figures and criticisms suffice to blow down the *Morning Post*'s childish house of cards," he wrote.[274] Robert Cecil initialed his concurrence and approved the recasting of Harwood's report for publication in the *Times*.[275] In so doing, however, Crowe and Cecil disregarded Harwood's prefatory remarks warning of "the extraordinary difficulty in considering statistics of this kind."[276] As an example, Harwood pointed out that U.S. trade figures for 1913 showed the exportation of 12.5 million bushels of wheat to Germany, yet the corresponding German import figures showed the arrival of no less than 40 million bushels of U.S. wheat. Which figure was correct, and what explained the enormous discrepancy?

Harwood confessed he could not say precisely. Obtaining even an approximation of the net flow into or out of a particular European country was an extraordinarily complicated undertaking that would require a comprehensive analysis of all wheat movements between Europe and the rest of the world—something that had not yet been attempted. Even then, he cautioned, the result of such calculations must to some extent remain conjectural because so much of the available data was based not upon movements of actual quantities but rather on tentative estimates of volume derived from cargo values. It should be noted, moreover, that Harwood believed that some of the statistical inferences made in the press, though not correctly drawn, were probably right in substance; for example, it could not be denied that Germany was obtaining a large quantity of meat from the United States and other countries. These warnings, however, went completely over the heads of both Cecil and Crowe. Consequently, in framing its repudiation of the press complaints, the Contraband Department made exactly the same analytical mistakes using similarly partial and inadequate data. As we shall see, this did not pass unnoticed.

Already, however, the government had accepted that it could no longer ignore the volume of outcry against blockade policy. "In this country the conviction is steadily spreading that the present system is largely ineffective," an editorial in the *Times* reported on 21 January.[277] The previous evening, the prime minister had at last bowed to demands from the Unionist Business Committee for a Commons debate.[278] It was scheduled for Wednesday evening, 26 January 1916.[279] In granting this concession, however, Asquith resolved to take no chances. The preceding afternoon, 25 January, at about 4:30 p.m., the prime minister took the extraordinary step of inviting to Downing Street some sixty owners and editors of the London and provincial newspapers for "a straight plain talk."[280] There can be little doubt that Asquith's objective was to blunt the severity of anticipated press criticism after the Commons debate. Lord Riddell, who was present as proprietor of the *News of the World,* noted that the prime minister deployed his entire arsenal of "artful" skills.[281] "We shall see what effect (if any) it produced, when we read on Thursday morning the comments on tomorrow night's debate," Asquith confided later that evening to Mrs. Henley.[282]

In presenting the government's case, the prime minister stuck more or less to the arguments contained in the recent white paper, emphasizing the legal obstacles standing in the way of more rigorous prosecution of economic warfare. His only departure was to admit, in sotto voce, that "All the neutral countries concerned, without a single exception, regard our action as oppressive and indefensible."[283] This was hardly news. The newspapermen were generally unimpressed by what they were told. Gwynne rejected the prime minister's claim that the government was doing all in its power to restrict leakage through the contiguous neutrals. Wickham Steed of the *Times* seemed to speak for the majority when he remarked, "Let the neutrals howl."[284]

Opening the parliamentary debate on 26 January 1916, Sir Edward Grey delivered a virtuoso performance. He bamboozled his critics by focusing upon the wildest accusations pitched at his blockade policy. He successfully glossed over past failures and disputed the authenticity of "reckless figures" circulated in the press, and in so doing refuted the negative inferences drawn from what he rejected as inadequate data. Grey's speech was widely reported, and the consensus was that he had demolished his critics.[285] Herbert Samuel, the home secretary, fairly gloated in a letter to the king that "the case against the Government melted away" and that Grey had successfully demonstrated "the misleading and untrustworthy character of many of the statistics on which his critics' case had been based."[286]

Better-informed commentators, however, contested this interpretation. The very next day, at the meeting of the WTAC, Sir Leo Money expressed his "indignation" at the "false impression" conveyed by Grey's speech.[287]

> The public not being well informed of the subject, would in respect of the answer of the WTD as supported in the House of Commons, be under the impression that a crushing reply had been made, but that reply, at least as far as tea, cocoa and other things were concerned, was based on a statement liable to a false interpretation.

Money hastened to clarify that he did not mean to criticize the foreign secretary; rather, he was aiming at those who had provided Grey with the false figures he used to build his case. Hastily moving on, Sir Leo regained his audience's sympathy in his condemnation of the Foreign Office's statement, recently published in the *Times*, refuting the statistics and arguments of the *Daily Mail* and *Morning Post*. Several WTAC members agreed it had been misleading and in places untruthful.[288] It might be added that a fortnight later, the head of the French statistical bureau, Jean Tannery, communicated to the Foreign Office his discomfort with the government's "deeply flawed" reply to the *Morning Post*'s figures.[289]

Within the WTAC there was general acknowledgment that in recent weeks all sides had been guilty of taking numbers out of context and of using incomplete and flawed data.[290] At the next meeting the continuing weaknesses in government statistics were reviewed.[291] It was also recognized that the combination of Grey's statement to the House and the recent Foreign Office press communiqué had produced "an important and unfortunate effect in neutral countries" that would hinder diplomatic efforts to tighten the blockade.[292] After a lengthy discussion on whether the government should formally withdraw the Foreign Office statement, everyone agreed that although a mistake had been made, the consequences of admitting such an error seemed worse. The WTAC resolved to say nothing.[293]

In the days that followed, the officers of the Admiralty trade division sifted the recent parliamentary speeches and press reports seeking fresh political ammunition.[294] Although they did not find anything useful, they concluded that the government had been injured by the recent attacks and had boxed itself into a position with little room for political maneuver.[295] At the Foreign Office, Lord Robert Cecil became more adamant that further concessions to the United States were out of the question. He reiterated to Spring Rice, as he had to Colonel House several weeks before, that Parliament and public opinion demanded the government stand firm. And if it did not, he might have added, the news surely would leak. Cecil told Spring Rice that "if a ballot were taken in the House of Commons, on the question of whether they had confidence in the present government, there would be an overwhelming majority against the government."[296] Albeit by a different route, Sir Edward Grey reached the same conclusion. On 15 February 1916, he wrote the prime minister:

> The confusion and want of guidance and policy in dealing with Contraband has reached a point at which I can no longer be responsible for the relations with neutral countries. We are now threatened with the complete alienation of Denmark and Norway, who are both undoubtedly friendly by nature[,] and I believe we are depriving both countries of things they really need. The complaint outside in this country is that the Foreign Office interferes too much.[297]

Asquith accepted that the need for a new approach had become irresistible. The next day at the cabinet meeting he proposed and it was agreed that a new Ministry of Blockade should be formed under the direction of Lord Robert Cecil to "coordinate the work of the War Trade Department, the Contraband Department of the Foreign Office and of all the different committees dealing with commercial questions."[298] To achieve this hitherto impossible goal, Cecil was given the authority to impose coherence upon government policy and, when necessary, arrogate the authority of the established departments of state. The search for a solution to administrative problems attending the enforcement of blockade policy was finally over. It now remained to be seen whether this solution would work and what would be the expected (and unexpected) consequences of creating this new machinery.

Conclusions

During the half century before the outbreak of the First World War, technological revolutions in communications, transportation, and financial services facilitated the global spread of market capitalism. The growth and intensification of international commerce had tremendous ramifications for the development of national power and the dynamics of national power relationships. Consequent structural modifications in the functioning of the global trading system produced other changes of great strategic significance. Innovations such as credit financing, freight forwarding, and the growing practice of what later became to be called just-in-time ordering, especially for food, increased commercial flexibility and efficiency and thus lowered economic costs. As a consequence, industrialized nations came to depend upon an uninterrupted flow of maritime trade, a condition with implications that most governments well understood.

Before 1914 there was considerable worry that war must cause a serious dislocation of global trade and on a scale that might well precipitate national economic crises of unparalleled dimensions, bringing in their train grave social disorder and ultimately political revolution. Following ideas advanced by French strategic theorists of the *jeune école,* contemporary commentators predicted that Great Britain, standing at the center of the new world economic system, was particularly vulnerable to such a catastrophe. Parliament's grudging recognition of this possibility lay behind Britain's heavy investment in naval defense during the final decade of the nineteenth century, a form of insurance against economic misfortune in the event of war. Between 1889 and 1900, effective spending on the Royal Navy doubled, eventually consuming more than a quarter of state revenue. Such concerns also gave impetus to a serious (albeit ill-conceived) attempt by the international community to create a universal governing code of maritime law and the first attempt to establish an international court with appellate jurisdiction over national courts.

Yet within the Admiralty the prospect of a meltdown in the global trading system appeared to offer Britain a strategic opportunity as well as a strategic danger. Consideration of the trade defense problem in light of the recent economic transformation led certain naval planners to contemplate the vulnerability of future enemies to such an Armageddon. They began toying with the possibility of harnessing Britain's naval supremacy to her effective monopoly control over the infrastructure of the global trading system (shipping, financial services, and global communications). If practicable, they thought, the Admiralty might intensify pressure upon the enemy's economy with potentially decisive results, while at the same time taking steps to mitigate the effects of war upon their own.

Between 1905 and 1908, the Admiralty conceived the broad outlines of an economic warfare strategy against Germany. Over the course of the next four years, the Committee of Imperial Defence extended and refined the concept. To a considerable extent, the strategy was the product of a remarkable partnership between the state and outside expert advice. Previous historians have noted the British government's success in exploiting civilian expertise to boost the war effort during the First World War. The present work shows this was a phenomenon rooted in prewar planning and preparation.

In 1912, Britain's political leaders approved the plan for economic warfare as the basis of strategic action in the event of war against Germany. This was reflected in the prime minister's decision to grant the Admiralty predelegated authority to act immediately at commencement of hostilities. The hope was that swift offensive action against Germany's trade would foment a financial crisis before her monetary institutions could apply effective countermeasures. The British objective was to wound severely, if not topple, the financial systems upon which depended her primary opponent's ability to prosecute the war.

On 5 August 1914, accordingly, Great Britain implemented economic warfare through a series of already drafted royal proclamations. Within a fortnight, however, political commitment to economic warfare began to crumble under protests from civilian departments that resented Admiralty control of issues they regarded as their bailiwick, from bankers distraught at the havoc already wreaked, and from businessmen upset at government interference with their trade. Further objections were raised by neutrals, irritated by Royal Navy threats of interference with their commerce.

After just three weeks of war, before any major clash of arms on the Continent, fearsome projections of the high political, diplomatic, and economic costs attending the implementation of the strategy broke the will of the cabinet. Irresolute ministers persuaded themselves that it was not in the national interest to endanger the security of the already weakened global trading system upon which national prosperity ultimately rested. This was coupled to the conviction that, anyway, it was unnecessary to resort to such drastic measures. Confidence in an early victory remained both high and widespread. Given the magnitude of the Entente's assumed military superiority over the Central Powers, this seemed plausible.

In late August, therefore, the British government first relaxed and then, at the end of October, in response to mounting pressure from the United States, effectively suspended the implementation of economic warfare. This action proved misjudged: within a matter of weeks it became apparent that the war would be protracted and thus would require greater—not lesser—exertion and sacrifice on Britain's part. By then, however, the theoretical opportunity to wreck the German war machine through the sudden imposition of an economic stranglehold had passed.

The British government did not entirely abandon the strategy of economic coercion. Under the direction of the Foreign Office, a new approach to economic action was hastily improvised, based upon a very different set of assumptions and mechanisms, and intended to be less disruptive to the world economic system. This became known as blockade. Though it promised far less with respect to the effect on the German economy, the blockade system was a much more complex administrative undertaking—so much so, indeed, that for at least the first eighteen months of the war it proved largely ineffectual. During the summer of 1915, indeed, the cabinet believed the blockade so ineffective, and possibly even counterproductive to Britain's war effort, that ministers seriously considered its abandonment. The failure to make the blockade effective was not a function of the Royal Navy's inability to carry it out, or the consequence of continued neutral resistance (which admittedly remained considerable); rather, it was largely a result of the incapacity of the British system of government to coordinate and integrate departmental action.

The government's attempts to implement blockade strategy generated domestic strife while offending many important and traditional political interests. What implementation of economic warfare (in either form) implied for the role of government was almost as much at the center of divisions raging within the ruling Liberal party as the well-known controversy over conscription was. It certainly touched more people more directly. In previous wars, the state's aim in applying sea power had been to deploy its navy to permit and encourage national trade to continue (thereby creating national wealth and thus revenue for the state) and to impede that of the enemy (thereby undermining their economic base). Subsequent to the nineteenth century transformation in the global trading system, effective implementation of sea power was no longer simply a function of naval power but required the state to subordinate what might be termed the informal elements of maritime power (shipping, financial services, and communications). But in seeking control over the infrastructure of the global trading system, the British state created enormous resistance by effectively compelling its nationals to act against their profit-maximizing instincts.

More generally, the economic dimension of war policy is a subject of far greater importance than has been allowed, directly affecting critical strategic decisions, most notably that to launch the campaign at the Dardanelles. At the administrative level, the numerous departments of government with a role in blockade management consisted of individuals with very individualistic—and incompatible—ideas on policy, as well as on what should, could, or even had been done. Ensuring all pulled in even approximately the same direction required tight supervision plus management and leadership skills of the highest order. Before 1916, this was simply not achieved.

Wartime experience also demonstrated that administration of the blockade required a level of information gathering and processing that far outstripped what was available to the British state. Incomplete, conflicting, and faulty information inhibited the implementation of strategy. Not until much later in the war, after the government had overcome internal political opposition about the power and size of the state, and after the adoption (and invention) of more advanced information management techniques, were blockade officials finally able to achieve something approaching the necessary degree of coordination. Until such time the effects of the blockade could not be measured with reasonable accuracy and action directed accordingly.

The objective of the present work has been, first, to establish the precise delineation of British strategic intent; second, to explain why the prewar plans were not followed; third, to show how the actual strategy adopted was formulated and the means improvised; and lastly, to explore some of the implications of these choices. This is surely a rich meal—yet some readers may be left feeling unsated.

If economic warfare had been fully implemented, as planned, would British action have produced a critical level of financial crisis in Germany? Could the German state have taken adequate countervailing action? Would an implosion of the German financial system have collapsed that country's war effort? Ultimately, would the full implementation of economic warfare have brought the war to a rapid and successful conclusion? Such counterfactual questions lie beyond the purview of the present work. It may be pointed out, furthermore, that answers to such questions demand a measure of quantification; yet as this work has shown, sufficient statistical data do not exist and likely never did. To a considerable extent, therefore, seeking answers to such questions appears to be unproductive speculation. The best evidence of genuine fear of an economic Armageddon is reflected in the level of pressure applied by financial and commercial interests upon the political leadership to avoid war and, after this failed, to abort economic warfare. As early twenty-first-century events remind us, moreover, the integrity of banking systems depends so very much upon the supremely subjective concept of confidence.

Similarly, though the effects of the blockade and its importance in Germany's defeat have been much discussed, unfortunately there is little hard evidence against which to test such assessments. Evaluating the extent to which the blockade worked its dire strangulation upon Germany after 1916 is a task for other historians. Economic warfare strategy may or may not have been practicable, might or might not have produced decisive results, but it undoubtedly was an intelligent and shrewd (though maybe not wise) attempt to solve a real strategic problem, and one that was based firmly upon the economic realities of the day.

The story told here of the abortive economic warfare plan has profound implications for our understanding of Britain's role in the First World War. What is established here, for the first time, is the huge political influence of economic interests generated by the dependence of national economies on the smooth functioning of the global economic system. An increasingly sophisticated appreciation of the vulnerabilities and advantages of the economic system underpinned British strategic planning and strategic execution. Recognizing the political, bureaucratic, and service rivalries at work as this process unfolded offers a new way of understanding Britain's First World War.

More specifically, it has long been held that prewar British strategic preparations and action subsequent to the outbreak of war were dictated primarily by military imperatives and diplomatic considerations. Previous historians could not see how Britain's supreme naval and financial strength could affect the outcome of a European land war within the anticipated time frame of hostilities. It was thought that the Royal Navy's leadership could offer nothing more than improbable amphibious strategies; a conventional blockade could not possibly have time to bite before hostilities would be over. Thus, it was thought, the cabinet saw only one option in August 1914, and that was to approve the Army General Staff plan to send all available troops to the Continent. With few exceptions, historians have generally accepted that this fateful decision determined the nature of British strategy for 1914, and consequently for the war as a whole.

This understanding of events now requires modification. Most important, the cornerstone of prewar British strategic preparations against Germany was economic warfare—not the Continental commitment. The character of British strategy for the war was defined by the cabinet's decision not to prosecute economic warfare rather than by the dispatch of the BEF to France. The margin in favor of this course was much closer than previously realized, one might add. Only as historical events unfolded did the blockade (characterized in all literature with adjectives such as "grim," "relentless," and "patient") become relegated to a subsidiary strategy and the Continental commitment move to the fore.

Another point of importance to note is that the cabinet retained far greater control over strategic policy formulation than has been previously allowed. For the period of this study, extending to the first eighteen months of the war, the cabinet remained paramount in setting the parameters of strategic choices—in other words, shaping what the so-called War Council might consider. Cabinet attitudes, furthermore, were heavily conditioned by political-economic considerations, attitudes, and prejudices. Nowhere was this more apparent than in the formulation and implementation of blockade policy.

The character and dynamics of British diplomatic relations with neutrals in general and the United States in particular have also been shown to be much different from what has been supposed. The breakdown of the global trading system caused by fear of war, combined with the measures initially implemented by Britain, inflicted significant collateral damage upon the American economy and threatened to plunge the United States into recession during a midterm election year. Fearing economic catastrophe, especially in the South, where cotton was still king, President Woodrow Wilson implemented measures that placed Britain and America on a diplomatic collision course. The British Foreign Office urged the cabinet not to mount a full-blooded challenge to the American actions. Believing in the likelihood of a short war, the British government yielded—then spent the next three years trying to retract the concessions granted.

Previous scholars of Wilson's diplomacy have not fully appreciated the complexity of the Anglo-American dispute in part because they have not understood how the dispute helped to wreck the Admiralty's plans for economic warfare. Nor have they understood the commercial and financial practices that bore heavily on the legal aspects of the dispute. Comprehension of these issues transforms our understanding of Anglo-American relations in the First World War. Far from displaying an attitude of benevolent neutrality toward Britain, the Wilson administration acted ruthlessly to protect America's national interests and in so doing secured from Britain very significant concessions, substantially robbing the weapon of economic coercion of its effectiveness. Stripped of rhetoric, ideological theory, and talk of principled commitment to the cause of neutral rights, the friction between London and Washington was not about blockade and its legality but rather over its impact upon American politics—and, of course, British politics as well.

In the introduction we briefly explored why naval historians of this period so badly misread the history and significance of the blockade. In the chapters that followed we reviewed evidence suggesting, albeit implicitly, that the problems with traditional narratives are much more extensive. Led by Julian Corbett, the official historian, and later Arthur Marder, naval historians have consistently underestimated the magnitude, complexity, and even direction of Britain's policy with respect to the employment of its sea power. Official censorship (as outlined in the introduction) and other difficulties encountered in establishing the main narrative provide only a partial excuse for this weakness. It is inescapable that the core histories of the First World War were written from a too narrow perspective and a generally inadequate grasp of wider considerations and events, especially the political and economic aspects of defense policy formulation.

The study of national strategic policy is an inherently treacherous historical subject, the true complexity of which is all too frequently underestimated. To divine the closest approximation of the true course of events demands comprehensive consideration of the diverse and very large body of extant and often contradictory evidence. Every facet must be assessed and tested against the context of the whole. To comprehend strategic decision making, it is not sufficient to examine the views of the military high command and the highest civilian officials in government. It is all too easy to assemble a coherent and plausible narrative based upon such a narrow range of sources. Invariably, many of these sources are deceptive, providing a misleading and even wholly false record of events. "We must state emphatically," General Carl von Clausewitz wrote nearly two hundred years ago, that "military history can well become a chronic lie and deception if critics fail to apply the required correctives." He warned:

> Fraudulence is not merely a matter of bad habit; its roots lie in the nature of the case. The counterweights that weaken the elemental force of war, and particularly the attack, are primarily located in the political relations and intentions of the government, which are concealed from the rest of the world, the people at home, the army, and in some cases even from the commander. For instance no one can and will admit that his decision to stop or to give up was motivated by the fear that his strength would run out, or that he might make new enemies or that his own allies might become too strong. That sort of thing is long kept confidential, possibly forever. Meanwhile, a plausible account must be circulated. The general is, therefore, urged, either for his own sake or the sake of his government, to spread a web of lies.[1]

The present work provides an object lesson in how important it is in any analysis of strategic policy to understand what Clausewitz termed "the political conditions of war."

Abbreviations

Notes

Primary Sources

Acknowledgments

Index

Abbreviations

Primary Sources

BD	G. P. Gooch and Harold Temperley, eds., *British Documents on the Origins of the War, 1898–1914,* 13 vols. (London: HMSO, 1926–1938)
DC	*Trading with the Enemy: Report and Proceedings* (Desart Committee), 1912, CAB.16/18A
FGDN	*Fear God and Dread Nought: The Correspondence of the Admiral of the Fleet Lord Fisher of Kilverstone,* ed. Arthur Marder, 3 vols. (London: Jonathan Cape, 1952–1959)
FLM	Secret: First Lord's Minutes, 1911–1915, 3 vols., copy at Naval Library Ministry of Defence
FP2	*The Papers of Admiral Sir John Fisher,* ed. Peter Kemp, vol. 2 (London: Naval Records Society, 1964)
FRUS	U.S. Department of State, *Foreign Relations of the United States* (Washington, DC: Government Printing Office, various years)
HC Deb	*House of Commons Debates* (Hansard), Official Report, 4th and 5th Series (London: Wyman and Sons for HMSO, various years)
HL Deb	*House of Lords Debates* (Hansard), Official Report, 4th and 5th Series (London: Wyman and Sons for HMSO, various years)
JMK	*The Collected Writings of John Maynard Keynes: Activities 1914–1919, The Treasury and Versailles,* ed., Elizabeth Johnson, vol. 16 (London: Macmillan, 1971)
JRUSI	*Journal of the Royal United Services Institute*
LVS	*H. H. Asquith, Letters to Venetia Stanley,* ed. Michael and Eleanor Brock (Oxford: Oxford University Press, 1985)
NN	"Naval Necessities," 4 vols. (Naval Library Ministry of Defence, Portsmouth Naval Base, UK)
PWW	*The Papers of Woodrow Wilson,* ed. Arthur S. Link, 69 vols. (Princeton, NJ: Princeton University Press, 1966–1994)
WSC	*Winston S. Churchill,* ed. Randolph Churchill and Martin Gilbert, 8 vols. and 8 companions (London: Heinemann, 1966–1998)

Secondary Works

BESP David French, *British Economic and Strategic Planning, 1905–1915* (London: Allen and Unwin, 1982)
BSWA David French, *British Strategy and War Aims, 1914–1916* (London: Allen and Unwin, 1986)
FDSF Arthur Marder, *From the Dreadnought to Scapa Flow: The Royal Navy in the Fisher Era, 1904–1919,* 5 vols. (London: Oxford University Press, 1961–1969)
FNR Nicholas A. Lambert, *Sir John Fisher's Naval Revolution* (Columbia: University of South Carolina Press, 1999)
HMS Stephen Roskill, *Hankey: Man of Secrets,* 3 vols. (London: Collins, 1970–1974)
IDNS Jon Sumida, *In Defence of Naval Supremacy: Finance, Technology, and British Naval Policy, 1889–1914* (London: Routledge, 1989)
PGS Samuel R. Williamson, *The Politics of Grand Strategy: Britain and France Prepare for War, 1904–1914* (Cambridge, MA: Harvard University Press, 1969)
SC Lord Hankey, *The Supreme Command 1914–1918,* 2 vols. (London: Allen and Unwin, 1961)
SPMS Julian Corbett, *Some Principles of Maritime Strategy* (London: Longmans, Green, 1911)

Other Abbreviations

Add.Mss. Additional Manuscripts (British Library Museum)
CID Committee of Imperial Defence
DMO Director of Military Operations
DNI Director, Naval Intelligence Department
DOD Director, Operations Division, Naval War Staff
DTD Director, Trade Division, Naval War Staff
ESRC Enemy Supplies Restriction Committee
IWM Imperial War Museum, London
MP Member of Parliament
NID Naval Intelligence Division
NLMD Naval Library of the Ministry of Defence, Portsmouth Naval Dockyard, UK
NMM National Maritime Museum, Greenwich, London
RNVR Royal Navy Volunteer Reserve
WTAC War Trade Advisory Committee

Notes

Introduction

Epigraph: Basil H. Liddell Hart, "Economic Pressure or Continental Victories," JRUSI 76, no. 50 (28 January 1931): 503.

1. On Germany: L. L. Farrar, *The Short-War Illusion: German Policy, Strategy, and Domestic Affairs* (Santa Barbara, CA: ABC-Clio, 1973). On France: Robert Doughty, *Pyrrhic Victory: French Strategy and Operations in the Great War* (Cambridge, MA: Harvard University Press, 2005).

2. Jan de Block (a.k.a. Ivan Stanislavovic Bloch), *Is War Now Impossible? Being an Abridgement of "The War of the Future in Its Technical, Economic and Political Relations,"* with a prefatory conversation with the author by William T. Stead (London: Grant Richards, 1899), xvii, lx–lxi.

3. Norman Angell, *The Great Illusion: A Study of the Relation of Military Power in Nations to Their Economic and Social Advantage,* 3rd ed. (London: William Heinemann, 1911; first privately published November 1909).

4. Jon Sumida, "Re-imagining the History of Twentieth Century Navies," in Daniel Finamore, ed., *Maritime History as World History* (Gainesville: University of Florida Press, 2004), 167–82; Sumida, "Geography, Technology, and British Naval Strategy in the Dreadnought Era," *Naval War College Review* 59 (Summer 2006): 89–102; Sumida, *Inventing Grand Strategy and Teaching Command: The Classic Works of Alfred Thayer Mahan Reconsidered* (Baltimore: Johns Hopkins University Press, 1997); see also Alfred Thayer Mahan, *Some Neglected Aspects of War* (London: Sampson Low, 1907), 190.

5. SPMS, 93, 261–62, 264–79.

6. Ibid., 99–100.

7. Ibid., 15–16, 93, 99–100, 185, 261–62, 264–79.

8. Ibid., 15–16; Paul Kennedy, *The Rise and Fall of British Naval Mastery* (London: Allen Lane, 1974), 211–12.

9. HC Deb, 28 June 1916, vol. 83, c.838–39, H. H. Asquith.

10. On details of the history project, see Donald Shurman, *Julian S. Corbett: Historian of British Maritime Policy from Drake to Jellicoe* (London: Royal Historical Society, 1981), 155–65.

11. Howard Weinroth, "Norman Angell and the Great Illusion: An Episode in Pre-1914 Pacifism," *Historical Journal* 17, no. 3 (1974): 551–74; Martin Ceadel, *Living the Great Illusion: Sir Norman Angell, 1872–1967* (Oxford: Oxford University Press, 2009). N.b.: Angell was sacked in August 1915 (p. 6).

12. See also Shurman, *Julian S. Corbett,* 164–66.

13. John F. Naylor, *A Man and an Institution: Sir Maurice Hankey, the Cabinet Secretariat and the Custody of Cabinet Secrecy* (New York: Cambridge University Press, 1984), 120–21.

14. Ceadel, *Living the Great Illusion,* 117–22.

15. Minute (6 November 1916) by Lord Robert Cecil, "Official History of the Blockade," file E.8075, T.162/296 (Treasury papers, The National Archives, Kew, UK); History of the Blockade, f.378, CO 323/715/56 (Colonial Office papers, The National Archives, Kew, UK); there is also a file in the Admiralty archives. See especially Guy Locock (Cecil's private secretary) to Webb, 30 October 1916, ADM.137/2737 (Admiralty papers, The National Archives, Kew, UK).

16. John R. H. Weaver, *Henry William Carless Davis, 1874–1928: A Memoir* (London: Constable, 1933), 35–39.

17. Ibid., 39. See also obituary by Frederick M. Powicke in *The English Historical Review* 43, no. 172 (October 1928): 582; Marion Siney, "British Official Histories of the Blockade of the Central Powers during the First World War," *Journal of the American Historical Association,* January 1963, 394.

18. Papers of H. W. C. Davis, Mss.Eng. C.6038–39, Bodleian Library, Oxford.

19. Keith Grieves, "Early Historical Responses to the Great War: Fortescue, Conan Doyle and Buchan," in Brian Bond, ed., *The First World War and British Military History* (Oxford: Clarendon Press, 1991), 18.

20. Schurman, *Julian S. Corbett,* 180–84.

21. HMS, 2:126. Walter Birbeck Wood and James E. Edmonds, *The Civil War in the United States, 1861–1865* (New York: G. P. Putnam, 1905).

22. Naylor, *A Man and an Institution,* 72, 122–23, esp. 121n31; Schurman, *Julian S. Corbett,* 182–85.

23. H. W. Carless Davis, *History of the Blockade: Emergency Departments* (printed for official information only, March 1921, copy at NLMD). Printer's marks show a run of 250.

24. Harold Temperley, "VII—The Nineteenth Century and After, 1789–1929," *Annual Bulletin of Historical Literature* 19, no. 1 (1931): 53; Siney, "British Official Histories," 392–93.

25. Notes by Lord Emmott addressed to the War Cabinet, 27 March 1919, K.16, CAB.15/6/4 (Cabinet Office papers, The National Archives, Kew, UK).

26. Copy held in ADM.186/603. W. E. Arnold Forster was the son of H. O. Arnold Forster, parliamentary secretary to the Admiralty (1901–1903) and secretary of state for war (1903–1905) in the Balfour administration.

27. C. Ernest Fayle, *Seaborne Trade,* 3 vols. (London: John Murray, 1920–1924).

28. Archibald C. Bell, *A History of the Blockade of Germany and the Countries Associated with Her in the Great War: Austria-Hungary, Bulgaria, and Turkey* (London: HMSO, 1961), iii.

29. Schurman, *Julian S. Corbett*; Andrew Gordon, *The Rules of the Game: Jutland and British Naval Command* (London: John Murray, 1996), 539–48.

30. Brian Tunstall, "History of the Great War: Naval Operations," *History: The Journal of the Historical Association* 19, no. 73 (January 1934): 25.

31. Minutes (18 and 21 January 1927) by Hotham, DNI, ff.139–46, 320, ADM.116/3423.

32. Ibid. See also attached minutes (5 March and 8 June 1927) by Oswyn Murray, permanent secretary, ff.145–46, ADM.116/3423; and minute (15 November 1935) by S. A. Phillips, head of M branch, on "CID sub committee on official history, 12 March 1931," ADM.116/3303.

33. Naylor, *A Man and an Institution*, 118–20, 205–9, 226, 272–77; Avner Offer, *The First World War: An Agrarian Interpretation* (Oxford: Clarendon Press, 1989), 228–29.

34. Winston S. Churchill, *The World Crisis, 1911–1918,* 5 vols. (New York: Scribner's, 1923–1931).

35. H. H. Asquith, *Memories and Reflections, 1852–1927,* 2 vols. (Boston: Cassell, 1928); Viscount Grey of Fallodon (Sir Edward Grey), *Twenty-Five Years: 1892–1916,* 2 vols. (New York: Frederick Stokes, 1925); David Lloyd George, *War Memoirs of David Lloyd George,* 6 vols. (London: Nicholson and Watson, 1933–1937).

36. Montagu Consett, *The Triumph of Unarmed Forces: An Account of the Transactions by Which Germany during the Great War Was Able to Obtain Supplies Prior to Her Collapse under the Pressure of Economic Forces* (London: Williams and Norgate, 1923).

37. HL Deb, 27 June 1923, vol. 54, c.647–54; see also HL Deb, 01 April 1925, vol. 60, c.860–76.

38. CID, Standing sub committee on the coordination of departmental action on the outbreak of war 533-B, 8 November 1924, CAB.16/79; CID, Technical advisory sub committee No. 5 Belligerent rights, CAB.62/67; Belligerent Rights at Sea Committee (BRL), 1929, CAB.16/82. For a general summary of pre–Second World War preparations, see William N. Medlicott, *History of the Second World War: The Economic Blockade,* 2 vols. (London: Longmans, 1952–1959), 1–23.

39. Minutes (26 March 1931) of sub-committee for the control of the Official Histories, 8th Meeting, p. 5, "Official History of the Blockade of Germany," ADM.116/3303. For original intent to publish, see Siney, "British Official Histories," 393.

40. Remarks by Frederick Captain Wake Walker, R.N. (Deputy Director of Training and Staff Duties), "CID sub committee on official history, 12 March 1931," ADM.116/3303.

41. Minutes (15 and 18 November 1936) by S. A. Phillips (M) and Oswyn Murray (secretary), ADM.116/3303.

42. Bell, *A History of the Blockade of Germany*, 23, 31–32.

43. Siney, "British Official Histories," 395.

44. Bell, *A History of the Blockade of Germany,* preface; Bell to Gasalee (FO librarian), 8 September, 18 October, and 11 November 1932, ff.105ff, L3778, FO.370/387 (Foreign Office papers, The National Archives, Kew, UK).

45. On official histories: HMS, 2:126; Naylor, *A Man and an Institution*, 72–73, 120–30, 226–27; David French, "Official but Not History? Sir James Edmonds and the Official History of the Great War," JRUSI 131, no. 1 (March 1986): 58–63; Jay Luvaas, "The First British Military Historians," *Military Affairs* 26 (Summer 1962): 49–58; Andrew Green, *Writing the Great War: Sir James Edmonds and the Official Histories, 1915–1948* (London: Frank Cass, 2003). On blockade: Marion Siney, *The Allied Blockade of Germany, 1914–1916* (Ann Arbor: University of Michigan Press, 1957); Offer, *The First World War;* Eric Osborne, *Britain's Economic Blockade of Germany, 1914–1919* (London: Frank Cass, 2004).

46. The best general history remains Paul Halpern, *A Naval History of World War One* (Annapolis, MD: Naval Institute Press, 1994), 47–50.

47. The historiography is well summarized in Lance Davis and Stanley Engerman, *Naval Blockades in Peace and War: An Economic History since 1750* (Cambridge: Cambridge University Press, 2006), 17, 159–60, 209–14.

48. Kennedy, *Rise and Fall,* 226–30; Kennedy, "Strategy versus Finance in Twentieth-Century Great Britain," *International History Review* 3, no. 1 (January 1981): 48–49.

49. FDSF, ii, 372–78; Halpern, *A Naval History,* 48–50, 291–99.

50. Hew Strachan, *The First World War,* vol. 1: *To Arms* (Oxford: Oxford University Press, 2001), 98, 397–403; David French, *British Economic and Strategic Planning, 1905–1915* (London: Allen and Unwin, 1982), 22; David Stevenson, *1914–1918: The History of the First World War* (London: Allen Lane, 2004), 243–48.

51. The first to suggest that the blockade was the decisive factor in the war seems to have been Basil Liddell Hart in *Strategy: The Indirect Approach* (London: Faber and Faber, 1941), 265.

52. Michael Howard, *The British Way in Warfare: A Reappraisal* (London: Jonathan Cape, 1975), 18.

53. Hankey died on 26 January 1963, Churchill on 24 January 1965.

1. The Emergence of Economic Warfare

Epigraph: Alfred Mahan, "Considerations Governing the Dispositions of Navies," *National Review,* July 1902, 701–19.

1. HC Deb, 24 March 1873, vol. 215, c.33, George Goschen; HC Deb, 21 March 1873, vol. 214, c.2010, Mr. William Rathbone; George Goschen (1831–1907), First Lord of the Admiralty 1871–1874 and 1895–1900; chancellor of the exchequer, 1887–1892, created viscount, 1900.

2. HC Deb, 3 April 1873, vol. 215, c.543, Mr. Thomas Brassey (1836–1918), Liberal MP for Hastings, 1868–1886; Civil Lord of the Admiralty, 1880–1882 and 1882–1884; Admiralty Parliamentary Secretary, 1884–1885; founded Naval Annual, 1886; created 1st Earl Brassey, 1911.

3. HC Deb, 13 March 1876, vol. 227, c.1917, Captain George Edward Price (1842–1926).

4. Ibid.

5. Examples: HC Deb, 21 February 1902, vol. 103, c.782, H. H. Asquith (prime minister); HC Deb, 11 March 1935, vol. 299, c.159, Sir John Simon (foreign secretary). Most recently: HC Deb, 1 February 1996, vol. 270, c.1155, Ms Rachel Swire.

6. Ronald Findlay and Kevin O'Rourke, *Power and Plenty: Trade, War, and the World Economy in the Second Millennium* (Princeton, NJ: Princeton University Press, 2007), 381–87, 395–407, 411–14; Daniel Headrick, *The Tentacles of Progress: Technology Transfer in the Age of Imperialism, 1850–1940* (New York: Oxford University Press, 1988), 23, citing Walter Rostow, *The World Economy: History and Prospect* (London: Macmillan, 1978), 669; on communications, see Byron Lew and Bruce Carter, "The Telegraph, Co-ordination of Tramp Shipping, and Growth in World Trade, 1870–1910," *European Review of Economic History* 10 (2006): 147–73.

7. Kevin O'Rourke and Jeffrey Williamson, *Globalization and History: The Evolution of a Nineteenth-Century Atlantic Economy* (Cambridge, MA: MIT Press, 1999), 29–55.

8. Ibid., 43.

9. Peter Cain and Anthony Hopkins, *British Imperialism: Innovation and Expansion, 1688–1914* (London: Longmans, 1993), 449–51; Peter J. Katzenstein, "International interdependence: Some Long-Term Trends and Recent Changes," *International Organization* 29, no. 4 (Autumn 1975): 1021–34.

10. Charles Feinstein, *Statistical Tables of National Income, Expenditure and Output of the United Kingdom, 1855–1965* (Cambridge: Cambridge University Press, 1972), table 3 (T10).

11. David Rowe, "World Economic Expansion and National Security in Pre–World War I Europe," *International Organisation* 53, no. 2 (Spring 1999): 195–231.

12. William Ashworth, *An Economic History of England, 1870–1939* (London: Methuen, 1960), 138; O'Rourke and Williamson, *Globalization,* 2.

13. Paul Kennedy, *The Rise and Fall of British Naval Mastery* (London: Allen Lane, 1974), 224.

14. Marcello De Cecco, *Money and Empire: The International Gold Standard, 1890–1914* (Oxford: Blackwell, 1974), 26.

15. Paul Kennedy, "Strategy versus Finance in Twentieth-Century Great Britian," *International History Review* 3, no. 1 (January 1981): 47; Kennedy, *Rise and Fall,* 218–19.

16. Ibid.

17. Peter Mathias, *The First Industrial Nation: An Economic History of Britain, 1700–1914* (New York: Scribner's, 1969), 320.

18. Ibid., 333; Kennedy, "Strategy versus Finance," 49.

19. Paul Kennedy, *The Rise and Fall of the Great Powers: Economic Change and Military Conflict from 1500 to 2000* (New York: Random House, 1987); Aaron Friedberg, *The Weary Titan: Britain and Experience of Relative Decline, 1895–1905* (Princeton, NJ: Princeton University Press, 1988), 212–14.

20. Keith Neilson, "'Great Exaggerated': The Myth of the Decline of Great Britain before 1914," and John Ferris, "The Greatest Power on Earth: Great Britain in the 1920s," both in *International History Review* 13, no. 4 (November 1991): 661–880.

21. IDNS; FNR; Norman Friedman, *Naval Firepower: Battleship Guns and Gunnery in the Dreadnought Era* (Annapolis, MD: Naval institute Press, 2008).

22. Niall Ferguson, *The Pity of War: Explaining World War I* (New York: Basic Books, 1999), 33–35.

23. For a recent empirical study, see Stefano Battilossi, "The Determinants of Multinational Banking during the First Globalization 1880–1914," *European Review of Economic History* 10 (2006): 361–88.

24. Mathias, *First Industrial Nation,* 308, 310–14.

25. Feinstein, *Statistical Tables,* esp. table 15 (T37), table 37 (T82), table 2 (T8), table 19 (T47); B. R. Mitchell, *Abstract of British Historical Statistics,* vol. 17 (Cambridge: Cambridge University Press, 1971).

26. Barry Eichengreen, *Globalizing Capital: A History of the International Monetary System,* 2nd ed. (Princeton: Princeton University Press, 2008), 22.

27. The strategic implications of Britain's effective monopoly over cable communications are explored in Jonathan Winkler, *Nexus: Strategic Communications and American Security in World War I* (Cambridge, MA: Harvard University Press, 2008), 17–28, 34–40, 59–60.

28. Cain and Hopkins, *British Imperialism,* 150–51, table 5.7, 170.

29. BESP, 13.

30. Arne Røksund, *The Jeune École: The Strategy of the Weak* (Leiden: Brill, 2007). A historian with a good grasp of *jeune école* theory (though it is not the subject of his work) is David Oliver; see his *German Naval Strategy, 1856–1888: Forerunners to Tirpitz* (London: Frank Cass, 2004).

31. FNR, 21–29. An excellent paper is the Minute (March 1903) by DNI, Captain Prince Louis of Battenberg, marked in pencil "Given to Prime Minister before receiving the Stafford House Committee," ADM.137/2872.

32. FNR, 21–24.

33. Goschen, "Navy Estimates and Shipbuilding Programme, 1898–99," 17 February 1898, CAB.37/46/20.

34. Avner Offer, *The First World War: An Agrarian Interpretation* (Oxford: Clarendon Press, 1989), 226–32.

35. "Home Productions and Importations of Cereals—1891–1901: Memorandum from the Director of Naval Contracts," encl. with M17336/02 (November 1902), ADM.137/2872.

36. Minute (4 March 1903) by Battenberg, marked in pencil "Given to Prime Minister before receiving the Stafford House Committee," ADM.137/2872.

37. Julian S. Corbett, *Some Principles of Maritime Strategy* (London: Longmans, Green, 1911; reprint, Annapolis, MD: Naval Institute Press, 1988).

38. Cain and Hopkins, *British Imperialism,* 449–52.

39. Arthur Marder, *The Anatomy of British Sea Power: A History of British Naval Policy in the Dreadnought Era, 1880–1905* (New York: Alfred A. Knopf, 1940), 84–104.

40. IDNS, 10–12.

41. Ibid., 15–17 and appendix table 3, column 4.

42. On the NID see Nicholas Black, *The British Naval Staff in the First World War* (Woodbridge, UK: Boydell Press, 2009).

43. For summary of the incomplete plans, see record of meeting held at the Admiralty on 31 April 1905, "The Protection of Ocean Trade in War Time," f.104ff, ADM.116/866B.

44. Bryan Ranft, "The Protection of British Seaborne Trade and the Development of a Systematic Planning for War, 1860–1906," in Brian Ranft, ed., *Technical Change and British Naval Policy, 1860–1939* (London: Hodder and Stoughton, 1977), 1–22; Kennedy, *Rise and Fall,* 215.

45. Admiralty (Custance), "Memorandum on Sea Power and the principles involved in it," [1901] f.196, Selborne Mss. 134 (2nd Lord Selborne papers, Bodleian Library, Oxford); Captain Battenberg's testimony to the Royal Commission on Food Supply, 5 November 1903, Q.12, 3. ADM.137/2872.

46. Fisher to A. K. Wilson, 12 February 1902, in FGDN, 1:226.

47. For an excellent case study of problems with contemporary British statistics generated to calculate the proportion of the agriculture workforce recruited into the Army during the First World War, see Peter Dewey, *British Agriculture in the First World War* (London: Routledge, 1989), 41–55.

48. Minute (3 March) by DNI, Captain Prince Louis of Battenberg, marked in pencil "Given to Prime Minister before receiving the Stafford House Committee," ADM.137/2872; see also Board of Customs to Admiralty, 1 October 1902, ADM.137/2872.

49. For Fisher's views that France would likely not be vulnerable, see Fisher to Earl Spencer, 12 December 1894, FGDN 1:124–25.

50. For early hints of thinking in this direction, see Offer, *The First World War,* 229–30.

51. Fisher to Mrs. Reginald Neeld (daughter), 23 March 1899, FGDN 1:139–40.

52. Interview with William Stead; he described this as "the most serious obstacle in the way of modern war." See Jan de Block (a.k.a. Ivan Stanislavovic Bloch), *Is War Now Impossible? Being an Abridgement of "The War of the Future in Its Technical, Economic and Political Relations,"* with a prefatory conversation with the author by William T. Stead (London: Grant Richards, 1899), 37. Fisher also met Captain Alfred Mahan and for many years thereafter maintained a correspondence.

53. Fisher to Stead, 4 February 1910, FGDN 2:240; see also Ruddock Mackay, *Fisher of Kilverstone* (Oxford: Clarendon Press, 1973), 179–80.

54. Bloch, *Is War Now Impossible?,* prefatory conversation with W. T. Stead, xliii.

55. Esher served as Liberal MP for Penryn and Falmouth, 1880–1885.

56. Nicholas d'Ombrain, *War Machinery and High Policy: Defence Administration in Peacetime Britain, 1902–1914* (Oxford: Oxford University Press, 1973), 235–37.

57. FNR, 90–94, 97–115.

58. Jon Sumida, "Geography, Technology, and British Naval Strategy in the Dreadnought Era," *Naval War College Review* 59, no. 3 (2006): 89–102.

59. Nicholas A. Lambert, "Strategic Command and Control for Maneuver Warfare: Creation of the Royal Navy's 'War Room' System, 1905–1915," *Journal of Military History* 69, no. 2 (2005): 361–410.

60. Mathew Seligmann, "Switching Horses: The Admiralty's Recognition of the Threat from Germany, 1900–1905," and "New Weapons for New Targets: Sir John Fisher, the Threat from Germany, and the Building of H. M. S. *Dreadnought* and H. M. S. *Invincible,* 1902–1907," both in *International History Review* 30, no. 2 (2008): 239–72.

61. Until 1805, the year of Nelson's famous victory, the nautical day for ships at sea began and ended at noon and ran twelve hours ahead of the civil day. Although by Admiralty letter of 11 October 1805 the Royal Navy discontinued this practice and a day was deemed to begin and end at midnight, this instruction did not reach Lord Nelson's fleet before the battle commenced. By old maritime reckoning, therefore, and according to the logs of the participating warships, the Battle of Trafalgar commenced before noon on 20 October and ended after noon on 21 October.

62. Mackay, *Fisher of Kilverstone,* 315; Fisher to Cecil Fisher (son), 23 October 1904, FGDN 2:44.

63. George Monger, *The End of Isolation: British Foreign Policy 1900–1907* (London: Nelson, 1963), 172–73; Keith Neilson, "A Dangerous Game of American Poker: Britain and the Russo-Japanese War," *Journal of Strategic Studies* 12, no. 1 (March 1989): 63–87.

64. Knollys to Hardinge, 15 November 1904, volume 7, Hardinge Mss., as cited in Monger, *End of Isolation,* 173; for Battenberg's encouragement of Selborne, see ch. 6.

65. Cabinet letter, 28 October 1904 (signed 29 October): "Russia; Dogger Bank Incident, Etc.; Decision Not to Mobilise the Fleet," CAB.41/29/33; Admiralty, for Cabinet [Disposition of ships to prevent the Russian Baltic Fleet from reaching Far East, German Battle Fleet], 2 November 1904, CAB.37/72/131.

66. Fisher to wife, n.d. [1 November 1904], FGDN 2:47.

67. Minute (21 November 1904) by Selborne, "First and Second Progress Report" of the committee appointed to consider the "Redistribution of the Fleet in Home and Foreign Waters," addressed to Admiralty Secretary, on draft of memorandum marked "secret and confidential," f.15, ADM.1/7736.

68. Ibid.

69. See FNR, ch. 3, and Lambert, "Strategic Command and Control."

70. The latest work is in Christopher Andrew and Paul Vallet, "The German Threat," in Richard Mayne, Douglas Johnson, and Robert Tombs, eds., *Cross Channel Currents: 100 Years of the Entente Cordiale* (London: Routledge, 2004), 23–33.

71. Monger, *End of Isolation,* 186–88.

72. Marder, *Anatomy,* 502.

73. Wilson to Selborne, 6 March 1904, f.9, Selborne Mss. 21.

74. Ottley to Fisher, 1 May 1905, FP164, ff.81–86, FISR 1/4 (Admiral Lord Fisher papers, Churchill College, Cambridge).

75. Ibid.

76. Admiralty to A. K. Wilson (CinC Channel), 6 May 1905, paras. 1, 6, 7; Admiralty to Beresford (CinC, Mediterranean), 30 August 1905, M.01036/05, ADM.116/900B.

77. Offered post ca. 3 August 1907 while serving at The Hague Peace Conference; see Ottley to Esher, 13 August 1907, in Maurice Brett, ed., *Journals and Letters of Reginald, Viscount Esher,* 4 vols. (London: Ivor Nicholson and Watson, 1934–1938), 2:243. To qualify for promotion, regulations required a captain to have at least six years of active service, of which at least three years must have been sea service. For Ottley's concern over personal finances motivating his career choices, see Ottley to Esher, 21 December 1911, and subsequent, ESHR 5/40 (2nd Viscount Esher papers, Churchill College, Cambridge).

78. Selborne to Balfour, n/d [May 1904], f.235, Add.Mss. 49707 (Additional Manuscripts, British Library, London); early career as mines and torpedo specialist; inventor of Ottley automatic mine.

79. This position was apparently first offered in February 1904 to Colonel George Aston, Royal Marines, but for some reason the offer was subsequently withdrawn. See Jim Beach, "The British Army, the Royal Navy and the 'Big Work' of Sir George Aston, 1904–1914," *Journal of Strategic Studies* 29, no. 1 (February 2006): 145–68.

80. Selborne to Balfour, 17 May 1904, Add.Mss. 49707, as cited in d'Ombrain, *War Machinery,* 187; Kerr to Selborne, 14 October 1904, f.296, Selborne Mss. 41. N.b.: Kerr notes the necessity of changing the retirement rules.

81. Ottley's character is discussed in d'Ombrain, *War Machinery,* 187–94.

82. Ibid., 189.

83. Fisher to Esher, 17 January 1909, FGDN, 2:220 (the irresistible urge to speak and a rage for writing).

84. D'Ombrain, *War Machinery,* 189.

85. Doubtless his finances were stretched by his son being commissioned into the Coldstream (Foot) Guards.

86. George Alexander Ballard (1862–1948): commander, December 1897; captain, December 1903; commodore, May 1914; rear-admiral, August 1914; vice-admiral, May 1919; joined NID in February 1902. See "The Protection of Commerce during War," JRUSI 42, no. 242 (April 1898): 365–405; "Gold Medal Prize Essay," JRUSI 44, no. 266 (April 1900).

87. Ottley to Esher, 8 October 1911, ESHR 4/3.

88. Ballard, Record of Business, 3 January 1907, Box 1, MS80/200, Ballard Mss. (George Ballard papers), NMM.

89. HMS *Terrible*, June 1906; HMS *Hampshire*, August 1907; HMS *Commonwealth*, December 1909; HMS *Britannia*, December 1910. For Ballard's appointment as DNI see Grant-Duff, diary entry 16 October 1911, AGDF 2/1 (Adrian Grant-Duff papers, Churchill College, Cambridge).

90. FNR, 265.

91. Churchill to Battenberg, 19 November 1911, Battenberg Mss. MB1/T9/43 (Admiral Prince Louis of Battenberg papers, Southampton University Library, UK); Asquith to Troubridge, 1 September 1910, A1, Troubridge Mss. (NMM) (Admiral Ernest Troubridge papers, NMM).

92. Grant-Duff, diary entry 25 April 1912, AGDF 2/2.

93. Arthur J. Marder, *The Anatomy of British Sea Power: A History of British Naval Policy in the Dreadnought Era, 1880–1905* (New York: Alfred A. Knopf, 1940).

94. Michael Howard, *The Continental Commitment: The Dilemma of British Defence Policy in the Era of the Two World Wars* (London: Temple Smith, 1972), 43n78; BESP, 22–24; PGS, 44–51, 47–52; Neil Summerton, "The Development of British Military Planning for a War Against Germany, 1904–1914," Ph.D. thesis, University of London, 1970, 27–32.

95. FDSF, 1:116–119, 384–85.

96. Lance Davis and Stanley Engerman, *Naval Blockades in Peace and War: An Economic History since 1750* (Cambridge: Cambridge University Press, 2006), 161.

97. FDSF, 1:116–19, 384–85. During the 1930s he was given only limited access to Admiralty archives, for which see Admiralty, "Professor Arthur J. Marder: Access to Admiralty Records," ADM.178/207. Lastly, the same cited file was referenced in a naval staff study dated 1929, and presented in very different light.

98. Ballard to Fisher 3 May 1909, enclosing "Remarks on the Framing of Certain Plans for War with German now at the Admiralty," ADM.1/8997. Ballard further stated that the 1901 appraisal was prepared by a/DNI Captain Charles Briggs.

99. Ibid.

100. Ibid.

101. CID, Minutes of 31st Meeting (Preparedness of Navy in Case of Intervention in Russo-Japanese War), 8 February 1904, CAB.38/4/8; War Office, "The Military Resources of Germany and Probable Method of Their Employment: II. Memorandum on the Military Policy to Be Adopted in a War with Germany," 23 February 1904, CAB.38/4/9; Minutes of 32nd Meeting (Combined Naval and Military Maneuvers; Indian Defence), 2 March 1904, CAB.38/4/11.

102. Marder, *Anatomy,* 502–3.

103. Ibid., 503; for a different interpretation, see Offer, *The First World War,* 227.

104. Ottley to Corbett, 1 June 1905, RIC 9/1 (Admiral Herbert Richmond papers, NMM).

105. Ottley to Cawdor, 6 July 1905, box 293, Cawdor Mss. (3rd Earl Cawdor Papers, Carmathanshire Record Office, UK).

106. G. A. Ballard, Review of Edward Bradford's *Life of Wilson, Naval Review,* 1924, 40–46. Ballard's authorship of this article is established by James Goldrick, "Author List for *The Naval Review,* 1913–1930," appendix C in James Goldrick and John Hattendorf, eds., *Mahan Is Not Enough: The Proceedings of a Conference on the Works of Sir Julian Corbett and Admiral Sir Herbert Richmond* (Newport, UK: Naval War College Press, 1993). Veiled reference to Fisher's strategic intentions in 1905 can be seen also in Wilson's testimony to the CID, Q.2527, 2528, 24 June 1909, CAB.16/9A; see also Esher to Clarke and Esher to Fisher, both 18 February 1906, in Brett, *Journals and Letters,* 2:144–45.

107. Fisher to Arnold White, 26 April 1906, FGDN 2:81.

108. Lambert, "Strategic Command Control," 377–83.

109. Ballard, Review of Edward Bradford's *Life of Wilson.*

110. Admiralty, Orders for Commander in Chief, Channel Fleet (enclosure No. 4), 6 May 1905, case 640, ADM.116/900B. According to Captain Ballard, this had not been Fisher's intention; it had been forced on him as the price of buying Wilson's political support. Ballard, Review of Edward Bradford's *Life of Wilson*; for reconfirmation, see reference to amended war orders dated 24 June 1905, in Marder, *Anatomy,* 503 and 512n.

111. Minute (26 May 1905) by Ottley to Fisher, cited in BR1875, Naval Staff Monograph, "The Naval Staff of the Admiralty: Its Work and Development," *Naval Staff,* September 1929, 45, NLMD.

112. Ibid. N.b.: Not cited by Marder.

113. Marder, *Anatomy,* 504.

114. Wilson to Selborne, 6 March 1904, f.9, Selborne Mss. 21.

115. Marder, *Anatomy,* 504.

116. Ibid., 505.

117. Ottley to Corbett, 3 July 1905, RIC 9/1.

118. Ottley, "Preparations of Plans for Combined Naval and Military Operations in War," printed July 1905, CAB.17/5.

119. Admiralty (Ottley), "British Intervention in the Event of France Being Suddenly Attacked by Germany," n.d., but the reference to Russia being involved in "the present war" indicates clearly it was written in late June or more likely early July 1905; f.67, Add.Mss. 49711. The suggestion to form a committee means it predates the CID discussions on the subject at midmonth. N.b.: This paper was transmitted to the prime minister by Fisher. Undated and unsigned copy in Admiralty files, ff.219–21, ADM.116/1043B2.

120. Ottley to Sir William May, 15 September 1907, 5, enclosed with May to Tweedmouth, 18 September 1907, 164, Tweedmouth Mss., NLMD.

121. Admiralty (Ottley), "British Intervention in the Event of France Being Suddenly Attacked by Germany," n.d., but internal content indicates late June or early July 1905, f.67, Add.Mss. 49711.

122. Ibid.

123. Marder, *Anatomy,* 505; FDSF, 1:115–9, 384–87.

124. For copies annotated by Sir George Clarke, see Ottley, "Preparations of Plans for Combined Naval and Military Operations in War," printed July 1905, CAB.17/5; "Copy Re-

turned with Remarks," dated 16 July 1905, CAB.17/95; there is yet another draft at ff.136–44; ADM.116/866B. N.b.: The front page is missing from this version, so it is not immediately obvious it is the same document; ff.137–44, ADM.116/866B.

125. Ottley, "Preparations of Plans for Combined Naval and Military Operations in War," printed July 1905, CAB.17/5.

126. Ibid.; Marder, *Anatomy,* 501–2. For Fisher's flippant remark about capturing Holstein within a week, see Fisher to Lansdowne, 22 April 1905, FGDN 2:55. Yet that same day Fisher wrote to the prime minister about the danger of war with France and Russia; see Mackay, *Fisher of Kilverstone,* 327–28. See also f.143 on Ottley Combined Operations Memo, July 1905, ADM.116/866B; for evidence the Schleswig plan was never "seriously entertained" and "put about for the purpose of a warning," see Thomas Sandarson (PUS Foreign Office) to Harold Termperley, 17 August 1922, Note 105(a), 87, BD, vol. 3.

127. General Sir John Grierson, "Military Policy in the Event of War—France," 2, n.d., but covering letter is dated 12 July 1905, in "War Plans: Mediterranean and Channel Fleets, 1903–1905," ADM.116/3111; Ottley Combined Operations memo, 5, ADM.116/866B.

128. Minute (3 January 1899) by Beaumont (DNI), "Military Operations in the Event of War with France—Requirements in East Indies (1888–1904)," details of plans first drawn up in 1886 to launch an amphibious operation to capture the French naval base of Diego Suarez in Madagascar, ADM.116/1228B.

129. Ottley Combined Operations Memo, f.137, ADM.116/866B.

130. Andrew Gordon, "Time after Time in the Horn of Africa," *Journal of Military History* 74, no. 1 (January 2010): 107–44.

131. This issue is touched upon in Hew Strachan, "The British Army, Its General Staff, and the Continental Commitment 1904–1914," in David French, ed., *The British General Staff: Reform and Innovation, c. 1890–1939* (London: Frank Cass, 2002).

132. Ottley, Combined Operations Memo, f.137, ADM.116/866B.

133. "Report on the Naval and Military Conference on Oversea Expeditions," 1905, 22–23, A973, WO.33/344 (War Office papers, The National Archives, Kew, UK).

134. Ottley to Churchill, 2 November 1911, CAB.17/8. For further evidence of disappointment at the results, see Beach, "The British Army," 150.

135. Clarke to Balfour, 11 July 1905, f.268, Add.Mss. 49701.

136. Clarke, "Proposed Subjects for Discussion at Meeting 13 July 1905," enclosed with Clarke to Balfour, 11 July 1905, f.268, Add.Mss. 49701.

137. Ibid.

138. Minutes of 75th (13 July 1905) and 76th (20 July 1905) meetings of the CID, CAB.38/9/60 and CAB.38/9/61. See also minutes of 77th meeting (26 July 1905), CAB.38/9/65.

139. Clarke to Balfour, 24 July 1905, f.276, Add.Mss. 49701. (Signed on 27 July 1905.)

140. PGS, 45–51; Ruddock Mackay, *Balfour, Intellectual Statesman* (Oxford: Oxford University Press, 1985). 184.

141. Esher to Balfour, 16 September 1905, in Brett, *Journals and Letters,* 2:110–11.

142. Grierson to Ottley, Winchester House, 12 July 1905, attached to uncataloged file enclosing copies of memoranda marked A, B, C, and D. A and C were attributed to Grierson; B and D to Ottley. Internal evidence (references to the Russo-Japanese War) dates these papers to early 1905. Ottley became DNI only in February 1905. File contained in case titled

"Military Policy in the Event of War—France," 12 July 1905, in "War Plans: Mediterranean and Channel Fleets, 1903–1905," ADM.116/3111.

143. Ibid., memorandum A, para. 1.

144. Ibid., conclusion.

145. Ibid., memorandum B, 2.

146. Ibid., 3.

147. Ibid., 4, 7–10.

148. Ibid., conclusion.

149. Ibid., memorandum C, "Further Memorandum on Military Policy in the event of War with France," (D.F. e.i.5).

150. Ibid., para. 5.

151. Ibid., paras. 3, 6.

152. Ibid., memorandum D.

153. It may be noted also that the prime minister too was disparaging of War Office ambitions in this direction, having remarked, "To keep on foot in time of peace an expeditionary force for no other purpose than to capture some outlying colony, if our enemy happened to possess one, is not worth the cost which it must necessarily entail." Balfour, Military Needs of the Empire: supplementary noted by the Prime Minister, 19 December 1904, CAB.3/1/28A.

154. For CID formation, see D'Ombrain, *War Machinery;* FNR, 56–67, 71–72, 116–21.

155. Balfour to Esher, 14 January 1904, f.60, Add.Mss. 49718; Esher to Campbell Bannerman, 1 March 1906, in Brett, *Journals and Letters,* 2:146–49; PGS, 48–52; Mackay, *Balfour,* 162–65, 180–95, esp. 186–87.

156. Fisher to Sandars, 10 October 1905, f.126, Add.Mss. 49711; see also Esher to Sandars, 17 September 1905, Add.Mss. 49719.

157. Fisher, "The Elaboration of Combined Naval and Military Preparation for War," 12 October 1905, f.122, Add.Mss. 49711; for Fisher's authorship, see Fisher to Clarke, 12 October 1905, FGDN, 2:29–30 (copy in ADM.116/984-B).

158. Ibid.

159. Generally: Rhodri Williams, *Defending the Empire: The Conservative Party and British Defence Policy, 1899–1915* (New Haven, CT: Yale University Press, 1991); Peter Fraser, *Lord Esher: A Political Biography* (London: Hart Davis, MacGibbon, 1973), 174–78.

160. Brett, *Journals and Letters,* 2:87–145, esp. Balfour to Esher, 16 May 1905, 87–88; Esher to Kitchener, 26 July 1905, 95; Esher to Balfour, 16 September 1905, 5 October 1905, and 13 October 1905, 110–11, 114–15, 117–18; Fisher to Clarke, 12 October 1905, FGDN, 3:29–30. See also John Gooch, "Sir George Clarke's Career at the Committee of Imperial Defence, 1904–1907," *Historical Journal* 18, no. 3 (1975): 555–69, esp. 558.

161. Mackay, *Balfour,* 187.

162. War Office (Grant-Duff), "British Military Action in Case of War with Germany," 28 August 1905, E2.10, WO.106/46; PGS, 48–52.

163. Ballard to Grant-Duff, 2 September 1905, E.2, 10; PGS, 48–50.

164. Major Adrian Grant-Duff (deputy a/DMO) to Ballard, 7 September 1905, and Callwell (a/DMO) to Ballard, 3 October 1905, enclosing memorandum "British Military Action in Case of War with Germany," ff.209, 217–18, ADM.116/1043B2; Slade to Corbett, 26 December 1905, RIC 9/1; for more details see PGS, 48–50; also John Gooch, *The Plans for War:*

The General Staff and British Military Strategy, c. 1900–1916 (London: Routledge and Kegan Paul, 1974), 279–80; Monger, *End of Isolation,* 230–31; Summerton, "Development of British Military Planning," 29–36.

165. PGS, 49, citing minute (26 September 1905) by Col. William R Robertson to Col. A. C. Hansard, E2, 10, WO.106/46.

166. Ottley to Fisher, 14 October 1905, f.127, Add.Mss. 49711.

167. PGS, 48, is correct in the chronology. Summerton, "Development of British Military Planning," assumes the NID took the initiative, 42–43. Offer, *First World War,* 226, recognizes the War Office initiated but speculates the Admiralty may have enticed them to do so; so does John Gooch, "Adversarial Attitudes: Servicemen, Politicians and Strategic Policy in Edwardian England, 1899–1914," in Paul Smith, ed., *Government and the Armed Foreces in Britain 1856–1990* (London: Hambledon Press, 1996) 63.

168. C. L. Ottley, "Submarine Automatic Mines," 11 February 1905, on "Memorandum by CL Ottley, DNI," 12 February 1905, ADM.116/866B.

169. Ibid., 8–9.

170. Ottley, "Supply of Automatic Submarine Mines to the Fleet," n.d. (printed May 1905) in NN, 89.

171. Ottley to Fisher, 14 October 1905, f.127, Add.Mss. 49711.

172. Marginalia by Fisher: "When Ottley says the Danube you know what river he means!" (the Elbe).

173. See esp. C. L. Ottley, "Submarine Automatic Mines," 12 February 1905, ADM.116/866B; also NN, 2:101, paras. 46, 51.

174. Fisher to Balfour, 20 October 1905, f.126, Add.Mss. 49711.

175. Grey to Haldane, 8 January 1906, f.10, Haldane Mss. 5907 (Richard Haldane papers, National Library of Scotland, UK).

176. Clarke to Esher, 15 December 1905, ESHR.10/37.

177. Clarke to Esher, 16 December 1905, ESHR.10/37.

178. PGS, 66.

179. CID, "Notes of Conferences Held at Whitehall Gardens," 2nd meeting, 6 January 1906, CAB.18/24. There is a good summary in William Phillpott, "The Strategic Ideas of Sir John French," *Journal of Strategic Studies* 12, no. 4 (December 1989): 461–64.

180. D'Ombrain, *War Machinery,* 81–98.

181. PGS, 64–67.

182. Ottley to Fisher, 13 January 1906, doc. 221(b), BD 3, 186. N.b.: A footnote states that all Ottley's "opinion" was excluded.

183. D'Ombrain, *War Machinery,* 85.

184. Grey to Tweedmouth, 16 January 1906, FO.800/87, as cited in Keith Neilson, "Great Britain," in Richard Hamilton and Holger Herwig, eds., *War Planning 1914* (Cambridge: Cambridge University Press, 2010), 175–97. Neilson offers the best explanation for Grey's position.

185. Mackay, *Fisher of Kilverstone,* 353.

186. D'Ombrain, *War Machinery,* 81–88; PGS, 66–81.

187. Clarke to Esher, 18 January and 21 January 1906, ESHR.10/37; for earlier expressions of doubt, see "Notes of a Conference," 19 December 1905, CAB.18/24.

188. For instance, it was found that shortages of artillery, medical, and logistical units meant that the "largest force which we could possible put in the field" was only about sixty thousand. See Esher to Clarke, 1 December 1906, ESHR.4/2.

189. PGS, 66; Mackay, *Fisher of Kilverstone,* 354–55.

190. Clarke to Esher, 2 January 1906, ESHR.10/37.

191. D'Ombrain, *War Machinery,* 83, 85; CID, "Notes on Conferences," CAB.38/11/4.

192. Clarke to Esher, 27 January 1906, ESHR.10/38. Borkum is an undefended islet off the German coast that commanded the Ems estuary.

193. Clarke to Chamberlain, 21 July 1905, AC7/5b/3, Chamberlain Mss. (Austen Chamberlain papers, Birmingham University Library, UK); Clarke to Esher, 10 February 1906, ESHR.10/38; FNR, 134–35; see also Gooch, "Sir George Clarke's Career," 567–68; Fisher to Tweedmouth, 9 July 1906, FGDN, 2:83. Ample evidence exists to support Fisher's complaint, for which see Clarke's correspondence with Campbell-Bannerman for 1906 and 1907, Add.Mss. 41213. Clarke felt much the same: Clarke to Ponsonby 30 July 1906, f.200, Campbell-Bannerman, Add.Mss. 41213.

194. Paul Haggie, "The Royal Navy and War Planning in the Fisher Era," in Paul Kennedy, ed., *The War Plans of the Great Powers, 1880–1914* (London: George Allen and Unwin, 1979), 118–32; PGS, 44–45; Gooch, *Plans for War,* 282; *John Coogan, The End of Neutrality: The United States, Britain and Maritime Rights, 1899–1915* (Ithaca, NY: Cornell University Press, 1981), 83; FDSF, 1:115–6; Offer, *First World War,* 226.

195. Mackay, *Fisher of Kilverstone,* 331–34.

196. FDSF, 1:116–19, 384–85.

197. NID appraisal, probably Ottley in early 1907, on copy M0171/07 attached to copy of Dumas to Lascalles, 29 January 1907, printed by the Foreign Office, February 1907, ff.255–69, ADM.116/1043B2.

198. For instance, see Wilson to Fisher, 9 March 1906, f.1, FISR 1/5.

199. Slade to Corbett, 16 and 26 December 1905, RIC 9/1.

200. Beach, "The British Army," 152; see also George Aston, "Combined Strategy for Fleets and Armies; or 'Amphibious Strategy,'" 15 July 1907, JRUSI 51, no. 3.

201. Slade to Corbett, 3 January 1908, file 6/e, Corbett Mss. (NMM) (Julian Corbett papers, collection held at National Maritime Museum, Greenwich, London).

202. Ottley to Esher, 8 October 1911, ESHR.4/3; Lewis Bayly, *Pull Together: The Memoirs of Admiral Sir Lewis Bayly* (London: Harrap, 1939), 131; FNR, 184.

203. Undated minute by unknown author on copy "Plan to Seize Heligoland," f.608, ADM.116/1043B2.

204. Minute (25 November 1907) by Slade, on correspondence relating to secret German-Russian agreement about making the Baltic a closed sea, HD 3/133 (Secret Intelligence Service papers, The National Archives, Kew, UK).

2. The Envisioning of Economic Warfare

Epigraph: Eyre Crowe to his wife, 21 August 1907, f.146/7, Ms.Eng. d.2901 (Sir Eyre Crowe Mss, Bodleian Library, Oxford).

1. Nicholas A. Lambert, "Strategic Command and Control for Maneuver Warfare: Creation of the Royal Navy's 'War Room' System, 1905–1915," *Journal of Military History* 69, no. 2 (2005): 380; Jon Sumida, "British Naval Administration and Policy in the Age of Fisher," *Journal of Military History* 54, no. 1 (January 1990): 1–26; Avner Offer, *The First World War: An Agrarian Interpretation* (New York: Oxford University Press, 1989), 230–31.

2. Memorandum by Captain Ballard RN [November 1911], B-17-0, "Naval War Staff 1911," CAB.17/8.

3. FNR, 157–64, 184–94.

4. Minute (8 March 1906) by Ottley on M.270/06 attached to Beresford to Admiralty, 5 February 1906 (Bulwark at Malta), "Mediterranean Stations: Remarks by the Commander in Chief on the War Standing Orders," ADM.116/900B; for Fisher's growing concern at Beresford's disloyalty, see Fisher to Tweedmouth, 24 April 1906, FGDN, 2:79.

5. Fisher to Cawdor, 2 March 1906, FGDN 2:68–9; Fisher to Fortescue, 14 April 1906, FGDN 2:71–2; minute (17 March 1906) by Fisher on Ottley minute, Mediterranean Station, ADM.116/900B.

6. Fisher to Corbett, 11 June 1906, FGDN 2:82 and note 2; for initial reference to the idea, see Corbett to Fisher, 13 May 1906, FGDN 2:81.

7. FNR, 134–36, 159–61; Fisher to Tweedmouth, 26 September 1906, FGDN 2:92; see also Clarke, "The Hague Conference—Arbitration and Reduction of Armaments," 20 April 1906, unnumbered CID paper, CAB.17/94.

8. Tweedmouth, "Memorandum Relative to Meeting, under Presidency of the Prime Minister, on Thursday, July 12, at 10, Downing Street," 17 July 1906, for cabinet, CAB.37/83/65.

9. Admiralty, "Remarks by the Board of Admiralty on the Attached Memorandum—Notes on Comparative Naval Strength," n.d. [July 1906], ADM.116/3095.

10. See discussion of issues by Kerr (1SL) to Selborne (1 Lord), 9 September 1904, f.238, Selborne Mss. 41; Cabinet Papers, "Proposals for 2nd Peace Conference," 8 November 1904, CAB.37/72/141.

11. For a good overview, see Keith Neilson, "The British Empire Floats on the British Navy: British Naval Policy, Belligerent Rights, and Disarmament, 1902–1909," in B. J. C. McKercher, ed., *Arms Limitation and Disarmament: Restraints on War, 1899–1939* (New York: Praeger, 1992).

12. Britain had declared food contraband in 1793 and 1795, for which see CID Paper 23-B, 2, "Papers Relating to Contraband of War: Memorandum on Russian Regulations Respecting Contraband of War," 20 May 1904, CAB.4/1/1.

13. Testimony of Captain Prince Louis of Battenberg, DNI, to the Royal Commission on Supply of Food and Raw Material in Time of War, Secret Session, 5 November 1903, Q.17, ADM.137/2872. Note further discussion on the subject of contraband, Q.89–103.

14. Hardinge to Nicholson, 18 March 1907, FO.800/339, as cited in Neilson, "The British Empire Floats."

15. Fisher to Capt. Seymour Fortescue, 14 April 1906, FGDN 2:72.

16. Minute (14 February 1906) by Ottley on "Recent Admiralty opinion on the 'right of search,'" ADM.1/8366/12; see also Lord Loreburn letter to the *Times,* 15 October 1905.

17. Fisher to Capt. Seymour Fortescue, 14 April 1906, FGDN 2:72.

18. Admiralty, "Contraband and Conditional Contraband," Remarks by Admiralty on XI and XII, dated 12 May 1906, enclosed in CID 75-B, 11, CAB.4/2.

19. Clive Parry, "Foreign Policy and International Law," in F. H. Hinsley, ed., British Foreign Policy under Sir Edward Grey (Cambridge: Cambridge University Press, 1977), 104.

20. Grey to Lord Desart, 1 December 1908 (final instructions), ff.135–41, 533/09, FO.371/794; emphasis added.

21. CID Paper 23-B, "Papers Relating to Contraband of War: Memorandum on Russian Regulations Respecting Contraband of War," 20 May 1904, CAB.4/1/1.

22. The point was reiterated more forcibly by the Admiralty in 1906; see Clarke, "The Hague Conference: Notes on Subjects," 15 May 1906, CAB.4/2/75B.

23. Neilson, "The British Empire Floats."

24. Keith Neilson, "A Dangerous Game of American Poker: Britain and the Russo-Japanese War," *Journal of Strategic Studies* 12, no. 1 (March 1989): 63–87.

25. CID Paper 23-B, "Papers Relating to Contraband of War: Memorandum on Russian Regulations Respecting Contraband of War," 20 May 1904, CAB.4/1/1; CID Paper 30-B, Joseph A. Choate, "Contraband of War: Note by the American Ambassador," 24 June 1904, CAB.4/1/1.

26. Gorst to Hardinge, 24 August 1904, vol. 7, Charles Hardinge Papers (Cambridge University Library, UK). I am indebted to Keith Neilson for this reference.

27. Arthur Link, *Wilson,* vol. 3: *The Struggle for Neutrality, 1914–1915* (Princeton, NJ: Princeton University Press, 1960), 685 and n6; Lance Davis and Stanley Engerman, *Naval Blockades in Peace and War: An Economic History since 1750* (Cambridge: Cambridge University Press, 2006), 118.

28. CID, Sir George Clarke, "The Value to Great Britain as a Belligerent of the Right of Search and Capture of Neutral Vessels," CID 41-B, 12 December 1904, CAB.4/1/1 (also CAB.38/6/120).

29. Ibid.

30. Ibid. See also Parry, "Foreign Policy and International Law," 102–4.

31. Eric Osborne, *Britain's Economic Blockade of Germany, 1914–1919* (London: Frank Cass, 2004), 26–31; John Coogan, *The End of Neutrality: The United States, Britain and Maritime Rights, 1899–1915* (Ithaca, NY: Cornell University Press, 1981), 73–75, 84–88.

32. FNR, 135–36.

33. Clarke to Giffen, 12 April 1906, 4/39–46, Giffen Mss. (Sir Robert Giffen papers, London School of Economics Library, UK). For Giffen's written appraisal referred to in this letter, see "Right of Search and Capture—Note by Sir R Giffen," ff.237–41, CAB.17/85.

34. Clarke, "The Capture of the Private Property of Belligerents at Sea: Memorandum Prepared by Direction of the Prime Minister," 4 May 1906, CID paper 73-B, CAB.4/2. N.b.: 73-B opens with a summary of the conclusions offered in 41-B. See esp. paras. 31, 32, and 37.

35. Ibid., concl. B + C.

36. Ibid., para. 54; on disarmament, see Clarke, "The Hague Conference—Arbitration and Reduction of Armaments," 20 April 1906, unnumbered CID paper, CAB.17/94.

37. Clarke, "Capture of Private Property at Sea—Note on Memorandum Address to the Prime Minister and Signed by 168 Members of the House of Commons," 19 December 1906, ff.273–74, CAB.17/85.

38. Fisher to Tweedmouth, 16 October 1906, FGDN 2:101.

39. SC 1:38.

40. Although working in different departments, both are listed as working from Room 43 OB from 1903 on. "Naval Intelligence Department, 1903, Distribution of Work," 137–39, BR 1875, Naval Staff of the Admiralty, NLMD.

41. HMS *Terrible* and HMS *Hampshire.*

42. SC 1:39. See also reference to three other officers in Ballard to Fisher, "Remarks on the Framing of Certain Plans for War with Germany Now at the Admiralty," 1909, ADM.1/8997.

43. FP2, 316, implies that Corbett and Slade were members, as do numerous others, including Barry Hunt, *Sailor-Scholar: Admiral Sir Herbert Richmond* (Montreal: Wilfred Laurier, 1982), 18–19; and Shawn Grimes, "The Baltic and Admiralty War Planning, 1906–1907," *Journal of Military History* 74, no. 2 (April 2010): 407–31. For Slade's minimal contribution, see Ballard to Fisher, "Remarks on the Framing of Certain Plans for War," 3.

44. SC 1:40.

45. Plans A, B, and C.

46. Ballard to Fisher, "Remarks on the Framing of Certain Plans for War," 1–2. Ballard indicates that his committee worked only on A, B, and C. The two founded upon previous papers were A (Ballard's own 1902 appraisal) and C (based upon A. K. Wilson's letter to the Admiralty of June 1905).

47. Memorandum (B.17.1) by Capt. Ballard RN, Naval War Staff, annotated October 1911, ff.1–15, CAB.17/8.

48. Offer, *First World War,* 235.

49. Ottley to Churchill, 1 November 11, B.17(4), ff.28–30, CAB.17/8. The archives contain an unsigned "Plan to Seize Heligoland" dating from this period, f.608, vol. 3, ADM.116/1043B2.

50. Hankey to Ballard, 5 December 1911, ff.20–23, CAB.17/95.

51. Even the finest historians have made this error. See summary in Michael Howard, *The Continental Commitment: The Dilemma of British Defence Policy in the Era of the Two World Wars* (London: Temple Smith, 1972), 44–45.

52. McKenna testimony, 25 May 1909, 2185, 2189, 245–46, CAB 16/9A. N.b.: At the War College does not mean using War College staff.

53. Paul Haggie, "The Royal Navy and War Planning in the Fisher Era," in Paul Kennedy, ed., *The War Plans of the Great Powers, 1880–1914* (London: Allen and Unwin, 1979), 123–24; "Notes on Attached War Plans," "1907/Ballard's Committee," ff.225–42, ADM.116/1043B2. Who wrote this appraisal is a matter of debate. Offer insists it was Hankey (p. 236), but Hankey was then serving in the Mediterranean Fleet, for which see Hankey to his wife, 30 May 1907, HNKY.3/15 (Lord Hankey papers, Churchill College, Cambridge). The tone suggests it was written by an officer of command rank, possibly even Captain Ottley; failing that, the most likely candidate is one of the assistant DNIs: Captains Henry Campbell, Osmond de Brock, or Herbert King-Hall. Another possibility is Captain Alexander Bethell, who was "unofficially" involved in war planning beginning in 1908.

54. The 188-page version was distributed in January 1908; it excludes AKW commentary. Ff.191–348, stamped RO May 1934 and signed E. W. Griffen, dated 26 April 1907, vol. 1, ADM.116/1043B.

55. FP2.

56. For Fisher's joint authorship of Part 1, see Christopher Martin, "The 1907 Naval War Plans and the Second Hague Peace Conference: A Case of Propaganda," *Journal of Strategic Studies* 28, no. 5 (October 2005): 833–56, esp. 835–39, 841.

57. Yet earlier versions written under the title "War with Germany," printed in September 1906, ADM.116/1036B.

58. Remarks on War Plans by Admiral of the Fleet Sir A. K. Wilson, marked No. 1, May 1907, printed 5 June 1907, stamped RO 1 May 1934, f.59, vol. 1, ADM.116/1043B.

59. Introductory remarks, para. 6, f.363, FP2.

60. FP2, 397, Plan B, para. 7; for Borkum being undefended in 1907 see Slade "War With Germany," 1 September 1906, 2–3, ADM.116/1036B. It is interesting to note that Britain had seized Borkum before; see Rory Muir, *Britain and the Defeat of Napoleon, 1807–1815* (New Haven, CT: Yale University Press, 1996), 306.

61. For questioning assumptions, see FP2, para. 11, 365; paras. 30–31, 370–71.

62. For distant blockade, see Ruddock Mackay, *Fisher of Kilverstone* (Oxford: Clarendon Press, 1973), 370; for close blockade, see BESP, 28–29; Haggie, "War Planning," 123–24; Coogan, *End of Neutrality,* 239; Offer, *First World War,* 235; PGS, 105; John Gooch, "Adversarial Attitudes: Servicemen, Politicians and Strategic Policy in Edwardian England, 1899–1914," in Paul Smith, ed., *Government and the Armed Forces in Britain 1856–1990* (London: Hambledon, 1996), 53–74; for more outlandish theories, see Paul Hayes, "Britain, Germany and the Admiralty's Plans for Attacking German Territory, 1906–1915," in Lawrence Freedman, Paul Hayes, and Robert O'Neill, eds., *War, Strategy and International Politics: Essays in Honor of Sir Michael Howard* (Oxford: Oxford University Press, 1992), 95–116.

63. SC 1:39.

64. Martin, "1907 Naval War Plans," 835–40.

65. Fisher to Corbett, 9 March 1907, FGDN 2:120.

66. Fisher to Corbett, 17 March 1907, Corbett Mss. (NMM).

67. Fisher to Corbett, 4 April 1907, Corbett Mss. (NMM), cited in Martin, "1907 Naval War Plans," 839. Fisher invited Corbett to assist on 9 March 1907; Fisher to Corbett, FGDN 2:120.

68. This point was made to me by Dr. Christopher Martin, and I remain grateful to him for so willingly sharing his thoughts and research. Martin, "1907 Naval War Plans," 835.

69. Ottley to Mr. Phillips, 4 April 1907, enclosing Corbett to Phillips, 2 April 1907, "an introduction to the war plans," corr. file 1900–1927, Crease Mss. (Captain Thomas Crease papers, NLMD); reference to a final draft in Fisher to Corbett, 21 April 1907, Corbett Mss. (NLMD); WP Part I: Some Principles of Naval Warfare, marked copy No. 1 and stamped R.O. 1 May 1934, ff.22–58, printed at FO, 1 May 1907, vol. 1, ADM.116/1043B; for the suggestion that Slade edited the final version, see Slade to Corbett, 22 April 1907, Corbett Mss. (NLMD); for evidence Corbett's paper was printed during the first week of May, see Beresford to Admiralty, 8 May 1907 (contains Beresford's critique of Corbett's "pedagogue" plan). Copy in Appendix 2, 84, Beresford Enquiry, CAB.16/9B.

70. Ottley to Esher, 8 October 11, ESHR.4/3; see also Ottley, "Note of a Conversation with Lord Fisher at the Admiralty—Dec. 1909," in "Naval War Staff, 1909," CAB.17/6.

71. McKenna testimony, Beresford Enquiry, 4th meeting, 852, CAB.16/9A.

72. Fisher to Beresford, 30 April 1907, FGDN 2:122. The eight ideas clearly refers to part III. See also McKenna's remarks to Beresford enquiry (Q.859 and 860), CAB.16/9A.

73. Admiralty, Preface to 1907 War Plans, f.331, ADM.16/1043B2. N.b.: Not included in NRS version.

74. Beresford to Admiralty, 8 May 1907, f.18, enclosing remarks on War Plans—general remarks parts 2, 3, and 4, ADM.116/1037; copy in Beresford Enquiry, Appendix 11, 93, CAB.16/B.

75. Ibid.

76. FNR, 188–93.

77. Copies of Beresford's official correspondence are contained in "Appendixes to Proceedings of a Sub-Committee of the Committee of Imperial Defence Appointed to Inquire into Certain Questions of Naval Policy Raised by Lord Charles Beresford, 1909," 22–44, CAB16/9B.

78. Tweedmouth to Fisher, 8 June 1907, FGDN 2:125–26. Note refusal to distribute Fisher's documents cited above.

79. Ibid.

80. Letter M-0636, Admiralty to CinC Channel Fleet, 14 June 1907, canceling war order issued 24 June 1905, ADM.116/1043B2.

81. Minute (16 July 1907) by Fisher on Beresford to Admiralty, 8 May 1907, f.18, ADM.116/1037; memo entitled "Most Secret" (transcript of meeting between Fisher, Beresford, and Tweedmouth, 5 July 1907), ff.234–53, Add.Mss. 49711. Covering letter marked "remarks thereon," f.254, is dated 5 July 1907.

82. Notes for War Plans, undated papers, MS82/006, Corbett Mss. (NMM); Printed Naval Papers from Sir John Fisher (undated), Harcourt Mss., Mss.Dep. 510 (Lewis Harcourt papers, Bodleian Library, Oxford); Fisher to Garvin, 8 June 1907, Fisher Recip., Box 1, file 1/12, Garvin Papers. (James L. Garvin papers, Harry Ransom Center, University of Texas at Austin).

83. "Notes of Conversation Between Mr. Haldane, Mr. McKenna and Colonel Repington," 8 May 1908, 7, MCKN.16/12 (Reginald McKenna papers, Churchill College, Cambridge).

84. A. J. A. Morris, *The Scaremongers: The Advocacy of War and Rearmament, 1896–1914* (London: Routledge, 1984); Jon Sumida, "The Historian as a Contemporary Analyst: Sir Julian Corbett and Admiral Sir John Fisher," in James Goldrick and John Hattendorff, eds., *Mahan Is Not Enough: The Proceedings of a Conference on the Works of Sir Julian Corbett and Admiral Sir Herbert Richmond* (Newport, UK: Naval War College Press, 1993), 125–41.

85. Martin, "1907 Naval War Plans," 835.

86. Fisher to Corbett, 8 July 1907, 246, FISR1/5. My thanks to Chris Martin for bringing this to my attention.

87. Fisher to Tweedmouth, 21 January 1908, 279, FISR.1/16; Fisher to Grey, 23 January 1908 and to Tweedmouth, 23 January 1908, FGDN, 2:155–59.

88. Copy, "War Plans," ADM.116/1043B. N.b.: This volume was received by the Record Office from M branch on 3 November 1932 for record and retention. See also FNR, 177–82; Mackay, *Fisher of Kilverstone,* 367–68.

89. Fisher to Leyland, 7 November 11, FGDN 2:411–2.

90. For veiled references, see FP2, paras. 15 and 16, 366. Also para. 28, 369.

91. Offer, *First World War,* 228–29, citing Hankey to Lloyd George, 2 December 1930, f.6, LG G/8/18/15 (David Lloyd George papers, Parliamentary Archive, London).

92. SC 1:40.

93. Ballard to Fisher, "Remarks on the Framing of Certain Plans for War," 2; see also PMS, 101.

94. "Notes on Attached War Plans," enclosed in file marked Ballard Committee, f.231, ADM.116/1043B2; emphasis added.

95. FP2, para. 12, 365.

96. Ibid, 363.

97. "Notes on Attached War Plans," enclosed in file marked Ballard Committee, f.231, ADM.116/1043B2.

98. FP2, 364.

99. Martin, "1907 Naval War Plans," 848.

100. FP2, para. 13, 365–67.

101. FP2, Plan B, paras. 1–3 (quote from para 3), 395; see also para. 49–50, 408.

102. FP2, para. 3, 365, and paras. 48, 49, 50, 408.

103. FP2, paras. 2 and 4, 433–34.

104. FP2, "General Outline" of Plan C1, para. 2, 436.

105. NID appraisal, probably Ottley in Early 1907 on copy M0171/07 attached to copy of Dumas to Lascalles, 29 January 1907, printed by the Foreign Office, February 1907, ff.255–69, ADM.116/1043B2 (cited hereafter as "Ottley Appraisal").

106. "Ottley Appraisal," f.259.

107. Ibid., f.260.

108. Ibid., f.261.

109. FP2, para. 33, 371–72; "Remarks on the Probable Results of Plan (A)," para. 41, 382–83.

110. "Ottley Appraisal."

111. Minute (16 June 1907) by Ottley, "Proposed Substitution of the Right of Sequestration for that of Capture of Belligerent Merchant Shipping," ADM.1/8366/12.

112. Julian Corbett, "The Capture of Private Property at Sea," *The Nineteenth Century* 61 (June 1907): 990–91.

113. FP2, "Remarks on the Probable Results of Plan (A)," para. 41, 382–83.

114. Exchange of views between Captain Charles Ottley (DNI) and General Sir John Grierson (DMI) on "Military Policy in the Event of War with France," enclosed in Grierson to Ottley, 12 July 1905, "War Plans: Mediterranean and Channel Fleets," ADM.116/3111. See especially Paper D therein (by Ottley), entitled "Remarks on 'C,' " 2.

115. G. A. Ballard, "The Protection of Commerce During War," *JRUSI* 42, no. 242 (April 1898): 366.

116. E. F. Inglefield (Lloyd's) to H. H. Campbell (a/DNI), 14 November 1907, ADM.137/2864. (Head of Trade Division, 1901 to August 1906; Second Secretary of Lloyd's, 1906–1918). I have removed the paragraph breaks.

117. Ottley, "The Capture of Private Property of Belligerents at Sea," 14 May 1906, 68, CO.537/349; also Ottley, "Statement Respecting Questions Raised in CID Paper No. 66B," 26, FO.881/9120, as cited in Martin, "1907 Naval War Plans," 847. Note refs at—CAB.4/2/66B, 26 October 1905.

118. Minute (27 January 16) by Greene on Foreign Office Memorandum on Blockade, dated 28 December 1915, f.184, ADM.137/1164.

119. Grey, [The Hague Conference: Immunity from Capture at Sea in Time of War], 3 June 1907, CAB.37/89/65.

120. Grey to Fry, 12 June 1907, No. 1, Treaty, 19160, FO.372/67.

121. Satow journal, entry for 16 June 1907, f.23, Satow Papers, PRO.30/33/16/10.

122. Martin, "1907 War Plans," 840.

123. *The Nation*, 4, Sir Henry Campbell Bannerman, 2 March 1907.

124. Coogan, *End of Neutrality*, 238–39; Arthur Marsden, "The Blockade," in F. H. Hinsley, ed., *Foreign Policy under Sir Edward Grey* (Cambridge: Cambridge University Press, 1977), 488; Clive Parry, "Foreign Policy and International Law," in Hinsley, *Foreign Policy under Sir Edward Grey*, 102.

125. Paraphrase of Coogan, *End of Neutrality*, 86; this is certainly true for the printed official proceedings, but for contradiction, see Crowe to his wife, 17 August 1907, f.135, Ms. Eng. d.2901.

126. Osborne, *The Blockade*, 40.

127. Fisher to Corbett, 23 May 1907, Corbett Mss. (NLMD). Forwarding copy of Chancellor's Cabinet Paper, "The Capture of Private Property at Sea."

128. Fisher to Esher, 17 October 1907, ESHR.10/42.

129. Crowe to his wife, 16 June 1906, f.7, Ms.Eng. d.2901.

130. Crowe to Mrs. Crowe, 16 June (f.7), 17 June (f.9), 18 June (f.10), 19 June (f.13), 2 July (f.36), 7 July (f.45), 8 July (f.49) 1907, all Crowe Ms.Eng.d.2901.

131. Crowe to his wife, 17 and 18 June 1907, ff.8–10, Crowe Ms.Eng. d.2901; Ottley to Tweedmouth, 16 July 1907, 188, Tweedmouth Mss.

132. Crowe to his wife, 7 July 1907, f.45, Crowe Ms.Eng. d.2901.

133. Ibid.

134. Letter of 2 July 1907, f.36, ibid.

135. Letter of 8 July 1907, f.49, ibid.

136. Ibid.

137. See letters between Tweedmouth and Grey, June and July 1907, f.100, FO.800/87.

138. Grey to Tweedmouth, 17 August 1907, f.126, FO.800/87; May to Tweedmouth, 11 September 1907, 161, Tweedmouth Mss. Informative on this point are Crowe's letters to his wife, 17 August 1907, f.135, and 21 August 1907, f.146, Ms.Eng. d.2901.

139. Coogan, *End of Neutrality*, 96.

140. Reay to Campbell Bannerman, 21 July 1907, Add.Mss. 52514, as cited in Coogan, *End of Neutrality*, 93.

141. What follows is substantially based upon the work of Dr. Christopher Martin. He is the first scholar to recognise the significance of the Italian initiative. I am indebted to him for many hours of discussion and allowing me to read early drafts of his paper on this subject, for which see Christopher Martin, "The Declaration of London: A Matter of Operational Capability," *Historical Research* 82, no. 218 (November 2009): 731–55.

142. Satow Journal, 16 August 1907, cited in Martin, "Declaration of London."

143. Tweedmouth to Grey, 24 August 1907, FO.800/87 as cited in Martin, "Declaration of London."

144. Satow Journal (26 January 1907–22 April 1909), f.58, entry for 29 August 1907, PRO.30/33/16/10 (Miscellaneous Series of papers, The National Archives, Kew, UK).

145. Fry to Grey, 5 September 1907, FO.881/9077, as cited in Martin, "Declaration of London."

146. May to Tweedmouth, 7 and 8 September 1907, 158 and 159, Tweedmouth Mss.

147. Adm. to FO, 12 September 1907, FO.881/9077.

148. Minute (27 January 1916) by Greene, "Foreign Office Memorandum of 28th December 1915," f.185, ADM.137/1164.

149. Ottley to Sir William May, 15 September 1907, Tweedmouth Mss.

150. Ibid.

151. Marginal comment on draft letter, Admiralty to Foreign Office, 20 September 1907, attached to May to Tweedmouth, 20 September 1907, 165, Tweedmouth Mss.

152. Memorandum (18 September 1907) by Slade, "Memorandum on Continuous Voyage and the Probable Result of Abandoning the Right," enclosed with May to Tweedmouth, 18 September 1907, 164, Tweedmouth Mss.

153. Telegram (14 September 1907) Fry to Grey, FO.881/9077, as cited in Martin, "Declaration of London."

154. Ottley to Sir William May, 15 September 1907, Tweedmouth Mss.

155. Ibid.

156. Slade, "Memorandum on Continuous Voyage and the Probable Result of Abandoning the Right," 18 September 1907, enclosed with May to Tweedmouth, 18 September 1907, 164, Tweedmouth Mss.

157. Copy of Telegram (17 September 1907) from Ottley to May, Tweedmouth Mss. This document is not cited by Martin.

158. May to Tweedmouth, 17 September 1907, 163, Tweedmouth Mss.

159. Ibid.; returned on 22 September, for which see Crowe to wife, 22 September 1907, f.36, Crowe papers, Ms.Eng. d.2902.

160. Slade, "Memorandum on Continuous Voyage and the Probable Result of Abandoning the Right," 18 September 1907, reel 2, Slade Mss.

161. Greene to Tweedmouth, 20 September 1907, 196, Tweedmouth Mss.; for May's unhappiness with the concessions already made, see also May to Tweedmouth, 20 September 1907, 165, Tweedmouth Mss.

162. Crowe to wife, 20 September 1907, f.31, Ms.Eng. d.2902.

163. Fry to Grey, 24 September 1907, No. 220, copy in ADM.116/1079.

164. Eyre Crowe to Sir Charles Dilke MP, 15 October 1907, FO.800/243, as cited in Coogan, *End of Neutrality,* 101; see also Crowe to Tyrell, 11 October 1907, BD, VIII, No. 254, 287.

165. Fisher to King Edward VII, 8 September 1907, FGDN 2:129–30.

166. Fisher to Tweedmouth, 1 October 1907, 143, Tweedmouth Mss.

167. Foreign Office to Admiralty, 14 January 1908, ADM.116/1079; see also minute (26 October 1908) by Greene, on report of Naval Conference Committee, ADM.116/1079, and reference to conversation between Slade, Ottley, and Crowe at the CID rooms, entry 8 January 1908, in Slade diary, Slade Mss.

168. Minute (17 February 1908) by Greene, attached to FO to Admiralty, 14 January 1908, ADM.116/1079.

169. Coogan, *End of Neutrality,* 112; see also Grey's final instructions to Lord Desart, 1 December 1908, esp. paras. 6 and 7, "Maritime Conference" ff.135–41, 533/09, FO.371/794.

170. Martin, "Declaration of London."

171. Ottley to Esher, 12 August 1907, in Maurice Brett, ed., *Journals and Letters of Reginald, Viscount Esher,* 4 vols. (London: Ivor Nicholson and Watson, 1934–1938), 2:243; see also John Gooch, "Sir George Clarke's Career at the Committee of Imperial Defence, 1904–1907," *Historical Journal* 18, no. 3 (1975): 568.

172. By Admiralty letter is dated 28 October 1907, Slade was appointed DNI effective 1 November 1908, reel 2, Slade Mss. During the interim, Captain Herbert King-Hall (a/DNI) served as acting head of the department.

173. Martin, "Declaration of London," 9; see Admiralty to FO, 31 August 1908, M8377, as well as original draft in Fisher's hand as well as copy of Fisher to Slade, all dated 3 August 1908, ADM.116/1079.

174. FNR, 176–77.

175. Minute (27 January 1916) by Greene, reply to "Foreign Office Memorandum of 28th December 1915," f.185, ADM.137/1164; see also Minute (26 October 1908) by Greene, on report of Naval Conference Committee, ADM.116/1079.

176. Ottley to Esher, 30 January 11, ESHR.5/40.

177. Fisher to Grey, 29 July 1908, FO.800/97, as cited in Martin, "Declaration of London," 735.

178. Slade, "Naval Conference Committee—Memorandum by the Director of Naval Intelligence," 29 September 1908, enclosed under docket NID 972, ADM.116/1079.

179. Minute (29 October 1908) by Fisher and (18 November 1908) by McKenna, on docket NID 972, ADM.116/1079; Slade diary entry, 12 November 1908, Slade Mss.

180. Coogan, *End of Neutrality,* 239.

181. Minute (19 October 1908) by Greene on NID 972, docket "Naval Conference on International Law"; see also text of Conference Committee memo, 25, para. 5, which reads: "Continuous voyage—we should endeavor to maintain the British doctrine as regards contraband; as regards blockade, it is not considered that it can be supported," all ADM.116/1079.

182. Grey to Desart, 1 December 1908, "Maritime Conference," ff.135–41, 533/09, FO.371/794. N.b.: Paras. 15, 25, and 26 clearly show the British delegates were instructed to retain continuous voyage; paras. 22 and 23 neatly summarize the Admiralty view of how the proposed new blockade laws would be interpreted.

183. The insertion by the Germans and Dutch of article 19, which provided "that the blockade must not prevent access to a non-blockaded port," seems intended to prevent this interpretation, but afterward the Admiralty (esp. R. A. Bethell) felt this article was sufficiently ambiguous to justify still regarding their "distant blockade lines" as an "effective blockade." See also Crowe, "Notes of Further Discussions with Dr. Kriege on December 12 and 13, 1908," n.d. [14 or 15 December 1908], FO.371/794.

184. Desart, "Memorandum by the Earl of Desart Respecting the Effect of Some of the Provisions of Declaration of London, 1909," 14 December 1910, Slade Mss.

185. FP2, 371.

186. "Naval Conference—Memoranda Setting Out the Views of His Majesty's Government, Founded upon the Decisions in the British Courts, as to the Correct Rules of International Law on the Points Enumerated in the Programme of the Conference," chapter 7,

"Transfer of Merchant-Vessels to a Neutral Owner during or in Contemplation of Hostilities," ADM.116/1079.

187. Ibid.

188. Slade, "Naval Conference Committee," 21.

189. Minute (4 December 1908) by Crowe, "Notes on Conversation with M. Kriege," FO.371/794; see also Grey to Desart, 1 December 1908, para. 5, "Maritime Conference," ff.135–41, 533/09, FO.371/794.

190. Crowe, "Notes of Further Discussions with Dr. Kriege on December 12 and 13, 1908," n.d., ff.135–41, 533/09, FO.371/794.

191. Slade, "Interim Report—the Naval Conference," 14 December 1908, ADM.116/1079; for Slade's early concern about the German "uncompromising attitude," see diary entry, 4 December 1908, Slade Mss.

192. Under subheading "Blockade," Articles 1, 18. and 19, see: Slade, "Interim Report—the Naval Conference," 14 December 1908, ADM.116/1079.

193. Slade diary, 8 December 1908, Slade Mss.

194. Minute (15 December 1908) by Greene, ADM.137/1164.

195. Slade, "Naval Conference Committee," 15 December 1908, f.194, ADM.137/1164. Present: Grey, McKenna, Lord Desart, Crowe, Hurst, Ottley, Slade, and Greene. N.b.: The version cited, ff.194–98, is the "final" version, dated 30 December 1908; another version exists in ADM.116/1079. The Foreign Office commentary on the meeting is entitled "Naval Conference: Record of Meeting with Mr. McKenna in Sir Edward Grey's Room at the House of Commons on Dec 15, 1909," signed Eyre Crowe, 24 December 1908, and can be found at ff.143–48, 564/09, FO.371/794.

196. McKenna, f.196. ADM.137/1164; Slade had made the same point about deterrent in his memo of 14 December 1908, 3.

197. Minutes of meeting, 15 December 1908, ADM.116/1079.

198. Minute (26 December 1908) by Grey, attached to notes on "Naval Conference," dated 15 December 1908; Greene to Crowe, 23 December and 30 December 1908; unsigned (McKenna) objections to Grey's insertion of para. A, 22 December 1908; notes by Vincent Badderly (private secretary to First Lord) on conversation with Mr. Crowe, 28 December 1908, all found in ADM.116/1079.

199. Minute (24 December 1908), "Record of Meeting with Mr. McKenna in Sir Edward Grey's Room at the HOC on Dec 15, 1908," f.146, FO.371/794.

200. Attached minute (26 December 1908) by Crowe, f.146, FO.371/794.

201. Minute (26 December 1908) by Grey, attached to notes on "Naval Conference," dated 15 December 1908, ADM.116/1079. N.b.: This case contains drafts and further correspondence relating to the "Naval Conference" document found in ADM.137/1164 and cited above.

202. McKenna to Grey, 1 January 1909, f.180, FO.800/87.

203. McKenna to Asquith, 3 January 1909, f.24, Asquith Mss. 21 (H. H. Asquith papers, Bodleian Library, Oxford).

204. Fisher, "War Plans and the Distribution of the Fleet," 1908, ADM.116/1043B1.

205. Fisher to Garvin, 5 November 1908, Recip. File, file 5/12, Gavin Mss.

206. Minute (24 December 1908), "Record of Meeting with Mr. McKenna in Sir Edward Grey's Room at the HOC on Dec 15, 1908," f.146, FO.371/794; for evidence that

Crowe believed Fisher was sincere, see Crowe to Satow (private), 11 April 1909, PRO.30/33/12/4.

207. Minute 13 May 1909) by Crowe on FO print, "London Conference on International Maritime Law," 18125, ADM.116/1236; for evidence of this, see copy, Selborne, "Memorandum by the Lord Chancellor," 24 April 1885, CID Paper 23-B, 4, "Papers Relating to Contraband of War: Memorandum on Russian Regulations Respecting Contraband of War," 20 May 1904, CAB.4/1/1.

208. Fisher to Jellicoe, 30 December 13, Add.Mss. 49006.

209. Hankey, "Memorandum of a Conference," 23 February 1911, McKenna, Ottley, and Hankey present, ff.22–25, CAB.17/87.

210. NID, "Note on Contraband" (unsigned), 3, n.d. (ca. 1907), "Rights and Duties of Neutral Powers in Maritime War—Miscellaneous Papers," ADM.116/1073.

211. Green to Tweedmouth, 20 September 1907, 196, Tweedmouth Mss.

3. The Exposition of Economic Warfare

1. Ottley to May, 15 September 1907, 164a, Tweedmouth Mss.

2. May to Tweedmouth, 17 September 1907, 163, Tweedmouth Mss.

3. FNR, 169–77.

4. Ibid.

5. Memorandum (May 1908) by Slade, as cited in Archibald C. Bell, *A History of the Blockade of Germany and the Countries Associated with Her in the Great War: Austria-Hungary, Bulgaria, and Turkey* (London: HMSO, 1961), 25. N.b.: Bell was given access in the 1930s to the original files, which have since been lost. Fragments exist in miscellaneous files (case 0073) created between 1932 and 1936, ADM.116/1043B-1 and /1043B-2.

6. Captain Robert F. Scott was appointed to command the battleship HMS *Albemarle* in January 1907.

7. Avner Offer, *The First World War: An Agrarian Interpretation* (New York: Oxford University Press, 1989), 230–32, 306–7.

8. Ibid., 231.

9. Ibid., 223–25.

10. Ibid., 306–7; BESP, 57–58.

11. See Chapter 5.

12. Unsigned memo [Campbell] enclosed in folder marked "German Trade and Shipping," entitled "Prepared When Admiral Campbell Was HTD," ADM.137/2864.

13. "Information Required as to the Nature of German Oversea Trade," 28 May 1908, f.211, FO.371/460.

14. Minutes (1 and 7 September 1908), 30085 f.268, by Crowe, 18395, FO.371/460.

15. Gerhard Ritter, *Der Schlieffenplan: Kritik eines Mythos* (Munich: Oldenbourg, 1956), 180, as cited in Marc Frey, "Trade, Ships, and the Neutrality of the Netherlands in the First World War," *International History Review* 19, no. 3 (August 1997): 541–62.

16. Replies from Antwerp, Rotterdam, and Amsterdam, 18395, FO.371/460. Admiralty copies in ADM.1347/2782.

17. Minute, Robert Craigie, on No. 26217 German Oversea Trade—28 July 1908. Reply by William Ward, Hamburg, f.251, FO.371/460.

18. Campbell, "German Trade in Time of War," July 1908, on docket "Memos on Trade as Affecting Germany by Local Vice Consuls," ADM.137/2872.

19. Ibid.; Offer, *First World War,* 231.

20. Trade Division Memorandum annotated "Prepared When Admiral Campbell Was HTD," n.d. [1908], ADM.137/2864.

21. Offer, *First World War,* 288–90.

22. BESP, 29.

23. Thomas Otte, "Between Hammer and Anvil: Sir Francis Oppenheimer, the Netherlands Overseas Trust and Allied Economic Warfare, 1914–1918," in Christopher Baxter and Andrew Stewart, eds., *Diplomats at War: British and Commonwealth Diplomacy in Wartime* (Leiden: Martinus Nijhoff, 2008), 85–108.

24. Oppenheimer Report, Section 2a, Foodstuffs, 37070, f.150, FO.371/673.

25. Copy: Campbell, "German Trade in Time of War: Effect of the Industrial Output of the Country Due to a Call to the Colours, and Due to a Scarcity of Raw Materials" [July 1908], ADM.137/2872; for contradictory opinion by the General Staff, see copy, War Office, "M.O.-3(B)," 28 September 1908, ADM.116/1073; for German studies on this question, see Offer, *First World War,* 342–51.

26. Oppenheimer Report, Section 1a and conclusions, 37070, f.150, FO.371/673.

27. Minute (8 October 1909) by Crowe, 37070, f.150, FO.371/673.

28. Minute (n.d.) by Sir Charles Hardinge, 37070, f.150, FO.371/673.

29. Minute (n.d.) by Bethell, ca. July 1909, reproduced in Bell, *Official History,* 27. This document is no longer in the archives.

30. Memo, "Prepared When Admiral Campbell Was HTD," n.d. [1908], ADM.137/2864; see also Board of Trade statistics in ADM.137/2782.

31. Robert Giffen, *Economic Inquires and Studies,* 2 vols. (London: George Bell and Sons, 1904); see also supplementary chapter to Lord T. H. Farrer, *The State in Its Relation to Trade* (London: Macmillan, 1902). Farrer had been permanent secretary to the Board of Trade.

32. Roger Mason, "Robert Giffen and the Tariff Reform Campaign, 1865–1910," *Journal of European Economic History* 25, no. 1 (1996): 171–88; Mason, *Robert Giffen and the Giffen Paradox* (Totowa, NJ: Barnes and Noble, 1989).

33. I am indebted for this reminder to my old economics tutor, Sir Richard Smethurst, now provost of Worcester College.

34. Robert Giffen, "On International Statistical Comparisons," *Economic Journal* 2, no. 6 (1892): 209–38.

35. George Goschen (First Lord of the Admiralty) to Giffen, 26 February 1898, 1/144, Giffen Mss.; Selborne to Giffen, 27 February 1901, 2/6, Giffen Mss. See references to Giffen's written opinions supplied to the Admiralty in "The Economic Effect of War on German Trade," CID E-4, 12 December 1908, printed as appendix 5 to Military Needs of the Empire Subcommittee, CAB.16/5.

36. H. Murray to Giffen, 6 April [1902], 2/27, Giffen Mss.

37. Clarke to Giffen, 24 June 1905 through 18 April 1906, Giffen Mss. 4/39–43 et seq.; see also arguments employed by Clarke in "Capture of Private Property at Sea—Note on Mem-

orandum Addressed to the Prime Minister and Signed by 168 Members of the House of Commons," 19 December 1906, ff.273–74, CAB.17/85.

38. Clarke, CID 73-B, 5, f.28, CAB.4/2.

39. Ottley, untitled memorandum [in reply to two questions from the Chancellor of the Exchequer], 21 June 1905, ADM.137/2749.

40. Sir Robert Giffen, "The Necessity of a War Chest in the Country, or a Greatly Increased Gold Reserve," 25 March 1908, *JRUSI* 52 (July–December 1908): 1329–53.

41. Ibid., 1329.

42. Milton Friedman and Anna Schwartz, *A Monetary History of the United States, 1867–1960* (Princeton, NJ: Princeton University Press, 1963), 156–88.

43. For the anticipation of a steep fall in bond prices consequent to war, see Niall Ferguson, "Political Risk and the International Bond Market between the 1848 Revolution and the Outbreak of the First World War," *Economic History Review* 59, no. 1 (2006): 70–112.

44. Barry Eichengreen, *Globalizing Capital: A History of the International Monetary System,* 2nd ed. (Princeton, NJ: Princeton University Press, 2008), 30–35.

45. Ibid., 7–44; Hew Strachan, *Financing the First World War* (Oxford: Oxford University Press, 2004), 5–23.

46. Harley Withers, *The Meaning of Money,* 2nd ed. (London: Smith, Elder, 1909), 37–55, 157–65.

47. Brand and Huth Jackson estimates made in 1912. DC, Huth Jackson, 26 November 1911, 91–92.

48. Charles H. Feinstein, *Statistical Tables of National Income, Expenditure and Output of the United Kingdom, 1855–1965* (Cambridge: Cambridge University Press, 1972), table 15 (T37); this number tallies with contemporary accounting, for which see Treasury (John Bradbury), "Limits of Borrowing Abroad and at Home," 9 September 1915, CAB.37/134/11.

49. Feinstein, *Statistical Tables,* table 15, showing exports of services less imports of services for the period 1902–1911.

50. Withers, *Meaning of Money,* 228–53.

51. Edgar Crammond, "British Investments Abroad," *Quarterly Review,* July 1911. Crammond was a notable economist and secretary to the Liverpool Stock Exchange and also the Liverpool Shipowners Association.

52. Peter Cain and Anthony Hopkins, *British Imperialism: Innovation and Expansion, 1688–1914* (London: Longmans, 1993), 146–47.

53. Robert H. Brand, "Lombard Street and War," March 1912, 11, reproduced in Robert H. Brand, *War and National Finance* (London: Edward Arnold, 1921).

54. Withers, *Meaning of Money,* 128.

55. Cain and Hopkins, *British Imperialism,* 171–72.

56. Giffen, "Necessity of a War Chest," 1334; Withers, *Meaning of Money,* 128–36. For the dynamics of London credit system, see Withers, *Meaning of Money,* 223–41.

57. Giffen, "Necessity of a War Chest," 1330.

58. Ibid., 1336–39.

59. Ibid. One such milestone was the promulgation of the 1882 Bills of Exchange Act, widely acknowledged by economic historians as one of the central pillars supporting the international trade system.

60. Ibid., 1330.

61. Ibid., 1332.

62. Admiralty, CID E-4, para. 20, CAB.16/5.

63. Slade, "The Defence of Commerce with Proposals for Its Organisation in Peace Time," 16 September 1908, paper A8, reel 1, Slade Mss.

64. Rhodri Williams, *Defending the Empire: The Conservative Party and British Defence Policy, 1899–1915* (New Haven, CT: Yale University Press, 1991), 161; see also Slade diary, 6 November 1908, Slade Mss.

65. Grey to McKenna, 5 November 1908, BD, VII, No. 129, as cited in PGS, 132.

66. John Gooch, *The Plans of War: The General Staff and Military Strategy, c. 1900–1916* (London: Routledge and Kegan Paul, 1974), 287; 100th CID meeting, 22 October 1908, CAB.38/14/10; see also Ottley to Esher, Sunday n.d. [October 1908] ESHR.5/28.

67. Ottley, "Preparations of Plans for Combined Naval and Military Operations in War," printed July 1905, CAB.17/5.

68. CID, Report (CID 109-B), 24 July 1909, para. 1, vii–xi, CAB.16/5; PGS, 108.

69. Fisher to Esher, 15 March 1909, FGDN 2:232–33.

70. Slade diary, 28 November 1908, Slade Mss.

71. Gooch, *Plans of War,* 287–89; Nicholas d'Ombrain, *War Machinery and High Policy: Defence Administration in Peacetime Britain, 1902–1914* (Oxford: Oxford University Press, 1973), 97.

72. For Fisher's relations with Slade, see Slade diary, 12 and 13 November 1908, Slade Mss.

73. For Fisher's distrust, see Fisher to Esher, 27 November 1908, FGDN 2:202; for McKenna's views, see Pamela McKenna, Journal of the HMS *Enchantress*, entry 5 September 1908, MCKN.12/1l; Pamela McKenna to McKenna, n.d., "Thursday," MCKN.8/2 part 1. Fourteen months later, 31 January 1910, the McKennas asked Fisher to stand as godfather for their firstborn son.

74. FNR, 171–77; Slade diary, 21 October 1908, Slade Mss. N.b.: The final report of the Overseas Attack Committee was signed on 22 October 1908, CAB.38/14/11.

75. FNR 181; Captain Osmond de Brock to Col. Count Gleichen, 19 October 1908, cited in Ruddock Mackay, *Fisher of Kilverstone* (Oxford: Clarendon Press, 1973), 405–7.

76. Fisher to Esher, 17 January 1909 and 15 March 1909, FGDN, 2:220, 232–33.

77. Military Needs of the Empire Subcommittee, 3rd Meeting, Sir John French, para. 1, 23 March 1909, CAB.16/5.

78. Mackay, *Fisher of Kilverstone,* 407.

79. Military Needs of the Empire Subcommittee, remarks by Sir William Nicholson, 3rd meeting, CAB.16/5.

80. PGS, 109; Gooch, *Plans of War,* 288; d'Ombrain, *War Machinery,* 94.

81. Fisher, autobiographical notes, c.1918, 24, 26–27, FP 5101, FISR 9/1.

82. Hankey to McKenna, 15 August 1911, ff.1–5, Hankey Mss. 7/3; emphasis added. See also Fisher to Hankey, 19 February 18, FGDN 2:511–12. A less plausible explanation is found in Reginald Bacon, *The Life of Lord Fisher of Kilverstone,* 2 vols. (London: Hodder and Stoughton, 1929) 2:182–83; see also Mackay, *Fisher of Kilverstone,* 404–8. For confirmation of the date of the outburst as 3 December 1908, see Fisher to Crease, 19 April 18, referencing notes of the meeting provided to Fisher by Lord Esher, FGDN, 3:579–80.

83. Military Needs of the Empire Subcommittee, remarks by Haldane, 1st meeting, 2, CAB.16/5.

84. Remarks by Admiral Slade, CAB.16/5.

85. Ottley to McKenna, 5 December 1908, 1a, MCKN.3/7.

86. John Coogan, *The End of Neutrality: The United States, Britain and Maritime Rights, 1899–1915* (Ithaca, NY: Cornell University Press, 1981), 113.

87. The minutes record that "Admiral Slade made a statement in which he drew attention to the following points of his Memorandum"; Slade also claims authorship in his diary entry, 6 December 1908, Slade Mss.

88. Military Needs of the Empire Subcommittee, 1st meeting, Mr. Richard Haldane, 3 December 1908, CAB.16/5; for Bethell's early assumption of many of the DNI's duties during the London Conference, see Testimony of Reginald McKenna, 1st Lord, 25 May 1909, Q.2191, 2192, Beresford Enquiry, CAB.16/9A.

89. Admiralty, "The Economic Effect of War on German Trade," 12 December 1908, appendix 5 (CID E-4), CAB.16/5; note similarity to argument in Norman Angell, *The Great Illusion: A Study of the Relation of Military Power in Nations to Their Economic and Social Advantage,* 3rd ed. (London: William Heinemann, 1911), 31, 46ff.

90. CID E-4, paras. 1–6.

91. Ibid., para. 13.

92. Ibid., paras. 6, 7–15; reinforced by Slade during 2nd meeting, 17 December 1908.

93. Ibid., para. 20. N.b.: Note similarity to Angell's argument, 31, 46ff.

94. Ibid., para. 18. See also Angel, *Great Illusion,* 57.

95. CID E-4, para. 31.

96. On this see Gerald Feldman, "Mobilizing Economies for War," in Jay Winter, Geoffrey Parker, and Mary Habeck, eds., *The Great War and the Twentieth Century* (New Haven, CT: Yale University Press, 2000), 166–87.

97. CID E-4, paras. 22, 24, 31.

98. Ibid., para. 24.

99. Ibid., para. 38.

100. Esher, "The Assistance to Be Given by Great Britain to France if She Is Attacked by Germany," 14 December 1908, paras. 5–8, CID E-5, CAB.16/5.

101. Esher, para. 7, CID E-5, CAB.16/5.

102. Note by the General Staff, 5 March 1909, Appendix VIII, CID E-11, CAB.16/5.

103. Note by General Sir John French in reply to Appendix VII, 5 January 1910, CID E-11, CAB.16/5; Fisher to Esher, 15 March 1909, FGDN 2:232–33.

104. Ottley to Esher, 18 October 1909, ESHR.5/34.

105. Sir Frederick Bolton, shipping magnate and former chairman of Lloyd's, wrote to the prime minister on 19 January 1909. See "Supplies in Time of War (1908–1909)," B.27(1), CAB.17/26; also Ottley to Asquith, 20 February 1909, enclosing "Note by Sir Charles Ottley on Sir F. Bolton's Letter to the Prime Minister," 10 February 1909, ff.41–43, CAB.17/26.

106. BESP, 53–58.

107. CID B-27 (1), copy of memorandum sent to the Prime Minister by Sir Frederic Bolton, 19 January 1909 16, CAB.17/26. See also attached correspondence, Ottley to Asquith,

20 February 1909, enclosing "Note by Sir Charles Ottley on Sir F. Bolton's Letter to the Prime Minister," 10 February 1909, ff.41–45, and Ottley to Fisher, 14 May 1909, f.48.

108. His thoughts are still cited today by political scientists, most recently by Williamson Murray, "History, War and the Future," *Orbis: A Journal of World Affairs* 52, no. 4 (Fall 2008): 544–63; also Jari Eloranta, "From the Great Illusion to the Great War: Military Spending Behavior of the Great Powers, 1870–1913," *European Review of Economic History* 2 (2007): 255–83. Alas, both misrepresent Angell's key argument as to the probability of future war.

109. Originally privately published in November 1909 under the title *Europe's Optical Illusion.*

110. Angell, *Great Illusion,* 46–47; also in synopsis, viii; reference to U.S. bank crisis, 65; fragility of credit, 103.

111. Kevin O'Rourke and Jeffrey Williamson, *Globalization and History: The Evolution of a Nineteenth-Century Atlantic Economy* (Cambridge, MA: MIT Press, 1999), 208–23.

112. Martin Ceadel, *Living the Great Illusion: Sir Norman Angell, 1872–1967* (Oxford: Oxford University Press, 2009), 90–91.

113. Ibid., 2.

114. LVS, 36; Offer, *First World War,* 261, 263. In June 1911, Fisher was in the process of reading *The Great Illusion* and was favorably impressed; see Fisher to Gerald Fiennes, 19 June 1911, FISR 1/10; Fisher to Esher, 25 April 1912, FGDN 2:453–54. In January 1912, Hankey attended a lecture by Angell: Hankey to Esher, 20 January 1912, ESHR.5/40.

115. Ceadel, *Norman Angell,* 93–113, 117–22.

116. Edgar Crammond, "Paper on the Finance of War—Read before the Institute of Bankers on Wednesday, April 20, 1910 at 5.30 pm," 11, Printed for the Committee of Defence, 1 June 1910, Financial Effects of Outbreak of War, CAB.17/81.

117. Ibid.

118. Discussion on Mr. Crammond's paper, the President, 14, CAB.17/81. Huth Jackson was the principal expert called to testify before the CID Desart Committee in 1911–1912, CAB.16/18A; F. Huth Jackson (1863–1921), partner, Frederick Huth and Co., Director of Bank of England, 1892; president, Institute of Bankers, 1909–1911; Privy Council, 1911.

119. Fisher to Esher, 15 March 1909, FGDN 2:232–33.

120. Military Needs of the Empire Subcommittee, 3rd meeting, 23 March 1909, conclusions (a) and (b), 8, CAB.16/5; also "Final Report" (CID 109-B), 10, para. 20, CAB.16/5.

121. Asquith to Grey, 7 September 1908, Grey Mss. FO.800/100, as cited in PGS, 103.

122. The best account is Williams, *Defending the Empire,* 78; also see R. J. Q. Adams and Philip Poirier, *The Conscription Controversy in Great Britain 1900–18* (London: Macmillan, 1987); Mathew Johnson, "The Liberal War Committee and the Liberal Advocacy of Conscription in Britain, 1914–1914," *Historical Journal* 51 (2008): 399–420.

123. PGS, 103.

124. Ibid., 110.

125. Ibid., 110–11.

126. Gooch, *Plans for War,* 288.

127. Military Needs of the Empire Subcommittee, Final Report, 109-B, 24 July 1909, paras. 10–13, CAB.16/5.

128. Ottley to Bethell, 16 January 1911, 5, "Principles of Home Defence," ADM.1/8896.

129. Wilson, "Remarks on the War Plans," April 1907, FP2, 455; see also Testimony by Admiral Wilson to Beresford Inquiry, Q.2539, 2540, 307–8, CAB.16/9A.

130. Wilson, questions 2586 and 2587, 2590, 313, CAB.16/9A.

131. Esher to Sanders, 18 August 1909, f.115, Sanders Mss. 759.

132. Morley to Sir George Clarke, 20 August 1909, f.113, Eur. D.573.47/49. Morley Mss. (Lord Morley Papers, India Office Library, London).

133. FNR, 193–94, 199–200.

134. Fisher to McKenna, 8 November 1909, MCKN.3/4.

135. Selborne to Balfour, 20 May 15, f.251, Add.Mss. 49707.

136. Bridgeman to Fisher, 21 November 1909, FGDN, 2:282.

137. FNR, 201–4.

138. Ibid.

139. Pamela McKenna to Reginald McKenna, n.d., "Monday," MCKN.8/2 part 1. The reference to Lambton's inheritance dates the letter to mid-1911.

140. Offer, *First World War,* 286–87.

141. Crowe to Slade, 3 January 1910, microfilm reel 3, Slade Mss.

142. Minute (6 December 1910) by Rear-Admiral H. King-Hall and (26 January 1911) by Greene advising consulting the Foreign Office; endorsement by McKenna dated 1 February 1911, all on "Arrangements in Case of Blockade of German Ports and Coast," ADM.116/1233; Foreign Office replies dated 25 March 1911 and 7 June 1911; see also minute (7 July 1911) by Greene on "List of Chief Local Authorities at the German North Sea Ports Where Foreign Consuls Are Stationed," ADM.116/1233.

143. Minute (30 July 1909) by Greene, "Forwarding Copies of the Draft Naval Prize Manual," ADM.116/1231A; Papers of the Naval Prize Law Committee, ADM.116/1231A; Proceedings of the Naval Prize Manual Committee, 1913–14, ADM.116/1232.

144. Christopher Martin, "The Declaration of London: A Matter of Operational Capability," *Historical Research* 82, no. 218 (November 2009): 731–55.

145. John Coogan, *The End of Neutrality: The United States, Britain and Maritime Rights, 1899–1915* (Ithaca, NY: Cornell University Press, 1981).

146. HC Deb, 28 June 1911, vol. 27, cols. 407, 548.

147. Minute (27 January 1916) by Greene, "Foreign Office Memorandum of 28th December 1915," f.185, ADM.137/1164.

148. Minutes (19 December 1911) by Oswyn Murray and Bethell, on "Addenda to Preliminary War Orders (Blockade of North Sea Coast)," ADM.1/8132.

149. Admiralty (Bethell), "Naval Considerations Regarding Military Action in Denmark" (CID E-8), 4 February 1909, para. 4, CAB.16/5.

150. Minute (6 December 1910) by Rear-Admiral H. King-Hall, DNM, on "Arrangements in Case of Blockade of German Ports and Coast," ADM.116/1233.

151. For the nonissue of the orders, see minutes (7 December 1911) by Alex Flint to DNM and (19 December 1911) by Oswyn Murray, on "Addenda to Preliminary War Orders," ADM.116/1233.

152. Minute (7 October 1911) by Bethell, on "Blockade of North Sea Coast of German Empire," Ady 30/12/10, ADM.1/8132.

153. Ibid.

154. For a contradictory view, see memorandum by G. A. Ballard, "Proposals Regarding the Use of Mines in Support of an Offensive Strategic Plan," 6 February 1913, ADM.116/3412.

155. Minute (10 October 1911) by Greene and "M Branch Remarks" by Alex Flint, 2 September 1911, and minutes (16 October 1911) by Wilson, ADM.116/3412.

156. Minute (16 October 1911) by Wilson, and especially minute entitled "DNM's Remarks" (8 September 1911) by Captain George Hope (a/DNM), both ADM.116/3412.

4. The Endorsement of Economic Warfare

Epigraphs: Balfour to Esher, 9 January 12, ESHR.5/40; DC, "A Note by the Chairman," 21 February 1912, appendix 22, 418–20.

1. Ottley to Esher, 4 January 1910, ESHR.5/33; Nicholas d'Ombrain, *War Machinery and High Policy: Defence Administration in Peacetime Britain, 1902–1914* (Oxford: Oxford University Press, 1973), 190.

2. Bruce Murray, *The People's Budget 1909/10: Lloyd George and Liberal Politics* (Oxford: Clarendon Press, 1980).

3. D'Ombrain, *War Machinery,* 190–92, 236–37, 240–51; Ottley to Esher, 7 January 1910, ESHR.5/33, reporting conversation with Haldane.

4. Ottley to Esher, 16 October and 18 October 1909, ESHR.5/34.

5. CID, 105th meeting, 24 February 1910, CAB.38/16/4.

6. This is discussed at length by d'Ombrain, *War Machinery,* but he assumes military strategy was the primary topic.

7. Ottley to Esher, 18 October 1909, ESHR.5/34.

8. SC, 1:85; but see also 1:119: where Hankey contradicts himself on the date (12 November 1909) and gives a great deal more credit to Ottley and Haldane; the paper is presumably the unsigned memorandum entitled "Proposed Sub-Committee on the War Organization of the British Empire," XV.3(31), January (or December) 1909, 1910, ff.1–8, CAB.17/98; see also Ottley, "Suggestions Regarding the Pay and Functions of the Secretariat of the Committee of Imperial Defence," 1 November 1909, CAB.17/97; Esher, "The Functions of Sub-Committees of the Committee of Imperial Defence," 21 January 1910, CAB.38/16/1; Ottley to Esher, 16 October 1909, ESHR.5/31.

9. Ottley's thoughts are most clearly articulated in Ottley, "Coordination of Departmental Action on Outbreak of War: Note by the Secretary," CID-121B, 4 November 1910, CAB.38/16/21.

10. Hardinge to Esher, 28 January 1910, ESHR.5/33.

11. Ibid.

12. CID, 105th meeting, 24 February 1910 (discussing 112B and 114B), CAB.38/16/4.

13. CID, "Sub-committee to Consider the Desirability of an Enquiry into the Question of the Local Transportation and Distribution of Food Supplies in Time of War," CID 113-B, 22 March 1910, CAB.38/16/5.

14. SC, 1:88; Terms of Reference (p. iv), dated 2 March 1910, attached to Hardinge, "Report of the Standing Sub Committee of the Committee of Imperial Defence Regarding the Treatment of Neutral and Enemy Merchant Ships in Time of War," 28 October 1910, CAB.16/11.

15. Hankey to Esher, 1 February 1910, ESHR.5/33.

16. Marginal note by Esher, ESHR.5/33; d'Ombrain, *War Machinery,* 251.

17. Ottley to McKenna, 28 February 1910, f.5, MCKN 3/7; Postscript in Ottley to Esher, 1 March 1910, ESHR.5/33.

18. SC, 1:90.

19. Admiralty (Bethell), Memorandum M-15, 61, para. 7, 28 June 1910, "Neutral and Enemy Merchant Ships in Time of War" (Hardinge Committee), CAB.16/11.

20. SC, 1:90–92.

21. Hardinge, "Report of the Standing Sub Committee of the Committee of Imperial Defence Regarding the Treatment of Neutral and Enemy Merchant Ships in Time of War," 28 October 1910, para. 87, CAB.38/19/19.

22. Ottley to Esher, 26 January 1911, ESHR.5/36.

23. CID, 108th meeting, 26 January 1911, CAB.38/17/5; Asquith's approval is noted explicitly in Hankey to Esher, 26 January 1911, ESHR.5/36.

24. Hankey to Esher, 30 January 1911, ESHR.5/36; see also postscript, Ottley to Esher, 26 January 1911, ESHR.5/36.

25. Cuffe, Hamilton John Agmondesham, fifth Earl of Desart (1848–1934). Further details of his life are given in a biography by his younger daughter: Sybil Lubbock, *A Page from the Past: Memories of the Earl of Desart* (London: Jonathan Cape, 1936).

26. Hankey to Esher, 30 January 1911, ESHR.5/36; see also postscript, Ottley to Esher, 26 January 1911, ESHR.5/36.

27. SC, 1:91.

28. Ibid., 92. The "War Book" more properly called *Coordination of Departmental Action on the Outbreak of War,* 30 May 1914, Secret, K-30, CAB.15/5.

29. Samuel R. Williamson, "Hankey's Committee of Imperial Defence Revisited" (review of d'Ombrain, *War Machinery*), *Reviews in European History* 1 (September 1974): 228–34.

30. HMS, 1:138.

31. HMS, 2:335, 533; HMS, 3:611, 613–21; John F. Naylor, *A Man and an Institution: Sir Maurice Hankey, the Cabinet Secretariat and the Custody of Cabinet Secrecy* (New York: Cambridge University Press, 1984), 272–77.

32. Comments by Hankey on memorandum by Winston Churchill enclosed in Grigg to Hankey, 16 February 1928, f.10ff., HNKY 5/1.

33. SC, 1:91–92.

34. D'Ombrain, *War Machinery,* 194–95. Armstrong's offered Ottley £4,000 per year for life, whereas his naval pension amounted to just £500 per year; see Ottley to Esher, 21 November 1911, ESHR.5/40.

35. SC, 1:87–88, 98–101.

36. Archibald C. Bell, *A History of the Blockade of Germany and the Countries Associated with Her in the Great War: Austria-Hungary, Bulgaria, and Turkey* (London: HMSO, 1961), 20, 31–32.

37. Avner Offer, *The First World War: An Agrarian Interpretation* (New York: Oxford University Press, 1989), 243n27, rejecting d'Ombrain's criticisms of Hankey's exaggeration of his own importance.

38. CID, "Proposed Sub-Committee on the War Organization of the British Empire," XV.3(31), January (or December) 1909, 1910, 5, CAB.17/98.

39. SC, 1:87; Minute (16 February 1911) by Hankey addressed to Ottley, attached to Hankey, secret, "The Declaration of London from the Point of view of War with Germany," 15 February 1911, ADM.116/1236. I am indebted to Chris Martin for this point.

40. Ibid.

41. Ibid.

42. "Remarks by Sir Charles Ottley on Captain Hankey's paper (attached herewith)," 17 February 1911, ADM.116/1236.

43. Minute (17 February 1911) by Ottley, 4, ADM.116/1236; biting criticism from page 4 onward. Also Ottley to McKenna, 17 February 1911, ADM.116/1236.

44. Ibid.

45. See Chapter 3.

46. Ottley to McKenna, 17 February 1911, ADM.116/1236; SC, 1:99.

47. Ottley to Esher, secret, 30 January 1911, ESHR.5/36.

48. Ibid.

49. Ibid. (marginalia by Esher).

50. Secret, "Memorandum of a Conversation Held on Feby 23rd 1911," present: McKenna, Ottley, Hankey, ff.22–26, CAB.17/87. Note reference to Britain's ability to buy off neutrals and also benefits she would derive as a neutral.

51. SC, 1:99–100.

52. Grant-Duff Diary, 22 and 24 February 1911, AGDF.2/1.

53. Hurst Memorandum, 27 April 1911, ff.429–31, FO.371/1278.

54. Ibid.

55. Hankey, Reply to Mr. Hurst, 8 March 1911, ff.109–115, CAB.17/87.

56. Ibid.

57. Grant-Duff diary, 8 March 1911, AGDF 2/1.

58. Offer, *First World War,* 298.

59. Zara Steiner, *Britain and the Origins of the First World War* (London: Cambridge University Press, 1969), 200; Keith Neilson, "Great Britain," in Richard F. Hamilton and Holger Herwig, eds., *War Planning 1914* (Cambridge: Cambridge University Press, 2009), 185–88.

60. PGS, 141–66.

61. War Office, "Memorandum by the General Staff," and Wilson, "Note by the Director of Military Operations," 12 August 1911, CAB.38/19/47; Keith Jeffery, *Field Marshal Sir Henry Wilson: A Political Soldier* (Oxford: Oxford University Press, 2006), 95–99; D. M. Rowe, D. H. Bearce, and J. McDonald, "Binding Prometheus: How the 19th Century Expansion of Trade Impeded Britain's Ability to Raise and Army," *International Studies Quarterly* 46 (2002): 551–78, esp. 553–54, 570, 573.

62. Hew Strachan, "The British Army, Its General Staff, and the Continental Commitment, 1904–1914," in David French, ed., *The British General Staff: Reform and Innovation* (London: Frank Cass, 2002), 75–95. Strachan presents much the best and nuanced explanation of Henry Wilson's case as well as placing it within the wider military context. Both Lloyd George and Churchill attached enormous importance to this meeting in their memoirs; see Winston S. Churchill, *The World Crisis, 1911–1918,* 5 vols. (New York: Scribner's,

1923–1931), 1:56–64; David Lloyd George, *War Memoirs of David Lloyd George,* 6 vols. (London: Nicholson and Watson, 1933–1937) 1:56.

63. Neilson, "Great Britain," 186–88.

64. Hankey to McKenna, 15 August 1911, ff. 1–5, HNKY.7/3.

65. Fisher to McKenna, 20 August 1911, FGDN 2:380–81.

66. Keith Wilson, "Hankey's Appendix: Some Admiralty Manoeuvres during and after the Agadir Crisis, 1911," *War in History* 1, no. 1 (1994): 81.

67. Admiralty, "Remarks by the Admiralty on Proposal (b) of the Memorandum by the General Staff," n.d. [August 1911], printed 18 September 1911, CAB.38/19/48. (Written by Wilson as Bethell was on vacation. See Hankey to Fisher, 24 August 1911, 530A, FISR.1/10.)

68. "Remarks by the Admiralty on Proposal (b)," 18 September 1911, CAB.38/19/48.

69. Ibid.

70. Hankey to McKenna, 15 August 1911, f.1, Hankey Mss. 7/3.

71. "Resources and Trade of Germany: Answers by Board of Trade to Questions Addressed by the War Office," X.3(27), ff.97–134, CAB.17/61; copy, Board of Trade, "Memorandum for the Army Council," 1910, WO.106/47.

72. Grant-Duff diary, 25 August 1911, describing events at meeting on the 23rd, AGDF.2/1. For his recording of the minutes, see entry for 11 September 1911.

73. SC, 1:81.

74. Haldane to Asquith, 31 August 11, f.140, Haldane Mss. 5909.

75. Grant-Duff diary, 25 August 1911, describing events of 23 August 1911, AGDF.2/1.

76. FNR, 205 n57.

77. Ottley to Churchill, 2 November 1911, CAB.17/8. A further account by Ottley is found in Dumas diary, 18 December 1911, Dumas Mss. (Captain Philip Dumas papers, Imperial War Museum, London).

78. FNR, 204–6, 240–43.

79. FNR, 265–66; Churchill to Battenberg, 19 November 1911, MB1/T9/43.

80. SC, 1:82. Yet for contradiction of this view, see Hankey to Esher, 31 July 14, ESHR.5/46.

81. Fisher impressed upon Hankey the political difficulties in obtaining political sanction with landing an army in France, for which see Fisher to Hankey, 8 April 1912, f.11, and 13 April 1912, f.13, HNKY.5/2A; Morley to Esher, 27 August 1911, ESHR.10/31; Ottley to Esher, 27 August 1911, ESHR.5/37; K. M. Wilson, "The Making and Putative Implementation of a British Foreign Policy of Gesture, December 1905 to August 1914," *Canadian Journal of History* 31 (August 1996): 227–55.

82. Michael Howard, *The Continental Commitment: The Dilemma of British Defence Policy in the Era of the Two World Wars* (London: Maurice Temple Smith, 1972), 31, 43; BESP, 33.

83. Neilson, "Great Britain," 186–88.

84. Grey to Asquith, 8 September 1911, FO.800/100, as cited in ibid.

85. Esher journal entry, 24 November 1911, ESHR.2/2.

86. Ibid.; see also McKenna, "Note of Conversation with HHA," 20 October 1911, f.3, MCKN.4/2.

87. Esher journal entry, 24 November 1911, ESHR.2/2; see also Asquith to Haldane, 9 September 11, f.146, Haldane Mss. 5909.

88. Hardinge, "Report of the Standing Sub Committee of the Committee of Imperial Defence Regarding the Treatment of Neutral and Enemy Merchant Ships in Time of War," 28 October 1910, para. 87, CAB.38/19/19.

89. For Hankey's treatise, written under the general supervision of Professor L. F. Oppenheim, Wherwell Professor of International Law at Cambridge University, see Hankey, "Trading with the Enemy during the Wars of the French Revolution and Empire," appendix V, "Trading with the Enemy," Memorandum 470M by the Oversea Sub-Committee of the CID, 17 November 1913, CAB.38/25/37.

90. CAB.16/14. Sir Mathew Nathen, soldier and colonial administrator. Lieutenant-Colonel, Royal Engineers. Former head of the Colonial Defence Committee and governor of Natal.

91. CAB.16/27; CAB.16/19; CAB.16/24; CAB.16/29; CAB.16/30; CAB.16/31.

92. CID, 120th meeting, 6 December 1912, CAB.38/22/42.

93. Offer, *First World War,* 297; see also BESP, 60–61.

94. DC, 2nd meeting (22 November 1911), 63, and reaffirmed at 4th meeting (29 January 1912), 72.

95. Col. G. M. W. Macdonogh to Ottley, 1 December 1911, f.188, and Ottley to Llewellyn Smith (Board of Trade), 6 December 1911, f.189, both CAB.17/89; DC, "Memorandum by Lord Esher," appendix 20, 12 February 1912, 411; also DC, Desart at 6th meeting (23 February 1912), remarks by Desart, 82.

96. DC, 6th meeting, remarks by chairman, 84.

97. Testimony of Lt-Colonel Sir Maurice Hankey before the Dardanelles Commission, 19 September 1916, paragraph 164, CAB.19/2.

98. Sir Hubert Llewellyn Smith (1864–1945), social reformer and disciple of John Ruskin. Appointed first labor commissioner of the Board of Trade, 1893.

99. In 1913 Chalmers temporarily left the Treasury to become governor of Ceylon. In 1916 he returned to the Treasury as joint permanent secretary and remained in this post till the end of the war.

100. Hankey to Chalmers, 8 May 1912, ff.322–23, Esher to Hankey, 19 July 1912, ff.378–79, both CAB17/89; also Hankey to Esher, n.d. but referring to letter dated 19 July 1912, ESHR. 5/40.

101. Esher to Hankey, 19 July 1912, f.378, CAB.17/89.

102. Ottley to Bethell, 14 November 1911, ff.168–70, "Trading with the Enemy," CAB.17/89.

103. DC, 2nd meeting, Admiral Bethell, 64.

104. Ottley to Bethell, 14 November 1911, CAB.17/89.

105. Ibid.

106. DC, Board of Trade, "The Probable Effect of a War with Germany on British Trade," appendix 7, 274.

107. DC, 5th meeting 79.

108. Ibid., 80.

109. DC, 4th meeting, 74–75.

110. DC, 6th meeting, remarks by Mr. Risley, 84.

111. DC, 4th meeting, "The Practicability of Prohibiting Exports from the British Empire from Reaching Germany through Neutral Countries," 73.

112. Ibid.

113. DC, 6th meeting, 83.

114. DC, Ottley, "Note by the Secretary," appendix 14, 381–82. This must have been written after the 3rd meeting (23 January 1912) but before the 4th meeting (29 January 1912), at which it was discussed.

115. DC, "Extract from the Report of the Sub-Committee of the Committee of Imperial Defence on the Military Needs of the Empire" (CID 109-B), and "II. Memorandum by the Admiralty on the Economic Effect of War on German Trade," appendix 15, 383.

116. DC, Ottley, "Note by the Secretary," appendix 14, 381–82; emphasis added.

117. Ibid., para. 7.

118. DC, 4th Meeting, Desart remarks, 73.

119. CID, secret, "Report of an Interdepartmental Conference between Representatives of the Admiralty, War Office and Board of Trade to Consider the Question of Restrictions on the Export of Warlike Stores in Time of War," 21 February 1912, ff.249–55, CAB.17/89; see also Ottley to Llewellyn Smith, 18 January 1912, f.216, CAB.17/89.

120. CID, secret, "Report of an Interdepartmental Conference between Representatives of the Admiralty, War Office and Board of Trade to Consider the Question of Restrictions on the Export of Warlike Stores in Time of War," 21 February 1912, ff.249–55, CAB.17/89, para. 9.

121. Ibid.

122. DC, fifth meeting, Chalmers, 79.

123. DC, Esher memorandum, 12 February 1912, appendix 21, 410–413; see also DC, fifth meeting, Esher, 80.

124. Ibid.

125. DC, "A Note by the Chairman," 21 February 1912, appendix 22, 418. For Lord Desart's explicit concurrence with Esher on this point, see opening remarks by Desart to 6th meeting, 23 February 1912, 82; also DC, Final Report, considerations of general policy, 2–3.

126. DC, 6th meeting, 83–84.

127. Hankey to Chalmers, 9 May 1912, f.322, CAB.17/89.

128. DC, 6th meeting, 86–87.

129. Marc Frey, "Trade, Ships, and the Neutrality of the Netherlands in the First World War," *International History Review* 19, no. 3 (August 1997): 541–62.

130. DC, Final Report, 6.

131. DC, Board of Trade Memorandum, Appendix 7, 275–76.

132. DC, 2nd meeting, 36.

133. DC, 6th meeting, remarks by Hurst, 84–85.

134. Ibid., Troubridge, 83.

135. DC, 5th meeting, 79.

136. DC, 6th meeting, 85.

137. DC, Esher paper, appendix 20, 410–13.

138. DC, 6th meeting, Esher, 85.

139. Foreign Office (Crowe), "Belgium: The Attitude of GB towards Belgium," April 1912, CAB.38/20/6; Col G. M. W. Macdonough (a/DMO) to Ottley, 1 December 1911, f.188, CAB.17/89.

140. CID, 117th meeting, 25 April 1912, CAB.38/20/9.

141. DC, Final Report, paras. 31–34, 6; DC, 6th meeting, 84.

142. DC, Final Report, 41.

143. DC, Memorandum by Board of Trade, Appendix 7, 274; DC, Final Report, 25.

144. DC, "Note by Sir H. Llewellyn Smith" (Board of Trade), n.d. [early 1911], appendix 24, 422–23.

145. DC, "A Note by Mr. CJB Hurst," 13 March 1912, appendix 26, 425–26.

146. Ibid.

147. Ibid.

148. Ballard, "The Protection of Commerce during War," *JRUSI* 42, no. 242 (April 1898): 365–405.

149. DC, Report of Sub-Conference, schedule 8, 41–42.

150. Ibid.

151. Ibid.

152. Ibid.

153. Ibid., paras. 30, 40; DC, Final Report, paras. 124, 20.

154. Esher to Fisher, 20 April 1912, in Maurice Brett, ed., *Journals and Letters of Reginald, Viscount Esher,* 4 vols. (London: Ivor Nicholson and Watson, 1934–1938), 3:88.

155. Fisher to Esher, 25 April 1912, FGDN 2:453–54.

156. Ibid.

157. DC, "A Note by Lord Esher," 9 May 1912, appendix XXVII, 427.

158. Fisher to Esher, 25 April 1912, FGDN 2:453–54.

159. DC, "Remark by Chairman (Desart) to Governor of Bank of England (AC Cole)," 1 February 1912, Q.98, Cole testimony, 104.

160. DC, evidence of F. Huth Jackson, 26 November 1911, 88–92; Lord Revelstoke, 19 December 1911; 93–104; A. C. Cole, 1 February 1912, 104–9; Sir Felix Schuster, 27 February 1912, 149–66. For further details on these bankers, see Youssef Cassis, *City Bankers, 1890–1914* (Cambridge: Cambridge University Press, 1994).

161. DC, 3rd meeting, 67; for Cole thinking the crisis would be limited, see Cole testimony, Q.108–10, 107; also Revelstoke testimony, Q.18, 93.

162. DC, Huth Jackson testimony, 92.

163. DC, Revelstoke testimony, Q.96, 103–4; but see Cole testimony, Q.110, 107.

164. DC, Schuster testimony, Q.693, 164.

165. Barry Eichengreen, *Globalizing Capital: A History of the International Monetary System,* 2nd ed. (Princeton, NJ: Princeton University Press, 2008), 17.

166. The figures Huth Jackson cited were £7 million per day and an average of 70 days on each bill. This gives a total of £350 million; DC. Brand says over £300 million; Robert Brand, "Lombard Street and War," *Round Table* 2, no. 6 (March 1912): 249. Schuster estimates between 300 and 400: DC, Schuster testimony, Q.574, 151, and Q.644, 158.

167. DC, Huth Jackson testimony, 90–91.

168. DC, Q.14, 91.

169. Ibid., paras. 1–7, 88–89. Revelstoke makes the same point at Q.42–3, 96. A. C. Cole is equally adamant that deliberate depletion of British gold was nearly impossible; Q100–108, 104–6.

170. DC, Q.14, 90–91.

171. Ibid.

172. DC, Q.99, 105; Q.69, 99.

173. Marcello De Cecco, *Money and Empire: The International Gold Standard, 1890–1914* (Oxford: Basil Blackwell, 1974), 86–87.

174. Ibid., 101.

175. DC, 4th meeting, 72; Schuster testimony, question by Desart, Q.703, 165.

176. DC, Revelstoke testimony, 19 December 1911, Q.42, 96.

177. DC, 4th meeting, 74.

178. Ibid., 72.

179. DC, Huth Jackson testimony, 92.

180. DC, Revelstoke, Q.71, 100; Schuster, Q.703, 165.

181. DC, Schuster, Q.644, 158; Q.703–704, 165.

182. On this point Huth Jackson and Robert Chalmers agreed. DC, Huth Jackson testimony, 26 November 1911, Q.8–13, 89–90; see also A. C. Cole, Q.98, 104. On the importance of retaining foreign balances in London, see Eichengreen, *Globalizing Capital,* 23, 35–39.

183. DC, Schuster testimony, Q.685, 162.

184. DC, 3rd meeting, Desart's summation of Huth Jackson's and Revelstoke's testimony, 67; see also Final Report, paras. 69–70, 11; 120th CID meeting, 6 December 1912, remarks by Desart, CAB.38/22/42.

185. DC, 4th meeting, Chalmers, 72.

186. DC, Final Report, 61, 68–69.

187. CID, 120th meeting, 6 December 1912, 5, CAB.38/22/42.

188. Brand, "Lombard Street and War."

189. Brand to Philip Kerr (later Lord Lothian), 27 May 1915, shows friendship with Alwyn Parker; FO, box 182. Vincent Badderley to Brand, 4 December 1912, box 26A; Eustace Percy, 4 February 1913, and 31 December 1914, box 26A, all Brand Mss. (Lord Robert Brand papers, Bodleian Library, Oxford).

190. Hubert Brand was chief of staff to Beatty and Second Sea Lord in Beatty's administration during the 1920s.

191. See "Lombard Street and a First Class War," *Times Review,* 29 February 1912; Kerr to Brand, 20 March 1912, box 182, Brand Mss.

192. Brand, "Lombard Street and War," 246.

193. DC, Final Report, para. 28, 5.

194. Ibid., para. 9, 2.

195. Ibid., para. 29, 5.

196. Ibid., para. 22, 4.

197. CID, 120th meeting, CAB.38/22/42; CID, 121st meeting, 7 January 1913, CAB.38/23/2.

198. Ibid.

199. Ibid., remarks by Haldane, Crewe, Harcourt, and Asquith.

200. Grant-Duff diary, entry 8 February 1913 (referring to CID meeting on 6 December 1912), AGDF.2/2.

201. Ibid.

202. CID, 120th meeting, CAB.38/22/42, Lloyd George.

203. Ibid., remarks by Haldane, Crewe, Harcourt and Asquith.

204. Ibid., 7.

205. Ibid., 2.

206. CID, 121st meeting, 7 January 1913, CAB.38/23/2.

207. Opening paragraph to CID, "Supplies in Time of War: Trade in General" [1913], f.1, CAB.17/32.

208. CID, 120th meeting, 6 December 1912, 8, CAB.38/22/42.

209. Ibid.

210. CID, "War Book, 1914," 30 May 1914, Secret, K-30, CAB.15/5.

211. Section 25, (a) and (c); also section 30 (a*), CAB.15/5 (Customs and Inland Revenues Act, 1879).

212. Admiralty (Murray) to Hankey, 3 January 1913, and reply of 7 January 1913, f.449, 451, CAB.17/89.

213. Not passed till 8 September 14.

214. Memorandum 470M by the Oversea Sub-Committee of the CID, 17 November 1913, CAB.38/25/37; see also remarks by Sir John Anderson (PUS Colonial Office), CID, 125th meeting, 3 March 15, section 4, CAB.38/26/11.

215. "Note Prepared for Mr. Runciman," 7 February 1913, f.18, CAB.17/32. For an idea of the limitations of contemporary databases, see Board of Trade, "The Probable Effect of a War with Germany on British Trade," appendix VII, 273, ca. 1911, CAB.16/18A.

216. For known problems with British trade figures, see Peter Mathias, *The First Industrial Nation: An Economic History of Britain, 1700–1914* (New York: Scribner's, 1969), 303. For a recent article, see Adam Tooze, "Trouble with Numbers: Statistics, Politics, and History in the Construction of Weimar's Trade Balance, 1918–1924," *American Historical Review* 113 (June 2008): 678–700.

217. Ballard, "Proposals Regarding the Use of Mines in Support of an Offensive Strategic Plan," 6 February 1913, f.495, ADM.116/3412. Minute (11 February 1913) by Jackson approving, ibid.

218. Ibid.

219. Minutes (11 February 1913) by Jackson, f.501, and (30 April 1913) by Ballard, f.504, and Draft of M0033/13, Admiralty to CinC, 23 April 1913, f.505, all ADM.116/3412. Note also minute (21 November 1913) f.500, 541, by Hydrographer of the Navy, referring to orders received 22 September to print "orders to mariners," ADM.116.3412.

220. FNR, 270–74.

5. "Incidentally, Armageddon Begins"

Chapter title: Rudyard Kipling, diary entry 4 August 14, as cited in Frank Field, *British and French Writers of the First World War: Comparative Studies in Cultural History* (Cambridge: Cambridge University Press, 1991), 161. I am indebted to Kathleen McDermott for this reference.

1. Except Niall Ferguson, *The Pity of War* (New York: Basic Books, 1999); Hew Strachan, The *First World War: To Arms* (Oxford: Oxford University Press, 2001).

2. Marcello De Cecco, *Money and Empire: the International Gold Standard, 1890–1914* (Oxford: Basil Blackwell, 1974), 127–70. For a still useful older account, see E. Victor Morgan,

Studies in British Financial Policy, 1914–23 (London: Macmillan, 1952); Brendan Brown, *Monetary Chaos in Europe* (New York: Croom Helm, 1988) provides a more recent though general summary. For a yet more recent historiographical review, see John Peters, "The British Government and the City-Industry Divide," *Twentieth Century British History* 4, no. 2 (1993): 126–48. Peters also offers a useful account of how the crisis impacted industry as distinct from the city. See also Christof Dejung and Andreaus Zangger, "British Wartime Protectionism and Swiss Trading Companies in Asia during the First World War," *Past and Present* 207 (May 2010): 181–213.

3. A review of economic crisis is missing from the otherwise excellent summary in Samuel Williamson and Ernest May, "An Identity of Opinion: Historians and July 1914," *Journal of Modern History* 79 (June 2007): 335–87.

4. Niall Ferguson, "Political Risk and the International Bond Market between the 1848 Revolution and the Outbreak of the First Word War," *The Economic History Review* 59, no. 1 (2006): 95, 98–99, notes that the assassination had "no discernable effect" upon the world bond markets.

5. David Stevenson, *Armaments and the Coming of War: Europe, 1904–1914* (Oxford: Clarendon Press, 2000), 378.

6. Grey to de Bunsen (British ambassador in Vienna), 24 July 1914, No. 5, "Correspondence Respecting the European Crisis," White Paper (Miscellaneous, No. 6), 1914.

7. Asquith to Stanley, 24 July 1914, LVS, 122–23. See also PGS, 344.

8. For the Russian view, see telegram, 24 July 1914, 5:40 p.m., Sir G. Buchanan to Grey, BD, 11:101.

9. Asquith to Stanley, 24 July 1914, LVS, 122–23.

10. Harcourt diary, Nuneham, 26 July 1914, Ms.Dep. 6231 (Lewis Harcourt papers, Bodleian Library, Oxford). N.b.: Diary was uncataloged when examined.

11. Notes of cabinet meeting, 7 August 1914, Ms.Dep. 6231. Harcourt was one of the five minutes who received "flimsies," Grey, Asquith, Churchill, and Kitchener being the others. Asquith to Stanley, 18 August 1914, LVS, 175–77.

12. Hobhouse diary, 23 March 1915, f.17, Add.Mss. 60507 (Sir Charles Hobhouse papers, the British Library, London).

13. Churchill's opinion in Winston S. Churchill, *The World Crisis, 1911–1918,* 5 vols. (New York: Scribner's, 1923–1931), 1:211; Harcourt diary, cabinet meetings 27 July (5:30 p.m.) and 29 July (11:30 a.m.) 1914, Ms.Dep. 6231. Harcourt lists the following ministers as supporting his peace party: Harcourt, Morley, Runciman, McKinnon Wood, Pease, McKenna, Beauchamp, Burns, Simon, Hobhouse, and Birrell (probably also Samuel and Masterman; see also Cameron Hazlehurst, *Politicians at War, July 1914 to May 1915: A Prologue to the Triumph of Lloyd George* (London: Jonathan Cape, 1971), 56–60.

14. Martin Horn, *Britain, France, and the Financing of the First World War* (Montreal: McGill–Queen's University Press, 2002), 28–31.

15. Rothschilds to NM de Rothschild Frères, 27 July 1914, X1/130A/8, Rothschild Archive; telegram, 24 July 1914, 8:15 p.m., Max Muller to Grey, BD, 11:106.

16. See Jeremy Adelman, "Prairie Farm Debt and the Financial Crisis of 1914," *Canadian Historical Review* 71, no. 4 (1990): 491–519; for discussion of the impact upon U.S. cotton growers, see Chapter 6.

17. Ferguson, *Pity of War,* 192.

18. Asquith to Stanley, 28 July 1914, LVS, 131; for the Rothschilds' refusal to ship gold to Paris, see Rothschilds to NM de Rothschild Frères, 28 July 1914, X1/130A/8, Rothschild Archive.

19. Walter Bagehot, *Lombard Street: A Description of the Money Market* (London: King, 1873), chapter 2; JMK, 4–42.

20. De Cecco, *Money and Empire,* 130–32.

21. Ferguson, "Political Risk," 99.

22. See remarks by Harcourt, "Cabinet Committee at Treasury on War Finance," 18 August 1914, 4:00 p.m., and minutes, "Cabinet Committee Board Room Treasury," 1 September 1914, 3:30 p.m., 3 and 4 September 1914, all Ms.Dep. 6231.

23. David Lloyd George, *War Memoirs of David Lloyd George,* 6 vols. (London: Nicholson and Watson, 1933–1937), 1:61.

24. William L. Silber, *When Washington Shut Down Wall Street: The Great Financial Crisis of 1914 and the Origins of America's Monetary Supremacy* (Princeton, NJ: Princeton University Press, 2007), 35. Silber provides an excellent explanation of how gold arbitrage worked on 29–32 and 90–92.

25. Ibid., 34.

26. Ibid., 10–15, 35–42; Horn, *Britain, France,* 62–66. See also remarks by Henry Lee Higginson to Woodrow Wilson, 20 August 1914, PWW 30:420–21.

27. Silber, *When Washington Shut Down Wall Street,* 70–81.

28. Robert H. Brand, "Lombard Street in War" (published in the *Round Table,* October 1914), reproduced in R. H. Brand, *War and National Finance* (London: E. Arnold & co., 1921) 54; very similar remarks in editorial in *Economist,* 1 August 1914, as cited in Ferguson, "Political Risk."

29. Asquith to Stanley, 31 July 1914, LVS, 138, 139n3. See also Harcourt, note, "4 p.m. at the House of Commons," Ms.Dep. 6231.

30. Barry Eichengreen, *Globalizing Capital: A History of the International Monetary System,* 2nd ed. (Princeton, NJ: Princeton University Press, 2008), 35; see also Michael Bordo, *The Gold Standard and Related Regimes: Collected Essays* (Cambridge: University Press, 1999, 2005), 27–124.

31. Harcourt, note, 31 July 1914, "4 p.m. at the House of Commons," Ms.Dep. 6231.

32. Harcourt diary, cabinet meeting, 1 August 1914 (on reverse of FO telegram), Ms.Dep. 6231. Harcourt's notes on the Finance Committee Meeting held on 1 August 1914 at 2:00 p.m. record that the committee included Lloyd George, Samuel, Haldane, Harcourt, Simon, McKenna, and Runciman, plus Edwin Montagu and Lord Emmott. Also the governor and deputy governor of the Bank of England, Sir Frederick Schuster, Sir E. Holden, and L. Currie, plus five or six others.

33. De Cecco, *Money and Empire,* 149–70.

34. Lloyd George, *Memoirs;* "How We Saved the City" is the title of chapter 4.

35. J. M. Keynes, "Memorandum against the Suspension of Gold," 3 August 1914, JMK, 7–14.

36. Asquith to Stanley, 1 August 1914, LVS, 139–41.

37. Harcourt, Banking Committee, 18 August 1914, Ms.Dep. 6231.

38. Horn, *Britain, France,* 29–35; see also J. M. Keynes, "The Proper Means for Enabling Discount Operations to Be Resumed," 5 August 1914, JMK, 16–19.

39. Peters, "The British Government," 139.

40. Lloyd George, *Memoirs,* 69.

41. Harcourt, notes on cabinet [finance] committee, Bd. Rm. 2:20 p.m., 1 September 1914, and cabinet notes, 2 September 1914, Ms.Dep. 6231.

42. HC Deb, 27 November 1914, vol. 68, c.1533, 1544–55, Lloyd George.

43. SC, 1:160–61.

44. Hazlehurst, *Politicians at War,* 63.

45. See also note passed between John Simon and L. V. Harcourt during cabinet meeting on 30 July 1914, Harcourt cabinet notes, Ms.Dep. 6231.

46. Harcourt, cabinet diary 31 July 1914, Ms.Dep. 6231.

47. Ibid.

48. John Viscount Morley, Memorandum on Resignation: August 1914, MS.Eng. d.3585 (published London, 16 August 1928).

49. Lloyd George, *Memoirs,* 62.

50. Ibid.; see also cabinet note dated 1 August 1914 passed between Harcourt and Simon, Ms.Dep. 6231.

51. Morley, Memorandum on Resignation.

52. Winston S. Churchill, *Great Contemporaries: John Morley* (London: Reprint Society, 1941), 89.

53. Ferguson, *Pity of War,* 191.

54. Harcourt cabinet notes, 31 July 1914, Ms.Dep. 6231.

55. Cambon to Viviani, 31 July 1914 and 2 August 1914, *Documents diplomatiques français* 11:375, 470, cited in Horn, *Britain, France,* 37; Asquith to Stanley, 31 July 1914, LVS, 138.

56. LVS, 139n3.

57. Churchill to his wife, 31 July 1914, in *Winston and Clementine: The Personal Letters of the Churchills,* ed. Mary Soames (London: Doubleday, 1998), 97. Crowe notes difficulty in obtaining cash: Crowe to wife, 4 August 1914, f.7, Crowe Mss., Ms.Eng. 3020.

58. Harcourt, note of meeting with Sir Thomas Robinson (agent-general for Queensland), 11:00 p.m., 2 August 1914; notes of cabinet meeting, 3 August 1914, Ms.Dep. 6231. See also notes of conversation with Andrew Bonar Law, 31 July 1914, cabinet notes, 4:00 p.m., Ms. Dep. 6231.

59. Memo by J. A. Simon on 10 Downing Street paper, dated at the bottom as 31 July 1914, Harcourt diary, Ms.Dep. 6231.

60. Ibid.

61. Grey to Bertie, 31 July 1914, BD, 11:367.

62. For Grey's diplomacy during the July crisis, see Zara Steiner and Keith Neilson, *Britain and the Origins of the First World War* (Basingstoke, UK: Palgrave MacMillan, 2003), 229–57; Stephan Valone, "There Must Be Some Misunderstanding: Sir Edward Grey's Diplomacy of August 1, 1914," *Journal of British Studies* 27 (1988): 405–24.

63. Keith Jeffery, *Field Marshal Sir Henry Wilson: A Political Soldier* (Oxford: Oxford University Press, 2008), 128; Keith Wilson, ed., *Decisions for War 1914* (London: UCL Press, 1995), 200. See also Sibyl Crowe and Edward Corp, *Our Ablest Public Servant: Sir Eyre Crowe, 1864–1925* (Brauton, UK: Merlin Books, 1993), 265; Zara Steiner, *The Foreign Office and Foreign Policy, 1898–1914* (London: Cambridge University Press, 1969), 162.

64. Viscount Grey of Fallodon (Sir Edward Grey), *Twenty-Five Years: 1892–1916,* 2 vols. (New York: Frederick Stokes, 1925), 1:302, 2:20.

65. Crowe memorandum enclosed in Crowe to Grey, 31 July 1914, BD, 11:369; Keith Neilson, *Britain and the Last Tsar: British Policy and Russia 1894–1917* (Oxford: Clarendon Press, 1995), 35.

66. Minute (31 July 1914) by Crowe on Oppenheimer to Goschen, 29 July 1914, BD, 11:322; see also Stephen Gross, "Confidence in Gold: German War Finance 1914–1918," *Central European History* 42 (2009): 223–52.

67. Peters, "The British Government," 133, cites J. M. Keynes as saying there had been a "general failure" to consider the implications, but Keynes knew nothing of the Desart Committee.

68. SC, 1:93; see also Sir Francis Oppenheimer, *Stranger Within: Autobiographical Pages* (London: Faber and Faber, 1960), 218.

69. Lloyd George, *Memoirs,* 62.

70. Asquith to Pamela McKenna, 1 August 1915, MCKN 9/3, 2 of 4.

71. Hazlehurst, *Politicians at War,* and Williamson, PGS remains the best; Keith Wilson, "The British Cabinet's Decision for War, 2 August 1914," *British Journal of International Studies* 1 (1975): 148–59.

72. Note by Harcourt, Sunday morning 2 August 1914, Harcourt Ms.Dep. 6231.

73. Cabinet finance committee, 1 August 1914, 2:00 p.m. to 6:15 p.m., Harcourt Ms.Dep. 6231. The measures were (1) a moratorium on settlement of all debts, (2) authority for the Bank of England to inject £45 million into the banking system, and (3) authority for the issuance of war risk insurance for all merchant vessels.

74. Harcourt, cabinet notes, 2 August 1914 (11:00 a.m.), Ms.Dep. 6231.

75. Samuel to wife, 2 August 1914, f.49, Samuel Mss. (Herbert Samuel papers, the Parliamentary Archive, London).

76. Asquith to Stanley, 2 August 1914, LVS, 140.

77. Samuel to wife, 2 August 1914, f.49, Samuel Mss.

78. HC Deb, 3 August 1914, vol. 65, c.1906–1932, Sir Edward Grey; emphasis added. For timing, see Churchill, précis of a conversation, 2 August 1914, WSC (companion part 1), 3:11–12. For zoo, see Hazlehurst, *Politicians at War,* 96. Telegram (2 August 1914, 4:50 p.m.), Bertie to FO, reproduced in BD, 11:487.

79. PGS, 355.

80. Asquith to Stanley, 31 July 1914, LVS, 138.

81. Note appended to record of cabinet meeting, 2 August 1914, 11:00 a.m. to 1:55 p.m., Harcourt Ms.Dep. 6231.

82. Harcourt, cabinet notes, 2 August 1914, 11:00 a.m.–1:55 p.m., Ms.Dep. 6231.

83. Mrs. Pease to Jack Pease, 4 August 1914, Gainford Mss., box 91, as cited in Keith Wilson, "The British Cabinet's Decision for War, 2 August 1914," *British Journal of International Studies* 1 (1975): 158.

84. Hazlehurst, *Politicians at War,* 92–100.

85. HC Deb, 3 August 1914, vol. 65, 1906–1932, Sir Edward Grey; see also remarks by Ramsey Macdonald, who described the speech and noted, "The echoes of which will go down in history" (c. 1829). Grey speech is reprinted in *25 Years,* 2:308–26.

86. Hazlehurst, *Politicians at War,* 43–48.

87. Grey, *25 Years,* 2:10, 11–18.

88. View shared by Avner Offer, *The First World War: An Agrarian Interpretation* (New York: Oxford University Press, 1989), 309. Offer treats Grey's words as a speech, not as a cabinet statement.

89. HC Deb, 3 August 1914, vol. 65, Sir Edward Grey, c. 1823.

90. Ibid., c. 1826.

91. Offer, *First World War,* 310.

92. Esher journal, 3 August 1914, 4, ESHR 2/13.

93. Harcourt, note of conversation, 11:15 a.m., 4 August 1914, Ms.Dep. 6231.

94. Record of cabinet meetings, 4 and 6 August 1914, Ms.Dep. 6231.

95. Samuel to wife, 4 August 1914, f.68, Samuel Mss.

96. Samuel to wife, 5 August 1914, f.71, Samuel Mss.

97. Samuel to wife, 4 August 1914, f.68, Samuel Mss.

98. Asquith to Stanley, 4 August 1914, LVS, 149–51.

99. Richmond diary, 5 August 1915, RIC.1/9.

100. Pease diary, 29 July 1914, as cited in Hazlehurst, *Politicians at War,* 72; Harcourt, cabinet notes, 29 July 1914 (11:30 a.m.), Ms.Dep. 6231.

101. Harcourt diary, cabinet meeting 29 July 1914, Ms.Dep. 6231.

102. Ibid.

103. Harcourt, cabinet notes, 1 August 1914, Ms.Dep. 6231.

104. Hazlehurst, *Politicians at War,* 87–91; see also Harcourt diary, cabinet meeting, 2 August 1914, Ms.Dep. 6231.

105. Asquith to Stanley, 2 August 1914, LVS, 145–47.

106. Harcourt note dated 3 August 1914, Ms.Dep. 6231.

107. For Churchill taking up half the meeting, see Asquith to Stanley, 1 August 1914, LVS, 140.

108. Churchill to LG, cabinet notes, [1 August 1914], WSC (companion part 2), 2:1996–7.

109. Hazlehurst, *Politicians at War,* 103.

110. Strachan, *To Arms,* 198–99; Stevenson, *Armaments and the Coming of War,* 394; BESP, 20–36.

111. Samuel to wife, 5 August 1914, f.71, Samuel Mss.

112. PGS, 362–64.

113. SC, 1:158; General Haig GOC II Corps notes receiving the order to mobilize at 5:30 p.m., 4 August 1914, for which see *Douglas Haig: War Diaries and Letters, 1914–1918,* ed. Gary Sheffield and John Bourne (London: Weidenfeld and Nicolson, 2005), 52.

114. Asquith to Stanley, 5 August 1914, LVS, 157–58.

115. Harcourt, cabinet notes, 5 August 1914, 10:30 a.m., Ms.Dep. 6231.

116. Admiral Prince Louis of Battenberg.

117. Kitchener was offered the post of secretary of state for war on the evening of 4 August but was not sworn in until the Privy Council meeting held after the cabinet meeting on 6 August, for which see Asquith to Stanley, 6 August 1914, Stanley Ms.Eng. 7093 (Venetia Stanley papers, Bodleian Library, Oxford). There is a suggestion that Asquith first asked Jack Seely to return to the War Office, but he refused.

118. Montagu to Asquith, 7 December 1914, enclosing memorandum on the War Office, AS6/9/19, Montagu Mss. (Edwin Montagu papers, King's College, Cambridge).

119. Runciman to Sir Robert Chalmers, 7 February 1915, Runciman Mss (Walter Runciman papers, Newcastle University Library, UK).

120. Sheffield and Bourne, *Douglas Haig,* 6; Strachan, *To Arms,* 203.

121. Asquith to Stanley, 2 August 1914, LVS, 146; Asquith to Bonar Law, 2 August 1914, cited in Hazlehurst, *Politicians at War,* 90; Jeffrey, *Field Marshal Sir Henry Wilson,* 126–27.

122. This excellent point was made in William Philpott, "The Strategic Ideas of Sir John French," *Journal of Strategic Studies* 12, no. 4 (December 1989): 458–78; see also Philpott, *Anglo-French Relations and Strategy on the Western Front* (Basingstoke, UK: Macmillan, 1996), 3–14.

123. Haig, diary, 4–5 August 1914, in Sheffield and Bourne, *Douglas Haig,* 52–53.

124. Churchill to Hankey, 15 October 1933, f.83, HNKY 7/11.

125. Minutes of War Council, 5 August 1914 [Secretary's Notes], CAB.42/1/2. See also Viscount French of Ypres, *1914* (London: Constable, 1919), 6; Henry Wilson diary as cited in Sheffield and Bourne, *Douglas Haig,* 6; PGS, 363–64.

126. Haig to Haldane, personal, 4 August 1914, Haldane Mss. 5910. See also Haig, diary, 4–5 August 1914, in Sheffield and Bourne, *Douglas Haig,* 52–53. Haig envisaged a force of 300,000; Hazlehurst, *Politicians at War,* 89n3.

127. Hazlehurst, *Politicians at War,* 89–90. For Hankey's doubts, see Corbett diary, 25 August 1914, as cited in Donald Shurman, *Julian S. Corbett: Historian of British Maritime Policy from Drake to Jellicoe* (London: Royal Historical Society, 1981), 157. Further details can be found in correspondence between Churchill and Hankey, 10 October 1933 (f.69), 13 October 1933 (f.70), 15 October 1933 (f.78), all in HNKY.5/1.

128. Secretary's Notes, 2nd War Council, 6 August 1914, CAB.42/1/3.

129. Asquith to Stanley, 6 August 1914, LVS, 158; Hobhouse says that McKenna stood out against dispatch of BEF, Hobhouse 60506.

130. Harcourt, note of meeting at 10 Downing Street, 11:15 p.m., Tuesday, 4 August 1914, Ms.Dep. 6231.

131. Pease diary, 6 August 1914, f.108, Gainford Mss. 39 (Lord Gainford papers, Nuffield College, Oxford).

132. Harcourt, cabinet notes, 6 August 1914, Ms.Dep. 6231.

133. Ibid.; also Pease diary, 6 August 1914, f.108, Gainford Mss. 39.

134. Minutes of War Councils, 5 and 6 August 1914, CAB.42/1/2–3.

135. For example, Strachan, *First World War,* 198, 203–4; Philpott, *Anglo-French Relations and Strategy,* 7–8.

136. Hankey to Esher, 31 July 1914, ESHR 5/46.

137. George Casser, *Kitchener's War: British Strategy from 1914 to 1916* (Washington, DC: Brassey's, 2004), 24–37; Roy Prete, "French Strategic Planning and the Deployment of the BEF to France in 1914," *Canadian Journal of History* 24 (1989): 42–62; A. J. P. Taylor, *War by Timetable: How the First World War Began* (London: Macdonald, 1969). See also Hazlehurst, *Politicians at War,* 63–64, 88–90, 121–22. See Kitchener for the cabinet, "The War," 31 May 1915, CAB.37/128/30.

138. Ibid. See also William Philpott, "Britain and France Go to War: Anglo-French Relations on the Western Front 1914–1918," *War in History* 2 (1995): 43–64.

139. CID, "Joint Naval and Military Committee for the Consideration of Combined Operations in Foreign Territory," 5 August 1914; "Proceedings of a Sub-Committee of the Committee of Imperial Defence, August 5, 1914," CAB.38/28/45. Further meetings held 6, 8, 14, 17, 25, 27, 29 August. Typescript copies of these two memoranda are contained in Harcourt's cabinet notes.

140. Asquith to Stanley, 6 August 1914, LVS, 158.

141. Jack Pease to Sir A. Pease (brother), 28 August 1914, Gainford Mss. 145.

142. Samuel to wife, 3 August 1914 (5:30 p.m.), f.63, Samuel Mss.; Harcourt's notes of cabinet discussions on 2, 3, and 4 August 1914 contain similar references, Ms.Dep. 6231.

143. The Greek alliance and the possibility of extending the alliance to Balkan countries may not have been considered until the week of 17 August, for which see Asquith to Stanley, 20 August 1914, LVS, 182.

144. Memorandum (3 August 1914) signed by Churchill, Battenberg, and Sturdee, addressed to Grey and Asquith, f.103, FO.800/88; copy CHAR.13/27 (Sir Winston Churchill papers, Chartwell Trust Collection, Churchill College, Cambridge).

145. Harcourt, note of meeting on Tuesday, 4 August 1914 (11:15 p.m. 3 August), Harcourt, cabinet notes, Ms.Dep. 6231.

146. Churchill to Grey, 5 August 1914, f.104, and Admiralty to Belgian Government via FO, 5 August 1914, f.107, both Grey, FO.800/88.

147. Samuel to wife, 5 August 1914, f.71, Samuel Mss.

148. Exception is BSWA, 28–36.

149. Neilson, *Last Tsar,* 343–44.

150. Churchill to Grey, 11 August 1914, CHAR.13/43/49.

151. Minute (5 August 1914) by Crowe, 36542, f.414, FO.371/2162.

152. Minutes (n.d.) by Grey, 35752/4 August 1914, ff.108–42, FO.371/2161. N.b.: The original drafts of these telegrams and instructions were omitted from the archive and the printed official copies.

153. Ibid., f.145.

154. Crowe, "Prosecution of the War," 5 August 1914, enclosed in "Question of endeavoring to bring into a system of fighting alliances a ring of Powers surrounding the enemies," 36542, FO.371/2162. See also attached minute (5 August 1914) by Grey, 36542, FO.371/2162; minute (7 August 1914) by Crowe, f.100, 36754, FO.371/2163.

155. Crowe to wife, 8:00 p.m., 5 August 1914, f.9, Crowe, Ms.Eng. 3020.

156. Telegram (4 August 1914) by Buchanan (ambassador, St. Petersburg), received 5 August, No. 215, f.326, and telegram (4 August 1914) by Bertie (ambassador, Paris) f.315, and also telegram (7 August 1914) by Findlay (Christiania), No. 49, f.103, all FO.371/2161; minutes (14 August 1914) by Wellesley and Olliphant 38555, MF35250, FO.372/600; for evidence of the French government's knowledge of the initiative, see Telegram No. 626 (4 August 1914, 3:25 p.m.), Bertie to Grey, BD, 11:626.

157. Telegram (4 August 1914) by Findlay to Grey, received 5 August, No. 36, f.311, 35932, FO.371/2161.

158. Crowe to wife, 6 August 1914 (past midnight so actually 7 August), f.12, Crowe Ms. Eng. 3020.

159. Report of Grey's conversation with Dutch minister, 7 August 1914, 36690, f.56, FO.371/2163.

160. Quote from Hobhouse, 8 September; Asquith to Stanley, 2 and 3 and 6 September 1914, LVS, 214–18, 224; Richmond diary, 9 August 1914 and 19 October 1914, in Arthur J. Marder, *Portrait of an Admiral: The Life and Papers of Sir Herbert Richmond* (London: Jonathan Cape, 1952), 96, 119; Hobhouse diary, 3 September 1914, f.58, and 8 September 1914, f.60, Hobhouse 60506; Harcourt, cabinet notes, 3 September 1914, Ms.Dep. 6231; Pease diary, 8 September 1914, f.124, Gainford Mss. 39; Churchill to Grey, 7 September 1914, FO.800/88.

161. Note (5 August 1914) by Crowe, on 36692, f.64, FO.371/2163. Grey may have felt justified in so doing after discussing the matter with Churchill, for which see Churchill to Grey, 5 August 1914, CHAR.13/44/98.

162. Telegram (7 August 1914) by Findlay (Christiania), No. 49, f.103, FO.371/2161.

163. Telegram (7 August 1914) by Howard (Stockholm), 36887, FO.371/2163.

164. Minute (7 August 1914) by Crowe, 36754, FO.371/2163.

165. Zara Steiner, "The Foreign Office and the War," in F. H. Hinsley, ed., *British Foreign Policy under Sir Edward Grey* (Cambridge: Cambridge University Press, 1977), 517.

166. Crowe to wife, 6 August 1914 (past midnight so actually 7 August), f.12, Crowe Ms. Eng. 3020.

167. Crowe to wife, 1 September 1914, f.82, Crowe Ms.Eng. 3020.

168. Riddle diary, conversations with Lloyd George and Reginald McKenna, 10 October 1914, ff.183–84, Add.Mss. 62974 (Lord Riddle papers, British Library, London).

169. For Asquith's complaint about Grey, see LVS, 8, 23, and 27 October 1914, 268, 283, 287–88.

170. Asquith to Stanley, 28 October 1914, LVS, 288.

171. Asquith to Stanley, 23 October 1914, LVS, 283.

172. Asquith to Stanley, 12 March 1915, LVS, 476–77.

173. Sir Laurence Collier, "Impressions of Sir Eyre Crowe," typescript, n.d. [1960], 7, Collier MISC.466 (Lawrence Collier Papers, London School of Economics, UK). I am indebted to Professor Keith Neilson for bringing this document to my attention. For further analysis, see Clive Parry, "Foreign Policy and International Law," in F. H. Hinsley, ed., *British Foreign Policy under Sir Edward Grey* (Cambridge: Cambridge University Press, 1977), 90–91.

174. Offer, *First World War,* 309–10, citing Grant-Duff diary entry, 5 May 1911, f.65, and 10 June 1911, f.75, AGDF.2/1.

175. War Book, Section 6, Admiralty, Part 25, "Censorship of and Control of Messages by Radio-Telegraphy," f.55, CAB.15/5.

176. SC, 1:118–23; CID "Coordination of Departmental Action," War Book—1914 ed., CAB.15/5.

177. "Second Supplement to the *London Gazette* of Tuesday, the 4th of August 1914," 5 August 1914, issue 28862.

178. Ibid., proclamation governing "the exportation from the United Kingdom of certain warlike stores, provisions and victual," 2–3.

179. CID, "Inter-Departmental Conference on Trading with the Enemy," 1 March 1915, para. 13, enclosed as section II to CID 216-B, 9 March 1915, f.49, CAB.4/5.

180. Agreed at second meeting of Trading with Enemy Committee, 22 November 1911, for which see report 29, "Restrictions on the export of warlike stores in time of war," 27 February 1912, f.74; see also Part 1, Final Report, Trading with the Enemy Committee, para. 118,

19, both CAB.16/18B; The meeting agreed that the list would be drawn up in conjunction with the War Office and Board of Trade, but in practice this was not done. See conclusion C, Final Report, Trading with the Enemy Committee, CAB.16/18B; see narrow recommendations by subconference, ff.37–39, schedule VIII.

181. Minutes (5 August 1914), "Cargo of Gas Coke for Norway," 35982, FO.372/600.

182. Extensions to the list were announced: *London Gazette,* 7 August 1914, issue 28864; 11 August 1914, issue 28867.

183. B. R. Mitchell, *Economic Development of the British Coal Industry, 1800–1914* (Cambridge: Cambridge University Press, 1984), table 5.2.

184. Runciman to Grey, 9 August 1914, ff.235–36, FO.800/89.

185. Nicholas A. Lambert, "Strategic Command and Control for Maneuver Warfare: Creation of the Royal Navy's 'War Room' System, 1905–1915," *Journal of Military History* 69, no. 2 (2005): 361–410.

186. Dumas diary, 1 August 1914, Dumas.65/23/1 (Captain Philip Dumas Papers, Imperial War Museum, London).

187. Appendix, "Administrative Measures for Securing Our Economic Position," 17, printed October 1914, CAB.1/10; also "Notes by Sir M. Hankey," October 1914, ff.6–7, CAB.1/11.

188. "Notes by Sir M. Hankey," October 1914, ff.6–7, CAB.1/11.

189. Jonathan Winkler, *Nexus: Strategic Communications and American Security in World War I* (Cambridge, MA: Harvard University Press, 2008), 41.

190. Telegram (4 August 1914, 5:55 p.m.) to all ships, f.331, ADM.137/987; C. Ernest Fayle, *Seaborne Trade,* 3 vols. (London: John Murray, 1920–1924), 1:47; notes by Sir Maurice Hankey, "Measure to Secure the Economic Equilibrium in the United Kingdom," f.14, CAB.1/11; for Admiralty notification of Foreign Office, see Admiralty to FO, 4 August 1914, f.154, 35820, FO.371/2161.

191. Minute (4 August 1914) by Webb to First Lord, f.341, ADM.137/987; Minute (5 August 1914) by Webb, "Diverted Cargo: Proposals for Dealing With," approved by Battenberg, 5 August 1914, ff.12–14, ADM.137/982. Again, the Admiralty could claim quasi-authority for this action, for which see DC, Final Report, para. 53, 8.

192. Overzealousness by the Customs officers found in Harcourt, cabinet notes, 21 August 1914, Ms.Dep.6231.

193. The barque *Chile,* case heard before Sir Samuel Evans, 4 September 1914, prize court transcripts, vol. 1, NR 341.362.1PRI, NLMD.

194. Charles Kersey (Canadian Pacific Railway) to Webb (DTD), 3 August 1914, f.10, ADM.137/982.

195. Admiralty to Board of Trade, 5 August 1914, "Diverted Cargo—Proposals for Dealing With," f.15, ADM.137/982.

196. Minute (16 August 1914) by Webb, "Deflection of British Ships from Rotterdam," and W/t signal to VA 2nd and 3rd Fleets, RA 7th CS, and Admiral of Patrols (16 August 1914), ff.348–50, ADM.137/987.

197. Fayle, *Seaborne Trade,* 1:182.

198. Statement by John Smith and Sons (coal exporters) of Glasgow, addressed to Admiralty, 26 August 1914, ff.361–63, ADM.137/987.

199. "Note of a Meeting at Lloyd's on 11 December [1914] between the Committee of Lloyd's and Mr. Leverton Harris," ADM.137/2804. N.b.: Leverton Harris was head of the T.11 section of the Naval Staff.

200. See ESRC reports, ADM.137/2988.

201. C. S. Denniss (Cardiff Railway Company) to Hopwood, 3 August 1914, f.74, ADM.137/988.

202. Hankey memo, ff.20–22, CAB.1/11. Arguably, the British action might be defended under the "right of angary."

203. Page to FO, 14 August 1914, and FO minute (16 August 1914) thereon by GHW (?), 39323/15 August 1914, FO.368/1158.

204. Telephone message received from Foreign Office (6:45 p.m., 16 August 1914) and minute thereon (16 August 1914) by Webb, f.42, ADM.137/982.

205. Esher journal, 31 August 1914, ESHR.2/13. See procurator general to Foreign Office, 26 August 1914, FO.372/600. For recommendation by the Food Committee to release the cargoes, see minute (25 August 1914) by W. E. Davidson, "Release of Grain Cargos," 41728, FO.368/1158.

206. Crowe to Greene, 30 July 1914, 34874, FO.372/588.

207. FO to Admiralty, 7 August 1914, ADM.116/1233; telegram (6 August 1914, 6:45 p.m.), Bertie (Paris) to FO, 36563, FO.372/588.

208. Minute (6 August 1914) by Grey, FO.372/588; FO to Admiralty, 7 August 1914, ADM.116/1233.

209. Grey to Barclay, 7 August 1914, 37140, 711, FO.372/588.

210. For Grey continuing to favor the Admiralty, see his approval of draft telegram enclosed in Churchill to Grey, 10 August 1914, f.79, 37812, FO.371/2164.

211. See minute (21 August 1914) by Crowe and accompanying FO to Admiralty, 26 August 1914, 38872, FO.372/588.

212. FO to J. W. Baird and Co., 9 August 1914, FO.372/600, as cited in John Coogan, *The End of Neutrality: the United States, Britain and Maritime Rights, 1899–1915* (Ithaca, NY: Cornell University Press, 1981), 154.

213. Memo (10 August 1914) by Hurst, FO.372/588.

214. For possible Conservative warning on this, see Austen Chamberlain to Harcourt, 10 August 1914, Ms.Dep.6231.

215. Minute (n.d.) by Simon, 38186, FO.372/588.

216. For details on the revised 1904 prize manual, see Minute (14 July 1913) by Rear-Admiral Edward Pakenham, on report of Admiralty committee appointed to revise naval prize manual, and Admiralty to FO, 15 August 1913, ADM.116/1232; see also "Report of Naval Prize Law Committee," 30 June 1913, ADM.116/1231A. Minute (7 August 1914) by Greene, on draft order-in-council, ADM.116/1233.

217. Additional minute (8 August 1914) by Slade, ADM.116/1233.

218. Initialed by Battenberg 9 August and by Churchill 10 August, ADM.116/1233; Admiralty to FO, 11 August 1914, 38186, FO.372/588.

219. FO to Admiralty, 14 August 1914, attached to file 36563, ADM.116/1233.

220. This is what Churchill meant when he wrote at the foot of the Admiralty docket enclosing the draft order-in-council, "We ought to know the result of the battle before taking a final decision." ADM.116/1233.

221. Cabinet letter, 12 August 1914. See also Marc Frey, "Trade, Ships, and the Neutrality of the Netherlands in the First World War," *International History Review* 19, no. 3 (August 1997): 544.

222. Harcourt, report of cabinet, 12 August 1914, Ms.Dep. 6231.

223. See Chapter 4.

224. Asquith, Lloyd George, Grey, Churchill, Haldane, Harcourt, and Crewe had been present at the 120th CID and were still members of the cabinet in August 1914. Of the two who had since left, Jack Seely had resigned after the Curragh Mutiny, and Sidney Buxton had been appointed governor-general of South Africa.

225. Esher journal, 14 August 1914, ESHR.2/13.

226. John Naylor, *Man and an Institution: Sir Maurice Hankey, the Cabinet Secretariat and the Custody of Cabinet Secrets* (Cambridge: Cambridge University Press, 1984), 19–21.

227. Cabinet letter, 13 August 1914, CAB.41/35/29.

228. Coogan, *End of Neutrality,* 155–56.

229. Simon to Grey, 14 August 1914, f.18, FO.800/89.

230. See minutes of conference held at the Foreign Office, "Declaration of London," 19 August 1914, 42063, FO.372/588. Copy in ADM.116/1233.

231. Simon to Grey, 14 August 1914, f.18, FO.800/89. This opinion was not formally recorded by the Attorney General's department, for which see volume of "Opinions," TS.25/2023 (Treasury Solicitor's Office, The National Archives, Kew); see also minute (16 August 1914) by Greene to Sturdee, ADM.116/1233. Greene noted that "it is not certain that a mere calculation of the quantity required for the Dutch population as compared with actual imports would be held as conclusive if the civil population of Germany also had to be considered." There are further hints of a policy based on rationing in Oppenheimer, *Stranger Within,* 234–35.

232. Harcourt, cabinet notes, 13 August 1914, Ms.Dep. 6231.

233. Simon, Harcourt, Hobhouse, Emmott, and Pease. Runciman was the sixth, but his motivations were somewhat different. See Asquith to Stanley, 21 August 1914, LVS, 184–86.

234. Emmott diary, 13 August 1914, 107, and 17 August, Emmott Mss. 2.

235. Hobhouse diary, 13 and 14 August 1914, f.51, Add.Mss. 60506.

236. Harcourt, cabinet notes, 13 August 1914, Ms.Dep. 6231.

237. Harcourt called it the Cabinet Committee on Contraband, for which see cabinet notes, 13 August 1914, Ms.Dep. 6231.

238. Minutes (13 August 1914) by Churchill to Grey, McKenna, Lloyd George, and Runciman, CHAR 13/27/B/9.

239. Asquith to Stanley, 19 August 1914, LVS, 178–80. Asquith listed Grey, Runciman, Lloyd George, Churchill, Kitchener, and Simon.

240. Memorandum (13 August 1914) on blockade, appendix E, in Churchill, *World Crisis,* 1:573; original handwritten and annotated by Grey, Runciman, Lloyd George, and McKenna, f.2, CHAR.13/27B/9.

241. Hankey, "The Co-ordination of the War Arrangements for Trade Restrictions, &c," 13 January 1915, 1, CID-203B, CAB.42/1/15.

242. Memorandum (13 August 1914) on blockade, appendix E, WC, 1:573.

243. ESCR, 1st Report, 15 August 1914, ADM.137/2988; telegram (31 August 1914), Grey to Johnston (No. 20 commercial), 44818, FO.368/1032; Oppenheimer, *Stranger Within,* 234–41.

244. Cabinet letter, 15 August 1914, CAB.41/35/30.

245. Harcourt, cabinet notes, 14 August 1914, Ms.Dep. 6231. The question mark is in the original.

246. Ibid.

247. Cabinet letter, 15 August 1914, CAB.41/35/30.

248. Asquith to Stanley, 17 August 1914, LVS, 170–72. Intriguingly, this was the first reference to the subject in their correspondence.

249. Ibid. See also cabinet letter, 17 August 1914, CAB.41/35/31.

250. Harcourt, cabinet notes, 14 August 1914, Ms.Dep. 6231; see also Emmott diary, 17 August 1914, f.108, Emmott Mss. 2.

251. Churchill to Grey, 10 August 1914, f.79, 37812, FO.371/2164; see also FNR 270–74.

252. Harcourt, cabinet notes, 7 August 1914, Ms.Dep. 6231.

253. For timing, see telephone message received from Foreign Office (6:45 p.m., 16 August 1914) and minute thereon (16 August 1914) by Webb, f.42, ADM.137/982. Note from Mr. Bryan.

254. Harcourt, cabinet notes, 17 August 1914, Ms.Dep. 6231.

255. Hobhouse diary, 14 August 1914, Add.Mss. 60506.

256. Emmott, 17 and 19 August 1914, 108–10, Emmott Mss. 2.

257. Ibid.

258. Hobhouse, 14 August 1914, f.51, Add.Mss. 60506.

259. Harcourt, cabinet notes, 14 August 1914, Ms.Dep. 6231.

260. Cabinet letter, 15 and 20 August 1914, CAB.41/35/30 and 41/35/34; for deletion of coal from the list, see Harcourt cabinet notes, 20 August 1914, Ms.Dep. 6231; *London Gazette*, issue 28876, 21 August 1914, 2.

261. HC Deb, 28 August 1914, vol. 66, c.350–52, Mr. Tickler (Exportation of Coal to Holland).

262. Harcourt, cabinet notes, 18 August 1914, Ms.Dep. 6231.

263. Board of Trade circular letter dated 19 August 1914. See memorandum by N. J. Highmore, "Some Suggestions in Reference to the Blockade," 7 July 1916, 138420, para. 2, FO.382/1100.

264. Asquith to Stanley, 19 August 1914, LVS, 178–80.

265. "Second Supplement to the *London Gazette* of Tuesday, the 4th of August 1914," 5 August 14, issue 28862, 3; see also various Minutes (5 August 14), "Cargo of Gas Coke for Norway," 35982, FO.372/600.

266. Cabinet letter, 19 August 1914, CAB.41/35/33.

267. Draft (not sent) of memo to HHA on food blockade of Germany, 20 August 1914, Emmott Mss. 5/195.

268. ESRC, 2nd Report, 21 August 1914, ADM.137/2988.

269. Ibid.

270. "Declaration of London—Conference Held at the Foreign Office, 19th August 1914," 42063/22, August 1914, FO.372/588; Harcourt, cabinet notes, 19 August 1914, Ms.Dep. 6231, confirms this meeting took place after the cabinet meeting.

271. Eric Osborne, *Britain's Economic Blockade of Germany, 1914–1919* (London: Frank Cass, 2004), 62–64.

272. Hurst to Greene, n.d. [14 August 1914], case 455, ADM.116/1234; also minutes (13 August 1914) by Davidson and (14 August 1914) by Hurst on "Netherlands and Goods

Consigned to Germany," 38332, FO.372/600. The point is that it removed restrictions; see "Memorandum on Paragraph 5," by Hurst, n.d., ADM.116/1233.

273. Minutes (15 August 1914) and (18 August 1914) by Slade on Hurst, "Memorandum," ADM.116/1233.

274. Minutes (16 August 1914) by Sturdee and (18 August 1914) by Slade, ADM.116/1233.

275. Minute (17 August 1914) by Churchill, ADM.116/1233.

276. "Declaration of London—Conference Held at the Foreign Office, 19th August 1914," 42063/22 August 1914, FO.372/588. Also present were Admirals Battenberg, Sturdee, and Slade, plus Greene and Hurst.

277. Ibid., 2.

278. "Memorandum of a Conversation held on Feby 23rd 1911," secret (present: McKenna, Ottley, Hankey), ff.22–26, CAB.17/87.

279. See also minute (29 August 1914) by Wellesley on "Article 3 of the Order in Council of 20th August," and Mellor (procurator general) to FO, 26 August 1914, 43595/35250, FO.372/600.

280. "(5) Notwithstanding the provisions of Article 35 of the said declaration, conditional contraband, if shown to have the destination referred to in Article 33, is liable to capture, to whatever port the vessel is bound and at whatever port the cargo is to be discharged."

281. Admiralty to FO, 23 August 1914, 42366, FO.372/600; copy of signal (19 August 1914) to all ships, "Confidential Admiralty Interim Orders," appended to revised instruction on "Contraband and Conditional Contraband," 47, issued 26 August 1914, ADM.137/2733; minute (19 August 1914) by Battenberg on draft telegram canceling "previous instructions to the fleet," ADM.116/1233.

282. Pease diary, 20 August, 114, Gainford Mss. 39; Asquith to Stanley, 20 August 1914, LVS, 182. According to Hurst, the cabinet revised para. 3, for which see minute (22 August 1914) by Hurst to Grey, "Destination and Continuous Voyage of Conditional Contraband," 41003, FO.372/600.

283. Cabinet letter, 20 August 1914, CAB.41/35/34; see also Harcourt cabinet notes, 20 August 1914, Ms.Dep. 6231.

284. Supplement to the *London Gazette*, 21 August 1914, issue 28877, 6673–74.

285. List of food in *London Gazette,* issue 28876, 21 August 1914, 2.

286. Diary, 21 August 1914, f.52, Hobhouse Add.Mss. 60506.

287. Pease diary, 1 March 1915, Gainford Mss. 40.

288. Hankey to Asquith, 20 July 1915, (31) CAB.63/5.

289. Minute (20 August 1914) by W. A. Sanderson, 41062, f.281, FO.372/578; draft letter by Crowe to Russian ambassador, 21 August 1914, 36781, FO372/588.

290. Minute (21 August 1914) by Crowe, 41194, FO.372/600; similar complaints in minutes (17 August 1914) by Wellesley on "Goods in Transit through Netherlands for Germany," 39263, FO.372/600.

291. Minute (20 August 1914) by Wellesley, Sanderson, Orde, and Hurst, and (21 August 1914) by Crowe, on "Dutch Differential Treatment as Regards Transit of Foodstuffs for Respective Belligerents," 41071, FO.372/588 (on Villiers 4T of 19 August).

292. Minutes (23 August 1914) by Crowe and Davidson on telegram from Johnstone to Grey, 22 August 1914 (No. 106, commercial), 42155, FO.368/1026; ESRC, 4th Report,

29 August 1914, ADM.137/2988; previous telegram (19 August 1914), No. 106, commercial, received 6:45 p.m.; also, "Destination and Continuous Voyage of Conditional Contraband," 41003, FO.372/588.

293. For the claim that the ban was in place, see urgent telegram No. 106 (19 August 1914) by Johnstone (The Hague), received 6:45 p.m., 41003, FO.372/600; for contradictory evidence, see telegram (19 August 1914) from Sir Edward Villiers (Brussels) to FO, copy in CHAR 13/43/53, and Churchill to Grey, 20 August 1914, CHAR 13/43/54; also, British naval attaché (The Hague) to Admiralty, 12 August 1914, on 38332, FO.372/600; Ernest Maxse (consul general, Rotterdam) to Grey, 13 August 1914 (received 15 August), 39363, FO.372/600.

294. British naval attaché (The Hague) to Admiralty, 12 August 1914, on 38332, FO.372/600.

295. Minute (n.d.; ca. 20 August 1914) by Greene, ADM.137/2988; see also minutes (20 and 21 August 1914) by Slade and W. F. Nicholson, f.52, ADM.137/982.

296. Frey, "Trade, Ships"; Thomas Otte, " 'Between Hammer and Anvil': Sir Francis Oppenheimer, the Netherlands Overseas Trust and Allied Economic Warfare, 1914–1918," in Christopher Baxter and Andrew Stewart, eds., *Diplomats at War: British and Commonwealth Diplomacy in Wartime* (Leiden: Martinus Nijhoff, 2008), 85–91.

297. Minute (23 August 1914) by Churchill to Grey, FLM, 2:37–38.

298. Frey, "Trade, Ships," 544nn1–2.

299. ADM to FO, 23 August 1914, 42366, FO.372/600.

300. Extract from Admiralty letter M.15498 of 26 August 1914, as reproduced in "Minutes of a Meeting of the Coordinating Committee Held in the Home Secretary's Room on Thursday, August 27, 1914, at 6:30 p.m.," 1 September 1914, CAB.17/88B. Copies in FO.372/600 and FO.368/1158.

301. Diary entry, 31 August 1914, Esher Mss. [2/13], cited in Coogan, *End of Neutrality,* 163; see also minute (25 August 14) by W. E. Davidson, "Release of Grain Cargoes," 41728, FO.368/1158.

302. Copy, Grey to Johnson (Hague) 25 August 1914, 4:05 p.m., ADM.116/1233.

303. FO to ADM, 26 August 1914, and attached minutes, 38872, FO.372/588.

304. Oppenheimer, *Stranger Within,* 238.

305. Asquith to Stanley, 20 August 1914, LVS, 181–83.

306. Harcourt's cabinet notes for these days contain no reference to discussion of this subject.

307. Cabinet letter, 26 August 1914, CAB.41/35/36. Present: McKenna, Runciman, Hopwood, Slade, Hurst, Hankey.

308. HMS, 1:145; McKenna, Memorandum, CID 197-B, 28 September 1914, CAB.38/28/38.

309. Hankey, "Minutes of Coordinating Committee," 1 September 1914, f.20, CAB 17/88B.

310. Ibid.

311. Minute (29 August 1914) by Grey, 43837/27 August 1914, FO.368/1158.

312. Minutes (2 September 1914) by Hurst and (5 September 1914) by Crowe, "Article 3 of the Order in Council of 20th August," 45395, FO.372/600.

313. Minutes (14 September 1914) of a meeting held at the CID, 12 September 1914, "Foodstuffs Diverted from Dutch Ports," CAB.17/88C.

6. The Problem with Americans

Epigraph: Oppenheimer diary, 24 March 1918, box 5, Oppenheimer Mss. (Sir Francis Oppenheimer papers, Bodleian Library, Oxford). I am indebted to Dr. Thomas Otte for this reference.

1. Telegram (26 August 1914), French to Kitchener, enclosed with Asquith to Stanley, nearly midnight, 24 August 1914, LVS, 192–93; cabinet letter, 26 August 1914, CAB.41/35/36.

2. Harcourt, journal, 24 August 1914, Ms.Dep. 6231; Hobhouse diary, 24 August 1914, Add.Mss. 60506.

3. Asquith to Stanley, 25 August 1914, LVS, 194–96. See also Harcourt, "Notes of Dinner Conversations," 24 August 1914, Ms.Dep. 6231; and see generally Robert Doughty, *Pyrrhic Victory: French Strategy and Operations in the Great War* (Cambridge, MA: Harvard University Press, 2005), 46–104. More specialized analysis of British military operations is in Terence Zuber, *The Mons Myth: A Reassessment of the Battle* (Stroud: History Press, 2010).

4. Harcourt journal, 25 August 1914, Ms.Dep. 6231.

5. Harcourt journal, 25 and 26 August 1914, Ms.Dep. 6231.

6. Emmott diary, 25 August 1914, f.114, Emmott Mss. 2.

7. Asquith to Stanley, 25 and 26 August 1914, LVS, 194–99; Harcourt, cabinet notes, 31 August 1914, Ms.Dep. 6231.

8. Harcourt, cabinet notes, 31 August 1914, Ms.Dep. 6231.

9. Asquith to Stanley, 1 and 2 September 1914, LVS, 212–14.

10. Dennis Showalter, *Tannenberg: Clash of Empires* (Hamden, CT: Archon Books, 1991; reprint, Washington, DC: Brassey's, 2004).

11. BESP, 124–35; Winston S. Churchill, *The World Crisis, 1911–1918,* 5 vols. (New York: Scribner's, 1923–1931). 1:253.

12. Viscount Grey of Fallodon (Sir Edward Grey), *Twenty-Five Years: 1892–1916,* 2 vols. (New York: Frederick Stokes, 1925), 2:71; Keith Neilson, "Kitchener: A Reputation Refurbished?" *Canadian Journal of History* 15, no. 2 (August 1980): 207–9.

13. George Cassar, *Kitchener's War: British Strategy from 1914 to 1916* (Washington, DC: Brassey's, 2004).

14. Esher on Kitchener's strategy, 9 October 1914, CAB.17/111; Page to House, 22 September 1914, in Burton J. Hendrick, *The Life and Letters of Walter H. Page,* vol. 1, part 2 (New York: Doubleday, 1924), 331; for discussion of Kitchener's timetable, see David French, "The Meaning of Attrition, 1914–1916," *English Historical Review* 103 (April 1988): 385–405.

15. Casser, *Kitchener's War,* xvi, 292–96.

16. French, "Meaning of Attrition," 385–405.

17. SC, 1:221.

18. Harcourt, cabinet notes, 6 August 1914, Ms.Dep. 6231.

19. Asquith to Stanley, 24 August 1914, LVS, 190–91; also Harcourt journal, 24 August 1914, Ms.Dep. 6231. Asquith claimed that 600,000 to 700,000 men was thirty divisions.

20. Harcourt, cabinet notes, 27 August 1914, Ms.Dep. 6231.

21. Asquith to Stanley, 1 and 2 September 1914, LVS, 212–14.

22. Asquith to Stanley, 3 September 1914, LVS, 217.

23. Very quickly ministers were irked by Kitchener's reticence. See Hobhouse diary, 3 September 1914, f.59, Add.Mss. 60506; generally, Hew Strachan, The *First World War: To Arms* (Oxford: Oxford University Press, 2001), 160.

24. Asquith to Stanley, 8 September 1914, LVS, 226, puts the number of divisions at fifty, as did Harcourt, journal, 8 September 1914, Ms.Dep. 6231. Hobhouse says Kitchener projected forty-six divisions; Hobhouse diary, 8 September 1914, f.60, Add.Mss. 60506.

25. Asquith to Stanley, 5 September 1914, LVS, 220–22.

26. Asquith to Stanley, 29 October 1914, LVS, 295–96.

27. Montagu to Asquith, 1 October 1914, AS1/7/32(1), Montagu Mss. (Edwin Montagu papers, Trinity College, Cambridge).

28. Ibid.

29. For chaotic War Office purchasing in the United States, see B. P. Blackett to Sir John Bradbury (Treasury), 24 November 1914, f.166, Asquith Mss. 26.

30. See also Montagu to Asquith, 7 December 1914, AS6/9/19, enclosing memorandum on the War Office, Montagu Mss.

31. Ibid.

32. Asquith to Stanley, 27 October 1914, LVS, 287–88.

33. Asquith to Stanley, 3 November 1914 (1), LVS, 306–7.

34. Runciman (BdT), "Unemployment Due to the War," for cabinet, 28 August 1914, and McKenna (Home Office), "State of British Industries One Month after Declaration of War," for cabinet, 8 September 1914, both ADM.116/3486.

35. BSWA, 89–91; BESP, 151–55; Martin Horn, *Britain, France, and the Financing of the First World War* (Montreal: McGill–Queen's University Press, 2002), 45.

36. Lloyd George, "Some Further Considerations of the Conduct of the War," 22 February 1915, CAB.37/124/40; see also Treasury, for cabinet, "The Financial Position in May: Report by Director of Financial Enquiries," 8 June 1915, CAB.37/129/23.

37. Emmott diary, 20 October 1914, f.122, and 1 December 1914, f.148, Emmott Mss. 2.

38. Minute (20 August 1914) by Davidson, on Telegram 7R (20 August 1914, 6:45 p.m.) to Findlay (Christiania), 35250/41017, FO.372/600.

39. John Coogan, *The End of Neutrality: The United States, Britain and Maritime Rights, 1899–1915* (Ithaca, NY: Cornell University Press, 1981), 169–70.

40. Signal (17 August 1914), Admiralty to 4th CS, CHAR.13/36/68 (copy in ADM.137/982); see also minute (17 August 1914) by Crowe on "Diversion to UK Ports of British vessels Carrying Foodstuffs," 39323, FO.368/1158.

41. Telegram (21 August 1914), Grey to Barclay (Washington, DC), 41679, FO.368/1158.

42. Minute (29 August 1914) by Grey, and telegram (1 September 1914) by Grey to Spring-Rice, 45253, FO.372/600; see also telegram (19 October 1914), Page to SECSTATE, FRUS, 1914, Su253.

43. Minute (29 August 1914) by Grey, 45253, FO.372/600.

44. Jellicoe to Admiralty, 25 September 1914, and attached minutes, f.195ff., ADM. 137/982.

45. Nearly all such figures are derived indirectly from a single source: Abraham Berglund, "The War and the World's Mercantile Marine," *American Economic Review* 10, no. 2 (June 1920): 227–58.

46. U.S. Department of Commerce, *Annual Report of the Commissioner of Navigation to the Secretary of Commerce for the Fiscal Year Ended June 30, 1915* (Washington, DC: Government Printing Office, 1915), 8.

47. Excluding the tonnage on the U.S. Great Lakes and the fleets of Austria, Germany, and Japan, the remainder is 35,249,000 GRT. This means the British merchant fleet accounted for 58.3 percent. Add the French and it comes to 64 percent.

48. Jerry Jones, "The Naval Battle of Paris," *Naval War College Review* 62, no. 2 (Spring 2009): 77–89 and n1. Table 1 shows 305 vessels on the American register in June 1915. We know that 96 vessels had been added since June 1914. Therefore in June 1914, the American merchant marine consisted of 209 vessels.

49. "Increased Ocean Transportation Rates, Letter from the Secretary of the Treasury and the Secretary of Commerce," 29 December 1914, 63rd Congress, 3rd session, Senate Doc. 673, part 1, 3–4; Arthur S. Link, *Wilson,* vol. 3: *The Struggle for Neutrality, 1914–1915* (Princeton, NJ: Princeton University Press, 1960), 82.

50. PWW, 30:325–26. British vessels accounted for 60 percent, Germany for 18 percent, and all neutrals for 17 percent, leaving U.S.-flagged vessels with just 5 percent.

51. Berglund, "The War and the World's Mercantile Marine." 239n31.

52. U.S. Department of Commerce, *Annual Report of the Commissioner of Navigation.*

53. Runciman to Grey, 25 March 1915, f.295, FO.800/89; Board of Trade, for cabinet, "Transfer of British Ships," 26 January 1915, CAB.37/123/53.

54. "The World Shipbuilding in 1914," enclosed in U.S. Department of Commerce, *Annual Report of the Commissioner of Navigation,* 109–16.

55. Admiralty, "Purchase of German Ships Abroad: Memorandum, with Tables, by Commander T. Fisher RN and Mr. T. Royden," table A, 23 July 1915, appendix 13, 111, CAB.16/35. The total number of German vessels in overseas ports exceeded 1,000, for which see CID, "Administrative Measures for Securing Our Economic Position," 17, October 1914, CAB.1/10; also "Notes by Sir M. Hankey," October 1914, ff.6–7, CAB.1/11.

56. CID report, "Transfer of Enemy Vessels Lying in Neutral Ports to Allied or Neutral Flags," 1915, containing "Memorandum by the Foreign Office with Appendixes," 8 July 1915, appendix (i), "Deviations from General Attitude of His Majesty's Government," 68–75, appendix 2, 35, CAB.16/35.

57. Declaration of London, Article 56; see also 1908 memo on this issue in ADM.116/1079.

58. Crowe, "Notes of Further Discussions with Dr. Kriege on December 12 and 13, 1908," n.d. [14 or 15 December 1908], ff.101–2, FO.371/794.

59. The most comprehensive statement of the legal position is found in Admiralty (trade division), for cabinet, "Transfer of Ships to Neutral Flag: The Dacia Case," 20 January 1915, CAB.37/123/35. See also Foreign Office, "Memorandum by the Foreign Office, with Appendixes," 8 July 1915, Appendix 2, 64, CAB.16/35.

60. "Transfer of Ships to Neutral Flag: The Dacia Case," 20 January 1915, CAB.37/123/35. See also minute (4 August 1914) by W. A. Stewart on French embassy to Foreign Office, 3 August 1914, 35471, FO.372/578; Lance Davis and Stanley Engerman, *Naval Blockades in Peace and War: An Economic History since 1750* (Cambridge: Cambridge University Press, 2006), 123.

61. FO, "Steamers of German Cosmos Co. in Chilean Ports," 8 August 1914, 36864, f.220, FO.372/578.

62. Minute (4 September 1914) to Grey, "Purchase of Kosmos Line by Chilean Government," 44824, f.401, FO.372/578.

63. "Transfer of 3 German Merchant Vessels to Spanish Flag," 12 August 1914, 38292, f.232, FO.372/578.

64. Note (13 August 1914) by Grey on telegram (same date), "Sale of Steamships in America," f.242, 38375, FO.372/578; "Steamers of German Cosmos Company," 38644/35471, f.245, FO.372/578. For evidence the Admiralty had already learned of this, see Cunard Shipping Company to Churchill and Hopwood (Admiralty) to Crowe, 12 August 1914, 39737, FO.372/578.

65. Minute (29 August 1914) by Crowe, f.384, 44392, 41498, FO.372/578.

66. Admiralty to Foreign Office, 12 August 1914, confidential and urgent, 35471, FO.372/578; the file is "Sale of German Steamships in America," 38375/35471, ff.234–41, FO.372/578.

67. Minutes (4 August 1914) by Stewart and Wellesley on French embassy to FO, 3 August 1914, 35471/35749, FO.372/578.

68. Minute (13 August 1914) by Hurst, f.236, FO.372/578; before the war, in 1912, Hurst had anticipated this action by the Americans, for which see DC, "A Note by Mr. C. J. B. Hurst," appendix XXVI, 13 March 1912, 435–36.

69. Link, *Wilson,* 3:83–85.

70. House to Wilson, 4 August 1914, PWW, 30:345; reply, 6 August 1914, PWW, 30:352.

71. Ibid.

72. Minute (12 August 1914) by Robert Sperling on "Sale of German Steamships in America," f.234, 38375, FO.372/578.

73. Minutes (13 and 14 August, 16 October 1914) by Crowe, 38375, ff.235–37, FO.372/578.

74. Minute (n.d.) by Grey, but sequence suggests 14 August 1914, FO.372/578; Hobhouse diary, 14 August 1914, f.51, Add.Mss. 60506.

75. Hobhouse diary, 19 August 1914, f.52, Add.Mss. 60506; Pease diary, 18 August 1914, f.113, Gainford Mss. 39.

76. Harcourt journal, notes of cabinet, 17 August 1914, Ms.Dep. 6231.

77. Harcourt journal, 17 and 18 August 1914, Ms.Dep. 6231.

78. Asquith to Stanley, 17 August 1914, LVS, 170–72.

79. Emmott diary, 17 August, f.108, Emmott Mss. 2.

80. For description of the problems faced by shipowners, see Royal Mail Steam Packet Company (Owen Philips) to Runciman, 24 August 1914, f.119, Runciman Mss. 124.

81. Arthur Salter, *Allied Shipping Control: an Experiment in International Administration* (Oxford: Clarendon Press, 1921), 38.

82. Cabinet letter, 18 August 1914, CAB.41/35/32; for British government connections with J. P. Morgan, see Roberta A. Dayer, "Strange Bedfellows: J. P. Morgan and Co., Whitehall and the Wilson Administration during World War I," *Business History* 18, no. 2 (1976): 125–51. Also essential is Kathleen Burk, "A Merchant Bank at War: The House of Morgan, 1914–1918," in L. Cottrell and D. E. Moggridge, eds., *Money and Power: Essays in Honour of L. S. Pressnell* (Houndmills, UK: Macmillan, 1988); Martin Horn, "A Private Bank at War: J. P. Morgan and Co. and France, 1914–1918," *Business History Review* 74, no. 1 (2000): 85.

83. Telegram (19 August 1914) by Barclay (Washington), f.298, 41129; minute (19 August 1914) by Orde, f.270, 40668; minute (21 August 1914) by Davidson, f.314, 41498, all FO.372/578.

84. Link, *Wilson,* 3:86–91.

85. Pease diary, 19 August 1914, f.114, Gainford Mss 39.

86. Ernest May, *The World War and American Isolation* (Cambridge, MA: Harvard University Press, 1959), 13–14.

87. This is very clear in Grey (Algernon Law) to Barclay, 29 Treaty, 21 August 1914, FO.115/1805.

88. J. P. Morgan to Woodrow Wilson, 21 August 1914, PWW, 30:426–27, and reply (22 August 1914), 431; copy in FRUS, *The Lansing Papers, 1914–1920,* 2 vols. (Washington, DC: U.S. Government Printing Office, 1939), 1:100–101.

89. Grey (Algernon Law) to Barclay, 29 Treaty, 21 August 1914, FO.115/1805.

90. Wilson to Lansing, 22 August 1914, PWW, 30:431.

91. Daniels to Wilson, 22 August 1914, enclosing report of Board of Neutrality on shipping bills (original given as in RG59 763.7211/7321), PWW, 30:435.

92. Asquith to Stanley, 19 August 1914, LVS, 179.

93. Churchill to Grey, 19 August 1914, FLM, 2:34–36. Also reproduced as appendix E in Churchill, *World Crisis,* 1:574–75; see also Admiralty to Foreign Office, letter, confidential and immediate, and minutes attached, 24 August 14, 35471/42734, FO.372/578.

94. For the resulting British protests, see Barclay to State Department, 4 August 1914 (second letter), and Barclay to State, 20 August 1914, FRUS, 1914 Supp., 594–95, 602–4.

95. Churchill to Grey, 19 August 1914, FLM, 2:34–36. Also reproduced as appendix E in Churchill, *World Crisis,* 1:574–75.

96. Telegram (20 August 1914) by Grey and Runciman to Spring-Rice, 41129, f.299, FO.372/578. Spring-Rice was en route from London to Washington, for which see Crowe to his wife, 13 August 1914, f.38, Ms.Eng. 3020.

97. Link, *Wilson,* 3:87.

98. Telegram 305R (20 August 1914) from Barclay, 41498, FO.372/578.

99. Minute (21 August 1914) by Wellesley, 41498, FO.372/578.

100. Link, *Wilson,* 3:84n33, notes the French warning to the United States on 4 August 1914. See Lansing to Wilson, 23 November 1914, FRUS, *Lansing Papers,* 1:107–9.

101. Minute (20 August 1914) by V. Wellesley, f.297, 41129, and (21 August 1914) f.314, 41498, FO.372/578.

102. Minutes (21 August 1914) by Davison and Crowe, ff.314–18, 41498, FO.372/578; telegram, 26 Treaty, Grey (Algernon Law) to Barclay, 21 August 1914, 42404, FO.372/578; telegram, 29 Treaty, Grey to Barclay, FO.115/1805. See also Harcourt journal, 21 August 1914, Ms.Dep. 6231. A copy of Grey's telegram to Barclay was handed to Robert Lansing and passed to Wilson, for which see Lansing to Wilson 21 August 1914, enclosing telegram (21 August 1914), Grey to Barclay, PWW, 30:435–36.

103. Harcourt, cabinet notes, 21 August 1914, Ms.Dep. 6231.

104. Lansing to Wilson, 24 August 1914, FRUS, *Lansing Papers,* 1:101–2; copy also in PWW, 30:447–49.

105. Ibid. Link, *Wilson,* 3:85–86, suggests Lansing and Wilson misinterpreted, but I disagree.

106. Lansing to Wilson, 24 August 1914, PWW, 30:447–49.

107. Admiralty to FO, confidential and immediate, 24 August 1914, 35471/42738, FO.372/578.

108. Link, *Wilson,* 3:87–88; see also Spring-Rice to Grey, 8 September 1914, f.251, FO.800/84. For the five-year period, see minute (27 June 1916) by Captain Webb, sheet 4 of NL 30571, ADM.116/1235.

109. Spring-Rice to Grey, 25 August 1914, f.229, FO.800/84.

110. Minute (16 October 1914) by Hurst, on telegram, No. 117 Treaty, from Spring-Rice, f.328, 60037, FO.372/601.

111. *Chicago Evening Post,* 25 August 1914, as cited in Link, *Wilson,* 3:87–89.

112. Spring-Rice to Grey, 8 September 1914, f.251, FO.800/84; see also Spring-Rice to Grey, 5 October 1914, FO.115/1770. For McAdoo's sponsorship, see Link, *Wilson,* 3:137.

113. Minute (5 September 1914) by W. A. Stewart on Spring-Rice to Grey, dispatch 39, 25 August 1914, 35471, FO.372/579. See minute (8 September 1914) by W. A. Stewart on telegram, No. 31 Treaty (7 September 1914), Spring-Rice to Grey; also telegram, No. 48 Treaty (7 September 1914), Grey to Spring-Rice, all 35471, FO.371/579.

114. Arthur S. Link, "The Cotton Crisis, the South, and Anglo-American Diplomacy, 1914–1915," in J. Carlyle Sitterson, ed., *Studies in Southern History* (Chapel Hill: University of North Carolina Press, 1957), 122–38.

115. Link, *Wilson,* 3:89–90.

116. FO, "Purchase of Kosmos Line by Chilean Gov't," f.394, 44824, and telegram (28 August 1914), FO to Stockholm, f.366, 42876, FO.372/578; Admiralty, "German Merchantmen Sailing under Flags of Other Countries," 28 August 1914, minute (29 August 1914) by Battenberg on copy of telegram, Howard to FO, 28 August 1914, ff.183–84, ADM.137/982. For evidence of German steamers transferred to the Mexican flag, see telegram, No. 4 Treaty (5 September 1914), Carden (minister in Mexico) to FO, 35471/46802, FO.372/579.

117. Minute (29 August 1914) by Crowe, f.384, 44392/41498, FO.372/578.

118. Link, *Wilson,* 3:90n54.

119. Minute (8 September 1914) by Wellesley, attached to telegram 31T (7 September 1914), Spring-Rice to Grey, 35471/47262, FO.371/579.

120. FO to Admiralty, 28 August 1914, Admiralty to FO, 9 September 1914, confidential Admiralty interim order, 6 September 1914, 55, "Suspicious Colors—Duty of Verifying," ff.187–92, ADM.137/982.

121. Runciman to Grey, 6 September 1914, f.396, 44824, 41498, FO.372/578.

122. Minute (3 September 1914) by Crowe, initialed same day by Nicholson, 41498, FO.372/578.

123. Minute (n.d.) by Grey and (4 September 1914) by Crowe, 41498, FO.372/578.

124. Sir Francis Bertie, memorandum, 19 December 1914, FO.800/163. I am indebted to Keith Neilson for this reference.

125. Zara Steiner, "The Foreign Office and the War," in F. H. Hinsley, ed., *British Foreign Policy under Sir Edward Grey* (Cambridge: Cambridge University Press, 1977), 518.

126. Llewellyn Smith to Chamberlain, 10 February 1915, AC 19/6/2, enclosing list of "Firms abroad suspected of acting as agents for the supply of necessaries as to the German government or German warships," AC 19/6/8, Chamberlain Mss (Sir Austen Chamberlain papers,

Birmingham University Library, UK); see also letter of complaint from Admiralty to FO, 2 December 1914, 36300/88294, FO.372/619.

127. CID report, "Transfer of Enemy Vessels Lying in Neutral Ports to Allied or Neutral Flags," 1915, containing "Memorandum by the Foreign Office with Appendixes," 8 July 1915, appendix (i), "Deviations from General Attitude of His Majesty's Government," 68–75, CAB.16/35.

128. Minute (16 September 1914) by Steward, attached to 53T, Spring-Rice to Grey, 5 September 1914, 35471/49554, FO.372/579; Runciman, "USA Ship Purchase Bill," 1 January 1915, f.245, Asquith Mss. 26; Hendrick, *Life and Letters of Walter H. Page,* vol. 1, part 2, 392–93.

129. Telegram 53T (21 September 1914), Spring-Rice to Grey, 35471/51656, FO.372/579.

130. File "SS. Corning, Petrolile and Leda," 19 January 1915, 147/7269, FO.372/728.

131. Supreme Court of Bermuda, the "Leda," before Chief Justice P. M. C. Sherriff, 20 November 1914, 2, Prize Transcripts, II, NLMD. She was released in April 1915. After the war the Admiralty petitioned that the Foreign Office action was incorrect, and their complaint was upheld by the Naval Prize Tribunal, for which see "Before the Naval Prize Tribunal, Derfflinger and Other Cases, 5 June 1919, Lloyd's Reports of Prize Cases, VIII, 458–83; for judgment, see 468–72. Grey incorrectly claimed he had Standard Oil's promise not to carry to Germany either directly or indirectly. See HC Deb, 2 November 1915, vol. 75, c.439.

132. Lansing to W. Wilson, 20 October 1914, PWW, 31:193; Spring-Rice to Grey, 20 October 1914, f.353, FO.800/84 (copy in FO.115/1770); Spring-Rice to President Wilson, 20 October 1914, personal, FO.115/1770. See telegram (13 October 1914, 4:55 a.m.), Rear-Admiral H. M. S. Lancaster, Halifax, Nova Scotia, to Admiralty, f.263, ADM.137/982.

133. Wilson to Lansing, 22 October 1914, PWW, 31:209.

134. Lansing to Wilson, 23 November 1914, FRUS, *Lansing Papers,* 1:107–9.

135. Ernest J. Moggridge (head of Marine Dept. Board of Trade) to FO, 5 September 1914; Foreign Office to Thomas Wilson Co. and Sons Ltd., 14 September 1914, ADM.137/2917.

136. The ten U.S. Steel vessels operated under C. G. Dunn and Co., the Isthmian Steamship Co., and New York and South American Line.

137. U.S. Department of Commerce, *Annual Report of the Commissioner of Navigation,* 14.

138. Minute (27 September 1914) by Leverton Harris, T.10 section, "Transfer of British Ships to American Flag," ADM.137/2917.

139. No Admiralty document has been found to this effect, though there is reference to its circulation in Board of Trade, for cabinet, "Transfer of British Ships," 26 January 1915, CAB.37/123/53. For complaints of damage to British interests, see ESRC, 28th Report, 5 December 1914, ADM.137/2989.

140. *London Gazette,* 25 December 1914, issue 29019, 11046–7. At the council chamber, 23 December 1914, item (3).

141. Admiralty (trade division), "Transfer of Ships to Neutral Flag: The Dacia Case," 20 January 1915, CAB.37/123/35; Board of Trade, "Transfer of British Ships," 26 January 1915, CAB.37/123/53. For revival of the issue, see minutes attached to telegrams subsequent to (4 January 1915) Spring-Rice to Grey, 955/955, 174/2149, 174/2369, FO.372/728.

142. U.S. Department of Commerce, *Annual Report of the Commissioner of Navigation,* appendix L.

143. For the evasive reply, see HC Deb, 20 December 1915, vol. 77, c.9/10. For answers, see HC Deb, "British Mercantile Marine (Transfer to Foreign Flags)," 12 January 1916, vol. 77, c.1605. Mr. [Ernest George] Pretyman (BdT), 247 vessels in fifteen months of war (507,830 GRT), of which only 37 sold since January 1915; HC Deb, "British Merchant Vessels (Sales to Foreign Owners)," 17 February 1916, vol. 80, c.237–38. For a complete list of the nearly 100 ships sold to foreigners in 1915 and their tonnages, see Runciman, "Ships Transferred from the British Register and Exported during the War," for cabinet, 4 January 1916, CAB.37/140/5.

144. ESRC, 43rd Report, 25 February 1915, 169, ADM.137/2989; also Runciman to Grey, 25 March 1915, f.295, FO.800/89.

145. Testimony by Sir Joseph Maclay to CID, 19 July 1915, "Transfer of Enemy Vessels Lying in Neutral Ports to Allied or Neutral Flags," 29, CAB.16/35.

146. Eric Rauchway, *Blessed among Nations: How the World Made America* (New York: Hill and Wang, 2007) is useful here.

147. William L. Silber, *When Washington Shut Down Wall Street: The Great Financial Crisis of 1914 and the Origins of America's Monetary Supremacy* (Princeton, NJ: Princeton University Press, 2007), 70–86. See also Horn, *Britain, France,* 62–69. For the annoyance of British authorities at the U.S. action, see Harcourt, notes on meetings of finance committee of cabinet, 3 and 4 September 1914, Ms.Dep. 6231.

148. Silber, *When Washington Shut Down Wall Street,* 102; Spring-Rice to Grey, 22 September 1914, f.271, FO.800/84.

149. Higginson to Wilson, 20 August 1914, PWW, 30:426–27.

150. Silber, *When Washington Shut Down Wall Street,* 118–21; in addition, Basil Blackett report 27 November 1914, mission to USA, f.175ff, Asquith 26.

151. Grey, *25 Years,* 2:115–19.

152. Average for period 1910–1914. *Federal Reserve Bulletin,* May 1923, 567.

153. Douglas A. Irwin, "Explaining America's Surge in Manufactures Exports, 1880–1913," *Review of Economics and Statistics* 85, no. 2 (May 2003): 364–76, table 1.

154. What follows is substantially taken from Link, "Cotton Crisis."

155. Telegram 45C (20 August 1914), Barclay to FO, 1117/41816, FO.368/1149.

156. The total was 17 million bales from 36 million acres.

157. Bruce E. Matthews, "The 1914 Cotton Crisis in Alabama," *Alabama Review* 46 (January 1993): 3–23; James L. McCorkle Jr., "Louisiana and the Cotton Crisis, 1914," *Louisiana History: The Journal of the Louisiana Historical Association* 18, no. 3 (Summer 1977): 303–21; Link, *Wilson,* 3:92–100.

158. Silber, *When Washington Shut Down Wall Street,* 101–3, 141–42. For the wider ambitions of U.S. bankers, see Priscilla Roberts, "'Quis Custodiet Ipsos Custodes?' The Federal Reserve System's Founding Fathers and Allied Finances in the First World War," *Business History Review* 72, no. 4 (1998): 585.

159. Telegram (23 October 1914), Harris Irby Cotton Co. to Senator T. P. Gore (D.-Okla.), forwarded (24 October 1914) to Secretary of State, FRUS, 1914 Supp., 287–88, 288–95.

160. Proclamation against reinsurance of cotton, *London Gazette,* 28932, 9 October 1914.

161. Silber, *When Washington Shut Down Wall Street,* 102. Silber makes no mention of these aspects of the problem—a weakness in his treatment of the subject.

162. ESRC, 7th Report, 12 September 1914; 8th Report, 19 September 1914; 10th Report, 26 September 1914; 13th report, 4 October 1914, all ADM.137/2988. For authorization of 12,000 tons of wheat to proceed, see minute (n.d. but sequence indicates 20 August 1914) by Grey, on "Dutch Differential Treatment as Regards Foodstuffs for Respective Belligerents," 41071/35250, FO.372/600.

163. According to an entry in Lord Esher's diary, 31 August 1914, the figure was 52 ships (cited in Coogan, *End of Neutrality,* 163). According to a report by the CID dated October 1914, the figure was 128 ships (but this figure may also include ships bound for Scandinavia), 22, CAB.1/10.

164. Minute (29 August 1914) by Grey, 45253, 1 September 1914, FO.372/600.

165. ESRC, 6th Report, 9 September 1914, ADM.137/2988.

166. Minutes (10 September 1914) by Nicholson and (8 September 1914) by Hurst to Grey, "Proposed Seizure of Neutral Steamers Carrying Oil to Rotterdam," 48050, master file 35250, FO.372/600.

167. ESRC, 9th Report, 22 September 1914, ADM.137/2988. It was taken into Falmouth on 21 September and held until 4 November. Other tankers detained included *Ocean, Charlois, New York, America,* and *Rotterdam,* for which see appendix 2, 10 September 1915, Page to Grey, 5 November 1915, CAB.37/137/7.

168. Harcourt journal, cabinet notes, 11 September 1914, Ms.Dep. 6231.

169. Bismuth is a rare mineral (atomic number 83) used in the manufacture of high-grade steel.

170. Minute (13 September 1914) by Wellesley on 48901, FO.372/600.

171. Note (18 September 1914) by Hurst on conference held at Admiralty, also minute (17 September) by Hurst citing Grey's approval, 50599, FO.372/600.

172. CID, secret (draft), "The Control of Supplies Proceeding to Dutch Ports," 1 October 1914, CAB.1/10.

173. Spring-Rice to Grey, 25 August 1914, ff.229–32, FO.800/84.

174. Telegram (3 September 1914), Spring-Rice to Grey, f.241, FO.800/84.

175. Asquith to Stanley, 5 September 1914, LVS, 222.

176. Robert W. Tucker, *Woodrow Wilson and the Great War* (Charlottesville: Univerity of Virginia Press, 2007), 88.

177. Coogan, *End of Neutrality,* 173–74; text in Lansing to Page, 26 September 1914, FRUS, 1914 Supp., 225–32.

178. Telegram 78T (29 September 1914, 11:10 p.m.), Grey to Spring-Rice, f.98, FO.372/601; see also telegram 65T (28 September 1914), Spring-Rice to Grey, FO.115/1770, and Lansing to Page, 26 September 1914, FRUS, 1914 Supp., 225–32. For instructions not to present the demarche until ordered, see T.227 (1 October 1914), Bryan to Page, FRUS, 1914 Supp., 239; Coogan, *End of Neutrality,* 174–77.

179. Scholars less preoccupied with the "Wilsonian" history convincingly suggest that House's influence and importance were far greater. See Philip Bobbit, *The Shield of Achilles: War, Peace, and the Course of History* (New York: Anchor Books, 2003), 367–410.

180. House diary, 28 September 1914, f.177, House Mss. (Yale).

181. Telegram, Spring-Rice to Grey, 66T, 28 September 1914, FO.800/84; Link, *Wilson,* 3:109–14; Coogan, *End of Neutrality,* 181; House diary, 27 and 28 September 1915, 175–80, House Mss.

182. House diary, 30 September 1914, House Mss.

183. Telegrams, Spring-Rice to Grey, 28 September 1914, 66T, and another marked "Private, Further to 65T," 28 September 1914, both FO.115/1770. I am indebted to Keith Neilson for this reference.

184. Spring-Rice to Grey, 1 October 1914, private letter, FO.115/1770.

185. Telegram (28 September 1914), Lansing to Page, 28 September 1914, FRUS, 1914 Supp., 232–33; Coogan, *End of Neutrality,* 176–77.

186. Telegram (28 September 1914), Spring-Rice to FO, 53883, FO.372/601.

187. Spring-Rice believed Lansing lacked authority and was no more than a mouthpiece for Wilson; see Spring-Rice to Grey, 20 October 1914 (second letter), f.363, FO.800/84; Tucker, *Wilson and the Great War,* 30–33.

188. Coogan, *End of Neutrality,* 172, 176, 178.

189. Spring-Rice to Grey, 20 October 1914, f.360, FO.800/84.

190. Page to House, 22 October 1914, reproduced in Hendrick, *Life and Letters of Walter H. Page,* vol. 1, part 2, 382.

191. Telegram 758 (29 September 1914), Page to State, FRUS, 1914 Supp., 233; copy, telegram (28 September 1914), Grey to Spring-Rice, handed to State Department 1 October 1914, FRUS, 1914 Supp., 236–37.

192. Minute (30 September 1914) by Hurst on telegram (29 September 1914), 66T, from Spring-Rice, ff.90–91, 54116, FO.372/601; also minutes (23 October 1914), by C. W. Orde and Grey, 62348, f.32, FO.372/602.

193. Minutes (29 September 1914) by Charles Orde and Victor Wellesley, 53883, f.75, FO.372/601.

194. "Anglo-American Prize Practice and the Declaration of London," 3 November 1914, 2, Article 18, citing cases of Stephan Hart, Bermuda, Springbok, and Peterhoff, 66753, FO.372/588; see also Spring-Rice to Lansing, 2 December 1914, f.116, 82319, FO.368/1162.

195. Minute (30 September 1914) by Hurst on telegram (29 September 1914) 66T from Spring-Rice, ff.90–91, 54116, FO.372/601.

196. Ibid.

197. Telegram 80T (30 September 1914), Grey to Spring-Rice, f.97, 54705, FO.372/601.

198. Runciman to Dutch ambassador, 30 September 1914, 62922, FO.368/1027.

199. Telegram 228 (1 October 1914, 5:00 p.m.), Bryan to Page, FRUS, 1914 Supp., 240.

200. Asquith to Grey, 21 October 1914, f.322, FO.800/100.

201. Note (21 October 1914) by Eyre Crowe reporting meeting with Dutch minister, 21 October 1914, 62922, FO.368/1027.

202. Minute (22 October 1914) by Crowe, 62068, FO.372/602. For a summary of the impasse, see cabinet memorandum, Foreign Office, "The Passage of Enemy Supplies through Countries Contiguous to Germany and Austria-Hungary," initialed O.G.S[argeant], 25 October 1914, CAB.1/10.

203. Minute (25 October) by Vansittart and endorsed by E. Grey, 62922, FO.368/1027.

204. Asquith to Stanley, 29 September 1914, LVS, 256.

205. Asquith to Stanley, 29 September and 1 October 1914, LVS, 256–58.

206. Ibid.

207. ESRC, 10th and 11th Reports, 26 and 29 September 1914, ADM.137/2988. For explicit evidence of Lloyd's cooperation, see "Note of a Meeting at Lloyd's on 11 December [1914] between the Committee of Lloyd's and Mr. Leverton Harris," ADM.137/2804.

208. Ballard, "Observation Force in the North Sea," 16 September 1912, f.290, ADM.116/866B; minutes (6 February 1913) by Ballard and (11 February 1913) by Jackson, on "Proposals for the Use of Mines in Anti-German War," f.493, ADM.116/3412; FNR, 270–73.

209. Asquith to Stanley, 29 September and 1 October 1914, LVS, 256–58.

210. FNR, 270–72; reference to Hague VIII, Article 2.

211. Asquith to Stanley, 29 September 1914, LVS, 256. Curiously, Harcourt notes a discussion on mines in the cabinet on 23 September 1914, Ms.Dep. 6231.

212. Asquith to Churchill, 29 September 1914, f.83, CHAR 13/44.

213. Cabinet letter, 30 September, CAB.41/35/47; Harcourt journal, 30 September 1914, Ms.Dep. 6231.

214. Asquith to Stanley, 30 September 1914, f.261, Ms.Eng. 7093. N.b.: Omitted from printed version.

215. Minute (1 October 1914) by Churchill to Sturdee, ADM.137/843.

216. Naval Staff Monograph No. 8, 171; Admiralty Press Release, 3 October 1914, 55558, FO.372/633.

217. See two dismissive minutes (25 September 1914) by Leveson and (25 September 1914) by Sturdee on Cmdr. D. Arnold Forster (2nd Minelaying Squadron), "Appreciation on Extensive Mining Operations in the Heligoland Bight," ff.31–34, ADM.137/843.

218. Richmond diary, in Arthur J. Marder, *Portrait of an Admiral; The Life and Papers of Sir Herbert Richmond* (London: Jonathan Cape, 1952), 118, 121–22.

219. Dumas diary, 1 October 1914, Dumas Mss. 65/23/1.

220. T. 758 (29 September 1914), Page to State, FRUS, 1914 Supp., 233.

221. Hobhouse diary, 9 October 1914, f.69, Add.Mss. 60506; see also cabinet paper by Grey, "Suggestions," 9 October 1914, CAB.17/111A.

222. Text of draft order-in-council contained in Telegram 806 (9 October 1914), Page to SECSTATE, FRUS, 1914 Supp., 244–46; Declaration of London, order-in-council, 29 October 1914, ADM.1/8400/394.

223. Telegram (19 October 1914), Page to SECSTATE, FRUS, 1914 Supp., 253–54.

224. Telegram (17 October 1914), Grey to Spring-Rice, f.329, 60037, FO.372/601.

225. Telegram (19 October 1914), Page to SECSTATE, FRUS, 1914 Supp., 253–54.

226. For U.S. recognition, see telegram (15 October 1914), Spring-Rice to Grey, reporting conversation with Lansing, f.331, and Grey's reply (17 October 1914), ff.329–30, both 60037, FO.372/601. Also Wilson to Lansing, same date, in FRUS, *Lansing Papers,* 1:251–52; Lansing, "Memorandum by the Acting Secretary of State," 29 September 1914, in FRUS, *Lansing Papers,* 1:234. For evidence of early negotiations with contiguous neutrals, see telegram (23 October 1914) from Henry Lowther (Copenhagen), 45480, FO.368/1103.

227. Minute by Charles W. Orde, 22 October 1914, reporting conversation with Frederick Leverton Harris, 62163, FO.372/602.

228. Telegram (16 October 1914, 3:00 p.m.), Lansing to Page, FRUS, 1914 Supp., 250–51. See also telegram (15 October 1914), Grey to Spring-Rice, forwarded from Wilson to Lan-

sing, same date, FRUS, *Lansing Papers,* 1:251–52, clause C, 254; also telegram (16 October 1914), Lansing to Page, FRUS, *Lansing Papers,* 1:253–55, para. 4.

229. ESRC, 17th Report, 17 October 1914, ADM.137/2988.

230. Foreign Office paper signed O. G. S[ergeant], "The Passage of Enemy Supplies through Countries Contiguous to Germany and Austria-Hungary," 25 October 1914, 2, CAB.1/10; dispatch by Sir Alan Johnson (The Hague), dated 23 October 1914, 63272, FO.368/1027.

231. Minute (31 October 1914) by Leveton Harris attached to telegrams, HSB283, ADM.137/2805; ESCRC, 23rd Report, 10 November 1914, ADM.137/2988.

232. Webb (DTD), "Copper Shipments at Gibraltar," 31 October 1914, ff.372–74, ADM. 137/982.

233. Appendix to ESRC, 20th Report, 29 October 1914. This issue is discussed also in Jonathan Winkler, *Nexus: Strategic Communications and American Security in World War I* (Cambridge, MA: Harvard University Press, 2008), 44–50, esp. 48–49.

234. Lansing to U.S. ambassador Rome, 15 October 1914, appended to ESRC, 20th Report, 29 October 1914, ADM.137/2988; emphasis in original.

235. See copy of message intercepted by cable censors. Telegram (14 October 1914, 5:00 a.m.), Holland America New York to Holland America Rotterdam, f.375, FO.800/84.

236. DTD (Webb) to FO, 4 December 1914, and reply dated 12 December 1914, both in ADM.137/2805. For FO disinterest, see minutes (19 and 24 February 1915) by A. Pearson and (24 February 1915) by Crowe on Trade Clearing House to FO, 15 February 1915, "Commercial Cables between Diplomatic and Consular Officials—Complaints of Abuse of Diplomatic Privileges in Assisting the Trade of the Enemy. Intercepted Messages," 18795, FO.382/442. For the eventual protest, see Winkler, *Nexus,* 49.

237. Telegram (12 October 1914), Spring-Rice to Grey, FO.372/601. For a hint of this in U.S. correspondence, see telegram (13 October 1914), Lansing to Page, FRUS, 1914 Supp., 247.

238. Cabinet letter, 13 October 1914, CAB.41/35/52.

239. Hobhouse diary, 14 October 1914, f.69, Add.Mss. 60506. The use of the French word *réclame* (meaning "advertisement" or "publicity") was quite deliberate.

240. Cabinet letter, 16 October 1914, CAB.41/35/53: 1,860 laid, 4,400 in stock, 3,000 being filled, and 15,000 on order. Harcourt cabinet notes, 15 October 1914, Ms.Dep. 6231: 1,860 laid, 5,000 in reserve, 3,090 being modified, and 15,000 on order.

241. Memorandum by W. S. Churchill for cabinet, "Notes on Mining," printed 19 October 1914, Battenberg papers, MB1/T38/367B.

242. Telegram (16 October 1914, 1:00 p.m.), Lansing to Page, FRUS, 1914 Supp., 249–50.

243. Coogan, *End of Neutrality,* 181, 190.

244. Link, *Wilson,* 3:117.

245. Lansing to Page, 2 and 4 October 1914, FRUS, 1914 Supp., 240–45; see also telegram 66.T (28 September 1914), Spring-Rice to Grey, FO.115/1770.

246. Minutes (23 October 1914) by Wellesley, Orde, Crowe, and Grey, 62348, f.32, FO.372/602. See also telegram (21 October 1914), Spring-Rice to Grey, 62001, f.8, FO.372/602.

247. Page to Wilson, 15 October 1914, FRUS, 1914 Supp., 248.

248. Page to House, 22 October 1914, cited in Hendrick, *Life and Letters of Walter H. Page,* vol. 1, part 2, 381.

249. Wilson to Page, 16 October 1914, FRUS 1914 Supp., 252–53.

250. Link, *Wilson,* 3:122.

251. Telegram (20 October 1914), Page to Lansing, FRUS, 1914 Supp., 253.

252. Spring-Rice to Grey, 20 October 1914 (second letter), f.362, FO.800/84 (copy in FO.115/1771).

253. Lansing to Wilson, 20 October 1914, PWW, 31:188–89.

254. House diary, 22 October 1914, f.202, House Mss.

255. Telegram (22 October 1914), 4:00 p.m., Lansing to Page, FRUS, 1914 Supp., 257–58; see also Grey to Spring-Rice, 23 October 1914, circulated at cabinet 28 October, FO.899/9/41.

256. Spring-Rice to Grey, 21 October 1914, 62001, FO.372/602.

257. Coogan stops his narrative on 21 October 1914; see *End of Neutrality,* 191–93. So does Link; see *Wilson,* 3:125–26 (but see 131). FRUS contains no further reference. See also John Milton Cooper Jr., *Walter Hines Page: The Southerner as American, 1855–1918* (Chapel Hill: University of North Carolina Press, 1977), 294–95.

258. Minutes (23 October 1914) by Crowe and Grey, on Spring-Rice to FO, 22 October 1914, f.32, 62348, FO.372/602.

259. See reference to meeting in Spring-Rice to Lansing, 26 October 1914, FRUS, 1914 Supp., 289–90.

260. Telegrams (24 October 1914) Lansing to Page, FRUS 1914 Supp., 288–89.

261. Spring-Rice to W. Wilson, 24 October 1914, PWW, 31:229–30. Full letter with further details is found in FO.115/1770.

262. Asquith to Stanley, 24 October 1914, Ms.Eng. 7094. Harcourt reported this was a cabinet subcommittee; see cabinet notes, 23 October 1914, Ms.Dep. 6231. See also HL Deb, 27 June 1923, vol. 54, c.651, Sir Edward Grey.

263. Telegram (26 October 1914), Page to Lansing; Spring-Rice to Lansing, 26 October 1914, FRUS 1914 Supp., 289–90. N.b.: Enclosed telegram from Grey dated 25 October 1915, 290. Original in telegram (25 October 1914), Grey to Spring-Rice, f.56, 63127, FO.372/602.

264. Matthews, "The 1914 Cotton Crisis in Alabama," 21. See also Woodrow Wilson press conference, 26 October 1914, PWW, 31:233–34.

265. Communiqué, Washington, DC, 26 October; *New York Times,* 27 October 1914, 1. See also "Passing of the Cotton Crisis," *New York Times,* 28 October 1914, 12.

266. Silber, *When Washington Shut Down Wall Street,* 145.

267. Wilson to Spring-Rice, 28 October 1914, PWW, 31:243 (copy enclosed with Spring-Rice to Grey, 5 December 1914, FO.115/1771).

268. Minutes (23 October 1914) by Orde and Grey, 62348, f.32, FO.372/602; see also telegram (21 October 1914), Spring-Rice to Grey, 62001, f.8, FO.372/602.

269. Sir Almeric Fitzroy, *Memoirs,* 2 vols. (London: Hutchinson, 1925), 2:575.

270. Runciman to Grey, 27 October 1914, f.257, FO.800/89.

271. Churchill to Grey, 27 October 1914, f.202, FO.800/88.

272. Memorandum (26 October 1914) by Webb (DTD) with attached minute (n.d., but probably same day) by Churchill to Grey, f.199, FO.800/88.

273. Arthur Marsden, "The Blockade," in F. H. Hinsley, ed., *British Foreign Policy under Sir Edward Grey* (Cambridge: Cambridge University Press, 1977), 488–516, esp. 494; Archibald C. Bell, *A History of the Blockade of Germany and the Countries Associated with Her in*

the Great War: Austria-Hungary, Bulgaria, and Turkey (London: HMSO, 1961), 58–59; Marion Siney, *The Allied Blockade of Germany, 1914–1916* (Ann Arbor: University of Michigan Press, 1957), 30–32; Eric Osborne, *Britain's Economic Blockade of Germany, 1914–1919* (London: Frank Cass, 2004) 69–70; Sir Francis Oppenheimer, *Stranger Within: Autobiographical Pages* (London: Faber and Faber, 1960), 240–41.

274. Coogan, *End of Neutrality,* 184–95; Lansing to Wilson, 15 October 1914, FRUS, *Lansing Papers,* 1:252–55; Keith G. Robbins, *Sir Edward Grey: A Biography of Lord Grey of Fallodon* (London: Cassell, 1971), 314.

275. May, *World War and American Isolation,* 19–21; Link, *Wilson,* 3:114–15.

276. Tucker, *Wilson,* 75–82, 220–21nn16–17. Tucker draws heavily on Coogan, *End of Neutrality,* esp. 181–82.

277. Coogan, *End of Neutrality,* 178; Tucker, *Wilson,* 78, 81–82.

278. Lansing to Wilson, 20 October 1914, PWW, 31:193, and reply, 22 October 1914, PWW, 31:209; see also Spring-Rice to Grey, 5 and 20 October 1914, FO.115/1770; Spring-Rice to Grey, 3 November 1914, f.391, FO.800/84; Link, *Wilson,* 3:108.

279. Wilson to Mrs. Crawford H. Toy, 15 October 1914, as cited in Link, "Cotton Crisis," 128.

280. Telegram (23 October 1914), Harris Irby Cotton Co. to Senator T. P. Gore (D.-Okla.), forwarded (24 October 1914) to Secretary of State, FRUS, 1914, 287–88; see also generally 285–95.

281. Dewey Grantham, *Hoke Smith and the Politics of the New South* (Baton Rouge: Louisiana State University Press, 1967), 277–82.

282. Matthews, "The 1914 Cotton Crisis in Alabama," 19–23; Bobbit, *Shield of Achilles,* 391–94.

283. Horn, *Britain, France,* 60–61.

284. McAdoo to Josephus Daniels (Secretary of Navy), 14 October 1914, Daniels Papers, Library of Congress, as cited in Link, "Cotton Crisis," 128.

285. Telegram 53C (19 September 1915), Spring-Rice to FO, 51220, FO.368/1159. See also Horn, *Britain, France,* 63–67.

286. Memorandum enclosed in Lansing to Wilson, 23 October 1914, PWW, 31:217–19.

287. House diary, 13, 14, and 17 October 1914, ff.192–97, House Mss.

288. Telegrams 65.T and 66.T (28 September 1914), Spring-Rice to Grey, FO.115/1770; also private letters, Spring-Rice to Grey, 1, 5, 20 October and 3 November 1914, all FO.115/1770.

289. Russian ambassador to Russian foreign minister, 7 October 1914, as cited in May, *World War and American Isolation,* 22n44.

290. Page to Wilson, 10 March 1915, PWW, 32:357–63.

291. Link, *Wilson,* 3:115.

292. Ibid., 131.

293. Kevin O'Rourke and Jeffrey Williamson, *Globalization and History: The Evolution of a Nineteenth-Century Atlantic Economy* (Cambridge, MA: MIT Press, 1999), ch. 3 generally, esp. 41–47.

294. Ibid., 43–55.

295. Explanatory paper handed to American ambassador by Foreign Office, enclosed in Page to State, 9 October 1914, FRUS, 1914 Supp., 246; see also minute (23 October 1914) by Slade, "Goods Consigned to Order—Meaning of Expression," f.466, ADM.137/982.

296. Minutes attached to letter, Frederick Huth Jackson to Crowe, 14 April 1915, "Bills of Lading for Conditional Contraband to Neutral Ports," 44404, FO.382/452.

297. Declaration of London, Article 32: "Where a vessel is carrying absolute contraband, her papers are conclusive proof as to the voyage on which she is engaged, unless she is found clearly out of the course indicated by her papers, and unable to give adequate reasons to justify such deviation."

298. The point is made in telegram (29 September 1914), Page to State, FRUS, 1914 Supp., 233; copy, telegram (28 September 1914), Grey to Spring-Rice, handed to State Department 1 October 1914, FRUS, 1914 Supp., 236–37.

299. H. W. Carless Davis, *History of the Blockade: Emergency Departments* (printed for official information only, March 1921, copy at NLMD), 4.

300. Memorandum (26 December 1914) by Richmond, "Considerations Affecting the Attitude of Holland," in "Holland: Attitude of—Pros and Cons," ADM.1/8407/494.

301. Minutes by chief of Naval Staff Henry Oliver (26 December 1914) and W. Churchill (31 December 1914), ADM.1/8407/494.

302. Jellicoe to Admiralty, 25 September 1914, f.195, ADM.137/982.

303. ESRC, 12th Report, 1 October 1914, ADM.137/2988.

304. ESRC, 13th Report, 4 October 1914, ADM.137/2988; see also Foreign Office paper signed O. G. S[ergeant], "The Passage of Enemy Supplies Through Countries Contiguous to Germany and Austria-Hungary," 25 October 1914, 3, CAB.1/10.

305. Consett to W. R. Hall, 7 November 1914, Hall Mss. (NLMD), (Captain Reginald William Hall papers, collection held at NLMD, UK).

306. DTD memorandum, "To Scandinavian Ports," ff.369–71, ADM.137/982; ESRC, 25th Report, 25 November 1914, 152, ADM.137/2988.

307. Spring-Rice to Grey, 3 November 1914, f.390, FO.800/84.

308. ESRC, 22nd Report, 9th November 1914, ADM.137/2988; C. Ernest Fayle, *Seaborne Trade*, 3 vols. (London: John Murray, 1920–1924), 1:295. The policy was actually in force beginning on 29 October; see Bennett (consul general, New York) to Spring-Rice, 29 October 1914, FO.115/1807.

309. Bennett (consul general, New York) to Spring-Rice, 29 October 1914, FO.115/1807.

310. ESRC, 23rd Report, 10 November 1914, ADM.137/2988.

311. Minute (26 November 1914) by O. G. Sargent, "Detention of American Ships: Agitation in United States Respecting Question of False Manifests," f.49, 75178, FO.368/1162.

312. Minute (4 December 1914) by Webb (DTD), ADM.137/2806.

313. Minutes (23 and 24 December 1915) by Sargeant, on "Contraband Negotiations with US Gov," f.253, f.257, 85657 and 86298, FO.368/1162.

314. Minute (26 November 1914) by O. G.Sargent, "Detention of American Ships: Agitation in United States Respecting Question of False Manifests," f.49, 75178, FO.368/1162.

315. Ibid.

316. Minutes (26 November 1914) by Pearson, Crowe, and Grey, 75178, FO.368/1162; telegram (1 December 1914), Grey to Spring-Rice, 109 Commercial, FO.115/1771.

317. Telegram 225.T (24 November 1914), Spring-Rice to FO, reporting conversation with Lansing, f.53, 75178, FO.368/1162; telegrams (13 December 1914), Grey to Spring-Rice, 136 Commercial and replies (15 and 22 December 1914), all FO.115/1771.

318. ESRC, 23rd Report, 10 November 1914, ADM.137/2988.

319. Minute (8 November 1914) by Cmdr. Frederick Leveton Harris (T.10 section), f.381, ADM.137/982.

320. Minute (17 December 1914) by Commercial Department, A. P[earson], "Holland as a Base for German Army Supplies," 83879, FO.368/1028.

321. Minutes (27 November 1914) by Sargent, Pearson, Hurst, and Crowe, on "Arrangements with Denmark as to Meat," 75770; see also minutes (4 December 1914) by Sargent on files 45480/78594, all FO.368/1103.

322. Telegram (1 December 1914, 6:00 p.m.), FO to Spring-Rice, 109 Commercial, f.57, 75178, FO.368/1162.

323. Ibid.

324. Telegram (1 December 1914), Grey to Lowther (Copenhagen), FO.368/1162.

325. Cable (4 December 1914) by Lowther (Copenhagen), 81549, FO.368/1103; ESRC, 25th Report, 25 November 1914, ADM.137/2988.

326. ESRC, 25th Report, 25 November 1914, ADM.137/2988.

327. Minute (26 November 1914) by Sargent, f.49, FO.368/1162.

328. ESRC, 25th Report, 25 November, ADM.137/2988. On the price of copper, see minute (4 December 1914) by Webb on Spring-Rice to Grey, 4 December 1914, ADM.137/2806.

329. Marion Siney, "British Negotiations with American Meat Packers, 1915–1917: A Study of Belligerent Trade Controls," *Journal of Modern History* 23, no. 4 (December 1951): 343–53.

330. ESRC, 27th Report, 1 December 1914, ADM.137/2989.

331. ESRC, 43rd Report, 25 February 1915, 167, ADM.137/2989.

332. ESRC memorandum (December 1914) by Hopwood reporting meeting with the chancellor of the exchequer and the lord chief justice, f.229, FO800/88.

333. The import of lard for Denmark in October 1914 was 1,005,000 pounds, as against 39,000 pounds for all of 1913. ESRC, 25th Report, 25 November 1914, 152, ADM.137/2988.

334. Remarks by Captain Richard Webb (DTD), ESRC, 29th Report, 19 December 1914, ADM.137/2989.

335. The problem of trading with the enemy was first reported in September. See ESRC, 10th report, 26 September 1914, ADM.137/2988. This will be discussed further in Chapter 8. See also John McDermott, "Total War and the Merchant State: Aspects of British Economic Warfare against Germany, 1914–16," *Canadian Journal of History* 21 (April 1986): 61–76.

336. For the creation of the Contraband Department, see G. M. Trevelyan, *Grey of Falloden* (London: Longmans, Green, 1937), 305–7. N.b.: This account is misleading, giving undue credit to Alwyn Parker (who advised the biographer) and misrepresenting Grey's motives at the time.

337. Minute (27 November 1914) by Crowe, 81549, FO.368/1103.

338. Minute (19 December 1914) by Crowe, 84794, and minutes (17 and 19 December 1914) by Pearson and Crowe on 83766, all FO.368/1103; also, minute (9 December 1914) by Crowe, f.90, FO.368/1162.

339. Minutes (21 December 1914) by Webb (DTD) and Oliver (COS), ADM.137/2806.

340. Minute (22 December 1914) by Hopwood, ADM.137/2806.

341. For a general survey and explanation of Danish policy, see Carsten Due-Neilsen, "Denmark and the First World War," *Scandinavian Journal of History* 10 (1985): 1–18. For an

opinion that Denmark outmaneuvered Britain on this, see Bent Bludnikow, "Denmark during the First World War," *Journal of Contemporary History* 24 (1989): 683–703.

342. Minute (25 December 1914) by Webb (DTD), ADM.137/2806.

343. File 88872, 31 December 1914, FO.368/1103.

7. Admiralty Infighting

Epigraph: Runciman to Sir Robert Chalmers, 7 February 1915, f.18, Runciman Mss. 136.

1. Memorandum (18 January 1919) by Captain Alan Hotham (Director of Trade Division) to Private Office (secretary to First Lord of the Admiralty) Walter Long, ADM.137/2737. Long became First Lord on 10 January 1919.

2. Ibid.

3. Minute (18 January 1927) by DNI (Rear-Admiral Alan Hotham), ff.139–141, ADM.116/3423. Hotham held the post from 1924 to 1927.

4. Stephan Roskill, *Churchill and the Admirals* (New York: William Morrow, 1978), 19–40.

5. Beatty to wife, 19 August 1914, f.34, BTY.17/28 (David Beatty papers, NMM, London).

6. Winston S. Churchill, *The World Crisis, 1911–1918,* 5 vols. (New York: Scribner's, 1923–1931), 1:258–59, 432.

7. Bridgeman to Sandars, 11 January 1914, f.17, Sandars, Ms.Eng.Hist. c.766.

8. These included Wilson, Bridgeman, Pakenham, Ballard, Bethell, Hood, and Troubridge. For Churchill's reluctance to combat Jellicoe, see Sandars to Balfour, 21 and 29 September 1914, f.90, f.106, Add.Mss. 49768.

9. For Jellicoe's views on this subject, see Jellicoe to Hamilton, 19 and 22 May 1915, HTN.125 (Frederick Hamilton papers, NMM, London).

10. Bridgeman to Sandars, 8 March 1916, f.62, Sandars, Ms.Eng.Hist. c.769; Fisher to Jellicoe, 22 May 1914, FGDN, 2:505–6.

11. The most recent biographical sketch is by John Hattendorf, "Admiral Prince Louis of Battenberg," in Malcolm Murfett, ed., *The First Sea Lords: From Fisher to Mountbatten* (Westport, CT: Praeger, 1995), 84–85.

12. Esher to Fisher, 20 April 1912, 569, FISR.1/11; see also Esher to Fisher, 31 December 1911, 551, FISR.1/11.

13. Beatty to wife, 16 April 1909, in Brian Ranft, ed., *The Beatty Papers: Selections from the Private and Offical Correspondence of Admiral of the Fleet Earl Beatty*, 2 vols. (Aldershot, UK: Naval Records Society, 1989, 1993), 1:23.

14. Fisher to Spender, 25 October 1911, FGDN, 2:398; Bridgeman to Sandars, 13 November 1914, f.134, Sandars, Ms.Eng.Hist. c.767; Hattendorf, "Admiral Prince Louis."

15. The mention of high regard is in Hattendorf, "Admiral Prince Louis of Battenberg"; for the low opinion, see Battenberg to Fisher, 24 July 1906, MB1/T93.

16. Lambton to Selborne, 10 June 1904, f.74, Selborne Mss 19.

17. Commander, 30 August 1885; captain, 31 December 1891. Richard Hough, *Louis and Victoria: The Family History of the Mountbattens,* 2nd ed. (London: Weidenfeld and Nicolson, 1984), 173.

18. Mark Kerr, *Prince Louis of Battenberg, Admiral of the Fleet* (London: Longmans, Green, 1934), 70.

19. Troubridge diary entries, 11 January and 24 January 10, 66/2/1, Troubridge Mss (IWM) (Ernest Troubridge papers, Imperial War Museum collection, London). It should also be remembered that at this time captains were automatically promoted to admiral according to seniority.

20. Battenberg was appointed director only after the sudden death of the successor designate (Rear-Admiral Burges Watson) and the disqualification of the second choice (Captain Henry May), for which see Greene to Selborne, 22 September 1902, f.37, Selborne Mss. 33; Kerr to Selborne, 1 July 1902, f.102, Selborne Mss. 31. Battenberg completed his tour as a/DNI in 1901 and had been in the Mediterranean Fleet (HMS *Implacable*) for less than one year.

21. King Hall diary, volume marked RCG (1902), 20 and 23 October 1902, King-Hall Mss. (George King Hall papers, private collection but copies held at Royal Navy Museum. Portsmouth, UK).

22. King Hall diary, volume marked HP2 (1909), 10 July 1909, King Hall Mss.

23. Battenberg to Cecil Fisher, 28 August 1921, MB1/T39/387.

24. Knollys to Hardinge, 15 November 1904, vol. 7, Hardinge Mss., as cited in George Monger, *The End of Isolation: British Foreign Policy 1900–1907* (London: Nelson and Sons, 1963) 173; see also Selborne to Balfour, 2 November 1904, Add.Mss. 49708.

25. Kerr, *Prince Louis,* 181, notes that the offer of 2CS, on 9 November 1904, came as a surprise.

26. After less than eight months commanding his cruiser squadron Battenberg wrote to Fisher begging to return to Whitehall; Battenberg to Fisher, 14 December 1905, 190, FISR.1/4.

27. Fisher to McKenna, 1 February 1910, FGDN, 2:302–3.

28. Diary of Major Adrian Grant-Duff (assistant secretary, CID), 25 April 1912, AGDF 2/2; further question marks over Battenberg's appointment in Admiral Percy Scott to Arnold White, n.d. [November 1911], naval correspondence, WHI.172 (Arnold White papers, NMM, London).

29. Earl of Balcarres to Sandars, 5 December 1912, Sandars, Ms.Eng.Hist. c.766; see printed copies of the private correspondence between Battenberg, Churchill, and Bridgeman, MB1/T22/167.

30. Fisher to McKenna, 1 February 1910, MCKN.6/3. Rear-Admiral Bacon had been offered and accepted the post and had been due to take over from Jellicoe in April 1910; see Bacon letter to the *Times* dated 15 April 1923, printed 17 April 1923.

31. For Custance's influence over Churchill, see Bridgeman to Sandars, 11 January 1914, f.17, Sandars, Ms.Eng.Hist. c.766; for Battenberg's disparagements of Custance, see Battenberg to Churchill, 24 October 1913, f.109, CAB.1/33.

32. King Hall diary, volume marked HP2, 10 July 1909, King Hall Mss.

33. Roskill, *Churchill and the Admirals,* 32.

34. James Goldrick, *The King's Ships Were at Sea: The war in the North Sea, August 1914–February 1915* (Annapolis, MD: Naval Institute Press, 1984).

35. Asquith to Stanley, 22 September 1914, LVS, 253; see generally Paul Halpern, *A Naval History of World War One* (Annapolis, MD: Naval Institute Press, 1994), 33–34. For Sturdee's responsibility in keeping the cruisers on station, see Keyes to Richmond, 4 June 1936, in Paul

Halpern, ed., *The Keyes Papers: Selections from the Private and Official Correspondence of Admiral of the Fleet Baron Keyes of Zeebrugge,* 3 vols. (London: Allen and Unwin for the Naval Records Society, 1979–1981), 2:353.

36. Fisher to Lord Rosebery, 11 September 1914, Rosebery Mss. 10124 (Lord Rosebery papers, National Library of Scotland, UK).

37. Beatty to his wife, 20 October 1914, in Ranft, *The Beatty Papers,* 1:144–45.

38. Sandars to Balfour, 21 and 29 September 1914, ff.90–106, Add.Mss. 49767. N.b.: Sandars was uncle to Captain Robert "Bubbles" James, and his friendship with Admiral Sir Francis Bridgeman gave him access to many serving officers.

39. Sandars to Balfour, 29 October 1914, f.119, Add.Mss. 49767, reporting conversation with Commander Bolton Eyres-Monsell, MP, staff officer, 2nd BS; see also remarks by Fisher to Mrs. McKenna, 3 October 1914, FGDN, 3:59–60. Eyres Monsell served as parliamentary secretary to the Admiralty, 1922–1923, and later as First Lord of the Admiralty, 1931–1936.

40. Fisher to Mrs. McKenna, n.d. (October 1914), FGDN, 3:61.

41. See copy of Vice-Admiral Cecil Burney to Churchill, 8 November 1914, 836, FISR.1/16.

42. WSC, 3:37; Richmond diary, in Arthur J. Marder, *Portrait of an Admiral: The Life and Papers of Sir Herbert Richmond* (London: Jonathan Cape, 1952), 96, 98–99; Roskill, *Churchill and the Admirals,* 29.

43. Minute (17 March 13), Jackson (COS) to Battenberg (1SL) and Churchill, and remarks thereon by DOD G. A. Ballard, 10 July 1913, ADM.137/452; remarks (27 July 1914) by Jackson, on Plan L (b), f.24, ADM.137/995.

44. Richmond diary, in Marder, *Portrait of an Admiral,* 95–97.

45. Ibid., 121.

46. Burney to Churchill, 8 November 1914, 836, FISR.1/16.

47. Richmond diary, in Marder, *Portrait of an Admiral,* 121.

48. Ibid., 107–8.

49. Richmond diary, 19 September 1914, RIC 1/9.

50. Richmond diary, in Marder, *Portrait of an Admiral,* 121.

51. Asquith to Venetia Stanley, 21 September 1914, f.245, Ms.Eng. c.7093.

52. For Duff's opinion, see Sandars to Balfour, 21 September 1914, f.90, Add.Mss. 49768; Hamilton to Fisher, 25 September 1914, FP 823 FISR.1/15; see also James Goldrick, "The Impact of War: Matching Expectation with Reality in the Royal Navy in the First Months of the Great War at Sea," *War in History* 14, no. 1 (2007): 31.

53. Asquith to Stanley, 17 and 22 September, 3 October, 4 and 5 December 1914, LVS, 325–27.

54. Balfour to Sandars, 22 September 1914, f.145, Sandars, Ms.Eng.Hist. c.766.

55. Bridgman to Sandars (reporting conversation with Bartolomé), 26 November 1914, f.171, Sandars, Ms.Eng.Hist. c.767.

56. Asquith to Stanley, 3 October 1914, LVS, 260. For "little army" quote, see Asquith to Stanley, 21 September 1914, f.245, Stanley, Ms.Eng. c.7093 (omitted from published version of letter); see also Violet Bonham Carter, *Winston Churchill as I Knew Him* (London: Eyre and Spottiswoode, 1965), 337–38. Violet was the sister of Arthur Asquith.

57. Asquith to Stanley, 5 and 7 October 1914, LVS, 263–66.

58. Ibid.; Harcourt, cabinet notes, 5 October 1914. Ms.Dep. 6231.

59. Asquith to Stanley, 13 October 1914, LVS, 275–76.

60. Ibid.

61. Asquith to Stanley, 7 October 1914, LVS, 266.

62. Lord Riddell diary, reporting conversation with Lloyd George, 10 October 1914, f.180, Add.Mss. 62974.

63. Asquith to Stanley, 6 October 1914, f.29, Stanley Mss., MSS.Eng. 7094. Omitted from the printed version.

64. Ibid.

65. Harcourt, cabinet notes, 6 October 1914, Ms.Dep. 6231.

66. Fisher to Lord Rosebery, 10 October 1914, Rosebery Mss. 10124.

67. Asquith to Stanley, 24 October 1914, LVS, 285.

68. Asquith to Stanley, 28 October 1914, LVS, 290; Haldane to Churchill, 19 October 1914, cited in WSC, 3:143–45. For evidence that Battenberg's dismissal was widely anticipated, see Bridgeman to Sandars, 24 October 1914, f.38, Sandars Mss., Ms.Eng.Hist. c.767; Beatty to his wife, 23 October 1914, in Ranft, *The Beatty Papers,* 1:148.

69. Violet Asquith, the prime minister's daughter, recalled her father's concern at replacing Battenberg. Bonham Carter, *Winston Churchill,* 343.

70. Haldane to Churchill, 19 October 1914, cited in WSC, 3:144. McKenna, one of Fisher's closest friends, opposed his recall, for which see Riddell diary, conversation with McKenna, 10 October 1914, f.181, and 31 October 1914, Add.Mss. 62974.

71. Bonham Carter, *Winston Churchill,* 345; see also John E. Wrench, *Geoffrey Dawson and Our Times* (London: Hutchinson, 1955), 43.

72. Churchill, *World Crisis,* 1:439–40. For contemporary comments on Fisher's health, see Beatty to his wife, 2 November 1914, in Ranft, *The Beatty Papers,* 1:151.

73. Douglas Brownrigg, *Indiscretions of the Naval Censor* (London: Cassell, 1920) 51; George Riddell diary, Add.Mss. 62968.

74. Sandars to Balfour, 4 November 1914, f.129, Add.Mss. 49768.

75. Sandars to Balfour, 29 October 1914, f.119, Add.Mss. 49768, citing conversation with Cmdr. Eyres Monsell; Reginald Hall biography, draft C of Strauss's biography, ch. 7, "Lord Fisher and Mr. Churchill," 2, Hall Mss(CCC).3/5 (W. R. Hall papers, Churchill College, Cambridge); Philip Dumas diary, 30 October 1914, Dumas Mss.; Richmond diary, 8 November 1914, in Marder, *Portrait of an Admiral,* 125.

76. Beatty to his wife, 30 October and 4 December 1914, in Ranft, *The Beatty Papers,* 1:149, 173.

77. Fisher testimony, 11 October 1916, 10th Day, 189, Q.3050, ADM. 137/1437B. On 20 October Asquith informed Venetia Stanley that "Winston has a grandiose scheme (entre nous) for bringing in both Fisher & Sir A. Wilson!" (cited in WSC, 3:147).

78. Asquith to Stanley, 29 October 1914, LVS, 295–96.

79. No actual list of candidates exists, but various sources indicate that candidates included Admiral Hedworth Meux (formerly Lambton), Admiral George Callaghan, Admiral Henry Jackson, Vice-Admiral Doveton Sturdee, and Admiral John Durnford (retired).

80. Fisher to George Lambert, 26 October 1914, FGDN, 3:39.

81. Asquith to Stanley, 28 and 29 October 1914, LVS, 290–96.

82. Churchill, *World Crisis,* 1:437. See Roskill, *Churchill and the Admirals,* 36; Richard Ollard, *Fisher and Cunningham: A Study of the Personalities of the Churchill Era* (London: Constable, 1991), 46. Marder was not among these. Oliver told him that the impetus came from the cabinet; see FDSF, 2:88.

83. Asquith to Stanley, 27 October 1914, LVS, 287.

84. Churchill, *World Crisis,* 1:435.

85. Bridgeman to Sandars, 13 November 1914, f.134, Sandars Mss., Ms.Eng.Hist. c.767. For evidence of this long-standing hostility within the service toward Battenberg, see King Hall diary, volume marked RCG, 23 October 1902, King Hall Mss.

86. Colville to Hamilton, 10 November 1914, HTN.124.

87. Sandars to Balfour, 30 October 1914, f.123, Add.Mss. 49767; Beatty to his wife, 30 October and 3–4 November 1914, in Ranft, *The Beatty Papers,* 1:148–53. Fisher claimed Battenberg had "utterly collapsed," for which see Fisher to Jellicoe, 30 November 1914, f.56, Jellicoe 48990.

88. WSC, 3:154; Ruddock Mackay, *Fisher of Kilverstone* (Oxford: Clarendon Press, 1973), 458; FDSF, 2:93.

89. Reginald Bacon, *The Life of Lord Fisher of Kilverstone,* 2 vols. (London: Hodder and Stoughton, 1929), 2:168–69; see also Fisher to Churchill, 16 May 1915, FGDN, 3:230–31.

90. Captain T. E. Crease, "Secret & Personal: Memorandum on Dardanelles," ADM.1/28268.

91. Garvin, Works, f.20, Notebook 147, Garvin Mss. (James L. Garvin papers, Harry Ransom Center, University of Texas at Austin).

92. Garvin, Notes on World Crisis, n.d. (ca. 1923), f.26, Notebook 147; Edward Goulding to Garvin, 6 March 1915, recip. Goulding (Wargrave), Garvin Mss.

93. Fisher to Cecil Fisher, 29 August 1914, FISR.15/1/3/3.

94. Fisher to Jellicoe, 29 August 1914, f.32, Add.Mss. 49006.

95. Bacon, *Life of Lord Fisher,* 2:161–62.

96. Ibid.

97. Admiralty, "Instructions for the DNI," 24 December 1903, ADM1/7663.

98. Churchill to Battenberg, 19 November 1911, MB1/T9/43.

99. Mackay, *Fisher of Kilverstone,* 458.

100. Bacon, *Life of Lord Fisher,* 2:161.

101. Fisher to Jellicoe, 20 December 1914, FGDN, 3:99–100.

102. At 5:00 p.m. on 4 November, Richmond was told that Leveson also was leaving and that he was promoted to DOD, but one hour later this instruction was countermanded. Richmond diary, 4 November 1915, in Marder, *Portrait of an Admiral,* 125.

103. HMS, 1:153.

104. Philip Dumas diary, 30 October 1914, Dumas Mss.; see also views of Captain W. R. (Blinker) Hall, Draft 'C' of Strauss's biography, ch. 7, "Lord Fisher and Mr. Churchill," 2, Hall Mss(CCC).3/5.

105. Churchill first offered Wilson the post on 29 or 30 October, on testimony to the Dardanelles Commission, 28 September 1916, 5th Day, 65, Q.1050, ADM.137/1437B. Wilson started in an unofficial capacity on 7 November; Richmond diary, 8 November 1914, in Marder, *Portrait of an Admiral,* 125.

106. Churchill, *World Crisis,* 1:439. On 14 October he was moved from DID to naval secretary and replaced by W. R. Hall.

107. Beatty to his wife, 11 December 1914, in Ranft, *The Beatty Papers,* 1:175.

108. Captain, HMS *Drake,* 1907–1909; flag captain, HMS *Indomitable,* Rear-Admiral Stanley Colville, 1909–1912; captain, HMS *Warspite,* 1917–1918; 3SL 1918–9.

109. Richmond diary, 1, 3, and 4 November 1914, in Marder, *Portrait of an Admiral,* 122–25. This is also the assessment of C. I. Hamilton, "Expanding Naval Powers: Admiralty Private Secretaries and Private Offices, 1880–1945," *War in History* 10, no. 2 (2003): 125–56, 143.

110. Fisher to Jellicoe, 19 November 1914, FGDN, 3:76; Fisher to Esher, 1 November 1914, WSC (companion part 2) 3:243; Roger Keyes, *Naval Memoirs,* 2 vols. (London: Thornton Butterworth, 1934), 1:129; Philip Dumas diary, 1 November 1914, Dumas Mss.

111. Fisher to Jellicoe, 20 December 1914, FGDN, 3:99–100.

112. "The Naval Staff of the Admiralty: Its Work and Development," Naval Staff Monograph, September 1929, 67–68, BR1875, NLMD.

113. Captain Charles Bartolomé (naval secretary to First Lord) also attended.

114. Richmond diary, 22 November 1914, in Marder, *Portrait of an Admiral,* 128.

115. Bacon, *Life of Lord Fisher,* 2:166, 168.

116. For instance, Stephen Roskill neither investigated nor questioned these assumptions, but instead relied upon Marder. HMS, 1:152n1.

117. Winston S. Churchill, *Great Contemporaries* (London: The Reprint Society, 1941), 300.

118. This is from his 1929 reply to Bacon. For the vagueness of Churchill's original account, see Churchill, *World Crisis,* 1:437–41, 479–501; FDSF, 3:93, citing Bacon, *Life of Lord Fisher,* 2:161–62; Halpern, *Naval History,* 36. Bacon may inadvertently cemented this view with his apocryphal tale at Bacon, *Life of Lord Fisher,* 2:238–39.

119. FDSF, 2:93–98; FGDN, 3:41–44. Mackay, *Fisher of Kilverstone,* 460.

120. Keyes, *Naval Memoirs,* 1:130; Gaddis Smith, *Britain's Clandestine Submarines, 1914–1915* (New Haven, CT: Yale University Press, 1964).

121. FDSF, 191–96; FGDN, 3:44–47.

122. WSC, 3:802–9; Mackay, *Fisher of Kilverstone,* 459–62.

123. Churchill to Garvin, 29 September 1916, et. seq., recip. file for Winston Churchill; also Goulding to Garvin, 8 October 1916, et. seq., recip. file for Edward Goulding, both Garvin Mss. Churchill concerted his evidence with others also, especially General Sir Ian Hamilton; see Jenny Macleod, "General Sir Ian Hamilton and the Dardanelles Commission," *War in History* 8, no. 4 (2001): 418–41.

124. Mackay, *Fisher of Kilverstone,* 459–62.

125. It seems significant that Arthur Marder never reviewed Mackay's biography of Fisher. Mackay exhibits more explicit criticism of Marder's scholarship in "Historical Reinterpretations of the Anglo-German Naval Rivalry, 1897–1914," in Gerald Jordan, ed., *Naval Warfare in the Twentieth Century 1900–1945: Essays in Honour of Arthur Marder* (London: Croom Helm, 1977), 32–45.

126. Mackay, *Fisher of Kilverstone,* 457–75. The sabotage remark is on 458.

127. Fisher to Lady Jellicoe, 16 August 1914, FGDN, 3:51.

128. Fisher to Jellicoe, 29 August 1914, Add.Mss. 48990.

129. Admiralty Training Division, "Naval Staff Monographs: Fleet Issue," vol. 8 (Naval Operations Connected with the Raid on the North Sea Coast), 174, copy at NLMD.

130. Asquith to Stanley, 2 November 1914, LVS, 305; see also Fisher to Jellicoe, 3 November 1914, FGDN, 3:65–66, referencing their meeting the previous day.

131. Fisher had wanted to ban all fishing vessels from the North Sea but was prevented from going this far; Fisher to Jellicoe, 28 December 1914, FGDN, 3:115.

132. Fisher to Rosebery, 11 September 1914, Rosebery Mss. 10124.

133. Asquith to Stanley, 2 November 1914, LVS, 305. For evidence that some of these ideas had been considered before but rejected, see FO Legal Department, 26 September 1914, 53220, FO.372/633.

134. Asquith to Stanley, 2 November 1914, LVS, 305.

135. Asquith to Stanley, 8 November 1914, LVS, 314.

136. Fisher to Grey, 7 November 1914, f.211, FO.800/88.

137. Admiralty, memo issued through Press Bureau, 2 November 1914, ADM.1/8403/425; Admiralty, "Closure of North Sea," 3 November 1914, ADM.137/977.

138. Fisher to Beatty, 30 November 1914, FGDN, 3:83–4; see also Fisher to Mrs. McKenna, 21 November 1914, FGDN, 3:79; Fisher to Jellicoe, 3 November 1914, FGDN, 3:65–66.

139. Admiralty to FO, 25 November 1914, 75534, FO.372/634.

140. Minute (27 November 1914) by Sanderson, on Admiralty to Foreign Office, 25 November 1914, 75534 (39810), FO.372/634.

141. Minutes (27 November 1914) by Wellesley and (29 November 1914) by Davidson, 75534 (39810), FO.372/634.

142. Minute (30 November 1914) by Crowe, 75534 (39810), FO.372/634.

143. Minute (30 November 1914) by Grey, 75534 (39810), FO.372/634. Reply sent 4 December 1914.

144. Minute (28 December 1914) by Sanderson on Admiralty to FO, 25 December 1914, 87141, 75534 (39810), FO.372/634.

145. Admiralty Training Division, "Naval Staff Monographs," vol. 8, 172–74.

146. Memoranda by Inspecting Captain of Mines (M. A. Cobbe), "Remarks on Mining (Existing Service Fittings)," 15 May, minute (6 November 1914) by Leverson, on f.418, f.188, and telegram (5 November 1914) by Buchanan (ambassador, St. Petersburg) to Admiralty, ADM.137/988.1914, f.22, and "Serious Defects in Our Mining Apparatus Requiring Urgently to be Remedied," 15 May 1914, f.24, ADM.137/843.

147. Minute (22 November 1914) by Dumas (director of mines) on G01589, 28/11/14, "Blockade Mines—as to Supply Of," 846, FISR.1/16.

148. Minutes (27 November 1914) by Oliver and Fisher (28 November 1914), FISR.1/16; see also Fisher to Churchill, 4 January 15, 901, FISR.1/16.

149. Hankey to Balfour, 29 December 1914, ff.126–27, Add.Mss. 49703.

150. Ibid.

151. Ibid.

152. Donald Shurman, *Julian S. Corbett: Historian of British Maritime Policy from Drake to Jellicoe* (London: Royal Historical Society, 1981), 160n2.

153. For details of destroyers fitted to carry fifteen mines each, see G branch, file G.01358/12, "Fitting of Mines in Torpedo Boat Destroyers," Important Questions dealt with by the Director of Naval Ordnance, vol. 3, f.318ff. (1914), NLMD.

154. See minute (2 January 1915) by Arnold Forster, attached to Jellicoe to Admiralty, 29 December 1914, ff.85–86, ADM.137/843. Canadian Pacific Rail Road steamship company, *Princess Irene, Princess Margret*, taken up December 1914.

155. Fisher to Churchill and reply, both 21 December 1914, FGDN, 3:104–5.

156. Ibid. At the meeting of the War Council on 1 December 1914, Churchill proposed a resolution to capture an island off the German coast; CAB.22/1. See also WSC (companion part 1), 3:290.

157. Churchill, "Memorandum on Capture of Sylt," 2 December 1914, ADM.137/452, as cited in WSC (companion part 1), 3:291–94; Balfour to Hankey, 5 December 1914, as cited in WSC (companion part 1), 3:297.

158. Churchill to Fisher, 22 December 1914, FISR.1/17.

159. Goldrick, *King's Ships*, 189–219.

160. Fisher to Jellicoe, 20 (two letters) and 21 (two letters), December 1914, FGDN, 3:99–103.

161. Churchill to Fisher, 23 December 1914, WSC (companion part 1), 3:326–327.

162. Contained in ADM.137/1943.

163. Admiralty to Jellicoe, 6 January 1915, ff.339–43, ADM.137/1943; also Julian S. Corbett and Henry J. Newbolt, *Naval Operations*, 5 vols. (London: Longmans, Green, 1920–1931), 2:51.

164. Corbett and Newbolt, *Naval Operations*, 2:43.

165. Telegram (20 December 1914), Admiralty to Jellicoe, f.4, Jellicoe Add.Mss. 49008.

166. Fisher to Leyland, 9 June 1916, FGDN, 3:354.

167. The impulse to move the battle cruisers came from Wilson, for which see Fisher to Churchill, 20 December 1914, WSC (companion part 1), 3:321; Goldrick, *King's Ships*, 216–19.

168. Corbett and Newbolt, *Naval Operations*, 2:51; Fisher to Jellicoe, n.d. (20–21 December 1914), FGDN, 3:102.

169. Fisher to Jellicoe, 26 December 1914, FGDN, 3:111–12.

170. Fisher to Churchill, 26 December 1914, 889, FISR.1/17; for evidence that Fisher threatened resignation, see Fisher to Jellicoe, 26 December 1914, f.94, Jellicoe Add.Mss. 49006.

171. Fisher to Churchill, 26 December 1914, 889, FISR.1/17; for reiteration of this key point, see Fisher to Jellicoe, 28 December 1914, FGDN:115.

172. Fisher to Churchill, 26 December 1914, 889, FISR.1/17; Fisher to Jellicoe, 27 and 28 December 1914, ff.96–99, Jellicoe Add. Mss. 49006. For evidence of support for sweeps, see FNR, 204; for opposition, see Beatty to Jellicoe, 7 May 1916, in Ranft, *The Beatty Papers*, 1:308; Jellicoe to Balfour, 25 January 1916, f.69, Jellicoe Add. Mss. 49714. Shortly after Fisher's resignation, Jellicoe petitioned for a lifting of this edict, for which see Jellicoe to Beatty, 4 June 1915 (two letters), Jellicoe NRS, 165–67. In early 1916 Jellicoe again petitioned for the restrictions to be lifted; Jellicoe to Balfour, 25 January 1916, f.69, Add.Mss. 49714.

173. Fisher to Mrs. McKenna, 29 December 1914, FGDN 3:116.

174. Asquith to Stanley, 12 March 1915, LVS, 475.

175. Runciman to his wife, 6 January 1915, f.18, Runciman Mss.; Balfour to Lansdowne, 9 February 1915, Lansdowne Mss., as cited in Cameron Hazlehurst, *Politicians at War, July 1914 to May 1915; a Prologue to the Triumph of Lloyd George* (London: Jonathan Cape, 1971), 160–61; HMS, 1:144.

176. Asquith to Balfour, 24 November 1914, f.146, Add.Mss. 49692.

177. Balfour to Sandars, 27 November 1914, f.175, Sandars, Ms.Eng.Hist. c.766.

178. Undated Emmott diary entries (January and March 1915) express unhappiness at the "inner circle" taking important decisions; f.167, f.181, Emmott Mss. 2.

179. Balfour in November 1914; Crewe in December 1915; Haldane in February 1915; McKenna and Harcourt in March 1915. Simon and Runciman were knocking on the door.

180. Montagu (chancellor of the Duchy of Lancaster) to Hankey, 22 March 1915, as cited in HMS, 1:172.

181. Asquith to Stanley, 30 December 1914, LVS, letter 241, 345–46.

182. Lloyd George, "Suggestions as to the Military Position," point 4. 1 January 1915, CAB.42/1/8; Riddell diary, conversation with Lloyd George, 2 January 1915, f.2, Add.Mss. 62975.

183. Balfour to Hankey, 2 January 1915, f.137, Add.Mss. 49703.

184. Kitchener to French, 2 January 1915, PRO.30/57/50; Kitchener to Sir John French, 9 January 1915, ff.207–14, Asquith Mss.26.

185. Asquith to Stanley, 30 December 1914, LVS, 345–47.

186. Churchill to Asquith, 29 December 1914, WSC (companion part 1), 3:343–44.

187. Asquith to Stanley, 1 January 1915, LVS, 356–58; Asquith to Churchill, 1 January 1915, CHAR.13/46.

188. Kitchener to French, 2 January 1915, PRO.37/57/50.

189. Hankey to Balfour, 2 January 1915, f.142, Add.Mss. 49703.

190. Hankey memo, 28 December 1914, para. 1 (introduction) and para. 32 (conclusion), CAB.37/122/194.

191. Ibid., paras. 6–12.

192. Ibid., para. 18.

193. Ibid., para. 16.

194. Ibid., para. 17.

195. Ibid., paras. 32 and 17.

196. SC, 1:353. Comments by Hankey on Memorandum by Churchill enclosed within Grigg to Hankey, 16 February 1928, f.10, HNKY.5/1.

197. Lloyd George, "Suggestions as to the Military Position," 1 January 1915, sec. 1 and 5, CAB.42/1/8.

198. Covering letter, Lloyd George to Asquith, 31 December 1914, C/6/11/24, Lloyd George Mss.

199. Lloyd George, "Suggestions as to the Military Position," sec. 5, CAB.42/1/8.

200. Ibid., sec. 6.

201. Ibid., sec. 8.

202. Minutes of War Council, "The General Policy of the War," 7 January 1915, CAB.42/1/11.

203. Lloyd George, "Suggestions as to the Military Position," conclusions, CAB.42/1/8.

204. Asquith to Stanley, 1 January 1915, LVS, 358; Lloyd George, "Suggestions as to the Military Position," CAB.42/1/8.

205. Lloyd George, "Suggestions as to the Military Position," point 4, CAB.42/1/8.

206. Ibid.

207. It was Asquith who classed Churchill's letter as a memo, for which see Asquith to Stanley, 30 December 1914, LVS, 345.

208. Churchill to Asquith, 29 December 1914, WSC (companion part 1), 3:343–45.

209. Ibid.

210. Churchill to Asquith, 31 December 1914, enclosing memorandum dated 31 December 1914, WSC (companion part 1), 3:346–49.

211. Ibid.

212. Ibid.

213. Asquith to Churchill, 1 January 1915, WSC (companion part 1), 3:357.

214. Fisher to Churchill, 2 January 1915, CHAR.13/56/2.

215. Ibid.

216. Ibid.

217. Fisher to Hankey, 2 January 1915, CAB.63/4.

218. Hankey to Balfour, 2 January 1915, f.142, Add.Mss. 49703; Fisher to Hankey, 2 January 1915, CAB.63/4.

219. Fisher to Churchill, 3 January 1915, FGDN, 3:117–18. Fisher made similar remarks to Jellicoe but no mention of the Turkey plan; Fisher to Jellicoe, 4 January 1915, FGDN, 3:120.

220. Fisher to Churchill, 3 January 1915, FGDN, 3:117–18; in this context see also Fisher to Balfour, 4 January 1915, FGDN, 3:118–19.

221. Many of the ideas Fisher listed (such as forcing the Dardanelles) were in fact Churchill's—thus, in effect, Fisher was throwing back at Churchill his own words and thoughts.

222. Churchill to Vice-Admiral Carden, 3 January 1915, 1:28 p.m., WSC (companion part 1), 3:367.

223. Churchill to Fisher, Wilson, and Oliver, 3 January 1915, WSC (companion part 1), 3:365–66. The original is in ADM.137/452; for use of the code name Sylt, see Churchill to Jellicoe, 11 January 1915, CHAR.13/46/10.

224. Churchill to Fisher, Wilson, and Oliver, 3 January 1915, WSC (companion part 1), 3:365–66; Fisher to Balfour, 4 January 1915, FGDN, 3:118–19. The offending memo is in ADM.137/452.

225. Ibid.

226. Churchill to Fisher, 4 January 1915, FGDN, 3:121.

227. Ibid., item (a). Note the salutation is not "My dear Winston" but "First Lord."

228. Ibid., item (b).

229. Lady Richmond diary, 5 January 1915, RIC 1/17, as cited in Robin Prior, *Gallipoli: The End of the Myth* (New Haven, CT: Yale University Press, 2009), 5.

230. This claim can be substantiated. In addition to the documents already cited above, see Fisher to Jellicoe, 28 October 1914, FGDN, 3:64, and Fisher to Leyland, 15 October 1914, FGDN, 3:63. See also letters from Fisher to Jellicoe, 26 and 29 December 1914, 1 January 1915, all Add.Mss. 49006; Fisher to Rosebery, 10 September 1914, Rosebery Mss. 10124.

231. Fisher to Churchill, 4 January 1915, 901, FGDN, 3:121.

232. Fisher, "Mine-Laying," 4 January 1915, attached to Fisher to Churchill, 4 January 1915, FGDN, 3:121–23.

233. Lord Fisher, *Memories and Records*, 2 vols. (New York: George Doran, 1920), 1:135–38.

234. Ibid.

235. See reference to Fisher's appeal for help in Hankey to Balfour, 29 December 1914, f.127, Add.Mss. 49703.

236. Jellicoe to Admiralty, 29 December 1914, stamped received 31 December 1914, 737/HF005, f.79, ADM.137/843. For Fisher request for political ammunition on other issues, see Fisher to Jellicoe, 23 December 1914, FGDN, 3:107–8.

237. Minutes (1 January 1915) by Dumas and (2 January 1915) by Morgan Singer, on Jellicoe letter of 29 December 1914, FGDN, 3:107–8.

238. Minute (2 January 1915) by D. Arnold-Forster, FGDN, 3:107–8. See also two appreciations by Arnold-Forster, "Appreciation on Extensive Mining Operations in the Heligoland Bight," 23 September 1914, f.31, and "Appreciation on Laying Mines of the Elbe, Weser, or Lister Deep, Using One, Two or Four Minelayers," 20 September 1914, f.28, ADM.137/843.

239. Minute (7 January 1915) by Oliver, ff.88–89, "Operation OQ: Laying Mines on the Route Lister Deep to the Elbe," ADM.137/837.

240. Minute (8 January 1915) by A. K. Wilson, ADM.137/837.

241. "Operation OQ: Laying Mines on the Route Lister Deep to the Elbe," f.8, and attached minute (11 January 1915) by CoS on "Reporting Operations on German Coast," SC1, 10 January 1915, ff.129–31, ADM.137/837.

242. Churchill to Jellicoe, 4 January 1915, ff.175–78, Add.Mss. 48990. See also Fisher to Jellicoe, 12 January 1915, FGDN, 3:128–29; Churchill to Jellicoe, 1 January 1915, CHAR.2/66/51.

243. Jellicoe to Churchill, 8 January 1915, f.9, and 15 January, f.11; also Churchill's replies 11 January 1915, f.10, and 18 January 1915, f.12, all CHAR.13/46.

244. Fisher to Jellicoe, 11 January 1915, ff.115–17, Add. Mss. 49006 (edited version available in FGDN, 3:129–30).

245. Fisher to Jellicoe, 12 January 1915, FGDN, 3:128–29; see also similar letter, n.d., FGDN, 3:181–82, and minute (12 January 1914) by Fisher on "Operation OQ: Laying Mines on the Route Lister Deep to the Elbe," f.91, ADM. 137/837.

246. For further expressions of Jellicoe's support for mine warfare, see Jellicoe to Jackson (1SL), 14, 15, and 19 August, 1 September 1916, Henry Jackson Mss., NLMD.

247. Jellicoe to Churchill, 15 January 1915, WSC (companion part 1), 3:417–18; Churchill to Jellicoe, 18 January 1915, ff.183–85, Add.Mss. 48990. For Fisher's original minute proposing the minefield, see Fisher to 1st Lord and CoS, 14 January 1915, ff.92–93, ADM.137/843.

248. Minute (21 January 1915) by Churchill on secret file, "Proposed Protection of Dover Straits by Mines," f.87, ADM.137/843.

249. Minute (21 January 1915) by Fisher underneath minute (21 January 1915) by Churchill on secret file, "Proposed Protection of Dover Straits by Mines," f.87, ADM.137/843.NB. Fisher submitted a supplementary, more forceful minute 21 January 1915, at f.103.

250. Hankey to Balfour, 17 January 1915, states that the 29th Division was available and would be sent to the Mediterranean within "9 or 10 days"; WSC (companion part 1), 3:425.

251. He expressed this view to Kitchener on 7 January and again on 19 January to his secretary Colonel Fitzgerald; FGDN, 3:48.

252. Asquith to Stanley, 13 January 1915, WSC (companion part 1), 3:412.

253. Fisher to Jellicoe, 19 and 21 and 23 January 1915, FGDN, 3:133, 141–42, 144–45.

254. Ibid.

255. Dawson, "Notes on a Luncheon with Lord Fisher, 18 January 1915," reproduced in Wrench, *Geoffrey Dawson and Our Times,* 117–18.

256. Ibid.

257. For support of Alexandretta and reasons for so doing, see Fisher to Churchill, 9 January 1915, WSC (companion part 1), 3:399–400; Fisher to Churchill, 18 January 1915, FGDN, 3:132. See also Fisher to Churchill, 6 January 1915, WSC (companion part 1), 3:384. On oth-

ers' support of the Alexandretta operation, see Churchill to Grey, 16 January 1915, enclosing a note to Comte de Saint-Seine, 16 January 1915, WSC (companion part 1), 3:421–23; Churchill to Fisher and Oliver, 20 January 1915, WSC (companion part 1), 3:432; Churchill to Kitchener, 20 January 1915, WSC (companion part 1), 3:433. For evidence of the wide circulation of this letter, see copy in Lloyd George C/3/16/16, Lloyd George Mss.

258. Asquith to Stanley, 20 January 1915, LVS, 387–88.

259. Asquith to Stanley, 22 January 1915, LVS, 271, 390–91; Churchill to Asquith, 22 January 1915, WSC (companion part 1), 3:439–42.

260. Fisher to Jellicoe, n.d. (20 January 1915), FGDN, 3:181–82. Marder misdates this letter as April 1915, but the internal evidence is inconsistent. The debate over mines occurred in January not April 1915. It is known that Jellicoe was summoned before 28 January 1915 but did not attend. Reference to Jellicoe's summons together with the mention of "today's meeting" of the cabinet indicates the letter must have been written on 20 January 1915. (See record of cabinet meeting, 20 January 1915, CAB.41/36/2.) The previous meeting of the cabinet was on 12 January, clearly too early, and the next one, on 3 February, was too late.

261. Fisher to Jellicoe, n.d. (20 January 1915), FGDN, 3:181–82. See also Fisher to Beatty, 20 January 1915, FGDN, 3:141.

262. Fisher to Lloyd George, 11 January 1915, papers, C4/11/2, Lloyd George Mss.

263. Julian Corbett, *England in the Seven Years' War,* 2 vols. (London: Longmans, Green, 1907), 2:373–74.

264. Fisher to Churchill, 22 January 1915, WSC (companion part 1), 3:438. For Fisher's contentment at the return of the battle cruisers from the Mediterranean this day, see Fisher to Jellicoe, 22 January 1915, FGDN, 3:143.

265. Minute (23 January 1915) by Churchill, f.112, ADM.137/843.

266. Fisher to Churchill, 23 January 1915, CHAR.13/57/54.

267. Fisher to Jellicoe, 23 January 1915, Add.Mss. 49006; see also Fisher to Churchill, 23 January 1915, WSC (companion part 1), 3:442–43.

268. Fisher to Churchill 23 January 1915, WSC (companion part 1), 3:442–43. It is not clear whether Fisher was present in the war room during the battle. Churchill states Fisher was, for which see *World Crisis,* 2:131. For suggestion of the First Sea Lord's absence, see Fisher to Churchill, 25 January 1915, WSC (companion part 1), 3:449.

269. The most accessible copy of this is found in WSC (companion part 1), 3:452–54. It is dated 25 January 1915. For Hankey's collaboration the previous days, see SC, 1:269–70.

270. SC, 1:269–70; Mackay, *Fisher of Kilverstone,* 482–85; WSC, 3:263–65.

271. Fisher, "Memorandum by the First Sea Lord on the Position of the British Fleet and Its Policy of Steady Pressure," 25 January 1915, CAB.42/1/24.

272. Ibid.

273. Mackay, *Fisher of Kilverstone,* 484–86.

274. Julian Corbett diary, 25 and 26 January 1915, reporting conversation with Hankey, as cited in Shurman, *Julian S. Corbett,* 160.

275. Churchill to Fisher, 26 January 1915, WSC (companion part 1), 3:458.

276. See Hankey to Balfour, 3 February 1915, f.157, Add.Mss. 49703.

277. Fisher to Asquith, 28 January 1915, WSC (companion part 1), 3:461; Fisher to Jellicoe, 29 January 1915, WSC (companion part 1), 3:470; Esher diary, 29 January 1915, in Maurice

Brett, ed., *Journals and Letters of Reginald, Viscount Esher,* 4 vols. (London: Ivor Nicholson and Watson, 1934–1938), 3:470; Fisher to Churchill, 28 January 1915, CHAR.13/56/23.

278. Fisher to Asquith, 28 January 1915, FGDN, 3:147–48; also WSC, 3:461–62.

279. Fisher to Asquith, 28 January 1915, FGDN, 3:147–48.

280. Asquith to Stanley, 28 January 1915, LVS, 405. Churchill chided Fisher for "light-heartedly" threatening resignation, for which see Churchill to Fisher, 28 January 1915, FGDN, 3:149.

281. Fisher to Jellicoe, 29 January 1915, FGDN, 3:149–50.

282. Asquith to Stanley, 28 January 1915, LVS, 404–7.

283. Useful here is Keith Neilson, "For Diplomatic, Economic, Strategy and Telegraphic Reasons: British Imperial Defence, the Middle East and India, 1914–1918," in Greg Kennedy and Keith Neilson, eds., *Far Flung Lines: Essays on Imperial Defence in Honor of Donald Mackenzie Shurman* (London: Frank Cass, 1996).

284. Churchill to Kitchener, 20 January 1915, PRO 30/57/72.

285. George H. Cassar, *The French and the Dardanelles: A Study of the Failure in the Conduct of War* (London: George Allen and Unwin, 1971), 51–61; see also telegram 619 (21 January 1915) from French ministry of marine to Churchill, f.45, CHAR.13/46/45.

286. Grey to Churchill, 24 January 1915, f.56, CHAR.13/46.

287. Ibid.

288. Cassar, *The French and the Dardanelles,* 59; Churchill to Grey, and reply, 26 January 1915, CHAR.13/54/15.

289. Asquith to Stanley, 28 January 1915, LVS, 405.

290. War Council minutes 28 January 1915, CAB.42/1/26.

291. Asquith to Stanley, 9 and 23 February 1915, LVS, 423, 445–46.

292. David French, "The Origins of the Dardanelles Campaign Reconsidered," *History,* July 1983, 210–24.

293. Riddell diary, conversation with Lloyd George, 2 October 1915, f.129, Add.Mss. 42976.

294. Asquith to Stanley, 23 February 1915, LVS, 445–46. For further evidence of Asquith uncertainties, see 9 February 1915 (ii), 3:00 p.m., letter 295, LVS, 421–23; 17 February 1915 (ii), 4:30 p.m., letter 310, LVS, 434–35.

295. Fisher, "Memorandum," 27 March 1915, WSC (companion volume part 1), 3:754–55, and reply by Churchill, 28 March 1915, WSC (companion volume part 1), 3:756; Fisher, "Memorandum," 8 April 1915, WSC (companion volume part 1), 3:781; Sandars to Lord Curzon, 4 November 1915 (copy) reporting conversation with Lord Fisher, f.96, Sandars, Ms.Eng.Hist. c.768.

296. Battenberg, "Statement Made to Me by Sir Francis Hopwood, Additional Civil Lord at Admiralty," 24 June 1916, MB1/T39/378.

297. Fisher to Jellicoe, 4 April 1915, FGDN, 3:186.

298. Fisher to Jellicoe, 28 March 1915, 4 April 1915, 20 April 1915, FGDN, 3:174–5, 186, 198–99.

299. Hankey to Balfour, 10 February 1915, Add.Mss. 49703.

300. HMS, 1:161–68.

301. Hankey to Esher, 15 March 1915, as cited in HMS, 1:167.

302. Fisher to Jellicoe, 27 February 1915, FGDN, 3:160–61.

303. Hankey diary, 19 March 1915, HNKY.1/1; Hankey to Fisher, 9 June 1915, 1049, FISR.1/20.

304. Asquith to Stanley, 28 and 30 January 1915, LVS, 405, 409–11; Riddell diary, conversation with Lloyd George, 2 October 1915, f.129, Add.Mss. 42976; Battenberg, "Statement Made to Me by Sir Francis Hopwood, Additional Civil Lord at the Admiralty," 24 June 1916, MB1/T39/378; diary entry, 18 May 1915, *Lady Cynthia Asquith: Diaries 1915–18* (London: Hutchinson, 1968), 22–23. Cynthia Asquith was the wife of Herbert Asquith, second son of H. H. Asquith.

305. HC Deb, v.75, 2 November 1915, c.509, Mr. Asquith.

306. George Riddell, diary entry for 3 February 1915, in *Lord Riddell's War Diary, 1914–1918* (London: Ivor Nicholson and Watson, 1933), 58.

307. George Riddell, diary entry for 11 February 1915, in *Lord Riddell's War Diary*, 62.

308. Fisher to Jellicoe, 25 February 1915, FGDN, 3:159–60.

309. See especially the series of minutes attached to Churchill to Wilson, 18 April 1915; A. K. Wilson to War Group, 21 April 1915; Oliver, 26 April 1915; Fisher, 27 April 1915, all in 983, FISR.1/19.

8. Vigorous Indecision

Epigraph: Runciman to his wife, 6 January 1915, f.18, Runciman Mss.

1. Emmott diary, 4 January 1915, f.164, Emmott Mss. 2.

2. Page to Bryant, 28 December 1914 (received by State 11 January 1915), in FRUS, *The Lansing Papers, 1914–1920,* 2 vols. (Washington, DC: U.S. Government Printing Office, 1939), 1:259–60.

3. Minutes of War Council, 7 January 1915, CAB.42/1/11.

4. Lloyd George, "Suggestions as to the Military Position," 1 January 1915, point 4, CAB.41/1/8.

5. Asquith to Stanley, 13 February 1915, LVS, 429.

6. Martin Horn, *Britain, France, and the Financing of the First World War* (Montreal: McGill–Queen's University Press, 2002), 78–89.

7. Lloyd George, "Some Further Considerations of the Conduct of the War," 22 February 1915, CAB.37/124/40.

8. Kathleen Burk, *Britain, America, and the Sinews of War, 1914–1918* (London: Allen and Unwin, 1985); Vincent Barnett, "Keynes and the Non-neutrality of Russian War Finance during World War One," *Europe-Asia Studies* 61, no. 5 (July 2009): 797–812. For review of British taxation policy during the war, see Martin Horn, "The Concept of Total War: National Effort and Taxation in Britain and France during the First World War," *War and Society* 18, no. 1 (2000): 1–22.

9. Harcourt, cabinet notes, 15 December 1914, Ms.Dep. 6231.

10. Lloyd George, "The Finances of the Allied Powers Etc.," minutes of War Council, 16 December 1914, CAB.42/1/6.

11. Harcourt, cabinet notes, 8 December 1915, Ms.Dep. 6231.

12. Horn, *Britain, France,* 44–45.

13. Minutes of War Council, 16 December 1914, CAB.42/1/6.

14. Hankey to Balfour, 19 December 1914, f.121, Add.Mss. 49703; minutes of War Council, 16 December 1914, CAB.42/1/6.

15. Ruddock Mackay, *Balfour, Intellectual Statesman* (Oxford: Oxford University Press, 1985), 230–31; The draft treatise is in the Balfour papers at the British Mueum, Add.Mss. 49945–56.

16. The paper was not actually printed until four days later; see Hankey to Balfour, 5 January 1915, f.145, Add.Mss. 49703.

17. Ibid. See also Horn, *Britain, France,* 24–25, 86–89, 94.

18. Burk, *Britain, America,* 62.

19. Balfour, "Limits of Enlistment," 1 January 1915, CID 200-B, f.289, CAB.4/5.

20. George Cassar, *Kitchener's War: British Strategy from 1914 to 1916* (Washington, DC: Brassey's, 2004), 68–76, 120–24.

21. Diary entry, 17 January 1915, in Frances Lloyd George, *Lloyd George: A Diary,* ed. A. J. P. Taylor (New York: Harper and Row, 1971), 22–23; see also Horn, *Britain, France,* 46, 52–53; BESP, 151–53; and Balfour to Sir Arthur Nicolson, 21 and 24 December 1914, Add.Mss. 49749, as cited in Keith Neilson, *Strategy and Supply: The Anglo-Russian Alliance, 1914–1917* (London: Allen and Unwin, 1984), 59.

22. Horn, *Britain, France,* 88–89.

23. Churchill, "Limits of Enlistment," 7 January 1915, printed 11 January 1915, CID 201-B, ADM.116/3486.

24. Callwell to Sir Henry Wilson, 2 January 1915, Wilson Mss. 73/1/18 [IWM, London], cited in David French, "The Meaning of Attrition, 1914–1916," *English Historical Review* 103, no. 407 (April 1988): 391. The document in question is War Office, "The War: A Comparison of the Belligerent Forces," 6 January 1915, CAB.42/1. Four weeks later Kitchener produced another paper reverting to his original position that the war must continue to 1917. See Kitchener, for cabinet, "Remarks on the Chancellor of Exchequer's Memorandum on the Conduct of the War," 25 February 1915, CAB.37/124/50.

25. Asquith to Stanley, 14 and 26 January 1915 (ii), LVS, 378, 396. N.b.: Asquith expressed these views on the very same days he was considering this very issue. General Staff, "The War: A Comparison of the Belligerent Forces," 6 January 1915, CAB.42/1/10.

26. Asquith to Stanley, 30 March 1915 (i), LVS, 520–21.

27. Asquith to Stanley, 12 January 1915, LVS, 371.

28. H. Llewellyn Smith (Board of Trade), "Limits of Enlistment," 11 January 1915, 1, CID 202-B, CAB.42/1/14.

29. John G. Little, "H. H. Asquith and Britain's Manpower Problem, 1914–1915," *History* 82, no. 267 (July 1997): 397–409, citing Parliamentary Accounts and Papers, Report on the State of Employment in the United Kingdom in February 1915 (1914–1916), xxviii, Cd.7939.

30. Graeme Thomson (Admiralty), "Report by the Director of Transports, Admiralty, on the Memorandum on the Shortage of Merchant Shipping Tonnage Prepared by the Board of Trade," 3, ADM.116/3486.

31. Lord Lucas, "Limits of Enlistment," CID 208-B, CAB.4/5.

32. Llewellyn Smith, "Limits of Enlistment," 11 January 1915, CID 202-B, CAB.42/1/14.

33. Ibid.

34. Runciman, "Shortage of Merchant Shipping Tonnage," 11 January 1915, CAB.37/123/21. Runciman drew most of his arguments from a paper by Llewellyn Smith reporting the views of Mr. E. G. Saltwood, a director of the Baltic Exchange; see "Retail Prices on 1 January 1915," n.d. (printed January 1915), T/4/14, J. M. Keynes Mss. (John Maynard Keynes papers, King's College, Cambridge); see also Montagu to McKenna, Runciman, and Lucas, 12 January 1915, AS1/6/18(1), Montagu Mss.

35. Arthur Salter, *Allied Shipping Control: An Experiment in International Administration* (Oxford: Clarendon Press, 1921), 45.

36. Admiralty, for cabinet, [Supplies of Wheat and Meat], 25 January 1915, CAB.37/123/49.

37. Asquith to Stanley, 12 January 1915, LVS, 371; cabinet letter, 13 January 1915, CAB.41/36.

38. Graeme Thompson (1875–1933), joined Admiralty 1900; director of transports, 1914–1917; director of shipping at Admiralty and Ministry of Shipping, 1917–1919; KCB 1919; colonial secretary of Ceylon, 1919–1922; governor of British Guiana, 1922–1925; governor of Nigeria, 1925–1931; governor of Ceylon, 1931–1933 (died in office). HC Deb, 15 February 1915, vol. 69, c.925, Winston Churchill. The remark is widely attributed to Churchill but undocumented. The earliest use is found in *Ashburton Guardian* (New Zealand) 35, no. 9131 (4 May 1915), 6.

39. Graeme Thomson (Admiralty), "Report by the Director of Transports, Admiralty, on the Memorandum on the Shortage of Merchant Shipping Tonnage Prepared by the Board of Trade," 3, ADM.116/3486.

40. Ibid. See also minute (17 January 1915) by Churchill, FLM 2:57–58.

41. Admiralty, [Supplies of Wheat and Meat], 25 January 1915, CAB.37/123/49.

42. Eventually Fisher made a personal appeal to Kitchener, which was honored for a short time. See Fisher to Jellicoe, 29 April 1916, copy, recip. file 10/12, Garvin Mss.

43. Graeme Thomson (Admiralty), "Report by the Director of Transports, Admiralty, on the Memorandum on the Shortage of Merchant Shipping Tonnage Prepared by the Board of Trade," 3, ADM.116/3486.

44. Ibid. See also Admiralty, [Supplies of Wheat and Meat], 25 January 1915, CAB.37/123/49.

45. Asquith to Stanley, 12 January 1915, LVS, 371–72; confirmed by Harcourt, cabinet notes, 12 January 1915, Ms.Dep. 6231.

46. Cabinet letter, 13 January 1915, CAB.41/36.

47. Harcourt, cabinet notes, 20 January 1915, Ms.Dep. 6231.

48. Board of Trade, "Prices of Principle Food Stuff," n.d., T/4/1, Keynes Mss.

49. Ibid. See also Kathy Burk, "Wheat and the State during the First World War," in Michael Dockrill and David French, eds., *Strategy and Intelligence: British Policy during the First World War* (London: Hambledon, 1996), 119–38.

50. Keynes, "Greatness of Risk as Compared with Smallness of Insurance," n.d. (May 1915), T/4/177; also Keynes, "Secret: A Note on the Wheat Position of the UK" (for cabinet Committee on Food Supplies), 1 May 1915, T/4/215, Keynes Mss.

51. Llewellyn Smith, Board of Trade Memorandum, 20 January 1915, T/4/50, Keynes Mss.

52. Note by Llewellyn Smith, 20 January 1915, T/4/55, Keynes Mss.

53. Confidential: Board of Agriculture and Fisheries, "The Wheat Position, 11 January 1915," 16 January 1915, T4/36, Keynes Mss.

54. Asquith to Stanley, 20 January 1915, LVS, letter 268, 387; Montagu to Asquith, 21 January 1915, AS1/7/33(1), Montagu Mss.

55. Memorandum (12 January 1915) by Edwin Montagu, addressed to McKenna, Runciman and Lucas, AS1/6/18(10, Montagu Mss.; general summary in Burk, "Wheat and the State," 122–23. Many historians have conflated the committees; for instance, see P. E. Dewey, *British Agriculture in the First World War* (London: Routledge, 1989), 23–24.

56. Montagu to McKenna, Runciman, and Lucas, 12 January 1915, AS1/6/18(1), and papers attached to W. Vernon and Sons to Runciman, 7 October 1914, AS1/4/18(1) (box 2), all Montagu Mss.

57. Appendix to Treasury [John Maynard Keynes], memorandum for cabinet, 25 January 1915, CAB.37/123/51. A copy of this document can be found in JMK, 16:57–65; see also L. Margaret Barnett, *British Food Policy during the First World War* (Boston: George Allen and Unwin, 1985), 27–30.

58. Asquith to Stanley, 22 January 1915, LVS, 390; 9 February 1915 (ii), 421–23; 29 January 1915 (ii), 408–9; 4 February 1915, 3:30 p.m., 415–16; 10 February 1915 (i), 424–25; HC Deb, 11 February 1915, series 5, vol. 69, "Necessaries of Life," c.756–867. The minutes of the first meeting (22 January) as well as those of the third and fourth meetings can be found in: T/4/111, T/4/115, T/4/116, all Keynes Mss.

59. Asquith to Stanley, 22 January 1915, LVS, 390.

60. Asquith to Stanley, 10 February 1915, LVS, 423–25. Technically, Keynes was assistant to Sir George Paish, special advisor to Lloyd George; for Asquith's respect for Keynes, see Horn, *Britain, France,* 47–50; Marcello De Cecco, *Money and Empire: The International Gold Standard, 1890–1914* (Oxford: Basil Blackwell, 1974), 138–39, 150–52.

61. JMK, 16:57.

62. HC Deb, 11 February 1915, vol. 69, c.756–867.

63. For the best summary of the Indian wheat problem, see memorandum (23 February 1915), McKenna to Asquith, AS1/4/30(1), Montagu Mss.; for warning by Indian government on 8 December 1914, see memorandum by T. H. W., undersecretary of state for the India Office, "Government of India's Proposal to Restrict Wheat Exports," 17 December 1914, T/4/59, Keynes Mss. This danger also figured prominently in the calculations by the cabinet Food Price Committee: Treasury [John Maynard Keynes], memorandum for cabinet, 25 January 1915, CAB.37/123/51; see also Keynes, "Notes on Lord Crewe's Minute and India," 22 February 1915, T/4/63–69, Keynes Mss.; HC Deb, 22 April 1915, vol. 71, c.427–8W, Sir J. D. Rees.

64. J. M. Keynes, "Meeting of Com[itt]ee on Wheat Prices and Freights, Friday January 22nd [1915], 11:30 a.m.–1:30 p.m.," T/4/111–115, Keynes Mss. N.b.: The minutes of this meeting are recorded in Keynes' hand.

65. Asquith to Stanley, 22 January 1915, LVS, 390.

66. Asquith to Stanley, 9 February 1915, LVS, 421–23.

67. Treasury [John Maynard Keynes], memorandum for cabinet, 25 January 1915, CAB.37/123/51.

68. The price of a quarter (480 lbs.) of Manitoba 1 (wheat) increased from 36s.3d. to 57s.11d. The freight portion was calculated at 3s.6d. See HC Deb, 11 February 1915, series 5, vol. 69, "Necessaries of Life," c.765.

69. "Directions from the Cabinet Committee on Food Prices to the Transport Department, Admiralty," conclusions I and II, 10 February 1915, f.28, Asquith Mss. 27.

70. Treasury [John Maynard Keynes], memorandum for cabinet, 25 January 1915, CAB. 37/123/51.

71. Ibid.

72. Minutes of War Council, 28 January 1915, CAB.41/1/28.

73. Balfour, "Notes on Lord Fisher's Memorandum of 25 January," 1 February 1915, ff.144–47, Add.Mss. 49712.

74. Hankey to Asquith, 2 February 1915, G-8, CAB.24/1. I am indebted to Keith Neilson for bringing this document to my attention.

75. Ibid. See also Fisher to Churchill, 16 February 1915, misdated 29 January 1915 in WSC (companion part 1), 3:471–72, advising, "Not a grain of wheat will come back from the Black Sea unless there is military occupation of the Dardanelles." Also, Hankey to Balfour, 17 February 1915, f.167, Add.Mss. 49703.

76. There exist additional explicit statements of the importance of wheat. For example, Kitchener, for cabinet, "The Dardanelles: A Note by the War Office," 28 May 1915, CAB.37/128/27; HC Deb, vol. 75, 2 November 1915, c.509.

77. Sir Alfred Edmund Bateman, KCMG (1844–1929). Barrister. Entered Board of Trade, 1865; rose to comptroller general of commerce, labour and statistics, 1897–1903 (in succession to Robert Giffen); president, Royal Statistical Society, 1897; Royal Commission on Food Supply, 1902–1905; chairman, Labor Exchange Committee, 1910–1917; British representative member, Dominions Royal Commission, 1913. My thanks to Cameron Hazlehurst for this information. In 1916, Bateman succeeded Leverton Harris as chairman of the Enemy Exports Committee.

78. See Montagu to Runciman, 12 November 1914, AS1/4/6, Montagu Mss.; secret, paper No. 18, "Meeting of the Interdepartmental Committee on Wheat and Flour Supplies," 13 March 1915, T/4/138; second proof of printed "Minutes of Meeting of the Interdepartmental Committee on Wheat and Flour Supply," T/4/218, Keynes Mss. Members: Sir Alfred Bateman; R. H. Rewe (Agriculture); Sir Frederick Black (Admiralty); Brigadier S. S. Long (War Office); Mr. F. Phillips (Treasury); E. J. Riley (War Office); A. S. Gage (Agriculture); J. M. Keynes (Treasury).

79. HC Deb, 22 April 1915, vol. 71, c.377–78, Mr. Houston.

80. See Barnett, *British Food Policy*, appendix 1: stocks of food in the United Kingdom. Stocks of wheat never fell so low than 1 July 1915.

81. Keynes, "Note on the Wheat Position of the United Kingdom: Greatness of Risk as Compared with Smallness of Insurance," 1 May 1915, T/4/177, Keynes Mss.

82. Ibid. See also JMK, 16:82–92.

83. Further details can be found in Barnett, *British Food Policy,* chapters 3–5; J. H. Thomson, *The Harvests of War: The Prairie West, 1914–1918* (Toronto: McClelland and Stewart, 1978) contains lots of statistical data on Canadian and world prices and yields during the war.

84. Hankey, "Limits of Enlistment: Note by the Secretary," 21 January 1915, CID 206-B, CAB.4/5.

85. Ibid. His source was Sir Charles Ottley, managing director of Armstrong's; Hankey to Balfour, 21 January 1915, f.151, Add.Mss. 49703.

86. Montagu to Asquith, 21 January 1915, AS1/7/33(1), Montagu Mss.

87. CID, minutes of the 131st Meeting, 27 January 1915, CAB.2/3.

88. Ibid., 2 (remarks by Kitchener).

89. Harcourt, notes on CID meeting, 27 January 1915 at 3:00 p.m., Ms.Dep. 6231.

90. BESP, 155–59.

91. Asquith to Stanley, 27 January 1915, LVS, 400.

92. Minutes of 131st CID, 27 January 1915, CAB.42/1/25; Llewellyn Smith, "Limits of Enlistment," 21 January 1915, CAB.42/1/20, and supporting memoranda submitted by Board of Trade and Board of Agriculture, CAB.42/1/21 and /22; minutes of 131st Meeting of CID, 27 January 1915, CAB.42/1/25. See also BESP, 156–67.

93. BESP, 159.

94. Grey to Sydney Buxton, 21 March 1915, Sydney Buxton Mss [privately held collection]. as cited by Keith G. Robbins, "Foreign Policy, Government Structure and Public Opinion," in F. H. Hinsley, ed., *British Foreign Policy under Sir Edward Grey* (Cambridge: Cambridge University Press, 1977), 536.

95. Asquith to Stanley, 30 March 1915(i), LVS, 520–21.

96. Ibid.

97. Lloyd George, "Some Further Considerations of the Conduct of the War," 22 February 1915, CAB.37/124/40. Also cited in WSC (companion part 1), 3:544–47. For even earlier suggestions, see Ottley to Hankey, 2 September 1914, and minutes thereon by Hankey and Churchill, Kitchener papers, PRO.30/57/82; HMS, 1:149.

98. HC Deb, 15 February 1915, vol. 69, c.913.

99. BESP, 153.

100. Kitchener, for cabinet, "Remarks on the Chancellor of Exchequer's Memorandum on the Conduct of the War," 25 February 1915, CAB.37/124/50.

101. Harcourt, cabinet notes, 2 March 1915, Ms.Dep. 6231.

102. Kitchener, for cabinet, "Remarks on the Chancellor of Exchequer's Memorandum on the Conduct of the War," 25 February 1915, CAB.37/124/50. For one study of trade union resistance to concessions (based on union records), see John Singleton, "The Cotton Industry and the British War Effort, 1914–1918," *Economic History Review* 47, no. 3 (1994): 601–18.

103. Asquith to Stanley, 6 March 1915, LVS, 462–63.

104. BESP, 160–62.

105. John Singleton, "The Cotton Industry and the British War Effort, 1914–1918," *Economic History Review* 47, no. 3 (1994): 609. British intelligence reports contain frequent accusations of the use of British-made fabric in German aircraft.

106. "Report on the Visit of Admiral Slade and Mr. Hurst to Paris, Decr. 19th–23rd 1914," 87327, FO.372/603.

107. John McDermott, "Total War and the Merchant State: Aspects of British Economic Warfare against Germany, 1914–16," *Canadian Journal of History* 21 (April 1986): 68. While Kitchener lobbied for Egyptian cotton, Harcourt did the same for African coffee; see Cassar, *Kitchener's War,* 45–48.

108. Hopwood to Runciman, 12 December 1914, f.221, FO.800/88; ESRC, 43rd Report, 25 February 1915, 162–63, 165, ADM.137/2989.

109. Kathleen Burk, ed., *War and the State: The Transformation of British Government, 1914–1919* (London: Allen and Unwin, 1982).

110. H. W. Carless Davis, *History of the Blockade: Emergency Departments* (printed for official information only, March 1921, copy at NLMD), 124.

111. John McDermott, "A Needless Sacrifice: British Businessmen and Business as Usual in the First World War," *Albion* 21, no. 2 (Spring 1989): 270.

112. Page to Bryant, 28 December 1914, FRUS, *Lansing Papers,* 1:259–60.

113. Hankey memo, 28 December 1914, para. 17, CAB.37/122/194.

114. Printed copy: Page to Sir Edward Grey, 28 December 1914, 88200, f.285, FO.368/1162. Although the letter is dated 28 December, Harcourt says it reached the Foreign Office on the morning of 30 December 1914, for which see cabinet notes, 30 December 1914, Ms. Dep. 6231.

115. Notes by Lansing (10 January 1915) on Grey to Bryant, 7 January 1915, FRUS, *Lansing Papers,* 1:262–63.

116. Page to Wilson, December 1914, reproduced in Burton J. Hendrick, *The Life and Letters of Walter H. Page,* 4 vols. (New York: Doubleday, 1924), 2:335.

117. State, "Note to Great Britain of December 26, [1914] Protesting against Seizures and Detentions Regarded as Unwarranted," FRUS, 1914 Supp., 372–75.

118. Arthur S. Link, *Wilson,* vol. 3: *The Struggle for Neutrality, 1914–1915* (Princeton, NJ: Princeton University Press, 1960), 174.

119. Grey to Page, 7 January 1915, FRUS, 1915 Supp., 299–302; Spring Rice to Grey, 13 March 1915, No. 121 Commercial, 36586, FO.382/442.

120. Leverton Harris to Grey, 5 January 1915 (2 letters), ff.260–64, FO.800/88.

121. Minute (25 December 1914) by Crowe, "Contraband Negotiations with the US Gov," f.258, 86298, FO.368/1162; see also Crowe (11 January 1915) on Spring Rice to Grey, 7 January 1915, FO.372/785.

122. Leverton Harris to Grey, 5 January 1915 (second letter), f.264, FO.800/88.

123. Hopwood to Grey, 30 December 1914, f.232, FO.800/88; see also John Coogan, *The End of Neutrality: The United States, Britain and Maritime Rights, 1899–1915* (Ithaca, NY: Cornell University Press, 1981), 204–9.

124. Asquith to Stanley, 30 December 1914, LVS, 345–47.

125. Sir John Simon, Attorney General's Opinion, n.d. (29 December 1914), FO.800/89.

126. Grey, "Draft Note," 2 January 1915, for cabinet, CAB.37/124/57.

127. Coogan errs considerably in his analysis: British did not "seize" U.S. contraband (211); sowing mines on the high seas was not illegal (214); and had the United States employed force to defend her "rights" (226), the Allied navies not only had plenty of resources to wage a maritime war but, arguably, likely would have inflicted far more damage on the U.S. economy than vice versa.

128. Coogan, *End of Neutrality,* 208.

129. Hankey, "The Coordination of the War Arrangements for Trade Restrictions, &c.," 13 January 1915 (CID 203-B), CAB.42/1/15.

130. Ibid.

131. Hankey, notes on opening, November 1914, CAB.1/11; undated ESRC memo (December 1914), f.229, FO800/88.

132. Runciman, "The Capture of Enemy Trade," 31 October 1914, CAB.37/122/198; for broader study, see McDermott, "Total War"; McDermott, "A Needless Sacrifice"; Jonathan Boswell and Bruce Johns, "Patriots or Profiteers? British Businessmen and the First World War," *Journal of European Economic History* 11, no. 2 (1982): 423–45.

133. Phillip Dehne, "From 'Business as Usual' to a More Global War: The British Decision to Attack Germans in South America during the First World War," *Journal of British Studies* 44 (July 2005): 516–35.

134. McDermott, "Total War," 64; McDermott, "A Needless Sacrifice," 266–73.

135. Dehne, "From 'Business as Usual,'" 522–29.

136. Davis, "History of the Blockade," 116–17, citing Treasury notice dated 22 August 1914.

137. J. S. Todd to Admiralty (DTD), 11 November 1914, "German Agents of British Steamship Companies," ADM.137/2828.

138. Minute (23 March 1915) by Hurst, FO.368/1232. N.b.: Cited by Dehne, but not found in this file.

139. Norman Hill (Harrison SS Co.) to Webb (DTD), 2 December 1914, ADM.137/2828, cited in Dehne, "From "Business as Usual," 524.

140. Hankey, "The Coordination of the War Arrangements for Trade Restrictions," para. 10, CAB.42/1/15.

141. Minute (21 December 1914) by Vansittart, FO.368/1028.

142. Ibid.

143. Ibid.

144. Minute (25 January 1915) by Crowe on Orme G. Sargent's minute dated 21 January 1915, "Shipment of Copper from Australia," 7759, FO.382/437.

145. Minute (27 January 1915) by Hurst on O. G. Sargent's minute dated 21 January 1915, "Shipment of Copper from Australia," 7759, FO.382/437.

146. Minutes (4 February and 16 March 1915) by Crowe on Sargent's minute dated 21 January 1915, "Shipment of Copper from Australia," 7759, FO.382/437.

147. Minutes of 130th CID (Trading Coordination Subcommittee), 14 January 1915, CAB.42/1/17.

148. Asquith to Stanley, 14 January 1915, LVS, 378.

149. Minutes of 130th CID (Trading Coordination Subcommittee), 14 January 1915, CAB.42/1/17.

150. Emmott, "Memorandum on the Trade Clearing House Section of the War Trade Department (for Circulation to Government Departments)," 1 March 1915, 29288, FO.382/445; Davis, "History of the Blockade," 144.

151. SC 1:354. For Hopwood's proposal to create a unified department under the authority of a single minister possessing executive authority, see Curzon to Asquith, "Mr. Montagu's Memorandum," n.d. (August 1915), f.200, Asquith Mss. 29.

152. Asquith to Stanley, 25 February 1915, LVS, 452; Emmott diary, 21 January 1915, f.168, Emmott 2; CID to Treasury, 21 January 1915, T2234, and 23 January 1915, T1/11862.

153. Webb memo, 10 August 1914, ADM.137/2863.

154. ESRC, "N.E.T. Index: Neutral and Enemy Trade Index," n.d. (ca. 1917), ff.2–5, ADM1/8408/1.

155. Bell to Gasalee, 28 June 1932, L 3434, FO.370/387.

156. Harris and Dixon, shipowners, London. Married to daughter of W. H. Smith. He was a shipowner and Lloyd's underwriter of more than thirty years' experience. See Leverton-Harris to McKenna, 18 April 1910, unpaginated bound case, ADM 116/1070.

157. *Oxford Dictionary of National Biography*, entry for "Harris, (Frederick) Leverton (1864–1926)" by H. S. Ede, rev. Marc Brodie, 2004.

158. Leverton Harris was Principal Private Secretary to Arnold-Forster at the War Office from 1903 to 1905.

159. For this information I am indebted to Captain Chris Page RN, Head of the Naval Historical Branch (staff).

160. Leverton-Harris to McKenna, 18 April 1910, unpaginated bound case, ADM 116/1070.

161. February 1915, commander; December 1919, honorary captain; 1916–1919, undersecretary at Ministry of Blockade.

162. Webb, "Clerical Work in the Trade Branch," 10 August 1914, ADM.137/2863.

163. Douglas Brownrigg, *Indiscretions of the Naval Censor* (London: Cassel, 1920), 10–11, 180.

164. For this information I am indebted to Dr. Nicholas Black and Miss Jenny Wraight, Admiralty Librarian, NLMD.

165. Page to Wilson, 30 December 1916, in Hendrick, *Life and Letters*, 3:311–12, as cited in *Oxford Dictionary of National Biography*, entry for "Harris, (Frederick) Leverton (1864–1926)."

166. For his declination of a baronetcy, see Leverton Harris to Bonar Law (May 1915), BL/50/3/58 (Andrew Bonar Law papers, Parliamentary Archive, London).

167. Inglefield to Campbell, 14 November 1907, ADM.137/2864.

168. Home Office (McKenna), "Trading with the Enemy," 25 January 1915, CID 209-B, CAB.42/1/23.

169. Ibid.

170. Customs, "Trading with the Enemy. Observations by the Board of Customs and Excise on Paper 209B," 3 February, CID 210-B, CAB.42/1/31; Board of Trade, "Trading with the Enemy. Note by the Board of Trade," 10 February 1915, CID 211-B, CAB.42/1/34; "Trading with the Enemy. Note by the Chairman of the Board of Customs and Excise," 22 February 1915, CAB.42/1/40.

171. Board of Trade, "Trading with the Enemy," 10 February 1915, CAB.42/1/34.

172. Runciman to Grey, 30 January 1915, enclosing extract of minute, f.289, FO800/89.

173. The War Trade Department was formed by Treasury minute dated 17 February 1915. Emmott, untitled memorandum and undated memorandum (August 1915), 5/307, Emmott Mss.

174. Minutes of Interdepartmental Committee on Trading with the Enemy, 24 February 1915, CAB.42/1/43; draft report by Interdepartmental Committee on Trading with the Enemy, 25 February 1915, CAB.42/1/46; Trading with the Enemy (1) note by secretary, (2) report of an interdepartmental conference, 9 March 1915, CID 216-B, CAB.42/2/4.

175. CID (Hankey), draft report of the Interdepartmental Committee on Trading with the Enemy, 27 February 1915, paras. 4, 7, 8, and 12, CAB.42/1/46.

176. John McDermott, "Trading with the Enemy: British Business and the Law during the First World War," *Canadian Journal of History* 32 (August 1997): 201–19.

177. Ibid.

178. Minutes (24 April 1915) by Vansittart, (27 April 1915) by Pearson, (28 April and 2 May 1915) by Crowe, and letter from NJ Highmore of War Trade Department, 22 April 1915, attached to "British Firms Suspected of Trading with Enemy," 29158, FO.382/448.

179. CID (Hankey), draft report of the Interdepartmental Committee on Trading with the Enemy, 27 February 1915, para. 23, CAB.42/1/46; also CID 216-B, para. 22, 8–9.

180. McDermott, "A Needless Sacrifice," 275.

181. Jonathan Winkler, *Nexus: Strategic Communications and American Security in World War I* (Cambridge, MA: Harvard University Press, 2008), 34–40, 59–60.

182. Bertram Dawson to Brand, 21 October 1914, uncataloged (General Corr box 26A), Brand Mss. I am indebted to Captain Chris Page, RN, for confirmation that Leverton Harris and Brand worked in the same section and indeed shared an office.

183. *Oxford Dictionary of National Biography*, entry for "Brand, Robert Henry. Baron Brand 1878–1963," by Kathleen Burk, 2004.

184. Brand to Lord Robert Cecil, 25 February 1916, uncataloged (box 114), Brand Mss.

185. Brand, "Memorandum A," 7 December 1914, uncataloged (box 19), Brand Mss. Handwritten drafts; typed copies in box 114.

186. "Memorandum B," 7 December 1914, uncataloged (box 19), Brand Mss.

187. ESRC memorandum by Hopwood, n.d. (apparently December 1914), f.229, FO.800/88.

188. Carless Davis, *History of the Blockade,* 156–74, 87–88.

189. Marion C. Siney, "British Official Histories of the Blockade of the Central Powers during the First World War," *American Historical Review* 68, no. 2 (January 1963): 392–401. Note 8 on 394 refers to the interview having taken place in 1939.

190. Dehne, "From "Business as Usual,'" 524–26, cites documents found in the archives of the Bank of London and South America showing how little this bank observed the spirit of the law.

191. Raymond Beck (chairman of Lloyd's) to Brand, 16 April 1915, uncataloged (box 114), Brand Mss.

192. Captain F. H. Brownrigg (comptroller, Trade Clearing House) to Brand, 10 and 14 April 1915, uncataloged (box 114), Brand Mss.

193. Cunliffe (Bank of England) to Chamberlain, 18 January 1915, suggesting first meeting be held on Friday, 22 January 1915; AC 19/6/3, Chamberlain Mss. See also "Cornhill Committee: Direct or Indirect Utilization of Credit Facilities in the United Kingdom for the Furtherance of Enemy Trade Conducted through Neutral Countries," T1/11777.

194. Richard Guinness to Brand, 6 July 1915, uncataloued (box 114), Brand Mss. Lord Inchcape joined at the second meeting.

195. Although Brand is not listed as secretary, his signature is clearly appended to a letter from the Cornhill Committee to Parker (Foreign Office, Contraband Department), 1 May 1915, 53586, FO.382/455. By the summer of 1915, Brand was also a member of the Prize Claims Committee.

196. Largest cache of documents found in Brand Mss. See also Llewellyn Smith to Chamberlain, 10 February 1915, AC 19/6/2, enclosing list of "Firms Abroad Suspected of Acting as Agents for the Supply of Necessaries as to the German Government or German Warships," which names five South American and two European firms; AC 19/6/8, all Chamberlain Mss.

197. Alwyn Parker, joined Foreign Office in 1900. Assistant clerk, 1912. Nominally senior clerk of the Contraband Department, though not promoted to this rank until 1916. Shunted to become FO librarian in 1919. Lord Inchcape, James Lyle Mackay (1852–1932), began with

the India-based trading house of Mackinnon, Mackenzie and Co. and later returned to Scotland in 1893 a nabob. In 1913 he was appointed chairman of the British India (BI) Steam Navigation Company and in 1914 was the driving force behind the merger of BI with Peninsular and Orient. In 1915 Lord Inchcape served as chairman of the Cornhill Committee, but relinquished the position upon becoming chairman of Peninsular and Orient at the end of 1915.

198. Parker to Crowe, 14 January 1915, 8762, FO.382/299.

199. M. Samuel and Co. to Austin Chamberlain, 25 February 1915, and M. Samuel and Co. to C. Paget (Bank of England), AC 19/6/9 and /10, Chamberlain Mss.; reference to HSBC in minute (14 June 1915) by W. E. Davidson (chief legal advisor to FO), attached to "Financing of Trade between German Trade + Neutral Countries," 76752, FO.382/455.

200. Agenda for Cornhill Committee meeting, 14 April 1915, uncataloged (box 114), Brand Mss.

201. H. W. Carless Davis (War Trade Department) to Mr. Richard Guinness (Cornhill), 17 August 1915 (attached to agenda for meeting of 19 August 1915, memorandum initialed HBB on Cornhill Committee letterhead "Grain Trade with Scandinavian Countries," 8 July 1915, uncataloged (box 114), Brand Mss.

202. Memorandum (18 February 1915) by Cornhill Committee to Lord Cunliffe, AC 19/6/6, Chamberlain Mss.

203. This report did not reach the Foreign Office till May 1915, for which see Brand (Cornhill Committee) to Parker, 1 May 1915, 53586, FO.382/455.

204. Cornhill Committee, 2, White Lion Court, Report, 2 March 1915, T7684, 24 March 1915, T1/11777.

205. Ibid., paras. 6 and 7.

206. Minute (12 March 1915) by H. P. Hamilton to Sir John Bradbury (Treasury permanent secretary), T7684, 24 March 1915, T1/11777.

207. Treasury, "Conference in the Cornhill Committee's Report on the Credit Facilities of London," 1 April 1915, T7684, 24 March 1915, T1/11777.

208. Brand (Cornhill Committee) to Alwyn Parker, 1 May 1915, 53586, FO.382/455. See also Treasury to Foreign Office, 12 June 1915, enclosure 2 in No. 1, circular Letter (confidential), 3 May 1915, 78752, FO.382/455.

209. Treasury circular letter dated 10 June 1915, 76752, FO.382/455.

210. Report on "The Trade Clearing House—a Brief Account of Its Development and Function," section "Finance Section," 16–18, 136095, 22 September 1915, FO.382/470. Some fragments ("Miscellaneous Papers Bearing on the Work and History of the Section") have survived in FO.902/37.

211. Cornhill Committee to Treasury, 28 July 1915, uncataloged (box 114), Brand Mss; Treasury to Foreign Office, 28 August 1915, enclosing circular letter dated 26 August 1915, 121666, FO.382/455. Note attached minute (28 February 1916) by Sir Adam Block, stating that this circular was "immediately withdrawn"; for evidence that it was the Treasury that initiated this withdrawal, see memorandum (24 March 1916) by Lord Eustace Percy (Foreign Office), "Abuse of London Credits: Offenders on the Statutory Lists," enclosed in Cornhill Committee to Brand, 3 April 1916, for discussion at meeting of Cornhill Committee meeting of 4 April 1916, uncataloged (box 114), Brand Mss.

212. Memorandum (24 March 1916) by Lord Eustace Percy (Foreign Office), "Abuse of London Credits: Offenders on the Statutory Lists," enclosed in Cornhill Committee to Brand, 3 April 1916, for discussion at meeting of Cornhill Committee meeting of 4 April 1916, uncataloged (box 114), Brand Mss.

213. Ibid.

214. Harcourt, cabinet notes, 27 January 1915, Ms.Dep. 6231.

215. Harcourt, cabinet notes, 3 February 1915, Ms.Dep. 6231.

216. Cabinet letter, 3 February 1915, CAB.41/36.

217. Hobhouse diary, 3 February 1915, f.5, Add.Mss. 60507.

218. For Asquith's skepticism, see Asquith to Stanley, 13 February 1915, LVS, 429.

219. Minute (7 January 1915) by Wellesley on telegram (6 January 1915), 8T, Spring Rice to Grey, 174/2149, FO.372/728; Link, *Wilson,* 3:179–87.

220. Hobhouse diary, 27 January 1915, f.3, Add.Mss. 60507.

221. Webb (DTD), "The Navy in Relation to the Food Supply of the Country," February 1915, ADM.1/8410/30. Marked as circulated to cabinet.

222. Horace Plunkett diary, 6 February 1915, reporting conversation with Grey, as cited in Link, *Wilson,* 3:335. Regrettably, I was denied permission to examine the original Plunkett diary.

223. Asquith to Stanley, 6 February 1915, LVS, 416. Proposals were framed and agreed by a meeting of Churchill, McKenna, Runciman, Simon, Hopwood, Leverton Harris, and Captain Richard Webb; see Churchill to Grey, 4 February 1915, CHAR.13/47/2.

224. Arthur S. Link, "The Cotton Crisis, the South, and Anglo-American Diplomacy, 1914–1915," in J. Carlyle Sitterson, ed., *Studies in Southern History* (Chapel Hill: University of North Carolina Press, 1957), 131.

225. Edward J. Clapp, *Economic Aspects of the War: Neutral Rights, Belligerent Claims and American Commerce in the Years 1914–1915* (New Haven, CT: Yale University Press, 1915), ch. 7.

226. Asquith to Stanley, 8:00 p.m., 10 February 1915, LVS, 425; cabinet letter, 10 February 1915, CAB.41/36/4.

227. Leverton Harris, "Effect of the Order in Council of March 11, 1915, upon German Exports to the United States of America," 27 August 1915, for cabinet, 358, FO.899/2.

228. Simon, "Note by the Attorney-General," 15 February 1915, 18193, FO.382/185; Harcourt, cabinet notes, 10 February 1915, Ms.Dep. 6231.

229. Harcourt, cabinet notes, 18 February 1915 (first meeting), Ms.Dep. 6231.

230. Churchill to Runciman, 12 February 1915, f.58, Runciman Mss. 301; see also Churchill to Runciman, 13 February 1915, f.61, and 16 February 1915, f.62, Runciman Mss. 301. Generally, see Cameron Hazlehurst, *Politicians at War, July 1914 to May 1915: A Prologue to the Triumph of Lloyd George* (London: Jonathan Cape, 1971), 188–89.

231. HC Deb, 15 February 1915, vol. 69, c.938.

232. Cabinet letter, 17 February 1915, CAB.41/36/5.

233. Hobhouse diary, 16 February 1915, f.6, Add.Mss. 60507.

234. Asquith to Stanley, 11:15 a.m., 18 February 1915, LVS, 437. Minutes of the War Council held on 19 February 1915 record no discussion of the reprisals policy, the session being devoted to discussion of the Dardanelles operation.

235. Asquith to Stanley, 7:30 p.m., 18 February 1915, LVS, 437–38.

236. Ibid.; Pease diary, 25 February 1915, Gainford Mss. 40; cabinet meeting, 18 February 1915, CAB.41/36/6; cabinet meeting, 24 February 1915, CAB.41/36/7.

237. Link, *Wilson,* 3:218. The first meeting between House and Grey took place on 7 February 1915.

238. Harcourt, cabinet notes, 25 February 1915, Ms.Dep. 6231.

239. Asquith to Stanley, 17 February 1915, LVS, 435; see also Admiralty, "Observations upon the United States Note of the 22nd February, 1915," 28 February 1915, CAB.1/11.

240. SC, 1:359–68; HMS, 1:157–58.

241. Arthur Nicholson to Grey, 24 February 1915, f.23, FO.800/95.

242. Hankey to Asquith, 25 February 1915, ff.177–79, FO.800/90.

243. ESRC, 43rd Report, 25 February 1915, 160–61, ADM.137/2989.

244. HC Deb., 1 March 1915, vol. 70, c.589–623, Mr. Asquith.

245. Ibid., c.600.

246. Ibid.

247. "Declaration Made by His Majesty's Government and Communicated to Neutral Governments," 1 March 1915, in Kenneth Bourne, D. Cameron Watt, and David Stevenson, eds., *British Documents on Foreign Affairs,* part II, series H, volume 5, part 1 (Frederick, MD: University Publications of America, 1989), docs. 27, 34.

248. Wilson remarks at press conference, 2 March 1915, PWW, 32:306–9.

249. Bryant to Wilson, 3 March 1915, enclosing draft telegram to Walter Page, PWW, 32:311–12; telegram 223 (5 March 1915, 5:00 p.m.), State to Page, FRUS, 1915 Supp., 132–33; Asquith to Stanley, 12 March 1915, LVS, letter 345, 474–75; Link, *Wilson,* 3:337.

250. Emmott diary, 3 March 1915, f.179, Emmott Mss. 2. The cabinet working paper (circulated 3 March 1915) was composed by Admiral Slade, Hopwood, and Captain Webb; see CAB.1/11/40.

251. Harcourt, cabinet notes, 2 March 1915, Ms.Dep. 6231.

252. Hobhouse Diary 4 March 1915, f.11, Add.Mss. 60507; Emmott diary 3 March 1915, f.179, Emmott Mss. 2.

253. Pease diary, 4 March 1915, Gainford Mss. 40.

254. Hobhouse diary, 2 March 1915, f.9, and 4 March 1915, f.11, Add.Mss. 60507; Diary 3 March 1915, f.179, Emmott 2; Grey to Churchill, 27 February 1915, f.315, FO.800/88.

255. Minute (3 March 1915) by Crowe, 23815, FO.382/185.

256. Churchill, "A Note on Blockade," for cabinet, 5 March 1915, CAB.37/125/16.

257. Ibid.

258. Note, "Proposed Destruction of German Harvest" and other topics, 24 February 1915, CAB.42/1/42. The idea was nevertheless revived in April 1915, for which see Hankey, "Proposed Devastation of the Enemy's Crops," 1 April 1915, CID 217-B, CAB.4/5.

259. Cabinet letter, 27 April 1915, CAB.41/36/18.

260. Hobhouse diary, 28 April 1915, f.23, Add.Mss. 60507.

261. Hankey, "Notes on Lord Crewe's Memorandum June 18, 1915," 23 June 1915, CAB.37/130/25; Hankey diary, 2 June 1915, HNKY.1/1.

262. Minute (9 March 1915) by Crowe, "Retaliatory Measures against Germany," 27501, FO.382/185.

263. Additional minute (11 March 1915) by Crowe on "Retaliatory Measures Against Germany," 27501, FO.382/185. This makes clear Britain told France she would wait no lon-

ger. The 12 March 1915 issue of the *Gazette* was not actually published until Monday, 15 March.

264. Grey, "Retaliation Policy against Germany," for cabinet, 17 July 1915, FO.899/2.

265. Minute (13 March 1915) by DTD, in "Effectiveness of Blockade," ADM.137/2734.

266. HC Deb, 1 March 1915, vol. 70, c.600–601.

267. Ibid.

268. Asquith to Stanley, 6 February 1915, LVS, 416. Proposals were framed and agreed by a meeting of Churchill, McKenna, Runciman, Simon, Hopwood, Leverton Harris, and Captain Richard Webb; see Churchill to Grey, 4 February 1915, CHAR.13/47/2.

269. Minute (31 July 1915) by Crowe, after interview with M. de Fleurian, in "The Maritime Policy of His Majesty's Government," 104590, FO.382/464.

270. Bonar Law's remarks reported in Page to Wilson, 10 March 1915, PWW, 32:357–63; for the support of Lansdowne and Bonar Law, see Harcourt, cabinet notes, 10 February 1915, Ms.Dep. 6231.

271. Balfour to Hankey, 17 February 1915, f.169, Add.Mss. 49703.

272. Ibid.

9. A Management Problem

Epigraph: Maurice Pascal Alers Hankey, *The Supreme Command, 1914–1918,* 2 vols. (London: Allen and Unwin, 1961), 1:355.

1. Hobhouse diary, 4 March 1915, f.11, Add.Mss. 60507; Emmott diary, 3 March 1915, f.179, Emmott Mss. 2.

2. Foreign Office, "Recommendations as to Carrying the Retaliation Policy into Effect" (for cabinet), 10 March 1915, FO.899/9.

3. Ibid.

4. Foreign Office (Maurice de Bunsen) to Cornhill Committee (RH Brand), 30 March 1915, box 114, Brand Mss.; Foreign Office to Cornhill Committee, 18 March 1915, enclosing copies of all correspondence between Grey and Spring Rice over special concessions given to cotton, esp. Telegram 190.C (10 March 1915), Brand Mss.; Arthur S. Link, "The Cotton Crisis, the South, and Anglo-American Diplomacy, 1914–1915," in J. Carlyle Sitterson, ed., *Studies in Southern History* (Chapel Hill: University of North Carolina Press, 1957), 133.

5. "Note by Mr. Hurst on the Question of Claims for Detention of Vessels and Goods," 30 July 1915, attached as appendix to "The Future Procedure as to the Terms upon Which Vessels and Goods Placed in the Prize Court Might Be Released," 9 August 1915, CAB.42/3/14.

6. Grey to Churchill, 27 February 1915, f.315, FO.800/88; the new orders are found in CMO.84/1915, NLMD.

7. H. W. Carless Davis, *History of the Blockade: Emergency Departments* (printed for official information only, March 1921, copy at NLMD), 7.

8. Commander M. Anderson, "Blockade: Stoppage of Goods of German Ownership," 5 July 1916, AWS (TD) 2233, ff.33–34, and attached minute (28 June 1916) by Anderson, ff.29–30, ADM.137/1212. Anderson was Admiralty liaison officer to the Foreign Office–based enemy export committee.

9. Ibid.

10. Viscount Grey of Fallodon (Sir Edward Grey), *Twenty-Five Years: 1892–1916,* 2 vols. (New York: Frederick Stokes, 1925), 2:107.

11. Ibid.

12. McKenna, "Confidential Memorandum by the Chancellor on the Financial Situation," 29 July 1915, MCKN.5/8. In addition, see Kathleen Burk, *Britain, America, and the Sinews of War, 1914–1918* (London: Allen and Unwin, 1985), 63–65; Martin Farr, "A Compelling Case for Volunteerism: Britain's Alternative Strategy, 1915–1916," *War in History* 9, no. 3 (2002): 279–306.

13. F. H. Hinsley, ed., *The Foreign Policy of Sir Edward Grey* (Cambridge: Cambridge University Press, 1977).

14. For the expansion in Admiralty personnel see Nicholas Black, *The British Naval Staff in the First World War* (Woodbridge, UK: Boydell Press, 2009).

15. Grant-Duff diary, 12 October 1910, AGDF.2/1.

16. Autobiographical notes, Hall Mss (CCC) 3/2.

17. CID (Hankey), "Draft Report of the Interdepartmental Committee on Trading with the Enemy," 27 February 1915, CAB.42/1/46.

18. Telegram (13 March 1915) 121.C, Spring Rice to Grey, 36586, FO.382/422; copy in ADM.137/2806.

19. Guy Gaunt, *The Yield of the Years* (London: Hutchinson, 1940).

20. This was not routine in October 1914. See Scott (Washington Embassy) to Bennett (CG New York), 13 October 1914, FO.115/1829; memo entitled "Naval Intelligence Organization Abroad," NID 10388/21, section A, "Outline 1893–1914," enclosed in Admiralty Intelligence Division to head of naval intelligence Australia, June 1921, MP1587/189D, Australian Archives. The prewar organization was severely understaffed, consisting of just fifteen officers and six clerks. During the war this organization was rapidly expanded into twenty-eight centers employing 170 staff; for details on the creation of a new center in September 1914 to service the eastern United States, see Admiralty to Foreign Office, 8 September 1914, "Naval Intelligence, New Center at St. John's Newfoundland," ff.142–55, 47595 and 55238, FO.371/2174.

21. McCormick-Goodhart, "Consideration of Ships—Manifests before Arrival of Most in UK Waters," 1 March 1915, ADM.137/2863; Spring Rice to Grey, 13 March 1915, 36586, FO.382/422.

22. Further minute (1 or 2 April 1915) by Davidson, on "Shipments of Contraband from the United States," 36586, FO.382/422; Foreign Office to War Trade Department, 17 March 1915, 29291, FO.382/449.

23. Minutes (28 July 1915) by Craigie, Sanderson, Hurst, and Crowe, on "Ships Manifests," 101289, FO.382/454; also minute (21 August 1915) by Craigie, on "Manifests," 116091, FO.382/454.

24. Board of Trade to Foreign Office, 19 August 1915, and reply dated 4 September 1915, both in 116091, FO.382/454.

25. Carless Davis, *History of the Blockade,* 200–210; Admiralty, office note on "The N.E.T. Index," ff.2–5, ADM.1/8408/1.

26. Minutes (14 May 1915) by Alwyn Parker and Eyre Crowe, on "Restriction Committee" report No. 49, 49845, FO.382/433.

27. Grey, "Memorandum," 26 July 1915, for cabinet, CAB.37/131/42.

28. Draft, "Minutes of the Meeting," chaired by Mr. Penson, discussing centralization of trade intelligence conference, 13 March 1916, ADM.137/2735.

29. Ibid., remarks by Mr. Simkin.

30. McCormick-Goodhart, "Consideration of Ships—Manifests before Arrival of Most in UK Waters," 1 March 1915, ADM.137/2863.

31. Further memorandum by McCormick-Goodhart to DTD, 3 March 1915, ADM.137/2863.

32. Ibid.

33. Minute (12 March 1915) by Webb, ADM.137/2863.

34. Minute (12 March 1915) by Lt. L. McCormick-Goodhart attached to agenda for meeting to be held in Room 9 (O.B.), signed by Webb, 12 March 1915, ADM.137/2863.

35. Minute (14 March 1915) by Webb, on memo by Commander Thomas Fisher (T.3 section) of 13 March 1915, ADM.137/2734.

36. "Note by Mr. Hurst on the Question of Claims for Detention of Vessels and Goods," 30 July 1915, attached as appendix to "The Future Procedure as to the Terms upon Which Vessels and Goods Placed in the Prize Court Might be Released," 9 August 1915, CAB.42/3/14.

37. Ibid. Demurrage charges alone were estimated in August 1915 at over £1 million.

38. Notes on meeting held on 13 April 1915 between Grey, Simon, Runciman, Hurst, and procurator general, 15 April 1915, f.129, Cave Papers, Add.Mss. 62465.

39. Victor Wellesley, *Diplomacy in Fetters* (London: Hutchinson, 1944).

40. Minute (12 March 1915) by O. G. Sargent addressed to Parker, 29291, FO.382/449.

41. See minutes attached to file "Shipments of Contraband from the United States," 36586, FO.382/422.

42. For timing, see footnote to minute (1 April 1915) by Davidson (referencing file 29291), 36586, FO.382/422.

43. Sargent to Parker, 12 March 1915, attached to "Weekly Return of Articles Imported and Exported," 13 March 1915, 29291, FO.382/449.

44. Consul General New York (C. Bennett) to Spring Rice, 25 March 1915, 52155, FO.382/442.

45. Robert Craigie, "Memorandum Respecting the Restriction of the Imports of Certain Neutral States to Their Normal Peace Time Requirements," 1 May 1915, 70127, FO.382/460.

46. Hall to Consett, 15 June 1915, Hall Mss. (NLMD).

47. Telegram (7 July 1915), Foreign Office to Howard, No. 687, copy in ADM.137/2872.

48. Craigie to Parker (n.d. but stamped 31070/17 March 1915), attached to memo by Leverton Harris (Admiralty), "Copper Licenses from the United Kingdom to Sweden," 10 March 1915, 28834, FO.382/448.

49. Admiralty, note on "The N.E.T. Index," ff.2–5, ADM.1/8408/1.

50. Carless Davis, *History of the Blockade,* 200–208.

51. Ibid., 208.

52. War Trade Statistical Department, 1st Report, 3 August 1915, TS.14/81.

53. Ibid.

54. Minute (21 August 1915) by Craigie, on "Manifests," 116091, FO.382/454; see also minutes (28 July 1915) by Craigie, Sanderson, Hurst, and Crowe, on "Ships Manifests," 101289, FO.382/454.

55. Cecil to Beatty, 27 February 1917, f.292, ADM.137/1933.

56. Paget to Crowe, 12 September 1916, f.24, Add.Mss. 51254. Paget made the same point is a letter addressed to Lord Robert Cecil, 20 August 1916, f.8, Paget papers, Add.Mss. 51254.

57. Treasury Minute, "Co-ordination of Arrangements for Trade Restrictions: Creation of the War Trade Department and Transfer of Other Work Hitherto Performed by the Committee on Trade with the Enemy to the Office of the Parliamentary Counsel—Provision of Accommodation, Selection and Pay of Staff, Financial Arrangements," and "Treasury Minute Dated the 17th February 1915," T4768/19, February 1915, T1/11862.

58. Carless Davis, *History of the Blockade,* 122.

59. Report, "The Trade Clearing House—a Brief Account of Its Development and Function," section "Finance Section," 20, 136095/ 22 September 1915, FO.382/470; by August 1915 the daily average had passed 1,900. See also Carless Davis, *History of the Blockade,* 122, 147.

60. Emmott to Hankey, 27 March 1915, reproduced as an appendix to CID paper 218-B, 12 April 1915, CAB.42/2/48.

61. Emmott diary, 5 April 1915, f.187, Emmott Mss. 2.

62. Harcourt, cabinet notes, 30 March 1915, Mss.Dep.6231.

63. Hobhouse diary, n.d. (March 1915), f.14, Add.Mss. 60507.

64. Emmott diary, 5 April 1915, f.187, Emmott Mss. 2. The antipathy between Churchill and Emmott dates to the 1899 Oldham by-election. I am indebted to Cameron Hazlehurst for this information.

65. Minutes of meeting held at 6:30 p.m. on 30 March 1915 in Mr. McKenna's room at the Home Office, CID 218-B, 12 April 1915, CAB.42/2/48.

66. Emmott to Hankey, 27 March 1915, reproduced as appendix to CID 218-B, 12 April 1915, CAB.42/2/48.

67. Minutes of meeting held at 6:30 p.m. on 30 March 1915 in Mr. McKenna's room at the Home Office, CID 218-B, 12 April 1915, CAB.42/2/48. Between the outbreak of war and 21 February 1915, about 66,000 export licenses were issued; see Carless Davis, *History of the Blockade,* 122.

68. Minutes of meeting held at 6:30 p.m. on 30 March 1915 in Mr. McKenna's room at the Home Office, CID 218-B, 12 April 1915, CAB.42/2/48.

69. Emmott diary, 5 April 1915, Emmott Mss. 2.

70. Minutes of meeting held at 6:30 p.m. on 30 March 1915 in Mr. McKenna's room at the Home Office, CID 218-B, 12 April 1915, CAB.42/2/48.

71. The evidence is reviewed in Skinner to Lansing, 11 October 1915, enclosing "Memorandum from the British Embassy to the Department of State," FRUS, 1915 Supp., 566–69.

72. Marion Siney, "British Negotiations with American Meat Packers, 1915–1917: A Study of Belligerent Trade Controls," *Journal of Modern History* 23, no. 4 (December 1951): 343–53; see also summary of memorandum by Treasury Solicitor's Department summarizing negotiations, contained at front of TS.13/15A.

73. Churchill to Grey, 23 April 1915, f.342, FO.800/88.

74. Emmott to Grey, 7 May 1915, f.552, FO.800/102.

75. Emmott to Asquith, 11 May 1915, Emmott Mss. 5/290; Emmott diary, 5 April 1915, f.187, Emmott Mss. 2.

76. Runciman to Emmott, 26 March 1915, Emmott Mss. 5/282.

77. Churchill to Grey, 23 April 1915, f.342, FO.800/88; Emmott to Balfour, 1 September 1915, Emmott 5/374.

78. Minute (24 July 1915) by Llewellyn Smith, on Barnes to Runciman, 23 July 1915, f.195, Asquith Mss. 29.

79. Grey to Rosebery, 7 February 1915, Rosebery Mss. I am indebted to Keith Neilson for this reference.

80. Crowe to Grey, 12 August 1915, attached to Board of Trade statistical report, 108933, FO.382/464.

81. Emmott to Runciman, 21 July 1915, f.17, Runciman Mss. 113.

82. Emmott to Asquith, 13 August 1915, f.173, Asquith Mss. 29.

83. Ibid.

84. "Memorandum Communicated to Swedish Minister," 38487, 12 April 1915, copy ADM.137/2791.

85. Runciman to Grey, 30 January 1915, enclosing extract of minute, f.230, FO800/89.

86. Carless-Davis, *History of the Blockade,* 127.

87. Emmott, memorandum, prepared for Lord Crewe, n.d. (ca. June 1915), Emmott 5/307. This paper is similar to a letter Emmott wrote to the cabinet about two months later: Emmott, "Policy of the War Trade Department," 6 August 1915, CAB.37/131/8.

88. Emmott, memorandum sent to Asquith, 13 August 1915, Emmott 5/357.

89. Ibid.

90. Hankey to Asquith, 21 May 1915, (37) "Memorandum on the War Trade Machinery," CAB.63/5.

91. Ibid.; see also minute (22 July 1915) by Asquith, on Montagu to Asquith, 19 July 1915, f.162, Asquith Mss. 29; Hankey to Asquith, 20 July 1915, f.120, Asquith Mss. 117.

92. Hankey to Asquith, 21 May 1915, para. 4, (37) "Memorandum on the War Trade Machinery," CAB.63/5.

93. Copy, minute (21 February 1915) by Phillpotts to Howard, miscellaneous folder, Trade Division Papers, ADM.137/2791.

94. Howard to Grey, 29 March 1915, 144 Commercial, copy, ADM.137/2791.

95. Crowe to Howard, 27 March 1915 (misdated 1914), Howard papers, DHW.4/Official/6 (Howard of Penrith papers, Cumbria Record Office, UK); see also B. J. C. McKercher and Keith Neilson, "The Triumph of Unarmed Forces: Sweden and the Allied Blockade of Germany, 1914–1917," *Journal of Strategic Studies* 7, no. 2 (June 1984): 178–99; for other evidence of Foreign Office awareness of Swedish duplicity, see minute (3 June 1915) by Crowe, 70924, FO.382/267.

96. Crowe to Howard, 27 March 1915 (misdated 1914), Howard papers, DHW.4/Official/6. See also minutes by Craigie (13 March 1915) and Parker (16 March 1915), on Vansittart, "Copper Licenses," 28834, FO.382/448.

97. Minute (10 January 1915) by Crowe, on 3581/113, FO.382/264.

98. Hopwood to Crewe, 15 June 1915, f.382, FO.800/88.

99. Ibid.

100. A selection can be found in file 113, FO.382/266. See also telegram (24 March 1915), Grey to Howard, and telegram (29 March 1915), Howard to Grey, in Kenneth Bourne, D. Cameron Watt, and David Stevenson, eds., *British Documents on Foreign Affairs,* part II, series

H, volume 5, part 1 (Frederick, MD: University Publications of America, 1989), docs. 54 and 55, pp. 63–64.

101. McKercher and Neilson, "The Triumph of Unarmed Forces," 178–99.

102. Jellicoe to Admiralty, 20 March 1915, ADM.137/1917.

103. Enclosure in Home Fleet letter 532/HF-0022 of 20 March 1915, ADM.137/1917; Grey, note to cabinet, 21 January 1915, CAB.37/123/44.

104. Admiralty to Jellicoe, 1 May 1915, ff.120–22, ADM.137/1917.

105. Jellicoe to Admiralty, 19 May 1915, ff.122–26, and also concurrence of Vice Admiral S. C. Colville (admiral commanding Orkneys and Shetlands) to Jellicoe, 18 May 1915, f.101, both ADM.137/1917.

106. The only reference to blockade in their entire correspondence for 1915 (private and official) is a single line in Fisher to Churchill, 27 April 1915, CHAR.13/57/17.

107. Fisher to Jellicoe, 4 April 1915 and n.d. (2 April 1915), FGDN, 3:183–86.

108. Keith Neilson, *Strategy and Supply: The Anglo-Russian Alliance, 1914–1917* (London: Allen and Unwin, 1984), 43–85.

109. Howard to Grey, 14 January 1915, reporting terms of Swedish Royal Proclamation of 9 January 1915, 4866/113, FO.382/264.

110. Telegram (26 February 1915), Buchanan to Grey, 113/22930, FO.382/264. This was sent in reply to telegram (20 January 1915) No. 33, 6406, FO.382/264.

111. Telegram (27 February 1915), Buchanan to Grey, 113/22930, FO.382/264.

112. Carless Davis, *History of the Blockade,* 207.

113. Minute (3 April 1915) by Vansittart, 36855/113, FO.382/265.

114. Howard to Grey, 13 April 1915, No. 180 commercial, 47312, in Bourne, Watt, and Stevenson, *British Documents on Foreign Affairs,* doc. 84, pp. 96–98.

115. Minute (14 April 1915) by Grey, "Contraband," 44370, copy, ADM.137/2791; Fisher to Jellicoe, 14 April 1915, 5:00 a.m., FGDN, 3:195; see also memorandum from Swedish minister dated 14 April 1915, 44370, FO.382/265; hearing of the High Court of Justice (Probate, Divorce and Admiralty Division) before the Rt. Hon. Sir Samuel Evans, Wednesday, 25 August 1915, in John Bridge Aspinall, ed., *Lloyd's Report of Prize Cases Heard before and Decided by the Right Honourable Sir Samuel Evans during the European War, Which Began in August 1914,* 6 vols. (London: Lloyd's, 1915–1920), copy in NLMD.

116. Telegram, urgent, Grey to Buchanan (St. Petersburg), 17 April 1915, 44370, in Bourne, Watt, and Stevenson, *British Documents on Foreign Affairs,* doc. 81, p. 90.

117. Minute (16 April 1915) by Grey, also minutes by Parker (15 April) and Crowe (16 April) recommending this action, 44370, FO.382/265. For the legation's distress, see Howard to Crowe, 10 June 1915, Howard DHW.5/6, and Crowe's reply dated 7 July 1915, DHW.4/official/7. See also McKercher and Neilson, "The Triumph of Unarmed Forces." The problem with Crowe's explanation is that the events he described took place in early March, for which see 28834, FO382/448; also Grey to Emmott, 15 March 1915, f.546, FO.800/102.

118. Money, "Memorandum on Sweden . . . ," 25 April 1915, 50914/113, FO.382/265. In December, Money produced another very similar memo: "Ministry of Munitions, Memorandum on German Imports through Holland and Scandinavia, by Sir Leo Chiozza Money, MP," 2 December 1915, distributed at 10th meeting of WTAC, 193053, FO.382/433.

119. Committee of Unionist MPs to Grey, 4 May, 27 May, and 5 June 1915, in "Restriction of Enemy's Supplies," 71048, FO.382/455. See also E. M. Pollock (committee of MPs) to Grey, 27 May 1915, 71048, and 5 June 1915, 74923, FO.382/455.

120. See, for instance, memorandum sent to the Foreign Office: Leverton Harris, "Copper Licenses from the United Kingdom to Sweden (and Neutral Countries)," 10 March 1915, 28834, FO.382/448.

121. See, for instance, Consett to Hall, 3 February 1915, T25180, Hall Mss. (NLMD).

122. Consett to Paget, 27 December 1916, f.145, Add.Mss. 51254.

123. Paget to Cecil, 15 October 1916, f.41, Add.Mss. 51254.

124. Consett to Hall, 26 July 1915, T25269, Hall Mss. (NLMD); Paget to Campbell, 22 November 1916, f.95, Paget papers, Add.Mss. 51254; Paget to Hardinge, 25 November 1916, f.121, Add.Mss. 51254.

125. See Minute (15 July 1915) by Crowe, on Findlay (Christiania) to Grey, 7 July 1915, No. 416 Commercial, enclosing memorandum by Captain Consett, 7 July 1915, 93622, FO.382/480.

126. Howard to Crowe, 10 June 1915, Howard Mss. DHW/5/6.

127. Howard to Hilaire Belloc, 15 September 1923, DHW/9/3.

128. Manfred Findlay (Minister in Christiania from 1914) and sir Ralph Paget (Minister in Copenhagen from 1916) both seemingly disliked though respected Consett. See Paget to Consett, 21 October 1916, f.57, and Paget to Cecil, 8 December 1916, f.128, Add.Mss. 51254; Paget to Cecil, 2 January 1917, f.4, and 16 January 1917, f.24, Add.Mss. 51255A; Findlay to Paget, 28 August 1916, f.15, Add.Mss. 51254.

129. Consett to Hall, 29 April 1915, Hall Mss. (NLMD).

130. Hall to Consett, 11 May 1915, Hall Mss. (NLMD).

131. Hall to Consett, 15 June 1915, Hall Mss. (NLMD).

132. First indications of concern are found in Grey to Emmott, 15 March 1915, f.546, FO.800/102.

133. Minute (19 May 1915) by Davidson, on Johnson (The Hague) to Foreign Office, No. 635, 11 May 1915, "Sources of German Supplies," 59664, FO.382/435. The subject of the paper was potatoes.

134. Minute (21 May 1915) by Crowe, 59664, FO.382/435.

135. Minutes by Hurst (21 May 1915) and by Sargent (24 May 1915), 59664, FO.382/435.

136. Minutes by Hurst (26 May), by Sargent (28 May), and by Pearson and Crowe (3 June 1915), 59664, FO.382/435.

137. Minute (26 May) by Hurst, 59664, FO.382/435.

138. Webb (DTD), "Note on Mr. Cohen's Letter to the First Sea Lord," 9 June 1915, ADM.137/2735; see also Hopwood to Crewe, 15 June 1915, f.382, FO.800/88.

139. Minute (3 June 1915) by Huggesson, "Raw Rubber from Malmo to Lubeck," 113/70924, FO.382/267.

140. Crowe to Howard, 7 July 1915, DHW/4/Official/7.

141. Minute (3 June 1915) by Parker, 71007, and minute (3 June 1915) by Sargent, 70924, both FO.382/267.

142. See Board of Trade to Foreign Office, 30 April 1915, 52575, and contrast with Board of Trade to Foreign Office, 4 May 1915, 54075, both in Bourne, Watt, and Stevenson, *British Documents on Foreign Affairs,* doc. 105, p. 128 and doc. 112, p. 144.

143. Minute (3 June 1915) by Crowe, 70924, both FO.382/267.

144. Hopwood to Crewe, 15 June 1915, f.382, FO.800/88.

145. HC Deb, 9 June 1915, vol. 72, c.274–5W, c.275–6W (written answers, "Cotton Imports, Scandinavia and Netherlands and Neutral Countries"). See also remarks on this subject by Mr. Pennefather in minutes of "Meeting of Unionist Business Men at the House of Commons," 23 June 1915, 85180, FO.382/455.

146. Minutes of "Meeting of Unionist Business Men at the House of Commons," 23 June 1915, 85180, FO.382/455.

147. Minute (10 June 1915) by Nicholson: similarly dismissive attitudes are displayed in minutes by Leslie (7 June), Pearson (9 June), and Crowe (10 June), all on "Restrictions of Enemy's Supplies," 71048 (also remarks 23 June 1915 on 85180), FO.382/455.

148. Norman Rose, *Vansittart: Study of a Diplomat* (London: Heinemann, 1978), 41.

149. Vansittart to Grey, 29 July 1915, 107118, FO.382/448.

150. Crowe to Howard, 7 July 1915, DHW.4/official/7.

151. Foreign Office, minute by Mr. Parker, 19 August 1915, for cabinet, CAB.37/132/31.

152. Minute (22 July 1915) by Frederick E. F. Adam (junior clerk in section 5 of contraband department), on "Treatment of American Trade," 98394, FO.382/464.

153. Notes by L. V. Harcourt, 30 July 1914, Mss.Dep.6231.

154. Cabinet letter, 15 August 1915, CAB.41/35/30.

155. Elliot to Vansittart, 26 April 1915, enclosing statistics on coal exports to various countries, August 1913 to March 1915, 50316, FO.382/453.

156. Harcourt, cabinet notes, 23 March 1915, Ms.Dep. 6231.

157. On this point, see minute (28 April 1915) by Vansittart, in "Monthly Exports of Coal from UK," 50316, FO.382/453.

158. Asquith to Stanley, 23 April 1915, LVS, 568.

159. HC Deb, 20 April 1915, vol. 71, c.173–74, Mr. Anderson, Mr. Duncan Millar. For a general overview, see Alan Redmayne, *The British Coal-Mining Industry during the War* (Oxford: Clarendon Press, 1923), 22–28.

160. Board of Trade (Fountain) to Foreign Office, 22 April 1915, in "Export of Coal from UK to Neutral Countries," 47826, FO.382/453.

161. Ibid.

162. Foreign Office to Board of Trade, 22 April 1915, 47826, FO.382/453. Membership included Russell Rea, MP (Liverpool merchant and shipowner), Sir Douglas Owen, Sir Richard Redmayne (chief inspector of mines and managing director of Durham colliery), and E. J. Elliot (secretary).

163. Foreign Office to Board of Trade, 22 April 1915, 47826, FO.382/453.

164. Minute (27 April 1915) by Huggessen to Crowe, in "Monthly Exports of Coal from UK," 50316, FO.382/453.

165. Minutes (28 April 1915) by Sargent, Vansittart, and Pearson, and (29 April 1915) by Crowe, 50316, FO.382/453.

166. Ibid.

167. Note list "How Disposed Of" on the front page of the docket, ibid.

168. See telegrams to ministers in Norway, Denmark, Holland, Italy, Spain, Portugal, and Greece annexed to Foreign Office Print (by E. J. H. Leslie), "Memorandum Respecting the

Treatment to Be Accorded to Certain Neutral Countries in Regard to the Export of Coal from the United Kingdom," 11 May 1915, 61207, FO.382/453.

169. Elliot (Coal Committee) to Leslie (Foreign Office), 18 May 1915, and minute (19 May 1915) by Leslie, on "Coal Committee," 62850, FO.382/453.

170. Minute by Vansittart (21 May 1915) and by G. S. Sanderson and Crowe (22 May 1915), 62850, FO.382/453.

171. Coal Export Committee to Foreign Office, 21 May 1915, 64405, FO.382/453.

172. Ibid.

173. See minutes by Leslie (n.d., ca. 23 May 1915), by Vansittart (25 May 1915), by Parker (26 May 1915), and by Crowe (27 May 1915), all on "Export of Coal to Neutral Countries," 64405, FO.382/453.

174. Crowe to Admiralty, 16 June 1915, 71360, FO.382/477; minutes by Sergeant (9 June 1915) and by Pearson (14 June 1915), on "Export of Coal to the Baltic Ports of Sweden," 71360, FO.382/477.

175. Coal Export Committee to War Trade Department, 1 June 1915, 71360, FO.382/477.

176. Ibid.

177. Minutes by Huggessen (15 June 1915), Vansissart (15 June 1915), and Parker (16 June 1915), all on "Export of Coal to the Baltic Ports of Sweden," 71360, FO.382/477. See also Foreign Office to Admiralty, 16 June 1915, 71360, FO.382/477.

178. Consett to Hall, 23 September 1915, Hall Mss. (NLMD).

179. Howard to Crowe, 4 December 1915, Howard Mss. DHW/5/6.

180. Consett to Hall, 7 July 1915, enclosing attaché report dated 7 July 1915, and Hall to Consett, 25 August 1915, Hall Mss. (NLMD) (note reference to previous report on this subject dated 8 June 1915); Montagu Consett, *The Triumph of Unarmed Forces: An Account of the Transactions by Which Germany during the Great War Was Able to Obtain Supplies Prior to Her Collapse under the Pressure of Economic Forces* (London: Williams and Norgate, 1923), 136.

181. Consett to Hall, 7 July 1915, enclosed with Findlay (Christiania) to Grey, 7 July 1915 (No. 416 Commercial), 93622, FO.382/480.

182. Report, 22 July 1915, FO.382/480.

183. Consett to Hall, 26 July 1915, Hall Mss. (NLMD).

184. Minute (13 July 1915) by Huggessen, on "Coal Supplies for Scandinavia," 93662, FO.382/480; also minute (29 July 1915) by Huggessen, "Supply of German Coal to Scandinavia via Stettin," 102341, FO.382/480.

185. Minutes by Alwyn Parker (14 July 1915) and by Crowe (15 July 1915), 93662, FO.382/480.

186. Minute (13 July 1915) by E. H. J. Leslie, on "Coal Supplies for Scandinavia," 93662, FO.382/480.

187. Grey, note to cabinet, 23 September 1915, on history of negotiations with Sweden, FO.899/9/188.

188. See Chapter 10.

189. Hall to Consett, 25 August 1915, Hall Mss. (NLMD).

190. Webb to Hall, 6 November 1915, Hall Mss. (NLMD).

191. Webb (DTD), "Note on Mr. Cohen's Letter to the First Sea Lord," 9 June 1915, ADM. 137/2735.

192. Ibid.

193. Ibid.

194. Admiralty to Foreign Office, 11 May 1915, 58439, FO.382/453; see also Admiralty to Foreign Office, 10 July 1915, in "SS Disa and SS Wilton and Bunker Coal at UK Ports," 93279, FO.382/477.

195. Minute (16 May 1915) by Crowe, on Admiralty to Foreign Office, 11 May 1915, on "Neutral Vessels Supplying Coal to and Trading on Behalf of Germans (as 'Etna' and 'Vulcano')," 58439, FO.382/453.

196. Minute (9 June 1915) by Sargent, on "Export of Coal to the Baltic Ports of Sweden," 71360, FO.382/477.

197. Minute (20 June 1915) by Vansittart, on "Bunkers for Norwegian Ships Visiting England," 79857, FO.382/480; Runciman to Balfour, 28 July 1915, f.7, and Webb to Runciman, 1 August 1915, "Memorandum," ff.9–13, Add.Mss. 49716.

10. The Summer of Discontent

1. Cameron Hazlehurst, *Politicians at War, July 1914 to May 1915: A Prologue to the Triumph of Lloyd George* (London: Jonathan Cape, 1971), 157–59.

2. Ibid., 188–91.

3. Michael J. Turner, *British Politics in an Age of Reform* (Manchester: Manchester University Press, 1999), 83–85.

4. Committee of Unionist MPs to Grey, 4 May, 27 May, and 5 June 1915, in "Restriction of Enemy's Supplies," 71048, FO.382/455.

5. Ibid.

6. David French, "The Origins of the Dardanelles Campaign Reconsidered," *History*, July 1983, 210–24.

7. Asquith to Stanley, 30 March 1915, LVS, 520–21.

8. Fisher to Jellicoe, 26, 29, 31 (two letters) March 1915, Fisher to Churchill, 27 and 28 March 1915, FGDN, 3:171–81; Fisher to Churchill, 28 March 1915, WSC (companion part 2), 3:757–58; Asquith to Stanley, LVS, 30 March 1915, 520; Fisher to Jellicoe, 4 April 1915, f.2, Add. Mss. 49007; Asquith to Stanley, 7 April 1915, LVS, 535; Churchill to Fisher, 11 April 1915, CHAR.13/57/8; Fisher to Churchill, 12 April 1915, CHAR.13/57/10; Hankey, diary entries 15, 18, 19, and 20 April 1915, SC, 1:302.

9. Hankey diary, 6 April 1915, cited in SC, 1:300.

10. BESP, 159–67; Hazlehurst, *Politicians at War,* 228–30.

11. BESP, 165.

12. Asquith to Stanley, 16 April 1915, LVS, 544.

13. HC Deb, 4 May 1915, vol. 71, c.1015, Lloyd George.

14. For Asquith's sensitivity to this campaign, see Asquith to Stanley, 4 and 7 May 1915, LVS, 419, 583, 586.

15. *Times,* 6 May 1915, editorial; *Times,* 11 May 1915, letter to the editor by Lord Selborne.

16. Derby to Kitchener, 10 April 1915, Kitchener papers, PRO.30/57/73, as cited in John Gordon Little, "H. H. Asquith and Britain's Manpower Problem, 1914–1915," *History* 82, no. 267 (July 1997): 403.

17. The clearest articulations of these beliefs are found in slightly later documents: Asquith to Balfour, 18 September 1915, f.157, Add.Mss. 49692; Montagu to Asquith, 14 August and 22 October 1915, AS5/1/1 and AS5/1/2, Montagu Mss.; Runciman to Asquith, 30 December 1915, f.47, Runciman Mss.

18. Runciman to McKenna, 19 May 1915, ff.1–2, MCKN.5/8; Hobhouse diary, 19 May 1915, f.27, Add.Mss. 60507.

19. For Asquith's lack of communication with his junior ministers during the crisis (12 May to 25 May), see Runciman to Emmott, 26 May 1915, Emmott 5/282; Runciman to McKenna, 19 May 1915, ff.1–2, with postscript referring to conversations with Grey and Haldane, McKenna Mss. 5/8.

20. Asquith, letter to cabinet, 17 May 1915, CAB.37/128/19.

21. See also passage in Asquith to Stanley, 14 April 1915, LVS, 539–42.

22. Turner, *British Politics,* 61–63.

23. Lord Beaverbrook, *Politicians and the War, 1914–1916* (London: Lane, 1928), sees Fisher's resignation as the decisive factor. More recently the focus has switched to the shell crisis. See Martin Pugh, "Asquith, Bonar Law and the First Coalition," *Historical Journal* 17, no. 4 (1974): 813–36; George Cassar, *Asquith as War Leader* (London: Hambledon Press, 1994), 93–99. See also review of historiography in the otherwise unconvincing article by Stephan Koss, "The Destruction of Britain's Last Liberal Government," *Journal of Modern History* 40, no. 2 (1968): 257–77. Koss's overall thesis, however, was demolished by Hazlehurst in *Politicians at War,* who at the same time provided the essential framework of understanding of events employed by all subsequent historians. An important new detail of McKenna's role is cited in Martin Farr, *Reginald McKenna: Financier amongst Statesmen* (New York: Routledge, 2007), 257–286.

24. For Asquith accusing Fisher of deserting his post, see Asquith to Balfour, 20 May 1915, f.149, Add.Mss. 49692.

25. Hazlehurst, *Politicians at War,* 166–67. As early as 19 November 1914, War Office permanent secretary Sir Reginald Brade claimed that Kitchener was "worn out and cannot take the strain"; *Lord Riddle's War Diary, 1914–1918* (London: Ivor Nicholson and Watson, 1933), diary entry 19 November 1914, 41.

26. Violet Bonham Carter, *Winston Churchill as I Knew Him* (London: Collins, 1965), 318–22.

27. Lord Stamfordham to King George V, 19 May 1915, WSC (companion volume 2), 3:911–12, says Asquith referred to Fisher as "somewhat unhinged," and Asquith viewed Fisher's demands as "signs of mental aberration."

28. Review of evidence in HMS, 1:173–75.

29. For many years Churchill was unsure if Fisher's act was premeditated. See General Sir Ian Hamilton to Churchill, 30 June 1915, WSC (companion volume 2), 3:1064–65. By 1933 his views were very different; see Churchill to Roger Keyes, 17 August and 29 December 1933, f.17, 31, CHAR.2/203.

30. Fisher to Hankey, n.d. (12 May 1915), HNKY.5/2A.

31. Stephen Koss, "The Destruction of Britain's Last Liberal Government," *The Journal of Modern History* 40, no. 2 (June 1968): 257–77.

32. The phrase "trial of strength" comes from Rear-Admiral Alexander Duff's diary, 20 May 1915, as cited in Hazlehurst, *Politicians at War,* 255.

33. Riddle war diary, notes of conversation with Lloyd George, 23 May 1915, 93. In his memoirs, written in the 1930s, Lloyd George presented a slightly different version of events; see David Lloyd George, *War Memoirs of David Lloyd George,* 6 vols. (London: Ivor Nicholson and Watson, 1933–1937), 1:225; also Bonham Carter, *Churchill as I Knew Him,* 389.

34. Hobhouse diary, 17 May 1915, f.26, Add.Mss. 60507; see also Fisher to Asquith, 15 May 1915, (copy) FISR.1/9. Typescript note, McKenna to Fisher, 16 May 1915, MCKN.4/7.

35. The best account, remain those by Ruddock Mackay, *Fisher of Kilverstone* (Oxford: Clarendon Press, 1973), 496–505; and Cassar, *Asquith as War Leader,* 91–99.

36. Ironically, Fisher wrote to Bonar Law on 19 May 1915: "It is impossible to explain by letter the chicanery in progress!" Did he serious expect more from Bonar Law? See Bonar Law Papers 50/3/1.

37. Mackay, *Fisher of Kilverstone,* 502.

38. Harcourt, aide-mémoire, 25 May 1915, Ms.Dep. 6231.

39. The faulty advice came from his old friend Lord Esher in a conversation on 17 May, and two letters dated 17 and 20 May 1915; Mackay, *Fisher of Kilverstone,* 499–501. Even so, afterward Selborne and McKenna (both former First Lords) continued to insist that despite his faults Fisher was still by far the best qualified officer for the post. See Selborne to Balfour, 19 May 1915 (two letters), ff.243, 248, Add.Mss. 49708.

40. Fisher to Hankey, 29 May 1915, f.6, HNKY.5/2B. For Fisher's apology, see Fisher to Asquith, n.d. (17 June 1915), encl. in Asquith to Sylvia Henley, 19 June 1915 (box 1), Ms.Eng. lett. c.542. (Sylvia Henley papers, Bodleian Library, Oxford).

41. Asquith to Sylvia Henley, 19 June 1915 (box 1), Ms.Eng. lett. c.542.

42. See Pugh, "Asquith, Bonar Law and the First Coalition."

43. Crewe to Lloyd George, 24 May 1915, Lloyd George Mss, C/4/1/22, as cited in Hazlehurst, *Politicians at War,* 278–79.

44. Pugh, "Asquith, Bonar Law and the First Coalition," 830–31.

45. Ibid.

46. My thanks to Cameron Hazlehurst for clarifying my understanding of these events.

47. Turner, *British Politics,* 62–63.

48. On the subject of Ireland, for instance, see Asquith to Sylvia Henley, 7 and 9 June (two letters) 1915 (box 1), Ms.Eng. lett. c.542.

49. Cabinet letter, 28 May 1915 (covering meetings 27 and 28 May), CAB.37/129/25.

50. Harcourt, cabinet notes, 28 May 1915, Ms.Dep. 6231. See also Selborne, "Note on National Organization," 27 May 1915, f.1, Selborne Mss. 80.

51. Selborne, "Note on National Organization," 27 May 1915, f.1, Selborne Mss. 80.

52. Cabinet letter, 8 and 23 June 1915, CAB.37/129/21 and CAB.37/130/24; see also Little, "H. H. Asquith and Britain's Manpower Problem," 405. On the pro-conscription lobby being furious, see Gwynne to Long, 2 July 1915, letter 72, in Keith Wilson, ed., *The Rasp of War: The Letters of H. A. Gwynne to the Countess Bathhurst, 1914–1918* (London: Sidgwick and Jackson, 1988), 106.

53. Remark by Lord Selborne, minutes of the Dardanelles Committee, 25 June 1915, CAB.42/3/5; see also Selborne to Bonar Law, 7 July 1915, as cited in D. G. Boyce, ed., *The Crisis of British Unionism: Lord Selborne's Domestic Political Papers,* 2 vols. (London: The Historians Press, 1987), 1:130–32.

54. Balfour to Curzon, 19 June 1915, f.1, Add.Mss. 49734.

55. Asquith, Lansdowne, Curzon, Bonar Law, Kitchener, Balfour, Churchill, Selborne, and Crewe.

56. Cabinet letter, 8 June 1915, CAB.37/129/21; decision taken at meeting of the Dardanelles Committee (renamed War Council), 7 June 1915, CAB.42/3/1. N.b.: Hankey was deliberately excluded from this meeting, which meant no notes were taken.

57. Churchill to John Churchill (brother), 12 June 1915 (marked not sent), CHAR. 1/392/28.

58. Asquith to Sylvia Henley, 18 June 1915 (box 1), Ms.Eng. lett. c.542.

59. Harcourt, cabinet notes, 17 June 1915, Ms.Dep. 6231.

60. Cabinet letters, 16 and 18 June, CAB.37/130/2 and CAB.37/130/14.

61. Board of Trade (Llewellyn Smith), for cabinet, "Statistical Note on the Limits of Enlistment," 29 May 1915, CAB.37/128/28.

62. Ibid.

63. Board of Trade (Runciman), "Effect of Diminished Exports on Foreign Exchanges," 2 June 1915, CAB.37/129/4.

64. For unreliability of trade statistics at this time because they do not include figures for government purchases, see H.W. (Treasury), "The Financial Position in May: Report by Director of Financial Enquiries," 8 June 1915, CAB.37/129/23.

65. Board of Trade (Runciman), "Effect of Diminished Exports on Foreign Exchanges," 2 June 1915, CAB.37/129/4.

66. Unsigned, for cabinet, "Food Supplies of Germany," 2 June 1915, CAB.37/129/7. Listed in Public Record Office catalog as Foreign Office. A copy in the Runciman papers, however, complete with a covering note signed W[alter] R[unciman], shows beyond contestation that it was circulated by the Board of Trade and from internal evidence was probably written by the foreign intelligence section. See covering note by W.R. to "Food Supplies of Germany," 2 June 1915, f.20, Runciman Mss. 89.

67. Hankey to Fisher, 22 April 1915, copy in ff.90–92, Asquith 27.

68. Covering note, ibid.

69. Cabinet letters, 4 June 1915, CAB.37/129/9.

70. Hankey to Asquith, 5 June 1915, CAB.17/118.

71. Ibid.

72. Harcourt, cabinet notes, 4 June 1915, Ms.Dep. 6231.

73. Hankey to Webb, 22 May 1915, ADM.137/2735.

74. Minute (n.d.) by Webb on Hankey to Webb, 22 May 1915 (written between 22 and 28 May 1915), ADM.137/2735.

75. Webb to Hankey, 28 May 1915, ADM.137/2735.

76. Ibid.

77. Ibid. See also endorsement (28 May 1915) by Captain Longden (Admiralty representative to the Contraband Department), ibid.

78. Viscount Grey of Fallodon (Sir Edward Grey), *Twenty-Five Years: 1892–1916,* 2 vols. (New York: Frederick Stokes, 1925) 2:107.

79. Page to Grey, 2 April 1915, enclosure 1, copy for cabinet, CAB.37/129/15. Also Enclosure 3, "Draft Reply to Mr. Page's Note of April 2, 1915," CAB.37/129/15.

80. Spring Rice to Grey, 11 December 1914, f.448, FO.800/84; telegram (10 December 1914), Spring Rice to FO, No. 171 Commercial, f.102, 81393, FO.368/1162; Spring Rice dispatch from Washington, DC, 21 July 1915, Confidential 339, 3, printed for the cabinet, FO899/2.

81. Keith Neilson, "Sir Cecil Spring Rice and the United States, 1914–1917," in Christopher Baxter and Andrew Stewart, eds., *Diplomats at War: British and Commonwealth Diplomacy in Wartime* (Leiden: Martinus Nijhoff, 2008), 65–83. See, for instance, memo by Lord Eustace Percy addressed to Mr. Clerk, 17 July 1915, f.195, Grey Papers, FO.800/95; minute (16 November 1915) by Crowe, f.437, 172186, FO.382/12.

82. Minute (3 March 1915) by Crowe, on telegram (28 February 1915) by Spring Rice to FO, 23815, FO.382/185.

83. Minute (18 November 1915) by Crowe, and attached minutes (19 November 1915) by Cecil, Lord Crewe, and Sir Edward Grey, f.437, 172186, FO.382/12; Minute (28 January 1916) by Crowe, on "America and the Blockade," 16535, FO.382/1099; minutes (n.d.) by Grey and (2 February 1916) by Nicolson, on 18183, FO.371/2848; Montagu to Drummond, 28 February 1916, AS1/5/88(1), Montagu Mss.

84. Percy to Mr. Clerk, 17 July 1915, f.195, FO.800/95.

85. Wilson to Bryan, 24 March 1915, in FRUS, *The Lansing Papers, 1914–1920,* 2 vols. (Washington, DC: U.S. Government Printing Office, 1939), 1:288–89; Arthur S. Link, *Wilson,* vol. 3: *The Struggle for Neutrality, 1914–1915* (Princeton, NJ: Princeton University Press, 1960), 342–48.

86. John Coogan, *The End of Neutrality: The United States, Britain and Maritime Rights, 1899–1915* (Ithaca, NY: Cornell University Press, 1981), 229–36.

87. Bryan to Wilson, 22 March 1915, FRUS, *Lansing Papers*, 1:285–87.

88. Link, *Wilson,* 3:379, 390, 594–98.

89. Harcourt, cabinet notes, 13 April 1915, Ms.Dep. 6231.

90. Link, *Wilson,* 3:390, 594–98.

91. Memorandum by Grey, 7 May 1915, FO.899/9/131.

92. Telegram (5 May 1915), Wilson to House, Wilson Mss., as cited in Link, *Wilson,* 3:390.

93. Asquith to Stanley, 11 May 1915, LVS, letter 423, 590.

94. FO, "Memorandum Respecting American Ships and Cargoes Detained at British Ports," 14 May 1915, f.3, Add.Mss. 62466. The *Joseph W. Fordney* had been intercepted on 8 April.

95. Minutes by Davidson (19 May 1915), by Crowe (21 May 1915), by Hurst (26 May 1915), by Orme Sargent (28 May 1915), and by Pearson and Crowe (3 June 1915), on Johnson (The Hague) to FO, No. 635, 11 May 1915, "Sources of German Supplies," 59664, FO.382/435; Crowe to Nicholson, 11 June 1915, f.65. 77371, FO.382/12. The first to point out the danger was the Admiralty, for which see Leverton Harris (Admiralty), "Copper Licenses from the United Kingdom to Sweden," 10 March 1915, 28834, 382/448.

96. Minutes by Crowe (21 May 1915), 59664, FO.382/435, table 1, f.18.

97. Spring Rice to Grey, 26 March 1915, No. 137 Commercial, enclosing statement of "Imports, Exports, and Balance of Trade for February 1915," 23 March 1915, both in Kenneth Bourne, D. Cameron Watt, and David Stevenson, eds., *British Documents on Foreign Affairs*, part II, series H, volume, 5 part 1 (Frederick, MD: University Publications of America, 1989), docs. 55 and 56, pp. 74–75.

98. Wilson to Bryant, 24 March 1915, as cited in Robert W. Tucker, *Woodrow Wilson and the Great War* (Charlottesville: Univerity of Virginia Press, 2007), 105.

99. Telegram (28 May 1915), Spring Rice to FO, 61821, FO.382/12.

100. Spring Rice to FO, 20 May 1915, enclosing figures extracted from U.S. Journal of Commerce, 69649, in Bourne, Watt, and Stevenson, *British Documents on Foreign Affairs,* vol. 5, doc. 159, p. 232.

101. For instance see Spring Rice to Grey, No. 225 Commercial, enclosing report Colville Barclay, 16 May 1915, 68440, enclosed with 51255, FO.382/442.

102. Minute (11 June 1915) by Crowe to Nicholson, f.65, 71683, FO.382/12.

103. Ernest May, *The World War and American Isolation, 1914–1917* (Cambridge, MA: Harvard University Press, 1959), 150–53.

104. Ibid., 372–73.

105. Wilson to Bryan, 20 May 1915, FRUS, *Lansing Papers,* 1:411.

106. Trade Division, Admiralty, copy of dictated note, 22 May 1915, HSB.214, ADM.137/2736.

107. SC, 1:359–68; HMS, 1:157–58.

108. Arthur Nicholson to Grey, 24 February 1915, f.23, FO.800/95.

109. Telegram (14 May 1915), House to Wilson, Wilson Papers, as cited in Link, *Wilson,* 3:392.

110. Telegram (20 May 1915), House to Wilson, cited in Link, *Wilson,* 3:393.

111. Telegram (21 May 1915), House to Wilson, FRUS, *Lansing Papers,* 1:412–13; also Link, *Wilson,* 3:394.

112. Telegram (25 May 1915), Ambassador Gerald (Berlin) to Bryan, FRUS, 1915 Supp., 415.

113. Link, *Wilson,* 3:395–96.

114. Wilson to Bryan, 27 May 1915, FRUS, *Lansing Papers,* 1:416.

115. Bernstorff to Chancellor Bethman-Hollweg, 2 June 1915, as cited in Tucker, *Wilson and the Great War,* 125–26.

116. Telegram (6 June 1915), Spring Rice to Grey, f.73, FO.800/95; see also Drummond to Crewe, 12 June 1915, f.94, FO.800/95.

117. Spring Rice to Grey, 11 December 1914, f.448, FO.800/84; telegram (10 December 1914), Spring Rice to FO, No.171 Commercial, f.102, 81393, FO.368/1162.

118. Spring Rice to Grey, 11 December 1914, f.448, FO.800/84.

119. Spring Rice to Grey, 259.C, 4 December 1914, FO.115/1771.

120. Spring Rice's remarks were reproduced in memorandum by Lord Crewe, for cabinet, 18 June 1915, CAB.37/130/15. A copy of Spring Rice's original text can be found also in FO.899/9/148, which was recirculated to the cabinet on 21 July 1915.

121. Drummond to Grey, 7 June 1915, f.76, FO.800/95. The draft telegram is attached (see ff.79–85, FO.800/95).

122. Marginal comment in Grey's hand (n.d.) on Drummond to Grey, 7 June 1915, f.76, FO.800/95.

123. Minute (4 June 1915) by Crowe, 71683, FO.382/12; also Viscount Grey of Fallodon (Sir Edward Grey), *Twenty-Five Years: 1892–1916,* 2 vols. (New York: Frederick Stokes, 1925), 2:106–7.

124. Drummond to Crewe, 12 June 1915, f.94, FO.800/95.

125. Grey to Crewe, 14 June 1915, f.107, FO.800/95.

126. "Memorandum by Lord Crewe," for cabinet, 18 June 1915, CAB.37/130/15; see also Grey to Crewe, 14 June 1915, f.107, FO.800/95. This letter makes quite clear Grey's conviction that the entire blockade should be renounced.

127. Memorandum by Lord Crewe, for cabinet, 18 June 1915, CAB.37/130/15; see also Drummond to Grey, 12 June 1915, f.94, FO.800/95.

128. Minute (31 July 1915) by Crowe, after interview with M. de Fleurian, in "The Maritime Policy of His Majesty's Government," 104590, FO.382/464.

129. Ibid.

130. O'Malley, Memorandum [on rationing], page 13, 87822, FO.382/461.

131. Memorandum of understanding, "Paris Conference—Rationing of Neutrals," 25 June 1915, 84242, FO.382/461.

132. Foreign Office to Board of Trade, 6 July 1915, ff.281–84, ADM.137/1915.

133. Report by O'Malley, in "Paris Conference—Rationing of Neutrals," 1, 84242, FO.382/461. Note references to private conversations.

134. Foreign Office to Board of Trade, 6 July 1915, ff.281–84, ADM.137/1915.

135. Minutes by Robert L. Craigie (3 July 1915) and by Hurst (n.d.; ca. 4 July 1915) on "Paris Conference," 84242, FO.382/461.

136. Foreign Office to Board of Trade, 6 July 1915, 86068/15, copy, f.281, ADM.137/1915.

137. Foreign Office to Board of Trade, 9 July 1915, signed by Algernon Law, 84242, FO.382/461.

138. Minute (26 July 1915) by Hurst, on "Rationing of Neutrals," 97667, FO.382/461.

139. Lt. W. E. Arnold-Forster, RNVR, "Normal Averages—the History of Rationing Policy," June 1915, ADM.137/2872. Arnold Forster was the junior naval representative on the Contraband Committee. For the lifting of rationing in January 1915, see minute (27 January 1915) by Hurst on "Shipment of Copper from Australia," 7759, FO.382/437.

140. Craigie, "Memorandum Respecting the Restriction of the Imports of Certain Neutral States to their Normal Peace-time Requirements," 1 May 1915, in "Imports of Neutral Countries," 70127, FO.382/460.

141. Ibid.

142. Foreign Office (Hurst), "Memorandum Suspecting the Rationing Policy," n.d. (ca. 30 July 1915), prepared for cabinet at instruction of Eyre Crowe (minute of 26 July 1915) but not clear if distributed, 97067, FO.382/460.

143. Memorandum (2 July 1915) by Craigie, 9–10, "The Rationing Policy," in "Paris Conference: Rationing of Contiguous Neutrals," 87822, FO.382/461, regarding the cases of *London* and *Vulcan*.

144. Lt. W. E. Arnold-Forster, RNVR, "Normal Averages—the History of Rationing Policy," June 1915, ADM.137/2872.

145. Ibid.

146. Foreign Office (Hurst or Craigie), "Memorandum Suspecting the Rationing Policy," n.d. (ca. 30 July 1915), prepared for cabinet at instruction of Eyre Crowe (minute of 26 July 1915) but not clear if distributed, 97067, FO.382/460.

147. Minute (8 June 1915) by Crowe on Craigie memo of 1 May 1915, "Imports of Neutral Countries," 70127, FO.382/460.

148. Board of Trade (Barnes) to Foreign Office, 19 July 1915, enclosing memorandum, 97967, FO.382/461.

149. Minutes by Hurst (26 July 1915), by Pearson (24 July 1915), and by Craigie (23 July 1915), 97967, FO.382/461.

150. Churchill, "A Further Note upon the General Military Situation," 18 June 1915, para. 1b, CAB.37/130/16.

151. Ibid., para 2.

152. Hopwood, "Retaliation Policy against Germany," 12 July 1915, for cabinet, and attached memorandum by Grey, 17 July 1915, for cabinet, FO.899/2; Captain R. Webb, "Effect of Order in Council on Imports to Europe," 30 July 1915, marked used in cabinet, ADM.137/2734; "Memorandum by Mr. Leverton Harris, MP," July 1915, for cabinet, 337, FO.899/2; earlier draft found in Admiralty staff Trade Division papers, ADM.137/2734.

153. Hankey diary, 25 June 1915, HNKY.1/1.

154. Hankey, notes on Lord Crewe's memorandum, 23 June 1915, CAB.37/130/25.

155. Corbett diary, 23 and 28 June 1915, as cited in Donald Shurman, *Julian S. Corbett: Historian of British Maritime Policy from Drake to Jellicoe* (London: Royal Historical Society, 1981), 171.

156. Hankey, "The Future Policy of the War," 26 June 1915, CAB.37/130/26 (n.b.: the correct date for this paper should be 24 June 1915). See also HMS, 1:182–83. Hankey credits assistance from Mark Bonham Carter and Eric Drummond (private secretaries to Asquith) as well as James Masterton Smith (private secretary to Churchill) and Lt. Colonel O. A. G. Fitzgerald (personal secretary to Kitchener).

157. Hankey restated his arguments more succinctly in a private letter to Esher, 24 June 1915, WSC (companion part 2), 3:1050–51.

158. Balfour, "The War Situation: Need for a Policy of 'Active Defence,'" 2 July 1915, CAB.37/131/4. For Hankey's communications with Kitchener, see David French, "The Meaning of Attrition, 1914–1916," *English Historical Review* 103, no. 407 (April 1988): 385–405. Cabinet letters, 2 and 3 July 1915, show that Generals French, Robinson and Wilson were present to discuss the strategic situation; CAB.37/131/3.

159. Harcourt, cabinet notes, 10 July 1915, Ms.Dep. 6231.

160. Hankey, "The Future Policy of the War," 26 June 1915, paragraph 29, CAB.37/130/26.

161. Martin Horn, *Britain, France, and the Financing of the First World War* (Montreal: McGill–Queen's University Press, 2002), 105–6. Horn sees this letter in the outcome of Montagu's private concerns rather than, as argued here, in the context of the Crewe and Hankey memoranda.

162. Ibid., 94; for reference to Montagu's attempt in May 1915 to get the cabinet to reform the War Trade Department, see Lady Gwendeline Churchill to Winston Churchill, 21 January 1916, WSC (companion part 2), 3:1386–87.

163. See, for instance, Lord Robert Cecil (undersecretary at the Foreign Office) to Churchill, 30 June 1915, WSC (companion part 2), 3:1063–64. Cecil was commenting upon a recent paper by Kitchener entitled "An Appreciation of the Military Situation in the Future," 26 June 1915, CAB.37/130/28.

164. Montagu to Asquith, 3 July 1915, ff.83–100, Asquith 14; see also Horn, *Britain, France,* 105–6.

165. Memorandum by Emmott, War Trade Department, 7 July 1915, copy ADM.137/2872.

166. Ibid.

167. Memorandum signed by Leverton Harris and dated 12 July 1915, attached to agenda for meeting of Cornhill Committee for 20 July 1915, (box 114) Brand Mss., R. H. Brand Papers; Admiralty copy (12 July 1915), endorsed by DTD, ADM.137/2872.

168. "Memorandum by Mr. Leverton Harris, MP," July 1915, for cabinet, 337, FO.899/2; earlier draft found in Admiralty staff Trade Division papers, ADM.137/2734.

169. Minute (12 July 1915) by Webb, ADM.137/2872. Figures for April and May.

170. Ibid.

171. Emmott to Balfour, 25 August 1915, Emmott 5/374.

172. HC Deb, 1 March 1915, vol. 70, c.600.

173. Mr. Peto on contraband (cotton), HC Deb, 14 April 1915, vol. 71, c.4–5; Sir John Lonsdale, HC Deb 20, April 1915, vol. 71, c.152; Sir Philip Magnus, HC Deb, 21 April 1915, vol. 71, c.257; Mr. Ronald McNeil (supplies to Germany), HC Deb, 28 April 1915, vol. 71, c.701–2; Sir J. D. Rees (cotton), HC Deb, 5 May 1915, vol. 71, c.1088–89; Sir J. Lonsdale (cotton as contraband), HC Deb, 19 May 1915, vol. 71, c.2322–24; Sir John Lonsdale (cotton imports), HC Deb, 9 June 1915, vol. 72, c.260; Mr. Joynson-Hicks (export of tins to Germany), HC Deb, 23 June 1915, vol. 72, c.1153–54; Mr. Thomas Williams (tinned plates exported), HC Deb, 23 June 1915, vol. 72, c.1178W; Sir Henry Dalziel, HC Deb, 19 July 1915, vol.73, c.1145–46.

174. For a technical explanation for the use of cotton in explosives, see printed letter, T. D. Barlow, for Messrs. Barlow and Jones, to Mr. Weakley, 9 August 1915, 110804, FO.382/445.

175. *Daily Mail,* 23 July 1915.

176. January–July 1914, 3,713,234 bales; 1915, January–July 1915, 5,937,361 bales. Reported in *New York Times,* 8 September 1915.

177. Admiralty Trade Division, copy of dictated note, 22 May 1915, ADM.137/2736.

178. Grey, for cabinet, "Cotton as Contraband," n.d. (copy in FO.382/444 is dated 3 July 1915, with cover note to cabinet dated 7 July 1915), CAB.37/131/5. For files of correspondence on this subject and especially an excellent memo by Sir Eyre Crowe (3 July 1915), see FO.382/435. Also see FO.382/444. Follow-up memorandum (on cotton as contraband), Foreign Office, 10 July 1915, CAB.37/131/13.

179. Link, *Wilson,* 3:600, 605.

180. Spring Rice to Grey, 21 July 1915, printed for cabinet August 1915, f.339, FO.899/2.

181. Testimony of Mr. A. Booth, 19 July 1915, 3rd meeting of CID committee appointed to investigate "transfer of enemy vessels lying in neutral ports to allied or neutral flags," CAB.16/35.

182. Leverton Harris to Grey, 12 July 1915, f.386, FO.800/88.

183. See covering letter by Balfour dated 14 July 1915, referring to "today's" cabinet, attached to memorandum for cabinet by Sir Francis Hopwood, "Retaliation Policy against Germany," 12 July 1915, CAB.37/131/15; Asquith's official letter to the king, 15 July 1915, CAB.41/36/33.

184. Asquith's official letter to the king, 15 July 1915, CAB.41/36/33.

185. Harcourt, cabinet notes, 14 July 1915, Ms.Dep. 6231.

186. Ibid.

187. Minute (22 July 1915) by Asquith attached to confidential memorandum by E. S. Montagu, 21 July 1915, f.164, Asquith 29. See also covering letter from Montagu to Asquith, 19 July 1915, f.162, Asquith 29.

188. Minute (22 July 1915) by Asquith, on Montagu to Asquith 19 July 1915, f.162, Asquith 29.

189. Hankey to Asquith, 21 May 1915, (37) "Memorandum on the War Trade Machinery," CAB.63/5.

190. Montagu to Asquith, 19 July 1915, enclosing memorandum, f.162, Asquith 29.

191. Grey, *25 Years,* 2:107.

192. Link, *Wilson,* 3:597–605.

193. Hankey to Asquith, 20 July 1915, (31) CAB.63/5. Link misidentifies this document as the product of a CID meeting. Link's narrative (*Wilson,* 3:605–628) is (understandably) weak on the British side of the story.

194. Asquith to Selborne, 26 July 1915, ff.36–39, Selborne Mss. 80.

195. Grey to Asquith, 20 July 1915, f.374, FO.800/100.

196. Ibid.

197. Ibid.

198. Asquith to Grey, 21 July 1915, f.376, FO.800/100.

199. Marion Siney, "British Negotiations with American Meat Packers, 1915–1917: A Study of Belligerent Trade Controls," *Journal of Modern History* 23, no. 4 (December 1951): 343–53.

200. Churchill to Grey, 23 April 1915, f.342, FO.800/88.

201. Telegram 2485 (17 July 1915), Page to Lansing, FRUS, 1915 Supp., 474–76, and note 3. Bryan's reasons for resigning are hazy. Most historians assert he did so arguing that Wilson was being too pro-British in his direction of U.S. foreign policy.

202. For analysis, see Records of Procurator General, "Report of H.M. Procurator General upon the Prize Work of His Department during the War 1914–1918," 28 November 1923, "The *Kim* Group," ff.80–84, TS.13/858. Negotiations *subsequent* to the trial are found in TS.13/15A and TS.13/15B.

203. Carson (as attorney general) to Grey, 17 July 1915, f.38, FO.800/89. For Grey's enduring fear of the meatpackers, see Grey to McKenna and Runciman, 25 February 1916, f.383, FO.800/89; for Mann's efforts on behalf of the meatpackers, see Herbert Margulies, *Reconciliation and Revival: James R. Mann and the House Republicans in the Wilson Era* (Westport, CT: Greenwood Press, 1996), 120–21.

204. For the receipt of these protests, see Foreign Office, for cabinet, copy of telegram from Mr. Maurice Low (Washington) dated 16 July 1915, CAB.37/131/23; Foreign Office, for cabinet, copy of Ambassador Page to Grey, 17 July 1915 (received 21 July), CAB.37/131/28.

205. Lansing remarks to O. G. Villard, 13 July 1915, as cited in Link, *Wilson,* 3:597; telegram 1852 (15 July 1915), Lansing to Page, FRUS, 1915 Supp., 472–73.

206. Telegram 1860 (16 July 1915, 5:00 p.m.), Lansing to Page, FRUS, 1915 Supp., 473–74.

207. Ibid.

208. Wilson to House, 19 July 1915, House papers, as cited in Arthur S. Link, "The Cotton Crisis, the South, and Anglo-American Diplomacy, 1914–1915," in J. Carlyle Sitterson, ed., *Studies in Southern History* (Chapel Hill: University of North Carolina Press, 1957), 135.

209. Telegram (19 July 1915), House to Sir Horace Plunkett, House Papers, as cited in Link, "Cotton Crisis," 135.

210. Telegram 2491 (19 July 1915, 6:00 p.m.), Page to Lansing, FRUS, 1915 Supp., 478–79. For the strength of U.S. opinion, see Grey, *25 Years,* 2:116; see also cipher telegram 877 (19 July 1915), Spring Rice to Grey, copy, D19/19, Lloyd George Mss.

211. Telegram 220.C (19 July 1915), Grey to Spring Rice, 98896, f.167, FO.382/12.

212. Telegram 2491 (19 July 1915, 6:00 p.m.), Page to State, FRUS, 1915 Supp., 478–79.

213. Cabinet letter, 19 July 1915, CAB.41/36/34; Harcourt, cabinet notes, 19 July 1915, Ms.Dep. 6231.

214. Link, "Cotton Crisis"; Harcourt notes, 19 July 1915, Ms.Dep. 6231; Link, *Wilson,* 3:606–7.

215. Telegram 1308 (20 July 1915) by Spring Rice (received 10:15 a.m. 21 July), "Treatment of American Trade," 98394; also Telegram 1327 (22 July 1915) by Spring Rice (received 9:45 a.m. 23 July), reporting conversation on the subject with Lansing, in "Increases in British Exports to Holland and Scandinavia," 99740, both FO.382/464.

216. Published as U.S. Department of Commerce Report 203, 30 August 1915. Enclosed with Spring Rice to Foreign Office, 13 September 1915, 130845, FO.382/465.

217. Minute (11 August 1915) by Frederick Adam; quote taken from Grey's letter to Page, 13 August 1915, FO.382/465.

218. Minute (23 July 1915) by Crowe, in "Treatment of American Trade," 98394, FO.382/464; see also minute (24 July 1915) by Craigie, "Increases in British Exports to Holland and Scandinavia," 99740, FO.382/464.

219. The figures were actually supplied by the Board of Trade and had been requested on 3 June and supplied on 16 June. See Page to Grey, 3 June 1915, 14199, FO.382/465.

220. Telegram (20 July 1915) by Spring Rice to Grey, in "Treatment of American Trade," 98394, FO382/464. The United States did not formally present Skinner's case until August, for which see telegram (4 August 1915), Spring Rice to Grey, Comm. T.395, 114354, FO.382/464.

221. Board of Trade, "Memorandum Respecting Increased Re-Exports from the United Kingdom," 9 August 1915, note to p. 7, 96992/108933, FO.382/464.

222. Minute (11 August 1915) by Frederick Adam, "Increase of British Exports to Neutral Countries," and minute thereon (12 August 1915) from Crowe to Grey, 96992/108933, 9 August 1915, FO.382/464. See also Spring Rice to Grey, 1 September 1915, 130845, FO.382/465; reply, British embassy, Washington, DC, memorandum, 12 October 1915, not signed (Sir Robert Crawford, commercial attaché), 149026, FO.382/465; Foreign Office to Page (drafted by Crowe), 24 September 1915, 130845, FO.382/465; press clipping and minutes attached to "United States Consul-General, London," 147627, FO.382/465; memorandum by Mr. Osborne of Washington embassy staff enclosed in Spring Rice to Grey, 1 October 1915, 149026, FO.382/465.

223. Hankey to Asquith, 20 July 1915, (31) CAB.63/5.

224. Ibid.

225. Cabinet letters, 19 and 22 July 1915, CAB.37/131/26 and CAB.37/131/34.

226. Harcourt, cabinet notes, 22 July 1915, Ms.Dep. 6231.

227. Grey, for cabinet, "Memorandum [on the Controversy with USA on Trade]," 22 July 1915, CAB.37/131/36. Contrast this with his previous memo on the subject: Grey, note to cabinet on justification of blockade system against Germany, 17 July 1915, CAB.37/131/24.

228. Grey, "Memorandum [on the Controversy with USA on Trade]," 22 July 1915, CAB.37/131/36. A note on the draft copy states this paper was circulated on 26 July but there was no meeting of the cabinet that day, but there was on 27 July, for which see: 100744, 24 July 1915, f.187, FO.382/12. The precise date seems not to matter, as Grey delivered essentially the same message on both 22 and 26 July.

229. Grey, "Memorandum [on the Controversy with USA on Trade]," 22 July 1915, CAB.37/131/36.

230. Chelwood to Balfour, 12 April 1916, f.15, Add.Mss. 49738; see also Foreign Office to Admiralty, 28 April 1916, f.367, ADM.137/1164. For Admiralty advice against this, see "Memorandum by Mr. Leverton Harris, MP," July 1915, for cabinet, 337, FO.899/2; earlier draft found in papers of DTD, ADM.137/2734.

231. Memo, H. W. C. Davis (Contraband Committee), 4 September 1915, FO.899/9/184.

232. Asquith to Grey, 21 July 1915, f.376, FO.899/9/184.

233. McKenna, "Confidential Memorandum by the Chancellor on the Financial Situation," printed for the cabinet, 29 July 1915, MCKN.5/8. N.b.: There is a pencil note attached to McKenna's copy stating that the accompanying memorandum was originally circulated only to Asquith, Balfour, and Kitchener. The distribution list also shows Grey.

234. McKenna, "Confidential Memorandum by the Chancellor on the Financial Situation," 29 July 1915, CAB.37/131/37.

235. Asquith to Sylvia Henley, 23 July 1915, f.278 (box 1), Ms.Eng. lett. c.542.

236. Kathleen Burk, *Britain, America, and the Sinews of War, 1914–1918* (London: Allen and Unwin, 1985) 63–65; Martin Farr, "A Compelling Case for Volunteerism: Britain's Alternative Strategy, 1915–1916," *War in History* 9, no. 3 (2002): 279–306.

237. Kitchener, "The Financial Situation: Note by the Secretary of State for War," 27 July, CAB37/131/44. Copy in MCKN.5/8.

238. Asquith to McKenna, 25 July 1915, f.3, MCKN.5/8.

239. Ibid.

240. McKenna to Asquith (copy), 25 July 1915, f.5, and Asquith to McKenna, 26 July 1915, f.6, MCKN.5/8; Horn, *Britain, France,* 102–3.

241. Grey to McKenna, 24 July 1915, f.1, MCKN.5/6.

242. Minutes by Llewellyn Smith (24 July) and G. S. Barnes (23 July 1915) to Runciman, ff.195–97, Asquith 29.

243. Crowe, note on "Proposed New War Trade Organization," 23 July 1915, FO.899/2.

244. Ibid.

245. Minute (24 July 1915) by E. Davidson on Crowe's memorandum, 335, CAB.37/131/40; copy f.335, FO.899/2.

246. Cabinet letter, 27 July 1915, CAB37/131/43; Harcourt, cabinet notes, 27 July 1915, Ms.Dep. 6231; Asquith to Sylvia Henley, 27 July 1915, f.286 (box 1), Ms.Eng. lett. c.542.

247. Grey, (draft note to United States on blockade), 26 July 1915, CAB.37/131/42.

248. Harcourt, cabinet notes, 27 and 29 July 1915, Ms.Dep. 6231.

249. Telegram 2573 (31 July 1915), Page to State, enclosing note received from Sir Edward Grey, FRUS, 1915 Supp., 495–96; see also Link, *Wilson,* 3:607.

250. Asquith to Sylvia Henley, 4 and 8 August 1915, f.299, f.317 (box 2), Ms.Eng. lett. c.542.

251. Harcourt, cabinet notes, 10 July 1915, Ms.Dep. 6231; Churchill to Kitchener, 15 June 1915, f.24, Kitchener Papers, PRO.30/57/62.

252. Asquith to Churchill, 16 July 1915, WSC (companion part 2), 3:1096.

253. Bonar Law to Selborne, 19 July 1915, f.27, Selborne Mss. 80; additional note by Harcourt, 19 July 1915, Ms.Dep. 6231.

254. HMS, 1:188.

11. The End of the Beginning

Epigraph: Churchill, "Memorandum," July 1915, WSC (companion part 2), 3:1088–95.

1. Asquith to Sylvia Henley, 4 August 1915, f.299, Ms.Eng. lett. c.542 (box 2).

2. Asquith to Sylvia Henley, 8 August 1915, f.317, Ms.Eng. lett. c.542 (box 2). Hankey's letter of 28 July 1915 is reproduced in SC, 1:378–80; see also HMS, 1:189–205.

3. Robin Prior, *Gallipoli: The End of the Myth* (New Haven, CT: Yale University Press, 2009), 171–81, 190–200.

4. Stamfordham to Esher, 11 August 1915, in WSC (companion part 2), 3:1124–25.

5. Minute (31 July 1915) by Crowe, "The Maritime Policy of His Majesty's Government," 104590, FO.382/464.

6. Statistics handed in by the French delegation (communicated by Board of Trade, August 14, 1915), 112994, confidential print, FO.382/464; see also Emmott, "Memorandum Regarding French Ambassador's Communications as to Imports into Holland from GB in April 1915," 19 August 1915, f.21, Runciman Mss. 113.

7. Telegram 1749 (5 August 1915, 6:00 p.m.), Foreign Office to Bertie (Paris) and Spring Rice (Washington, DC), 104590, FO.382/464; minute (7 August 1915) by Crowe, "Maritime Policy of His Majesty's Government," 107565, FO.382/464.

8. Crowe to Mrs. Crowe, 10 August 1915, f.137, Ms.Eng. 3020.

9. Crowe to Fountain, 11 August 1915, 109039, FO.382/464.

10. Craigie, "Memorandum Respecting the Introduction of the Rationing Policy," 10 September 1915, 129355, FO.382/461.

11. Louis Guichard, *The Naval Blockade, 1914–1918,* trans. and ed. Christopher Turner (London: Philip Allan, 1930), 59–62.

12. The minutes are contained in telegram 1090 (14 August 1915, 3:00 p.m.), Grey to Spring Rice, CAB.37/132/20.

13. Telegram (19 July 1915), House to Sir Horace Plunkett, House Papers, as cited in Arthur S. Link, "The Cotton Crisis, the South, and Anglo-American Diplomacy, 1914–1915," in J. Carlyle Sitterson, ed., *Studies in Southern History* (Chapel Hill: University of North Carolina Press, 1957), 135.

14. Arthur S. Link, *Wilson,* vol. 3: *The Struggle for Neutrality, 1914–1915* (Princeton, NJ: Princeton University Press, 1960), 606.

15. Ibid.

16. Telegram (27 July, 3:45 p.m.), Wilson to Lansing, in FRUS, *The Lansing Papers, 1914–1920,* 2 vols. (Washington, DC: U.S. Government Printing Office, 1939), 1:301; see also Skinner to State, 28 July 1915, FRUS, 1915 Supp., 502–3. This report shows that the U.S. government was aware that U.S. exports of cotton were higher in 1915 than they had been in 1914.

17. Lansing to Wilson (28 July 1915, noon), FRUS, *Lansing Papers,* 1:301–2; telegram (28 July 1915), Spring Rice to Foreign Office, 105722, 31 July 1915, FO.382/464.

18. Telegram (31 July 1915), Spring Rice to Foreign Office, 104511, FO.382/464.

19. Acreage sown: 1914, 36,832 acres; 1915, 31,412 acres. *The Cotton Growing Countries: Production and Trade* (Rome: Statistical Bureau of International Institute of Agriculture, 1922), 29.

20. Runciman to Grey, 6 August 1915, f.328, FO.800/89.

21. Charles H. Burr to Richard S. Guinness, 9 August 1915 (copy sent to R. H. Brand, 10 August) (box 114), Brand Mss. Guiness was senior partner of Higgenson & Co., British branch of U.S. bankers Lee Higgenson & Co. In 2009 prices, $100 million is equivalent to more than $2 billion.

22. Grey to House, 10 August 1915, House papers, as cited in Link, "Cotton Crisis," 136; what follows relies substantially upon Link, *Wilson,* 3:606–16.

23. Harcourt, cabinet notes, 20 August 1915, Ms.Dep. 6231. N.b.: Harcourt says the price agreed was 9 cents.

24. Emmott to Asquith, 13 August 1915, ff.190, Asquith 29; drafts in Emmott 5/357.

25. Minute (22 July 1915) by Asquith, on Montagu to Asquith, 19 July 1915, f.162, Asquith 29.

26. Emmott [policy of the War Trade Department], 6 August 1915, CAB.37/132/8.

27. Emmott diary, 8 August 1915, f.219, Emmott Mss. 2 (Asquith's letters to Mrs. Henley show he was in Scotland on 8 August); Emmott to Hopwood, 8 August 1915, Hopwood Mss. 11. Emmott's memorandum is in Emmott Mss. 5/307.

28. Emmott to Asquith, 13 August 1915, plus attached memorandum, Emmott Mss. 5/357. Emmott's reasoning is more clearly explained in a letter to Balfour, for which see Emmott to Balfour, 1 September 1915, Emmott Mss. 5/374.

29. Emmott to Asquith, 13 August 1915, f.176, Emmott Mss. 5/357.

30. Ibid; see also draft memorandum by Emmott in Emmott Mss. 5/307.

31. Emmott to Asquith, 13 August 1915, ff.190, Asquith Mss. 29.

32. Ibid.

33. Curzon to Asquith, 10 August 1915, ff.199–202, Asquith Mss. 29. N.b.: According to Emmott, Curzon was offered the head of the new department with cabinet approval on Friday, 6 August 1915, for which see Emmott to Asquith, 13 August 1915, f.170, Asquith Mss. 29; see also Emmott to Hopwood, 8 August 1915, Hopwood Mss. 11 (Francis Hopwood, Lord Southborough papers, Bodelian Library, Oxford).

34. Curzon to Asquith, 10 August 1915, ff.199–202, Asquith Mss. 29.

35. Ibid.

36. Ibid.

37. For a suggestion Asquith may also have approached Lord Milner, see G. M. Trevelyan, *Grey of Falloden* (London: Longmans, Green, 1937), 309.

38. Emmott to Asquith, 20 August 1915, Emmott Mss. 5/365. The idea is presented at the end of his letter to Asquith dated 13 August 1915. See also Emmott diary entry 15 August 1915, f.215, Emmott Mss. 2.

39. Emmott diary, 15 August 1915, f.215, Emmott Mss. 2.

40. Asquith to Emmott, 20 August 1915, Emmott Mss. 5/371.

41. SC, 1:391–92.

42. Prior, *Gallipoli,* 160–89, 190–209.

43. Harcourt, cabinet notes, 11 August 1915, Ms.Dep. 6231; see also John Churchill to Winston Churchill, 11 August 1915, WSC (companion part 2), 3:1125–26.

44. Runciman to wife, 11 August 1915, f.26, Runciman Mss. 160.

45. Asquith to Sylvia Henley, 13 August 1915, f.332 (box 2), Ms.Eng. lett. c.542.

46. Asquith to Sylvia Henley, 15–16 August 1915, f.339 (box 2), Ms.Eng. lett. c.542. Hankey tried to notify Asquith the previous evening, but evidently his telegram went astray. See

Telegram 991 (14 August 1915, 8:15 p.m.), Hankey to Asquith, f.74, Asquith Mss. 28; SC, 1:376–405.

47. Asquith to Sylvia Henley, 15–16 August 1915, f.348 (box 2), Ms.Eng. lett. c.542.

48. Asquith to Kitchener, 20 August 1915, Kitchener Papers, PRO.30/57/63.

49. Joint Admiralty–War Office memorandum, "An Appreciation of the Existing Situation in the Balkans and Dardanelles, with Remarks as to the Relative Importance of This Situation in Regard to the General Conduct of the War," 9 October 1915, ADM.137/1145 and WO.106/708.

50. Minutes of the Dardanelles Committee, 20 August 1915, CAB.22/2; Kitchener to Asquith, 17 August 1915, as cited in Keith Neilson, *Strategy and Supply: The Anglo-Russian Alliance, 1914–1917* (London: Allen and Unwin, 1984), 96–97. Neilson provides further evidence in "Kitchener: A Reputation Refurbished?" *Canadian Journal of History* 15, no. 2 (August 1980): 222–23.

51. Harcourt, cabinet notes, 1 September 1915, Ms.Dep. 6231.

52. Asquith to Sylvia Henley, 15–16 August 1915, f.348 (box 2), Ms.Eng. lett. c.542.

53. Neilson, *Strategy and Supply,* 105–7; BSWA, 121; Kathleen Burk, *Britain, America, and the Sinews of War, 1914–1918* (London: Allen and Unwin, 1985), 63–64; Martin Horn, *Britain, France, and the Financing of the First World War* (Montreal: McGill–Queen's University Press, 2002), 102–3.

54. Harcourt, cabinet notes, 18 August 1915, Ms.Dep. 6231.

55. The best summary of the financial problems is found in J. M. Keynes, untitled memorandum [The Alternatives], 23 August 1915, in JMK, 16:110–15.

56. Michael J. Turner, *British Politics in an Age of Reform* (Manchester: Manchester University Press, 1999), 4–5, 64–58; Cameron Hazlehurst, *Politicians at War, July 1914 to May 1915: A Prologue to the Triumph of Lloyd George* (London: Jonathan Cape, 1971), 264–69; BSWA, 116–23. Grey is often excluded from the list, but see Grey to Asquith, 23 November 1915, f.394, FO.800/100.

57. Horn, *Britain, France;* Burk, *Sinews of War,* 30–35, 63–76; See also Roberta A. Dayer, "Strange Bedfellows: J. P. Morgan & Co., Whitehall and the Wilson Administration during World War I," *Business History* 18, no. 2 (1976): 125–51.

58. There is no monograph on the establishment of the Canadian (imperial) Munitions Board even though there exists a wealth of material in the Canadian national archives. W. Lionel Hichens was chairman of the shipbuilders Cammell Laird. Brand was apparently recruited through his friendship with George Macaulay Booth, a Liverpool shipowner and the original "man of push and go" who was prominent in the Ministry of Munitions. I am indebted to Keith Neilson for this information.

59. Gwynne to Bonar Law, 27 July 1915, enclosing Gwynne to Asquith, 26 July 1915, in *The Rasp of War: The Letters of H. A. Gwynne to the Countess Bathurst 1914–1918,* ed. Keith Wilson (London: Sidgewick & Jackson, 1988), 108–13.

60. Runciman to wife, 11 August 1915, f.26, Runciman Mss. 160.

61. CID paper G-27, "War Policy: Report and Supplementary Memoranda of a Cabinet Committee," printed 12 October 1915, CAB.21/1.

62. John G. Little, "H. H. Asquith and Britain's Manpower Problem, 1914–1915," *History* 82, no. 267 (July 1997): 397–409.

63. See CID paper G-27, "War Policy: Report and Supplementary Memoranda of a Cabinet Committee," 6 September 1915, CAB.24/1/27. Membership included Crewe, Curzon, Chamberlain, Churchill, Selborne, and Arthur Henderson; see also Burk, *Sinews of War,* 63–66, 78–79.

64. CID G-27, "War Policy," 6 September 1915, CAB.24/1/27, paras. 25, 32.

65. BSWA, 119–23.

66. Turner, *British Politics,* 64–90; BSWA, 119–23; most recently in Matthew Johnson, "The Liberal War Committee and the Liberal Advocacy of Conscription in Britain, 1914–1916," *Historical Journal* 51, no.2 (2008): 399–420.

67. Hankey diary, 3 September 1915, HNKY.1/1; McKenna, memorandum to cabinet, 13 September 1915, CAB.37/134/17; Keynes, "The Financial Prospects of the Financial Year," 9 September 1915, CAB.37/134/12; John Bradbury, "Limits of Borrowing Abroad and at Home," 9 September 1915, CAB.37/134/11.

68. Bonar Law to Balfour, 25 October 1915, CAB.37/136/30.

69. Harcourt, cabinet notes, 8 September 1915, Ms.Dep. 6231.

70. Best expressed in Bonar Law's reply to Balfour, 25 October 1915, CAB.37/136/30. Balfour's views are set out in "Finance and the War," 17 October 1915, CAB.37/136/18, and Balfour, "War and Finance No. 2," 26 October 1915, CAB.37/136/31.

71. Harcourt, cabinet notes, 14 September 1915, also 28 September 1915, Ms.Dep. 6231.

72. Neilson, *Strategy and Supply,* 95–134.

73. Carson to Churchill, 19 September 1915, WSC (companion part 2), 3:1179–80. Carson ultimately resigned on 12 October 1915.

74. BESP, 159.

75. Winston Churchill to Clementine Churchill, 3 December 1915, WSC (companion part 2), 3:1308–9.

76. Asquith to Emmott, 20 August 1915, Emmott Mss. 5/371.

77. Foreign Office, "Memorandum Respecting the Introduction of the Rationing Policy," 10 September 1915, ADM.137/2872; originally by Craigie, for which see same title, 10 September 1915, 129355, FO.382/461; Board of Trade to Foreign Office, 13 September 1915, 131121, FO.382/461.

78. Harcourt, cabinet notes, 1 September 1915, Ms.Dep. 6231.

79. Ibid.

80. Ibid.

81. Copy of Sir Alfred Hopkinson to Lord Emmott, n.d., enclosed in Emmott to Grey, 30 August 1915, "Present System of Prohibition of Exports from UK," 122758, FO.372/469.

82. WTAC, 15th meeting, 6 January 1916, Cecil, ff.125–26, CO.323/727.

83. Phillip Dehne, "From 'Business as Usual' to a More Global War: The British Decision to Attack Germans in South America during the First World War," *Journal of British Studies* 44 (July 2005): 516–35.

84. WTAC, 15th meeting, 6 January 1916, Money, f.123, CO.323/727.

85. WTAC, 15th meeting, 6 January 1916, Hopwood, f.136, and Money, ff.123–25; WTAC, 16th meeting, 13 January 1916, Lord Islington, f.267, both CO.323/727.

86. Harcourt, cabinet notes, 1 September 1915, Ms.Dep. 6231.

87. Published as U.S. Department of Commerce Report No. 203, 30 August 1915.

88. Kitchener had left and Asquith did not vote, for which see Harcourt, cabinet notes, 1 September 1915, Ms.Dep. 6231.

89. Minute (2 September 1915) by Craigie, "Present System of Prohibition of Exports from UK," 122758, FO.382/469.

90. Minute (6 September 1915) by Crowe, endorsed same day by Lord Crewe, on "Present System of Prohibition of Exports from UK," 122758, FO.382/469. N.b.: The covering letter from Emmott to Grey, 30 August 1915, claims Runciman asked him to forward the report.

91. Harcourt, cabinet notes, 3 September 1915, Ms.Dep. 6231; see also memorandum of meeting under presidency of Lord Robert Cecil, 3 September 1915, signed A[lwyn] P[arker], printed for cabinet, CAB.37/134/4 (copy in FO.899/9), and minute (4 September 1915) by Alwyn Parker on "Present System of Prohibition of Exports from UK," 122758, FO.382/469.

92. Grey, [Imports of Coffee into Germany], signed Robert Cecil, 11 September 1915, para. 6, CAB.37/134/16.

93. Corbett diary, 29 November 1915, as cited in Donald Shurman, *Julian S. Corbett: Historian of British Maritime Policy from Drake to Jellicoe* (London: Royal Historical Society, 1981), 171.

94. Diary entry, 11 September 1915, f.225, Emmott Mss. 2.

95. ESRC, "Use of 'N.E.T. Index: Neutral & Enemy Trade Index,'" n.d. (ca. 1917), ff.2–5, ADM.1/8408/1.

96. The seven were Cecil Hurst (Foreign Office), Sir Francis Hopwood, Vice-Admiral Edmond Slade, Commander Frederick Leverton Harris (Admiralty), Captain Ernest Pretyman and G. J. Stanley (Board of Trade), and H. H. Fawcett (War Office). L. C. Liddle became secretary after Maurice Hankey declined the position; Hankey, diary entry, 17 September 1915, HNKY.1/1. They were joined by W. C. Bridgeman (deputy, War Trade Department), George Cave (solicitor general), A. D. Steel Maitland, MP (undersecretary, Colonial Office), Brigadier Cockerill (War Office), and J. R. Murray (Board of Trade).

97. WTAC, "Appointment of Members," CAB.39/1.

98. John Dickson-Poynder (1866–1936): Conservative member for Chippenham, 1892–1910; created 1st Baron Islington, 1910; governor-general of New Zealand, 1910–1912; undersecretary of state for the colonies, 1914–1915; undersecretary of state for India, 1915–1919. Son of Rear Admiral John Bourmaster Dickson.

99. Arthur D. Steel Maitland (1876–1935): Conservative MP for Birmingham East (1910–1918); chairman of Conservative party, 1911–1916; undersecretary for colonies, 1915–1917; secretary for overseas trade, 1917–1919; minister of labor, 1924–1929. Elected Fellow of All Souls, 1900. Created baronet, 1917.

100. WTAC, 1st meeting, 29 September 1915, 1, CAB.39/2.

101. WTAC, 17th meeting, 20 January 1916, Hopwood, ff.300–301, CO.323/727.

102. WTAC, 10th meeting, 2 December 1915, 193053, FO.382/433.

103. WTAC, 1st Meeting, 29 September 1915, CAB.39/2.

104. "Report of the Work on the Restrictions of Enemy Supplies Committee and the War Trade Advisory Committee," 15 April 1919, CAB.15/6/5.

105. Lloyd George to Crewe, n.d. (October 1915), LG/D/16/9/5; Francis Stevenson to Sir H. Llewellyn Smith, 9 October 1915, LG/D/1/2/22, Lloyd George Mss.

106. For Pollock's appointment, see WTAC, 8th meeting, 18 November 1915, CAB.39/9. For Cecil becoming responsible for blockade matters, see reference in Lord Robert Cecil to Captain Richard Webb (DTD), 17 June 1916, ADM.137/2737.

107. WTAC, 2nd meeting, 6 October 1915, 1, CAB.39/3; WTAC, 5th meeting, 26 October 1915, Crewe, CAB.39/6; WTAC, 6th meeting, 4 November 1915, CAB.39/7; WTAC, 7th meeting, 11 November 1915, CAB.39/8.

108. Minutes attached to WTAC, 9th meeting, 25 November 1915, 193051, FO.382/433.

109. WTAC, 10th meeting, 2 December 1915, CAB.39/11.

110. HL Deb, 13 January 1916, vol. 20, c.919–30, cocoa exports.

111. Archibald Bell, *A History of the Blockade of Germany and the Countries Associated with Her in the Great War: Austria-Hungary, Bulgaria, and Turkey* (London: HMSO, 1961), ch. 15.

112. Crowe to Fountain, 11 August 1915, 109039, FO.382/464.

113. Board of Trade to Foreign Office, 13 September 1915, 131121, FO.382/461; Foreign Office, "Memorandum Respecting the Introduction of the Rationing Policy," 10 September 1915, ADM.137/2872; Emmott to Foreign Office, 23 September 1914, enclosing memorandum by R. J. Thompson, Board of Agriculture, 21 September 1915, 137640, FO.382/461; see also in Kenneth Bourne, D. Cameron Watt, and David Stevenson, eds., *British Documents on Foreign Affairs,* part II, series H, volume 5, part 1 (Frederick, MD: University Publications of America, 1989), doc. 91, pp. 117–19.

114. Foreign Office, "Memorandum Respecting the Introduction of the Rationing Policy," 10 September 1915, 129355, FO.382/461; distribution list shows copies sent to Board of Trade, Admiralty, War Trade Department, Procurator General, India Office, Colonial Office, and British embassies in Paris and Rome. See also minute (14 September 1915) by Craigie referring to conversations with Crowe, 129355, FO.382/461.

115. Mellor (procurator general) to Crowe (Foreign Office), 4 October 1915, 14362, FO.382/461.

116. Minutes (11 September 1915) by Parker and (13 September 1915) by Hurst, on Craigie, "Rationing Policy," 129355, FO.382/461.

117. WTAC, 4th meeting, 14 October 1915, CAB.39/5.

118. Minute (20 October 1915) by Hurst, "Rationing Policy," 129355, FO.382/461.

119. Ibid.

120. Ibid. Membership of subcommittee: George Cave, Lord Emmott, Captain Pretyman, Admiral Slade, and Hurst. Crowe agreed to attend; see minute (22 October 1915) at foot of page tight inside the binding, 129355, FO.382/461.

121. WTAC, 5th meeting, 26 October 1915, CAB.39/6.

122. Link, *Wilson,* 3:685–86.

123. Spring Rice to Grey, 6 August 1915, 11379, f.229, FO.382/12.

124. The entire text is contained in FRUS, 1915 Supp., 578; also in a cabinet memorandum dated 5 November 1915, CAB.37/137/7. N.b.: The attached note states it was circulated to the cabinet Monday morning, 8 November 1915.

125. Lansing to Wilson, 9 October 1915, PWW, 35:45. The first draft was completed on 15 July 1915, for which see Ernest May, *The World War and American Isolation* (Cambridge, MA: Harvard University Press, 1959), 327n5.

126. Lansing to Wilson, 21 October 1915, PWW, 35:91–92.

127. Link, *Wilson,* 3:682–93.

128. Note by Grey, 5 November 1915, f.391, FO.382/12. Note also instructions to Page to present the note "in the sense of the following," FRUS, 1915 Supp., 578.

129. Grey, cabinet memorandum, 5 November 1915, CAB.37/137/7.

130. House to Wilson, 19 October 1915, PWW, 35:85.

131. Mary Kihl, "A Failure in Ambassadorial Diplomacy," *Journal of American History* 57 (December 1970): 636–53.

132. House diary, 14 October 1915, as reproduced in PWW, 35:61–65.

133. Telegram (14 October 1915), Spring Rice to Grey, FO.115/1921.

134. Grey, note to cabinet, 4 January 1916, CAB.37/140/6, circulated 5 January 1916.

135. May, *World War and American Isolation,* 326–27.

136. Link, *Wilson,* 3:686; Arthur S. Link, *Wilson,* vol. 4: *Confusions and Crises, 1915–1916* (Princeton, NJ: Princeton University Press, 1964), 101.

137. May, *World War and American Isolation,* 327; Robert W. Tucker, *Woodrow Wilson and the Great War* (Charlottesville: University of Virginia Press, 2007), 140.

138. Grey to House, 11 November 1915, enclosed with House to Wilson, 25 November 1915, PWW, 35:254–56.

139. House diary, 27 November 1915, PWW, 35:257–62.

140. Plunkett diary, 3 December 1915, PWW, 35:311n1; generally, Kihl, "Ambassadorial Diplomacy," 649.

141. House diary, 15 December 1915, PWW, 35:355–61; Wilson to House, 17 December 1915, PWW, 35:364.

142. Telegram (7 January 1916), House to Wilson, PWW, 35:453.

143. Minute (18 November 1915) by Crowe, and attached minutes (19 November 1915) by Cecil, Lord Crewe, and Sir Edward Grey, f.437, 172186, FO.382/12.

144. Minute (28 January 1916) by Crowe, on "America and the Blockade," 16535, FO.382/1099.

145. Ibid.; see also Keith Neilson, "Sir Cecil Spring Rice and the United States, 1914–1917," in Christopher Baxter, ed., *Diplomats at War: British and Commonwealth Diplomacy in Wartime* (Leiden: Martinus Nijhoff, 2008), 73–75.

146. Drummond to Grey, 24 January 1916, f.36, FO.800/96.

147. Montagu to Drummond, 28 February 1916, AS1/5/88(1), Montagu Mss.

148. Minutes (n.d.) by Grey and (2 February 1916) by Nicolson, on 18183, FO.371/2848; Neilson, "Sir Cecil Spring Rice and the United States," 65.

149. Foreign Office (U.S. note of 21 October—Page to Grey, 5 November 1915), paras. 14 and 30, CAB.37/137/7.

150. A. Pearce Higgins, "The Policy of Rationing Neutral States Adjoining Germany and Its Relation to International Law," 19 November 1915, printed 7 December 1915 as appendix to CAB.37/137/37. The first paragraph of this document makes clear the request for opinion emanated from the WTAC; the second paragraph makes equally clear the request came after the delivery of the U.S. protest. N.b.: Higgins makes frequent reference to the U.S. note in the text of his opinion, especially in sections I and II.

151. Ibid.

152. WTAC, "Report of Sub-Committee of the War Trade Advisory Committee on Proposal for Rationing Neutral Countries," 7 December 1915, CAB.37/139/18; the Foreign Office

copy is dated 17/21 December 1915, and especially minute (17 December 1915) by Hurst and is found in 195598, FO.382/461.

153. For strong dissent, see Crewe, "Some Observations upon the Report of the Sub-Committee on the Proposal for 'Rationing' Neutral Countries," and a note by Leo Chiozza Money dated 14 December 1915, circulated 25 January 1916, CAB.37/141/30. N.b.: The Money memorandum predates the WTAC subcommittee report.

154. Hurst, "Limitations of Certain Imports into Holland," 7 November 1915, 165784, FO.382/203; see also Thomas Otte, "Between Hammer and Anvil: Sir Francis Oppenheimer, the Netherlands Overseas Trust and Allied Economic Warfare, 1914–1918," in Christopher Baxter and Andrew Stewart, eds., *Diplomats at War: British and Commonwealth Diplomacy in Wartime* (Leiden: Martinus Nijhoff, 2008), 102–3. The understanding was reached 23 September 1915.

155. Not ratified till 2 February 1916; see H. Richie, *The Navicert System during the World War* (Washington, DC: Carnegie Foundation, 1938), Annex C.

156. WTAC, 8th meeting, 18 November 1915, CAB.39/9.

157. WTAC, 9th meeting, 25 November 1915, CAB.39/10.

158. Ibid., remarks by Pollock; also file 193051, FO.382/433.

159. Marc Frey, "Trade, Ships, and the Neutrality of the Netherlands in the First World War," *International History Review* 19, no. 3 (August 1997): 547.

160. Ibid.

161. WTAC, 9th Meeting, 25 November 1915, Pollock, CAB.39/10.

162. Ibid., remarks by Leverton Harris.

163. Sir Leo Chiozza Money, "Memorandum on German Imports through Holland and Scandinavia," attached to WTAC, 10th meeting, 2 December 1915, CAB.39/11.

164. Ibid.

165. WTAC, 15th Meeting, 6 January 1916, f.123, CO.323/727.

166. Curzon to Churchill, 30 November 1915, cited in WSC, 3:601, 872.

167. The answer may lie in Sir Reginald Plunkett's diary, held by the Plunkett Foundation, Dublin, Ireland; unfortunately, the diary was not available to me at time of writing.

168. Balfour to Emmott, 30 August 1915, Emmott Mss. 5/374.

169. Ibid.

170. Emmott to Balfour, 1 September 1915, Emmott Mss. 5/374.

171. Admiralty to secretary, Cornhill Committee, 30 August 1915, 142610, FO.382/470.

172. Cornhill Committee to Admiralty, 1 October 1915, 142610, FO.382/470.

173. Minute (4 October 1915) by O. G. Sargent, "Insurance of Cargoes Consigned to Holland and Scandinavia," 142610, FO.382/470; see also report of meeting by H. H. Lamb dated 5 October 1915, FO.382/470.

174. Admiral Stanley Colville to Jellicoe, 18 May 1915, f.101, ADM.137/1917; Jellicoe to Admiralty, 19 May 1915, ff.122–26, ADM.137/1917.

175. Jellicoe to Beatty, 16 July 1915, as reproduced in A. Temple Paterson, ed., *The Jellicoe Papers*, 2 vols. (London: The Naval Records Society, 1966, 1968), 1:172.

176. Edward Hilton Young (Baron Kennett), *The System of National Finance* (London: Smith, Elder, 1915).

177. Emmott to Crewe, 29 January 1916, Emmott Mss. 6.

178. Jellicoe to Admiralty, 19 June 1915, ADM.137/1915; Jellicoe to Admiralty, 4 August 1915, f.252, ADM.137/1911.

179. Jellicoe to Admiralty, 3 August 1915, ADM.137/2734; see also comments thereon by the Trade Department in the minute (13 August 1915) by Webb, ADM.137/2734.

180. Jellicoe to Admiralty, 4 August 1915, f.252, ADM.137/1911.

181. Jellicoe to Admiralty, 27 August 1915, f.285, ADM.137/1911.

182. Jellicoe to Admiralty, 1 September 1915, ADM.137/1915.

183. Ibid., appendix: "Denmark, Sweden, Norway and Holland, 1 April–1 September 1915, f.20.

184. Minute (13 August 1915) by Webb and Oliver, ADM.137/2734.

185. Lieutenant W. E. Arnold Foster, "Rationing—Notes on Memorandum by Lieutenant E. Hilton Young MP," n.d., ADM.137/2872.

186. Minute (16 August 1915) by Hopwood, ADM.137/2734.

187. Ibid.

188. Minute (16 August 1915) by Jackson, "Interception of Neutral Shipping," from Cinch, 4 August 1915, ADM.137/2734.

189. Minute (20 August 1915) by Balfour, ADM.137/2734.

190. George Cave, "Minute by Chairman of Contraband Committee," 30 August 1915, ADM.137/2734.

191. Jellicoe to Admiralty, 14 September 1915, ff.41–44, ADM.137/1915.

192. Minute (27 September 1915) by Webb, ADM.137/2734. The Admiralty formally replied to Jellicoe on 3 October 1915, copy in ADM.137/1915. See also minute (n.d.) by Commander Longden (naval liaison officer to Foreign Office Contraband Committee), ADM.137/2734.

193. Jellicoe to de Chair, 15 September 1915, box P39, de Chair Papers, IWM.4/2/d.

194. Jellicoe to de Chair, 21 October 1915, IWM.4/2/d.

195. Fisher to Cecil Fisher (his son), 22 September 1915, FISR.15/1/3/3.

196. Churchill to wife, 2 February 1916, as cited in WSC, 3:699–705. For Hamilton's fear that Jackson must be replaced, see Hamilton diary 20 November 1915, HTN.106.

197. Hamilton diary, entry 3 November 1915, HTN.106.

198. See, for instance, "British Blockade of Germany," Admiralty to Foreign Office, 3 October 1915, enclosing correspondence from Jellicoe, 143545, FO.382/470; "Vessels Bound for Scandinavia, Holland," Admiralty to Foreign Office, 16 December 1915, enclosing Jellicoe to Admiralty, 16 November 1915, 192190, FO.382/474; Jellicoe to Admiralty, 6 December 1915, f.57, ADM.137/2736.

199. Minute (17 December 1915) by W. E. Davidson, on "Vessels Bound for Scandinavia, Holland," 192190, FO.382/474.

200. Minute (7 October 1915) by Craigie, on "British Blockade of Germany," enclosing Admiralty to Foreign Office, 3 October 1915, 143545, FO.382/470.

201. Crowe to Greene, 2 October 1915, in "Contraband Committee Minutes," 138208, FO.382/470.

202. Crowe to Runciman, 19 November 1915, f.148, Runciman Mss. 136.

203. Ibid.

204. See Jellicoe to Admiralty, 14 September 1915, ff.41–44, ADM.137/1915.

205. Jellicoe to Admiralty, 16 November 1915, copy in 192190, FO.382/474.

206. WTAC, 9th meeting, 25 November 1915, CAB.39/10.

207. Minute (18 December) by E. Leslie, on "Vessels Bound for Scandinavia and Holland," 192190, FO.382/474.

208. Minute (20 December 1915) by Alywn Parker, initialed Crowe, 21 December 1915, 192190, FO.382/474.

209. Cecil to Crewe, n.d., enclosing record of meeting, f.71, FO.800/196.

210. See Jellicoe to Admiralty, 6 February 1916, f.90, ADM.137/2736.

211. Lady Randolph Churchill to Winston Churchill, 19 December 1915 and 23 January 1916, WSC (companion part 2), 1337–38, 1392.

212. Page to Wilson, 31 December 1915, PWW, 35:412–14. Note Page's reference to previous letter on same subject.

213. May, *World War and American Isolation,* 315.

214. HC Deb, 2 November 1915, vol. 75, c.503–37, Asquith and Carson. Carson resigned 18 October 1915.

215. BSWA, 159.

216. HC Deb, 2 November 1915, vol. 75, c.600–619, Lord Charles Beresford and Cecil.

217. HC Deb, 2 November 1915, vol. 75, c.620, Sir Alfred Markham.

218. HC Deb, 2 November 1915, vol. 75, c.612, Lord Robert Cecil.

219. HL Deb, 16 December 1915, vol. 20, c.670–72, Lord Strachie; c.674–75, 677–78, Earl of Portsmouth; c.680–84, Lord Devonport.

220. Gwynne was close to Sir Edward Carson; see J. M. McEwen, "The Press and the Fall of Asquith," *Historical Journal* 21 (1978): 863–83.

221. Gwynne to Lady Bathurst, 20 December 1915, letter 106, in *Rasp of War,* 154–55. Selected MPs were also shown the treaty; see HL Deb, 16 December 1915, vol. 20, c.683, Lord Devonport.

222. Cecil to Lady Cecil, 12 December 1915, CHE.5/148 (Lord Robert Cecil papers, Hatworth House Collection, Herts, UK).

223. HL Deb, 16 December 1915, vol. 20, c.670–72. Lord Strachie: former Liberal MP, 1911; paymaster general (no. 3 in Treasury) in Asquith government until coalition.

224. HC Deb, 23 December 1915, vol. 77, c.647–784; c.719, Sir Henry Dalziel.

225. Ibid.

226. HC Deb, 23 December 1915, vol. 77, c.727, Sir Richard Cooper Bt. (Walsall-C).

227. Asquith to Montagu, 28 December 1915, Montagu Mss. AS1/1/45.

228. Asquith to Sylvia Henley, 29 December 1915, f.509 (box 2), Ms.Eng. lett. c.542. Generally: Turner, *British Politics,* 73–83; BSWA, 158–80; Michael Fry, "Political Change in Britain, August 1914 to December 1916: Lloyd George Replaces Asquith: The Issues Underlying the Drama," *Historical Journal* 31, no. 3 (1988): 609–27.

229. Granted royal assent on 27 January 1916.

230. HMS, 1:240–41, 243–46. Hankey emphasizes in his diary the hours he spent alongside Asquith, first in defusing the crisis and second as chairman of the Military and Finance Committee. The Committee's papers are in CAB.37/141/38.

231. Memorandum by Edward Grey, 14 January 1916, f.18, FO.800/96.

232. Foreign Office, [British Measures for Intercepting German Sea-borne Trade], 28 December 1915, CAB.37/139/62.

233. Ibid., 18.

234. Ibid., 20.

235. HC Deb, 4 January 1916, vol. 77, c.785; "Statement of the Measures Adopted to Intercept the Sea Borne Commerce of Germany," in "German Sea Borne Commerce (Miscellaneous, No. 2, 1916)" [Command Paper 8145]; "British Blockade Policy—Official Statement," *Times,* 5 January 1916, 7.

236. In his memoirs Grey quoted from the first version: Viscount Grey of Fallodon (Sir Edward Grey), *Twenty-Five Years: 1892–1916,* 2 vols. (New York: Frederick Stokes, 1925), 2:105.

237. Foreign Office, [British Measures for Intercepting German Sea-borne Trade], 28 December 1915, para 29, CAB.37/139/62.

238. Minute (27 January 1915) by Greene, on Foreign Office memorandum dated 28 December 1915, ff.183–99, ADM.137/1164; another copy is found in ADM.137/2733.

239. Jellicoe to Admiralty, 10 January 1916, ADM.137/1164.

240. Ibid; See also letter of 13 January 1916, ADM.137/1164.

241. Jellicoe to Cecil, 17 January 1916, encl. Jellicoe to Admiralty, 13 January 1916, 13353, FO.382/1099.

242. Jellicoe to Fisher, 20 January 1916, FGDN 3:291.

243. Fisher to Jellicoe, 12 February 1916, FGDN 3:306–7.

244. *Morning Post,* 17–19, 27, and 28 January 1915.

245. *Morning Post,* 18 January 1916.

246. *Times,* 5, 12, 14–15, 17, 19–22, 24–29, and 31 January 1916.

247. HL Deb, 13 January 1916, vol. 20, c.919–30, cocoa exports.

248. Ibid., c.922. See also subsequent speech: HL Deb, 22 February 1916, vol. 21, c.72–128, Lord Sydenham.

249. Cecil to Cordert, 19 January 1916, f.262, FO.800/196.

250. Ibid.

251. Telegram (13 January 1916) No. 4, House to Wilson, PWW, 35:471. See also House's telegrams to Wilson No. 1 of 7 January 1916 and No. 6 of 16 January 1916, PWW 35:453, 87–88; for Hankey reading the House-Wilson correspondence, see HMS, 1:247; for the contrary view, see Link, *Wilson,* 4:115–16.

252. Skinner to State, 17 January 1916, No. 1083, and Page to State, 20 January 1916, No. 2878, FRUS, 1916 Supp., 340–43.

253. Cecil to Grey, 12 January 1916, f.15, FO.800/96.

254. Ibid.

255. The minute on this letter from Grey to Asquith is undated.

256. Appointed 11 January 1916.

257. Lady Gwendeline Churchill to Winston Churchill, 21 January 1916, WSC (companion part 2), 3:1386–7.

258. Harcourt, cabinet notes, 25 January 1916, Ms.Dep. 6231.

259. WTAC, 16th meeting, 13 January 1916, ff.277–78, CO.323/727.

260. WTAC, 17th meeting, 20 January 1916, ff.307–9, CO.323/727; previous reference to this in 16th meeting at f.277, CO.323/727. N.b.: The only surviving copy of these minutes is the Colonial Office archive; they are missing from CAB, ADM, BT, WO, and T.

261. WTAC, 17th meeting, 20 January 1916, ff.307–9, CO.323/727.

262. Ibid., remarks by Money, f.299.

263. Ibid., remarks by Hopwood, f.303.

264. Ibid., ff.302–3.

265. WTAC, 16th meeting, 13 January 1916, ff.274–75, remarks by Slade, CO.323/727.

266. Ibid., f.278.

267. Minute (19 February 1916) by DTD on report of WTAC, 17th meeting, 20 January 1916, ADM.137/1164. Pretyman (Board of Trade) and Leverton Harris (Admiralty) agree, f.303. See also memorandum by Commander Tarleton, 4 February 1916, f.226, ADM.137/1164.

268. Minute (24 January 1916) by Crowe on "Transmits Copy of Letter Sent to Admiralty Enclosing Diagrams Showing Monthly Imports of Certain Commodities by Countries Contiguous to Germany," 13353, FO.382/1099.

269. Minute (22 January 1916) by Craigie, 13353, FO.382/1099.

270. Minutes (22 January 1916) by Craigie and Parker, 13353, FO.382/1099.

271. Minute (24 January 1916) by Crowe, 13353, FO.382/1099.

272. Emmott to Crewe, 29 January 1916, Emmott Mss. 6.

273. "Export of Certain Articles from USA," 20 January 1916, enclosing Harwood, "Memorandum on the Statistics of Exports of Certain Articles from the United States of America Quoted in the *Morning Post* of 18th January, 1916," 19 January 1916, 11926, FO.382/1099.

274. Minute (20 January 1916) by Crowe, FO.382/1099.

275. For Harwood's more considered response, see Harwood to Locock, 4 February 1916, enclosing Harwood to Cecil, 4 February 1916, 23317, FO.382/1099; *Times,* 26 January 1916, 6, col. A.

276. Harwood, "Memorandum on the Statistics of Exports of Certain Articles from the United States of America Quoted in the *Morning Post* of 18th January, 1916," 19 January 1916, 11926, FO.382/1099, paras. 1 and 2.

277. *Times,* 21 January 1916, 33, col. A.

278. Ibid., col. E; see also *Times,* 26 January 1916, 9, cols. C, D.

279. For the likelihood that Asquith took this decision on 25 January, see Jackson to Jellicoe, 25 January 1916, f.20, Add.Mss. 49009.

280. "Conference between the Prime Minster (the Right. Hon. H. H. Asquith, KC, MP) and the Editors of the Principal London and Provincial Newspapers on the Subject of the Blockade and the Restriction of Trade with Neutral Countries," in "The Blockade + Restriction of Trade with Neutral Countries," Tuesday 25th January 1916, 17418, FO.382/1099. For an alternative interpretation of this meeting, see Greg Kennedy, "Strategy and Power: The Royal Navy, the Foreign Office and the Blockade, 1914–1917," *Defence Studies* 8, no. 2 (2008): 190–206.

281. *Lord Riddle's War Diary, 1914–1918* (London: Ivor Nicholson and Watson, 1933) 151.

282. Asquith to Sylvia Henley, 25 January 1916, f.554 (box 3), Ms.Eng. lett. c.542.

283. Remarks by Asquith, in "Conference between the Prime Minster (the Right. Hon. H. H. Asquith, KC, MP) and the Editors of the Principal London and Provincial Newspapers," 9.

284. Ibid.

285. *A Speech Delivered by the Rt. Hon. Sir E. Grey, Secretary of State for Foreign Affairs, in the House of Commons, on the 26th January, 1916* (London: Hodder and Stoughton, 1916).

286. Report to the king, 26 January 1915, A.51/1, Samuel Mss.

287. WTAC, 18th Meeting, 27 January 1916, ff.345–46, CO.323/727.

288. Ibid., opening remarks by Crewe; also Emmott to Crewe, 29 January 1916, Emmott Mss. 6.

289. Jean Tannery, "Le Blocus: Le Memorandum War Trade Department (*Times* du 26 janvier 1916," 20 January 1916, enclosed in "M. Tannery's Reply to Mr. Harwood," 45904, FO.382/1100. See also minute (20 March 1916) by Crowe, FO.382/1100. Tannery was *chef de la section de contrôle* in Paris. Additional material can be found in a file titled "The *Morning Post*, 25 January 1916, 'The Blockade Farce—A Reply to FO Criticisms,'" 15850, FO.382/1099.

290. Commander Anderson, "Memorandum on the Debate of Blockade Policy in the House of Lords, Feb 22nd & 23rd, 1916," file reference 126z, ADM.137/2737. On serious errors found in a WTD report underestimating Scandinavian copper imports by at least 50 percent, see WTAC, 21st meeting, 21 February 1916, f.527, CO.323/727.

291. WTAC, 19th meeting, 3 February 1916, f.429, CO.323/727.

292. Ibid.

293. Ibid.

294. Memorandum by Commander M. H. Anderson (4 February 1916), ff.225–36, ADM.137/1164; see also copies and minutes attached inside docket marked "Copy of AWS (TD) No. 1515, House of Commons Debate (Jan 26th) on Subject of Blockade. Analysis and Remarks on Speeches," ADM.137/2737.

295. In addition to the two documents cited in note 294 see also minutes (19 February 1916) by Lieutenants (RNVR) F. McCormick Goodhart and W. Ginman on Jellicoe to Admiralty, 16 February 1916, ADM.137/2734.

296. Cecil to Spring Rice, 25 February 1916, f.135, FO.800/196.

297. Grey to Asquith, 15 February 1916, f.408, FO.800/100.

298. Memorandum, signed HHA, 16 February 1916, f.409, FO.800/100; Harcourt, cabinet notes, 16 February 1916, Ms.Dep. 6231.

Conclusions

1. Carl von Clausewitz, *On War,* ed. and trans. Michael Howard and Peter Paret (Princeton, NJ: Princeton University Press, 1984), book 6, ch. 8, 387–88.

Primary Sources

Archive and Manuscript Collections

UNITED KINGDOM

The National Archives (formerly Public Record Office, Kew)

Admiralty (ADM)
Board of Trade (BT)
Cabinet Office (CAB)
Colonial Office (CO)
Committee of Imperial Defence (CAB)
Foreign Office (FO)
Secret Intelligence Services (HD)
Treasury (T)
Treasury Solicitor and Attorney General (TS)
War Office (WO)
War Trade Advisory Committee (CAB)
War Trade Department (CAB)
Also private papers of:
Lord Robert Cecil (Viscount Chelwood) FO 800
Sir Edward Grey FO 800
Field Marshall Lord Kitchener (PRO 30)
James Masterton Smith (CAB 1)

Birmingham University Library

Austen Chamberlain (AC.7)

Bodleian Library, Oxford

Herbert H. Asquith (Asquith Mss.)
Margot Asquith (MSS.Eng.)
Robert H. Brand (Brand Mss.) (Uncataloged at time of use)
Sir Eyre Crowe (Ms.Eng.)

Howell A. Gwynne (Gwynne Mss.)
Lewis Harcourt (Mss.Dep. 510 and Mss.Dep. 6123) (Uncataloged at time of use)
Sylvia Henley (Mss.Eng. lett.)
Sir Francis Hopwood (Lord Southborough) (Hopwood Mss.)
William Palmer, 2nd Earl Selborne (Selborne Mss.)
John S. Sandars (Ms.Eng.Hist.)
Sir John Simon (Simon Mss.)
Venetia Stanley (MSS.Eng.)

British Library

H. Oakley Arnold-Forster (Add.Mss.)
Arthur J. Balfour (Add.Mss.)
John Burns (Add.Mss.)
Sir Henry Campbell-Bannerman (Add.Mss.)
Sir George Cave (Add.Mss.)
Lord Robert Cecil (Viscount Chelwood) (Add.Mss.)
Sir George Clarke (Baron Sydenham) (Add.Mss.)
Charles Hobhouse (Add.Mss.)
Admiral John R. Jellicoe (Add.Mss.)
Admiral Roger S. Keyes (Keyes Mss.)
George A. Riddle (Add.Mss.)
James A. Spender (Add.Mss.)

Carlisle Record Office

Esme Howard (Lord Penrith) (Howard Mss., DHW)

Carmarthenshire Record Office

Frederick Campbell, 3rd Earl Cawdor (Cawdor Mss.)

Churchill Archives Center, Churchill College, Cambridge

Reginald Brett, Viscount Lord Esher (ESHR)
Sir Winston S. Churchill (CHAR)
William F. Clarke (CLKE)
Alexander G. Denniston (DENN)
Major Adrian Grant Duff (AGDF)
Admiral John A. Fisher (FISR)
Admiral William Reginald Hall (Hall Mss., CCC)
Maurice Hankey (HNKY)
Reginald McKenna (MCKN)
William T. Stead (STED)
Admiral Frederick Doveton Sturdee (SDEE)

Gloucester Record Office

Sir Michael Hicks-Beech (Lord St. Aldwyn) (Hicks-Beach Mss.)

The Parliamentary Archive (formerly House of Lords Records Office)

Andrew Bonar Law (Bonar Law Mss.)

David Lloyd George (Lloyd George Mss.)
Herbert Samuel (Samuel Mss.)

Imperial War Museum
Captain Philip Dumas (Dumas Mss.)
Admiral Trevelyan Napier (Napier Mss.)
Admiral Ernest Troubridge (Troubridge Mss., IWM)
Field Marshal Sir Henry Wilson (Wilson Mss.)

Naval Library Ministry of Defence, Portsmouth Naval Base
Admiral Roger Backhouse (Backhouse Mss.)
Frederick Campbell, 3rd Earl Cawdor (Cawdor Mss., NLMD)
Winston S. Churchill, Secret: First Lord's Minutes, 2 volumes (FLM)
Captain Montagu Consett—Captain William R. Hall correspondence (Hall Mss., NLMD)
Julian S. Corbett (Corbett Mss., NLMD)
Captain Thomas Crease (Crease Mss.)
Admiral Sir Henry Jackson (Jackson Mss.)
Admiral George King Hall (King Hall Mss.)
Edward Marjoribanks, 2nd Baron Tweedmouth (Tweedmouth Mss.)

Nuffield College, Oxford
Alfred Emmott (Lord Emmott) (Emmott Mss.)
Joseph A. Pease (Lord Gainford) (Gainford Mss.)
John E. B. Seely (Lord Mottistone) (Mottistone Mss.)

Hartley Centre, Southampton University Library
Admiral Prince Louis of Battenburg (MB1/T)
Sir Ernest Cassell (MB1/T)

Newcastle University Library
Walter Runciman (Runciman Mss.)

India Office Library
John Morley (Morley Mss.)

National Library of Scotland
Richard B. Haldane (Haldane Mss.)
Fifth Lord Rosebery (Rosebery Mss.)

National Maritime Museum
Admiral George Ballard (Ballard Mss.)
Admiral David Beatty (BTY)
Julian S. Corbett (Corbett Mss., NMM)
Sir William G. Greene (GEE)
Admiral Frederick T. Hamilton (HTN)
Admiral Charles Madden (MAD)
Admiral William H. May (MAY)
Admiral Gerald Noel (NOE)

Admiral Herbert Richmond (RIC)
Admiral Edmond Slade (Slade Mss.)
Admiral Ernest Troubridge (Troubridge Mss., NMM)

British Telecom, Freeling House, Mount Pleasant Complex, London
The Post Office Archives (POST)

Guildhall City Library, London
Lloyd's of London

Liddell Hart Centre, Kings College London
Admiral Alexander Bethell (Bethell Mss.)
Julian S. Corbett (Corbett Mss., KCL)

London School of Economics
Sir Robert Giffen (Giffen Mss.)

King's College, Cambridge
John Maynard Keynes (Keynes Mss.)

Trinity College, Cambridge
Edwin S. Montagu (Montagu Mss.)

UNITED STATES

Harry Ransom Centre, University of Texas at Austin
James L. Garvin (Garvin Mss.)

Stirling Library, Yale University
Edward M. House (House diary)

Published Government Documents

Kenneth Bourne and D. Cameron Watt, eds., *British Documents on Foreign Affairs: Reports and Papers from the Foreign Office Confidential Print; Part II, Series H: The First World War, 1914–1918* (Frederick, MD: University Publications of America, 1981).

U.S. Department of State, *Foreign Relations of the United States* (Washington, DC: Government Printing Office, 1914–1928).

Acknowledgments

This book has been a long time in the making. During that time, I have incurred numerous debts of gratitude. In particular, I would like to thank the following for scrutinizing the entire manuscript and making invaluable comments: Professors Cameron Hazlehurst, Samuel R. Williamson, Keith Neilson, Daniel E. Rogers, Jon Sumida, Katherine Epstein, and Jonathan Winkler; Captain Jeremy Read RN and Captain Christopher Page RN; and Drs. Bruce Taylor, Timothy Dottridge, and Lawrence Burr. None, of course, are responsible for what follows, and any errors of fact or interpretation are my own. I have also received valuable criticism and suggestions from Drs. Norman Friedman, Nicholas Black, and Christopher Martin. For their assistance, I am especially grateful to Helen Langley and Mike Webb of the Bodleian Library; Jenny Wraight, the Admiralty librarian; John E. Davies of the Carmarthenshire Record Office; and the "paragraph fairy." Thanks are due also to Professors Sir Michael Howard, John Gooch, William Roger Louis, Art Eckstein, Paul Pickering, Christopher Woolgar, Andrew Gordon, Thomas Otte, Greg Kennedy, and Paul Halpern; Commander Mike Codner RN; Drs. Anne-Louise Antonoff and David Stevens; Rear Admiral James Goldrick RAN; Jock Gardner, Peter and Emmy Nash, Becky Yang, and Terry Lindell; Dr. Roderick Sudderby at the Imperial War Museum; Melanie Wood of the Robinson Library at Newcastle University; Clare Kavanagh at Nuffield College Oxford archives; Caroline Herbert at the Churchill Archives Centre, Churchill College, Cambridge; Ivana Fryan in the Department of Special Collections, University of Birmingham; Tom Robson at the Carlisle Record Office; Paul Banfield at the Queen's University, Kingston; and Sophia Saeed Khan at Harvard University Press. For endeavoring to hammer in to me some economic history, I wish to thank my former tutor, the late Professor Charles Feinstein. For supplying the map, I am indebted to Philip Schwatzberg of Meridian Mapping. Lastly, I am grateful to Kathleen McDermott, my editor at Harvard, for remaining undaunted by the length of this book.

The following have graciously allowed me permission to quote from the material to which they own the copyright: Sir Brian Crowe (Sir Eyre Crowe papers); Professor

C. M. Woolgar and the Trustees of the Broadlands Archives (Admiral Prince Louis of Battenberg papers); the curators of the Bodleian Library (collections owned by the Bodleian Library); the Bonham Carter trustees (H. H. Asquith papers); Mrs. Anna Mathias (Venetia Stanley papers); Richard Ford (Robert Brand papers); the Harcourt family (Sir Lewis Harcourt papers); Garry Runciman and also the librarian, Robinson Library, Newcastle University (Runciman papers); Sir Charles Hobhouse (Hobhouse papers); the Parliamentary Archives (David Lloyd George and Andrew Bonar Law papers); Christopher Arnander (Reginald McKenna papers); Edward Sandars (John S. Sandars papers); the master, fellows, and scholars of Churchill College, Cambridge (Lord Hankey papers); the fifth Lord Esher (Lord Esher papers); the third Lord Fisher (Admiral of the Fleet Lord Fisher papers); Philip Howard (Lord Howard of Penrith papers); Susan Worrall (Austen Chamberlain Papers); the Trustees of the British Library (Arthur James Balfour and Robert Gascoyne-Cecil, Viscount Cecil of Chelwood, papers); the master and fellows of Trinity College, Cambridge (Edwin Montagu papers); the third Lord Gainford (Lord Gainford papers); and the Admiralty Librarian (Hall-Consett Papers). For permission to quote from the unpublished writings of J. M. Keynes, I thank the provost and scholars of King's College, Cambridge; to quote from *The Collected Writings of John Maynard Keynes,* I thank Palgrave Macmillan and also Professor Donald Winch, the publications secretary of the Royal Economics Society. Crown copyright material at the National Archives is quoted by permission of the controller of Her Majesty's Stationery Office. Although every effort has been made to trace the holders of the copyright in the letters and other documents quoted in this book, the search in some cases has been unsuccessful. I trust that anyone whose copyright has been unwittingly infringed will accept sincere apologies.

For the past six years I have benefited from an associate fellowship at the Royal United Services Institute for Defence and Security Studies. I should like to thank the director, Dr. Michael Clarke, and all the staff for their unfailing assistance and encouragement over so many years. Consultation of the James L. Garvin papers was made possible by a visiting fellowship awarded by the Harry Ransom Center, the University of Texas at Austin. Since 2010 the Europe Center, Australian National University, has allowed me a visiting fellowship, providing an office, support, and access to a library while finishing this manuscript.

Lastly, I wish to acknowledge an unquantifiable debt I owe two scholars. Samuel R. Williamson's *The Politics of Grand Strategy* (1969) and Cameron Hazlehurst's *Politicians at War* (1971) set a standard of archival research and historical analysis that has seldom been equaled. Their work on Edwardian politics and defense policy was far ahead of its time and after more than forty years remains unsurpassed. I profited from the archival trails they pioneered. My use of their work, ideas, and insights cannot be adequately acknowledged in the notes in this book. It is my pleasure to thank them for their guidance and encouragement.

Index

Harvard University Press is a member of Green Press Initiative (greenpressinitiative.org), a nonprofit organization working to help publishers and printers increase their use of recycled paper and decrease their use of fiber derived from endangered forests. This book was printed on recycled paper containing 30% post-consumer waste and processed chlorine free.